R. ARCHIBALD - #259

Management Accounting
Text and Cases

**The Willard J. Graham Series
in Accounting**

Consulting Editor
ROBERT N. ANTHONY   *Harvard University*

Management Accounting

Text and Cases

ROBERT N. ANTHONY, D.B.A.
Ross Graham Walker Professor of Management Control
Graduate School of Business Administration
Harvard University

and

JAMES S. REECE, D.B.A.
Associate Professor of Business Administration
Graduate School of Business Administration
University of Michigan

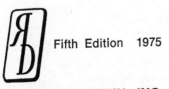 Fifth Edition 1975

RICHARD D. IRWIN, INC. Homewood, Illinois 60430
Irwin-Dorsey International Arundel, Sussex BN18 9AB
Irwin-Dorsey Limited Georgetown, Ontario L7G 4B3

Fifth Edition

First Printing, June 1975
Second Printing, January 1976

Case material of the Harvard Graduate School of Business Administration is made possible by the cooperation of business firms who may wish to remain anonymous by having names, quantities, and other identifying details disguised while basic relationships are maintained. Cases are prepared as the basis for class discussion rather than to illustrate either effective or ineffective handling of administrative situations.

ISBN 0-256-01648-8
Library of Congress Catalog Card No. 74-31593

Printed in the United States of America

LEARNING SYSTEMS COMPANY—
a division of Richard D. Irwin, Inc.—has developed a
PROGRAMMED LEARNING AID
to accompany texts in this subject area.
Copies can be purchased through your bookstore
or by writing PLAIDS,
1818 Ridge Road, Homewood, Illinois 60430.

PREFACE

The intended audience of this book is a person who wants to understand accounting so that he or she can use accounting information. Such a person needs to know something about accounting techniques in order to appreciate the meaning of accounting reports, and the book describes the technical material needed for this purpose. Its main focus, however, is on the use of this information.

This book is used in the following types of courses:

1. An introductory course for students with no background in accounting. For a thorough coverage, such a course is usually two semesters or three quarters in length, although the material can be covered in a one-semester course in less depth and with omission of most of the cases. The book is used in both upper level undergraduate courses and in graduate programs.

2. A half-year course that builds on an introductory course in accounting principles.

3. The accounting or control sequence in a management development program.

The title of the book dates from 1956 when "management accounting" meant any accounting that was of interest to managers. Today, the "management accounting" subject area is restricted to the internal uses of accounting, and "financial accounting" deals with reports prepared for external users. Notwithstanding its title, the book covers *both* financial accounting and management accounting in the current meaning of these terms, in approximately equal amounts.

Although designed for beginning students, the book does not contain enough "pencil-pushing" material to meet the needs of many instructors in beginning courses. Such instructors may want to use the companion volume, *Management Accounting Workbook*[1], which, in addition to

---

[1] James S. Reece and Robert N. Anthony, *Management Accounting Workbook* (Homewood, Ill.: Richard D. Irwin, Inc., 1975).

key terms and discussion questions, has much problem material, a short practice set, and some cases which are not in this volume.

Many instructors also assign, or recommend, the programmed text, *Essentials of Accounting*[2], either as preliminary to study of the subject (it is often sent in advance to participants in management development programs), or as a review device. This book is a self-study introductory treatment of financial accounting, geared to this text.

The Cases

As in previous editions, the cases have been selected because of their interest and educational value as a basis for class discussion. They are not necessarily intended to illustrate either correct or incorrect handling of management problems. Skill in the management use of accounting information can be acquired, we believe, only through experience. Thinking about a case, and discussing it in the classroom and in informal discussion groups, can help to provide such experience. In preparing to discuss a case in class, the student is required to *do* something—to analyze a problem, to weigh various factors involved in it, to make some calculations, to take a position, and so on. In class, the student is required to explain his or her point of view, to defend it, to understand and appraise the arguments of colleagues, and to decide what arguments are the strongest. Practice in doing these things helps to increase skill and understanding; in fact, many educators believe that the really important parts of a subject can be learned only by experience of some sort, as opposed to merely hearing or reading about them. Thus, although the case material comprises less than half the pages in this book, the discussion of these cases is by far the more important part of the educational process.

Although some professors have suggested that each case should be accompanied by a set of detailed questions, others feel that such questions would tend to channel the preparation and discussion of the case too narrowly. We have decided to continue, for most of the cases, the practice of giving only a few broad questions, with the thought that those who prefer the other approach can easily supplement these when making assignments.

Changes in the Fifth Edition

Developments in accounting in the last five years have been rapid, and they have resulted in many changes in the text, not only in its details, but also in the overall approach to certain topics.

The financial accounting material herein incorporates pronouncements of the Accounting Principles Board and of the Financial Account-

---

[2] Robert N. Anthony, *Essentials of Accounting* (Reading, Mass.: Addison-Wesley Publishing Co., Inc.).

ing Standards Board through December 1974. We have not only described the substance of relevant pronouncements, but also have adopted terminology that the FASB indicates it prefers.

Because of the increased emphasis given to these topics, we have: expanded the discussion of revenue recognition in Chapter 5 (and have included a section on credit cards because their use has become so widespread); included new sections on deferred income taxes, foreign currency adjustments, extraordinary gains and losses, and discontinued operations (Chapter 8); and incorporated new material on debt and shareholders' equity, in Chapter 9. The material on acquisitions and consolidated statements has been placed in a separate chapter, Chapter 10. Chapter 11 on the Statement of Changes in Financial Position is entirely rewritten, both to incorporate APB *Opinion No. 19*, and also to simplify the presentation of this complicated subject. In all these changes, our objective has been to incorporate the essence of the new developments at a level appropriate for beginning students and at the same time to improve the clarity of the presentation.

We have eliminated the chapter on income measurement in manufacturing companies, and have incorporated the material in Chapter 6 on inventories, omitting some of the mechanical details.

Part II on management accounting has been entirely restructured. The central pedagogical problem of management accounting always has been that students learn that there are several types of cost constructions and several purposes for which costs are used, but they are confused as to how many types there are and as to which type is appropriate for a given purpose. We take the position that there are three types of cost: (1) conventional full costs, (2) differential costs, and (3) responsibility costs. To emphasize the distinctions, we discuss full cost accounting in Chapters 15 and 16, differential accounting in Chapters 17–19, and responsibility accounting in Chapters 20–22. The uses of each type of cost information are discussed after the nature of the cost construction has been described. We think this approach lessens the students' confusion. The approach is discussed in more detail in Chapter 14.

In the chapters on full cost accounting, we have incorporated pronouncements of the Cost Accounting Standards Board through December 1974. We have added material on learning curves, economic order quantity, expected value and measures of uncertainty, decision trees, linear programming, the discounted payback method, and forecasting, always at a level appropriate for a first course.

The former Chapter 20 on automated data processing has been eliminated; its essential points have been incorporated in Chapter 4.

Approximately 35 cases in this Fifth Edition did not appear in the Fourth Edition, and most of those carried over from the Fourth Edition have been revised.

In earlier editions we inadvertently used "sexist" words and phrases. In the current revision, we have eliminated most references to "he," "men," and similar terms. In those few places where the masculine gender is retained, our reason is either that an alternative construction is awkward ("he" rather than "he or she" when it is clear that the reference is to a person of unspecified gender) or that predominant usage sanctions it ("businessman" instead of "businessperson").

Acknowledgments

As can be seen from the detailed list in the Index and Sources of Cases, many people participated in the process of preparing the cases included herein. We appreciate the permission that both those at Harvard and those at other institutions have given us to use their cases in this book. For ourselves and on behalf of the other authors of cases, we express our gratitude to the businessmen who were willing to give their time and the benefit of their experience in the development of these cases.

We are grateful to many persons who have made suggestions for improving the book. Colleagues who have taught the Control course at the Harvard Graduate School of Business Administration have contributed many new ideas. From other schools, we appreciate the comments of Paul R. Berney, Yale University; Yezdi Bhada, Georgia State University; James D. Blum, University of Delaware; Homer Brown, University of Oklahoma; Charles G. Carpenter, Pennsylvania State University; Eugene E. Comiskey, Purdue University; Joseph R. Curran, Northeastern University; Ubaldo de Dominicus, Instituto di Studi Aziendali, Genoa, Italy; G. F. Dominiak, Texas Christian University; Doyle A. Eilen, Cornell University; Albert A. Ewald, Temple University; Douglas Garbutt, Cranfield School of Management; James S. Hekimian Northeastern University; Yvonne R. Knight, Colby College; Brenda Mallouk, York University; Major T. Roger Manley, Air Force Institute of Technology; W. H. Patterson, Old Dominion University; Robert T. Sprouse, Financial Accounting Standards Board; Jose M. Tejoro, Colegio Universitario de la Rabida, Spain; L. M. Wallace, Jr., Chowan College; Glenn A. Welsch, University of Texas at Austin; and Walter H. Zukowski, Colby College.

Bonnie B. Reece did extensive work on revision of the cases. Ann B. Carter was in charge of secretarial work. Each did a superb job.

May 1975   ROBERT N. ANTHONY
                                                 JAMES S. REECE

CONTENTS

Realization Concept: *Distinction between Receipt and Revenue. Amount of Revenue.* The Matching Concept: *Relation of Cost and Expense. Nature of the Matching Concept. Expenses and Expenditures.* The Consistency Concept. The Materiality Concept. The Income Statement: *Revenues. Cost of Goods Sold. Gross Margin. Expenses. Net Income. Retained Earnings. Relation between Balance Sheet and Income Statement.* Other Concepts of Income: *Cash-Basis Accounting. Income Tax Accounting.*

4. Accounting Records and Systems   85

Bookkeeping: *The Account. Debit and Credit. The Ledger. The Chart of Accounts. The Journal. The Trial Balance.* The Adjusting and Closing Process: *Need for Adjusting Entries. Types of Adjusting Entries. Closing Entries. Ruling and Balancing Accounts. The Work Sheet. Summary of the Accounting Process.* Accounting Systems: *Special Journals. Control Accounts and Subsidiary Ledgers. Imprest Funds. Internal Control. Significant Bookkeeping Ideas.* Computer-Based Accounting Systems: *What a Computer Is. Relationship to Manual Accounting. Service Bureaus.* Appendix: *Locating Errors Revealed by the Trial Balance.*

5. Revenue and Monetary Assets   125

Timing of Revenue Recognition: *General Considerations. Installment Sales. Long-term Contracts. Consignments. Bad Debts. Credit Cards. Warranty Costs. Revenue Adjustment versus Expense.* Monetary Assets: *Certificates of Deposit. Marketable Securities.*

6. Cost of Goods Sold and Inventories   153

Overview of the Problem: *Types of Companies.* Merchandising Companies: *Acquisition Cost. Periodic Inventory Method. Perpetual Inven-*

tory Method. Comparison of Periodic and Perpetual Methods. Manufacturing Companies: *Inventory Accounts. Raw Materials Used. Cost of Goods Manufactured. Cost of Goods Sold. Alternative Income Statement Format. Cost Accounting. Product Costs and Period Costs.* Inventory Costing Methods: *Specific Identification Method. Average Cost. First-In, First-Out (Fifo). Last-In, First-Out (Lifo). Comparison of Fifo and Lifo.* Cost or Market Rule.

7. Fixed Assets and Depreciation   194

Acquisition of Fixed Assets: *Items Included in Cost. Measurement of Acquisition Cost. Acquisitions Recorded at Other than Cost.* Depreciation of Fixed Assets: *Judgments Required. Service Life. Depreciation Methods. Choice of a Method. Accounting for Depreciation. Reporting in Financial Statements. The Investment Credit.* Disposal of Fixed Assets: *Debits to Accumulated Depreciation.* Group and Composite Depreciation. Significance of Depreciation: *Concluding Comment.* Other Aspects of Fixed Assets: *Depletion. Accretion and Appreciation.* Intangible Assets: *Acquisition of Intangibles. Amortization of Intangibles. Deferred Charges. Research and Development Costs. Investments.*

8. Other Expenses and Net Income   232

Personnel Costs: *Payroll Transactions. Pensions.* Income Tax Allocations: *Permanent Differences and Timing Differences. Accounting for Timing Differences. Accounting Entries. Nature of Deferred Income Taxes Liability.* Foreign Currency Adjustments. Extraordinary Items: *Definition of Extraordinary Items. Accounting Treatment.* Discontinued Operations: *Accounting Treatment.* Net Income. Price Level Adjustments: *Nature of the Problem. Supplementary Financial Statements. General Approach. Illustration of the Calculation.* Direct Costing.

9. Liabilities and Owners' Equity   264

Nature of Liabilities: *Current Liabilities. Deferred Income Taxes. Contingent Liabilities.* Long-Term Liabilities: *Recording a Bond Issue. Balance Sheet Presentation. Bond Interest. Retirement of Bonds. Refunding a Bond Issue.* Forms of Business Organization: *Sole Proprietorship. Partnership. Corporations.* Accounting for Owners' Equity: *Proprietorship and Partnership Equity. Ownership in a Corporation. Recording the Issue. Treasury Stock. Surplus Reserves. Retained Earnings. Dividends. Stock Options and Warrants.* Earnings per Share. Balance Sheet Presentation.

10. Acquisitions and Consolidated Statements   296

Acquisitions and Mergers: *Accounting for Business Combinations. Earnings Impact.* Consolidated Statements: *Basis for Consolidation. Unconsolidated Investments. Consolidation Procedure. Asset Valuation. Minority Interest. Concluding Comment.*

11. The Statement of Changes in Financial Position   315

The Concept of Flow Statements. Statement of Changes in Financial Position—Cash Basis. Statement of Changes in Financial Position—Working-Capital Basis: *Misconceptions about Depreciation.* Preparation of the SCFP: *The SCFP Work Sheet. Work Sheet Entries. Preparing the SCFP. Summary of Preparation Procedures.* Uses of the SCFP.

12. Financial Statement Analysis   345

Business Objectives: *Return on Investment. Sound Financial Position.* Structure of the Analysis: *Overall Measures. Investment Turnover and*

Profit Margin. Tests of Profitability. Tests of Investment Utilization. Tests of Financial Condition. Difficulties in Making Comparisons: *Deciding on the Proper Basis for Comparison. Differences in the Situations Being Compared. Changes in the Dollar Measuring Stick. Differences in Definition. Hidden Short-Run Changes. The Past as an Indication of the Future.* Possible Bases for Comparison: *Experience. Goals. Historical Standards. External Standards.* Use of Comparisons.

13. Understanding Financial Statements 382

Additional Information in Annual Reports: *The Auditor's Opinion. Notes to Financial Statements. Full Disclosure. Comparative Statements. SEC Reports. Interim Reports.* Review of Criteria and Concepts: *Criteria. Concepts. Importance of the Concepts. Misconceptions about Concepts.* Accounting Alternatives: *Regulatory Requirements. Latitude in the Principles. Judgment in the Application of Principles. Implications of These Differences. Inherent Limitations.* Meaning of the Financial Statements: *The Income Statement. Statement of Changes in Financial Position. The Balance Sheet.*

Part II
MANAGEMENT ACCOUNTING

14. The Nature of Management Accounting 413

Management Accounting as One Type of Information: *Information. Operating Information. Management Accounting.* Types of Management Accounting Information and Their Uses: *Full Cost Accounting. Differential Accounting. Responsibility Accounting. Relation to Planning and Control.* Contrast between Management Accounting and Financial Reporting: *Differences. Similarities. Source Disciplines.* Some General Observations: *Different Numbers for Different Purposes. Accounting Numbers Are Approximations. Working with Incomplete Data. Accounting Evidence Is Only Partial Evidence. People, Not Numbers, Get Things Done.*

15. Essentials of Full Cost Accounting   435

The Concept of Cost: *General Definition. Cost Objective. Full Cost. Applicable Accounting Principles. Elements of Cost.* Systems for Cost Accumulation: *The Account Flowchart. Flow of Costs.* Job Order Costing and Process Costing: *Job Order Costing. Process Costing. Choice of a System. Variations in Practice.* Measurement of Direct Costs: *Direct Labor Cost. Direct Material Cost.* Allocation of Indirect Costs: *Distinction between Direct and Indirect Costs. Nature of Allocation. Cost Centers. Calculation of Overhead Rate. Standard Volume. Allocation to Products. Why Overhead Rates Are Predetermined. Unabsorbed and Overabsorbed Overhead.*

16. Additional Aspects of Full Cost Accounting   485

Standard Costs: *Variations in the Standard Cost Idea. Uses of Standard Costs.* Illustration: Black Meter Company: *Description of Company. Overview of System. Setting up Standard Costs. Developing Standard Product Costs. Accounting Entries. Sales and Cost of Goods Sold.* Joint Products and By-Products: *Joint Products. By-Products.* Nonmanufacturing Costs: *Residual Expenses.* Validity of Full Costs: *Tendencies toward Uniformity.* Uses of Full Cost: *Financial Reporting. Analysis of Segment Profitability. What Did It Cost? Setting Regulated Prices. Normal Pricing.*

17. Differential Accounting: The Behavior of Costs   515

The Differential Concept: *Cost Constructions for Various Purposes. Differential Costs. Differential Revenues.* Variable and Fixed Costs. Contribution Analysis: *Contrasts between Full Costs and Differential Costs.* Relation of Costs to Volume: *Cost-Volume Diagrams. Behavior of Total Costs. Cost Assumptions. Equation for the Cost Line. Unit Costs. Estimating the Cost-Volume Relationship. Measures of Volume.* The Profitgraph and Break-Even Analysis: *Interpretation of the Profitgraph. Improving Profit Performance. Several Products. Other Influences on Costs. Learning Curves.* Sources of Differential Cost Data. Appendix: *The Least-Squares Method.*

18. Alternative Choice Decisions 562

Nature of Alternative Choice Problems: *Business Objectives*. Steps in Analysis: *Steps 1 and 2. Definition of the Problem and of Alternative Solutions. Step 3. Weighing and Measuring the Quantitative Factors. Step 4. Evaluating the Unmeasured Factors. Step 5. Reaching a Decision.* Differential Costs: *Mechanics of the Calculation. Danger of Using Full Cost. Fringe Benefits. Opportunity Costs. Other Terminology. Estimates of Future Costs. Importance of the Time Span. Example: Operating an Automobile.* Types of Alternative Choice Problems. Problems Involving Costs. Problems Involving Both Revenues and Costs: *Supply/Demand/ Price Analysis. Contribution Pricing. Other Product Decisions. Benefit/ Cost Analysis.* Some Practical Pointers. Useful Decision Models: *Economic Order Quantity. Expected Value. Measuring Uncertainty. Decision Trees. Linear Programming.*

19. Capital Investment Decisions 613

What Is Present Value? *Finding Present Values. Application to Investment Decisions. Return on Investment. Stream of Cash Inflows. Other Present Value Tables.* Estimating the Variables: *Required Rate of Return. Cash Inflow. Economic Life. Investment. Nonmonetary Considerations. Nonuse of Discounting. The Overall Analytical Process.* Other Methods of Analysis: *Discounted Cash-flow Method. Payback Method. Discounted Payback Method. Unadjusted Return on Investment Method.* Preference Problems: *Criteria for Preference Problems. Comparison of Preference Rules.*

20. Responsibility Accounting: The Management Control Process   **660**

Characteristics of Organizations: *Management. Organization Hierarchy. Environment.* Behavioral Aspects of Management Control: *Behavior of Participants. Incentives. Goal Congruence. Cooperation and Conflict. Top Management Sponsorship. Participation and Understanding. Focus on Line Managers.* The Management Control Process: *Steps in the Management Control Process. Management Control System Characteristics.* Responsibility Centers: *Expense Centers. Profit Centers. Transfer Prices. Investment Centers.* Responsibility Accounting: *An Example: Computer Costs.* Controllable Costs: *Contrast with Variable Costs. Converting Noncontrollable Costs to Controllable Costs. Reporting Noncontrollable Costs.*

Cases
Gillette Safety Razor Company, 690
Birch Paper Company, 695
South American Coffee Company, 698
Empire Glass Company, 701

21. Programming and Budgeting   **714**

Engineered Costs. Discretionary Costs. Committed Costs. Programming: *Zero-Base Review.* Uses of the Budget. Types of Budgets. The Operating Budget: *Program Budgets and Responsibility Budgets. Variable Budgets. Nonfinancial Objectives.* Preparing the Operating Budget: *Organization for Preparation of Budgets. Budget Timetable. Setting Budget Guidelines. Making the Sales Budget. Initial Preparation of Other Budget Components. Negotiation. Coordination and Review. Final Approval and Distribution. Variations in Practice. Revisions.* The Cash Budget. The Capital Expenditure Budget. Appendix: Some Forecasting Techniques.

Cases
Società Rigazio, 740
Mammoth Manufacturing Company, 744
Whiz Calculator Company, 749

22. Analyzing and Reporting Performance   **755**

Overview of the Analytical Process: *Structure of the Analysis.* Gross Margin Variance: *Selling Price and Sales Volume Variances. Mix Variance.* Production Cost Variances: *Direct Labor Variances. Direct Material Variances. Overhead Variances.* Other Variances. Complete Analysis: *Gross Margin Variances. Cost Variances.* Control Reports: *Types of Reports. Content of Control Reports. Criteria for Control Reports. Use of Control Reports.* The Control Process: *Identification. Investigation.* Summary of Cost Constructions.

INDEX AND SOURCES OF CASES

The cases published in this book are listed below in alphabetical order, together with their authors and the institution with which they were associated when they wrote them. These institutions are the copyright owners. Cases without identification were written by, or under the supervision of, the authors of this book and are copyrighted by the President and Fellows of Harvard College. No case may be reproduced, in whole or in part, without the written permission of the copyright owner.

PART I

Financial Accounting

CHAPTER 1

THE NATURE AND PURPOSE
OF ACCOUNTING

Most of the world's work is done through organizations, rather than by people working as individuals. An organization is a group of people who work together to accomplish one or more objectives. In doing its work, an organization uses resources—material, labor, and various types of services. In order to work effectively, the people in an organization need information about these resources and about the results achieved through using them. Parties outside the organization need similar information in order to make judgments about the organization. The system that provides this information is called accounting.

Organizations can be classified broadly as either profit oriented or nonprofit. As these names suggest, a dominant purpose of organizations in the former category is to earn a profit, while organizations in the latter category have other objectives, such as governing, providing health care, providing education, and so on. Of the employed persons in the United States approximately two thirds work in profit-oriented organizations and one third in nonprofit organizations. Although accounting is basically similar in both types of organizations, in this book we shall focus on profit-oriented organizations.

THE NEED FOR INFORMATION

In its specifics, the information that is needed about an organization differs greatly among organizations of various types, but viewed broadly there are common characteristics that relate to the information needs of most profit-oriented, i.e. business, organizations. We shall outline these general information needs and illustrate them by referring to the Morgan Ford Company, an automobile dealership.

3

The Morgan Ford Company seeks to earn a profit. It does this by selling new and used automobiles, and parts and accessories for them, and by providing repair service on automobiles. It is an organization of 52 people, headed by Mr. Carroll, its President.

It owns a building in which are located the showroom, the service shop, a storeroom for spare parts and accessories, and office space. It also owns a number of new automobiles and used automobiles, which it offers for sale; a stock of spare parts, accessories and supplies; and cash in the bank. These are examples of the resources which the company needs to have in order to conduct its business.

What information is needed about the resources used in this organization and the results achieved by their use? We can classify this information into three categories: (1) operating information, (2) management accounting information, and (3) financial accounting information. Each is described briefly below.

Operating Information

A considerable amount of information is required simply to conduct day-to-day operations. Employees must be paid exactly the amounts owed them, and the government requires that payroll records be maintained for each employee, showing amounts earned by them and paid to them, as well as various deductions. The sales force needs to know what automobiles are available for sale and the cost or the selling price, or both, of each of them. When an automobile is sold, a record must be made of that fact. The person in the stockroom needs to know what parts and accessories are on hand, and if the stock of a certain part becomes depleted, this fact needs to be known so that an additional quantity can be ordered. Amounts owed by the company's customers need to be known, and if a customer does not pay his bill on time, this fact needs to be known so that appropriate action can be taken.

The company needs to know the amounts it owes to others and when these amounts should be paid. The company needs to know how much money it has in the bank.

In a very small business, the owner or manager could conceivably carry much of this information in his head, but if several people are involved in the organization, and if the detailed information is at all complicated, written records are necessary. Even a one-person business, such as a barbershop, needs some type of written records.

Management Accounting

The president, the vice president in charge of automobile sales, the supervisor of the service shop and other managers of the Morgan Ford

Company do not have the time to examine the details of the operating information. Instead they rely on summaries of this information, and they use these summaries, together with other information, to carry out their management responsibilities. The functions for which they use this information can be categorized as control, coordination, and planning. The accounting information specifically intended for these purposes is called management accounting.[1]

CONTROL. In the Morgan Ford Company, most of the automobile sales are made by sales people, and most of the service work is done by mechanics. It is not the responsibility of Mr. Carroll and the other managers to do this work themselves; rather it is their responsibility to see to it that it is done, and done properly, by the employees of the organization. The process they use for this purpose is called control. Accounting information is used in the control process as a means of communication, of motivation, of attention-getting, and of appraisal.

As a means of *communication*, accounting reports can assist in informing employees about management's plans and policies and in general the types of action that management wishes the organization to take. As a means of *motivation*, accounting reports can induce members of the organization to act in a way that is consistent with the overall goals and objectives of the company. As a means of *attention-getting*, accounting information signals that problems exist that require investigation and possibly action. As a means of *appraisal*, accounting helps to show how well members of the organization have performed, and thus provides a basis for a salary increase, promotion, reassignment, corrective action of various kinds, or, in extreme cases, dismissal.

COORDINATION. The several parts of the organization must work together to achieve the organization's objectives, and this requires that the activities of each unit must be coordinated with activities of other units. The stockroom must have the parts that are needed to service automobiles. The new car manager cannot order more automobiles than the company has resources to finance. Accounting aids in this coordination process.

PLANNING. Planning is the process of deciding what action should be taken in the future. The area covered by one plan may be a tiny segment of the enterprise, or it may be the whole enterprise. Thus, a decision as to whether the price of one product should be increased 10 cents tomorrow is a plan, and so is a decision to merge the company with another company.

Some businesses have planning staffs whose full-time job is to assist in making plans. The planning function, however, is much broader than the

---

[1] Some persons prefer the term "managerial accounting" rather than "management accounting." The choice turns on a fine point of grammar and is of no practical consequence.

work done by these staffs; it is performed at all levels in the organization and in all organizations, whether or not they have separate planning staffs. When the service shop foreman decides the order in which automobiles will be repaired and which mechanic will work on each of them, he is engaged in planning in the same sense as, but on a smaller scale than, the president when the latter decides to build a new showroom.

One important form of planning is called budgeting. Budgeting is the process of planning the overall activity of the enterprise for a specified period of time, usually a year. An important objective of this process is to fit together the separate plans made for various segments of the enterprise so as to assure that these plans harmonize with one another and that the aggregate effect of all of them on the whole enterprise is satisfactory. For example, the budgeting process might reveal that the sales manager has planned a considerable increase in the sales of automobiles and that the service department manager has planned for a corresponding increase in service department work, but that the parts manager has not planned to order the additional parts that will be needed for this additional activity. In a very small business, top management may have a sufficient personal awareness of overall plans so that formal, written budgets are unnecessary, but a business of any considerable size is likely to be so complex that some systematic process of formulating and balancing the plans for the separate parts of the enterprise is essential.

Planning involves making decisions. Decisions are arrived at essentially by recognizing that a problem exists, identifying alternative ways of solving the problem, analyzing the consequences of each alternative, and comparing these consequences so as to decide which is best. Accounting information is useful especially in the analysis step of the decision-making process.

Financial Accounting

Another type of accounting information is intended both for managers and also for the use of parties external to the business, including shareholders, bankers and other creditors, government agencies, and the general public. Shareholders who have furnished capital to the Morgan Ford Company want information on how well the company is doing, so that if the management is not performing satisfactorily, they can initiate corrective action. If they should decide to sell their shares, they need information that helps them judge how much their investment is worth. A prospective buyer of these shares needs similar information in order to decide how much he is willing to pay. If the company wants to borrow money, the bank or other lender wants information that will show that the loan is sound, that is, that there is a high probability that it will be repaid when it falls due.

Only in rare instances can these outside parties insist that a business furnish information that is tailor-made to their specifications. In most cases they must accept the information that the business chooses to supply. They could not conceivably understand this information without knowing the ground rules that governed its preparation. Since the typical outsider uses accounting information from many different businesses, there is a clear need for having basic ground rules that apply to all businesses, both so that the information from one business can be compared with that of another and also to obviate the necessity of learning a separate set of ground rules for each business. These ground rules are the subject matter of financial accounting.

When an outside party reads information that has been prepared in accordance with these ground rules, it is meaningful to him, provided, of course, that he understands what the ground rules are. Without such rules, clear communication between a business and the outside world would be practically impossible.

> EXAMPLE: When a person familiar with accounting sees on an accounting report the item "Inventory at Fifo Cost or Market, $1,435,655," he understands that this refers to a certain category of property, and that the amount of this property has been measured according to certain prescribed rules; and he can rely on this understanding even though he has had no personal contact with the accountant who reported this information.

The ground rules of financial accounting therefore facilitate communication between a business and outside parties who need information about that business.

Definition of Accounting

All of the activities described above are related to accounting. More formally, accounting has been defined as follows:

> Accounting is the art of recording, classifying, and summarizing in a significant manner and in terms of money, transactions and events which are, in part at least, of a financial character, and interpreting the results thereof.[2]

FOCUS OF THE BOOK

Accounting can be approached from either of two directions: from the viewpoint of the accountant, or from the viewpoint of the user of accounting information. One approach emphasizes the concepts and techniques that are involved in collecting, summarizing, and reporting accounting information, while the other emphasizes what the user needs to know about accounting. The difference between these two approaches is only one of emphasis. The accountant needs to know how information

---

[2] APB *Statement No. 4*, paragraph 9.

is to be used because he should collect and report information in a form that is most helpful to those who make use of it. The user needs to know what the accountant does; otherwise he is unlikely to understand the real meaning of the information that is provided.

This book focuses on accounting from the viewpoint of the user. We shall not, however, discuss the uses of accounting information to any great extent until after we have described carefully what accounting information is.

Preconceptions about Accounting

The reader has already been exposed to a great deal of accounting information. The cash register receipt at the stores where he trades, the checks that he writes or (hopefully) that he receives, his bank statement, the bills which he is expected to pay, all these are parts of accounting systems. He reads in his newspaper about the profit of a company or of an industry, about dividends, about money being spent to build new buildings, and this information comes from accounting systems. Even before he begins a formal study of the subject, therefore, the reader has accumulated a number of ideas about accounting.

The trouble is that some of these ideas are likely to be incorrect. For example, it seems intuitively sensible that accounting should report what a business is "worth," but accounting does not in fact do this, or even attempt to do it. As another example, there is a general notion that the word "asset" refers to valuable things, good things to have; but the skill and ability of the chief executive of a company is not an asset in the accounting sense, even though it may be a principal determinant of the company's success.

Thus, as is the case with many other subjects, the student of accounting must be wary of his preconceptions. He will discover that accounting "as it really is" may be different in important respects from what he surmises it to be, or from what common sense tells him it should be. He will find that there are sound reasons for these differences, and it is important that he understand these reasons. In order to achieve such an understanding, he needs to know enough about accounting concepts and techniques to understand the nature and limitations of the information that they produce. He does not, however, need the detailed knowledge that the accountant must have.

Approach to Accounting

The approach to accounting taken here is something like that used by an airplane pilot in learning to use his instruments. The pilot needs to know the meaning of the message conveyed by each of his instruments;

that is, he needs to know such things as the fact that a clockwise movement of a certain arrow probably means one thing and that a counterclockwise movement probably means another thing, that the flashing of a red light probably means that a certain component is not functioning, that a certain sound in his earphones probably means that he is on course, and so on. The word "probably" is used because, for one reason or another, an instrument may not always give the reading that it is supposed to give; the pilot must realize this, and he must also understand something of the likelihood of, and the reasons for, these abnormalities. On the other hand, the pilot does not need to know how to design airplane instruments, how to construct them, how to check them for accuracy, how to maintain them, or how to repair them. Specialists are available for these important functions.

Similarly a person who is to make intelligent use of accounting information must understand what a given accounting figure probably means, what its limitations are, and the circumstances in which it may mean something different from the apparent "signal" that it gives. He does not, however, need to know how to design, construct, operate, or check on the accuracy of an accounting system. He can rely on accountants for these important functions.

Plan of the Book

Earlier, we described three types of accounting information: operating information, management accounting information, and financial accounting information. Since our viewpoint is that of the user, and particularly the management user, we shall not describe operating information in any great detail. We shall refer to it only as needed to explain the source, the raw material, from which financial accounting information and management accounting information are derived. The book is therefore divided into two approximately equal halves, one on financial accounting and the other on management accounting.

The discussion of financial accounting comes first because the structure of financial accounting underlies all accounting. This structure consists of a few basic principles and concepts, a set of relationships among the elements comprising the accounting system, a terminology, and a number of rules and guides for the application of the principles and concepts to specific situations. We shall describe the complete financial accounting structure, in a general way, in Chapters 2, 3 and 4, and we shall then go over the same ground again in more detail in Chapters 5 through 11. The uses of financial accounting information will be discussed in Chapters 12 and 13.

In the second half of the book, we discuss the nature and use of management accounting information. The management of a business can establish whatever ground rules it wishes for the accounting information collected for internal use. Thus, although the rules of financial accounting are applicable to all businesses, the rules of management accounting are tailor-made to meet the needs of the management of a specific business.

There is nevertheless a similarity in the management accounting of most businesses, for two reasons. First, there are obvious economies in using financial accounting information wherever possible for management accounting purposes, rather than devising two completely different systems for the two purposes; thus the rules of financial accounting have a great influence on management accounting. Second, there are principles of management accounting that have wide applicability, and these tend to shape the management accounting practices of a great many companies.

The terms "financial accounting" and "management accounting" are not precise descriptions of the activities they comprise. All accounting is *financial* in the sense that all accounting systems are in monetary terms, and *management* is responsible for the content of financial accounting reports. (This is the first of many problems in terminology that will be noted throughout this book. The reader is cautioned against drawing inferences from the labels alone; he must learn the concepts that the labels represent.)

THE FINANCIAL ACCOUNTING FRAMEWORK

Suppose you were asked to keep track of what was going on in a business so as to provide useful information for management. One way of carrying out such an assignment would be to write down a narrative of important events in a diary or in a log similar to that kept by the captain of a ship. After some experience with your log or diary, you would gradually develop a set of rules to guide your efforts. For example, since it would be impossible to write down every action of every person in the business, you would frame rules to guide you in choosing between those events that were important enough to record and those that should be omitted. Thus, if your business was a retail automobile dealership, you certainly would want a record of each car sold, but you might well decide not to make a record of every person who came into the showroom.

You would also find that your diary would be more valuable if you standardized certain terminology. People who studied it would then have a clearer understanding of what you meant. Furthermore, if you standardized terms and definitions of these terms, you could turn the job of keeping the diary over to someone else and have some assurance that this person's report of events would convey the same information that you would have conveyed had you been keeping the diary personally.

In devising these rules of keeping a diary, you would necessarily be somewhat arbitrary. There might be several ways of describing a certain event, all equally good; but in order to have a common basis of understanding, you would select just one of these for use in your record-keeping system. Thus, since the products handled by your automobile dealership could be called "vehicles," "autos," "cars," or "trucks," some of which are synonyms and others not, it would clearly be desirable to agree on a standard nomenclature.

All the foregoing considerations were actually involved in the development of the accounting process. Accounting has evolved over a period of several hundred years, and during this time certain rules and conventions have come to be accepted as useful. If you are to understand accounting reports—the end products of an accounting system—you must be familiar with the rules and conventions lying behind these reports.

Accounting as a Language

Accounting is often called "the language of business." In an important sense this is an apt phrase since accounting provides the principal formal means by which information about a business is communicated (although of course there are many other types of business communication). In any event, the task of learning accounting is essentially the same as the task of learning a new language.

This task is complicated by the fact that many of the words used in accounting mean almost, but not quite, the same thing as the identical words mean in everyday, nonaccounting usage. If you are an American learning French, you realize from the beginning that the words and the grammar in French are completely new to you and must therefore be learned carefully. The problem of learning accounting, however, is more like that of an American learning to speak English as it is spoken in Great Britain. Unless he is careful, the American will fail to recognize that words are used in Great Britain in a different sense from that used in America.

> EXAMPLE: The grain that Americans call "wheat" is called "corn" by the British, and the British use the word "maize" for the grain that Americans call "corn." To complicate the matter further, a grain grown in certain parts of America is called "maize," and it is almost, but not quite, like American corn. Unless they understand these differences in terminology, Americans and Englishmen will not communicate what they intend when talking with each other.

Moreover, certain terms used in accounting have different meanings in different circumstances, and the context must be understood in order to comprehend the meaning. The problem is similar to that of the word "ton." A ton is most commonly thought of as a measure of weight, 2,000 pounds. But a ton in certain circumstances may mean 2,240 pounds, which is called a long ton. A "six-ton truck" to some people means a truck that weighs 12,000 pounds fully loaded; to others it means the weight of the load alone. A measurement ton is not even a measure of weight; it is a measure of volume, 40 cubic feet. The tonnage of a ship may be calculated according to any of several methods, but often refers to the weight of the sea water that the ship displaces.

Perhaps the greatest difficulty that a beginning student of accounting encounters is that of distinguishing between the accounting meaning of certain terms and the meaning that he has attached to these terms in their nonaccounting, everyday usage.

> EXAMPLE: An amount labeled "net worth" appears on many accounting reports. The commonsense interpretation is that this amount refers to what something is "worth"—what its value is—but such an interpretation is incorrect. For the correct meaning, see p. 43.

As is the case with language, accounting has many dialects. There are differences in terminology and practice among industries and among companies within industries. In this introductory treatment, we shall not attempt even to list all these differences, although the principal ones will be mentioned.

Accounting also resembles a language in that some of its rules are definite, whereas others are not; and there are differences of opinion among accountants as to how a given event should be recorded, just as there are differences of opinion among grammarians as to many matters of sentence structure, punctuation, and choice of words. Nevertheless, there are many practices that are clearly "poor English," and there are also many practices that are definitely "poor accounting." In these chapters, therefore, an attempt is made to describe the elements of "good accounting" and to indicate areas in which there are differences of opinion as to what constitutes good practice.

Finally, languages evolve and change in response to the changing needs of society, and so does accounting. The rules described here are currently in use, but some of them will probably be modified to meet the changing needs of business.

Nature of Principles

The rules and conventions of accounting are commonly referred to as "principles." The word "principle" is here used to mean "a general law or rule adopted or professed as a guide to action; a settled ground or basis of conduct or practice."[3] Note that this definition describes a principle as a *general* law or rule that is to be used as a *guide* to action. This means that

---

[3] *Accounting Terminology Bulletin No. 1*, p. 9. (See also, footnote 4, p. 15.)

accounting principles do not prescribe exactly how each detailed event occurring in a business should be recorded. Consequently, there are a great many matters in accounting practice that differ from one company to another. In part, these differences are inevitable, because a single detailed set of rules could not conceivably apply to every company. In part, the differences reflect the fact that accountants have considerable latitude within the "generally accepted accounting principles" in which to express their own ideas as to the best way of recording and reporting a specific event.

Readers should realize, therefore, that they cannot know the precise meaning of many of the items on an accounting report unless they know which of several equally acceptable possibilities has been selected by the person who prepared the report. The meaning intended in a specific situation requires knowledge of the context.

Criteria

Accounting principles are man-made. Unlike the principles of physics, chemistry, and the other natural sciences, accounting principles were not deduced from basic axioms, nor is their validity verifiable by observation and experiment. Instead, they have evolved. The process of evolution is essentially as follows: a problem is recognized; someone works out what he thinks is a good solution to this problem; if other people agree that this is a good solution, its use gradually becomes widespread, and then it becomes an accounting principle. Moreover, some hitherto accepted principles fall from favor with the passage of time. This evolutionary process is going on constantly; accounting principles are not "eternal verities."

The general acceptance of an accounting principle or practice usually depends on how well it meets three criteria: relevance, objectivity, and feasibility. A principle is *relevant* to the extent that it results in information that is meaningful and useful to those who need to know something about a certain business. A principle is *objective* to the extent that the information is not influenced by the personal bias or judgment of those who furnish it. Objectivity connotes reliability, trustworthiness. It also connotes verifiability, which means that there is some way of ascertaining the correctness of the information reported. A principle is *feasible* to the extent that it can be implemented without undue complexity or cost.

We shall illustrate and expand on the significance of these criteria in connection with the discussion of the principles themselves. At this point it is sufficient to point out that these criteria often conflict with one another. The most relevant solution is likely to be the least objective and the least feasible.

> EXAMPLE: The development of a new product may have a significant effect on a company's real value—Xerography and Polaroid cameras being spectacular recent examples. Information about the value of new

products is most useful to the investor. It is indeed relevant. But the best estimate of the value of a new product is likely to be that made by management, and this is a highly subjective estimate; that is, some persons would make extremely optimistic estimates, whereas others would be equally extreme on the conservative side. Furthermore, many managements have a natural tendency to make the figures look as good as possible. Accounting therefore does not attempt to record such values. It sacrifices relevance in the interests of objectivity.

The measure of the value of the owners' interest in the Xerox Corporation obtained from the stock market quotations (i.e., multiplying the price per share of stock times the number of shares outstanding) is a much more accurate reflection of the true value than the amount at which this item appears in the corporation's accounting records. As of December 31, 1973, the marketplace gave this value as $9.7 billion; the accounting records gave it as $1.5 billion. The difference does not indicate that there is an error in the accounting records. It merely illustrates the fact that accounting does not, and does not attempt to, report market values.

In developing new principles, the essential problem is to strike the right balance between relevance on the one hand and objectivity and feasibility on the other. Failure to appreciate this problem often leads to unwarranted criticism of accounting principles. It is easy to criticize accounting on the grounds that accounting information is not as relevant as it might be; but the critic often overlooks the fact that proposals to increase relevance almost always involve a sacrifice of objectivity and feasibility. On balance, such a sacrifice may not be worthwhile.

Source of Accounting Principles

The foundation of accounting consists of a set of what are called "generally accepted accounting principles." Currently, these principles are established by the Financial Accounting Standards Board (FASB) which was created in 1973. The FASB consists of seven leading accountants who work full time on developing new or modified principles. The Board is supported by a professional staff, which does research and prepares a discussion memorandum on each problem that the Board addresses. The Board acts only after interested parties have been given an opportunity to suggest solutions to problems and to comment on proposed pronouncements. The FASB is a nongovernmental organization financed by contributions from business firms and from the accounting profession.

The FASB superseded the Accounting Principles Board (APB) of the American Institute of Certified Public Accountants (AICPA). The APB had the same functions as the FASB, but its members did not devote full time to Board activities. In one of its first actions, the FASB adopted the principles that had been developed by the Accounting Principles Board, and published as its *Opinions*. Thus, in this description of accounting we shall refer to *Opinions* of the Accounting Principles Board as being authoritative, and we shall refer to them as Financial Accounting Standards Board pronouncements, even though they were made by a predecessor organization.[4]

Companies are not legally required to adhere to the generally accepted accounting principles (GAAP) established by the Financial Accounting Standards Board. As a practical matter, however, there are strong pressures for them to do so. This is because the accounting reports of most companies of any substantial size are audited—that is, examined—by certified public accountants (CPAs) who are members of the AICPA. Although the AICPA does not require its members to force companies to adhere to GAAP as promulgated by the Financial Accounting Standards Board, it does require that if the CPA finds that the company has used a different principle, the difference must be called to public attention. Since companies usually do not like to go counter to the FASB— even though they may feel strongly that the FASB principle is not appropriate in their particular situation—they almost always conform to the FASB pronouncements.

Another source of pressure to conform to GAAP is the U.S. Securities and Exchange Commission (SEC). This agency exists to protect the interests of investors, and it has jurisdiction over nearly all corporations whose securities are traded in interstate commerce. It requires these companies to file accounting reports, and these reports must be prepared in accordance with GAAP. In its *Regulation S–X* and its *Accounting Series Releases*, the SEC spells out acceptable accounting principles in more detail than, but generally consistent with, the pronouncements of the FASB.

The American Accounting Association also publishes statements of accounting principles, but these are to be regarded as normative rather than descriptive; that is, they state what accounting principles *should be*, rather than what they *are*. Thus, they are not necessarily a guide to current practice.

Various regulatory bodies also prescribe accounting rules for the companies they regulate. Among those subjected to such rules are banks and other financial institutions, insurance companies, railroads, airlines,

---

[4] Because these earlier statements have not yet been codified in a publication of the Financial Accounting Standards Board, we must cite the pronouncements of the earlier bodies. They are referred to here as *Accounting Terminology Bulletins*, *Accounting Research Bulletins*, *APB Opinions* and *APB Statements*. (APB Statements have not been officially approved, and are in the nature of recommendations or suggestions, rather than mandates.) All of these documents are brought together in the book *APB Accounting Principles*, published in 1973 by Commerce Clearing House, Inc., for the American Institute of Certified Public Accountants.

pipelines, radio and television companies, and electric and gas companies. These rules are not necessarily consistent with the principles of the Financial Accounting Standards Board, although there is a tendency in recent years to change the accounting rules of regulatory agencies so that they do conform.

> EXAMPLE: The Baltimore & Ohio Railroad reported that in 1973 its net income, measured in accordance with generally accepted accounting principles, was $31.8 million. Measured in accordance with rules prescribed by the Interstate Commerce Commission, its net income was $23.6 million.

The authority of the FASB and other agencies exists, of course, only in the United States of America. Accounting principles in other countries differ in some respects from American GAAP, but there is a basic similarity throughout the world, including the USSR. The notable exception is the Chinese Peoples Republic, whose principles differ in some significant respects. In 1973, efforts were begun to codify a set of accounting principles that would apply internationally.

The most convenient source of the various accounting practices used by American companies is *Accounting Trends and Techniques* published annually by the American Institute of CPAs. It summarizes the practices of 600 companies. Since these are relatively large companies, the summaries do not necessarily reflect the practices of all companies, large and small. This qualification should be kept in mind when data from this report are given in this text.

FINANCIAL STATEMENTS

The end product of the financial accounting process is a set of reports which are called financial statements. GAAP require that three such reports be prepared: (1) a balance sheet, (2) an income statement, and (3) a statement of changes in financial position. As we examine the details of the accounting process, it is important that the reader keep in mind the objective toward which the process is aimed, namely the preparation of financial statements.

Most reports, in any field, can be classified into one of two categories called, respectively, (1) reports of *stocks* or *status* and (2) reports of *flow.* The amount of water in a reservoir at a given moment of time is a measure of stock, whereas the amount of water that moves through the reservoir in a day or other time period is a measure of flow. Reports of stocks are always as of a specified instant in time; reports of flow always cover a specified period of time. Reports of stocks are like snapshots; reports of flows are more like motion pictures. One of the accounting reports, the balance sheet, is a report of stocks. It shows information about the resources of a business at a specified moment of time. The other two reports, the income statement and the statement of changes in financial position, are reports of flow. They report activities of the business for a period of time, such as a month or a year.

In the next two chapters we shall describe the balance sheet and income statement. We shall defer a description of the statement of changes in financial position until Chapter 11. We do this because this report is derived by rearranging data that were originally collected for the other two reports, and it is inappropriate to discuss the statement of changes in financial position until the balance sheet and income statement have been thoroughly explained.

SUMMARY

A business has three types of accounting information: (1) operating information, which has to do with the details of operations; (2) management accounting information, which is used internally for control, coordination and planning; and (3) financial accounting information, which is used both by management and by external accounting parties.

Financial accounting is governed by ground rules which are referred to as generally accepted accounting principles. These ground rules may be different than the student believes them to be, based on his previous exposure to accounting information. They are prescribed by the Financial Accounting Standards Board, and attempt to strike the optimum balance between the criterion of relevance on the one hand and the criteria of relevance and feasibility on the other hand.

The end products of the financial accounting process are three financial statements: the balance sheet, the income statement, and the statement of changes in financial condition. The balance sheet is a report as of a moment of time, and the other two statements summarize flows over a period of time.

CASES

CASE 1–1. CONAN COMPANY

The Conan Company manufactured an inexpensive grade of men's clothing which it sold through house-to-house salesmen. A salesman took the measurements of the customer and entered them on the order blank, which the company used as a cutting order. Since the company found from experience that the measurements were usually of approximately regular sizes, it cut the garments from regular-sized patterns with only slight changes. The wool worsted goods used by the Conan Company cost approximately $4.50 per yard.

In order to insure very quick delivery the company made out cutting tickets for each garment as fast as orders were received and distributed them to the cutters together with a record of the standard yardage allowance for cutting that size of that style garment. It was expected that cutters would try to cut garments out of the least amount of cloth possible in order to keep down costs. They were, of course, also expected to cut as many garments as possible in a day. Each cutter earned $2.70 per hour and worked eight hours per day.

A careful record was kept of the garments cut each day. A transcript of the cutting record for one day is shown in Exhibit 1[1] given on page 19. Yardage figures are given to the hundreth of a yard for ease in computation.

Questions

1. What conclusions can you draw from a cross-classification of yardage lost or saved according to cutters and styles? (By cross-classification is meant an orderly arrangement of the figures, grouped in column and row according to cutter, or style, or some other factor.) Who is apparently the fastest cutter? The most careful cutter? The best cutter?

---

[1] The sample used in this case is too small to be adequate. A small sample is used, however, to bring out certain points without requiring the reader to spend time on mere mechanical handling of a large number of figures. For purposes of class discussion, you may assume that this record is representative.

Exhibit 1

CUTTING RECORD

Cutting Ticket Number	Cutter	Style	Cloth	Color	Size	Yards Saved	Yards Lost
1	A	102	1073	Grey	37	...	0.10
2	B	101	1116	Blue	39	...	0.02
3	C	104	1178	Blue	37	...	0.10
4	D	103	1241	Brown	38	0.04	...
5	A	102	1073	Brown	40	...	0.14
6	B	101	1116	Brown	38	0.04	...
7	C	104	1178	Blue	38	...	0.06
8	A	103	1241	Brown	36	0.08	...
9	D	103	1241	Grey	35	0.10	...
10	B	104	1178	Grey	37	0.06	...
11	C	101	1116	Blue	36	...	0.06
12	A	101	1116	Grey	40	0.02	...
13	B	104	1178	Brown	37	0.00	0.00
14	D	104	1178	Blue	39	0.06	...
15	C	101	1116	Blue	36	...	0.08
16	A	103	1241	Brown	38	0.04	...
17	C	102	1073	Brown	40	...	0.18
18	D	103	1241	Blue	42	0.02	...
19	B	103	1241	Grey	36	...	0.04
20	A	102	1073	Brown	37	...	0.08
21	C	102	1073	Grey	37	...	0.16
22	B	102	1073	Brown	36	...	0.10
23	C	103	1241	Brown	38	0.02	...
24	A	104	1178	Grey	38	0.06	...
25	D	101	1116	Brown	36	0.04	...
26	B	104	1178	Brown	37	0.08	...
27	C	104	1178	Blue	39	0.02	...
28	A	101	1116	Grey	37	...	0.06
29	D	101	1116	Blue	42	0.08	...
30	B	104	1178	Grey	38	0.04	...
31	C	103	1241	Blue	37	...	0.12
32	A	103	1241	Grey	40	...	0.02
33	B	103	1241	Blue	38	0.02	...
34	C	101	1116	Blue	36	...	0.04
35	D	102	1073	Brown	39	...	0.06
36	B	101	1116	Grey	35	0.06	...
37	C	104	1178	Blue	44	...	0.06
38	A	102	1073	Grey	37	...	0.18
39	D	103	1241	Brown	40	0.02	...
40	C	103	1241	Brown	38	...	0.04

2. Comment on the reliability and adequacy of the standards used to measure performance.
3. Should the most careful cutter specialize on the style for which losses are most frequent?
4. Before taking any action, what additional information would be needed?

CASE 1–2. CHARLES MAVIOLI

In the fall of 1974, Charles Mavioli, a general carpenter living in one of the suburbs, decided to invest a part of his savings in wood-working machinery and in a building which had formerly been used as a small garage. His plan for some time had been to prepare himself for contracting work of a modest sort, including small-home construction. He had always wanted to build low-priced dwellings "all on his own." Such an activity would be limited, he knew, by his ability to carry his share of the total investment load necessary for such an undertaking. So far in his career, Mavioli had been extraordinarily successful as a general carpenter, working at a wide variety of jobs. At times he had been hired as "boss carpenter" on large and important constructions. For this kind of work he had received a very good salary, a large part of which he and his wife had been able to save against the time when he could have a business of his own.

By October 1974, Mavioli had his shop completely fitted and had hired two mill hands and a shop mechanic to help him in his new undertaking. As a "fill-in" between big jobs, it was his expectation to be able to provide fairly uniform employment for these people through making window and door frames, kitchen cabinets, and similar construction parts both for stock and on order.

In that same month, in connection with a substantial order for cabinets requiring six to eight weeks of shop activity, Mavioli talked with the credit officer of his bank about his need for some temporary financial assistance in the purchase of necessary materials and supplies. This assistance the bank was glad to extend to him. In granting the loan, however, the credit officer suggested that Mavioli would now need to spend more time and money on financial and operating records than had been necessary when his work was almost entirely a matter of personal services. "More paper work will be a painful necessity from now on," he said, "not only to make it easier for you to do a good job in managing your new business, but also in making your tax returns and in later dealings with this or other banks." The banker suggested that Mavioli talk with some qualified person about this problem. Mavioli said that he had a friend who was controller of a manufacturing business, and that he was sure this friend would give him some practical suggestions.

A week or so after the conference at the bank, Mavioli had a long and satisfactory talk with his friend about his need for additional records. At the outset he emphasized that up to this point he had gotten along pretty well with the stubs of his checkbook, plus some odds and ends of memoranda which he and his wife had been careful to keep for reference purposes. The controller agreed that it is easy to overdo "this business of keeping records," and said that in his opinion it would be best for them to make a small start and feel their way along for a few months before attempting anything that would call for much work.

He suggested that, as a starter, Mavioli and his wife might well spend an evening drawing up a list of the properties used in operating their shop and contracting business, and a corresponding list of the debts which had grown out of this business, together with the amounts of money that Mavioli had invested in it. The controller explained that the list of "properties used" should be confined to things having a money value in this particular business. "With these two lists," he said, "we can draw up a beginning financial statement of your assets and liabilities, which should be helpful in talking over your need for figures." To this he added: "Generally speaking, the problem of useful and understandable accounting information is built around this statement, and the job is to keep such a statement (or its supporting records) more or less continuously adjusted to what takes place in the affairs of the business it represents, with enough supplementary facts about resulting changes to help the owner be a better manager than would be possible without such tools to help him."

The controller assured Mavioli that he did not believe the cost of keeping the necessary records would be a very important consideration. He pointed out that he knew of experts in accounting procedures who specialized in making periodic visits to small concerns such as Mavioli's for the very purpose of relieving their clients of much of the clerical burden of keeping operating records. But he said it would nevertheless be necessary for Mavioli or his wife to keep a memorandum record or daybook of transactions practically as they occurred. The controller suggested that as time went on Mavioli might want to give some attention to the accepted ways of keeping accounting records; but, he said, there was no need for Mavioli to be apprehensive about the cost of supplying his simple requirements.

Questions

1. Why did Mavioli need any records? What did he need?
2. See what you can do to draw up a list of Mavioli's assets and liabilities, as the controller suggested, making any assumptions you consider useful. How should Mavioli go about putting a value on his assets?

3. Among the changes in the assets, liabilities, and proprietary claims of a business which the controller spoke of as the subject matter of accounting is an important variety growing out of "profit and loss" or "trading" operations. What would be the general construction of a profit and loss analysis for Mavioli's new business? How frequently would he wish to provide himself with such an analysis?

4. What other kinds of changes in assets, liabilities, and proprietary claims will need careful recording and reporting if Mavioli is to keep in control of his job as manager?

CHAPTER 2

BASIC ACCOUNTING CONCEPTS: THE BALANCE SHEET

In this chapter we describe six of the basic concepts from which principles of accounting are derived. We describe, in a preliminary way, the nature of the balance sheet and the principal categories of items that appear on the balance sheet. Finally, we show how amounts that appear on the balance sheet are changed to reflect events that affect business resources.

BASIC CONCEPTS

The principles of accounting are built on a foundation of a few basic concepts. They are so basic that most accountants do not consciously think of them; they are regarded as being self-evident, obvious, to be taken for granted. Nonaccountants will not find these concepts to be self-evident, however. Accounting could be constructed on a foundation of quite different concepts, and indeed some accounting theorists argue that certain of the present concepts are wrong and should be changed. In order to understand accounting as it now exists, however, one must understand what the underlying concepts currently are; different concepts would lead to different accounting results. As is the case with a language, one can criticize the way certain words are spelled (e.g., "dough," "bough," "cough"), but the fact remains that the words *are* spelled in a certain way. In order to use the language effectively, a person must understand what the rules actually are.

The Financial Accounting Standards Board has not published a list of basic concepts, and indeed no authoritative list exists. Various authors and committees have published lists that range in length from four to about

23

a dozen items.¹ Furthermore, other names are used for the notions that are here labelled "concepts:" postulates, basic assumptions, basic features, underlying principles, fundamentals or conventions. These differences in number and terminology do not reflect basic disagreement as to what the foundations of accounting are, but rather differences in personal judgments as to which ideas are really basic, which should be taken for granted, which should be stated separately rather than being subsumed under another concept, and so on. In this book, we shall use ten concepts, as follows:

1. Money measurement	6. Conservatism
2. Entity	7. Realization
3. Going concern	8. Matching
4. Cost	9. Consistency
5. Dual aspect	10. Materiality

The first six of these are discussed below, and the other four are discussed in Chapter 3.

1. The Money Measurement Concept

In financial accounting, a record is made only of those facts that can be expressed in monetary terms. The advantage of expressing facts in monetary terms is that money provides a common denominator by means of which heterogeneous facts about a business can be expressed as numbers that can be added and subtracted.

> EXAMPLE: Although it may be a fact that a business owns $10,000 of cash, 6,000 pounds of raw material, six trucks, 10,000 square feet of building space, and so on, these amounts cannot be added together to produce a meaningful total of what the business owns. Expressing these items in monetary terms—$10,000 of cash, $5,000 of raw material, $20,000 of trucks, and $100,000 of buildings—makes such an addition possible.

This concept imposes a severe limitation on the scope of an accounting report. Accounting does not record the state of the president's health; it does not record the fact that the sales manager is not on speaking terms with the production manager; it does not report that a strike is beginning; and it does not reveal that a competitor has placed a better product on the market. Accounting therefore does not give a complete account of the happenings in a business or an accurate picture of the condition of the business. It follows, then, that the reader of an accounting report should

---

¹ *A Statement of Basic Accounting Theory* (American Accounting Association, 1965), lists four "basic standards" and five "guidelines."
APB *Statement No. 4* lists 12 "basic features."

not expect to find therein all, or perhaps even the most important, facts about a business.

Money is expressed in terms of its value at the time an event is recorded in the accounts. Subsequent changes in the purchasing power of money do not affect this amount. Thus, material purchased in 1974 for $10,000 and land purchased in 1954 for $10,000 are both listed in the 1974 accounting records at $10,000, although the purchasing power of the dollar in 1974 was only about 50 percent of what it was in 1954. It is sometimes said that accounting assumes that money is an unvarying yardstick of value, but this statement is not quite accurate. Accountants know full well that the purchasing power of the dollar does change; they do not, however, attempt to reflect such changes in the accounts.

2. The Entity Concept

Accounts are kept for business entities, as distinguished from the persons who are associated with these entities. In recording events in accounting, the important question is, How do these events affect the business? not, How do they affect the persons who own, operate, or otherwise are associated with the business? When the owner takes cash out of his business, for example, the accounting records show that the business has less cash than previously, even though the real effect of this event on the owner himself may have been negligible. Although he has taken cash out of his business "pocket" and put it into his personal "pocket," it remains his cash.

It is sometimes difficult to define with precision the business entity for which a set of accounts is kept. Consider the case of a married couple who run a small unincorporated retail store. In *law* there is no distinction between the financial affairs of the store and those of the people who own it; a creditor of the store can sue and, if successful, collect from the owners' personal resources as well as from the resources of the business. In *accounting*, by contrast, a set of accounts is kept for the store as a separate business entity, and the events reflected in these accounts must be those of the store; the nonbusiness events that affect the couple must not be included in them. In accounting, the *business* owns the resources of the store, even though the resources are legally owned by the couple. In accounting, debts owed by the *business* are kept separate from personal debts owed by the couple. The expenses of operating the store are kept separate from the couple's personal expenses for food, clothing, shelter and the like.

The necessity for making such a distinction between the business entity and its owners can create problems. Suppose, for example, that the couple lives on the business premises. How much of the rent, the electric light bill, and the property taxes of these premises are properly part of the expenses of the business, and how much are personal expenses of the family? Because of questions like these, the distinction between the business entity and outside interests is a difficult one to make in practice in those businesses in which there is a close relationship between the business and the people who own it.

In the case of a corporation, the distinction is often quite easily made. A corporation is a legal entity separate from the persons who own it, and the accounts of many corporations correspond exactly to the scope of the legal entity. There may be complications, however. In the case of a group of legally separate corporations that are related to one another by stockholdings, the whole group may be treated as a single business entity for reporting purposes, giving rise to what are called "consolidated" accounting statements. Conversely, within a single corporation, a separate set of accounts may be maintained for each of the principal divisions of the corporation, especially when they are physically separated from the home office.

One reason for making a distinction between the business entity and the outside world is the fact that an important purpose of financial accounting is to provide the basis for reporting on stewardship. The managers of a business are entrusted with funds supplied by owners, banks, and others. Management is responsible for the wise use of these funds, and financial accounting reports are in part designed to show how well this responsibility, or stewardship, has been discharged.

An entity is any organization or activity for which accounting reports are prepared. Although our focus in this book is on business companies, accounting entities include governments, churches, universities, and other nonprofit organizations.

One entity may be part of a larger entity. Thus, a set of accounts may be maintained for an individual elementary school, another set for the whole school district, and still another set for all the schools in a state. There even exists a set of accounts, called the national income accounts, for the entire economic activity of the United States. In general, detailed accounting records are maintained for the lowest entity in the hierarchy, and reports for higher levels are prepared by summarizing the detailed data for the several entities of which the aggregate consists.

3.   The Going-Concern Concept

Unless there is good evidence to the contrary, accounting assumes that the business will continue to operate for an indefinitely long period in the future. The significance of this assumption can be indicated by contrasting it with a possible alternative, namely, that the business is about to be liquidated or sold. Under the latter assumption, accounting would attempt to measure at all times what the business is currently worth to a buyer; but under the going-concern concept there is no need to do this, and it is in fact not done. Instead, a business is viewed as a mechanism for creating values, and its success is measured by the difference between the value of its outputs (i.e., sales of goods and services) and the *cost* of the resources used in creating those outputs. Resources which have been acquired but not yet used in creating outputs are shown on the accounting records, not at their current value to an outside buyer, but rather at their cost. Their current resale value is irrelevant, since it is assumed that they will not be sold as such, but rather that they will be used in the creation of future output values.

> EXAMPLE: At any given moment (say December 31, 1974), a shoe manufacturing company has shoes in various stages of the manufacturing process. If the business were liquidated at that moment, these partially completed shoes might well have little if any value. Accounting does not attempt to value these shoes at what they are currently worth. Instead, accounting assumes that the manufacturing process will be carried through to completion, and that the amount which the partially completed shoes could be sold for if the company were liquidated at that moment is therefore irrelevant.

If, however, the accountant has good reason to believe that the business, or some part of it, is going to be liquidated, then the resources would be reported at their liquidation value. Such circumstances are uncommon.

4. The Cost Concept

The resources that a business owns are called its *assets*. They consist of money, land, buildings, machinery and other property and property rights, as will be described in a subsequent section. A fundamental concept of accounting, closely related to the going-concern concept, is that an asset is ordinarily entered on the accounting records at the price paid to acquire it—that is, at its cost—and that this cost is the basis for all subsequent accounting for the asset.

Since, for a variety of reasons, the real worth of an asset may change with the passage of time, the accounting measurement of assets does not necessarily—indeed, does not ordinarily—reflect what assets are worth, except at the moment they are acquired. There is therefore a considerable difference between the accounting concept of cost and the everyday, nonaccounting concept of value. In ordinary usage, "value" means what something is currently worth.

> EXAMPLE: If a business buys a plot of land, paying $5,000 for it, this asset would be recorded in the accounts of the business at the amount of $5,000. Subsequent changes in the market value of this land would ordi-

narily not be recorded in the accounts. If a year later the land could be sold for $10,000, or if it could be sold for only $2,000, no change would ordinarily be made in the accounting records to reflect this fact. (The word "ordinarily" is used since there are some situations in which accounting records are changed to reflect changes in market value; these will be described subsequently.)

Thus, the amounts at which assets are listed in the accounts of a company do *not* indicate what the assets could be sold for. One of the most common mistakes made by uninformed persons reading accounting reports is that of believing that there is a close correspondence between the amount at which an asset appears on these reports and the actual value of the asset.

Such a correspondence does exist for what are called *monetary assets*. These are assets which are either money itself or which can be converted into money at an amount that can be ascertained with reasonable certainty, such as securities that are traded on a securities market. For other assets, however, any correspondence between the accounted amount and the real worth of the item is a matter of happenstance. In general, it is safe to say that the longer an asset has been owned by a company, the less likely it is that the amount at which it appears on the accounting records corresponds to its current market value.

The cost concept does not mean that all assets remain on the accounting records at their original purchase price for as long as the company owns them. The figure for an asset that has a long, but nevertheless limited, life is systematically reduced over that life by the process called *depreciation*, as discussed in more detail in Chapter 7. The purpose of the depreciation process is systematically to remove the *cost* of the asset from the accounts and to show it as a cost of operations; depreciation has no necessary relationship to changes in market value or in the real worth of the asset to the company.

It follows from the cost concept that if the company pays *nothing* for an item it acquires, this item will usually *not* appear on the accounting records as an asset. Thus, the knowledge and skill that is built up as the business operates, the teamwork that grows up within the organization, a favorable location that becomes of increasing importance as time goes on, a good reputation with its customers—none of these appears as an asset in the accounts of the company.

On some accounting reports the term "goodwill" appears. Reasoning from everyday definition of this word, you may conclude that it represents the accountant's appraisal of what the company's name and reputation are worth. This is not so. Goodwill appears in the accounts of the company only when the company has *purchased* some intangible and valuable property right. A common case is when one company buys another company and pays more than the fair value of its tangible assets.

The amount by which the purchase price exceeds the value of the tangible assets may be called goodwill, representing the value of the name, the reputation, the location, or other intangible possessions of the purchased company. Unless the business has actually purchased such intangibles, however, no item for "goodwill" is shown in the accounts. If the item does appear, it is shown initially at the purchase price, even though the management may believe that its real value is considerably higher.

It also follows from the cost concept that an event may affect the true value of a business without having any effect on the accounting records. To take an extreme case, suppose that several key executives are killed in a plane accident. To the extent than "an organization is but the lengthened shadow of a man," the real value of the company will change immediately, and this will be reflected in the market price of the company's stock, which reflects investors' appraisal of value. The accounting records, however, will not be affected by this event.

To emphasize the distinction between the accounting concept and the ordinary meaning of worth, the term "book value" is used for the amounts as shown in the accounting records and the term "market value" for the actual value of the asset as reflected in the market place.

RATIONALE FOR THE COST CONCEPT. The cost concept provides an excellent illustration of the problem of applying the three basic criteria discussed in Chapter 1: relevance, objectivity, and feasibility. If the *only* criterion were relevance, then the cost concept would not be defensible. Clearly, investors and others are more interested in what the business is actually worth today rather than what the assets cost originally.

But who knows what a business is worth today? The fact is that any estimate of current value is just that—an estimate—and informed people will disagree on what is the right estimate. (For illustrations, see the judgments about companies that are reported in the financial press. On the same day, some people will say that the stock of a given company is overpriced and others will say that it is underpriced.) Furthermore, accounting reports are prepared by the management of a business, and if they contained estimates of what the business is actually worth, these would be management's estimates. It is quite possible that such estimates would be biased.

The cost concept, by contrast, provides a relatively objective foundation for accounting. It is not *purely* objective, for, as we shall see, judgments are necessary in applying it. It is much more objective, however, than the alternative of attempting to estimate current values. Essentially, readers of an accounting report must recognize that it is based on the cost concept, and they must arrive at their own estimate of current value, partly by analyzing the information in the report and partly by using nonaccounting information.

Furthermore, a "market value" or "current worth" concept would be difficult to apply, because it would require that the accountant attempt to keep track of the ups and downs of market prices. The cost concept leads to a system that is much more feasible.

In summary, adherence to the cost concept indicates a willingness on the part of those who developed accounting principles to sacrifice some degree of relevance in exchange for greater objectivity and greater feasibility.

5.   The Dual–Aspect Concept

As stated above, the resources owned by a business are called "assets." The claims of various parties against these assets are called "equities." There are two types of equities: (1) *liabilities*, which are the claims of creditors, i.e., everyone other than the owners of the business; and (2) *owners' equity* (or "capital," or "proprietorship"), which is the claim of the owners of the business. Since all of the assets of a business are claimed by someone (either by the owners or by some outside party) and since the total of these claims cannot exceed the amount of assets to be claimed, it follows that

$$\text{Assets} = \text{Equities.}$$

This is the fundamental equation, and, as we shall see, all accounting procedures are derived from it.

Accounting systems are set up in such a way that a record is made of *two aspects* of each event that affects these records, and in essence these aspects are changes in assets and changes in equities. Because of the two different types of equities, the equation is also often expressed as

$$\text{Assets} = \text{Liabilities} + \text{Owners' Equity.}$$

Suppose that Mr. Jones starts a business and that his first act is to open a bank account in which he deposits $10,000 of his own money. The dual aspect of this action is that the business now has an asset, cash, of $10,000, and Mr. Jones, the owner,[2] has a claim against this asset, also of $10,000, or

$$\text{Assets (Cash), \$10,000} = \text{Equities (Owner's), \$10,000.}$$

If the business borrowed $5,000 from a bank, the accounting records would show an increase in cash, making the amount $15,000, and a new claim against this cash by the bank in the amount of $5,000. At this point the accounting records of the business would show the following:

Cash...................	$15,000	Owed to bank............	$ 5,000
		Owner's equity............	10,000
Total Assets........	$15,000	Total equities.......	$15,000

---

[2] Recall from the entity concept that the accounts of the business are kept separate from those of Mr. Jones as an individual.

Every event that is recorded in the accounts affects at least two items; there is no conceivable way of making only a single change in the accounts. Accounting is therefore properly called a *double-entry system.*

An accounting system conceivably could be set up with some concept other than the one stated here. As a matter of fact, there is a system called *"single-entry" accounting* that records only one aspect of a transaction, very much like the record maintained in a ship's log or a diary. However, as will become apparent in later chapters, there are many advantages, both mechanical and conceptual, in the dual-aspect concept, and this is so universally accepted that no further mention will be made of any other possibility.

6. Conservatism

The conservatism concept means that when the accountant has a reasonable choice as to how a given event should be recorded, he ordinarily chooses the alternative which results in a lower, rather than higher, asset amount, or owners' equity amount. This concept is often stated as follows: "Anticipate no profit, and provide for all possible losses." It is especially important as a modifier of the cost concept. To illustrate, inventories (material held for sale, supplies, and so forth) are ordinarily reported, not at their cost, which is what one would expect in accordance with the cost concept, but rather at the *lower* of their cost or their current replacement value. The conservatism concept affects principally the category of assets called "current assets" (see page 37). It is ordinarily not applied to noncurrent assets.

The conservatism concept is applied much less strongly now than was the case a few decades ago when it was a common practice to report some assets at far less than either their cost or their current market value. Nevertheless, the concept still has an important influence on accounting. Many informed persons would say that this concept is illogical and that the accountant should attempt to report the figures either consistently on the basis of cost or consistently on the basis of market value rather than choosing the more conservative of these two possible approaches. Nevertheless, few would question the fact that the concept does exist and that it is important.

THE BALANCE SHEET

A balance sheet shows the financial position of an accounting entity as of a specified moment of time;[3] in fact, it is sometimes labelled as a

---

[3] A balance sheet dated "December 31" is implicitly understood to mean "at the close of business on December 31." Sometimes the identical balance sheet may be dated "January 1," meaning "at the beginning of business on January 1," which,

"statement of financial position." It is therefore a status report, rather than a flow report.

A balance sheet for a hypothetical corporation is shown in Illustration 2–1. Let us first examine this balance sheet in terms of the basic concepts listed above. The figures are *expressed in money* and reflect only those matters that can be measured in money amounts. The *entity* involved is the Garsden Corporation, and the balance sheet pertains to that entity rather than to any of the individuals associated with the corporation. The statement assumes that the Garsden Corporation is a *going concern*. The asset amounts stated are governed by the *cost concept*. The *dual-aspect* concept is evident from the fact that the assets listed on one side of this balance sheet are equal in total to the equities (liabilities and shareholders' equity) listed on the other side.

It should be emphasized that the fact that the two sides add up to the same total necessarily follows from the dual-aspect concept; this equality does not tell anything about the company's financial health. The label "balance sheet" can give the impression that there is something significant about the fact that the two sides balance. This is not so. The two sides always balance, and the label therefore has only a superficial meaning.

Next look at the general format of the balance sheet. Assets are listed on the left-hand side, and equities are listed on the right-hand side. An alternative practice is to list assets at the top of the page and to list equities underneath them. The former format is called the *account* form, and the latter is called the *report* form of balance sheet.

In the United States, when the account form is used, assets are always listed on the left-hand side. In certain other countries, assets are listed on the right-hand side and equities on the left-hand side. None of these differences has any real significance.[4]

An Overall View

The balance sheet is the fundamental accounting statement in the sense that *every* accounting transaction can be analyzed in terms of its effect on the balance sheet. In order to understand the information that a balance sheet conveys, and in order to understand how economic events affect the balance sheet, it is essential that the reader be absolutely clear as to the

---

from the standpoint of accounting, is the same moment of time. Ordinarily, the "close of business" connotation is the correct one because the balance sheet is ordinarily dated as of the end of the year or other period for which accounting reports are prepared.

[4] Most of the balance sheets in this book are given in the report form for the simple reason that this fits better on a printed page. Most balance sheets typed on regular 8½ × 11 paper are in the report form for the same reason. In published annual reports, the balance sheet is often in the account form since this makes an attractive two-page spread.

Illustration 2-1

GARSDEN CORPORATION
Balance Sheet
As of December 31, 1974

ASSETS

Current Assets:

Cash...............................		$ 3,448,891
Marketable securities (market value, $248,420).......		246,221
Accounts receivable...........		5,943,588
Inventories...................		12,623,412
Prepaid expenses and deferred charges.............		388,960
Total Current Assets...		$22,651,072

Fixed Assets:

Land, buildings, and equipment............	$26,945,848	
Less: Accumulated depreciation.............	13,534,069	13,411,779

Other Assets:

Investments...................	$ 110,000	
Goodwill......................	63,214	173,214
Total Assets.........		$36,236,065

LIABILITIES AND SHAREHOLDERS' EQUITY

Current Liabilities:

Accounts payable.............		$ 6,601,442
Estimated tax liability......		1,672,000
Accrued expenses payable...		640,407
Deferred income..........		205,240
Total Current Liabilities.................		$ 9,119,089

Other Liabilities:

Mortgage bonds payable......		3,000,000

Shareholders' Equity:

Capital stock................	$15,000,000	
Retained earnings............	9,116,976	24,116,976
Total Equities.........		$36,236,065

meaning of its two sides. They can be interpreted in either of two ways, both of which are correct.

One way has already been indicated. The items listed on the asset side are the resources owned by the entity as of the date of the balance sheet, and the amounts stated for each asset are recorded consistent with the basic concepts described above. Equities are claims against the entity as of the balance sheet date. The liabilities are the claims of outside parties, that is, the amounts that the entity owes to banks, vendors, its employees and creditors; and the owners' equity shows the claim of the owners. The fact is, however, that the owners do not have a claim in the same sense that the creditors do. In the Garsden Corporation illustration it can be said with assurance that the mortgage bondholders have a claim of $3,000,000 as of December 31, 1974—that the Corporation owes them $3,000,000, neither more nor less. The amount of $24,116,976 shown for the Shareholders' Equity is more difficult to interpret as a claim, however. If the Corporation were liquidated as of December 31, 1974, if the assets were sold for their book value, and if the creditors were paid the $12,119,089 due them, the shareholders would get what was left, which would be $24,116,976. These conditions are unrealistic, however. According to the going-concern concept, the Corporation is not being liquidated, and according to the cost concept, the assets are not shown at their liquidation values. The shareholders' claim might actually be worth considerably more or considerably less than $24,116,976.

Because of the difficulty of understanding the meaning of shareholders' equity in the approach described above, the second way of interpreting the balance sheet has considerable appeal. In this view the right-hand side of the balance sheet lists the sources from which the business has obtained the capital with which it currently operates, and the left-hand side shows the form in which that capital is invested on a specified date. On the right-hand side, the several liability items describe how much capital was obtained from trade creditors (accounts payable), from banks (notes payable), from bondholders (bonds payable), and from other outside parties. The owners' equity section shows the capital supplied by the owners. If the business is a corporation, the owners are shareholders and their contribution consists of two principal parts: capital directly supplied (capital stock) and capital which the shareholders provided by permitting earnings to remain in the business (retained earnings).

Capital obtained from various sources has been invested according to the management's best judgment of the optimum mix, or combination, of assets for the business. A certain fraction is invested in buildings, another fraction in inventories, another fraction is in the form of cash, and so on. The asset side of the balance sheet therefore shows the result of these management judgments as of the date of the balance sheet.

It should be emphasized that both of these views of the balance sheet are correct. In certain circumstances, the former is easier to understand, and in other circumstances, the latter is easier.

Note, incidentally, that the amounts in Illustration 2–1 are rounded to dollars. Pennies are eliminated in many published statements. In reports prepared for internal purposes, the amounts may be rounded even further, to thousands of dollars, or in large corporations to millions of dollars, so as to highlight the important figures.

Account Categories

Although each individual asset or equity—each building, each piece of equipment, each bank loan, and so on—could theoretically be listed separately on the balance sheet, it is more practicable and more informative to summarize and group related items into categories or *account classifications*. There is no fixed pattern as to the number of such categories or the amount of detail reported; rather, the format is governed by the accountant's opinion as to the most informative way of presenting significant facts about the status of the business.

As in any classification scheme, the categories are defined in such a way that (1) the individual items included in a category resemble one another in some essential and significant respect, and (2) the items in one category are essentially different from those in all other categories. Although the items included in a category are similar to one another, they are not identical.

EXAMPLE: The category labeled "Cash" usually includes money on deposit at savings banks as well as money on deposit in checking accounts. These two types of money are *similar* in that they both are in highly liquid form, but they are not *identical* because certain restrictions may apply to withdrawals from savings banks that do not apply to checking accounts. If an accountant thought this difference was important enough to report, he would show separate categories, one for cash in checking accounts and the other for cash in savings accounts. This would, however, increase the amount of detail shown on the balance sheet.

The balance sheet in Illustration 2–1 gives a minimum amount of detail. The terms used on this balance sheet are common ones, and they are described briefly below. These descriptions are preliminary, approximately correct definitions of balance sheet terms. More detailed descriptions are given in Chapters 5 through 10.

Assets

We shall now supersede the short definition of "asset" given in the preceding section by the following more exact statement: *Assets are economic resources owned by an entity whose cost at the time of acquisition can be objectively measured.* The three key points in this definition are the following: (1) an asset must be an economic resource; (2) the resource must be owned; and (3) its value at the time of acquisition must be objectively measurable.

ASSETS

A resource is an *economic* resource if it provides future benefits to the entity. Resources provide future benefits under any of three conditions: (1) they are money or can be converted to money; (2) they are goods which are expected to be sold; or (3) they are expected to be used in future activities of the entity.

> EXAMPLES: The Garsden Corporation is a manufacturing company. The cash that it has on deposit in banks is an asset because it is money which can be used to acquire other resources. The goods which it has manufactured and still has on hand are assets because they are expected to be sold. The equipment and other manufacturing facilities which it owns are assets because they are expected to be used to produce additional goods.
>
> Amounts due from customers are assets, to the extent that customers are likely to pay their bills. An insurance policy is an asset, since the insurance provides a valuable protection against losses from future misfortunes. Merchandise that, because of damage or obsolescence, cannot be sold is not an asset, even though it is owned by the business.

Ownership is a legal concept which is to be distinguished from possession or control. The accounting concept is close to, but not exactly the same as, the legal concept. Thus, when a business buys an automobile on the installment plan, the business may not own the car, in the legal sense, until the last installment has been paid; nevertheless, the automobile is regarded as substantially owned by the business and is shown as an asset. But possession or control, without substantial ownership, is not enough to qualify the item as an asset.

> EXAMPLES: A leased piece of equipment is not ordinarily an asset of the lessee even though it is in his possession and he has complete control over its use. (An exception that applies to certain types of leases is discussed in Chapter 7.) Goods on consignment are assets of the consignor who owns them, not of the consignee who has possession of them.

The *objective acquisition value* test is usually clear-cut, but in some instances is difficult to apply. If the resource was purchased for cash or for the promise to pay cash, it is an asset. If the resource was manufactured by the business, then money was paid for the costs of manufacture, and it is an asset. If the resource was acquired by trading-in some other asset or by issuing shares of capital stock, then the item is an asset, although there may be problems in measuring its amount because of the difficulty in valuing the traded-in item or the stock. Ordinarily, the solution to this problem is to determine what the asset would have cost had cash been paid for it; but when evidence of this amount cannot be found, the best possible estimate is made from whatever information is available. On the other hand, as already pointed out (p. 28), a valuable reputation or an efficient organization is not an asset if it arose gradually over a period of time, rather than being acquired at a specifically measurable cost.

EXAMPLE: Both "Schick" and "Gillette" are valuable trade names. Nevertheless, the February 28, 1973 balance sheet for Schick Electric, Inc. shows a zero amount for this item, whereas the December 31, 1973 balance sheet for Gillette Company shows $53,090,000, for "Goodwill, Trademarks, and Patents."

Assets are recorded at their total cost, not the company's "equity" in them.

EXAMPLE: If a business buys land for $100,000, pays $30,000 cash, and gives a $70,000 mortgage, the asset is recorded at $100,000, not $30,000.

On most business balance sheets, assets are listed in decreasing order of their liquidity; that is, in order of the promptness with which they are expected to be converted into cash. On some balance sheets, notably those of public utilities, the order is reversed, and the least liquid assets are listed first.

Assets are customarily grouped into categories. Current assets are almost always reported in a separate category. All noncurrent assets may be grouped together, or various groupings may be used, such as "Fixed Assets" and "Other Assets" as shown on the Garsden Corporation balance sheet.

Current Assets

Current assets include cash and other assets that are reasonably expected to be realized in cash or sold or consumed during the normal operating cycle of the business or within one year if the normal operating cycle is within one year.[5]

The distinction between current assets and noncurrent assets is important since much attention is given by lenders and others to the total of current assets. The essence of the distinction is *time*. Current assets are those that will be owned only for a short period of time, usually not more than a year from the balance sheet date. Although the usual time limit is one year, exceptions occur in companies whose normal operating cycle is longer than one year. Tobacco companies and distilleries, for example, include their inventories as current assets even though tobacco and liquor

---

[5] APB *Statement No. 4,* par. 198.

remain in inventory for an aging process that lasts two years or more.

Cash consists of funds that are immediately available for disbursement without restriction. Usually, most of these funds are on deposit in checking accounts in banks, and the remainder are in cash registers or other temporary storage facilities on the company's premises.

Marketable securities are investments which are both readily marketable and which are expected to be converted into cash within a year. They are investments made so as to earn some return on cash that otherwise would be temporarily idle. According to generally accepted accounting principles, marketable securities are reported on the balance sheet at their cost or their current market value, whichever is lower, unless the decline in market value is believed to be only temporary. When reported at cost, a parenthetical note of the current market value is customarily given. Many insurance companies, banks, investment companies, and other financial institutions report marketable securities at market value.

Accounts receivable are amounts owed to the company, usually by its customers. Sometimes this item is broken down into *trade* accounts receivable and *other* accounts receivable; the former refers to amounts owed by customers, and the latter refers to amounts owed by employees and others. Accounts receivable are reported on the balance sheet at the amount owed less an allowance for that portion which probably will not be collected. Methods of estimating this "allowance for doubtful accounts" are described in Chapter 5. If the amount owed is evidenced by a note or some other written acknowledgement of the obligation, it would ordinarily appear under the heading *notes receivable* rather than accounts receivable.

As defined by the FASB the term *inventory* means "the aggregate of those items of tangible personal property which (1) are held for sale in the ordinary course of business, (2) are in process of production for such sale, or (3) are to be currently consumed in the production of goods or services to be available for sale."[6] Inventory is reported at the lower of its cost or its current market value.

The item *prepaid expenses and deferred charges* represents certain assets, usually of an intangible nature, whose usefulness will expire in the near future. An example is an insurance policy. A business pays for insurance protection in advance, often for a three-year or a five-year period. Its right to this protection is an asset—a valuable, owned resource —but this right will expire within a fairly short period of time.

Prepaid expenses and deferred charges are reported at the cost of the unexpired service. Thus, if a business has purchased insurance protection for a three-year period, paying $1,200, and one year has expired as of the

---

[6] *Accounting Research Bulletin No. 43*, Chapter 3.

balance sheet date, the asset is reported at two thirds of its cost, or $800. The $800 represents the cost of the protection for the next two years. The distinction between "prepaid expenses" and "deferred charges" is not important.

Fixed Assets

Fixed assets are tangible, relatively long-lived resources. The term *Property, Plant and Equipment* is also frequently used for this category, and is more descriptive of its nature. The business has acquired these assets, ordinarily, in order to use them in the production of other goods and services. If the assets are held for resale they are classified as inventory, even though they are long-lived assets.

> EXAMPLE: A truck that is owned by a truck manufacturer which intends to sell it, is inventory. A similar truck that the manufacturer uses for transportation is a fixed asset.

In the balance sheet shown in Illustration 2–1 fixed assets are lumped together into the single item "land, buildings, and equipment," but in the balance sheets of many companies the figures for land, for buildings, and for various kinds of machinery and equipment are shown separately. In accordance with the cost concept, the figure $26,945,848 on the Garsden Corporation balance sheet represents the cost of these assets to the company at the time they were purchased. The next item, "accumulated depreciation," means that a portion of the original cost, amounting to $13,534,069, has been already allocated as a cost of doing business. Depreciation will be discussed in detail in Chapter 7.

Other Assets

Investments are securities of one company owned by another in order either to control the other company or in the anticipation of earning a return from the investment. They are therefore to be distinguished from "marketable securities," which is an item in the current asset section of the balance sheet, and which is intended to reflect the temporary use of excess cash. Investments are reported at cost if they represent a small proportion of the other company's stock; otherwise a special accounting procedure is used, as described in Chapter 10.

Intangible assets include goodwill (which was briefly described earlier in this chapter), patents, copyrights, leases, licenses, franchises, and similar valuable but nonphysical things owned by the business. They are distinguished from prepaid expenses, which are intangible current assets, in that they have a longer life-span than prepaid expenses.

Liabilities

In general, liabilities are the entity's obligations to pay money or to provide goods or services. (Some items that appear in the liabilities section of the balance sheet do not fit this definition, but we shall defer a discussion of these until later chapters.) Liabilities are claims against the entity's assets. Unless otherwise noted, the individual liabilities shown on the balance sheet are not claims against any *specific* asset or group of assets. Thus, although accounts payable typically arise through the purchase of material for inventory, accounts payable are claims against all the assets, not merely against inventories.

Even if a liability is a claim against a specific asset, as in a mortgage note, it is shown separately on the right-hand side of the balance sheet, rather than as a deduction from the asset amount to which it relates.

> EXAMPLE: If land is purchased for $100,000, and a $70,000 mortgage is given, secured by the land, the balance sheet reports land at $100,000 on the asset side, and the mortgage payable of $70,000 on the equities side, *not*—

$$
\begin{array}{lr}
\text{Land}\dots\dots\dots\dots\dots\dots\dots & \$100,000 \\
\text{Less: Mortgage}\dots\dots\dots\dots\dots & 70,000 \\
\text{Net Amount}\dots\dots\dots\dots\dots & \$\ 30,000
\end{array}
$$

Liabilities are reported at the amount owed as of the balance sheet date, including interest accumulated to that date. Interest that will be owed subsequent to the balance sheet date is excluded. Note that it is the amount *owed* that governs, not the amount *due* as of the balance sheet date. A loan is a liability even though it is not required to be repaid for another 10 years.

Current Liabilities

Current liabilities are obligations which are expected to be satisfied either by the use of assets classified as current in the same balance sheet, or by the creation of other current liabilities or obligations that are expected to be satisfied within a relatively short period of time, usually one year.[7]

If it is reasonably certain that an obligation which becomes due in the near future will be replaced by a noncurrent liability, rather than being paid in cash, the obligation is classified as a noncurrent liability. This is the case when a maturing bond issue is to be refunded, that is, replaced by another bond issue.

Accounts payable represent the claims of vendors and others. Usually these claims are unsecured. If the claim was evidenced by a note or some

---

[7] APB *Statement No. 4*, par. 198.

other written acknowledgment of debt, the item would be called *notes payable, bank drafts payable,* or some other term that describes the nature of the obligation.

Estimated tax liability is the amount owed the government for taxes. It is shown separately from other obligations both because of its size and because the amount owed is not precisely known as of the date of the balance sheet. Often, the liability for federal and state income taxes is shown separately from other tax liabilities.

Accrued expenses are the converse of prepaid expenses. They represent valid obligations, but they are not evidenced by an invoice or other document submitted by the person to whom the money is owed. An example is the wages and salaries owed to employees for work they have performed but for which they have not been reimbursed.

Deferred income represents the liability that arises because the company has received advance payment for a service it has agreed to render in the future. An example is precollected rent, which represents rental payments received in advance, for which the owning company agrees to permit the tenant to use a specified building (or other property) during some future period.

Other Liabilities

Other liabilities are obligations which do not fall due within one year. Evidently the mortgage bonds of the Garsden Corporation do not mature within the next year, nor do any fraction of them; otherwise all or part of this liability would appear as a current liability (unless, as stated above, it is planned to refund them).

Owners' Equity

The owners' equity section of the balance sheet shows the amount the owners have invested in the entity. The terminology used in this section of the balance sheet varies with different forms of organization.

In a corporation, the ownership interest is evidenced by shares of stock, and the owners' equity section of its balance sheet is therefore usually labelled *Shareholders' Equity* or *Stockholders' Equity*. The shareholders' equity is divided into two main categories. The first category, called *paid-in capital* or *contributed capital*, is the amount which the owners have invested directly in the business. Paid-in capital in most corporations is further subdivided. Each share of stock has a stated value, and one item in the category, called capital stock, shows the stated value per share times the number of shares. If investors actually paid into the corporation more than the stated value per share, the excess is shown separately, with a caption *Other Paid-in Capital*.

EXAMPLE: The Maxwell Corporation issued 1,000,000 shares of common stock with a stated value of $10 per share. Investors actually paid into the corporation $15,000,000 for these shares. The balance sheet would appear as follows:

Paid-in capital
Common stock......................	$10,000,000	
Other paid-in capital................	5,000,000	
Total.........................		$15,000,000

The second category of shareholders' equity is labelled Retained Earnings. The owners' equity increases through *earnings* (i.e., the results of profitable operations) and decreases when earnings are paid out in the form of dividends. The difference between the total earnings to date and the total amount of dividends to date is *retained earnings;* that is, it represents that part of the total earnings which have been retained for use in the business.[8] If the difference is negative, the item is labeled *deficit.*

Note that the amount of retained earnings on a given date is the *cumulative* amount that has been retained in the business from the beginning of the corporation's existence up to that date.

Note also that the amount of retained earnings does not indicate the *form* in which the earnings were retained. They may be invested in any type of resources. The resources in which equities of all types are invested appear on the assets side of the balance sheet, not the owners' equities side. This fact is emphasized because there is a common misconception that there is some connection between the amount of retained earnings and the amount of cash. That no such connection exists should be apparent from the fact that the Garsden Corporation balance sheet shows over $9 million of retained earnings, but only $3.4 million of cash.

EXAMPLE: In a magazine article,[9] Philip Moore wrote: "It (General Motors Corporation) has $8 billion of cash surplus on deposit in some 380 banks around the world." When a reader pointed out that the GM balance sheet showed only $550 million of cash as an asset, Moore replied, "The $8 billion figure refers to what I understand to be General Motors' current capital surplus, which I assumed to be either in cash or highly liquid form such as treasury bills, most of which would be on deposit either in cash or as nominee in the 380 banks."[10] If Mr. Moore had taken a course in accounting he would have realized that "capital surplus" on the equities side of the balance sheet (which is GM's terminology for other paid-in capital) has no relationship whatsoever to any specific asset, such as cash, or "highly liquid assets."

---

[8] Shareholders' equity is also affected by events other than the accumulation of earnings and the withdrawal of these earnings. Examples are donations of capital, revaluation of stock, and the creation of special reserves. Some of these events will be discussed in Chapter 9.

[9] "What's Good for the Country is Good for GM," *Washington Monthly,* December, 1970, pp. 10–18.

[10] *Washington Monthly,* March, 1971, p. 4.

The term "surplus" was formerly used instead of "retained earnings," and is still used by some companies. The word "surplus" is apt to be misleading, since to the uninitiated a surplus is something tangible, something "left over." There is, in fact, nothing tangible about retained earnings. All the tangible things owned by the business appear on the assets side of the balance sheet. It is because of this misleading connotation that use of this word is no longer recommended. The word "surplus" is sometimes used with appropriate modifiers (capital surplus, paid-in surplus, and so forth) for certain special items that will be described in Chapter 9.

"Net worth" is another obsolete term. It was formerly used as a synonym for owners' equity, but is being abandoned because of the connotation that the amount states what the owners' interest is "worth," in the ordinary sense of this word. Such a connotation is completely erroneous.

In unincorporated businesses, different terminology is used in the owners' equity section. In a *proprietorship*, which is a business owned by one person, it is customary to show the owner's equity as a single figure, with a title such as "John Jones, capital," rather than making a distinction between the owner's initial investment and the accumulated earnings retained in the business.

In a *partnership*, which is an unincorporated business owned jointly by several persons, there is a capital account for each partner, thus:

```
James Smith, capital...................... $15,432
John Smith, capital...................... 15,432
     Total Partners' Equity............. $30,864
```

In addition to these basic owners' equity items, a proprietorship or a partnership may, for convenience, use a temporary item called a *drawing account* in which amounts withdrawn from the business by the owner(s) are recorded. Periodically, the total accumulated in the drawing account is subtracted from the capital item, leaving the net equity of the owner(s). For example, a balance sheet might show the following:

```
John Jones, capital............. $25,000
     Less: Drawings............... 2,400
     Net Proprietorship Equity..       $22,600
```

After the two items have been combined, the balance sheet would read simply:

```
John Jones, capital............. $22,600
```

The reader may have heard of the terms "partnership accounting" and "corporation accounting," and from these he may have formed the impression that different accounting systems are used for different forms of business organization. As a matter of fact, the treatment of assets and liabilities is generally the same in all forms of organization; differences occur principally in the owners' equity section as noted above.

BALANCE SHEET CHANGES

At the moment a business starts, its financial status can be recorded on a balance sheet. From that time on, events occur that change the numbers on this first balance sheet, and the accountant records these changes in accordance with the concepts given above. Full-fledged accounting systems provide a means of accumulating and summarizing these changes and of preparing new balance sheets at prescribed intervals, such as the end of a month or a year. The balance sheet shows the financial condition of the entity at that time after giving effect to all of these changes.

Although in practice a balance sheet is prepared only at prescribed intervals, in learning the accounting process it is useful to consider the changes one by one. This makes it possible to study the effect of individual events without getting entangled with the mechanisms used in practice to record these events. The technical name given to an event that affects an accounting number is *transaction*. An example of the effect of a few transactions on the balance sheet will now be given. For simplicity, they are assumed to occur on successive days.

Jan. 1.   John Smith starts a business, called Glendale Market, by depositing $10,000 of his own funds in a bank account which he has opened in the name of the business entity. The balance sheet of Glendale Market will then be as follows:

GLENDALE MARKET
Balance Sheet as of January 1

ASSETS		EQUITIES	
Cash..................	$10,000	John Smith, capital....	$10,000

Jan. 2.   Glendale Market borrows $5,000 from a bank giving a note therefor. This transaction increases the asset "cash," and the business incurs a liability to the bank, which is called Notes Payable. The balance sheet after this transaction will appear as follows:

GLENDALE MARKET
Balance Sheet as of January 2

ASSETS		EQUITIES	
Cash..................	$15,000	Notes payable..........	$ 5,000
		John Smith, capital....	10,000
Total...........	$15,000	Total...........	$15,000

Jan. 3. The business buys inventory, that is, merchandise which it intends to sell, in the amount of $2,000, paying cash. The balance sheet is as follows:

GLENDALE MARKET

Balance Sheet as of January 3

ASSETS		EQUITIES	
Cash...................	$13,000	Notes payable..........	$ 5,000
Inventory..............	2,000	John Smith, capital....	10,000
Total...........	$15,000	Total...........	$15,000

Jan. 4. The store sells, for $300 cash, merchandise that cost $200. The effect of this transaction is that inventory has been decreased by $200, cash has been increased by $300, and John Smith's own equity has been increased by the difference, or $100. The $100 is the profit on this sale. The balance sheet will then look like this:

GLENDALE MARKET

Balance Sheet as of January 4

ASSETS		EQUITIES	
Cash...................	$13,300	Notes payable..........	$ 5,000
Inventory..............	1,800	John Smith, capital....	10,100
Total...........	$15,100	Total...........	$15,100

These illustrations could be extended indefinitely. As we delve more deeply into the mechanics of accounting, it is worth remembering that every accounting transaction can be recorded in terms of its effect on the balance sheet.

Concluding Comment

In subsequent chapters we shall expand considerably on the concepts and terms introduced here. We shall describe modifications and qualifications to certain of the basic concepts, and we shall introduce many additional terms that are used on balance sheets. We shall not, however, discard the basic structure that was introduced in this chapter. The reader should be able to relate all the new material to this basic structure.

SUMMARY

The basic concepts discussed in this chapter may be briefly summarized as follows:

1. *Money Measurement.* Accounting records only those facts that can be expressed in monetary terms.

2. *Entity.* Accounts are kept for entities as distinguished from the person(s) associated with those entities.
3. *Going Concern.* Accounting assumes that an entity will continue to exist indefinitely and that it is not about to be sold.
4. *Cost.* An asset is ordinarily entered in the accounts at the amount paid to acquire it, and this cost, rather than market value, is the basis for subsequent accounting for the asset.
5. *Dual Aspect.* The total amount of assets equals the total amount of equities.
6. *Conservatism.* An asset is recorded at the lower of two reasonably possible amounts, or a transaction is recorded in such a way that the owners' equity is lower than it otherwise would be.

The balance sheet shows the financial condition of an entity as of a specified moment in time. It consists of two sides. The assets side shows the resources which are expected to provide future benefits to the business and which were acquired at objectively measurable amounts. The equities side shows the liabilities, which are obligations of the business, and the owners' equity, which are amounts invested by the owners. Liabilities are claims against the business as a whole, not against specified assets.

Each transaction can be recorded in terms of its effect on the balance sheet. It is recorded in such a way that the basic equation, Assets = Equities, is always maintained.

SUGGESTIONS FOR FURTHER READING ON ACCOUNTING PRINCIPLES
(For Chapters 2–13)

There are several excellent textbooks, any of which may be useful either for additional information or to obtain a different viewpoint on topics discussed here. In addition, the following are useful:

Eric L. Kohler. *A Dictionary for Accountants.* 4th ed.; Englewood Cliffs, N.J.: Prentice-Hall, Inc., 1969. Much more than a dictionary, it contains a good discussion of many terms and concepts, and because of its dictionary format provides a quick way of locating desired information.

Rufus Wixon (ed.). *Accountants' Handbook.* 5th ed.; New York: Ronald Press Co., 1970. A standard source for detailed information.

Publications of the AICPA, American Accounting Association, and U.S. Securities and Exchange Commission, referred to in the text, are important sources of the latest information on what constitutes "generally accepted accounting principles." *APB Accounting Principles,* published by Commerce Clearing House, Inc., contains all pronouncements of the former Accounting Principles Board. In Volume 1, these are classified by topics, and in Volume 2 they are reproduced chronologically. *A Statement of Basic Ac-*

counting Theory, American Accounting Association, 1966, gives the standards proposed by that organization. *Accounting Trends and Techniques*, published annually by the American Institute of Certified Public Accountants, gives detailed information on the accounting practices of 600 leading corporations as revealed in their annual reports.

CASES

CASE 2–1. PROBLEM IN BALANCE SHEET CONSTRUCTION

As of December 31, 1974, the accounts of the Fintley Corporation showed the following balances (000 omitted):

Accounts payable.......................................	$ 131
Accounts receivable....................................	526
Accrued expenses......................................	243
Accumulated depreciation on plant and equipment...........	840
Bank notes payable.....................................	5
Bonds payable...	300
Capital stock..	438
Cash...	69
Deferred income (progress payments from customers).........	229
Dividends payable......................................	43
Estimated tax liability..................................	254
Inventories..	610
Investments in other companies...........................	157
Marketable securities...................................	409
Other assets...	164
Other liabilities.......................................	126
Plant and equipment (at original cost)....................	1,553
Retained earnings......................................	879

Question

1. Prepare a balance sheet as of this date, in proper form.

CASE 2–2. PROBLEM IN BALANCE SHEET CHANGES

On a sheet of paper, set up in pencil the balance sheet of Glendale Market as it appears after the last transaction described in the text, page 45, leaving considerable space between each item. Record the effect, if any, of the following events on the balance sheet, either by revising ex-

48

isting figures (cross out, rather than erase) or by adding new items as necessary. At least one of these events does not affect the balance sheet. The basic equation, Assets = Equities, must be preserved at all times. Errors will be minimized if you make a separate list of the balance sheet items affected by each transaction and the amount (+ or −) by which each is to be changed.

After you have finished recording these events, prepare a balance sheet in proper form. Assume that all these transactions occurred in January and that there were no other transactions in January:

1. The store purchased and received merchandise for inventory for $2,000, agreeing to pay within 30 days.
2. Merchandise costing $500 was sold for $800, which was received in cash.
3. Merchandise costing $600 was sold for $900, the customer agreeing to pay $900 within 30 days.
4. The store purchased a three-year fire insurance policy for $200, paying cash.
5. The store purchased two lots of land of equal size for a total of $10,000. It paid $2,000 in cash and gave a 10-year mortgage for $8,000.
6. The store sold one of the two lots of land for $5,000. It received $1,000 cash, and in addition, the buyer assumed $4,000 of the mortgage; that is, Glendale Market became no longer responsible for this half.
7. Smith received a bona fide offer of $15,000 for the business, and although his equity was then only $10,700, he rejected the offer. It was evident that the store had already acquired goodwill of $4,300.
8. Smith withdrew $500 cash from the store's bank account for his personal use.
9. Smith took merchandise costing $400 from the store's inventory for his personal use.
10. Smith learned that the man who purchased the land (No. 6 above) subsequently sold it for $8,000. The lot still owned by Glendale Market was identical in value with this other plot.
11. The store paid off $2,000 of its note payable (disregard interest).
12. Glendale Market was changed to a corporation, Glendale Market, Inc. Smith received common stock with a par value of $9,800 in exchange for his equity in the store. (Disregard costs of organizing the corporation. Note that this event creates a new entity.)
13. Smith sold one fourth of the stock he owned in Glendale Market, Inc., for $3,000 cash.
14. Merchandise costing $300 was sold for $450, which was received in cash.

CASE 2–3.   SMOKY VALLEY CAFE[1]

On August 12, 1946, three people who had previously been employed to wait on tables in one of the cafes in Baxter, Oregon, formed a partnership. The eldest of the three was Mrs. Bevan, a middle-aged widow. The other two were Mr. and Mrs. Elmer Maywood. The partnership lasted for slightly more than four months, and in connection with its dissolution the preparation of a balance sheet became necessary.

Each of the partners contributed $2,000 cash, a total of $6,000. On August 12, the partnership purchased the Smoky Valley Cafe for $16,000. The purchase price included land valued at $2,500, improvements to land at $2,000, buildings at $10,500, and cafe equipment at $1,000. The partnership made a down payment of $4,500 (from its $6,000 cash) and signed a mortgage for the balance of the $16,000. The doors of the cafe were opened for business shortly after August 12.

One of the things that made this particular piece of property attractive to them was the fact that the building contained suitable living accommodations. One of these rooms was occupied by Mrs. Bevan, another by the Maywoods.

The Maywoods and Mrs. Bevan agreed that Mrs. Bevan would operate the kitchen, Mrs. Maywood would have charge of the dining room, and Mr. Maywood would attend the bar. Mrs. Bevan agreed to keep the accounting records. She was willing to perform this task because she was vitally interested in making the business a success. She had invested the proceeds from the sale of her modest home and from her husband's insurance policy in the venture. If it failed, the major part of her financial resources would be lost.

A beer license was granted by the state authorities. On August 15, the partnership sent a check for $35 to the distributor who supplied beer. This $35 constituted a deposit on bottles and kegs necessary for the operation of the bar and would be returned to the Smoky Valley Cafe after all bottles and kegs had been returned to the beer distributor.

In October, the partners decided that to continue to offer their patrons quality food, they would have to add to their equipment. This new equipment cost $415.95, and because the supplier of the equipment was unimpressed with the firm's credit rating, the equipment was paid for in cash.

The month of November did not improve the cash position of the business. In fact, the cash balance became so low that Mrs. Bevan contributed additional cash in the amount of $400 to the business. She had hopes, however, that the future would prove to be more profitable.

The Smoky Valley Cafe was located on a major highway, and a great

---

[1] Based on a case argued before the Supreme Court of the State of Oregon, March 28, 1950. See 216 P2d 1005.

deal of business was obtained from truck drivers. One of these truck driver patrons, Fred Mead, became a frequent customer. He soon gained the friendship of Mrs. Maywood. On the night of December 12, Fred Mead stopped in the cafe. Shortly after he left, Mrs. Maywood retired to her room. A few hours later, Mr. Maywood came in and asked for her, and after a brief search discovered that she had departed through a window. Her absence led him to the conclusion that she had departed with Fred Mead, and he thereupon set out in pursuit of the pair.

On December 16, Mrs. Bevan decided that the partnership was dissolved because she had not heard any word from either of the Maywoods. (The courts subsequently affirmed that the partnership was dissolved as of December 16, 1946). Although she had no intention of ceasing operations, she realized that an accounting would have to be made as of December 16. She called in Mr. Bailey, a local accountant, for this purpose.

Mrs. Bevan told Mr. Bailey that they had been able to pay $700 on the mortgage while the partnership was operating. Cash on hand amounted to $65.35, but the bank balance was only $9.78. Mr. Bailey found bills owed by the cafe totaling $92.01. Mrs. Bevan said that her best estimate was that there was $100 worth of food on hand.

Mr. Bailey estimated that a reasonable allowance for depreciation on the fixed assets was as follows:

Assets	Depreciation Allowance
Land improvements	$ 44.45
Buildings	233.45
Cafe equipment	44.19

Questions

1. Draw up a balance sheet for the Smoky Valley Cafe as of August 12, 1946, taking into account the events described in the first two paragraphs of the case.

2. Draw up a balance sheet as of December 16, 1946.

3. What were the equities of the Maywoods and Mrs. Bevan, respectively? (In partnership law, the partners share equally in profits and losses unless there is a specific provision to the contrary. Each partner in the Smoky Valley Cafe, therefore, would have an equity in one third of the profits, or his equity would be decreased by one third of the losses.)

4. Do you suppose that the partners received these amounts? Why?

CHAPTER 3

BASIC ACCOUNTING CONCEPTS: THE INCOME STATEMENT

This chapter introduces the idea of income as used in financial accounting, and describes the income statement, the financial statement which reports income and its determinants.

In the course of this discussion, the last four of the ten basic concepts listed in Chapter 2 are explained, namely:

7. The realization concept.
8. The matching concept.

9. The consistency concept.
10. The materiality concept.

THE NATURE OF INCOME

In Chapter 2, we described the balance sheet, which reports the financial condition of an entity as of one moment in time. In Chapter 3, we describe a second financial statement, the income statement. The income statement summarizes the results of operations for a period of time. It is therefore a *flow* report, as contrasted with the balance sheet which is a *status* report.

The nature of the "income" which is the focus of the income statement can be clarified if a business is thought of as an organization that uses inputs to produce outputs. The outputs are the goods and services that the business entity provides to its customers. The values of these outputs are basically the amounts that customers pay for them. In accounting, these amounts are called *revenues*. The inputs that the business uses in providing these goods and services are economic resources. In accounting, the cost of the resources used in providing goods and services during a period are called *expenses*. Income is the amount by which the revenues earned during a period exceed the expenses incurred during that period.

52

Since the word "income" is often used with various qualifying adjectives, the term *net income* is used to refer to the net excess of all the revenues over all the expenses of a period. If total expenses exceed total revenues, the difference is a *net loss.*

The Accounting Period

It is relatively easy to measure net income for the whole life of a business. This is simply the difference between the money that comes in and the money that goes out (excluding, of course, money invested by the owners or paid to the owners).

EXAMPLE: John Wainwright operated a boys' camp for one summer, renting all the necessary facilities and equipment. Before the camp opened, he invested $4,000 of his own money for food, the initial rental payment, and certain other costs. At the end of the summer, after all affairs were wound up, he had his $4,000 back and $2,179 additional. This $2,179 was the net income of the camp business. It was the difference between the fees he received from parents and the money he paid out for food, wages, and other costs. The income statement for the business looked like this:

Campers' fees		$21,400
Less expenses:		
Food	$6,252	
Wages	8,645	
Rental	2,500	
Other costs	824	
Total expenses		18,221
Net Income		$ 2,179

Relatively few business ventures have a life of only a few months, as was the case with John Wainwright's summer camp. Most of them operate for many years; indeed, in accordance with the going-concern concept, it is usually assumed that the life of a business is indefinitely long. Management and other interested parties are unwilling to wait until the business has terminated before obtaining information on how much income has been earned. They need to know at frequent intervals "how things are going." Therefore, accountants choose some convenient segment of time and they measure the net income for that period of time. The time interval chosen is called the *accounting period.*

For the purpose of reporting to outsiders, one year is the usual accounting period. Pacioli, the first author of an accounting text, wrote in 1494: "Books should be closed each year, especially in a partnership, because frequent accounting makes for long friendship."[1] Most corporate

---

[1] Lucas Pacioli, *Summa de Arithmetica Geometria Proportioni et Proportionalita,* from the translation by John B. Geijsbeck.

bylaws require an annual report to the shareholders, and income tax reporting is also on an annual basis.

In the majority of businesses, the accounting year, or *fiscal* year, corresponds to the calendar year, but many businesses use the *natural business year* instead of the calendar year. For example, nearly all department stores end their fiscal year on January 31, which is after the Christmas rush and its repercussions in the form of returns and clearance sales.

Management invariably needs information more often than once a year, and income statements for the use of management are therefore prepared more frequently. The most common period is a month, but the period may be as short as a week or even a day. The Securities and Exchange Commission requires quarterly income statements from companies over which it has jurisdiction. These reports are called *interim* reports to distinguish them from the annual reports.

Businesses are living, continuing organisms. The act of chopping the stream of business events into time periods is therefore somewhat arbitrary since business activities do not stop or change measurably as one accounting period ends and another begins. It is this fact that makes the problem of measuring income in an accounting period the most difficult problem in accounting.

> EXAMPLE: If, instead of a summer camp, John Wainwright operated a year-round hotel, his income for a year could not be measured simply as the difference between the money taken in and the money paid out. As of the end of the year, some of his guests would not have paid their bills, but these unpaid bills are an asset, accounts receivable, which surely increase the "well-offness" of the business, even though the cash has not yet been remitted. Conversely, some of the cash paid out may have been for the purchase of an asset, such as the hotel itself, and this asset still has value at the end of the accounting period; it would be incorrect to conclude that his income has been decreased by the amount of such payments.

Relation between Income and Owners' Equity

As explained in Chapter 2, the net income of an accounting period increases owners' equity. In order to understand the implication of this relationship, let us refer back to the January 4 transaction of Glendale Market (p. 45). On that day, merchandise costing $200 was sold for $300 cash. Looking first at the effect of this transaction on assets, we note that although inventory decreased by $200, cash increased by $300, so that the total assets increased by the difference, $100. From the dual-aspect concept, which states that the total of the assets must always equal the total of the equities, we know that the equities side of the balance sheet must also have increased by $100. Since no liabilities were affected, the increase must have occurred in the owner's equity item. In summary, because assets were sold for more than was paid for them, the owner's equity increased. Such increases in owner's equity are called income.

In understanding how this income came about, it is useful to consider two aspects of this event separately: the $300 received from the sale, and the $200 decrease in inventory. If we look only at the $300, we see that it is an increase in cash, and a corresponding *increase* in the owner's equity. The $200, taken by itself, is a decrease in the asset, inventory, and a corresponding *decrease* in the owner's equity. These two aspects illustrate the only two ways in which business operations can affect owner's equity: they can increase it, or they can decrease it.

It follows that revenues and expenses can also be defined in terms of their effect on owners' equity: a *revenue* is an increase in owners' equity resulting from the operation of the entity, and an *expense* is a decrease. Restating the transactions described above in these terms, there was revenue of $300, expense of $200, and income of $100.

The basic equation

$$\text{Revenues} - \text{Expenses} = \text{Net Income}$$

clearly indicates that income is a *difference*. Sometimes the word *income* is used improperly as a synonym for *revenue*. This is because the approved definitions as given above are of relatively recent origin and some companies have not kept up with the latest developments. For example, Western Electric Company, Incorporated, reported "gross income" in 1973 of $7,073,061,000; the term should have been "revenue."

On an income statement, no misunderstanding is caused by such an error because revenue, however it is labelled, appears at the top and income at the bottom; but in other contexts confusion can be created. For example, if someone says Company X had an income of a million dollars, he gives a completely false impression of the size of the company if he actually meant that Company X had *revenues* of a million dollars.[2]

Income Not the Same as Cash Receipts

It is extremely important to recognize that income is associated with changes in owners' equity, and that it has no necessary relation to changes in cash. Income connotes "well-offness." Roughly speaking the bigger the income, the better off are the owners. An increase in cash, however, does not necessarily mean that the owners are any better off—that their equity has increased. The increase in cash may merely be offset by a decrease in some other asset or by an increase in a liability, with no effect on owners' equity at all.

---

[2] The income tax Form 1040 still contains the phrases "dividend income," "interest income," and "pension and annuity income" for items that actually are *revenues*. The government is not always quick to change its ways.

Again, reference to the transactions of Glendale Market may help to clarify this point. When Glendale Market borrowed $5,000 from the bank on January 2 (p. 44), its cash was increased, but this was exactly matched by an increase in the liability to the bank. There was no change in owner's equity. No income resulted from this transaction; the $5,000 was not revenue. Similarly, the purchase of inventory for $2,000 cash on January 3 (p. 45) resulted in a decrease in cash, but there was an exactly corresponding increase in another asset, inventory, and owner's equity was not changed.

As we have already seen, the sale for $300 of inventory costing $200 *did* result in income, but it should be noted that the income was $100, whereas cash increased by $300, so even here the income is different from the amount by which the cash changed. In short, although individuals typically measure their personal income by the amount of money they receive, this concept of income is not correct when applied to a business entity.

In sorting out the transactions that affect net income during an accounting period from those that do not, and in measuring the amount of revenue or expense associated with each such transaction, the basic guides are the realization concept and the matching concept.

THE REALIZATION CONCEPT

Revenues result from providing goods and services to customers. In order to measure the revenues in a given accounting period, we need the answers to two questions:

1. When should revenues be recognized? More formally, in what accounting period should the increase in owners' equity arising from the sale of goods or services be recorded?

2. At what amounts should revenues be recognized?

The *realization concept* provides answers to these questions:

1. Revenues are generally recognized in the period in which goods are delivered to the customer or the period in which services are rendered. This is the period in which revenue is said to be realized.

2. The amount of revenue is the amount that customers are reasonably certain to pay.[3]

We shall defer to Chapter 5 a discussion of the application of the realization concept to complicated situations that arise in practice, and shall limit the discussion here to the basic ideas.

---

[3] The realization concept is described in more detail in APB *Statement No. 4*, paragraphs 148–153.

The problem we address now arises from the fact that although business activities take place continuously through time, the income statement measures revenues and expenses for one portion of that flow, which is the accounting period, as is shown in Illustration 3–1.

Illustration 3–1

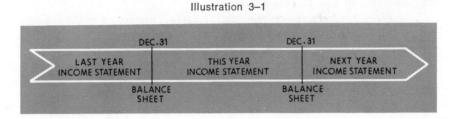

Our problem is to measure the revenues of "this year," so as to distinguish them from the revenues of "last year" and also from those of "next year."

Distinction between Receipt and Revenue

The realization concept refers to the delivery of goods or the rendering of services, and these actions must be clearly distinguished from the receipt of cash. For many transactions, of course, cash is received at the same time that goods are delivered to the customer. This is the case with most supermarkets, and for many transactions in other retail stores. It can happen, however, that the cash is received in either an earlier period or a later period than that in which the revenue is realized. Examples of each are given below.

PRECOLLECTED REVENUE. Most newspaper and magazine companies sell subscriptions that the subscriber pays for in advance; that is, the company receives the cash before it renders the service of providing the newspaper or the magazine. Referring to Illustration 3–1, if subscription money is received this year for magazines to be delivered next year, the revenue belongs in next year, not this year. The amount is therefore recorded, not as revenue for this year, but rather as a liability on the balance sheet as of the end of this year. The liability represents the claim that subscribers have to receive the magazine next year. Similarly, rent on property is often paid in advance, and when this happens, the revenue is properly recognized in the period in which the services of the rented property are provided, not the period in which the rent is received.

ACCOUNTS RECEIVABLE. The converse of the above situation is illustrated by sales made on credit, that is, the customer agrees to pay for the goods or services sometime following the date on which he actually receives them. In this case, the revenue is recognized in the period in which the sale is made, and if the payment is not due until the following period, an asset, accounts receivable, is shown on the balance sheet as of the end of the current period. When the customer pays his bill, the amount is not revenue; rather, it reduces the amount of accounts receivable outstanding and increases cash.

The difference between revenue and receipts is illustrated in the following tabulation that shows various types of sales transactions and classifies the effect of each on cash receipts and sales revenue for "this year":

| | | | This Year | |
		Amount	Cash Receipts	Sales Revenue
1.	Cash sales made this year................	$200	$200	$200
2.	Credit sales made last year;			
	cash received this year................	300	300	0
3.	Credit sales made this year;			
	cash received this year................	400	400	400
4.	Credit sales made this year;			
	cash received next year................	100	0	100
	Total.............................		$900	$700

Note that in the above illustration the total cash receipts do not equal the total sales revenue for the period. The totals would be equal in a given accounting period only (1) if the company made all its sales for cash, or (2) if the amount of cash collected from credit customers in an accounting period happened to equal the amount of credit sales made during that period.

ACCRUED REVENUE.   Another example of a transaction in which cash is received in a period following "this year" is interest revenue on amounts loaned this year with payments not due until next year. Such interest is recorded as revenue for this year, and there is an asset, accrued interest revenue, on the balance sheet as of the end of this year.

Amount of Revenue

The realization concept states that the amount that is recognized as revenue is the amount that is "reasonably certain" to be realized. There is room for differences of judgment as to how certain "reasonably certain" is, but the concept does indicate clearly that the amount of revenue recorded for a period may well be less than the sales value of the goods and services sold during that period. One obvious situation is the sale of merchandise at a discount, that is at an amount that is less than its normal price. In such cases, revenue is recorded at the lower amount, not the normal price.

EXAMPLE: Most television sets have a list price which is quoted in the manufacturer's catalog and set forth in advertisements. Many dealers sell television sets at less than the list price. In these circumstances, revenue is the amount at which the sale is made, rather than the list price. If the list price is $250 and the set is actually sold for $210, the revenue is $210.

A less obvious situation is the sale of merchandise on credit. When a company makes a credit sale, it expects that the customer will pay the bill. Experience may indicate. however, that not all customers do pay their bills. In measuring the revenue for a period, the amount of sales made on credit should be reduced by the estimated amount of credit sales that will never be realized, that is by the estimated amount of *bad debts*.

EXAMPLE: If a store makes credit sales of $100,000 during a period, and if experience indicates that 5 percent of credit sales will eventually become bad debts, the amount of revenue for the period is $95,000, not $100,000.

THE MATCHING CONCEPT

Relation of Cost and Expense

Before discussing the matching concept, which governs the measurement of expenses, we need to distinguish carefully between "cost" and "expense." The use of resources for any purpose is a cost. An expense is an item of cost that is subtracted from revenue in a given accounting period. Thus an expense is one type of cost. Resources are also used to acquire assets. Thus, the acquisition of assets is another type of cost. It is important to distinguish between assets and expenses because if a certain item of cost is classified as an asset, income at that time is unaffected; whereas if it is classified as an expense, income is reduced.

Expenses always relate to a specified accounting period. Many items that are originally classified as assets become expenses in subsequent accounting periods.

EXAMPLES: Merchandise purchased for resale but still on hand at the end of the accounting period is an asset (inventory) as of that time. If the merchandise is sold in the next accounting period, its cost becomes an expense in that period. If it is not sold and still is in good condition at the end of the accounting period it remains as an asset as of that time. Furniture, fixtures, and other equipment in a retail store are purchased with the intention that they will be used for several years. At the time of purchase, they are assets. Each year, a portion of the cost becomes an expense of that year, and the remainder continues to be recorded on the balance sheet as of the end of the year as an asset.

Nature of the Matching Concept

The matching concept provides guidelines for deciding which items of cost are expenses in a given accounting period. The *matching concept* is that, to the extent feasible, costs are reported as expenses in the period in which the associated revenue is reported. When the sales value of a certain television set is reported as revenue in "this year," the cost of that television set is reported as an expense in "this year." Note the order in which the realization concept and the matching concept are stated: First, revenues are measured in accordance with the realization concept, and *then* costs are associated with these revenues. Costs are matched with revenues, not the other way around.

Not all elements of cost can be directly associated with specific revenues. The expenses reported for an accounting period include costs for which the association is only indirect. More specifically, costs are reported as expenses in a given accounting period under any one of three circumstances:

1.   When there is a direct association between costs and revenues.
2.   When costs are directly associated with activities of the period itself, even though they are not associated with specific revenues reported in that period.
3.   When costs cannot be associated with the revenue of a future period.

DIRECT ASSOCIATION WITH REVENUES.   As already indicated, the costs of goods that are sold are reported as expense in the same period as the sales value of these goods is reported as revenue. Similarly, if salespersons are paid a commission, the commission is reported as expense in the same period as the revenue arising from these sales is reported. This period may be earlier or later than the period in which the commission is received.

EXAMPLE: If a salesman receives an advance commission this year for booking an order that is to be shipped and recognized as revenue next year, the commission is an expense of next year, not of this year. Conversely, if commissions are actually paid next year for sales that were made this year, they are nevertheless recorded as expenses of this year.

DIRECT ASSOCIATION WITH THE PERIOD.   Some items of expense are associated with a certain accounting period, even though they cannot be traced to any specific revenue transactions occurring in that period. In general, these expenses are the costs of "being in business." In a retail store, they include the expenses of operating the store during the period, even though these expenses cannot be traced directly to the specific products sold.

EXAMPLE: If salespersons are paid a salary, rather than a commission as in the previous example, the salary is reported as an expense in the period in which it is earned. Although the amount of the salary is not affected by the volume of sales, and hence there is no direct relationship between the cost and the revenue, the salary is one of the costs of operating the business during the period and hence is related in a general way to the revenue of the period.

Costs Not Associated with Future Revenue. Even if a cost item is not associated with the operations of a period, it is reported as an expense of that period if it cannot be associated with the revenue of some future period. This principle is in accordance with the dichotomy between assets and expenses that has already been mentioned. An item of cost must be either an asset or an expense.

If it is an asset, it must be an item that can be matched against revenue of some future period. If it does not qualify as an asset by this test, it must be an expense of the current period.

EXAMPLE: Employee training programs are intended to provide benefits to future periods, in that the trained employees are expected to perform better as a result of the training. The future benefits of this training cannot be objectively measured, however, so training costs are charged as an expense of the current period, rather than being set up as an asset.

Under this general principle, many items of cost are charged as expenses in the current period even though they have no connection with the revenues of that period, or even with the operations of the period. If assets are destroyed by fire or lost by theft, for example, the amount of the loss is an expense of the current period. In general, if a cost is incurred, and there is no reasonable basis for classifying the cost as an asset, it is reported as an expense.

If, during the period, an item that once was classified as an asset is found to have no value for future periods, the asset amount is removed from the balance sheet and becomes an expense of the period. This can happen, for example, when goods held in inventory are found to have deteriorated, become obsolete, or otherwise become unsaleable.

This principle also governs the treatment of errors that are discovered in the current period and that affect the income of prior periods. Suppose that in 1975 a company receives a bill for services performed for it by a lawyer in 1974, but the cost of these services had been overlooked when the 1974 financial statements were prepared. This cost is a cost of doing business in 1974, and a logical procedure, therefore, would be to make the deduction in owners' equity directly rather than to report it as an expense of 1975. Until recently, such a procedure was followed by many companies, but the Financial Accounting Standards Board now adheres to the concept of the *all-inclusive income statement,* which is that almost all changes in owners' equity, other than dividend payments and changes in capital structure, should be reported on the current year's income statement.

There is room for wide latitude in applying this principle, as we shall see in more detail in later chapters.

Expenses and Expenditures

An *expenditure* takes place when an asset or service is acquired. The expenditure may be made by cash, by the exchange of another asset, or by incurring a liability. When such expenditures are made, costs are incurred. As already noted, these costs can be either assets or expenses. Over the entire life of a business most expenditures made by a business become expenses, and there are few expenses that are not represented by an expenditure. In any time segment *shorter* than the life of a business, however, there is no necessary correspondence between expense and expenditure.

> EXAMPLE: In 1974, $1,000 of fuel oil was purchased for cash. This was an expenditure of $1,000, which was the exchange of one asset for another. If none of this fuel oil was consumed in 1974, there was no *expense* in 1974; rather, the fuel oil was an asset as of the end of 1974. If the fuel oil was consumed in 1975, there was an *expense* of $1,000 in 1975.

Just as it is important to distinguish between revenue and cash receipts, it is also important to distinguish between expenses and expenditures. The expenses of "this year" include the cost of the products *sold* during the year, even though these products were purchased or manufactured in a prior year. Expenses include the wages and salaries *earned* by employees who sold these products, whether or not the employees were paid during the year. Expenses include the supplies, telephone, electricity, and other assets or services *consumed* or *used* during the year in connection with the production of this revenue, whether or not the bills for these items were paid.

Four types of events need to be considered in distinguishing between amounts that are properly considered as expenses of a given accounting period, and the expenditures made in connection with these items. Focusing on "this year" in the diagram in Illustration 3–1, these are as follows:

1. Expenditures this year that are also expenses of this year.
2. Expenditures made prior to this year that become expenses during this year. These appeared as assets on the balance sheet at the beginning of this year.
3. Expenditures made this year that will become expenses in future years. These will appear as assets on the balance sheet at the end of this year.

4. Expenses of this year that will be paid for in a future year. On the balance sheet at the end of this year, these will appear as liabilities.

EXPENDITURES THAT ARE ALSO EXPENSES. This is the simplest type of event, and the least troublesome to account for. If an item is acquired during the year, it is an expenditure; if it is consumed during the same year, it is also an expense of the year.

ASSETS THAT BECOME EXPENSES. On January 1, the balance sheet shows certain assets. During "this year" some of these assets are used up and hence are transformed into expenses. The three principal types of such assets are described below.

First, there are *inventories* of products; these become expenses when the products are sold.

Second, there are *prepaid expenses* and *deferred charges.* These represent services or other assets purchased prior to "this year" but not yet used up when the year begins. They become expenses in the year in which the services are used or the assets are consumed. Insurance protection is one such item; the premium on most types of insurance policies is paid in advance, and the insurance protection bought with this premium is an asset until the accounting period in which the insurance protection is received, at which time it becomes an expense. Prepaid rent follows the same pattern, with the expense being associated with the year in which the company receives the benefit of occupying the rented premises.

> EXAMPLE: A company purchased three-year insurance protection on December 31, 1973 for $900. The $900 appears as an asset on the balance sheet of December 31, 1973. In 1974, $300 becomes an expense and $600 remains as an asset on the balance sheet of December 31, 1974. In 1975, $300 more becomes an expense, and so on.
>
> EXAMPLE: A company paid $12,000 to its landlord on October 1, 1974, representing an advance payment of one year's rent. Of this amount $3,000 is rent expense of 1974. On the balance sheet of December 31, 1974, $9,000 appears as an asset, and this amount becomes rent expense in 1975.

The third category of assets that will become expenses is long-lived, or *fixed* assets. Most fixed assets (with the exception of land) have a limited useful life; that is, they do not last forever. They are purchased with the expectation that they will be used in the operation of the business in future periods, and they will become expenses in these future periods. The principle is exactly the same as that of the insurance policy previously mentioned, which also was purchased for the benefit of future periods. An important practical difference between a fixed asset, such as a building, and an insurance policy, however, is that the life of a building is usually difficult to estimate, whereas the life of an insurance policy is known precisely. It follows that estimating what portion of a building's cost is an expense in a given accounting period is a more difficult task than that of determining the insurance expense of a period. The mechanism used to convert the cost of fixed assets to expense is called *depreciation* and is described in Chapter 7.

EXPENDITURES THAT ARE NOT YET EXPENSES. As the preceding examples show, some expenditures made to acquire assets "this year" are not expenses of "this year" because the assets have not yet been used up. These include not only the purchase of assets as such, but also expenditures incurred in connection with the *manufacture* of goods that are to be sold in some future year. Thus, wages and salaries earned by production personnel and all other costs associated with manufacturing become part of the cost of the goods manufactured and remain as part of the cost of an asset, inventory, until the product is sold. The distinction between manufacturing costs, which initially are added to inventory amounts, and other operating costs, which are expenses of the current period, will be discussed in more detail in Chapter 6.

EXPENSES NOT YET PAID. Some expenses which were incurred "this year" are not paid for by the end of the year. The parties who furnished these goods or services have a claim against the business for the amounts owed them, and these amounts are therefore liabilities of the company as of December 31. The liability for wages earned but not yet paid is an example that has already been mentioned. Several other types of obligations have the same characteristic; namely, that although services were rendered in an accounting period prior to that for which the balance sheet is prepared, these services have not yet been paid for. The *incurrence* of these expenses reduces owners' equity; the subsequent *payment* of the obligation does not affect owners' equity.

For all obligations of this type, the transaction involved is essentially the same: the expense is shown in the period in which the services were used, and the obligation that results from these services is shown on the liability section of the balance sheet as of the end of the period.

> EXAMPLE: In 1974 an employee earned $50 that was not paid him. This is an expense of $50 in 1974, and there is a corresponding liability of $50 (called accrued wages) on the balance sheet as of December 31, 1974. In 1975, when the employee is paid, the liability is wiped out, and there is a corresponding reduction in cash.

Note that in these examples, the basic equality, Assets = Equities, is always maintained. The earning of wages resulted in an expense of $50, which was a decrease in owners' equity, and there was an equal increase in the liability, accrued wages, so the total of the equities was unchanged. The payment of the $50 resulted in a decrease in cash and a decrease in the liability, accrued wages; that is, both assets and equities were reduced by $50.

Another common item of this type is *interest*. Interest is the cost of using borrowed money, and it is an expense of the period during which the money was used. Interest rates are usually stated on an annual basis. The treatment is different depending on whether the interest is paid when the loan *matures* (i.e., falls due) or whether it is paid in advance. The latter practice is called *discounting* and is customary for short-term bank loans. An example of each will be given.

EXAMPLE: On December 1, 1974, a company borrowed $1,000 for four months at 9 percent interest, the interest and principal to be paid on March 31, 1975. The loan itself results in an increase of cash, $1,000, and creates a liability, loans payable, of $1,000. The total interest cost is $1,000 × $4/12$ × 0.09 = $30. One fourth of this interest, $7.50, is an expense of 1974. Since it has not been paid, $7.50 also appears as a liability item, interest payable, on the December 31, 1974, balance sheet. The remaining $22.50 interest is an expense of 1975. When the loan is repaid on March 31, 1975, cash is reduced by $1,030, and this is balanced by the decrease in loans payable of $1,000, the decrease in interest payable of $7.50, and the interest expense for 1975 of $22.50.

EXAMPLE: On December 1, 1974, a company borrowed $1,000 for four months at 9 percent discounted. The company received $970. Interest expense for 1974 is $7.50, as in the preceding example, but now there is an asset, prepaid interest, of $22.50 on the December 31, 1974, balance sheet, representing the interest cost that will not become an expense until 1975. Thus, the following items are affected by this transaction in 1974: cash has increased by $970; there is an asset, prepaid interest, of $22.50; owners' equity has decreased by the applicable $7.50 of interest expense; and there is a liability, notes payable, of $1,000. Note that, as always, the change in assets ($970 + $22.50) equals the change in equities ($1,000 − $7.50).

THE CONSISTENCY CONCEPT

The eight concepts that have been described in this and the preceding chapters are so broad that there are in practice several different ways in which a given event may be recorded in the accounts. For example, when a company takes a cash discount in paying bills to its vendors, this discount may be treated as being revenue; it may be treated as a reduction in the purchase price of the goods purchased; or the cash discounts *not* taken may be treated as an expense. The *consistency concept* requires that once a company has decided on one method, it will treat all subsequent events of the same character in the same fashion unless it has a sound reason to do otherwise. If a company made frequent changes in the manner of handling a given class of events in the accounting records, comparison of its accounting figures for one period with those of another period would be difficult.

Because of this concept, changes in the method of keeping accounts are not made lightly. A company's auditors invariably include in their opinion (i.e., a letter summarizing the results of their annual examination of accounting records) the statement that the figures were prepared "in conformity with generally accepted accounting principles *applied on a basis consistent with that of the preceding year*"; or if there were changes in practice, these are spelled out in the opinion.

Note that consistency as used here has a narrow meaning. It refers only to consistency over time, not to *logical* consistency at a given moment of time. Some people argue that it is inconsistent to measure inventory at the lower of cost or market, but to measure fixed assets at cost. Whatever the merits of this argument may be, it does not involve the accounting concept of consistency. This concept does not mean that the treatment of different categories of transactions must be consistent with one another, but only that transactions in a given category must be treated consistently from one accounting period to the next.

THE MATERIALITY CONCEPT

In law, there is a doctrine called *de minimis non curat lex*, which means that the court will not consider trivial matters. Similarly, the accountant does not attempt to record a great many events which are so insignificant that the work of recording them is not justified by the usefulness of the results. An example of these trivialities is the accounting treatment of pencils. A brand new pencil is an asset of the company. Every time someone writes with the pencil, part of this asset is used up, and the owners' equity decreases correspondingly. Theoretically, it would be possible to ascertain daily the number of partly used pencils that are owned by the company and to correct the records so as to show that fractional amount of the asset amount that remains, but the cost of such an effort would obviously be gigantic, and no accountant would attempt to do this. He would take the simpler, even though less exact, course of action and consider that the asset was used up at the time the pencils were purchased or at the time they were issued from inventory to the user.

There is no agreement as to the exact line separating material events from immaterial events. The decision depends on judgment and common sense. It is natural for the beginning student, who does not have an appreciation of the cost of collecting accounting information, to be more meticulous in recording events in the accounts than would the practicing accountant. For example, the reader may have noticed that in Chapter 2, the cost of insurance protection for two future years was stated to be a current asset, even though the definition of current asset refers to *one* year. In accordance with the strict definition, one year's worth of insurance protection would be recorded as a current asset and the other year would be recorded as a noncurrent asset, but this is not done in practice because such a breakdown is not material.

The materiality concept is important in the process of determining the expenses and revenue for a given accounting period. Many of the expense items are necessarily estimates, and in some cases they are not very close estimates. There is a point beyond which it is not worthwhile to attempt to refine these estimates. Telephone expense is a familiar example. Telephone bills, although rendered monthly, often do not coincide with a calendar month. It would be possible to analyze each bill and classify all the toll calls according to the month in which they were made. This would be following the matching concept precisely. Few companies bother to do this, however. They simply consider the telephone bill as an expense of the month in which the bill is received, on the grounds that a system that would ascertain the real expense would not be justified by the accuracy gained. Since in many businesses the amount of the bill is likely to be relatively stable from one month to another, no significant error may be involved in this practice. Similarly, very few businesses attempt to match the expenses of making telephone calls to the specific revenues that might have been produced by those calls.

Materiality is also used in another sense in accounting. The principle of *full disclosure* requires that all material information about the financial condition and activities of a business must be disclosed in reports prepared for outside parties. In this sense also there is no definitive rule that separates material from immaterial information. This topic is discussed further in Chapter 13.

THE INCOME STATEMENT

The accounting report that summarizes the revenues and the expenses of an accounting period is called the *income statement* (or the "profit and loss statement," "statement of earnings," or "statement of operations"). In a technical sense the income statement is subordinate to the balance sheet in that it shows in some detail the items that together account for the change arising from operations during an accounting period in one balance sheet category, owners' equity, and more specifically in one item in that category, retained earnings. Nevertheless, the information on the income statement is usually much more important than information on the balance sheet, because the income statement reports the results of operations and indicates reasons for the business's profitability or lack thereof. The importance of the income statement is illustrated by the fact that in situations where accountants in recording an event must choose between a procedure which distorts the balance sheet or one which distorts the income statement (a choice which is unfortunately necessary on occasions), they usually choose the former.

There is in practice considerable variation among companies in the format used for the income statement. The Financial Accounting Standards Board has suggested a format along the lines shown in Illustration 3–2, but makes it clear that this is not mandatory. Illustration 3–2 indi-

Illustration 3–2

ABLE CORPORATION

Statement of Income
Years Ended December 31, 1974, and December 31, 1973

	1974	1973
Net sales	$84,580,000	$75,650,000
Other revenue	80,000	100,000
Total revenues	$84,660,000	$75,750,000
Costs and expenses:		
Cost of goods sold	60,000,000	55,600,000
Selling, general, and administrative expenses	4,200,000	3,900,000
Research and development expense	800,000	700,000
Interest expense	100,000	100,000
Other deductions	80,000	90,000
Income tax	9,350,000	7,370,000
Total costs and expenses	$74,530,000	$67,760,000
Income before extraordinary items	$10,130,000	$ 7,990,000
Extraordinary items	(2,040,000)	(1,280,000)
Net Income	$ 8,090,000	$ 6,710,000
Retained earnings at beginning of year	$25,680,000	$23,350,000
Plus: Net Income	8,090,000	6,710,000
	$33,770,000	$30,060,000
Cash dividends on common stock, $0.75 per share	4,380,000	4,380,000
Retained earnings at end of year	$29,390,000	$25,680,000
Per share of common stock:		
Income before extraordinary items	$1.73	$1.37
Extraordinary items	(0.34)	(0.22)
Net Income	$1.39	$1.15

Source: Adapted from Exhibit A of APB *Opinion No. 9* (December 1966).

cates the amount of detail that appears in typical published financial statements (with a few exceptions to be discussed in Chapters 9 and 13). In statements prepared for the use of management, more detailed information is usually shown.

The income statement in Illustration 3–2 gives information for the prior year, as well as for the current year, to provide a basis for comparison. The FASB requires such a practice, both for the income statement and for the balance sheet.

Comments about the items listed on this income statement and variations often found in practice are given in the following paragraphs.

Revenues

An income statement often shows several separate items in the revenue section, the net of which is the *net sales* figure. For example:

Gross sales............................		$15,400
Less: Returns and allowances...........	$450	
Sales discounts....................	350	800
Net sales..............................		$14,600

Gross sales is the total invoice price of the goods shipped (or services rendered) during the period. It does not ordinarily include *sales taxes* or *excise taxes* that may be charged the customer. Such taxes are not revenues, but rather represent collections which the business makes on behalf of the government. They are a liability to the government until paid. Similarly, postage, freight, or other items billed to the customer at cost are not revenues; they appear not in the sales figure but as an offset to the costs the company incurs for these items. Exceptions are made to these rules when it is not feasible to disentangle the revenue and nonrevenue portions of the transaction.

Sales returns and allowances represent the sales value of goods that were returned by customers or on which customers were given a credit because the goods were not as specified or for some other reason. The amount could have been subtracted from the sales figure directly, without showing it as a separate item on the income statement, but it is often considered as being important enough information to warrant reporting it.

Sales discounts are the amount of *cash* discounts taken by customers for prompt payment. For example, if the business sells merchandise for $1,000 on terms 2/10, n/30 (2 percent off if payment is made in 10 days, and the net, or total, amount due in 30 days), and the customer takes advantage of the discount by paying within 10 days, the business receives only $980 cash and records the other $20 as a sales discount. On some income statements, sales discounts are listed as an operating expense rather than as a deduction from sales; but showing them as an adjustment to the billed price, as above, is probably more common and is more indicative of their character. *Trade discounts,* which are formulas used in figuring the actual selling price from published catalogues or price lists (e.g., "list less 40 percent"), do not appear in the accounting records at all.

Other revenue is revenue earned from activities not associated with the sale of goods and services. Interest or dividends earned on marketable securities owned by the company is an example. The amount is shown separately from net sales so as to facilitate the calculation of gross margin, as explained below.

Cost of Goods Sold

At the identical moment that income is increased by the sales value of merchandise sold, it is also decreased by the cost of that merchandise. Indeed, were it not for the fact that the separate amounts for sales revenue and the cost of goods sold are useful to management, a record could be made only of the net increase in owners' equity that results from a sale.

Some businesses, especially those that sell high unit value merchandise (such as automobiles), keep a record of the cost of each individual item sold. In these businesses, the cost of each item sold is recorded as an expense when the sale is made, and the cost is also subtracted from the asset, inventory, so that at all times the asset item shows the cost of merchandise still on hand. This method is referred to as the *perpetual inventory* method.

If the business does not have such a direct method for ascertaining the cost of the products sold during an accounting period, it must deduce the cost by indirect means. The procedure for doing this is described in Chapter 6. The measurement of cost of goods sold in a manufacturing business involves special problems that are also discussed in Chapter 6.

If a company sells services, rather than goods, or if it sells both goods and services, the item would be labelled *cost of sales* rather than cost of goods sold. The cost of services are the costs associated with providing the service. The cost of sales in a television repair company, for example, would include the labor costs of the repairmen and the cost of parts used, but not the costs of operating the office, nor of advertising, nor of other selling, general and administrative costs.

Gross Margin

The difference between sales revenue and cost of goods sold is the *gross margin* or *gross profit*. On many income statements this amount appears as a separate item.

Conversely, some companies do not show cost of goods sold as one item on the income statement, but instead list individual expenses by *object*, such as salaries and wages, purchases of goods and services, and interest. In such an income statement it is impossible to calculate the gross margin.

Expenses

The classifications given in Illustration 3–2 are a minimum. In many income statements, especially those prepared for internal use, the "selling, general, and administrative expense" category is broken down so as to show separately the principal items of which it is composed.

The separate disclosure of *research and development expense* is a relatively recent requirement. Formerly, most companies included this expense as part of general and administrative expenses. Because the amount spent on research and development can provide an important clue as to how energetic the company is in keeping its products and processes up to date, the FASB requires that this amount be reported separately if it is material.

Extraordinary items are also set forth separately so as to distinguish them from the more-or-less recurring costs of normal operations. The nature of extraordinary items is discussed in Chapter 8.

Net Income

Net income is colloquially referred to as "the bottom line" for obvious reasons.

In Illustration 3–2, income tax is listed with the other expenses. In many income statements, the item "income before income tax" is given and income tax expense is then subtracted. The term used is "net income," with no qualification or modification. Net income is reported not only in total but also per share of stock. The per share amount is obtained by dividing the dollar amount of net income by the number of shares outstanding. The income before extraordinary items and the extraordinary items are also shown on a per share basis.

Retained Earnings

Strictly speaking, the income statement ends with the item "Net Income." Illustration 3–2 goes beyond this to show the changes in retained earnings other than from net income that have occurred during the period. This final section links the income statement to the retained earnings item on the balance sheet. It shows that during the year 1974 retained earnings was increased by the amount of net income (for 1974, $8,090,000) and was decreased by the amount of dividends (for 1974, $4,380,000), so that at the end of the year 1974 it was $29,390,000. Many companies report this calculation separately from the income statement, in which case it is called a *statement of retained earnings*.

Relation between Balance Sheet and Income Statement

The balance sheet and income statement are said to *articulate*, that is, there is a definite relationship between them. More specifically, the amount of net income reported on the income statement, together with the amount of dividends, explains the change in retained earnings between the two balance sheets prepared as of the beginning and the end of the accounting period. This relationship is shown in Illustration 3–3. (The

Illustration 3–3

A "PACKAGE" OF ACCOUNTING REPORTS

Balance Sheet
As of December 31, 1974

ASSETS

Current assets......	$23,839,904
Fixed assets........	14,255,720
Other assets........	180,535
Total Assets....	$38,276,159

EQUITIES

Current liabilities.	$12,891,570
Other liabilities...	3,000,000
Common stock........	15,000,000
Retained earnings...	7,384,589
Total Equities..	$38,276,159

Income Statement
For the Year 1975

Net sales............	$75,478,221
Less: Cost of sales..	52,227,004
Gross margin.........	$23,251,217
Less: Expenses.......	10,784,830
Income before taxes..	$12,466,387
Provision for income taxes.	6,344,000
Net income...........	$ 6,122,387
Retained earnings, beginning........	7,384,589
	$13,506,976
Less: Dividends......	4,390,000
Retained Earnings, Ending..	$ 9,116,976

Balance Sheet
As of December 31, 1975

ASSETS

Current assets......	$22,651,072
Fixed assets........	13,411,779
Other assets........	173,214
Total Assets....	$36,236,065

EQUITIES

Current liabilities.	$ 9,119,089
Other liabilities...	3,000,000
Common stock........	15,000,000
Retained earnings...	9,116,976
Total Equities..	$36,236,065

same December 31, 1974 balance sheet is shown in more detail in Illustration 2–1.)

OTHER CONCEPTS OF INCOME

We have described how income is measured and reported in accordance with generally accepted accounting principles. Not all income statements are prepared in accordance with these principles, however. As noted in Chapter 1, some regulatory bodies prescribe different principles which they require be used by companies within their jurisdiction. Two other types of variation are discussed below: cash-basis accounting and income tax accounting.

Cash-Basis Accounting

The measurement of income as described in this chapter is often called *accrual accounting*. Accrual accounting measures flows in terms of revenues and expenses rather than in terms of receipts and expenditures. Some business entities use a different approach to the measurement of income which is called *cash-basis accounting*. In cash-basis accounting, "income" is regarded as the difference between cash receipts and cash outlays. This approach has the great advantage of simplicity; most of the measurement problems discussed in this chapter do not even arise. In companies in which revenues and expenses do not closely coincide with cash receipts and cash outlays, it has the great disadvantage of not measuring the change in owners' equity in a meaningful way. Cash-basis accounting is used in many small businesses, particularly in those where cash receipts and outlays are good approximations of revenue and expense, for example, retail stores that do not sell on credit and in which inventory is relatively constant. Most individuals use cash-basis accounting in measuring their personal income. Cash-basis accounting is *not* permitted by generally accepted accounting principles.

Income Tax Accounting

Most business entities must calculate their taxable income and pay a federal tax, and in some cases a state or local tax, that is based on this income. The amounts of revenue and expense used to determine federal taxable income are usually similar to, but not identical with, amounts measured in accordance with generally accepted accounting principles. The differences are sufficiently significant so that it is unwise to rely on income tax regulations as a basis for solving business accounting problems.

Unless tax rates applicable to the business are expected to increase in the future, a business usually reports the minimum possible amount of taxable income in the current year, thus postponing tax payments as much as possible to future years. It does this generally by recognizing expenses as soon as legally possible, but postponing the recognition of revenue for as long as possible. Note that this is a process of shifting revenue and expense from one period to another; over the long run in most businesses there is little difference between the total expenses and revenues computed for tax purposes and the total expenses and revenues computed for financial accounting. The objective of minimizing current taxes is, as the Supreme Court has pointed out, entirely legal and ethical, provided it is done in accordance with the tax regulations. It is also legal and proper under most circumstances to figure income one way for tax purposes and another way for financial accounting purposes.

The objective of minimizing current taxes is not by any means the same as the objective of financial accounting, which is to inform management and others as to the income earned. Therefore, the two measurements of income may well be different. For example, income tax regulations permit the cost of certain types of fixed assets to be charged as expenses over a shorter time period than the estimated life of these assets and at amounts in the early years that are greater than the cost of the services consumed in those years. These practices result in higher expenses, and correspondingly lower taxable income, in the early years of an asset's life, and therefore encourage businesses to invest in new fixed assets. Many businesses use these practices in calculating their taxable income, but they use different practices for financial accounting.

As a practical matter, many businesses choose to pattern their accounting practices after the tax regulations. This policy is convenient in that it reduces somewhat the number of separate records that must be maintained. If it is carried to the point of complete subservience to the tax regulations, however, serious distortions in accounting reports can result. In constructing a business income statement, the accountant should not use the authority of a tax regulation as a substitute for careful thinking about the best way of measuring income in accordance with accounting principles.

Although tax regulations are not described in detail in this book, references are made to accounting practices which are or are not consistent with them. The manager learns early the importance of becoming thoroughly familiar with the principal tax rules that affect his operations and also the importance of consulting an expert when unusual situations arise.

SUMMARY

Revenues are the value of goods sold and services supplied to customers during an accounting period. Expenses are the cost of the resources used, either directly or indirectly, in providing these goods and services. Net income is the amount by which revenues exceed expenses. Stated another way, revenues are increases in retained earnings resulting from operations during an accounting period, and expenses are corresponding decreases.

In measuring revenues, the basic guide is the realization concept, which is that revenues are generally recognized in the period in which they are realized, that is, in the period in which goods are shipped to customers or in which services are rendered. The amount recognized is the amount that customers are reasonably certain to pay.

In measuring expenses, the basic guide is the matching concept, which is that costs become expenses in a given accounting period under any of three circumstances: (1) when there is a direct association between costs and revenues, (2) when costs are directly associated with activities of the period itself, or (3) when costs cannot be associated with revenues of any future period.

The consistency concept requires that once a company has decided on a certain method of accounting for a given class of events, it will use the same method in accounting for all subsequent events of the same character unless it has a sound reason to do otherwise.

The materiality concept permits departures from the other concepts, in the interest of simplicity, when the effect of such departures is not material.

The income statement summarizes the revenues and expenses for an accounting period. The "official" accounting period is one year, but interim income statements are usually prepared on a monthly or quarterly basis.

Accounting for revenues and expenses according to the concepts stated above is called accrual accounting. Accrual accounting differs from cash-basis accounting and, in certain respects, from the accounting used in calculating taxable income.

CASES

CASE 3–1. ELMER KUPPER

In 1973, Elmer Kupper opened his own retail store. At the end of 1974, his first full year of operation, he thought he had done moderately well, and he was therefore somewhat chagrined when the trade association to which he belonged sent him figures which indicated that he had operated at a loss.

Mr. Kupper had been employed as manager of the local unit of a chain store for several years. In 1973 he had received an inheritance, and this, together with his savings, provided him with enough funds to buy a small store building on the main street of his town for $45,000.

He joined the trade association to which several thousand independent retailers in the same line of business belonged. One of the services furnished by this association was the annual compilation of typical operating figures of member firms. These figures were prepared by Hartje & Mees,

Exhibit 1
INCOME STATEMENT FOR 1974, AS PREPARED BY MR. KUPPER

Gross sales		$102,891
Less: Returns and allowances to customers		3,639
Net Sales		99,252
Cost of merchandise sold		64,129
Gross margin		$ 35,123
Expenses:		
Salaries and wages	$10,848	
Advertising	1,773	
Supplies and postage	1,189	
Taxes, insurance, repairs, and depreciation on building	2,020	
Heat, light, and power	639	
Business and social security taxes	1,488	
Insurance	708	
Depreciation on equipment	562	
Interest expense	360	
Miscellaneous expense	2,640	
Income taxes	1,830	$ 24,057
Net Income		$ 11,066

76

a large public accounting firm. Early in 1975, Hartje & Mees sent Mr. Kupper a standard form and requested that he report his revenue and expenses on this form and return it so that his figures could be averaged in with those of other member stores. Exhibit 1 shows the figures which, with some difficulty, Mr. Kupper entered on this form.

Subsequently, he received a request from Hartje & Mees for information on his salary and on the rental value of his building. Mr. Kupper answered substantially as follows:

I own my own business, so there is no point in my charging myself a salary. I drew $14,000 from the business in 1974 for my personal use. My annual salary as a manager of a Mogell store in recent years was $12,000, although I don't see what bearing this has on the figures for my own store.

I thought I made it clear in my original submission that I own my own building. It would cost me $5,400 a year to rent a similar building, and you can see from the figures that I save a considerable amount of money by not being forced to rent.

On the basis of the information in this letter, Hartje & Mees revised Mr. Kupper's figures and sent him the income statement shown in Exhibit 2. Mr. Kupper was considerably upset by this revised statement.

Exhibit 2
INCOME STATEMENT FOR 1974, AS REVISED BY HARTJE & MEES

Gross sales		$102,891
Less: Returns and allowances to customers		3,639
Net sales		99,252
Cost of merchandise sold		64,129
Gross margin		$ 35,123
Expenses:		
Salaries and wages	$22,848	
Advertising	1,773	
Supplies and postage	1,189	
Rent	5,400	
Heat, light, and power	639	
Business and social security taxes	1,488	
Insurance	708	
Depreciation on equipment	562	
Interest expense	360	
Miscellaneous expense	2,640	37,607
Net Loss		$ 2,484

He showed it to a friend and said:

These fancy accountants have gotten my figures all mixed up. I want to know the profit I have made by operating my own business rather than by working for somebody else. They have turned my profit into a loss by calling part of it salary and part of it rent. This is merely shifting money from one pocket to another. On the other hand, they won't even let me show my income tax as an expense. I realize that the tax is levied on me as an individual rather than on the business as such, but my only source of income is my store, and I therefore think the tax is a legitimate expense of my store.

Questions

1. How much profit did Mr. Kupper's store earn in 1974? How do you explain the difference between the profit shown on Exhibit 1 and the loss shown on Exhibit 2? What, if any, accounting principles are violated in either statement?
2. Should Mr. Kupper continue to operate his own store? Has he been successful?
3. Does the income statement that would be most useful to Mr. Kupper differ from the income statement that would be most useful in compiling average figures for use by the trade association membership?

CASE 3–2.   VITAR ELECTRONICS, INC.

After six months of operation, Victor Peterson and Harold Corning met to decide what to do next with their "baby," Vitar Electronics, Inc. The company seemed to be off to a profitable start, and they were intrigued by the possibility of changing it from a part-time to a full-time venture.

Mr. Peterson, 29, was a production engineer for the Davis Machine Company, a large manufacturer; Mr. Corning, 32, was on the sales promotion staff of the same company. Each earned a salary of $12,000 per year. They were neighbors and close friends. Mr. Peterson had an inventive bent, and among his ideas was a new type of stepping switch. A stepping switch is a device which activates a number of electrical circuits in sequence automatically, one after the other. One of its uses is in product inspection and testing.[1] On his own time, Mr. Peterson developed a working model and applied for a patent. He interested the Davis quality control department in his stepping switch, and after tests and negotiation, the Davis Company, on May 1, agreed to purchase 20 units at $565 each.

Messrs. Peterson and Corning thereupon formed Vitar Electronics, Inc. Each took 200 shares of stock in exchange for $3,000 cash, a sizable

---

[1] A more complete description is: The Vitar Stepping Switch M–1 consists of 20 single-pole switching positions and can be wired through a plug board to perform any programming of switching forward, backward, or in any preselected pattern, up to 200 impulses per second. It can be wired to advance one position on each successive impulse fed into it or can be timed to complete the entire switching cycle automatically. There are no moving parts except for vacuum-sealed mercury whetted magnet-operated relays—each guaranteed to perform 4 million times. The controlling circuit is transitor powered and can operate at a speed of 7,000 impulses per second.

Exhibit 1

VITAR ELECTRONICS, INC.

Financial Statements as of October 31

Balance Sheet

ASSETS

Current Assets:		
Cash..	$ 610	
Accounts receivable................................	1,130	
Inventory of parts and components..................	3,543	
Completed stepping switches........................	1,752	
Total Current Assets.............................		$ 7,035
Equipment (at cost)..................................	$4,319	
Patent rights..	7,500	11,819
Total Assets..................................		$18,854

EQUITIES

Liabilities:		
Accounts payable..................................		$ 1,480
Notes payable.....................................		7,500
Total Liabilities.................................		$ 8,980
Capital:		
Capital stock.....................................	$6,000	
Retained earnings.................................	3,874	
Total Capital.................................		9,874
Total Equities................................		$18,854

Income Statement for Six Months

Sales...		$14,125
Cost of sales.....................................		7,203
Gross margin......................................		$ 6,922
Advertising.......................................	$2,193	
Other expenses....................................	855	3,048
Net Income.......................................		$ 3,874

fraction of their savings. Mr. Peterson also assigned his rights in the invention to the corporation in exchange for a noninterest-bearing 10-year note in the amount of $7,500.

The manufacture of the stepping switch involved principally assembly and wiring. The two men did this themselves in Mr. Corning's basement, working evenings and weekends. The 20 units were completed, and payment received, by September.

Meanwhile, Mr. Corning wrote and placed free "product announcements" and a small amount of paid advertising in trade publications. These resulted in inquiries that led to orders for additional units from other companies. The owners were thereby encouraged to seek sales more vigorously, so in September they placed larger advertisements costing a total of approximately $1,500. In order to be able to fill promptly the orders expected to result from this advertising, they continued to assemble stepping switches in September and October, and by the end of October had six completed units on hand. They also had on hand a supply of printed circuits and other component parts, most of which were made to Vitar's specifications by outside companies.

During the entire six-month period from May 1 to October 31, Messrs. Peterson and Corning each worked about 10 hours a week making stepping switches, plus some additional time in preparing promotional material, answering inquiries, talking with prospective customers, and handling other Vitar problems. During this time they had paid themselves no salary, since Vitar's available cash was needed to buy components and to pay for equipment, most of which was built to their design in a local machine shop. They decided that the time had come to think about devoting full time to Vitar. As part of their appraisal of where they stood, Mr. Corning prepared the financial statements shown in Exhibit 1. In addition to the component parts shown on the balance sheet, Vitar had also ordered $2,731.00 of printed circuits and other components, with delivery expected some time in November.

Mr. Peterson, upon seeing these statements, remarked: "Not bad for a starter. Even with our organization costs and advertising expenses deducted, we show an excellent profit, and a very gratifying return on our investment."

Questions

1. Comment on the performance of Vitar Electronics, Inc., and its status on October 31.
2. What additional information, if any, would you need before recommending a course of action for Messrs. Peterson and Corning?

CASE 3–3. JOHN BARTLETT (A)

John Bartlett was the inventor of a hose-clamp for automobile hose connections. The clamp would soon be given a patent, whose legal life was 17 years. Having confidence in the clamp's commercial value, but possessing no excess funds of his own, he sought among his friends and acquaintances for the necessary capital to put the hose-clamp on the market. The proposition which he placed before possible associates was that a corporation, Bartlett Manufacturing Company, should be formed with capital stock of $25,000 par value.

The project looked attractive to a number of the individuals to whom the inventor presented it, but the most promising among them—a retired manufacturer—said he would be unwilling to invest his capital without knowing what uses were intended for the cash to be received from the proposed sale of stock. He suggested that the inventor determine the probable costs of experimentation and of special machinery, and prepare for him a statement of the estimated assets and liabilities of the proposed company when ready to begin actual operation. He also asked for a statement of the estimated transactions for the first year of operations, to be based on studies the inventor had made of probable markets and costs of labor and materials. This information Mr. Bartlett consented to supply to the best of his ability.

After consulting the engineer who had aided him in constructing his patent models, Mr. Bartlett drew up the following list of data relating to the transactions of the proposed corporation during its period of organization and development:

1. The retired manufacturer would pay the corporation $10,000 cash for which he would receive stock with a par value of $10,000. The remaining stock (par value, $15,000) would be given to Mr. Bartlett in exchange for the patent on the hose-clamp.
2. Probable cost of incorporation and organization, including estimated officers' salaries during developmental period, $1,650.
3. Probable cost of developing special machinery, $5,000. This sum includes the cost of expert services, materials, rent of a small shop, and the cost of power, light, and miscellaneous expenditures.
4. Probable cost of raw materials: $500, of which $300 is to be used in experimental production.

On the basis of the above information, Mr. Bartlett prepared the estimated balance sheet shown in Exhibit 1.

Exhibit 1

BARTLETT MANUFACTURING COMPANY

Estimated Balance Sheet as of Date Company Begins Operations

ASSETS		EQUITIES	
Cash	$ 2,850	Shareholders' equity	$25,000
Inventory	200		
Machinery	5,000		
Organization costs	1,650		
Experimental costs	300		
Patent	15,000		
Total Assets	$25,000	Total Equities	$25,000

Mr. Bartlett then set down the following estimates as a beginning step in furnishing the rest of the information desired:

1. Expected sales, all to be received in cash by the end of the first year of operation, $84,000.
2. Expected additional purchases of raw materials and supplies during the course of this operating year, all paid for in cash by end of year, $27,000.
3. Expected borrowing from the bank during year but loans to be repaid before close of year, $2,000. Interest on these loans, $150.
4. Expected payroll and other cash expenses and manufacturing costs for the operating year: $33,000 of manufacturing costs (excluding raw materials and supplies) plus $6,000 for selling and administrative expenses, a total of $39,000.
5. New equipment to be purchased for cash, $1,000.
6. Expected inventory of raw materials and supplies at close of period, at cost, $5,000.
7. No inventory of unsold hose-clamps expected as of the end of the period. All products to be manufactured on the basis of firm orders received; none to be produced for inventory.
8. All experimental and organization costs, previously capitalized, to be charged against income of the operating year.
9. Estimated depreciation of machinery, $600.
10. Dividends paid in cash, $3,000.
11. Estimated tax expense for the year, $4,225. This amount would not be due until early in the following year.

It should be noted that the transactions summarized above would not necessarily take place in the sequence indicated. In practice, a considerable number of separate events, or transactions, would occur throughout the year, and many of them were dependent on one another. For example, operations were begun with an initial cash balance and inventory of raw materials, products were manufactured, and sales of these products provided funds for financing subsequent operations. Then, in turn, sales of the product subsequently manufactured yielded more funds.

Questions

1. Trace the effect on the balance sheet of each of the projected events appearing in Mr. Bartlett's list. Thus, Item 1, taken alone, would mean that cash would be increased by $84,000 and that (subject to reductions for various costs covered in later items) shareholders' equity would be increased by $84,000. Notice that in this question you are asked to consider all items in terms of their effect on the balance sheet.
2. Prepare an income statement covering the first year of planned operations and a balance sheet as of the end of that year.
3. *Assume* that the retired manufacturer received capital stock with a par

value of $8,000 for the $10,000 cash he paid to the corporation, John Bartlett still receiving stock with a par value of $15,000 in exchange for his patent. Under these circumstances, how would the balance sheet in Exhibit 1 appear?

4. *Assume* that the management is interested in what the results would be if no products were sold during the first year, even though production continued at the level indicated in the original plans. The following changes would be made in the 11 items listed above: Items 1, 6, 7, 10, and 11 are to be disregarded. Instead of Item 3, assume that a loan of $78,000 is obtained, that the loan is not repaid, but that interest thereon of $9,350 is paid during the year. Prepare an income statement for the year and a balance sheet as of the end of the year. Contrast these financial statements with those prepared in Question 2.

CASE 3–4. JAMES STANTON

James Stanton took his savings, some money his parents had left him, some material he found in his parent's garage, and started business for himself. It wasn't a large business, but it did give him the pleasure of being his own boss, and combined the inside work of manufacturing with the outside work of selling. His product was a painted wooden toy train that was priced at retail at $20.30 each. It was a well-built toy, designed to be reminiscent of the hand-made toys of his grandfather's generation. Stanton was an energetic person and he soon had output rolling. This had been accomplished despite difficulties, chiefly with paint, but at last Mr. Stanton had found a supplier who promised to provide him with the necessary quality.

At the end of the first six months' experience, James Stanton took pride in his first profit and loss statement. He hoped it would be the forerunner of a long series of reports showing operations "in the black."

Income Statement for Six Months Ending December 31

Net Sales....................................			$11,620.49
Beginning inventory, July 1....................		$ 210.00	
Purchases of material........................	$ 7,007.00		
Labor.......................................	11,347.63		
Rent of machines and space..................	2,926.14	21,280.77	
		$21,490.77	
Less: Inventory at end of period, December 31..		16,086.70	
Cost of goods sold...........................			5,404.07
Gross margin................................			$ 6,216.42
Advertising and other selling expenses..........	$ 2,114.32		
Interest.....................................	73.50		$ 2,187.82
Net Income.................................			$ 4,028.60

Mr. Stanton's "balance sheet" as of December 31 appeared as follows:

Assets:

Cash..	$ 428.26	
Inventory, at cost.............................	16,086.70	$16,514.96

Less: Liabilities:

Note payable, L. K. Stanton......................	$ 4,200.00	
Accounts payable...............................	3,835.30	8,035.30
Leaving James Stanton's Net Worth as..............		$ 8,479.66

Question

Comment on Mr. Stanton's performance to date and on his prospects for the future.

CHAPTER 4

ACCOUNTING RECORDS
AND SYSTEMS

Up to this point, the effect on the financial statements of each individual transaction has been described separately. Thus, starting with the item "Cash, $10,000" on a balance sheet, a transaction involving an increase of $5,000 in cash would be recorded, in effect, by erasing the $10,000 and putting in the new number, $15,000. This procedure was appropriate as an explanatory device in view of the small number of transactions with which we have been dealing. Clearly, however, such a technique is not a practical way of handling the large volume of transactions that occur in actual business operations. This chapter describes some of the bookkeeping procedures that are used in practice. It should be emphasized that *no new accounting concepts are introduced;* the devices described here are no more than the mechanical means of increasing the facility with which transactions can be recorded and summarized.

We first describe the procedures used in a manual system, that is one in which the numbers are recorded by hand. We then show the similarities and the differences between this manual system and a computer-based system.

BOOKKEEPING

We are not here concerned with bookkeeping procedures for the purpose of training bookkeepers. Some knowledge of these procedures is nevertheless useful for at least two reasons. First, as is the case with many subjects, accounting is something that is best learned by doing—by the actual solution of problems—and although any accounting problem can be solved without the aid of the tools discussed in this chapter, their

85

use will often speed up considerably the problem-solving process. Secondly, the debit-and-credit mechanism, which is the principal technique discussed here, provides a framework for analysis that has much the same purpose, and the same advantages, as the symbols and equations of elementary algebra. This mechanism can often be used to reduce an apparently complex, perhaps almost incomprehensible, statement of facts to a simple, specific set of relationships. Thus, the debit-and-credit mechanism provides a useful way of thinking about many types of business problems—not only strictly accounting problems but also problems of other types.

The Account

Consider again a balance sheet on which the item "Cash, $10,000" appears. Subsequent cash transactions can affect this amount in only one of two ways: they can increase it, or they can decrease it. Instead of increasing or decreasing the item by erasing the old amount and entering the new amount for each transaction, considerable effort can be saved by collecting all the increases together and all the decreases together and then periodically calculating, in a single arithmetic operation, the net change resulting from all of them. This can be done by adding the sum of the increases to the beginning amount and then subtracting the sum of the decreases. The difference is the new cash *balance*, reflecting the net effect of all the separate increases and decreases.

In accounting, the device called an *account* is used for just this purpose. The simplest form of account, called a *T account*, looks like this:

Cash

(Increases)		(Decreases)	
Beginning balance	10,000		2,000
	5,000		600
	4,000		400
	100		1,000
	2,700		
	800		
	22,600		4,000
New balance	18,600		

All increases are listed on one side, and all decreases are listed on the other. Also note that the dollar sign ($) is omitted; this is the usual practice in most accounting procedures.

The saving in effort can be seen even from this brief illustration. If the balance were changed for each of the nine transactions listed, five additions and four subtractions would be required. By using the account device, the new balance is obtained by only two additions (to find the 22,600 and 4,000) and one subtraction (22,600 − 4,000).

In actual accounting systems, the account form is set up so that other useful information, in addition to the amount of each increase or decrease, can be recorded. A common arrangement of the columns is the following:

CASH

January 1975

Date	Explanation	(R)	Amount	Date	Explanation	(R)	Amount
	Balance		10,000	3	Accts. Pay.	2	2,000
2	Sales	1	5,000	4	Supplies	2	600
2	Accts. Rec.	1	4,000				

The essence of this form of the account is the same as that of the T-account; in fact, the T can be observed in the double-ruled lines. Its headings are self-explanatory except that of "R" (standing for "reference") under which is entered a simple code showing the source of the information recorded. This is useful if it is necessary to check back to the source of the entry at some future time.

Debit and Credit

The left-hand side of any account is arbitrarily called the *debit* side, and the right-hand side is called the *credit* side. Amounts entered on the left-hand side are called debits, and amounts on the right-hand side, credits. The verb "to debit" means "to make an entry in the left-hand side of an account,"[1] and the verb "to credit" means "to make an entry in the right-hand side of an account." *The words debit and credit have no other meaning in accounting.* The preceding sentence is emphasized because in ordinary usage these words do have other meanings. Credit has a favorable connotation (such as, "She is a credit to her country.") and debit has an unfavorable connotation (such as "Chalk up a debit against him."). In accounting, these words do not imply any sort of value judgment; they mean simply "left" and "right." Debit and credit are usually abbreviated to Dr. and Cr.

If each account were considered by itself, without regard to its relationship with other accounts, it would make no difference whether increases were recorded on the debit side or on the credit side. In the 15th century a Franciscan monk, Lucas Pacioli, described a method of

---

[1] The verb "to charge" is often used as a synonym for "to debit."

arranging accounts in such a way that the dual aspect that is present in every accounting transaction would be expressed by a debit amount and an equal and offsetting credit amount. This made possible the rule, *to which there is absolutely no exception*, that for each transaction the debit amount (or the sum of all the debit amounts, if there are more than one) must equal the credit amount (or the sum of all the credit amounts). This is why accounting is called *double-entry* accounting. It follows that the recording of a transaction in which debits do not equal credits is incorrect. It also follows that, for all the accounts combined, the sum of the debit balances must equal the sum of the credit balances; otherwise, something has been done incorrectly. Thus the debit and credit arrangement used in accounting provides a useful means of checking the accuracy with which the work has been done.

The equality of debits and credits is maintained in the accounts simply by specifying that asset accounts are increased on the debit side while liabilities and owners' equity accounts are increased on the credit side. The account balances, when they are totalled, will then conform to the two equations:

(1)   Assets = Liabilities + Owners' Equity
(2)   Debits = Credits.

This arrangement gives rise to three rules:

1. Increases in *asset* accounts are debits; decreases are credits.
2. Increases in *liability* accounts are credits; decreases are debits.
3. Increases in *owners' equity* accounts are credits; decreases are debits.

We can derive the rules for expense and revenue accounts if we recall that expenses are decreases in owners' equity and revenues are increases in owners' equity. Since owners' equity accounts decrease on the debit side, expense accounts increase on the debit side; and since owners' equity accounts increase on the credit side, revenue accounts increase on the credit side. In summary, the rules are:

4. Increases in *expense* accounts are debits.
5. Increases in *revenue* accounts are credits.

These rules are illustrated in the diagram shown in Illustration 4–1. Note that assets, which are "good" things, and expenses, which are "bad" things, both increase on the debit side, and that liability and revenue accounts both increase on the credit side. This is another illustration of the fact that "debit" and "credit" are neutral terms; they do not connote value judgments.

Debits and credits to certain special accounts are not covered by these rules, but they can be deduced from them. As an example, consider the account, Sales Discount, which is a deduction from sales revenue. We know that Sales is a revenue account and that increases are therefore recorded on the credit side. Since Sales Discount is a deduction from Sales, it must be treated in the opposite way from Sales. Sales Discount, therefore, increases on the debit side.

Illustration 4–1

RULES OF DEBIT AND CREDIT

Assets	=	Liabilities	+	Owners' Equity
Example:		*Example:*		*Example:*
Cash		**Accounts Payable**		**Retained Earnings**

Dr.	Cr.		Dr.	Cr.		Dr.	Cr.
+	–		–	+		–	+

	Expenses	Revenues
	Example:	*Example:*
	Wage Expense	**Sales**

Dr.	Cr.		Dr.	Cr.
+				+

Debit Balances = Credit Balances

The Ledger

A ledger is a group of accounts. The reader has probably seen a bound book with the word "ledger" printed on the cover. All the accounts of a small business could be maintained in such a book. Or, the business might have an "Accounts Receivable Ledger," an "Accounts Payable Ledger," and a "General Ledger," each containing the group of accounts suggested by the title. The ledger is not necessarily a bound book; it may consist of a set of loose-leaf pages, a set of punched cards, or, with the advent of electronic computers, a set of impulses on a reel of magnetic tape. No matter what its form may be, the essential character of the account and the rules for making entries to it remain exactly as stated above.

The Chart of Accounts

Prior to setting up an accounting system, a list is usually prepared showing each item for which a ledger account is to be maintained. This list is called the *chart of accounts*. Each account on the list is numbered in a way that facilitates arrangement. For example, the group of asset accounts might be numbered 1 – – –; current assets, 11 – –; cash, 111 –, and Cash in First National Bank, 1111. Only the last of these, Account 1111, is an actual account in which entries are made; the others are account categories.

There will be at least as many separate accounts as there are items on the balance sheet and income statement. Usually there are many more accounts than this minimum number so that detailed information useful to management can be collected. The number of accounts is governed by management's need for information. For example, although the single item "accounts receivable" ordinarily appears on the balance sheet, a separate account for each customer is often maintained in a ledger so as to show how much is owed by each.

There is no limit, other than the cost of record keeping, to the proliferation of accounts that may be found in practice. Take, for example, transactions concerned with sales revenue. In the simplest ledger, there would be one account, sales revenue. If management wanted information of sales by geographic regions, there would be a number of accounts, one for sales made in each region. The sum of the balances in all these accounts would equal total sales revenue. Going a step further, if management wanted information classified both by sales region and by product class, there would be an account for sales of each product class within each region. Each sales transaction is recorded in one and only one account. With such a chart of accounts, sales revenue for a region can be obtained by adding up all the product class accounts in that region, and sales revenue for a product class can be obtained by adding up all the regional accounts for that product class.

When such multidimensional classifications are desired, the number of separate accounts increases rapidly, for there must be a separate account for the smallest unit of information that is to be aggregated.

> EXAMPLE: A manufacturing company divides its sales territory into nine regions. It sells products which it groups into ten classes. In order to obtain information on sales both by region and by product class, it must have, not 19 ($= 9 + 10$) sales revenue accounts, but rather 90 ($= 9 \times 10$) accounts.

With a manual system, the sheer bulk of the number of ledger pages constrains the proliferation of accounts that results from the desire for information that is classified in various ways. In a computer-based system, as we shall see, these constraints are much less severe.

The Journal

A journal is a chronological record of accounting transactions showing the names of accounts that are to be debited or credited, the amounts of the debits and credits, and any useful supplementary information about the transaction. A simple form of the journal is shown in Illustration 4–2. It helps in understanding these transactions if the reader reasons out the events that gave rise to each of them.

With respect to format, note that the debit entry is listed first, that the debit amounts appear in the first of the two money columns, that the account to be credited appears below the debit entry and is indented, and that credit amounts appear in the second money column. "LF" is an abbreviation for "ledger folio," that is, the page reference to the ledger account where the entry is to be made; these references are inserted at the time the entry is recorded in the account, and their

Illustration 4–2

JOURNAL

1975		Accounts	LF	Debit	Credit
Jan.	2	Cash.....................	1	5,000.00	
		Sales..................	41		4,900.00
		Sales tax liability.....	21		100.00
	2	Accounts Receivable.......	2	1,711.50	
		Sales..................	41		1,650.00
		Sales Tax Liability.....	21		49.50
		Postage................	32		12.00
	2	Cash.....................	1	4,000.00	
		Sales Discount...........	43	60.00	
		Accounts Receivable.....	2		4,060.00
	3	Sales Returns and Allow- ances................		47.00	
		Accounts Receivable.....			47.00

presence indicates that the entry has been recorded. (In the illustration, the first ten items have been recorded in the accounts, and the remaining two have not yet been recorded.) In some businesses, a brief explanation is written beneath each entry.

The journal contains explicit instructions as to the changes that are to be made to the balances in the accounts. The process of making these changes is called *posting*. No account balance is ever changed except on the basis of a journal entry. (The balance in the account is computed and recorded periodically, but this process does not in any way *change* the balance in the account.)

Thus, the ledger is a device for *reclassifying* and *summarizing*, by accounts, information originally listed in chronological order in the journal. Entries are first made in the journal; they are later posted to ledger accounts.

The Trial Balance

The trial balance is simply a list of the account names and the balances in each account as of a given moment of time, with debit balances in one column and credit balances in another column. The preparation of the trial balance serves two principal purposes: (1) it shows whether the equality of debits and credits has been maintained, and (2) it provides a convenient transcript of the ledger record as a basis for making adjusting and closing entries (to be described in the next section) or in the preparation of financial statements.

To maintain the relationship "Total Assets = Total Liabilities + Owners' Equity," debits and credits must be kept in balance. Although the fact that totals on a trial balance are equal does indicate that the integrity of the accounting equation has been maintained, it does not prove that errors have not been made. Entries may have been omitted entirely; they may have been posted to the wrong account; offsetting errors may have been made; or the transaction may have been analyzed incorrectly. For example, when a debit for the purchase of a truck is made incorrectly to an expense account rather than correctly to a fixed asset account, the totals of the trial balance are not affected. Nevertheless, errors that result in unequal debits and credits are common, and the fact that such errors exist is evident when a trial balance does not balance; that is, when the debit column does not add to the same total as the credit column.

A trial balance may be prepared at any time. A *preadjustment* trial balance is one prepared after the original entries for the period have been posted, but prior to the adjusting and closing process. A *postclosing* trial balance is prepared after the closing process.

THE ADJUSTING AND CLOSING PROCESS

Need For Adjusting Entries

Most of the entries that are to be made in accounts come to the accountant's attention easily and obviously. When checks are drawn against the company's bank account, it is obvious that an entry must be made crediting Cash and debiting some other account. When invoices are sent out, a credit to Sales and a debit to Accounts Receivable is obviously generated. Entries of this type are called *original entries* or *spot entries*.

Some events that affect the accounts are not evidenced by such obvious documents. The effects of these events are recorded at the end of the accounting period by means of what are called *adjusting entries*. The purpose of the adjusting entries is to modify account balances so that they will reflect fairly the situation as of the end of the period.

CONTINUOUS TRANSACTIONS.   Most adjusting entries are made in connection with events that are, in effect, continuous transactions. Consider a tank of fuel oil purchased for $1,000. On the day of delivery, the $1,000 of fuel oil was an asset, but each day thereafter some fuel oil was consumed in the furnace, whereupon part of the $1,000 became an expense. Rather than record this consumption daily, a single adjusting entry is made at the end of the accounting period to show how much of the fuel oil is still an asset at that time and how much has become expense during the period. There are two ways of handling these events, both of which give the same result. Under one method, the fuel oil is originally recorded as an asset, and at the end of the accounting period the asset account is adjusted by subtracting the cost of fuel oil consumed, thus:

```
dr.*    Fuel Expense............................ 600
   cr.     Fuel Oil Inventory...................     600
```

Under the other method, the $1,000 expenditure for fuel oil is originally recorded in an expense account, and the fuel oil remaining at the end of the period is subtracted and shown as an asset, thus:

```
dr.    Fuel Oil Inventory...................... 400
   cr.     Fuel Expense........................     400
```

Although neither method reflects the correct facts *within* the period (with the trivial exception that the first method does reflect the facts on the first day), both reflect a correct statement of the facts as of the *end* of the accounting period, namely, that the fuel oil inventory is $400 and that fuel oil expense for the period was $600. Since accounting focuses on deriving the proper amounts for the statements that are prepared at the end of the accounting period, and since both methods result in the correct final amounts, the choice between these methods depends solely on which is more convenient.

Types of Adjusting Entries

Events that require adjusting entries essentially relate to the differences between expense and expenditure and between revenue and receipts discussed in Chapter 3. Four types of such events together with examples of each, are given below:

1. *Recorded costs to be apportioned among two or more accounting periods:*
   a. The fuel oil example given above is one example.
   b. For insurance protection, originally recorded as Prepaid Insur-

---

* As a reminder to the reader, the notations dr. and cr. are used in Chapters 4 and 5 to designate the debit and credit portions of each journal entry. These notations are not used in practice since the accountant distinguishes debits from credits on the basis of the order and indentation of the accounts.

ance (an asset), $300 of which becomes an expense in the current period:

```
dr.    Insurance Expense........................ 300
   cr.     Prepaid Insurance.....................        300
```

c. For rent paid in advance and originally recorded as an expense, $5,000 of which is an asset at the end of the period since it represents the right to use the property for the next period:

```
dr.    Prepaid Rent........................ 5,000
   cr.     Rent Expense....................        5,000
```

d. For $200 of supplies consumed in the period:

```
dr.    Supplies Expense........................ 200
   cr.     Supplies Inventory...................        200
```

2. *Unrecorded expenses:*
   a. For $50 of wages earned by an employee during the period but not yet paid to him:

```
dr.    Wages Expense............................. 50
   cr.     Accrued Wages Payable.................        50
```

   b. For interest expense of $5 which has not yet been paid:

```
dr.    Interest Expense............................. 5
   cr.     Accrued Interest Payable.................        5
```

   c. For interest (i.e., discount) deducted from a loan in advance and originally recorded as Prepaid Interest (an asset), $7 of which becomes an expense of the current period:

```
dr.    Interest Expense............................. 7
   cr.     Prepaid Interest..........................        7
```

3. *Recorded revenues to be apportioned among two or more accounting periods:*
   a. For rent collected during the period, and recorded as rent revenue, $600 of which is applicable to the next period and hence is a liability at the end of the current period:

```
dr.    Rent Revenue............................. 600
   cr.     Deferred Rent Revenue.................        600
```

4. *Unrecorded revenues:*
   a. For $20 of interest earned by the business during the period, but not yet received:

```
dr.    Accrued Interest Receivable................. 20
   cr.     Interest Revenue.....................        20
```

DEPRECIATION. Most fixed asssets are continuously being converted to an expense, just like fuel oil, prepaid insurance, and supplies. The item that shows the portion of fixed asset costs that have become expense during an accounting period is called *Depreciation Expense*. Instead of subtracting the amount of expense for the period directly from the asset amount, however, a separate account, *Accumulated Depreciation*, is used. This account shows the total of such subtractions to date and is deducted from the cost of fixed assets on the balance sheet, thus:

```
Equipment (at cost)........................ $1,000
   Less: Accumulated depreciation...........   400
      Net Equipment...........................         $600
```

The adjusting entry to record the depreciation expense for a period is therefore of the following form:

```
dr.    Depreciation Expense........................ 200
   cr.    Accumulated Depreciation.................         200
```

This process is described in more detail in Chapter 7.

OTHER ADJUSTMENTS. The accountant may make a variety of other adjusting entries in his attempt to make the accounts reflect fairly the results of operations and the status of the business. An example, discussed in more detail in Chapter 5, is *bad debt expense*, an adjustment made in order to recognize the likelihood that not all credit customers will pay their bills and that therefore the Accounts Receivable account may overstate the collectible amount of the company's claims against its customers. An adjusting entry that records the estimated amount of bad debts is as follows:

```
dr.    Bad Debt Expense........................... 300
   cr.    Allowance for Doubtful Accounts..........         300
```

On the balance sheet, Allowance for Doubtful Accounts is subtracted from Accounts Receivable, thus:

```
Accounts receivable (gross)........................ $1,000
   Less: Allowance for doubtful accounts............    50
      Net Accounts Receivable......................         $950
```

A CAUTION. When the student is given a problem involving the preparation of accounting statements, he must be told the precise nature of the original entries since he has no way of finding them out for himself. He will not necessarily be told about the adjusting entries, however; and he, like any accountant, is expected to be on the lookout for situations that require adjustment. For example, if the balance sheet at the beginning of a period shows the asset, prepaid insurance, accountants know that they must make an adjusting entry at the end of the period to show the expired cost, even though no routine document tells them to do so.

Closing Entries

Revenue accounts and expense accounts are called *temporary* (or "nominal") accounts, as distinguished from asset, liability, and owners' equity accounts, which are called *permanent* (or "real") accounts. The temporary accounts are actually subdivisions of owners' equity. They are a convenient means of classifying the various revenue and expense transactions that occur during an accounting period so as to provide the information needed to prepare the income statement for the period. The temporary accounts are periodically *closed* to owners' equity in order to determine the net effect (i.e., the profit or the loss) of all the revenue and expense transactions.

Closing procedures differ from company to company. Under all closing methods, however, revenue and expense accounts are ultimately closed to an account called *Income Summary* (also called *Profit and Loss* or *Loss and Gain* or *Expense and Revenue Summary*). This account reflects the net income or loss for a given accounting period. Income Summary is a temporary account which in turn is closed to Retained Earnings to complete the closing process. In many businesses, the revenue and expense accounts are not closed directly to Income Summary. Instead, one or more additional temporary or *clearing* accounts are set up, such as Cost of Goods Sold, and Trading (an account which shows the gross margin for the period), and successive closings are made to these accounts. The purpose of these intermediate clearing accounts is to show separately some or all of the elements comprising Income Summary (e.g., cost of goods sold and gross margin). The ultimate effect, however, is the same as a direct closing to Income Summary.

The closing process consists of transferring the balance of each temporary account to the same side of a clearing account. This is done by making a journal entry debiting the account to be closed if it has a credit balance (or crediting it if it has a debit balance) in an amount equal to the balance. The entry has the effect of reducing the balance in the account to zero, thereby closing it. Note that each entry is made on the opposite side from the side with the balance. The other half of this entry is made to Income Summary or to one of the intermediate clearing accounts.

EXAMPLE: If the credit balance in the Sales account at the end of an accounting period is $174,000, the account is closed by the following entry:

```
dr.   Sales........................... 174,000
    cr.    Income Summary................          174,000
```

EXAMPLE: If the Salaries and Wages expense account has a debit balance of $21,000, it is closed by the following entry:

```
dr.    Income Summary..................... 21,000
   cr.     Salaries and Wages..............        21,000
```

At the completion of the closing process, all temporary accounts have zero balances; the only accounts remaining open are the permanent accounts—the assets, liability, and owners' equity accounts.

It would be possible to close the revenue and expense accounts simply by drawing lines at the bottom of each account, rather than by making journal entries as described above. This would, however, violate the rule that all changes in account balances must be made by journal entries. The journal entry lessens the chances that an error or omission will be made, and facilitates the task of finding the error if the accounts do not balance.

Ruling and Balancing Accounts

At the end of the accounting period, each permanent account is ruled and balanced so that it is in a convenient form for the preparation of financial statements and ready to begin accumulating entries for the coming period. The procedure is as follows: First, a balancing amount is written in the appropriate column so as to make equal totals in both columns. The totals are then shown and double-ruled to indicate the end of the accounting period sequence. Finally, the new balance is "brought down" on the opposite side from that in which it was first written, as the initial figure for the new period. The account then appears as follows:

CASH

Balance	10,000		2,000
	5,000		600
	4,000		400
	100		1,000
	2,700	To Balance	18,600
	800		
	22,600		22,600
Balance	18,600		

The Work Sheet

A work sheet is a preliminary compilation of figures that facilitates recording or analysis. A work sheet is often used as a preliminary to the formal journalizing and posting of the adjusting and closing process. Its use permits the accountant to make a "dry run" of the whole process. Since a pencil is ordinarily used, any errors detected on the work sheet can be easily corrected, whereas alterations to the formal records are to be avoided wherever possible. The work sheet also classifies account balances according to the financial statements in which they are to be used.

The form of the adjusting-and-closing work sheet varies depending upon the procedure followed in closing the accounts, the form of the statements to be prepared, and the preference of the accountant. The work sheet consists of several pairs of columns. In each pair, the first column is used for debits and the second column for credits. On most adjusting-and-closing work sheets the first pair of columns contains the preadjustment trial balance. The next pair of columns is used for the adjustments for the period. These are followed by a pair of columns for the income statement items and another pair for the balance sheet items. In some cases there are additional pairs of columns for principal subdivisions of the income statement, such as the cost of goods sold section.

A work sheet is often used *in lieu of*, rather than as a preliminary to, the process of adjusting and closing the accounts. Many companies close their books only once a year, but nevertheless prepare monthly financial statements. These interim statements are prepared from a work sheet on which are listed the account balances at the end of the month together with the adjustments necessary to reflect revenue and expense in that month. Statements are prepared from the adjusted account balances that are developed on this work sheet. The income statement figures on such a work sheet would be cumulative for the year to date. An income statement for the current month can be derived from the cumulative figures simply by subtracting the corresponding figures on the preceding month's work sheet.

A sample work sheet for a merchandising company is shown in Illustration 4–3. The five adjustments shown thereon reflect:

a. Cost of merchandise sold, $121,300 (dr. Cost of Goods Sold, cr. Inventory). During the period all purchases of merchandise had been debited to inventory, but no entries had been made to show the movement of merchandise out of inventory.
b. Expired insurance of $300 (dr. Insurance Expense, cr. Prepaid Insurance).
c. Accrued interest expense of $100 (dr. Interest Expense, cr. Accrued Interest Payable).
d. Accrued wages of $1,000 (dr. Salaries and Wages, cr. Wages Payable).
e. Accrued employer's tax on wages of $30 (dr. Social Security Tax Expense, cr. Withholding and Social Security Taxes Payable).

Illustration 4-3
ILLUSTRATIVE WORK SHEET
(in round numbers)

	Trial Balance December 31 Dr.	Cr.	Adjustments Dr.	Cr.	Income Statement Dr.	Cr.	Balance Sheet Dr.	Cr.
Cash	18,600						18,600	
Inventory	156,300			121,300 (a)			35,000	
Prepaid insurance	900			300 (b)			600	
Accounts payable		8,700						8,700
Employee taxes payable		570		30 (e)				600
Notes payable		4,000						4,000
Capital stock		20,000						20,000
Retained earnings		1,300						1,300
Sales		174,000				174,000		
Rental and other space costs	8,300				8,300			
Salaries and wages	20,000		1,000 (d)		21,000			
Social security tax expense	670		30 (e)		700			
Advertising expense	2,100				2,100			
Miscellaneous expenses	1,900				1,900			
Nonoperating revenue		400				400		
Interest expense	200		100 (c)		300			
	208,970	208,970						
Cost of goods sold			121,300 (a)		121,300			
Insurance expense			300 (b)		300			
Accrued interest payable				100 (c)				100
Wages payable				1,000 (d)				1,000
Income tax expense			5,400 (f)		5,400			
Income tax liability				5,400 (f)				5,400
			128,130	128,130	174,400	174,400	54,200	13,100
Net income					13,100			
					174,400	174,400	54,200	54,200

f. Estimated income tax for the year of $5,400 (dr. Income Tax Expense, cr. Income Tax Liability).

Note that additional accounts are added as needed at the bottom of the work sheet.

The last item on this work sheet, $13,100, is the net income for the period. It is found by subtracting the sum of the other debits to "Income Statement" from the sum of the credits to "Income Statement." Showing the same amount in the credit column of "Balance Sheet" has the effect of closing the net income to retained earnings. After this amount is entered, each column of a pair should add to the same total, which is a check on the arithmetic accuracy of the whole closing process.

So that the connection between the adjusting and closing process and the financial statements will be clear, financial statements prepared from Illustration 4–3 are shown in Illustration 4–4.

Illustration 4–4

FINANCIAL STATEMENTS

Balance Sheet as of December 31

ASSETS		EQUITIES	
Cash...................	$18,600	Accounts payable.........	$ 8,700
Inventory............	35,000	Employee taxes payable...	600
Prepaid insurance.....	600	Wages payable...........	1,000
		Notes payable...........	4,000
		Accrued interest payable.	100
		Income tax liability.....	5,400
		Total Liabilities......	$19,800
		Capital stock............	20,000
		Retained earnings........	14,400
Total Assets......	$54,200	Total Equities.......	$54,200

Income Statement for the Year

Sales...		$174,000
Less: Cost of goods sold..............................		121,300
Gross margin...		$ 52,700
Expenses:		
Rental and other space costs................	$ 8,300	
Salaries and wages.........................	21,000	
Social security tax expense.................	700	
Advertising expense........................	2,100	
Insurance expense..........................	300	
Miscellaneous expense......................	1,900	
Interest expense...........................	300	34,600
		$ 18,100
Other revenue....................................		400
Income before income taxes......................		$ 18,500
Provision for income taxes......................		5,400
Net Income......................................		$ 13,100

Summary of the Accounting Process

1. The first, and by far the most important, part of the accounting process is the *analysis of transactions,* that is, the process of deciding which account or accounts should be debited, which should be credited, and in what amounts, in order to reflect events in the accounting records. This requires judgment.

2. Next comes the purely mechanical step of *journalizing original entries,* that is, recording the result of the analysis.

3. *Posting* is the process of recording changes in the ledger accounts, exactly as specified by the journal entry. This is another purely mechanical step.

4. At the ending of the accounting period, judgment is involved in deciding on the *adjusting entries,* and these are journalized and posted in the same way as are original entries.

5. The *closing entries* are journalized and posted. This is a purely mechanical step.

6. *Financial statements* are prepared. This requires judgment as to the best arrangement and terminology, but the numbers that are used result from the judgments made in Steps No. 1 and No. 4.

ACCOUNTING SYSTEMS

The simple journals, ledgers, and work sheets, together with the rules for using them, described in the preceding pages, constitute *an* accounting system, but such a system would not usually be the *best* system for an actual business. The best system is that one which best achieves the following objectives:

1. To process the information efficiently, that is, at low cost.
2. To obtain reports quickly.
3. To insure a high degree of accuracy.
4. To minimize the possibility of theft or fraud.

Designing a good accounting system is a specialized job requiring a high degree of skill. Only a few of the principles and techniques are noted here.

Special Journals

The journal form illustrated on page 91 is called a *general journal.* This form requires that the title of each account affected by each entry be written down. If there are a large number of entries made to a single account, time can be saved, both in journalizing and in posting, by using a *special journal* or *register.* In the special journal there are several columns, each headed with the name of an account that is to be debited or credited plus, usually, a "miscellaneous" column in which entries to other accounts may be recorded. Entries to the accounts indicated by column headings are made simply by entering the proper amount in these columns. At the end of the accounting period, all the amounts in each column are added, and the total is posted as one figure to the appropriate account. Entries in the "miscellaneous" column are posted individually. Illustration 4–5 is an

Illustration 4–5

CHECK REGISTER

| Date | To Whom Drawn | Cash Cr. | Accounts Payable Dr. | Miscellaneous Dr. | |
				Account	Amount

example of a check register, which is a special journal used to record credits to Cash and debits to various accounts. Columns are provided for the accounts in which entries are likely to be made frequently (here, Cash and Accounts Payable), and a miscellaneous column is provided for other debits.

The special-journal device illustrates one of the important considerations in systems design: to keep to a minimum the amount of *manual copying* of information from one document to another. Copying not only requires effort, and hence costs money, but it also increases the likelihood of making errors. In the simple check register shown, the amount of copying required is reduced, as compared with the general journal, in that all the credits to Cash and all the debits to Accounts Payable are posted to the ledger as single totals. The special journal also reduces the amount of writing effort, since the name of the account at the head of the column does not have to be written for each entry.

The same idea can be extended further by the use of bookkeeping machines. In recording sales on credit, for example, the use of a machine makes it possible to make the journal entry and post the debit to the customer's ledger account in the same operation. The operator positions the journal form and the ledger account form properly in the machine, and the amounts are entered on both forms simultaneously.

Control Accounts and Subsidiary Ledgers

Most businesses use one or more *subsidiary ledgers,* which are groups of related accounts taken out of the general ledger. For example, all the separate accounts for individual customers may be kept in an accounts receivable ledger. One advantage of this practice is that several bookkeepers can be working on the ledger accounts simultaneously. Moreover, it facilitates the process of localizing errors, since each ledger can be made the responsibility of a specific individual. If there are three bookkeepers working on accounts receivable, for example, there can be three accounts receivable ledgers.

In order to keep the general ledger in balance, a *control account* takes the place of the individual accounts removed to the subsidiary ledgers. A control account shows in summary form debits and credits that are shown in detail in a subsidiary ledger. When subsidiary ledgers are used, each amount is, in effect, posted twice. It is posted, often daily, to the proper account in the subsidiary ledger, and it also becomes a part of the total which is posted at the end of the period to the control account in the general ledger. In a large business, most if not all of the general ledger accounts are control accounts.

The use of various *ledgerless bookkeeping* devices should also be noted. The accounts receivable "accounts," for example, may consist not of actual ledger records but rather of copies of the invoices themselves. Or, bills for vendors may be kept in an "accounts payable" file, with the accounting entry made when the bill is paid rather than when it is received. The total of bills in the file at the end of the accounting period constitutes the accounts payable liability for the balance sheet and is recorded by an adjusting entry, crediting Accounts Payable and debiting various expense and asset accounts. In the latter situation, work is saved, but the possibility of verifying the accounts against the invoices is sacrificed.

Imprest Funds

The imprest fund is another device for saving work. An imprest fund consists of cash advanced to a responsible person and periodically replenished by additional cash that equals the amounts expended by this person.

The operation of an imprest fund may be illustrated by its most common version, the *petty cash* fund. The fund is established by drawing a check on the regular bank account. The person responsible for the fund cashes the check and puts the money in a separate place, a petty cash box. This transaction is recorded by the following entry:

```
dr.    Petty Cash............................... 50
   cr.    Cash...................................        50
```

The petty cash is used to pay small bills until it is nearly exhausted. At that time, these bills are summarized, and a check is drawn for the amount they total. The journal entry for this check debits the various expense or asset accounts represented by the bills, for example:

```
dr.    Office Supplies......................... 21
dr.    Miscellaneous Expense.................... 25
   cr.    Cash.................................        46
```

Note that the credit is to the regular Cash account. Once established, the Petty Cash account in the ledger is not changed unless the size of the fund is changed.

This procedure saves the effort involved in drawing checks and making separate journal entries for small bills. It also provides a safeguard, since the petty cash box should at all times contain cash and receipted bills which together total the amount shown in the Petty Cash account.

The imprest device is by no means limited to petty cash. Many government disbursing agencies operate on the same principle, but in amounts that run into millions of dollars. These agencies are advanced funds by the U.S. Treasury Department, they disburse these funds to pay properly authorized bills, and they submit these bills to the Treasury Department as a basis for replenishing the fund. The accounting entries are essentially the same as those given above for petty cash.

Internal Control

Two of the objectives of an accounting system stated above—accuracy and protection against theft or fraud—cannot be attained absolutely without conflicting with the other two—speed and economy. A system that "can't be beaten" would be prohibitively expensive and time-consuming. A basic principle of internal control therefore is that the system should make it *as difficult as is practical* for people to be dishonest or careless. Such a principle is based not on a cynical view of people in general but rather on the realistic assumption that a small fraction of people will be dishonest or careless if it is easy for them to do so.

Some of the devices used to insure reasonable accuracy have been touched on already—the idea of verifying one set of figures against another, for example. The idea of divided responsibility is another important one. Whenever feasible, one person should not be responsible for recording all aspects of a transaction, nor should the *custodian* of assets (e.g., the storekeeper or the cashier) be permitted to do the *accounting* for these assets. Thus, one person's work is a check on another's, and although this does not eliminate the possibility that two people will steal through collusion, the likelihood of dishonesty is greatly reduced.

The *voucher system* is another commonly used internal control device.

Under this system, every incoming bill is inserted in a voucher, or folder, which contains spaces in which authorized people write their initials to signify their approval of the appropriateness of the charge and the accounting entries made. Under this system, all bills, even those that are paid immediately in cash, are credited to Accounts Payable (or to Vouchers Payable) and debited to the appropriate asset or expense account. For cash payments, putting the bill through Accounts Payable involves additional work, but this is often warranted in the interest of having a single, uniform procedure through which all bills must pass and a prescribed set of approvals to assure that the business makes only proper payments.

These brief comments indicate only the nature of the problem of internal control, which is a big subject. Furthermore, a study that focuses on accounting principles, as this one does, leads to incorrect impressions of the complexities involved in operating accounting *systems*. Cash transactions, for example, are very easy to analyze, whereas textbooks on auditing may contain a dozen or more pages of questions that should be considered in connection with the internal control of the single item, cash.

Significant Bookkeeping Ideas

At least two significant ideas should emerge from this description of the bookkeeping process and of accounting systems.

The first is the idea of debit and credit equality—"every debit must have an equal credit." This idea is much more than a mechanical requirement of bookkeeping. It is a way of thinking that is extremely useful in analyzing what is going on in a business. There is a natural human tendency to think only about part of the consequences of a decision and to overlook some equally important part. For example, although a growing cash balance superficially looks good, this is only half of the story. It makes considerable difference whether the credits offsetting these debits to cash reflect income from profitable operations or whether they reflect emergency bank loans.

The second significant idea is that of *balancing*, the notion that one total should always equal some other total. Three balancing techniques have been described: (1) the fundamental debit-credit structure; (2) the control-subsidiary relationship, in which the total of the subsidiary items must always equal a control total; and (3) the imprest technique, in which the sum of cash and paid bills must always equal a predetermined total. As noted above, these devices provide a check on arithmetic accuracy, they lessen the risk of loss through dishonesty, and they lessen the chance that some part of a transaction will be overlooked. Numbers derived from a system that does *not* contain such balancing mechanisms should be regarded skeptically; the likelihood of errors or omissions is great.

COMPUTER-BASED ACCOUNTING SYSTEMS

Most large businesses and an increasing number of small businesses do their accounting work with an electronic computer, rather than with the manual methods described above. We explained the process initially in terms of manual methods both because the forms and records used in manual systems are visible, whereas the operations that go on inside a computer are invisible, and also because in solving problems of the type encountered in an accounting course, students usually will find it more convenient to use manual methods, even if they have access to a computer. In this section we describe the similarities and the differences between a computer-based system and a manual system.

What a Computer Is

Illustration 4–6 shows the main components of an electronic computer and the relationships between them. Each is described below.

Illustration 4–6

Schematic of an Electronic Computer

Data are entered into a computer by means of an *input* device. The data may be originally prepared in the form of a punched card or a paper tape, the computer may obtain them by reading an invoice or other source document with an optical scanning device, or they may come from cash registers or other machines which are wired so that they automatically transmit data to the computer. As soon as data are inputted, the computer translates them into a code, which is a combination of electrical states. Thereafter, the computer works with these coded data.

Storage units (or memory units) hold data until the computer needs to work on them. Internal storage, which is inside the computer itself, is arranged in such a way that the computer can locate a needed piece of data very rapidly, but such storage is relatively expensive. Therefore, most data are held in external storage devices until just prior to the time the computer needs to use them. These devices may be disks, which resemble phonograph records in appearance; reels of magnetic tape; or other devices on which data can be coded. External storage is less expensive than internal storage, but data retrieval from external storage is slower.

The *processing unit* consists of three parts: the internal storage, a control unit, and an arithmetic unit. The *control unit* instructs the computer to operate as specified in the program; that is, it instructs the computer to move data into and out of storage, to perform operations on these data, and to send the results either back to storage or to the output unit. The *arithmetic unit* performs the actual calculations. These are the usual arithmetic operations of addition, subtraction, multiplication, and division, plus the special operation of comparison, that is, examining two numbers and determining whether they are equal and, if unequal, which is the larger.

The *output unit* provides the results of the calculation. These may be in the form of hard copy, such as a printed report, or in the form of a cathode ray tube display, which is the same as the tube on a television set.

Relationship to Manual Accounting

By means of the devices briefly described above, the computer does the following:

1. It stores data.
2. It retrieves data from its storage.
3. It performs arithmetic operations on data.
4. It compares two items of data for equality or inequality.
5. It sorts data, that is, it rearranges data.
6. It prepares reports or causes some other machine to perform in a prescribed way.

An accounting system operated by human beings performs exactly the same functions. In order to show the correspondence, we shall relate the terms used in the description of a manual system to the terms used in a computer-based system.

The rules for debit and credit are exactly the same in a computer-based system as in a manual system. The storage units in a computer-based system serve the same purpose as the ledger in a manual system. The account numbers which are listed in the manual chart of accounts are called file numbers in a computer-based system, and each amount is called a file. Because computer storage is inexpensive and reusable, and because locating and using data held in storage is also inexpensive, it is much more feasible to have a large number of account classifications and cross classifications in a computer-based system, and it is much easier to make summaries of various types from these files.

The input in a computer-based system corresponds to the journal in a manual system. The program contains the information on the proper files to be debited and credited for nearly all types of transactions, the same function that is performed by the special journals in a manual system.

The computer will make adjusting entries, provided it is given the necessary information as input. It will make closing entries and prepare financial statements without human intervention, provided it has been programmed to do so. It will perform these functions without the equivalent of a trial balance or a work sheet because its program causes it to perform automatically and without error the same steps that a human being follows in preparing a work sheet.

Because of its ability to do arithmetic very rapidly, and its ability to sort and rearrange data, the computer can add up the amounts in individual files, provide summaries and various cross classifications that management may desire, and calculate percentages and other useful statistics much more rapidly than is feasible in a manual system.

From these characteristics, the following comparisons between a manual system and a computer-based system can be made:

1. The computer operates much more rapidly. Although entering data is, in many applications, relatively slow, once data are translated into computer code, operations are performed thereafter at the speed of electricity, which is approximately the speed of light. As a result, for example, large supermarket chains can provide managers with a detailed report of the preceding day's activities in each store and for the whole company, on the following morning.

2. The computer is essentially 100% accurate. Unlike humans, it does not make arithmetic errors, and it does not make copying errors. (The humans who prepare input data or who write the computer programs may make errors, however.)

3. The computer performs operations much less expensively. However, the cost of programming the computer to perform a certain operation is much greater than the cost of teaching a human to perform the same operation. Unless the number of operations of a given type is fairly large, the low cost per operation is more than offset by the high initial programming cost.

4. The computer and its related equipment cost more than the cost of the journals and ledgers in a manual system.

5. The computer does not use judgment; it does exactly what it is told to do by its program, and no more.

Service Bureaus

A small business cannot afford its own computer. Moreover, an expensive part of a computer-based system is the preparation of the program, and in a business with a relatively small number of transactions, this cost more than offsets the savings in operating cost. Even a small business can take advantage of the computer's capabilities, however, by using a service bureau. Service bureaus operate computers and have programs that are applicable to a number of businesses. Each of its clients shares these costs by paying a fee for the work done. Drug stores, for example, send to a service bureau sales invoices and remittances from customers, and the service bureau does the accounts receivable work for each store, including the preparation of the statement that customers need to support claimed income tax deductions or Medicare payments for drugs purchased. Similarly, the records required for a company's payroll are fairly complicated but, because of government requirements, they are in many respects identical for all companies. Many quite small companies therefore find it economical to have their payroll records prepared by a service bureau. Many accounting firms use a computer to prepare complete financial statements on the basis of invoices, bills received and other raw data submitted by a company.

SUMMARY

The account is a device for collecting information about each item that is to be accounted for. It has two sides, the left-hand, or debit, side and the right-hand, or credit, side. The rules are such that asset and expense accounts increase on the debit side, whereas liabilities, owners' equity and revenue accounts increase on the credit side. This maintains both the equation Assets = Liabilities + Owners' Equity, and the equation Debits = Credits.

A ledger is a group of accounts. Entries are made to ledger accounts on the basis of instructions given in a journal.

At the end of an accounting period adjusting entries are made so that, after adjustment, the revenue and expense accounts will show the appropriate amounts for the period. These temporary accounts are then closed to an income summary account, which in turn is closed to retained earnings.

In manual accounting systems, special journals, subsidiary ledgers, and other devices facilitate the process of recording accounting data. A computer-based system performs the same functions more rapidly, more accurately, and, if the volume of repetitive transactions is large, at lower cost.

APPENDIX

Locating Errors Revealed by the Trial Balance

Following are four suggested aids in detecting errors revealed by differences in the totals of the trial balance:

1. If the difference between the totals is 0.01, 1.00, 100, 1,000, etc., the error is probably in addition. Such an error is usually detected by re-adding the columns of the trial balance, or, if necessary, the columns in the ledger accounts.

2. When the discrepancy is an even number, the error may be the result of making a debit entry in a credit column, or vice versa. Divide the difference in totals by 2, and look, first, through the trial balance and, then, the ledger accounts for an amount corresponding to the quotient secured. The difference is divided by 2 because an item placed in the wrong column results in a difference of twice its amount.

3. If the difference is divisible by 9, the error is probably either a transposition or a transplacement, and the search can be narrowed down to numbers where these errors might have been made. A *transposition* occurs when 79 is written for 97, 318 for 813, and so on. A *transplacement* or *slide* occurs when the digits of the number are moved to the left or right, as when $6,328.00 is written as $632.80 or $63.28.

4. When the source of error is not readily discernible, it is advisable to check the trial balance against the ledger to determine whether all the account balances have been copied properly. This check may reveal that certain accounts have been omitted. As a last resort, it may be necessary to check all of the figures in the ledger with the journal and to check all additions and subtractions in the several accounts.

Care in making the entries, such as writing legibly, double-checking additions and subtractions as journalizing and posting proceeds, and making sure all entries are entered properly, will save much time otherwise spent in hunting for errors.

SUGGESTIONS FOR FURTHER READING

BLUMENTHAL, SHERMANN. *Management Information Systems.* Englewood Cliffs, N.J.: Prentice-Hall, Inc., 1969.

DEARDEN, JOHN; McFARLAN, F. WARREN; and ZANI, WILLIAM M. *Managing Computer-Based Information Systems.* Homewood, Ill.: Richard D. Irwin, Inc., 1971.

GILLESPIE, CECIL. *Accounting Systems: Procedures and Methods.* 3d ed. Englewood Cliffs, N.J.: Prentice-Hall, Inc., 1971.

MEIER, ROBERT C.; NEWELL, W.; and POZER, H. *Simulation in Business and Economics.* Englewood Cliffs, N.J.: Prentice-Hall, Inc., 1969.

MURDICK, ROBERT G., and ROSS, JOEL E. *Information Systems for Modern Management.* Englewood Cliffs, N.J.: Prentice-Hall, Inc., 1971.

SANDERS, DONALD H. *Computers and Management.* New York: McGraw-Hill Book Co., 1969.

CASES

CASE 4–1. KAYDENCE

Kaydence was a small yarn and needlework shop which sold manufacturers' kits and patterns as well as original designs. The store was opened by Kay Devlin, a young woman who had previously been an art teacher.

Exhibit 1

GENERAL JOURNAL

Entry Number	Account	Amount Dr.	Amount Cr.
(1)	Cash.............................	13,000	
	Bank Loan Payable................		3,000
	Proprietor's Capital.............		10,000
(2)	Rent Expense (August).............	400	
	Cash............................		400
(3)	Merchandise Inventory.............	6,300	
	Accounts Payable.................		6,300
(4)	Furniture and Fixtures............	2,400	
	Cash............................		2,400
(5)	Advertising Expense...............	350	
	Cash............................		350
(6)	Wages Expense.....................	220	
	Cash............................		220
(7)	Office Supplies Expense...........	371	
	Cash............................		371
(8)	Interest Expense	18	
	Cash............................		18
(9)	Utilities Expense.................	49	
	Cash............................		49

Warned by her friends of the danger of trying to operate without adequate records, Ms. Devlin engaged Fred Cole, a local accountant, to set up her bookkeeping system.

Mr. Cole wrote up the earlier financial transactions in journal form to serve as an example, and then asked Ms. Devlin to write up the store's financial transactions for the current month of September for his review.

Mr. Cole's journal for August, when Ms. Devlin and her assistant were preparing the store for its opening, appears in Exhibit 1.

At the end of September, Ms. Devlin had the following items to record:

10)	Cash sales for September.....................................	$2,650
11)	Credit sales for September...................................	840
12)	Bills paid for merchandise...................................	4,100
13)	Wages paid to assistant.....................................	330
14)	New merchandise received on credit from supplier..............	2,154
15)	Cash received from credit customers..........................	420
16)	Wages earned but unpaid at the end of September..............	110
17)	Petty cash fund established..................................	50
18)	Rent paid for September.....................................	400
19)	Telephone bill paid...	46
20)	Bills received but unpaid:	
	Gas and light from utility company........................	61
	Weekly cleaning of store..................................	64
21)	Ms. Devlin ascertained the cost of merchandise sold was.........	1,695
22)	Depreciation for September..................................	20
23)	September interest paid.....................................	24

Questions

1. Explain the events that probably gave rise to journal entries 1 through 9, of Exhibit 1.
2. Set up a ledger account (in T account form) for each account named in the general journal. Post entries 1 through 9 to these accounts, using the entry numbers as a cross-reference.
3. Analyze the facts listed as 10 through 23, resolving them into their debit and credit elements. Prepare journal entries and post to the ledger accounts. (Do not prepare closing entries.)
4. Prepare an income statement for the period ending September 30 and a balance sheet as of September 30.

CASE 4–2. LEGGATT COMPANY

The account balances in the ledger of the Leggatt Company on February 28 (the end of its fiscal year), before adjustments, were as follows:

Debit Balances		*Credit Balances*	
Cash......................	$ 30,970	Accumulated depreciation on	
		store equipment............	$ 5,610
Accounts receivable...........	44,700	Notes payable................	32,500
Merchandise inventory........	352,300	Accounts payable.............	37,250
Store equipment..............	28,400	Common stock...............	50,000
Supplies inventory............	6,750	Retained earnings.............	1,030
Prepaid insurance.............	4,800	Sales........................	375,000
Selling expense...............	4,200		
Sales salaries............... ..	18,200		
Miscellaneous general expense..	7,310		
Sales discounts...............	1,290		
Interest expense............. ...	1,780		
Social security tax expense.....	690		
Total..................	$501,390	Total..................	$501,390

The data for the adjustments are:

1. Cost of merchandise sold, $224,700.
2. Depreciation on store equipment, $4,260.
3. Supplies inventory, February 28, $1,650. (Purchases of supplies during the year were debited to the Supplies Inventory account.)
4. Expired insurance, $2,500.
5. Interest accrued on notes payable, $150.
6. Sales salaries earned but not paid to employees, $750.
7. Interest earned on savings account, but not recorded, $35.

Questions

1. Set up T accounts with the balances given above.
2. Journalize and post adjusting entries, adding other T accounts as necessary.
3. Journalize and post closing entries.
4. Prepare an income statement and balance sheet.

CASE 4–3.   OLYMPIC LUMBER COMPANY*

Jason Cornfield reread the letter that his new boss had given him that morning:

As your agent, I am indeed happy that you agreed to insure Olympic Lumber's building and inventory with a $1,000,000 fire insurance policy. The policy, which was effective November 1, 1970, will cover the loss from the untimely fire, and will continue to provide coverage through the end of 1974. While I am of course sincerely sorry that you incurred the loss, I am sure

---

* © 1971 by the Board of Trustees of the Leland Stanford Junior University. Used by permission.

you will agree that the expenditure of $25,000 for the policy was one of Olympic's more prudent decisions. Please call me when you have reconstructed your financial statements.

Jason Cornfield had been hired to replace Olympic's accountant, who had been fired for incompetence in early January 1971. Jason gazed out at the bleak February day and reviewed the events that had led up to his predecessor's dismissal. Until early 1971, Jason had operated a small but successful accounting practice. Shortly after the first of the year he had been offered the job of accountant for Olympic by Bill Woodstock, president of Olympic Lumber Company. Woodstock explained to him that the company had been doing very well, and in fact had had a record sales and profit performance in 1970. To celebrate the success, the company had hosted a party for its suppliers and customers on New Year's Eve. The guests became overly festive in their celebrations and began lighting firecrackers. Unfortunately, a skyrocket landed in the rough two-by-four inventory and burned Olympic's entire inventory and building. Because of the suddenness of the fire, all financial records had been lost.

Woodstock informed Jason that his accountant, Leonard Firebird, had been unable to reconstruct financial statements for the fiscal year that had just ended. He said, "Firebird was O.K. for the routine stuff, but this assignment, and the challenge of rebuilding Olympic, require real creative talent. That's why I'm counting on you."

Investigating the background of Olympic, Cornfield learned that the company had been formed in early 1966 and that the building, which contained the office and plant, had been purchased and occupied on May 1 of that year. Cornfield next came across a letter to Woodstock from a major supplier, who wrote, "I certainly enjoyed your party and was sorry it ended so abruptly. I appreciated receiving the first installment on the note with which you financed the inventory purchase from us. As we agreed that you will make payments every six months, unless I hear otherwise, I will expect your next payment of $50,000 on June 1 plus the 6 percent interest over the six month period."

Cornfield next asked Woodstock if he had any records that would help him in his work. The latter searched his briefcase and finally found a balance sheet (see Exhibit 1). Woodstock observed that expenditures for salaries and licenses in 1970 had been a third higher than their 1969 levels of $60,000 and $750, respectively. He commented that over the years freight expense had averaged $1,000 per month, that advertising had been 7 percent of sales, and selling expenses had been 20 percent of sales. Utilities had been some 15 percent higher than the previous year's $800 bill.

As Cornfield turned to leave, Woodstock remarked, "One more thing. I found a scrap of paper among the ashes and it said 'Closing entries to be

Exhibit 1

OLYMPIC LUMBER COMPANY

Balance Sheet, June 30, 1970

Assets

Cash...		$ 150,000
Accounts Receivable...........................		213,172
Supplies.....................................		14,427
Inventory—lumber............................		290,500
Land...		90,000
Building.....................................	$500,000	
Less accumulated depreciation.................	75,000	425,000
Total Assets..............................		$1,183,099

Liabilities

Accounts payable.............................		$ 72,047
Note payable................................		200,000
Total Liabilities............................		$ 272,047

Owners' Equity

Capital Stock.................................		$ 800,000
Retained Earnings.............................		111,052
Total Owners' Equity.....................		$ 911,052
Total Liabilities and Owners' Equity...........		$1,183,099

made: Sales, DR 921,000; Supplies, CR 8210.' The rest was unintelligible. I don't know what that means but maybe it will be helpful to you."

The new accountant then learned that the company had had a physical inventory on December 31, and Cornfield called the auditors who informed him that the lumber inventory on that date had been $414,000. They were also able to supply him with a list of all of Olympic's customers and suppliers. Calling the suppliers, he learned that all of the monies previously owed them had been paid in cash (except for the note referred to above) and that a third of the inventory acquired over the last six months of the year was still owed on account. Cornfield next discovered that total purchases of inventory in the second half of 1970 had been $159,500 more than the amount of the June 30 inventory level. Then he found out that no supplies had been purchased during 1970.

After considerable pencil-pushing, Cornfield was still unable to calculate his cash balance. He knew Woodstock was growing impatient for the statements and consequently was startled to see the latter charge brusquely into his cluttered cubicle and drop an envelope on the desk. Opening it, Cornfield realized to his relief that it was Olympic's bank statement, dated December 31, with a balance of $200,000.

Cornfield's phone rang and he heard Woodstock's secretary ask him when he would complete the financial statements. He replied, "I realize my answer is due and I will have the statements ready in a few minutes."

Question

Prepare an income statement for the six months ended December 31, 1970, and a balance sheet as of December 31, 1970. (Ignore income taxes, and assume that the sales and supplies figures are for the last six months of 1970 only.)

CASE 4–4. HARRY ERNEST

On March 15, Mr. Harry Ernest signed a lease agreement to operate a gasoline service station which was owned by the Octane Oil Company. Mr. Ernest had contacted the regional sales manager of the Octane Oil Company in response to an advertisement which solicited applicants "with $5,000 to invest" to lease and operate a newly-erected Octane Oil Company gasoline service station in a large city. Mr. Ernest had been able to accumulate approximately $6,000 for investment purposes as a result of a $4,000 inheritance and small savings on the salary of $140 per week which he earned as manager of a service station operated as a separate department of an automobile agency. Most of this $6,000 was held in government bonds.

The regional sales manager for the Octane Oil Company was impressed with Mr. Ernest's personal and financial qualifications and, after several interviews, a lease agreement was signed. During one of these meetings, the sales manager informed Mr. Ernest that the new porcelain-exterior service station would be completed and ready for occupancy on May 1 at a total investment cost of $120,000. Of this amount, $30,000 had already been paid for land and a total of $90,000 would be spent for a building which would be "good for about 40 years." In discussing profit potentiality, the sales manager pointed out that the national advertising program of the Octane Oil Company and the consumer appeal generated by the attractive station "will be worth at least $6,000 a year to you in consumer goodwill."

The lease agreement stipulated that Mr. Ernest pay a rental of $200 per month for the station plus $.02 for each gallon of gasoline delivered to the station by the Octane Oil Company.[1] A separate agreement was also signed whereby the Octane Oil Company agreed to sell and Mr. Ernest agreed to buy certain minimum quantities of gasoline and other automotive products for the service station operation.

---

[1] The lease, which covered a period of one year beginning May 1, was automatically renewable unless notice of cancellation was given by either party at least 30 days prior to an anniversary date. The regional sales manager of the Octane Oil Company estimated that approximately 150,000 gallons of gasoline would be delivered to Mr. Ernest's service station during the first 12 months of operation. Subsequently, Mr. Ernest's records revealed that 27,000 gallons were actually delivered during the first two months of operation.

As both an evidence of good faith and as a prepayment on certain obligations which he would shortly incur to the Octane Oil Company, Mr. Ernest was required to deposit $4,000 with the Octane Oil Company at the time the lease was signed. Mr. Ernest raised the cash for this deposit by liquidating government bonds. The Octane Oil Company used most of this money to defray certain obligations incurred by Mr. Ernest to the oil company prior to the opening of the new station. The deductions from the $4,000 deposit were applied as follows:

1. Opening inventories of gasoline, oil, grease, tires, batteries and accessories....................................... $2,950
2. Rental fee ($200 flat rental for the month of May and $90 figured at $.02 per gallon on the gasoline delivered in the opening inventory..................................... 290
3. Down payment (on Ernest's behalf) on equipment costing $1,260.. 260
$3,500

The equipment, including floor and hydraulic jacks, a battery charger, tune-up sets, and oil and grease guns, became the property of Mr. Ernest. A representative of the oil company stated that this equipment would last about five years. The unpaid, noninterest-bearing balance of $1,000 due for equipment to the Octane Oil Company was to be paid in five semiannual installments of $200 each. The first such payment was due October 30. The $500 remaining from the $4,000 originally deposited with the Octane Oil Company was returned to Mr. Ernest on April 30. He deposited this money in a special checking account he had set up for his service station venture.

Just before opening for business on May 1, Mr. Ernest converted some additional government bonds into $1,000 of cash which he also placed in the service station checking account. Prior to May 1, he wrote the following checks: $240 for office furniture which had an expected life of 10 years, and $120 for a fire and casualty insurance policy extending coverage for a one-year period beginning May 1. On April 30, Mr. Ernest transferred $100 from the service station checking account to the cash drawer at the service station. It was Mr. Ernest's intention to deposit in the bank all but $100 of the cash on hand at the close of each business day. The balance in the service station checking account at the start of business was, therefore, $1,040. In addition, Mr. Ernest had $850 in a savings account.

On May 1, the service station was opened for business. In his effort to build up a clientele, Mr. Ernest worked approximately 60 hours per week compared with 40 in his previous job. In addition, three other people were employed on either a full- or part-time basis. Mr. Ernest was reasonably well satisfied with the patronage he was able to build up during the first two months the station was open. At the end of June, however, he felt it would be desirable to take a more careful look at how he was making out in his new business venture. Mr. Ernest felt that he should record his progress and present position in a form which would be useful not only at the present time but also for comparative purposes in the future, perhaps at six-month intervals ending on June 30 and December 31.

Mr. Ernest maintained a simple record-keeping system in which cash receipts and cash payments were itemized daily in a loose-leaf notebook. Separate pages were reserved for specific items in this notebook. During the months of May and June, the following cash receipts and payments had been recorded:

Cash Receipts (May and June)

Sales of gasoline, motor oils, new and second-hand tires, batteries, and accessories and the revenue from lubrications, washing and polishing, and miscellaneous sales and services............................	$15,946
Rental from parking area on service station land.....................	120
	$16,066

Cash Payments (May and June)

Purchases (includes gasoline, motor oils, lubes, greases, new tires, batteries and accessories).......................................	$ 9,932
Rent (does not include $290 deduction from $4,000 deposit)..........	610
Payroll (does not include any payments to Mr. Ernest)..............	1,720
Utilities...	114
Advertising..	160
Miscellaneous...	86
Withdrawals by Mr. Ernest (June 1 and June 19)..................	1,200
	$13,822

The $120 listed in Cash Receipts as rental from parking area had been received from an adjacent business establishment that used one portion of the service station site as a parking space for certain of its employees. The rental received covered a period extending from May 15 to July 15.

In addition to the record of cash receipts and payments, a detailed listing was kept of the amounts of money which were due from or owed to other individuals or companies. An analysis of these records revealed that $72 was due the business for gas, oil, and car servicing from a wealthy widow friend of the Ernest family who preferred to deal on a credit basis. Also, on the evening of June 30, one of the employees completed the waxing of a car for a regular customer who was out of town and would be unable to call for his car until July 3. Mr. Ernest had quoted a price of $28 for this job. Mr. Ernest recalled that when he was working at the automobile agency, he had heard that setting up a reserve for bad debts equal to 2% of all outstanding accounts was a good idea.

Mr. Ernest had also jotted down the fact that he and his family had used gas and oil from the service station worth $46 at retail prices, for which no payment had been made. Approximately $36 had been paid to the Octane Oil Company for this merchandise.

A further summary of his records revealed the following unpaid bills resulting from operations in June:

Octane Oil Company for merchandise	$802
Rent payable (figured at $.02 per gallon on most recent delivery of gasoline)	40
Utilities for the month of June	110
	$952

The employees had last been paid on Saturday, June 28, for services rendered through Saturday evening. Wages earned on June 29 and 30 would amount to $42 in the following Saturday's payroll.

Mr. Ernest took a physical inventory on the evening of June 30, and he found gasoline, motor oils, lubes, greases, tires, batteries and accessories on hand which had cost $2,226. While Mr. Ernest was figuring his inventory position, he compared his recorded gallonage sales of gasoline from daily readings of the pump meters plus the volume of gasoline on hand at the end of the period against the volume of gasoline in the beginning inventory plus deliveries. In this manner, Mr. Ernest ascertained that shrinkage due to evaporation, temperature changes, waste, and other causes amounted to 302 gallons of gasoline which he estimated had cost $118.

Late in June, Mr. Ernest's married son realized that he would be unable, because of a prolonged illness, to make a payment of $96 for interest expense and $400 for principal repayment on a $1,200 bank loan. Mr. Ernest who had acted as cosigner on the note, would be obliged to meet this payment on July 1.

Question

Prepare a May 1 and a June 30 balance sheet for Mr. Ernest's service station and a profit and loss statement for the intervening period.

CASE 4–5. SUNAPEE MOTEL

Mr. and Mrs. William Bucks had purchased the Sunapee Motel in 1969 with their life savings, supplemented by a loan from a close personal friend. The motel consisted of 15 units (i.e., rentable rooms), and was located near a vacation area which was popular during both the summer and winter seasons. The Bucks had entered the motel business because Mr. Bucks had long wanted to run a business of his own.

Both Mr. and Mrs. Bucks felt that they had been successful. Each year saw a growth in revenue from room rentals. Furthermore, their bank balance had increased. They noted that many of their customers returned year after year. This was attributed to their location and their efforts to provide consistently clean rooms and up-to-date furnishings. Fortunately, no significant competition had arisen along the route on which the Sunapee Motel was situated.

Mr. Bucks had no formal business training, but he felt his experience since acquiring the motel had alerted him to the management problems involved. Both Mr. and Mrs. Bucks devoted their full time to operating the motel. In addition, they hired part-time help for cleaning and chambermaid work. They had no dining facilities, but had installed coffee, cigarette, and candy vending machines to supplement room rentals. The vending machines posed no inventory or maintenance problem as the vending machine company provided servicing and maintenance.

A frequent guest at Sunapee Motel was Mr. Rodney Burkhart, controller of a large company. Mr. Burkhart visited a company branch plant near the motel several times a year. As he stayed at the motel during these trips, he became acquainted with the Bucks.

In August 1974, Mr. Bucks showed Mr. Burkhart the July issue of the *Motel/Motor Inn Journal,* a trade journal which contained operating percentages of motels for the calendar year 1973. Data were given for motels with 20 or fewer units. Mr. Bucks commented: "These figures show a profit of 21 percent. Our profit last year was $22,451 on sales of $40,789, or 55 percent. We think 1973 was our best year to date, but we can't make our figures jibe with those in the magazine, and we wonder if we really are 34 percent ahead of the industry average. Can you help us?"

Mr. Burkhart was interested and willing to help. He told Mr. Bucks to get the available figures for 1973 so that he could look them over that evening. The principal records Mr. Bucks kept to reflect the motel's financial transactions were a record of receipts, taken from the cash register, and a checkbook describing cash paid out. In addition, certain rough notations of other expenses incurred were available.

That evening Mr. Bucks showed Mr. Burkhart the cash summary for the year 1973, as given in Exhibit 2. Mr. Burkhart immediately noted that the difference between receipts and expenditures was $7,951, and asked Mr. Bucks to explain why he had stated the profit was $22,451. Mr. Bucks replied, "Oh, that's easy. Our drawings aren't expenses; after all, we are the owners. My wife and I have consistently taken only $14,500 a year out because we want the rest of the profits to accumulate in the business. As I said, our bank balance has steadily risen. Furthermore, I have a local accountant make out the annual income tax statements so I don't have to worry about them. That income tax business is so complicated that I avoid it."

Mr. Burkhart worked with the *Motel/Motor Inn Journal* figures (Exhibit 1) and the cash summary (Exhibit 2) that evening and quickly found he needed more informaton. He told Mr. Bucks that he was returning to the home office the next morning but would be back in two weeks for another visit to the branch plant. Meanwhile, he wanted Mr. Bucks to get together some additional information. Mr. Burkhart suggested to Mr. Bucks that an important noncash expense was depreciation. Mr. Buckhart also wanted to know about expenses that had been incurred in 1972 but not paid until 1973. He told Mr. Bucks to check up on wages and salaries, insurance, advertising, taxes, utilities, and any other items paid in 1973 but applicable to 1972.

In addition, Mr. Burkhart instructed Mr. Bucks to try to find items of expense properly chargeable to 1973 but not paid by December 31, 1973. Mr. Bucks told Mr. Burkhart the same types of expenses were involved, that is, wages and salaries, insurance, advertising, taxes, and so forth. Also

Exhibit 1

OPERATING DATA FOR MOTELS WITH 20 OR FEWER UNITS, 1973 AND 1972*

(expressed as percentages of total income)

	1973	1972
Income:		
Room rentals	90.98	90.25
Other income	9.02	9.75
Total income	100.00	100.00
Operating expenses:		
Salaries and wages	9.83	10.73
Executive salaries	1.83	2.53
Laundry	2.99	2.90
Linen, chinaware, glassware	1.75	1.32
Advertising, printing, stationery	2.38	2.65
Payroll, taxes, insurance	0.97	1.42
Heat, light, and power	7.64	6.84
Repairs and maintenance	4.56	4.52
Cleaning and other supplies	3.60	3.26
Telephone and telegraph	2.56	2.31
Other operating expenses	3.86	3.77
Total operating expenses	41.97	42.25
Gross operating profit	58.03	57.75
Capital expenses:		
Real estate and property taxes	5.07	4.42
Insurance	2.45	2.19
Interest	11.00	9.01
Rent	1.54	0.80
Depreciation	16.90	15.62
Total capital expenses	36.96	32.04
Net Profit	21.07	25.71

* Copyright July 1974 issue of *Motel/Motor Inn Journal*, Temple, Texas. Further reproduction in part or in whole prohibited unless written permission obtained from the copyright owner.

Exhibit 2

CASH REGISTER AND CHECKBOOK SUMMARY DURING 1973

Receipts

From rooms	$39,420
From vending machines	1,369
Total	$40,789

Checks Drawn

Owners' drawings	$14,500
Salaries and wages	4,380
Paid to laundry	1,465
Replacement of glasses, bed linens and towels	276
Advertising	389
Payroll taxes and insurance	485
Fuel for heating	2,032
Repairs and maintenance	1,495
Cleaning and other supplies	1,136
Telephone and telegraph	464
Electricity	934
Real estate and property taxes	1,587
Insurance	1,929
Interest	1,766
Total	$32,838

Exhibit 3

ADDITIONAL INFORMATION ABOUT THE BUSINESS

Chargeable in 1972, but paid in January, 1973:

Wages and salaries	$168
Advertising	140
Fuel for heating	212
Telephone and telegraph	23
Electricity	84
Real estate and property taxes	234
Insurance	482
Interest	160
Payroll taxes and insurance	18

Chargeable in 1973, but not paid by December 31, 1973:

Wages and salaries	252
Advertising	232
Fuel for heating	196
Cleaning and other supplies	18
Telephone and telegraph	32
Electricity	115
Real estate and property taxes	261
Interest	135
Payroll taxes and insurance	28

Also 1973 depreciation charges of $5,150.

Also, 1973 cash receipts included a $275 payment from a company which had rented several units during December 1972 for a convention in the nearby city. There were no such uncollected rentals as of December 31, 1973.

Mr. Burkhart inquired about income from room rentals. He asked if any of the cash receipts during 1973 related to rentals during 1972 and if there were any rentals during 1973 that had not been collected.

During the two weeks Mr. Burkhart was back at the home office, Mr. Bucks checked his records and compiled the additional information requested by Mr. Burkhart. The evening Mr. Burkhart returned to the Sunapee Motel, Mr. Bucks gave him a summary of the information he had gathered (Exhibit 3). With all the additional information, Mr. Burkhart constructed an operating statement that matched in form the one appearing in the *Motel/Motor Inn Journal*. He calculated both the dollar amounts and percentage composition of each expense for more useful comparison with the *Journal* figures.

Questions

1. Prepare an operating statement such as Mr. Burkhart prepared.
2. As Mr. Burkhart, what comments would you make to the Bucks regarding their progress to date?

CHAPTER 5

REVENUE AND
MONETARY ASSETS

This and the next five chapters discuss more thoroughly certain balance sheet and income statement items that were treated in an introductory fashion in Chapters 2 and 3. In Chapter 5 we discuss the application of the two aspects of the realization concept; namely the timing of revenue recognition and the amount of revenue recognized in a given accounting period. Because of the close connection of these matters with the measurement of monetary assets, we also discuss monetary assets.

TIMING OF REVENUE RECOGNITION

One basic part of the realization concept is that revenues are generally recognized in the accounting period in which goods are shipped or services rendered. Some of the problems that arise in applying this concept and some important exceptions to it are discussed in this section.

General Considerations

Presumably, most of the activities in a business company are intended to contribute to its profit-seeking objective. These activities include what may be a fairly long sequence of events: the purchase of material, the manufacture of goods from this material, efforts to sell these goods, shipment of goods to the customer, and the collection of amounts due from the customer. In accounting, revenue is recognized at a single point in this sequence.

The basic reason for choosing a single point, rather than attempting to measure the separate profit contributions of each part of the process, stems from the criterion of objectivity. There is no objective way of knowing how much profit is created during the manufacturing process. The outcome of the whole production and sales cycle is known with reasonable certainty only when the buyer and the seller have agreed on a price, the goods have been delivered, and legal title has passed. Also, at this time there is usually an invoice or some other documentary evidence of the transaction, evidence that can be verified by some outside party. This "test of the marketplace" or "arm's-length agreement" provides an objective measure of the amount of revenue.

Arguments can be advanced for recognizing revenue either earlier or later than the date of shipment. If the sale were not recognized until the customer actually paid his bill, there would be an even greater degree of certainty that revenue actually was realized. Conversely, it could be argued that when the company receives a firm order for goods, the revenue-generating process has essentially been completed, and that the actual shipment of the goods to the customer is relatively incidental. Certainly, this is the way a salesman feels after he has succeeded in booking an order. Neither of these views prevails in general, however.

PRECIOUS METALS AND AGRICULTURAL COMMODITIES. An exception to the general rule occurs in companies that mine precious metals, such as gold, silver, and uranium. Many of these companies recognize revenue in the period in which the metal is mined, rather than in the period in which it is shipped. They reason that once the metal has been refined, it is as readily exchangeable as is cash, and that the revenue process has essentially ended at that time. Some farmers recognize revenue on wheat, corn, peanuts, cotton, and similar commodities in the period in which their crop is harvested, even though it may be sold in a later period. They feel that because the government guarantees a certain price for these commodities under its price support programs, revenue is assured at the earlier time.

Installment Sales

Consumers who pay for their purchases in installments (so much a month or so much a week) are, as a class, below-average credit risks; a significant number of them do not complete their payments, and the seller accordingly repossesses, or tries to repossess, the merchandise. When this happens, the face amount of the installment contract overstates the amount of revenue that actually is earned on the transaction. In a company which has many such installment contracts, it may not be conservative to measure revenue as the amount of the sales price shown on the contract, for it is likely that a significant amount of such revenue will never be received as cash. Under these circumstances, some companies use the *installment method* of accounting; that is, they recognize revenue only when the installment payments are received. The FASB states that sales revenue should "ordinarily" be accounted for when the sale is made, and that the installment method is acceptable only when "the circumstances are such that the collection of the sales price is not reasonably assured."[1] If the installment method is used in measuring revenue, the relevant expense is that fraction of the product's cost that corresponds to the fraction of installment payments received during the period.

The effect of the installment method is to postpone the recognition of revenue and income to later periods, as compared with the method that recognizes the full amount of revenue when the sale is made. If a company wants to report as much income as it legitimately can in the current period, it will therefore prefer to record the full amount of the transaction at the time of sale. If it wants to postpone the recognition of taxable income for as long as feasible, it will prefer the installment method. For this reason, many companies use the installment method for income tax purposes.

> EXAMPLE: A jeweler sells a watch in 1973 for $100, and the customer agrees to make payments totalling $50 in 1973 and $50 in 1974. (The customer would ordinarily pay interest in addition to the payments for the watch itself, but this is a separate revenue item which is disregarded here.) The watch cost the jeweler $60. If the whole amount of the sale is recognized as revenue in 1973, revenue is $100, cost of goods sold is $60, and gross margin is $40. If the installment method is used, revenue in 1973 is $50, costs of goods sold is $30, and gross margin is only $20. If expenses are otherwise unaffected by the transaction, and if the income tax rate is 50 percent, net income would be affected correspondingly as shown below:

	Effect on 1973 Income Statement	
	Usual method	*Installment method*
Sales...............................	$100	$50
Cost of goods sold...................	60	30
Gross margin.......................	$ 40	$20
Income tax.........................	20	10
Net Income.........................	$ 20	$10

CONDITIONAL SALES CONTRACTS. Most installment sales are technically conditional sales contracts. In conditional sales contracts, the title to the goods does not legally pass to the buyer until he makes the final payment. It could be argued that the final exchange has not taken place until that time, and that revenue should therefore be recognized only when the

---

[1] APB *Opinion No. 10* (December 1966) par. 12.

final payment is made. This practice is *not* ordinarily followed, however. Although the time at which title passes is one important factor to be considered in deciding when revenue is to be recognized, it is not the only one. If there is a reasonable certainty that an exchange of assets (i.e., goods from the seller, and a valid promise to pay from the buyer) has occurred earlier, then it is proper to recognize the revenue earlier.

LAND DEVELOPMENT SALES. An extreme form of installment sales is the sale of undeveloped parcels of land. Some land development companies sell such parcels on contracts which require only a small down payment, say 5 percent, with the balance being paid in monthly or quarterly installments over a long period, say 30 years. Until recently, some land development companies recorded the full amount of such sales as revenue in the period in which the sale was made, even though experience in the industry showed that a significant number of purchasers defaulted after making a few payments. However, the American Institute of CPAs currently requires that no revenue be recognized until at least 10 percent of the purchase price has been received.

INTEREST COMPONENT OF A SALE. When buyers purchase goods on an installment plan, they pay both for the goods themselves and for the interest which the seller charges on the amount of the unpaid balance. Revenue from the sales value of the merchandise should be recorded separately from interest revenue. In most sales to consumers, this separation is easy to recognize since Federal regulations require that the amount of interest be specified in the sales contract. Although the full sales value may be recorded at the time of the sale (unless the installment method is used), the interest revenue is recorded in the period to which it applies, that is, it is spread over the life of the installment contract.

In some sales agreements, the buyer gives a note promising to pay several years in the future, but the note does not indicate on its face that an interest charge is involved. Since any rational businessman expects to receive more money for a sale that is not completed for several years in the future than for a cash sale, it is apparent that the amount stated in the note includes both the sales value of the goods and an interest charge. In recording the transaction these two components must be shown separately. If the face amount of the note were recorded as revenue in the period in which the transaction took place, revenue for that period would be overstated by the amount of the interest component. The interest that is implicit in such a transaction is calculated by applying the going rate of interest for transactions of this general type.[2] The same principle is used for notes which state a rate of interest that is significantly below the going rate.

---

[2] See APB *Opinion No. 21* (August 1971) for details as to how the rate of interest is determined.

EXAMPLE: Company X buys a machine from Company Y and gives a note payable in three years, at no interest, for $10,000. If the going rate of interest is 8 percent, it can be determined that the interest charge implicit in this transaction is $2,060. Sales revenue in the current period is therefore recorded as $7,940, and the $2,060 is recorded as interest revenue over the three-year period.

Long-Term Contracts

When, under a firm contract, a business works for several years on a single product, a portion of the revenue is often recognized in each of these years rather than solely in the year in which the product is completed and shipped. Shipbuilding and major construction projects are examples of situations in which this *percentage-of-completion* method is used. The revenue recognized for a period can easily be estimated when the product is constructed under a straight *cost-plus* contract, since the revenue is a specified percentage of the costs incurred in the period. In the case of fixed-price contracts, and certain other types of contracts, the total amount of profit, and hence the amount applicable to each accounting period, cannot be known exactly until the total costs have been determined at the completion of the job. In these situations, an estimated revenue may nevertheless be assigned to each of the accounting periods in the same proportion to the cost for the period that total revenue is expected to be of total cost, the proportion being estimated conservatively so as to avoid overstatement of interim profits.

In accordance with the matching principle, when revenue is measured by the percentage-of-completion basis, the expenses for the period are the costs associated with the revenue.

The alternative to the percentage-of-completion method is the *completed-contract* method, under which all revenue is recognized at the time the contract is completed. Until that time, the costs incurred are held on the balance sheet as an asset, *construction in progress*. A company can use either the completed contract method or the percentage-of-completion method, as it chooses.

Consignments

Shipments on *consignment* are not sales, and no revenue should be recognized at the time merchandise is shipped to the consignee.[3] The consignor, that is, the manufacturer, retains title to consignment merchandise, and the sale is not consummated until the consignee, who is

---

[3] Nevertheless, some businesses treat consignment shipments as if they were sales on the grounds that they have learned through experience that the consigned merchandise ordinarily is not returned, and that the sale for all practical purposes is therefore consummated at the time of shipment.

usually a retailer, sells to the final customer. A consignment shipment therefore represents only the movement of the asset, inventory, from one place to another. In order to show the amount of merchandise out on consignment, it may be desirable to reflect this movement by a journal entry, at cost:

```
dr.    Inventory on Consignment................ 100
   cr.    Merchandise Inventory................          100
```

In the period in which the goods are sold, the effect on the accounts would be as in the following entries (although these amounts would probably be recorded, in practice, as a part of other summary entries for revenues and expense):

```
dr.    Cost of Goods Sold..................... 100
   cr.    Inventory on Consignment............          100
          To record the cost of consigned goods
          sold.

dr.    Accounts Receivable.................... 140
   cr.    Sales.............................          140
          To record the sales value.
```

AMOUNT OF REVENUE RECOGNIZED

We have discussed the timing aspect of the realization concept. The other aspect is that the amount of revenue recognized in a period is the amount that is reasonably certain to be collected from sales transactions that are properly recorded in that period. This concept requires that certain adjustments be made to the gross sales value of goods sold. Two of these adjustments, those for sales discounts and for sales returns and allowances, were discussed in Chapter 3. Two others, for bad debts and warranties, are discussed below.

Bad Debts

The main source of revenue in many businesses is the sale of merchandise to customers for credit, that is, "on account." These sales may involve a single payment, or they may involve a series of payments, as in the installment sales transactions discussed above. They give rise to the sales revenue and also to the asset, Accounts Receivable. Let us assume that the Essel Company began operations in 1973 and that during the year the company made sales of $262,250, all on credit. In the interest of simplicity, let us further assume that none of the customers had paid his bill by the end of 1973. The record made of these transactions would show Accounts Receivable in the amount of $262,250 and Sales Revenue of $262,250. It would be correct to report $262,250 as an asset on the balance sheet as of the end of 1973 and $262,250 as sales on the income statement for 1973 if, *but only if*, it is believed that every customer eventually will pay the full amount of his obligation to the Essel Company. The unfortunate fact is, however, that some of these customers may never pay their bills; if they do not, their accounts become *bad debts*.

Consider the extreme case: the person who purchases merchandise with no intention of paying for it and who in fact does not pay for it. In this case, the company has not actually made a sale at all. Although the fact was not known at the time, no revenue was actually earned, and nothing valuable was added to the asset, Accounts Receivable, as a result of this transaction. If this event is recorded as an increase in Sales and as an increase in Accounts Receivable, both of these accounts will be overstated.

In the more usual bad debt situation, the customer fully intends to pay his bill, but for one reason or another he never actually does make payment. The effect is the same as that in the extreme case. Such a sale is also recorded initially by debiting Accounts Receivable and crediting Sales at the sales value of the merchandise. In these situations, another entry must be made to show that the amount debited to Accounts Receivable does not represent a valid asset and that owners' equity has not in fact increased by the amount of the sale.

ACCOUNTING RECOGNITION OF BAD DEBTS. When the company made the sale, the fact that the customer would never pay his bill was not known; otherwise the sale probably would not have been made. Even at the end of the accounting period, the company probably does not know which of the obligations carried as accounts receivable will never be collected. An estimate of the amount of bad debts can nevertheless be made, and it is customary to adjust the accounting records at the end of each accounting period to reflect this estimate.

One method of making this adjustment is by a *direct write-off*. Accounts that are believed to be uncollectible are simply eliminated from the records by subtracting the amount of the bad debt from Accounts Receivable and showing the same amount as an expense item on the income statement. The entry to accomplish this would be as follows:

```
dr.    Bad Debt Expense...................... 200
   cr.    Accounts Receivable................       200
```

The direct write-off method, however, requires that the specific uncollectible accounts be detected, whereas this usually is not possible. An alternative procedure, therefore, is to estimate the *total* amount of uncollectible accounts, and to show this estimated amount as a deduction from Accounts Receivable on the balance sheet, and as an expense on the income statement. Instead of reducing the Accounts Receivable figure directly, the estimate is often shown as a separate number on the balance sheet, so that the reader can observe both the total amount owed by customers and that portion of the amount which the company believes will not be collected.

ACCOUNTS INVOLVED. An account used to record deductions in the amount shown in some other account is called a *contra* account. The balance sheet contra account for Accounts Receivable is labeled *Allowance for Doubtful Accounts* or *Allowance for Uncollectible Accounts*. At one time it was often labeled "Reserve for Bad Debts," but this caused confusion since the word "reserve" connotes to many people that a sum of money has been set aside, and such is not the case.[4] The Allowance for Doubtful Accounts is in the nature of a decrease in Accounts Receivable for specific, but as yet unknown, customers. The corresponding item on the income statement is called *Bad Debt Expense* or *Loss on Bad Debts*.

METHODS OF MAKING THE ESTIMATE. Any one of several methods may be used to estimate the amount of bad debt expense in an accounting period. One method is to examine each of the customer accounts and to set up an amount that is large enough to equal the balances in those accounts that seem to be uncollectible. In companies with hundreds, or thousands, of customer accounts, an analysis of each individual account may not be feasible. A common practice, therefore, is to rely on some overall formula developed on the basis of experience over a period of years. Some of the methods commonly used are as follows:

1. Estimate bad debt expense as a *percentage of total sales* for the period. This method can logically be used only when cash sales are either negligible or a constant proportion of total sales, for bad debt expense is not, of course, related to cash sales.
2. Estimate bad debt expense as a *percentage of credit sales*.
3. Adjust the Allowance for Doubtful Accounts so that it equals a prescribed *percentage of accounts receivable* outstanding at the end of the period.

The percentage used in each case depends in part on what the records show as to experience in the past and in part on management's judgment as to the extent to which past experience reflects the current situation. The allowance for doubtful accounts should be sufficient at all times to absorb the accounts that prove to be uncollectible. Because business conditions fluctuate, the amount may well turn out to be too large in some periods and too small in others. In practice, because of the concept of conservatism, it is common to find that the allowance is too large rather than too small. On the other hand, there have been some cases

---

[4] Notwithstanding the recommendation that the term "Reserve for Bad Debts" not be used, 62 of the 600 companies analyzed in *Accounting Trends and Techniques* did in fact use this term in 1972.

where the allowance for doubtful accounts turned out to be woefully inadequate.

AGING ACCOUNTS RECEIVABLE. Sometimes different percentages are applied to accounts outstanding for various lengths of time. This requires the preparation of an *aging schedule*, which is also a useful device for analyzing the quality of the asset, accounts receivable. An example is shown in Illustration 5–1.

Illustration 5–1

AGING SCHEDULE FOR ESTIMATING BAD DEBTS

Status	Amount Outstanding	Estimated % Uncollectible	Allowance for Doubtful Accounts
Current.....................	$207,605	1	$2,076
Overdue:			
Less than 1 month..........	26,003	1	260
1 up to 2 months...........	10,228	5	511
2 up to 3 months...........	7,685	10	768
3 up to 4 months...........	3,876	20	775
Over 4 months.............	6,853	40	2,741
Total................	$262,250		$7,131

THE ADJUSTING ENTRY. Once the amount has been determined, it is recorded as one of the adjusting entries made at the end of the accounting period. If Essel Company management estimated the Allowance for Doubtful Accounts on the basis of the above aging schedule, the entry would be as shown below:

```
dr.   Bad Debt Expense................... 7,131
   cr.   Allowance for Doubtful Accounts..        7,131
```

The accounts receivable section of the December 31, 1973 balance sheet would then appear as follows:

```
Accounts receivable........................... $262,250
   Less: Allowance for doubtful accounts........   7,131
      Accounts Receivable, Net................ $255,119
```

The income statement for 1973 would show bad debt expense in the amount of $7,131.

For reasons to be described, the Allowance for Doubtful Accounts usually will have a balance even before the adjusting entry is made. In these circumstances the amount reported as Bad Debt Expense on the income statement will be different from the amount reported as allowance for doubtful accounts on the balance sheet. (In the Essel Company example just given, this did not occur because the company was organized in 1973, and the above entry was the first one made to Allowance for Doubtful Accounts.)

When the Allowance for Doubtful Accounts has a balance, care must be taken in applying the methods listed above. Methods No. 1 and No. 2, which are related to sales, give the amount of bad debt *expense* for the period; this same amount is credited to whatever balance existed in Allowance for Doubtful Accounts prior to the entry. Method No. 3, which is related to accounts receivable, gives the amount that is to appear as the Allowance for Doubtful Accounts; the journal entry is made in an amount that brings the Allowance for Doubtful Accounts *up to* the desired balance.

> EXAMPLE: If at the end of 1974, in the Essel Company, Allowance for Doubtful Accounts had a credit balance of $1,000, and if it was decided that the allowance should be 2 percent of accounts receivable, which at that time amounted to $300,000, the balance must be increased *to* $6,000, which is an increase of $5,000. The journal entry would therefore be the following:

```
dr.    Bad Debt Expense................... 5,000
   cr.    Allowance for Doubtful Accounts..        5,000
```

The balance sheet as of December 31, 1974 would then show:

```
Accounts receivable............................ $300,000
   Less: Allowance for doubtful accounts.........    6,000
   Accounts Receivable, Net.................... $294,000
```

WRITE-OFF OF AN UNCOLLECTIBLE ACCOUNT. When the company decides that a specific customer is never going to pay his bill, Accounts Receivable is reduced by the amount he owes and a corresponding reduction is made in the Allowance for Doubtful Accounts. This entry is made whenever it is recognized that a specific account is bad, which may be either during the accounting period or at the end of the period. This entry has *no* effect on Bad Debt Expense.

> EXAMPLE: If sometime in 1975 the Essel Company decided that John Jones was never going to pay his bill of $200, the following entry would be made:

```
dr.    Allowance for Doubtful Accounts......... 200
   cr.    Accounts Receivable.................        200
```

A balance sheet prepared immediately after this transaction had been recorded (assuming no other changes since December 31) would appear as follows:

```
Accounts receivable........................... $299,800
   Less: Allowance for doubtful accounts.........   5,800
   Accounts Receivable, Net................... $294,000
```

Note that the *net* amount of accounts receivable is unchanged by this entry.

COLLECTION OF A BAD DEBT WRITTEN OFF. If, by some unexpected stroke of good fortune, John Jones should subsequently pay all or part of the amount he owed, cash would be increased (i.e., debited) and a corresponding credit would be recorded to have one of the following effects:

1. Add back the amount to Allowance for Doubtful Accounts on the balance sheet;
2. Show as Bad Debts Recovered, a separate item of revenue on the income statement; or,
3. Decrease Bad Debt Expense on the income statement.

The first method has the effect of reversing the previous entry, and it is often used. The second method is rarely used because the amount involved is ordinarily too small to warrant reporting it as a separate item. The third method is not entirely logical but is often used in practice since it provides a convenient way of handling the transaction.

Still another common procedure is, first, to reverse the entry by which the account was written off (i.e., debit Accounts Receivable and credit Allowance for Doubtful Accounts) and, then, to treat the collection just like any other payment on account (i.e., debit Cash and credit Accounts Receivable). This has the advantage of showing a complete record of the transaction in the account for the customer.

SUMMARY. Let us summarize the handling of events described above by showing the effect of hypothetical transactions in 1975 on the Essel Company accounts:

1. *Write-off of $5,000 more of bad debts during the year:*

```
dr.    Allowance for Doubtful Accounts..... 5,000
   cr.    Accounts Receivable............          5,000
          The balance in Allowance for
          Doubtful Accounts becomes $800.
```

2. *Recovery of $500 previously written off:*

```
dr.    Cash.................................... 500
   cr.    Allowance for Doubtful Accounts*....          500
          The balance in Allowance for Doubtful
          Accounts becomes $1,300.
```

* As mentioned, this is only one of several possible treatments.

3. *Adjustments at end of 1975* assuming allowance is to be maintained at 2 percent of accounts receivable, which are $400,000 as of December 31, 1975:

```
dr.    Bad Debt Expense........................... 6,700
   cr.      Allowance for Doubtful Accounts........        6,700
            This brings the allowance up to $8,000,
            which is 2 percent of accounts receivable.
```

Credit Cards

Hundreds of thousands of retailers and service establishments who sell on credit have contracted with an outside agency to handle all, or some, of their accounts receivable. There are two types of these credit card plans.

The first type is called a bank plan. Master Charge and Bank-Americard are examples. In this plan, the merchant sends the credit slips to his bank along with other bank deposits. The bank arranges to have the charges collected from the customer. If the customer's account is with another bank, the sales slip is sent to that bank for collection. So far as the merchant is concerned, this type of transaction is not a credit sale at all. No accounts receivable appear in the merchant's accounts. The sales slip (assuming it is properly made out) is the same as cash, and is credited to the merchant's account by the bank as soon as it is deposited, just like a check or other cash item. The only difference between a credit card sales slip and a check is that in the former case the bank deducts a fee for the service of handling the accounts receivable paperwork and assuming the risk of bad debts. This fee is in the nature of a sales discount, and is recorded as such in the merchant's accounts, thus:

```
dr.    Cash................................ 960
       Sales Discount (Credit Cards).........  40
   cr.      Sales...........................      1,000
```

In the other type of plan, the merchant sends the sales slips to a credit card company and receives reimbursement from this company within 30 days, 60 days, or whatever period is agreed upon. American Express and Diner's Club are examples. Because of the interval that elapses between the submission of sales slips and the receipt of cash, in this plan the merchant does have accounts receivable. There are no bad debts, however, because the credit card company assumes the risk of loss, provided the merchant follows instructions in making out and approving the sales slip. When the slips are sent in, the entry is:

```
dr.    Accounts Receivable................. 960
       Sales Discount (Credit Cards)....... 40
   cr.      Sales...........................      1,000
```

When cash is received from the credit card company, Accounts Receivable is credited.

Warranty Costs

Many companies agree to repair or replace merchandise that the customer finds to be defective. When this agreement is an explicit part of the sales contract, it is called a *warranty*. Other companies may respond to a customer's complaint, even though they have no legal obligation to do so. In either case, the amount of revenue originally recorded for the sales transaction turns out to be an overstatement of the amount of revenue that ultimately results. If it is estimated that a significant amount of costs will be incurred in a future period in order to repair or replace merchandise sold in the current period, the realization concept requires that an adjustment be made to the current period's revenue with an entry such as:

```
dr.    Estimated Warranty Expense......... 1,000
  cr.    Allowance for Warranties........          1,000
```

When costs are incurred in the future in order to carry out the warranty obligation, the Allowance for Warranties is debited and Cash, Accrued Wages, Inventory, or a similar account is credited.

Revenue Adjustment versus Expense

The transactions described above have been analyzed in accordance with the realization concept, that is, they were adjustments made in order to show the net amount of revenue "almost certainly" to be realized in an accounting period. Two alternative treatments of these transactions are possible.

First, adjustments to revenue of the current period can be disregarded, on the grounds that they are not material enough to warrant the bookkeeping effort required. This is common practice for sales returns and allowances and for warranties in situations in which these amounts either are likely to be small or are likely to be relatively constant from one period to the next. The amount actually allowed when merchandise is returned, or the amount actually spent on account of warranties, is recorded in the period in which these events occur. This practice is consistent with the concept of materiality.

Second, companies may analyze some or all of these transactions in accordance with the matching concept, rather than in accordance with the realization concept; that is, they may conclude that these are events that should be matched against recorded revenue, rather than as adjustments *to* revenue. If the matching concept is used, the items are listed as expenses. Either approach affects net income in exactly the same way. The difference between them is in the way they affect revenue and gross margin. The consistency concept requires that a company follow the same method from one year to the next, so comparisons within a company are not affected by these differences in practice. They can have a significant effect when the income statements of companies that use different methods are being compared, however.

EXAMPLE: Following are income statements for Company A, which treats all items of the type discussed in this section as adjustments to revenue, and Company B, which treats them as expenses. Otherwise, the firms are identical.

Income Statements (000 omitted)

	Company A		Company B	
	Amount	*%*	*Amount*	*%*
Gross sales............................	$1,000	110.0	$1,000	100.0
Less: sales discounts..................	20	2.2	0	
bad debts........................	40	4.4	0	
returns..........................	30	3.3	0	
Net sales..............................	$ 910	100.0	$1,000	100.0
Cost of goods sold....................	600	65.9	600	60.0
Gross margin.........................	$ 310	34.1	$ 400	40.0
Other expenses.......................	210	23.1	210	21.0
Discounts, bad debts, returns...........	0		90	9.0
Net Income......................	$ 100	11.1	$ 100	10.0

Note the differences between the two income statements, not only in the dollar amounts of net sales and gross margin, but also, and more importantly, in the percentages for all items. (In reporting percentage relationships on an income statement, net sales is customarily taken as 100 percent; that is, the percentages for other items are calculated by dividing each by the amount of net sales.) Various combinations of these alternatives would produce still different amounts and percentages.

MONETARY ASSETS

Monetary assets are assets that are cash or items that will be converted into cash, as contrasted with nonmonetary assets, which are items that will be used in the future in the production and sale of goods and services. No separate classification for monetary assets appears on the balance sheet; the important distinction on the balance sheet is between current assets and noncurrent assets. The reason for calling attention to the distinction between monetary and nonmonetary assets is that the concepts governing the amounts at which they appear on the balance sheet differ for these two categories.

In general, and with the notable exception of inventory which is discussed in Chapter 6, *nonmonetary* assets appear on the balance sheet at *unexpired cost;* that is, when acquired, they were recorded at cost, and the amount shown on the balance sheet at any time thereafter is the amount that has not yet been written off as an expense. If a building was acquired in 1960 at a cost of $1,000,000 and if $400,000 of its cost has been written off as depreciation expense in the intervening period, the balance sheet for December 31, 1975, will report the asset amount of this building at $600,000, *regardless of its market value at that time.*

For *monetary* assets, the idea of "unexpired cost" is not appropriate. As we have seen above, the accounts receivable item is in effect reported at its estimated realizable value. This is the effect of the adjustment for the estimated amount of bad debts that are included in the accounts receivable. Cash, of course, is reported at its face amount, whether on hand or deposited in banks. In the following paragraphs we describe the treatment of two other monetary assets, certificates of deposit and marketable securities.

Certificates of Deposit

By Federal law, a commercial bank is prohibited from paying interest on checking accounts, that is, on demand deposits. If the company has a temporary excess of cash, it can nevertheless loan the money to a commercial bank and receive interest on the amount loaned. The most common evidence of such a loan is a document called a certificate of deposit. Such loans are usually for a fairly short period of time, such as 90 days.

If the amounts are material, certificates of deposit should be reported separately from the amount of cash in checking accounts. They are reported at their face amount because of the high probability that the loan will be repaid at this amount.

Marketable Securities

Marketable securities are stocks and bonds of other companies which are traded on a securities market, and which are held for the purpose of producing income in the form of interest, dividends, or capital gains. They are to be distinguished from *investments* which are stocks in another company held for the purpose of exercising some control over that company, or stocks and bonds not traded on a securities market, whether held for control or for income-producing purposes. Investments are recorded at cost or at "equity," as described in Chapter 10. Marketable securities are monetary assets because they can be, and presumably will be, converted into cash. They may be classified on the balance sheet either as current assets or as noncurrent assets, depending on whether the company's intention is, or is not, to convert them to cash within the next year or other operating cycle.

Marketable securities are reported either at their cost or at their current market value, whichever is lower. This is consistent with the conservatism concept. In deciding whether the market value is lower than cost, the whole portfolio of stocks and bonds is considered as a group, rather than item by item; that is, if the cost of the whole portfolio was $100,000, and its total market value is more than $100,000, the balance sheet amount would be $100,000, even though some individual stocks or bonds in the portfolio may currently have a market value that is lower than cost. Also, marketable securities are reported at cost, rather than market value, if the decline below cost is judged to be temporary. (Since the balance sheet as of December 31 is ordinarily not published until two or three months thereafter, the accountant has an opportunity to find out whether a dip below cost on December 31 is, or is not, temporary.)

When marketable securities are reported at market value, the amount of cost is also reported in parentheses, viz:

```
Marketable Securities (Cost, $100,000)............. $95,000
```

The amount in parentheses does not affect the totals on the balance sheet. If marketable securities are reported at cost, their market value at the balance sheet date is also shown in parentheses.

SUMMARY

The realization concept states that revenues are generally recognized in the accounting period in which goods are shipped or services are rendered. When goods are sold on an installment plan, however, and when the likelihood that a significant number of installment contracts will not be completed is quite high, revenues may be recognized when installment payments are received; this is the installment method. As another exception, in the case of a long-term construction contract, revenue may be recognized over the life of the contract; this is the percentage-of-completion method.

The realization concept also states that the amount of revenue recognized in a period is the amount that is reasonably certain to be earned. Accordingly, the gross sales revenue is reduced by the estimated amount of bad debts that are hidden in credit sales. A corresponding reduction is made in the asset, accounts receivable. Similar reductions may be made for warranty costs and for sales returns and allowances.

Monetary assets are assets other than unexpired costs. They are reported on the balance sheet in various ways. Cash, certificates of deposit, and accounts receivable are reported at realizable amounts (which in the case of cash and certificates of deposit is the same as the face amount). Marketable securities are reported at the lower of cost or current market value unless the decline below cost is temporary.

CASES

CASE 5-1. PALMER CORPORATION (A)

On December 31, 1974, before the yearly financial statements were prepared, the controller of the Palmer Corporation reviewed certain transactions that affected accounts receivable and the allowance for

Exhibit 1

PALMER CORPORATION

Balance Sheet as of December 31, 1973

ASSETS

Current Assets:

Cash..		$ 358,050
Accounts receivable...................................	$ 527,071	
Less: Allowance for doubtful accounts..................	15,812	511,259
U.S. Treasury securities at cost.......................		143,299
Inventories...		925,013
Total Current Assets...............................		$1,937,621
Investments...		$ 219,892

Fixed Assets:

Land..		$ 98,836
Building..	$1,282,805	
Less: Accumulated depreciation........................	353,802	929,003
Factory machinery.....................................	$1,826,979	
Less: Accumulated depreciation........................	875,924	951,055
Furniture and fixtures................................	$ 30,125	
Less: Accumulated depreciation........................	21,546	8,579
Automotive equipment.................................	$ 31,093	
Less: Accumulated depreciation........................	19,817	11,276
Office machines......................................	$ 22,690	
Less: Accumulated depreciation........................	14,936	7,754
Tools...		32,690
Patent..		30,000
Total Fixed Assets.................................		$2,069,193
Prepaid expenses......................................		$ 56,963
Total Assets......................................		$4,283,669

142

Exhibit 1—(*continued*)

LIABILITIES AND CAPITAL

Current Liabilities:

Accounts payable..	$ 270,001
Unpaid taxes...	380,323
Accrued salaries, wages, and interest......................	75,455
Long-term debt, due within one year......................	36,960
Total Current Liabilities.............................	$ 762,739

Fixed Liabilities:

Long-term debt..	$ 665,263

Capital:

Common stock...	$1,335,082
Retained earnings......................................	1,520,585
Total Capital..	$2,855,667
Total Liabilities and Capital........................	$4,283,669

doubtful accounts. The controller first examined the December 31, 1973, balance sheet, Exhibit 1. His subsequent review of the year's transactions applicable to accounts receivable revealed the items listed below:

1. Sales on account during 1974 amounted to $5,267,412.
2. Payment received on accounts receivable during 1974 totaled $5,062,798.
3. During the year accounts receivable totaling $14,323 were deemed uncollectible and were written off.
4. Two accounts which had been written off as uncollectible in 1973 were collected in 1974. One account for $1,022 was paid in full. A partial payment of $750 was made by the King Company on another account which originally had amounted to $1,205. The Palmer Corporation was reasonably sure this account would be paid in full because reliable reports were circulating that the trustee in bankruptcy for the King Company would pay all obligations 100 cents on the dollar.
5. The allowance for bad debts was adjusted to equal 3 percent of the balance in accounts receivable at the end of the year.

Questions

1. Analyze the effect of each of these transactions in terms of their effect on accounts receivable, allowance for doubtful accounts, and any other account that may be involved, and prepare necessary journal entries.
2. Give the correct totals for accounts receivable and the allowance on doubtful accounts, as of December 31, 1974, after the transactions affecting them had been recorded.

CASE 5–2. MACDONALD'S FARM

Early in 1973, Dennis Grey was notified by a lawyer that his recently deceased uncle had willed him the ownership of a 2,000-acre wheat farm in East Central Iowa. The lawyer requested information as to whether Dennis wanted to keep the farm or sell it.

Mr. Grey was an assistant vice president in the consumer credit department of a large New York bank. Despite the distance between New York and Iowa, Grey was interested in retaining ownership of the farm if he could determine its profitability. During the last ten years of his life, Jeremiah MacDonald had hired professional managers to run his farm while he remained in semi-retirement in Florida.

Keeping the farm as an investment was particularly interesting to Dennis for the following reasons:

1. Recent grain deals with Communist countries had increased present farm commodity prices substantially; many experts believed these prices would remain high for the next several years.
2. While the number of small farms had decreased markedly in the last 20 years, large farms such as MacDonald's using mechanization and new hybrid seed varieties could be extremely profitable.
3. The value of good farm land in Iowa was appreciating at about 10 percent to 15 percent a year.

Included in the lawyer's letter were data on revenues and expenses for 1972 and certain information on balance sheet items, which are summarized below:

Inventory:

Beginning inventory	0 bushels
1972 wheat production	210,000 bushels
Sold to grain elevator	180,000 bushels
Ending inventory	30,000 bushels

Prices:

The average price per bushel for wheat sold to the grain elevator operator in 1972 was $2.20. The price per bushel at the time of the wheat harvest was $2.10. The closing price per bushel at December 31, 1972 was $2.28.

Accounts Receivable:

At year end, the proceeds from 20,000 bushels had not yet been received from the elevator operator. The average sales price of this wheat had been $2.22 per bushel. There were no uncollected proceeds at December 31, 1971.

Cash:

The farm has a checking account balance of $5,800 and a savings account totalling $15,000.

Land:

The original cost of the land was $250,000. It was appraised for estate tax purposes at $700 per acre.

Buildings and Machinery:

Buildings and machinery with an original cost of $275,000 and accumulated deprecia-
tion of $200,000 are employed on the farm. The equipment was appraised at book value.

Current Liabilities:

The farm has notes payable and accounts payable totalling $22,000.

Owner's Equity:

Common stock has a par value of $5,000 plus additional paid-in capital of $300,000.
There was no record of retained earnings although it was known that Jeremiah MacDonald
withdrew most of the earnings in the last few years in order to continue the life style to
which he had become accustomed in Florida.

1972 Expenses for the MacDonald Farm

A. Variable costs per bushel:

Seed	$.035
Fertilizer and chemicals	.210
Machinery costs, fuel and repairs	.065
Part-time labor and other costs	.025
Variable cost per bushel	$.335

B. Annual costs not related to the volume of production:

Salaries and wages	$ 45,000
Insurance	4,000
Taxes*	15,000
Depreciation	19,000
Other expenses	30,000
Total	$113,000

* This figure excludes income taxes since the corporation was taxed
as a sole proprietorship.

Looking over the data on revenues and expenses Mr. Grey discovered
that there were no numbers for total revenues for the year or for the
beginning or ending inventory. The lawyer's letter explained that there
was some doubt in his mind about when revenue for the farm should be
recognized and about the appropriate way to value the grain inventory.
There are at least three alternative stages in the wheat growing cycle at
which revenue could be counted.

First, the *production method* could be used. Since wheat has a daily
valuation on the Chicago Commodity Exchange, any unsold inventory
as of December 31 could be valued at market price very objectively. In
this way, revenue can be counted for all wheat produced in a given year,
regardless of whether it is sold or not. A decision not to sell this wheat
before December 31 is based on speculation about future wheat price
increases.

Second, the *sale method* could be used. This would recognize revenue
when the grain is purchased from the farm by the grain elevator operator
in the neighboring town. In this instance, the owner of the grain elevator
had just sold control to a Kansas City company with no previous experience in running such a facility. The manager of the MacDonald Farm
had expressed some concern about selling to an unknown operator.

Third, the *collection method* could be used. Under this approach revenue is counted when the cash is actually received by the farm from the grain elevator operator. Full collection often took several months because a grain elevator operator might keep wheat for a considerable time in the hope that prices would rise so he could sell at a greater profit.

Questions

1. Prepare the 1972 income statement and related ending balance sheet for the MacDonald Farm recognizing revenue by the:
   a. production method
   b. sales method
   c. collection method
   Which method would you recommend?
2. Assume that the MacDonald Farm had received a firm offer of $150,000 for 100 acres of the farm which would be used as the site of a new housing development. This development would have no effect on the use of the remaining acreage as a farm, and Mr. Grey planned to accept it. How would you account in the 1972 financial statements for the economic gain represented by this appreciation in land values?
3. Should Grey retain ownership of the farm?

CASE 5–3.   ROCKY MOUNTAIN CONSTRUCTION COMPANY

During a meeting of the board of directors of the Rocky Mountain Construction Company in early February 1970, Mr. Roy Benthall, president and chief operating officer, expressed his concern over an operating statement which had been presented at the meeting (see Exhibit 1). A discussion of this statement ensued in which several of those present took opposing views concerning the proper presentation of income for the firm's land development department. The company's statements were sent to the company's stockholders, and also were going to be presented either to a potential investor or to a commercial bank in order to raise the capital necessitated by the company's recent expansion into the field of land development.

Company Background

Mr. Benthall and his two sons had incorporated the Rocky Mountain Construction Company in 1956 as a small masonry and general home improvements construction organization located in Boulder, Colorado. The company had grown rapidly during its first few years and had expanded its operations into residential and small plant construction. As additional financing became necessary, Mr. Benthall had sold stock to several local

Exhibit 1

LAND DEVELOPMENT DEPARTMENT

Modified* Cash Operating Statement

For the Year Ending December 31, 1969

Sales Revenue:

Plot Number	Amount Received		
1	$632,000		
3	158,945		

Total Sales Revenue		$790,945	

Other Income:

Purchase option on Plot Number 9	5,000	
Total Income for Period		$795,945

Less Cost of Sales:

Original Purchase Price of Land	$500,000	
Land Development Costs to Dec. 31, 1969 (see Exhibit 2)	299,564	
Total Land Costs		$799,564

Operating Expenses:

Advertising	$ 475	
Commissions to Outside Brokers	665	
Park Dedication and Press Conferences	1,140	
Purchase of Signs and Office Equipment	6,226	
Inspection Fees	928	
Legal and Accounting	7,850	
(Includes Legal Fee, Title Fee, and Insurance Premium Incurred on Original Land Purchase)		
Photographs and Renderings	2,113	
Salaries—Salesmen	12,695	
Salaries—Office	6,620	
Salaries—Engineering	3,113	
Salaries—General Manager Land Department	10,000	
Sales Commissions	3,480	
Taxes	5,315	
Direct Operating Expense		60,620
Expense Allocation (from the Construction Department)†		8,533
Total Expenses for Period		$868,717
Net Cash Loss for Year Ending December 31, 1969		$ 72,772

* All operating expenses have been computed on an accrual basis and thus include not only cash expenditures made during 1969, but also include some 1968 expenditure and those 1969 expenses due but not paid as of December 31, 1969.

† Allocated on the basis of each department's total sales revenue. This includes heat, light, and power, rent on the office building, telephone and telegraph, and other joint expenses.

Boulder businessmen, but he and his sons retained 65 percent ownership and desired to maintain a controlling interest if possible. However, the need for cash was so pressing that Mr. Benthall and his sons had agreed to seek additional equity investors, if this was the only alternative. The company's income before taxes had been in excess of $50,000 every year since 1961, and had reached $70,000 in 1968. The company was expecting annual profits of $75,000 from its construction operations during the next few years.

Boulder Industrial Park

The population of Boulder, located 30 miles from Denver via a turnpike, had increased dramatically in the last eight years, and the number of industrial plants in the city had increased over 40 percent. Many national companies had indicated their interest in building local branch plants and offices in Boulder because of its ideal location and pleasant living conditions at the foot of the Rocky Mountains.

In late 1968, Mr. Benthall and his sons decided to establish a land development department which was to develop raw land into plots suitable for industrial plant construction. If this operation proved to be profitable, they planned further industrial land development undertakings of this same nature in the Denver-Boulder area. Accordingly, the company purchased for $500,000 a 64-acre tract of land adjoining a major highway leading into Boulder, and began planning Boulder Industrial Park.

During 1969, the company began to develop the raw farm land into tracts suitable for the construction of industrial plants. Some of the work was performed by the land development department itself, and other phases of the work were subcontracted to specialists. The work involved surveying and laying corner markers, site clearing, grading, the installation of temporary haul roads and storm ditches or drains, and finally, permanent access roads, storm drains, sewers, and water mains. Exhibit 2 lists the total improvement costs incurred as of December 31, 1969, for each of the major land development phases, and indicates the cost to complete each improvement phase as estimated by the individual project or operation superintendent or contractor.

Two parcels of land were completed and disposed of during 1969 as indicated in Exhibit 3. One was sold to Arapahoe Development Corpora-

Exhibit 2
LAND DEVELOPMENT DEPARTMENT

Improvement Costs to December 31, 1969

	Account	*Actual*	*Estimated*
500	Site Work*	84,835	–0–
520	Roads	77,087	38,690
540	Storm Drains	24,028	28,180
550	Sewerage	31,301	59,395
560	Water Mains	27,441	71,752
570	Open Drainage Ditch	34,315	–0–
580	Engineering	8,712	2,036
590	Indirect General Conditions†	11,845	11,049
	Grand Totals	299,564	211,102

* Includes site work chargeable directly to specific plots.
† Includes field supervision, watchman's salary, temporary toilets, rain gear and field telephone.

Exhibit 3

LAND DEVELOPMENT DEPARTMENT

Plot Number	Square Footage		Anticipated Sales Price (at start of development)			Sold to	Price Received	Comments
	Feet	Percent	Per Foot	Total Price	Percent			
1	746,532	30.5	$1.70	$1,270,000	36.2	Arap. Development Corp.	$632,000	First plot sold. Sold at discount since the proposed shopping center is expected to increase other land values.
2	180,127	7.3	1.50	270,000	7.7	Rocky Mountain Construction Company	158,945	All land used by the construction department is priced at a set rate of $1 per square foot.
3	158,945	6.5	1.20	190,000	5.4			
4	157,270	6.5	1.30	200,000	5.7	Rocky Mountain expects to use this plot for plant construction at some future time.		
5	152,790	6.2	1.40	215,000	6.1			
6	227,110	9.2	1.40	320,000	9.1			
7	454,829	18.5	1.20	550,000	15.6			
8	255,120	10.4	1.20	310,000	8.8			
9	120,000	4.9	1.60	190,000	5.4	Arap. Development Corp.	170,000	Sold purchase option for $5,000. Option must be exercised by January 1, 1972, its expiration date.
Totals	2,452,723	100.0%		$3,515,000	100.0%			

tion for a shopping center site, and the other was transferred to the construction department for construction of a plant which would then be sold or leased by the company to an industrial concern desiring to locate in the Boulder area.

Mr. Rowen, accountant and office manager of the land development department, prepared an operating statement for 1969, reproduced as Exhibit 1, and presented it to Mr. Benthall and the board of directors for approval at their February meeting. The ensuing discussion is summarized below.

Meeting of the Board of Directors

ROY BENTHALL: As Mr. Rowen has explained it to me, this statement (Exhibit 1) is essentially a cash statement, with certain normal accruals and deferrals. Our problem now is to decide how to adjust this statement, if at all, to arrive at the land development department's profit or loss for the year. I'd be very loath to present this statement as it is because combining this department's $73,000 loss with the construction department's 1969 profit of $68,000 would result in a net loss for the year of $5,000. Not only will our present shareholders be quite concerned, but the probability of selling additional stock or of obtaining a bank loan would be substantially reduced.

FRANK REED (Director of Rocky Mountain and owner of Ledgewood Realty Co.): Of course, it doesn't make any sense to use cash flow as a measure of profit or loss; that completely ignores the fact that the department has a large inventory of partially improved plots on hand as of the end of the year. Some of the improvement costs should be deferred as the cost of land that is still available for sale. If certain land costs are deferred, the department will show a profit rather than a loss for 1969.

ROY BENTHALL: Two points about that approach bother me. First, what happens to these deferred costs if our expected future sales don't materialize? We might not sell all of those plots for two or three years yet, even though we have spent the money. And second, how do you propose to allocate the total land costs to the plots which were sold? Mr. Rowen couldn't keep track of the costs by individual plots, and the plots are at various stages of completion.

JAMES HICKMAN (Director of Rocky Mountain and vice president of construction contracting): Roy, I think that Frank is making a mistake when he only looks at individual plots. I think we should consider the Park as a complete entity in itself, and recognize income from it based on the percentage-of-completion method used in our construction operation. From the figures Mr. Rowen gave you, (Exhibit 2) you can estimate the completed cost of the development. You could then reestimate the total income which you expect to receive from the development based on sales to date. Then the profit recognized this year would be the percentage of estimated total profit that incurred costs to date bear to estimated total costs.

FRANK REED: The only profit we are entitled to show is that profit which we made on actual sales during 1969. Jim's method would have us showing income this year on plots which may not be sold for two years. That just isn't good accounting. Not only that, think of the additional income tax you would have to pay under his method.

BILL COLLINS (Rocky Mountain stockholder):   You're right, Frank, that Jim's method would show a higher profit figure, but it is not allowed by the tax authorities. The tax code clearly specifies the method of accounting that land development companies are required to use in computing taxable income. The Prentice Hall tax guide, paragraph 10,163, states, "the cost should be equitably apportioned to the several lots, and gain or loss calculated on each lot sold. This rule implies that there will be an individual gain or loss on every lot sold and not that the taxpayer shall wait until the capital on the entire tract has been recovered through sales receipts before any taxable income is to be returned. Development costs, including future development costs, may be included in computing gain or loss on sale of lots. Cost apportionment must be made equitably and not ratably, e.g., on market price rather than a square-foot basis, since front lots would ordinarily bear a greater portion of the cost than those in the rear of the development."

BOB ALLEN (Director of Rocky Mountain and executive vice president of the First National Bank of Boulder):   We don't have to prepare our published statements in accordance with the tax code. Jim's and Bill's methods assume that all the land will eventually be sold, and at a profit. I think you have to look at the Park as one complete entity, not as nine separate units. I don't think you should show any profit until you have fully recovered all your costs. I think that all income and all expense from the development should be deferred until the entire project is finished and then you can decide how much profit you made. This is the method my bank uses in recasting submitted corporate statements, since it doesn't want to loan money to a company on the basis of unearned profits which may never be realized. As you know, Roy, there is considerable risk that actual future costs will not be the same as the estimated costs.

CAMERON BENTHALL (Mr. Benthall's eldest son and executive vice president of Rocky Mountain):   The plain fact is that we went into this deal knowing that it was risky, but that if we won we'd win big. Well, we've won. That is to say, now that Arapahoe has come in, a lot of the risk is gone. We didn't do as well as we expected on plot number one, but we'll do better than expected on the others, now that the Park is an established success. I think we will make two million bucks; no, I think we *have* made it already. The city of Boulder has just quadrupled the assessed valuation, now that it's developed land. I think we have an obligation to inform our stockholders as to just how well we've done. If anybody else wants to buy stock now, they're going to have to pay a price based on the current value of this Park, not just a prorata share of the original cost of the plots we haven't sold yet.

BRADLEY BENTHALL (Mr. Benthall's youngest son and general construction manager):   The land costs could be allocated to the plots sold in 1969 on the basis of expected market price, just as the tax regulations require. These plots should also bear some portion of the general operating expenses which will be incurred during the next two years, the time we anticipate it will take to dispose of all the plots. It seems likely to me that these expenses will remain relatively constant during the life of the development, regardless of the percent of completion or degree of sales saturation. Finally, I think estimated profit should be recognized on those plots which are held under a sales option contract or intended for use by the construction department. It appears likely that these options will be taken up, since land prices are constantly increasing. All costs not allocated to the plots sold in 1969, or under option, should be deferred until future years. The consistent use of this method will provide our stockholders and potential investors with stable revenue and earnings figures on which year-to-year operating comparisons can be based.

Questions

1. Using the plot price information contained in Exhibits 1 and 3, prepare income statements for the land development department for 1969 using the following accounting principles:
   a. The percentage-of-completion method, as suggested by Mr. James Hickman, and
   b. The cost allocation method, and related proposals, suggested by Mr. Bradley Benthall.
2. Applying either of these two methods requires a set of assumptions and decisions about how to handle certain items. Identify these items and appraise the relative importance of each in terms of its impact on the profit calculation.
3. Which, if any, of the four major proposals (the two above, plus Mr. Allen's and Mr. Cameron Benthall's) would you recommend that Rocky Mountain adopt for reporting to its stockholders?

CHAPTER 6

COST OF GOODS SOLD
AND INVENTORIES

This chapter describes the principles and procedures for measuring the cost of goods sold in merchandising companies and in manufacturing companies and the related measurement of inventory on the balance sheet. These costs may be accounted for either by the periodic inventory method or the perpetual inventory method; each method is described. The cost of individual units of inventory and of individual goods sold can be measured by any of several methods, including specific identification, average cost, Fifo, and Lifo; each of these methods is described, and they are compared.

OVERVIEW OF THE PROBLEM

Because the topics discussed in this chapter are interrelated, we start with a brief general description of cost of sales and inventory procedures in three types of companies: service companies, merchandising companies, and manufacturing companies. Next we shall describe in detail the procedure in merchandising companies. Since the procedure in manufacturing companies starts with the same steps used in merchandising companies and incorporates additional aspects associated with the manufacturing process, in describing manufacturing companies we shall focus primarily on these additional matters.

Types of Companies

A single company may conduct service, merchandising and/or manufacturing activities. For convenience, we shall assume that each company

153

described here conducts only one type. If a company does conduct more than one type of activity, for each type it will use the appropriate accounting method.

SERVICE COMPANIES.   A service company, such as a motel or a beauty parlor, provides intangible services rather than tangible goods. It therefore reports no cost of goods sold, as such, on its income statement, and no inventory of goods on its balance sheet. Some service companies report as cost of sales the costs directly associated with the services they provide, such as the labor costs of beauticians in a beauty shop. Others do not separate these costs from other operating expenses; instead, they report individual items of operating expense in a single list. Companies that follow the latter practice cannot develop a gross margin number, which is the difference between sales and cost of sales.

> EXAMPLE: If a plumbing company collects the labor costs of its plumbers and the costs of pipe and other material as its cost of sales, it can develop a gross margin. It would subtract management and office salaries, sales expenses, office costs, other general and administrative expenses, and income taxes from the gross margin in order to obtain net income. Alternatively, the plumbing company could list expense items in one list without classifying those related to cost of sales separately from the others. In the latter case it does not develop a gross margin.

We shall not discuss further the measurement of cost of sales in a service company.

MERCHANDISING COMPANIES.   A merchandising company sells goods in substantially the same physical form as that in which it acquires them. Its cost of goods sold is therefore the acquisition cost of the goods that are sold. On the balance sheet, a current asset, merchandise inventory, shows the cost of goods that have been acquired but not yet sold as of the balance sheet date.

MANUFACTURING COMPANIES.   A manufacturing company converts raw material into finished goods. Its cost of goods sold includes the conversion costs as well as the raw material costs of the goods that it sells. A manufacturing company has three types of inventory accounts:

1. Raw materials inventory;
2. Goods in process inventory; and
3. Finished goods inventory.

SUPPLIES.   In addition to inventory accounts for goods directly involved in the merchandising or manufacturing process, a company may have one or more inventory accounts for supplies. *Supplies* are tangible items such as fuel, office supplies, and repair parts for machinery, that will be consumed in the course of normal operations. They are distinguished from merchandise in that they are not sold as such, and they are distinguished from raw materials in that supplies are not accounted for separately as an element of the cost of goods manufactured. Paper offered for sale is merchandise inventory in a stationery store; paper is raw material inventory in a company that manufactures books; and paper intended for use in the office is supplies inventory in any company. Supplies will not be discussed further in this chapter.

MERCHANDISING COMPANIES

Retail stores, wholesalers, distributors and similar companies that offer tangible goods[1] for sale are merchandising firms. Illustration 6–1 should help the reader to visualize the problem of measuring merchandise inventory and the flow of goods.

Illustration 6–1

MERCHANDISE INVENTORY AND FLOWS

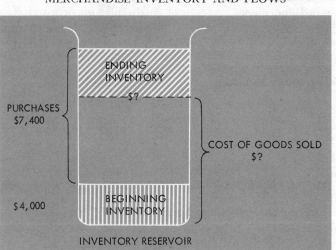

Think of merchandise inventory as a tank or a reservoir. At the beginning of an accounting period, there is a certain amount of goods in the reservoir; this is the beginning inventory. During the period additional merchandise is purchased and added to the reservoir. Also, during the period merchandise sold is withdrawn from the reservoir. At the end of the accounting period, the amount of goods remaining in the reservoir is the ending inventory. The flows through the reservoir during the period and the amount of inventory in the reservoir at the end of the

---

[1] The word *products* is often used when *goods* is intended. For clarity, we use *goods* for tangible items sold or offered for sale, *services* for intangibles, and *products* for the *sum* of goods and services. In other words, the outputs of a firm, whether tangible or intangible, are its products.

period can be accounted for by either of two methods, the periodic inventory method or the perpetual inventory method. Before describing these methods, we shall discuss the measurement of acquisition cost.

Acquisition Cost

Goods are added to inventory at their cost, in accordance with the basic cost concept. Cost includes the expenditures made to make the goods ready for sale, so merchandise cost includes not only the invoice cost of the goods purchased, but also the freight and other shipping costs required to bring the goods to the point of sale, and cost of unpacking and price marking. Since the bookkeeping task of attaching these elements of cost to individual units of merchandise may be considerable, some or all of them may be excluded from merchandise costs and reported as operating expenses when the amounts are immaterial.

The word "purchases" refers not to the placing of a purchase order, but rather to the receipt of merchandise purchased. No accounting entry is made when merchandisie is ordered, only when it is received.

Periodic Inventory Method

Look again at Illustration 6–1. It shows that there was $4,000 of goods in the reservoir at the beginning of the period and that $7,400 was added during the period. Of these $11,400 of goods available, some were shipped to customers and hence became cost of goods sold and others remain in the reservoir at the end of the period as ending inventory. How can we determine each of these two amounts? There are two approaches:

1. We can find the amount of ending inventory (i.e., the amount in the reservoir at the end of the period) and obtain cost of goods sold by subtraction. This is the periodic inventory method. Or,
2. We can measure the amount actually delivered to customers, and obtain the ending inventory by subtraction. This is the perpetual inventory method.

In the periodic inventory method, a physical count is made of merchandise in the ending inventory, that is, the amount remaining in the reservoir at the end of the period. Assume this amount is $2,000. Cost of goods sold is obtained by subtracting the ending inventory from the amount of goods available for sale, thus:

```
Beginning inventory.............................. $ 4,000
  Plus: Purchases...............................    7,400
  Equals: Goods available for sale..............  $11,400
  Less: Ending inventory........................    2,000
     Cost of Goods Sold.........................  $ 9,400
```

The amount of beginning inventory in the above calculation is, of course, the amount found by the physical inventory taken at the end of the *preceding* period.

Some companies show such a calculation in the cost of goods sold section of the income statement itself. Others, although deducing cost of goods sold by the method shown above, do not present the details. Still others report additional detail. For example, if there are freight charges and the return of purchased merchandise, the income statement might show:

```
Beginning inventory.....................      $ 4,000
    Plus: Purchases, gross................ $7,000
        Freight-in........................    600
                                         $7,600
    Less: Purchase returns................    200
Net purchases............................               7,400
Goods available for sale.................             $11,400
    Less: Ending inventory................              2,000
        Cost of Goods Sold................             $ 9,400
```

ACCOUNTS. When the cost of goods sold is deduced by the method described above, a separate account is established for each element in the calculation. Thus, a Purchases account is established, and the invoice cost of merchandise purchased is debited to this account, rather than directly to Inventory. Accounts are also established for Freight-In, Purchase Returns, and any other items involved in the calculation.

Rules for debiting and crediting these accounts can be deduced from their relationship to other accounts. Since Purchases shows additions to the asset account, Merchandise Inventory, it increases on the debit side. Purchase Returns is a reduction in Purchases and hence must have the opposite rule; it increases on the credit side. Freight-In adds to the cost of purchases and therefore increases on the debit side. (The rules can also be deduced by thinking of the offsetting part of the transaction. Whenever possible, it is simplest to assume that the other account is Cash. Thus, a cash purchase involves a decrease in Cash, which is a credit; therefore, the entry to Purchases must be a debit.)

ADJUSTING AND CLOSING. The accounts described above are temporary accounts which must be closed at the end of each accounting period. Furthermore, when these accounts are used, no entries are made during the accounting period to the Merchandise Inventory account; therefore the amount shown in Inventory when the adjusting process begins will be the amount of *beginning* inventory. The Merchandise Inventory account must be adjusted to show the proper inventory amount as of the end of the period. These adjusting and closing entries are customarily made in a certain order, which is more in the nature of a ritual than something of fundamental significance. It is as follows:

(1) Transfer the beginning inventory to Cost of Goods Sold.
(2) Close Freight-In, Purchase Returns, and similar accounts to Purchases, thereby showing the amount of net purchases in the Purchases account.
(3) Close Purchases to Cost of Goods Sold.
(4) Enter the ending inventory by debiting Merchandise Inventory and crediting Cost of Goods Sold.
(5) Close Cost of Goods Sold to Income Summary.

EXAMPLE: Using the numbers given above, these entries would be as follows:

(1)

```
dr.    Cost of Goods Sold.................. 4,000
    cr.     Merchandise Inventory..............        4,000
```

(2)

```
dr.    Purchases..........................   600
    cr.     Freight-In.......................        600
dr.    Purchase Returns...................   200
    cr.     Purchases........................        200*
```

(3)

```
dr.    Cost of Goods Sold.................. 7,400
    cr.     Purchases........................        7,400
```

(4)

```
dr.    Merchandise Inventory............... 2,000
    cr.     Cost of Goods Sold...............        2,000
```

(5)

```
dr.    Income Summary...................... 9,400
    cr.     Cost of Goods Sold...............        9,400
```

* This entry is shown in this form for clarity. In practice, the two parts of this entry would be combined, thus saving some work, as follows:

```
    dr.    Purchase ........................................................ 400
           Purchase Returns................................................. 200
        cr.    Freight-In....................................................        600
```

Perpetual Inventory Method

In the perpetual inventory method, a record is maintained of each item carried in the inventory, similar to the sample shown in Illustration 6–2. In essence, this record is a subsidiary ledger account (see Chapter 4 for description), and Merchandise Inventory is its control account. Purchases are entered directly on this record and also debited to Merchandise Inventory. Shipments are entered on this record and are credited to

Illustration 6–2

PERPETUAL INVENTORY CARD

Date	Receipts			Shipments			Balance		
	Units	Unit Cost	Total	Units	Unit Cost	Total	Units	Unit Cost	Total
Jan. 2							30	40	1,200
12				10	40	400	20	40	800
14				5	40	200	15	40	600
25	24	40	960				39	40	1,560
27				(2)	40	(80)*	41	40	1,640

Item: Chairs, Secretarial #1872   Unit: Each

* This item is a sales return

Merchandise Inventory; the offsetting debit is to Cost of Goods Sold. The balance at the end of the period is the amount of that item in the ending inventory, and the sum of the balances for all the items is the ending inventory for the business.

Assuming, for simplicity, that the company had only the one item shown in Illustration 6–2, the journal entries for the transaction listed there would be:

1. For purchases:
   dr. Merchandise Inventory......................... 960
       cr. Accounts Payable............................   960
2. For shipments to customers:
   dr. Cost of Goods Sold........................... 600
       cr. Merchandise Inventory......................   600
3. For returned sales:
   dr. Merchandise Inventory......................... 80
       cr. Cost of Goods Sold.........................   80

These entries would be posted to the ledger account as follows:

Merchandise Inventory

Beginning Balance	1,200			
(1)	960	(2)		600
(3)	80	To close		1,640
	2,240			2,240
Beginning Balance	1,640			

In this method, no separate purchases account is needed; purchases are debited directly to Merchandise Inventory.

Comparison of Periodic and Perpetual Methods

Both inventory methods match the cost of goods sold with the sales revenue *for those same goods*. It is essential that this matching occur.

The perpetual inventory method requires that a record be maintained for each item carried in inventory. It therefore requires additional recordkeeping, and such recordkeeping is not worthwhile in stores that sell low-cost items in small quantities, such as grocery stores and drug stores.

In other circumstances, the perpetual inventory method has three important advantages. First, the detailed record for each item is useful in deciding when and how much to reorder, and in making analyses of the customer demand for the item. Second, the perpetual inventory record has a built-in check that is not possible with the periodic method. In the periodic method, the physical inventory at the end of the period is an integral part of the calculation of cost of goods sold; the difference between the goods available for sale and the goods on hand is *assumed* to be the cost of goods sold. This assumption is not necessarily correct because some of the goods may have been pilfered, lost, thrown away, or overlooked when the physical inventory was taken. Collectively, these goods which are not in inventory but which were not sold make up the period's *inventory shrinkage*. In the perpetual inventory system, an actual count of the goods on hand can be used as a check on the accuracy of the inventory records. Third, with a perpetual inventory system, an income statement can be prepared without taking a physical inventory. Thus, an income statement can be prepared every month, with the accuracy of the underlying records being checked by an annual or semi-annual physical inventory.

MANUFACTURING COMPANIES

A manufacturing company has as a major function the conversion of raw materials into finished goods. In any company, cost of goods sold is the total of the purchase price plus conversion costs, if any, of the products that are sold. The manufacturer, therefore, includes in cost of goods sold the cost of raw material used, the cost of labor, and other costs incurred in the manufacture of the goods that are sold. The difference between accounting for the cost of goods sold in a merchandising company and in a manufacturing company arises because the merchandising company usually has no conversion costs; its cost of goods sold is practically the same as the purchase price of these goods.

The measurement of cost of goods sold is therefore more complicated in a manufacturing company than in a merchandising company. In a merchandising company, this cost is normally obtained directly from invoices. In a manufacturing company it must be obtained by collecting and aggregating the several elements of manufacturing cost.

Inventory Accounts

A manufacturing company has three types of inventory accounts. Their names and the nature of their content as of a balance sheet date are as follows:

1. *Raw Materials Inventory:* Items of material which are to be used in the manufacturing process. They are costed at acquisition cost, with the same types of adjustments as those made in calculating the net purchase cost of merchandise inventory, described above.

2. *Goods in Process Inventory:* Goods that have started through the manufacturing process but which have not yet been finished. They are costed as the sum of (1) the raw materials used in them plus (2) the labor and other manufacturing costs incurred on these items up to the end of the accounting period.

3. *Finished Goods Inventory:* Goods whose manufacture has been completed but which have not been shipped to customers as of the balance sheet date. They are costed at the total cost incurred in manufacturing them. This account is essentially the same as the Merchandise Inventory account in a merchandising company, except that the items are costed at the cost of manufacturing them rather than at their acquisition cost.

For all U.S. manufacturing companies combined, each of these three types of inventory was approximately the same size, about $40 billion, in 1974, but there are wide variations in their relative size among individual companies. Companies with a short production cycle may have so little work in process at the end of the accounting period that they do not have a separate goods in process inventory item. Companies that ship to the customer as soon as the product is completed have little or no finished goods inventory.

A diagram of these accounts and the flow of costs from one to another is shown in Illustration 6–3. We shall trace the flow of costs through these accounts, using the periodic inventory method. Each step is described by giving the relevant journal entries. The effect on ledger accounts is shown in Illustration 6–4.

In describing the procedure in a merchandising company, we established a separate account to show the Cost of Goods Sold. We could use

Illustration 6–3

MANUFACTURING INVENTORIES AND FLOWS

similar accounts in a manufacturing company to show separately the Raw Materials Used, Cost of Goods Manufactured, and Cost of Goods Sold. In the following description, however, we have not used these accounts, and instead arrive at the amounts by calculations made outside the accounts. There is no substantive difference between the two

Illustration 6–4

FLOW OF COSTS THROUGH INVENTORIES
(000 omitted)

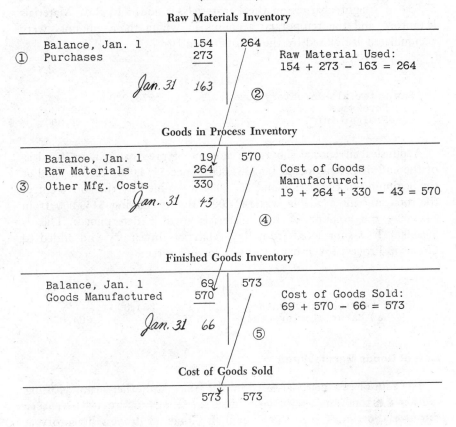

Raw Materials Inventory

Balance, Jan. 1	154	264	
① Purchases	273		Raw Material Used:
			154 + 273 – 163 = 264
Jan. 31	*163*		
		②	

Goods in Process Inventory

Balance, Jan. 1	19	570	
Raw Materials	264		Cost of Goods
③ Other Mfg. Costs	330		Manufactured:
Jan. 31	*43*		19 + 264 + 330 – 43 = 570
		④	

Finished Goods Inventory

Balance, Jan. 1	69	573	
Goods Manufactured	570		Cost of Goods Sold:
			69 + 570 – 66 = 573
Jan. 31	*66*		
		⑤	

Cost of Goods Sold

573	573

methods; both arrive at the same results. The method described below requires fewer journal entires than does the alternative.

Raw Materials Used

In determining the cost of raw materials used, the assumption is made that the amount of raw materials used is the difference between the materials available for use during the period (which is the total of the beginning inventory and the net purchases) and the ending inventory. This assumption does not take into account any waste or spoilage of material that might have occurred. In practice, waste and spoilage is either disregarded or is collected separately and removed from material costs by crediting Raw Materials Inventory and debiting a separate manufacturing cost account.

We shall make this calculation in the Raw Materials Inventory account. First, the amount of purchases made during the period, which includes $266,000 as the invoice cost of raw materials received plus $7,000 of freight charges on these materials, is added to Raw Materials Inventory and the temporary accounts in which these amounts were accumulated are closed by the following entry:

(1)

```
Raw Materials Inventory................ 273,000
    Purchases..........................          266,000
    Freight-in.........................            7,000
```

A physical inventory shows the amount of raw materials on hand as of the end of the period to be $163,000. Since $154,000 was on hand at the beginning of the period and $273,000 was added by the above entry, the total amount available was $427,000. By subtracting $163,000 from $427,000, the amount of raw materials used is determined. This is $264,000. It is subtracted from Raw Materials Inventory and added to Goods in Process Inventory by the following entry:

(2)

```
Goods in Process Inventory............ 264,000
    Raw Materials Inventory............          264,000
```

Cost of Goods Manufactured

The sum of raw materials used, direct labor, and other manufacturing costs is the total amount of cost added to Goods in Process Inventory during the period. Given the amount in Goods in Process Inventory at the beginning of the period and the amount remaining at the end of the period, the *cost of goods manufactured*, that is, the goods completed and transferred to Finished Goods Inventory, can be deduced.

The cost of raw materials used was added by the preceding entry. Other manufacturing costs incurred during the period are added to Goods in Process Inventory by the following entry:

(3)

```
Cost of Goods Manufactured............. 330,000
    Direct Labor......................          151,000
    Indirect Labor....................           24,000
    Factory Heat, Light, and Power....           90,000
    Factory Supplies Used.............           22,000
    Insurance and Taxes...............            8,000
    Depreciation, Plant and Equipment..          35,000
```

A physical inventory shows the amount of goods in process inventory as of the end of the period to be $43,000. Since $19,000 was on hand at the beginning of the period, and $264,000 of raw materials and $330,000 of other manufacturing costs were added by entries (2) and (3), the total amount available was $613,000. By subtracting $43,000 from $613,000, the cost of goods manufactured during the period is determined. This is $570,000. It is subtracted from Goods in Process Inventory and added to Finished Goods Inventory by the following entry:

(4)

```
Cost of Goods Sold..................... 570,000
      Cost of Goods Manufactured........              570,000
```

Cost of Goods Sold

Having determined the cost of goods manufactured, the cost of goods sold is found by adding this amount to the beginning Finished Goods Inventory so as to find the total amount available for sale, and then subtracting the ending Finished Goods Inventory. As with a merchandising company, the assumption is that if the merchandise is not in inventory, it has been sold.

A physical inventory shows the amount of finished goods inventory as of the end of the period to be $66,000. Since $69,000 was on hand at the beginning of the period, and $570,000 of manufactured goods were completed during the period and added to finished good inventory, the total amount available was $639,000. By subtracting $66,000 from $639,-000, the cost of goods sold is determined. This is $573,000. It is subtracted from Finished Goods Inventory and recorded as Cost of Goods Sold by the following entry:

(5)

```
Cost of Goods Sold..................... 573,000
      Finished Goods Inventory...........              573,000
```

The balance in the Cost of Goods Sold account is then closed to Income Summary by the following entry:

(6)

```
Income Summary......................... 573,000
      Cost of Goods Sold................              573,000
```

An income statement derived from the entries given above is shown in Illustration 6–5.

Illustration 6–5

ALFMAN MANUFACTURING COMPANY

Income Statement, January

Net sales..			$669,000
Cost of goods sold:			
Raw materials cost:			
Raw materials inventory, January 1............		$154,000	
Purchases....................................	$266,000		
Plus: Freight–in............................	7,000		
Total purchases...........................		273,000	
Material available......................		$427,000	
Less: Raw materials inventory, January 31.....		163,000	
Cost of materials used.....................			$264,000
Direct labor cost...............................			151,000
Manufacturing overhead cost:			
Indirect labor..............................		$ 24,000	
Factory heat, light, and power...............		90,000	
Factory supplies used........................		22,000	
Insurance and taxes.........................		8,000	
Depreciation—plant and equipment............		35,000	
Total manufacturing overhead cost...........			179,000
Total manufacturing costs................			$594,000
Add: Goods in process inventory, January 1......			19,000
Total...................................			$613,000
Less: Goods in process inventory, January 31....			43,000
Cost of goods manufactured.....................			$570,000
Add: Finished goods inventory, January 1........			69,000
Cost of goods available for sale................			$639,000
Less: Finished goods inventory, January 31......			66,000
Cost of goods sold..............................			573,000
Gross margin....................................			$ 96,000
Selling and administrative expenses:			
Selling expense................................		$ 39,000	
Depreciation—selling..........................		3,000	
Administrative expense.........................		32,000	74,000
Operating profit................................			$ 22,000
Other revenue...................................			15,000
Income before income taxes......................			$ 37,000
Provision for income taxes......................			13,000
Net Income......................................			$ 24,000

Alternative Income Statement Format

The income statement shown in Illustration 6–5 is useful in showing the steps involved in calculating the cost of goods sold. It is, however, a cumbersome and complicated appearing set of numbers. Illustration 6–6 recasts the cost of goods sold section of the income statement in a format that is both shorter and better suited to analysis. Instead of showing separately the amounts of beginning and ending inventories, this statement shows only the *changes* in the inventory balances between the beginning and the end of the period. These changes account for the difference between the costs incurred in manufacturing and the cost of goods sold. It is suggested that the reader reason out why inventory increases are subtracted and why inventory decreases are added.

Cost Accounting

The foregoing entries assumed the use of the periodic inventory method. The same transactions could be accounted for using the per-

Illustration 6–6

ALTERNATIVE FORMAT FOR COST OF GOODS SOLD

Manufacturing costs:		
Raw material costs:		
Purchases......................................	$273,000	
Increase in raw materials inventory.................	9,000	
Cost of materials used........................		$264,000
Direct labor cost.................................		151,000
Manufacturing overhead cost:		
Indirect labor..................................	$ 24,000	
Factory heat, light, and power....................	90,000	
Factory supplies used...........................	22,000	
Insurance and taxes.............................	8,000	
Depreciation–Plant and Equipment...................	35,000	179,000
Total manufacturing costs.....................		$594,000
Changes in inventory:		
Increase in goods in process......................	$ 24,000	
Decrease in finished goods.......................	3,000	21,000
Cost of goods sold...............................		$573,000

petual inventory method. In a manufacturing company, the perpetual inventory method is called a *cost accounting* system. In such a system, the cost of each product is accumulated as it flows through the manufacturing process, and the amounts involved in the journal entries are obtained directly from the cost records, rather than being deduced in the manner described above. The mechanism used for collecting this information is described in Chapter 15.

Product Costs and Period Costs

The items of cost that are included in the cost of manufacturing a product in the accounting process described above are called *product costs*. Other items of cost that are charged against revenue in a given accounting period are called *period costs,* and are reported on the income statement of the period under a caption such as Selling, General and Administrative expense.

In accordance with generally accepted accounting principles, the cost of each product includes (1) raw materials cost, (2) labor costs incurred directly in manufacturing the product, and (3) a fair share of the other manufacturing costs. These other costs are called *indirect costs* or *overhead.* Since some items of overhead cost apply to many products (e.g., the costs of heating and lighting a factory building apply to all the products made in the building), there must be a method of assigning a fair share of the total overhead costs to each product. Methods for doing this are discussed in Chapter 15. For our present purpose, the important point is that product cost includes all the items of cost incurred in manufacturing the product, that is, the *full factory cost.*

There is room for considerable difference of opinion as to whether specific items should be treated as product costs or as period costs. Some companies include the cost of such functions as manufacturing administration, personnel and industrial relations, plant protection, and accounting as manufacturing overhead and hence in product costs; other companies include the cost of some or all of these functions as period costs.

The way in which a manufacturing company classifies its costs into period costs and product costs can have an important effect on its reported net income.

Period costs are expenses in the accounting period in which they are incurred, whereas product costs add to the cost of the product and do not have an impact on net income until the product has been sold, which may well be a later accounting period than the period in which the costs were incurred.

To take the extreme case, all of the costs of a merchandising company, except the cost of the merchandise itself, are period costs. Thus, all labor costs and other operating costs incurred in a certain period affect the net income of that period. In a manufacturing company, on the other hand, those labor and other costs that are associated with the manufacturing process affect, initially, the value of inventory; they affect net income only *in the accounting period in which the products containing these costs are sold.* This may be a later accounting period than that in which the product was manufactured. The larger the inventory in relation to sales, the longer the time interval that elapses between the incurrence of a manufacturing cost and its impact on net income.

> EXAMPLE: Consider a wage increase amounting to $50,000 per year. In a merchandising company, income would be reduced $50,000 in the year in which the increase becomes effective, other things being equal. In a manufacturing company, however, that part of the increase paid to manufacturing employees would first go to increase the inventory value of the products they worked on, and income would not receive the full impact of the increase until these products were sold.

INVENTORY COSTING METHODS

One important topic remains to be discussed, namely, the measurement of inventory amounts and cost of goods sold when there is a change in the unit cost of the goods during the accounting period. Several acceptable methods of handling this situation exist, and they can have a significant effect on net income. We shall discuss four widely used methods:

1. Specific identification
2. Average cost
3. First-in, first-out (Fifo)
4. Last-in, first-out (Lifo)[2].

We shall illustrate these methods with an example from a merchandising company, but the same principles apply to a manufacturing company. As an illustration we shall assume the following for a month:

	Units	*Unit Cost*	*Total Cost*
Inventory, January 1	100	$ 8	$ 800
Purchased January 10	60	9	540
Purchased January 20	80	10	800
Goods available for sale	240		$2,140
Goods sold during January	150	?	?
Ending inventory	90	?	?

Specific Identification Method

When there is a means of keeping track of the purchase cost of each item, such as with a code on the price tag affixed to the item, it is possible to ascertain the actual cost of each item sold. This is common practice with certain "big-ticket" items, such as automobiles, and with unique items such as paintings, expensive jewelry, and custom-made furniture. However, for an item of which there is a substantial number sold, all physically similar, this method can be unsatisfactory, because the cost of goods sold depends on what items happen to be sold. Indeed, a merchant can deliberately manipulate the cost of goods sold by selecting items that have a relatively high cost or a relatively low cost, as he chooses:

> EXAMPLE: If the merchant selected the 100 items that had a unit cost of $8 and 50 of the items that had a cost of $9, his cost of goods sold would be $1,250. If he selected the 150 items with the highest cost, his cost of goods sold would be $1,420.

Average Cost

With this method, the average cost of the goods available for sale is computed, and the units in both cost of goods sold and ending inventory are costed at this average cost. In the periodic inventory method, this average is computed for the whole period. In the perpetual inventory method, a new average unit cost is calculated after each purchase.

---

[2] *Accounting Trends and Techniques* (1973) reports that of the 920 mentions of inventory methods in the 600 companies surveyed, 377 used Fifo, 242 used average cost, 150 used Lifo, 26 used specific identification, and the others used labels that could not be classified specifically under the above headings. Note that a company may use one method for one type of material or product, and another method for another type.

EXAMPLE: Assuming the periodic inventory method, the 240 units available for sale have a total cost of $2,140; hence the average cost is $8.917. The calculations are:

	Units	Unit Cost	Total*
Cost of goods sold	150	$8.917	$1,338
Ending inventory	90	8.917	802
Total	240		$2,140

* Rounded.

The average cost method gives results that are in between the next two methods to be described and is therefore a compromise for those who do not find the arguments for one or the other of these methods to be compelling. The average cost is representative of the cost of all the items that were available for sale during the period.

First-In, First-Out (Fifo)

In the Fifo method, it is assumed that the oldest goods are sold first and that the most recently purchased goods are in the ending inventory. In the illustrative situation, for the 150 units sold during January, it is assumed that the 100 units in beginning inventory were sold first and that the other 50 units sold were from the purchase made on January 10.

EXAMPLE:

	Units	Unit Cost	Total Cost
From beginning inventory	100	$ 8	$ 800
From purchase of January 10	50	9	450
Cost of goods sold	150		$1,250
From purchase of January 10	10	$ 9	$ 90
From purchase of January 20	80	10	800
Ending Inventory	90		$ 890
Total Available for Sale			$2,140

We shall contrast the Lifo and Fifo methods below. For the moment, it is sufficient to note that with Fifo (1) cost of goods sold is likely to approximate the *physical* flow of the goods because most companies sell their oldest merchandise first, and (2) the ending inventory approximates the current cost of the goods since it is costed at the amounts of most recent purchases.

Last-In, First-Out (Lifo)

The Lifo method is the opposite of the Fifo method. Cost of goods sold is calculated on the basis of the most recent purchases, and ending inventory is costed at the cost of the oldest units available.

EXAMPLE:

	Units	Unit Cost	Total Cost
From purchase of January 20	80	$10	$ 800
From purchase of January 10	60	9	540
From beginning inventory	10	8	80
Cost of Goods Sold	150		$1,420
Ending Inventory	90	$ 8	$ 720

At this point, it should be noted that with Lifo (1) cost of goods sold does not reflect the usual physical flow of merchandise, and (2) the ending inventory, a balance sheet asset, may be costed at prices prevailing several years ago which, in an era of inflation, are far below current prices.

LIFO DOLLAR VALUE METHOD.   Originally, Lifo was used only by companies whose inventory consisted of fungible products, such as wheat, each unit of which is physically like every other unit. Other companies, however, argued that this was unfair to them, and Lifo may now be used for almost any kind of inventory. It is applied to an inventory of physically unlike items by the so-called *Lifo dollar value method*. In this method, items whose prices tend to move together are grouped into an *inventory pool*. A pool may consist of all the items in the hardware department of a department store, for example, or it may consist of a store's entire inventory. The dollar amount invested in such a pool is treated as a unit in figuring the Lifo inventory value and cost of goods sold, and changes in the value of the dollar during the accounting period are allowed for by the application of index numbers of price changes.

As an illustration, assume that the beginning inventory in a pool had an actual invoice cost of $780,000, and that the inventory at the end of the year had an actual invoice cost of $880,000. Without additional information, we do not know how much of the $100,000 increase in the amount of inventory represents an increase in the *physical size* of the inventory and how much results from the same quantity being valued at a higher price because of inflation. By the use of an index number of price changes, the change associated with size can be separated from the change associated with price movements. Thus, if an appropriate price index increased from 100 at the beginning of the year to 110 at the end of the year, the year-end inventory can be *deflated* to the beginning price level by multiplying it by the ratio of the index change, or $100/110$. The value of the ending inventory expressed in beginning prices is therefore $100/110$ of $880,000, or $800,000. Since $800,000 exceeds the beginning inventory of $780,000 by $20,000, we estimate that the physical size of the inventory has increased by $20,000 during the year. This $20,000 is expressed in beginning prices, however, and under the Lifo method it must be added to inventory at the most recent prices, so it is *reinflated* by multiplying by the ratio $^{110}\!/_{100}$, to give \$22,000. The ending inventory thus is valued at \$802,000, which is the sum of the beginning inventory, \$780,000, plus the increase in physical inventory, \$22,000. Cost of goods sold is then found by the deduction formula—beginning inventory, plus purchases, less ending inventory—which results in a difference of \$78,000 between the invoice cost and the Lifo cost of ending inventory going into cost of goods sold.

In applying the dollar value method, department stores use price indexes especially computed for this purpose by the government. Other companies compute their own index from the movement of prices of all, or a sample of, items in inventory.

DECREASES IN INVENTORY. In a year when the physical size of the inventory increases above the amount on hand at the beginning of the year, in a Lifo system the inventory account is increased by the additional quantity valued at the costs existing during that year. During a period of growth, the inventory account will therefore consist of a number of *layers*, a new layer being added each year. If subsequently the physical inventory should decrease in size, these layers in effect are stripped off, taking the most recently added layer first, in accordance with the basic Lifo rule. This process can have a peculiar effect on the income statement. If, for example, inventory is decreased even below its original size when the Lifo system started, inventory items will be moving into cost of goods sold at costs established several years previously; and if there has been constant inflation during the interim, such a shrinkage in inventory can result in a significant increase in reported income. Some people assert that in a recession some companies deliberately eat into their Lifo inventories in order to increase reported income in a lean year.

VARIATIONS. In applying the general idea of Lifo to a particular situation, several alternatives are possible:

1. Lifo may be applied to all inventories, or only to the raw materials inventory, or only to certain items in inventory.
2. Products may be run through the cost accounting mechanism at Lifo values, or the detailed cost records may show Fifo or specific invoice values, with an adjustment to Lifo being made only at the end of the accounting period.
3. Inventory changes may be calculated annually, or monthly, or even daily.

Usually the differences in results between the several methods of applying Lifo are small compared with the basic difference between Lifo and Fifo, but the fact that these differences in the application of Lifo exist is one reason why Lifo is criticized. It is difficult to compare the earnings of a company that uses Lifo with the earnings of a company that uses Fifo; variations within the general Lifo idea make "confusion worse confounded."

Comparison of Fifo and Lifo

The following table summarizes the results of three of the four methods described above (the specific identification method depends on the specific items selected):

	Cost of Goods Sold	Ending Inventory
Fifo	1,250	890
Average cost	1,338	802
Lifo	1,420	720

It has been estimated that if in 1973 all companies had used the Lifo method, the net income of all U.S. companies would have been 25 percent less than the amount actually reported. The choice of a method is therefore important. All of the methods described are in accordance with generally accepted accounting principles, and all are acceptable for calculating taxable income.[3]

COST OF GOODS SOLD. Although the Lifo inventory method normally does not correspond to the *physical* flow of material, its advocates contend that in certain industries Lifo does match the *economic* flow of values since, they claim, the profit margin that actually influences business pricing decisions is the margin between sales prices and *current* costs, not the margin between sales prices and cost levels that existed at the time the inventory was purchased.

If this contention is correct, the Fifo system results in the reporting of false "inventory profits" during periods of rising prices. During these periods goods are sold at sales prices commensurate with current costs, while cost of goods sold reflects earlier, lower costs rather than current costs. (Lifo only *approximates* current costs since it shows the cost of *most recent* purchases, and this is not necessarily the same as current cost.)

A frequently used example of what is meant by this economic flow is the following excerpt from the Report of the Special Committee on Inventories of the AICPA (1936), a report which had much to do with the adoption of Lifo as a generally accepted principle:

A wagon maker has a wagon in stock which cost him $50, the selling price of which is $65 to yield him his desired profit of $15 per wagon. Before he sells the wagon he learns from the concern supplying him with his material of a price increase, the result of which is to make the reproduction cost of his wagon $60. By reason of this knowledge the wagon maker "marks up" his wagon to $75, at which figure he sells it for cash and builds a new wagon costing him $60. The net change resulting from the whole transaction is that his till shows $15 more cash than he had before.

Now the advocate of "Lifo" says to the wagon maker: The profit you made is $15, and the proper inventory price for the present wagon you have

---

[3] If a company uses the Lifo method for tax calculations, it must also use this method in its financial accounting system.

in stock is $50. That is the number of dollars of your capital invested in your stock-in-trade; the only change that you have effectively realized in that investment is the substitution of one wagon for another exactly like it—the same wagon, in fact, except only as regards physical identity.

On the other hand, the advocate of "first-in, first-out" says to the wagon maker: Your profit is $25, although you may have only $15 more in cash to show for it. The other $10 is contained in the increased cost and value of the new wagon—$60 as against the old one at $50. You must not fail to recognize and to give effect to the price level change.

Considering the other side of the problem, let us assume that after the above transaction the price level reverted to its original status, thus consummating the economic cycle; accordingly the wagon at present in stock, which actually had cost $60 to build (but was inventoried at either $50 or $60, according to the procedure followed) is sold for $65 and replaced in stock by one which cost $50 to build. Now, under either procedure the latest wagon will be inventoried at $50. The profit on the second transaction, however, will have been $15 according to the "Lifo" advocate, or $5 according to the "first-in, first-out" advocate. The aggregate profit on the two transactions, of course, will be the same in either case but the periodic distribution will differ.

One virtue of the Lifo method is its tendency to limit the amount of reported net income to an amount which might be made available to shareholders without impairing the scope and intensity of the operations of a going concern. Advocates also argue that such restrictions in reported income serve to conserve funds by reducing income taxes.

No one argues that Lifo is applicable to every company; rather it is recommended only when there is a definite relationship between selling price and *current* cost. For example, if a retailer sets his selling price by adding a fixed markup to the invoice cost of specific units of merchandise, and if he usually can sell the merchandise at this price, his profit is based on his invoice cost, and he should use the Fifo method. If, on the other hand, he finds it necessary or possible to change his retail prices as soon as, or shortly after, a change in wholesale prices occurs, his cost may be considered to be the Lifo cost.

A close correspondence between changes in selling prices and changes in current costs may reflect a general change in the value of money in the economy. If this is the case, it is argued that it makes little sense to state the revenue component of profit at the current value of the dollar while stating the principal expense component, cost of goods sold, in terms of a different kind of dollar. On the other hand, if the facts are that in a particular company the profit margin has really changed, for reasons having nothing to do with fluctuations in price levels, the use of Lifo may conceal such changes.

In addition to companies whose selling prices are related to invoice costs rather than to current costs, Lifo is also not appropriate for companies which eliminate inventory profits or losses by the practice called "hedging," nor for companies which are in the business of speculating on price changes, as are certain companies that trade in grain and other commodities.

The relative importance of inventory profits varies among companies, and Lifo has a more important influence on profits when—

1. Material cost constitutes a relatively large part of total cost.
2. The inventory is relatively large.
3. The manufacturing process is relatively long.

INVENTORY. Opponents of Lifo point out that under Lifo, the initial quantity of inventory is valued forever in terms of whatever the price level happened to be at the time Lifo was introduced. As time goes on and price levels change, the inventory figure under Lifo departs further and further from reality, becoming neither a reflection of actual purchase costs nor of current costs. In periods of prolonged inflation, the amount of inventory reported on the balance sheet is far below current material costs. Thus Lifo may make the inventory figure on the balance sheet of dubious usefulness.

In short, Lifo may result in a more meaningful income statement but a less realistic balance sheet, whereas Fifo may result in a more meaningful balance sheet but a less realistic income statement.

EXAMPLE: Illustration 6–7 illustrates the effect of the Lifo method on profit and on inventory valuation, as contrasted with the Fifo method.

Illustration 6–7

GROSS MARGIN CALCULATION UNDER FIFO AND LIFO

Year	(1) Inventory, January 1	(2) Purchases	(3) Inventory, December 31	(4) Cost of Sales*	(5) Sales†	(6) Gross Margin
		UNDER FIFO				
19X1........	1,000 at $1.00	1,000 at $1.00	1,000 at $1.00	$1,000	$2,000	$1,000
19X2........	1,000 at 1.00	1,000 at 1.50	1,000 at 1.50	1,000	2,500	1,500
19X3........	1,000 at 1.50	1,000 at 2.00	1,000 at 2.00	1,500	3,000	1,500
19X4........	1,000 at 2.00	1,000 at 0.50	1,000 at 0.50	2,000	1,500	(500)
19X5........	1,000 at 0.50	1,000 at 1.00	1,000 at 1.00	500	2,000	1,500
	Total Five-year Gross Margin.		....	....		$5,000
		UNDER LIFO				
19X1........	1,000 at $1.00	1,000 at $1.00	1,000 at $1.00	$1,000	$2,000	$1,000
19X2........	1,000 at 1.00	1,000 at 1.50	1,000 at 1.00	1,500	2,500	1,000
19X3........	1,000 at 1.00	1,000 at 2.00	1,000 at 1.00	2,000	3,000	1,000
19X4........	1,000 at 1.00	1,000 at 0.50	1,000 at 1.00	500	1,500	1,000
19X5........	1,000 at 1.00	1,000 at 1.00	1,000 at 1.00	1,000	2,000	1,000
	Total Five-year Gross Margin.		....	....		$5,000

* Beginning inventory, plus purchases, less ending inventory, each being assumed in this example to be 1,000 units. With an inventory turnover of 1, cost of sales under Fifo will equal the value of the beginning inventory, since it is assumed that the units sold were the oldest units on hand and equal in units to purchases. Under Lifo, cost of sales will equal the value of purchases, since it is assumed that the units sold were the units most recently purchased.
† 1,000 units times sales price per unit, which is assumed to be the current purchase price plus $1.

The situation illustrated is the simplest possible, namely, where:

1. Selling price is immediately and exactly adjusted for changes in material cost.
2. There is no change in inventory quantity, that is, as soon as a unit is sold, it is replaced in inventory by another unit.
3. Sales *volume* each year is constant (at 1,000 units).
4. One hundred percent of the product cost is material cost.
5. Inventory turnover is 1; that is, inventory consists of 1,000 units.

In the example, prices are assumed to go through a complete cycle; that is, they rise and then fall back to the starting point. The following points can be noted from these calculations:

1. There is no difference in total profits under Lifo and under Fifo over the complete cycle.
2. Under the conventional Fifo method, profits are high in years of high prices and low in years of low prices, even though the quantity sold and the margin between selling price and current material cost remains constant; also inventory values fluctuate widely, and inventory is at its highest price at the very top of the cycle.
3. Under the Lifo method, profit and inventory values are the same in each year; in one year 19X4, inventory was valued at more than "market."

COST OR MARKET RULE

All the foregoing had to do with measuring the *cost* of inventory. The Lifo and Fifo methods are alternative ways of measuring cost. The general principle is, however, that inventory is reported on the balance sheet at the *lower* of its cost or its market value.

In the ordinary situation, inventory is reported at its cost. It is reduced below cost (i.e., "written down") only when there is evidence that the value of the items, when sold or otherwise disposed of, will be less than cost. Such evidence may reflect physical deterioration, obsolescence, changes in price level, or other causes. When this evidence exists, inventory is stated at "market."

Since the goods in inventory have not in fact been sold, their true market value is not ordinarily known and must therefore be estimated. The FASB states that this estimate should be the current *replacement* cost of the item; that is, what it would cost currently to purchase or manufacture the item. The FASB further sets upper and lower boundaries on "market":

1. It should not be higher than the estimated selling price of the item less the costs associated with selling it. This amount is called the *net realizable value.*

2. It should not be lower than the net realizable value less a normal profit margin.[4]

SUMMARY

The objectives of inventory accounting are to match the cost of goods sold with the revenue earned from the sale of those goods in an accounting period and to measure the cost of inventory on hand at the end of the period, which is an asset.

A merchandising company has one inventory account. The separation of total costs into the amount determined to be cost of goods sold and the amount determined to be merchandise inventory can be accomplished either by the periodic inventory method or the perpetual inventory method. In the former, ending inventory is obtained by a physical count, and cost of goods sold is obtained by deduction. In the latter, both amounts are obtained directly from inventory records.

A manufacturing company has three inventory accounts: raw materials, goods in process, and finished goods. In the periodic inventory method, the amount in each account is counted, and the cost of raw materials used, the cost of goods manufactured, and the cost of goods sold are obtained by deduction. In a perpetual inventory system, also called a cost accounting system, these costs are obtained directly from the accounting records.

Inventory is ordinarily measured at its cost. In a merchandising company cost is essentially the amount expended to acquire the goods. In a manufacturing company, product costs include, in addition to raw materials costs, the labor cost and other factory costs incurred in converting the raw material into a finished product. Other operating costs, in either type of company, are called period costs; they are expenses of the current period.

The flow of costs can be measured by any of several methods, including specific identification, average cost, First-in, first-out, and Last-in, first-out. The best method is not necessarily the one that corresponds to the physical flow of goods, but rather the one which most closely matches the economic flow, as reflected in the company's pricing practices.

If the market value of inventory is below cost, the inventory is reported at its market value.

---

[4] *Accounting Research Bulletin No. 43*, Chapter 4.

CASES

CASE 6–1. PROBLEM IN INCOME STATEMENT PREPARATION

Listed below in alphabetical order are certain accounts of the Exco Manufacturing Company with balances for the year ended December 31. You are asked to prepare a detailed income statement on the basis of this information:

Administrative expense	$ 42,470
Customer returns and allowances	63,050
Depreciation—plant and equipment	41,600
Depreciation—selling	3,780
Direct labor cost	207,320
Dividends	13,000
Factory heat, light, and power	92,800
Factory supplies cost	26,500
Finished goods inventory, 1/1	78,650
Finished goods inventory, 12/31	82,130
Freight-in	8,580
Gain on disposal of machinery	13,600
Goods in process inventory, 1/1	30,970
Goods in process inventory, 12/31	31,920
Income tax expense	24,000
Indirect labor	26,150
Insurance and taxes (factory)	13,860
Interest expenses	9,350
Purchases	303,050
Raw materials inventory, 1/1	186,210
Raw materials inventory, 12/31	163,100
Sales	913,250
Selling expense	41,480

CASE 6–2. MARRETT MANUFACTURING COMPANY (A)

The management of the Marrett Manufacturing Company prepared annually a budget of expected financial operations for the ensuing calendar year. The completed budget provided information on all aspects of the coming year's operations. It included a projected balance sheet as of the end of the year and a projected income statement.

The final preparation of statements was accomplished only after care-

178

ful integration of detailed computations submitted by each department. This was done to insure that the operations of all departments were in balance with one another. For example, the finance department needed to base its schedules of loan operations and of collections and disbursements on figures that were dependent upon manufacturing, purchasing, and selling expectations. The level of production would be geared to the forecasts of the sales department, and purchasing would be geared to the proposed manufacturing schedule. In short, it was necessary to integrate the estimates of each department and to revise them in terms of the over-all effect on operations to arrive at a well-formulated and profitable plan of operations for the coming year. The budget statements ultimately derived from the adjusted estimated transactions would then serve the company as a reliable guide and measure of the coming year's operations.

At the time the 1976 budget was being prepared, in November of 1975, projected 1975 financial statements were compiled for use as a comparison with the budgeted figures. These 1975 statements were based on nine months' actual and three months' projected transactions. They appear as Exhibits 1, 2, and 3.

Exhibit 1
MARRETT MANUFACTURING COMPANY

Projected Balance Sheet,
December 31, 1975

ASSETS

Current Assets:		
Cash..		$ 68,900
Accounts receivable (net of allowance for doubtful accounts)....		123,000
Inventories:		
Raw materials...	$119,000	
Goods in process.....................................	47,000	
Finished goods..	15,500	
Supplies..	33,000	214,500
Prepaid taxes and insurance................................		9,000
Total Current Assets................................		$415,400
Fixed Assets:		
Manufacturing plant at cost..............................	$620,000	
Less: Accumulated depreciation..........................	210,000	410,000
Total Assets..		$825,400

LIABILITIES AND SHAREHOLDERS' EQUITY

Current Liabilities:		
Notes payable..	$ 64,000	
Accounts payable.......................................	27,000	
Income taxes payable...................................	5,000	
Total Current Liabilities..............................		$ 96,000
Shareholders' Equity:		
Contributed capital.....................................	$670,000	
Retained earnings......................................	59,400	729,400
Total Liabilities and Shareholders' Equity................		$825,400

Exhibit 2

MARRETT MANUFACTURING COMPANY

Projected Statement of Cost of Goods Sold
1975

Finished goods inventory, 1/1/75.....................			$167,000
Goods in process inventory, 1/1/75...................		$ 52,000	
Raw materials used...............................		181,000	
Plus: Factory expenses:			
Direct manufacturing labor........................		97,000	
Factory overhead:			
Indirect manufacturing labor....................	$39,500		
Power, heat, and light.........................	27,000		
Depreciation of plant..........................	29,000		
Social security taxes..........................	5,500		
Taxes and insurance, factory...................	5,000		
Supplies.....................................	15,800	121,800	
		$451,800	
Less: Goods in process inventory, 12/31/75........		47,000	
Cost of goods manufactured (i.e., completed)..........			404,800
			$571,800
Less: Finished goods inventory, 12/31/75..........			15,500
Cost of Goods Sold...............................			$556,300

Exhibit 3

MARRETT MANUFACTURING COMPANY

Projected Income Statement
1975

Sales..			$730,000
Less: Sales returns and allowances..................		$ 5,600	
Sales discounts allowed........................		14,000	19,600
Net sales..			$710,400
Less: Cost of goods sold (per schedule)..............			556,300
Gross margin.....................................			$154,100
Less: Selling and administrative expense..............			120,200
Operating income.........................,...........			$ 33,900
Less: Interest expense.............................			2,000
Income before federal income tax......................			$ 31,900
Less: Estimated income tax expense..................			9,000
Net Income.......................................			$ 22,900

Below is the summary of expected operations for the budget year 1976 as finally accepted:

1. *Sales:* All on credit, $815,000; sales returns and allowances, $7,000; sales discounts taken by customers, $15,000. (The sales figure is net of expected bad debts.)

2. *Purchases of goods and services:*
   a. New assets:
      Purchased for cash: manufacturing plant and equipment, $33,-000; prepaid manufacturing taxes and insurance, $12,000.
      Purchased on accounts payable: raw materials, $227,000; supplies, $25,000.
   b. Services used to convert raw materials into goods in process,[1] all purchased for cash: direct manufacturing labor, $152,000; indirect manufacturing labor, $56,000; social security taxes on labor, $9,400; power, heat, and light, $41,600. (Accrued payroll was ignored in these estimates.)
   c. Sales and administrative service, purchased for cash: $234,000.
3. *Conversion of assets into goods in process:* This appears as an increase in the "value" of goods in process and a decrease in the appropriate asset accounts. Depreciation of building and equipment, $26,000; expiration of prepaid taxes and insurance, $8,000; supplies used in manufacturing, $29,000; raw materials put into process, $259,000.
4. *Transfer of goods in process into finished goods:* This appears as an increase in finished goods and a decrease in goods in process. Total cost accumulated on goods that have been completed and transferred to finished goods inventory, $549,000.
5. *Cost of finished goods sold to customers:* $499,000.
6. *Financial transactions:*
   a. $180,000, borrowed on notes payable to bank.
   b. Bank loans paid off (i.e., retired), $210,000.
   c. Cash payment to bank of $3,000 for interest on loans.
7. *Cash receipts from customers on accounts receivable:* $810,500.
8. *Cash payments of liabilities:*
   a. Payment of accounts payable, $249,000.
   b. Payment of 1975 income tax, $5,000.
9. *Estimated federal income tax on 1976 income:* $28,000, of which $10,000 is estimated to be unpaid as of December 31, 1976.
10. *Dividends declared for year and paid in cash:* $11,000.

This summary presents the complete cycle of the Marrett Manufacturing Company's budgeted yearly operations from the purchase of goods and services through their various stages of conversion to completion of the finished product to the sale of this product. All costs and cash receipts and disbursements involved in this cycle are presented, including the provision for federal income tax and the payment of dividends.

---

[1] In a manufacturing company, inventory is assumed to increase in value by the amounts spent to convert raw material into salable products. These amounts include the items listed in 2(b) plus the items listed in 3.

Questions

1. Journalize each of the projected transactions. Set up T accounts with balances as shown on the balance sheet for December 31, 1975, and post the journal entries to these accounts.
2. Prepare a projected statement of cost of goods sold for 1976, a projected income statement for 1976, and a projected balance sheet as of December 31, 1976.
3. Describe the principal differences between the 1976 estimates and the 1975 figures as shown in Exhibits 1, 2, and 3. In what respects is 1976 performance expected to be better than 1975 performance, and in what respects is it expected to be poorer?

CASE 6–3. BRADFORD PRESS

In the 1930's, Bradford Press had acquired a tract of land on the outskirts of Craneville, a large city, with the intention eventually of constructing a branch warehouse thereon. Over the years, however, the company's marketing practices had changed, and by mid-1974 the management concluded that a warehouse would never be needed at Craneville. Consequently, the company sought to dispose of this land.

Bradford Press had paid $3,000 for the land and had made permanent improvements on it at a cost of $1,600, so that it was carried on the accounts of Bradford Press at $4,600. The best cash offer that could be found in 1974 was $200,000. Since an independent appraiser, hired by Bradford Press, had appraised the land at $250,000, the management was unwilling to accept this offer.

As it happened, the Craneville land was located adjacent to a warehouse owned by the Birch Paper Company, one of Bradford's four regular suppliers of paper. Birch expressed an interest in acquiring the property so that it could later expand its own facilities. Birch was unwilling to pay cash but offered instead to exchange 6,000 cwt. (hundredweight) of 70-pound machine-coated paper, to be delivered at the rate of 1,000 cwt. per month for six months. In addition, Bradford was to pay the freight on this paper, in accordance with usual practice. The going market price for this grade of paper was at that time $46 per cwt., plus freight.

Bradford Press typically used more than 1,000 cwt. of 70-pound machine-coated paper per month in the manufacture of booklets, brochures, and similar items, but Bradford Press ordinarily placed orders for delivery not more than two months in the future, unless it had firm contracts from its own customers that required such paper. It had no such contracts in the summer of 1974. After considerable discussion among Bradford executives as to the risk involved in the unusually large commitment for paper, the Bradford management finally decided to accept Birch's offer.

The contract was signed on June 21, 1974, and as of that date the following journal entry was made by Bradford's accountant, recording the paper at its market price, and showing the difference between this amount and the book value of the land as profit:

```
dr.    Inventory Due from Supplier..... 276,000
   cr.    Craneville Land..............         4,600
          Profit on Sale of Land.......       271,400
```

During the next three months of 1974, 3,000 cwt. of the paper was received from Birch as promised, and in the aggregate the entries made to record this receipt had the following effect:

```
dr.    Paper Inventory................ 138,940
   cr.    Inventory Due from Supplier..       138,000
          Cash (for freight charges)...          940
```

When he was examining the accounts of Bradford Press for fiscal year 1974, which had ended on September 30, 1974, the company's auditor raised questions about this transaction. He pointed out that the net effect of the above entries was that the entire profit on the transaction was shown in fiscal 1974, despite the fact that only 3,000 cwt. of paper had actually been delivered, and of this only about 2,000 cwt. had actually been used in the manufacture of products. (The physical inventory as of September 30 showed 1,000 cwt. of this paper as still on hand.)

A suggested alternative treatment was to split the profit into two parts. One part, $195,400, was the difference between the book value of the land and the best cash offer; this was to be called "profit on price-level changes" and shown on the 1974 income statement. The remainder, $76,000, was to be called "profit on sale of land" and divided one third to 1974 and two thirds to 1975, representing the fraction of the total paper consumed in each fiscal year. The auditor stated that such a separation was not usually made, but neither was this an ordinary transaction.

Bradford Press management disliked the implication in the above treatment that they had not made the $271,400 profit in 1974, especially since the price of 70-pound machine-coated paper had risen to $48 per cwt. as of September 30, 1974.

Questions

1. How do you think this transaction should be handled?
2. How would you answer the arguments of those who think it should be handled differently?

3. Would your answer be different if the market price had decreased to $44 as of the end of fiscal 1974?

CASE 6–4. PRENTISS DRESS SHOP

For over 20 years, Mr. Murray Prentiss had owned and operated a women's specialty shop in a suburban town. Early in 1975 Mr. Milton Wilcox, a representative of Dynamic Stores Inc., discussed with Mr. Prentiss the possibility of selling his business to Burroughs Stores, which owned 16 specialty shops in the same metropolitan area. Over the past several years, several other chains had approached Mr. Prentiss with similar propositions, but the Dynamic proposal was the first one that he seriously considered.

After a series of conversations, Mr. Prentiss told Mr. Wilcox that he would consider selling his business provided they could agree on a fair price and provided Dynamic would agree to employ him as store manager. Mr. Wilcox assured him that Dynamic would certainly be happy to have Mr. Prentiss continue as manager of the store, and the discussion then turned to the problem of deciding the selling price.

Mr. Wilcox asked what financial information was available, and Mr. Prentiss replied:

The only formal statements I have are balance sheets and my income tax returns, which I have a tax expert prepare for me. I expect him to work up the returns for 1974 within the next month. I know what is going on in the business well enough so that I don't need other statements. Of course, I have a checkbook, a file of charge slips showing what customers owe me, and a file of unpaid invoices from suppliers. On New Year's day, or the preceding afternoon, I take a physical inventory and determine the purchase cost of goods on hand.

I have two salespersons helping me, but I am at the store most of the time, and I try to keep a close tab on everything that takes place. There are two cash registers which everyone uses regardless of the kind of merchandise sold. None of us specializes in the sale of any particular kind of goods.

Mr. Wilcox replied that the lack of financial statements for 1974 probably would not prove to be any great obstacle to the conclusion of negotiations. All that was necessary was permission from Mr. Prentiss to examine whatever records were available, from which it was highly probable that Dynamic could ascertain all the operating facts about the business that were needed. Mr. Prentiss agreed with this arrangement.

Mr. Wilcox was able to gather the data presented in Exhibits 1 and 2. In going over this information with Mr. Prentiss, Mr. Wilcox commented: "If Dynamic takes over this store, even if you stay on as manager, we will need more figures than you have been gathering for yourself."

Exhibit 1

PRENTISS DRESS SHOP

Balance Sheet as of December 31, 1973

ASSETS

Current Assets:

Cash........................	$12,919
Notes receivable.............	2,000
Accounts receivable...........	8,562
Merchandise inventory........	22,601
Total Current Assets.....	$46,082

Fixed Assets:

Furniture and fixtures.	$6,870	
Less: Accumulated depreciation.....	3,913	2,957
Office equipment.....	$1,920	
Less: Accumulated depreciation.....	1,920	0
Total Assets..........		$49,039

EQUITIES

Current Liabilities:

Salaries payable..............	$ 820
Notes payable...............	7,600
Accounts payable............	4,188
Total Current Liabilities....	$12,608

Owner's Equity:

M. W. Prentiss, prop..........	16,500
Retained earnings............	19,931
Total Equities..........	$49,039

Exhibit 2

INFORMATION COLLECTED BY MR. WILCOX

Cash Record for 1974

Receipts:

Cash sales...............	$ 69,762
Collection of accounts receivable.............	39,118
Total receipts......	$108,880

Expenditures:

Payroll.................	$ 26,489
Rent..................	4,300
Advertising............	2,432
Taxes.................	1,741
Supplies..............	3,890
Travel...............	810
Telephone.............	912
Repairs to building.......	710
Insurance..............	450
Miscellaneous expenses..	978
Paid on accounts payable for merchandise.......	74,291
Total expenditures..	$117,003

Plus cash balance, December 31, 1973..........	12,919
Total.............	$121,799

Plus cash balance, December 31, 1974..........	4,796
Total..........	$121,799

Other Information

The expenditure for payroll includes Mr. Prentiss' salary of $16,000. Social security and withholding taxes may be disregarded since the expense portion was included in the payroll figure and amounts due to the government were immediately deposited in a separate bank account that does not appear on the financial statements.

Wages payable (including taxes thereon) as of December 31, 1974......	$ 1,448
Accounts payable represented only invoices for merchandise purchased on credit. As of December 31, 1974, these unpaid invoices amounted to....	9,896
Amounts due from customers on December 31, 1974, totaled...........	17,310
Merchandise inventory, December 31, 1974........................	37,936

Exhibit 2 (*continued*)

The note receivable carried a 9 percent rate of interest. The note payable carried an 8 percent rate of interest. The note receivable was not collected in 1974, nor was the note payable paid in 1974.

Miscellaneous expenses included $600 paid to Ajax Truck Rental for a three-month lease on a delivery truck. The lease began on December 1, 1974.

Depreciation on furniture and fixtures was computed at 10 percent of cost.

Questions

1. From the information given in Exhibits 1 and 2, determine (*a*) sales, (*b*) the cost of merchandise sold, and (*c*) the expenses for the year.
2. Prepare an income statement for 1974 and a balance sheet as of December 31, 1974.
3. Why should more figures apparently be justifiable under chain responsibility than when the store was owned by Mr. Prentiss?
4. How should the parties proceed to decide on a fair selling price for the business?

CASE 6–5. WORLEY COMPANY

On December 2, 1974, the audit committee of the board of directors of Worley Company met to discuss the advisability of shifting additional amounts of inventory to the Lifo method of accounting. The full board was scheduled to act on this matter the following day. The board usually relied heavily on the recommendation of the audit committee on accounting policy issues and in any event could not devote much time to this topic since it was 1 of about 20 issues that were on the agenda for the three-hour meeting. The audit committee consisted of three outside directors.

Worley Company was a multinational manufacturer of a wide variety of industrial products ranging from industrial chemicals which sold from a few cents a pound to machinery which sold for many tens of thousands of dollars a unit. Approximately 50,000 items were carried in its inventories. The company was organized into 20 domestic divisions, each responsible for the manufacture and sale of a family of related products, and an international division. Its stock was traded on the New York Stock Exchange. Condensed financial statements are given in Exhibits 1 and 2.

Inventory Accounting

As of December 31, 1973, the inventories of ten domestic divisions were reported on the Lifo basis. Inventories of these divisions had been switched to Lifo in 1950. Inventories of the other domestic divisions

Exhibit 1

CONDENSED CONSOLIDATED BALANCE SHEET
(thousands of dollars)

	December 31	
	1973	*1972*
Assets:		
Cash	$ 14,428	$ 25,694
Marketable securities	25,701	13,293
Accounts receivable	94,335	73,526
Inventories	90,035	70,340
Prepaid expenses and other	7,999	4,649
Total Current Assets	$232,498	$187,502
Investments and other assets	$ 29,397	$ 23,573
Properties, plants and equipment, at cost	$294,959	$284,928
Less depreciation and amortization	161,107	151,285
Total Properties, Plants and Equipment, net	$133,852	$133,643
Total Assets	$395,747	$344,718
Liabilities and Shareholders' Equity:		
Total Current Liabilities	$100,700	$ 76,967
Total Long-Term Debt and Other Liabilities	$ 57,900	$ 50,049
Deferred Taxes on Income	$ 12,045	$ 9,297
Shareholders' Equity		
Common stock at par value	$ 12,408	$ 12,384
Capital in excess of par value	23,120	22,785
Retained earnings	189,574	173,236
Total Shareholders' Equity	$225,102	$208,405
Total Liabilities and Shareholders' Equity	$395,747	$344,718

Exhibit 2

CONSOLIDATED STATEMENT OF INCOME
(thousands of dollars)

Year Ended December 31	*1973*		*1972*	
Sales	$460,729	100.0%	$377,245	100.0%
Cost of products sold	295,998	64.2	244,385	64.8
Gross margin	$164,731	35.8	$132,860	35.2
Selling, administrative and general expenses	$110,233	24.0	$ 88,797	23.5
Research and development expense	9,382	2.0	8,208	2.2
	$119,615	26.0	$ 97,005	25.7
Operating income	$ 45,116	9.8	$ 35,855	9.5
Total other income and (expense)	(211)	—	(983)	(0.3)
Income before taxes on income	$ 44,905	9.8	$ 34,872	9.2
Taxes on income	$ 22,004	4.8	$ 16,828	4.4
Net income	$ 22,901	5.0%	$ 18,044	4.8%
Net income per average outstanding common share	$6.19		$4.91	
Dividends per share	1.78		1.72	

and of the international division were reported on the Fifo basis. In general, the divisions on Fifo were those that had been acquired or organized since 1950. For all divisions on Lifo the dollar-value method was used, with the entire inventory of a division being treated as a single pool. Because of the very large number of products, it was not considered feasible to use a unit Lifo basis.

In 1973 and 1974 price levels increased rapidly; in 1974 the consumer price index rose at an annual rate well in excess of 10 percent. Costs of both raw materials and finished goods of the Worley Company had corresponding increases during this period, with some items considerably higher than the average and some items less. (In a few cases, costs of finished goods decreased because of improved manufacturing methods.) In view of this inflation, which was greater than for any period since the 1940s, the president of Worley decided early in 1974 that the possibility of extending the use of the Lifo method should be studied.

July 1974 Report to the Audit Committee

In July 1974 a report was submitted to the audit committee, and then to the full board, which read as follows:

Analysis of our inventory pricing policy leads us to recommend no change at this time.

At present, Lifo is in use for domestic inventories amounting to approximately 32 percent of gross inventory value, or $44.7 million. Since 1950, the year in which Lifo was adopted for these inventories, the Company has deferred the payment of approximately $6.7 million in taxes. Correspondingly, this same amount has not been included in earnings.

Of the $95.7 million in inventories not on Lifo, we believe that approximately $27.7 million or 29 percent would be eligible for Lifo treatment. Others are excluded primarily because the countries in which they are located prohibit the use of Lifo as a valuation technique.

Our recommendation to continue the present policy is based on the following considerations:

1. Abandonment or decreased use of the traditional Fifo method would generate too large an adjustment in income for 1974. Lower reported earnings as a result of adopting Lifo where allowable at this time could reduce the market value of the Company's stock or constrain its credit, thus increasing our cost of capital.
2. An analysis of other U.S. corporations indicates that less than 20 percent of all inventories are accounted for by the Lifo method.
3. Our most significant direct competitors use Fifo accounting. Our use of Lifo accounting tends to depress our earnings relative to theirs.
4. The use of Lifo accounting tends to increase the variability of our earnings. In particular, if we had no Lifo inventories, we would not

have shown an earnings decline in 1970, and our 1971 decline would have been moderated. [Earnings per share were $4.53 in 1969, $4.41 in 1970, $4.08 in 1971, $4.91 in 1972, and $6.19 in 1973.]

The full board accepted this recommendation. One director questioned the validity of the argument that a shift to Lifo would depress the market price of the company's stock. He pointed out that in 1973 the stock had sold at about $72 per share, which was 12 times earnings, whereas currently it was selling at less than $30 per share, or about 4 times earnings, despite the fact that sales and net income for each of the last several quarters set new records and the fact that earnings for 1974 were budgeted at $7.70 per share. Many other well regarded companies, particularly manufacturers of industrial products, had equally low price/earnings ratios in 1974. This director doubted that under these circumstances the change in the amount of reported earnings resulting from a switch to Lifo would have any material affect on the stock price.

During the discussion several board members urged management to continue to study the problem, especially since the rate of inflation showed no signs of subsiding.

December 1974 Report to the Audit Committee

In the second half of 1974, price levels continued to rise at an increasing rate. The press carried announcements that a number of companies were shifting to the Lifo method. Accordingly, in the fall, Grant Kelly, financial vice president, had another study made, and this led to the report that he presented to the audit committee on December 2. The report was as follows:

It is recommended that Worley extend the use of the Lifo (Last-in, first-out) method of inventory valuation to additional domestic inventories which are now on the Fifo (First-in, first-out) method.

By converting additional selected domestic inventories to Lifo, Worley's percentage of inventories on Lifo would increase from 30 percent to 45 percent.

GROSS CONSOLIDATED INVENTORIES BY VALUATION METHOD
(thousands of dollars)

	Present (9/30/74)		With Proposed Conversions	
	Amount	Percent	Amount	Percent
Domestic				
Fifo	$ 40,240	27	$ 17,279	12
Lifo	44,171	30	67,132	45
Total	$ 84,411	57	$ 84,411	57
Foreign	$ 64,646	43	$ 64,646	43
	$149,057	100	$149,057	100

All inventories carried on the Fifo method have been reviewed, including foreign. Countries where the majority of our foreign inventories are located do not allow Lifo for tax purposes. It is proposed that all domestic inventories be converted to Lifo, except for four divisions. Two of these were formed to carry out major construction projects and will be liquidated when these projects are completed. In the other two, substantial unit cost reductions are anticipated because of productivity improvements.

The Lifo method of inventory valuation is finding an increasing amount of acceptance because Lifo provides a better matching of current costs to current revenues in a period of rising prices. Thus, Lifo results in depressed earnings (as compared to Fifo), lower tax payments and increased cash flow.

Adoption of Lifo in 1974 will result in reduced taxes of $655,000 and a decline in earnings per share of 16 cents. Forecasts for 1975 indicate reduced taxes of $477,000 and a decline in earnings per share of 12 cents. Projections for the next six years, 1974–79, assuming a 5 percent inflation rate and constant inventory quantities, result in tax savings of $3,591,000 (with a present value of $2,620,000) and a decline in earnings per share of 92 cents for that period.

Kelly explained to the audit committee that the inventory amounts stated in this report were those used in the internal accounting system and were at standard costs. Unit standard costs were established at the beginning of each calendar year and were based on estimated costs to be incurred during the year. These amounts therefore did not correspond to inventory amounts as reported on the published financial statements, which were at actual costs (on either the Lifo or Fifo basis, depending on the division), reduced in some cases to estimated market value. Standard unit costs were not changed during the year.

Kelly presented the data in Exhibit 3 as an explanation of how the 16 cents decrease in earnings per share in 1974 was derived. Since the inventories were carried in the internal records at standard costs, the effect of valuing them at either Fifo or Lifo could be calculated by using the standard cost as a benchmark and measuring the change that resulted from changing them to each method. The net difference in the change in inventories was a corresponding difference in income before income taxes (IBT).

If inventories were valued at Fifo, the calculation showed that the beginning inventory would be increased by $405,000, representing the difference between the beginning inventory priced at actual and at the same quantity priced at standard. Similarly, the difference between the ending inventory priced at actual and at standard was $1,304,000. The sum of these two amounts, $1,709,000, was the net increase in inventory, which would result from a shift from standard to actual. There would be a corresponding increase in 1973 IBT. (On the published financial statements for 1973, the inventories for these divisions were reported at standard, rather than actual, because the $405,000 difference between actual and standard was not regarded as being material.)

Exhibit 3

COMPARISON OF LIFO VERSUS FIFO
(thousands of dollars)

Fifo:

Inventories as of 12/31/73—actual.............	$17,408	
Inventories as of 12/31/73—standard..........	17,003	
Difference.............................		$ 405
Inventories as of 12/31/74—actual.............	$22,721	
Inventories as of 12/31/74—standard..........	21,417	
Difference.............................		1,304
Total Fifo Revaluation..................		$1,709

Lifo:

Inventories as of 12/31/73—actual.............	$17,408	
Inventories as of 12/31/73—standard..........	17,003	
Difference.............................		$ 405
Inventories as of 12/31/73 (1974 standards)......	$17,663	
Inventories as of 12/31/74 (1974 standards)......	21,417	
Difference.............................	$ 3,754	
Inflation (standard versus actual).............		72
Total Lifo Revaluation..................		$ 477

Recap:

Impact from Fifo		
Income before taxes......................	$1,709	
Earnings per share.......................	22¢	
Impact from Lifo		
Income before taxes......................	$ 477	
Earnings per share.......................	6¢	
Lifo versus Fifo		
Income before taxes......................	$1,232	
Earnings per share.......................	16¢	

If inventories were valued at Lifo, there would be two effects. First, there would be the same $405,000 adjustment resulting from shifting the beginning inventory from standard to actual that was required in the Fifo method.

Second, there would be a $72,000 adjustment for the additional increment in inventory quantities in 1974. This inventory increment, measured at standard cost, amounted to $3,754,000. Income tax regulations gave the company the option of valuing this increment at either the average actual cost of the first quarter, the average actual cost of the whole year, or the average actual cost of the fourth quarter. Since Worley had used the first quarter average for divisions already on Lifo, the same basis was used in Exhibit 3. In the first quarter, the average actual cost of purchases was 1.9 percent below standard costs, so the increment was valued at 1.9 percent below the $3,754,000, a difference of $72,000. (The remainder of the $3,754,000 inventory increase was omitted from the calculation since its effect on earnings would be the same under Lifo as under Fifo, and Exhibit 3 measured only differences between the two methods.)

The sum of these two amounts, $477,000, was the total amount by which inventory and IBT would increase by the adjustment of standard costs to the Lifo basis.

The difference between the $1,709,000 increase in IBT under Fifo and the $477,000 increase under Lifo was the impact on IBT of shifting to Lifo. This was converted to earnings per share (EPS), by applying a 50 percent income tax rate and dividing by the number of common shares outstanding.

Since the committee members found this calculation difficult to follow, Kelly's assistant, who was present at the meeting, worked up an alternative set of numbers which he then put on a blackboard. It is shown in Exhibit 4.

Exhibit 4
ALTERNATIVE METHOD OF SHOWING IMPACT
(thousands of dollars)

Inventory Increase under Fifo		
Inventory 12/31/74	$22,721	
Inventory 12/31/73	17,408	
Increase		$5,313
Inventory Increase under Lifo		
Inventory 12/31/74	$21,084	
Inventory 12/31/73	17,408	
Increase		$3,676
Greater Increase under Fifo		$1,637
Less 1973 adjustment of standard to actual		405
Net Impact		$1,232

A committee member asked whether the pricing policy in the divisions involved corresponded more closely to a Fifo or a Lifo assumption as to cost flows. Kelly responded that it was impossible to give a general answer to this question. For many products, these divisions were not price leaders. For other products the policy was to recover current costs plus normal profit margins.

In response to a question, Kelly stated that the inventories at December 31, 1973 priced at 1974 standard unit costs amounted to $17,663,000. A committee member observed that this indicated to him that in 1974 there was a surprisingly large increase in inventory quantities and a surprisingly small increase in unit costs. Kelly responded that the 1974 year-end inventory estimates were derived from budgets that had been revised as of October 1, and that they were believed to be reasonably close approximations. Because of a recession forecast for 1975, inventory amounts were tightly controlled, and the increase reflected only the amount required to support increased sales volume. Furthermore, the calculations made by his staff had been double checked by the company's outside accountants. The partner of the outside accounting firm, who was present at the meeting, verified that this firm agreed with the accuracy of the calculations, subject to the estimates of year-end inventory amounts made by the company. In any event, it was not feasible to make new calculations prior to the board meeting on the following morning.

Another committee member asked whether a decrease in inventory quantities was likely in 1975, pointing out that if such a decrease occurred, some or all of the high-cost 1974 "layer" of inventory at Lifo would affect 1975 income. Kelly indicated that in all of the divisions involved, the order backlog was high, business was expanding, and no decrease in inventory quantities was foreseen, unless there was a much more severe recession than was currently anticipated. He had made a calculation that assumed a decrease in inventory quantities of 10 percent for each year, 1975 through 1979, and this showed total tax savings of $2,345,000 compared to the $3,591,000 given in the report. Even if inventory quantities decreased by a more substantial amount in 1975, the recession was expected to end by 1976, and the trend was for an increase in inventories, because of the expanding business of these divisions.

A question was also raised about the possibility of a decrease in unit costs in 1975 or subsequently. Kelly answered that anticipated continued inflation made such decreases unlikely as a general rule, but that in one sizable product line, significant unit cost decreases were possible because of the development of new production methods. He had calculated the maximum possible effect of such decreases in this inventory on earnings under Lifo to be less than 1 cent per share, as compared to the effect under Fifo.

The board meeting on December 3 was the last meeting prior to the end of the year. Advance approval of the change by the Internal Revenue Service was not required, but if a change to Lifo was made, IRS permission would have to be obtained if the company should desire to shift back to Fifo in some later year. It was believed that if the company requested such a shift in a year in which prices were falling, the request would be denied.

Questions

1. What is the basis for the committee member's comment that during 1974 "there was a surprisingly large increase in inventory quantities and a surprisingly small increase in unit costs."?
2. As an audit committee member, what would you recommend to the full board?

CHAPTER 7

FIXED ASSETS AND DEPRECIATION

This chapter discusses accounting for fixed assets and intangible assets, and the related charges for depreciation, depletion and amortization. The first section deals with fixed assets and discusses accounting for the acquisition, depreciation or depletion, and disposal of these assets. Later sections deal with intangible assets.

ACQUISITION OF FIXED ASSETS

A fixed asset is an asset that is expected to provide service for more than one year, usually for several years. A tangible asset is one that has physical substance, such as a building or a machine, as contrasted with stocks, bonds, patent rights or other intangibles. Although long-lived assets can actually be either tangible or intangible, when the term "fixed asset" is used without qualification, the reference usually is to tangible assets, and more specifically to property, plant, and equipment.

When an expenditure is recorded as a fixed asset, rather than as an expense, it is said to be *capitalized*. In accordance with the concept of materiality, items that have a low unit cost are not capitalized even though they have a long life. Each company sets its own criteria for capitalization, generally in the form of a monetary lower limit, which may range from $25 to $500 or more in different companies.

Items Included in Cost

As is the case with any productive asset, the cost of a fixed asset is the amount expended to make the asset ready to use. In many cases this amount can be determined easily. For example, the cost of a truck purchased for cash is simply the amount of cash paid. In other cases, the problem is more complicated. The cost of a parcel of land includes the purchase price, broker's commission, legal fees, and the cost of grading or tearing down existing structures so as to make the land ready for its intended use; the cost of some of these items may be difficult to ascertain. The cost of machinery includes the purchase price, sales tax, transportation costs to where the machinery is to be used, and installation costs.

Despite the principle stated above, many companies do not capitalize the costs incurred to make the asset ready to provide service. Instead they capitalize only the purchase price. They do this both because it is simpler and in order to minimize property taxes.

When a company constructs a machine or a building with its own personnel, the amount to be capitalized includes all the costs incurred in construction, including the material, the labor, and a fair share of the indirect costs incurred in the company.

A fixed asset may include the cost of the initial outfit of small items which do not individually meet the criteria for capitalization. Examples are the cost of small tools in a factory, the books in a library, and the tableware and kitchen utensils in a restaurant. When these items are subsequently replaced, the cost of replacing them is charged as an expense.

BETTERMENTS. Repair and maintenance is work done to keep an asset in good operating condition or to bring it back to good operating condition if it has broken down. Repair and maintenance costs are ordinarily expenses of the accounting period in which the work is done; they are *not* added to the cost of the asset. A *betterment* is added to the cost of the asset. The distinction between maintenance expenses and betterments is simple to state: maintenance work keeps the machine in good condition, but in no better condition than when it was purchased; a betterment makes the machine better than it was when it was purchased. In practice, the line between the two is difficult to draw. A new accessory designed to make the machine operate more efficiently or perform new functions is a betterment; an overhaul during which worn-out parts are replaced with new ones is maintenance. In the interests of conservatism some work which strictly speaking should be considered as a betterment is charged as an expense of the current period.

REPLACEMENTS. Replacements may be either assets or expenses, depending on how the asset unit is defined. The replacement of an entire asset results in the writing off of the old asset and the booking of the new. The replacement of a component part of an asset is maintenance expense. Thus, if one company treats a complete airplane as a single asset unit and another company treats the airframe as one unit and the engine as another, then the replacement of an engine results in a maintenance charge in the first company and in a new asset in the second. In general, the broader the definition of the asset unit, the greater will be the amount of costs charged as maintenance and hence expensed in the year the replacement parts are installed.

LEASED ASSETS. Ordinarily, when a company leases or rents an item of property or equipment, it has the right to use the item for a stated period of time, such as a month, a year, or a period of years, but it does not have any other rights with respect to the item itself. Such leases are called *operating leases*. Items used under such lease agreements are not assets of the lessee; rather, they are fixed assets on the accounts of the lessor. By contrast, some lease agreements cover a relatively long period of time and provide to the lessee almost as many rights in the property or equipment as if he owned the asset outright. Such leases are called *financial leases*. Assets acquired under financial leases are capitalized, just as if they were owned.[1]

LEASEHOLD IMPROVEMENTS. Improvements made to leased property are capitalized if they otherwise meet capitalization criteria, whether or not the property itself is capitalized.

Measurement of Acquisition Cost

In the great majority of cases, an asset is acquired for cash, or for a note or other obligation whose cash equivalent is easily determined. In other cases, the general principle is that, first, the fair market value of the consideration given in exchange for the fixed asset should be determined, and, second, if it is not feasible to determine this fair market value, the fair market value of the fixed asset itself should be estimated.

EXCHANGES. When a new fixed asset is acquired in exchange for another, the old asset is part of the consideration given; therefore its trade-in value is part of the cost of the new asset. The amount used as the value of this exchange depends on whether or not the asset traded is similar to the new asset. If the trade-in is *similar*, its value is assumed to be its book value, that is, its cost less the amount depreciated to date. If the asset traded is *dissimilar*, its value is its estimated fair market value.[2]

> EXAMPLE: Assume a company trades in two automobiles, each of which cost $5,000 of which $3,000 has been depreciated, so each has a book value of $2,000. Each has a fair market value as a used car of $2,500.
>
> The first automobile is traded for another automobile, with a list price of $6,000, and $3,000 cash is given to the dealer in addition to the trade-in. In this case the cost of the new automobile is recorded as

[1] See APB *Opinion No. 5* (September 1964) for detailed criteria on capitalization of financial leases, and methods of arriving at the amount to be capitalized.

[2] See APB *Opinion No. 29* (May 1973)

$5,000, that is, the sum of the $3,000 cash and the $2,000 book value of the trade-in.

The second automobile is traded for a machine tool which also has a list price of $6,000, and $3,000 cash is given in addition to the trade-in. In this case, the cost of the new machine tool is recorded as $5,500, that is, the sum of the $3,000 cash and the $2,500 market value of the trade-in.

In neither case does the list price enter into the determination of acquisition cost. The list price would be used only if there were no way of determining the fair market value of the asset exchanged.

The reason for the different treatment of the two types of exchanges will become clearer when we discuss the disposal of fixed assets.

BASKET PURCHASES. If a company acquires in one transaction fixed assets which are to appear in more than one balance sheet category, it must divide the cost of the acquisition between the categories on some reasonable basis. Usually this requires an appraisal of the relative value of each asset included in the "basket purchase."

> EXAMPLE: A parcel of land with a factory building thereon is purchased for $300,000. An appraiser states that the land is worth $35,000 and the building is worth $315,000, a total of $350,000. Since the appraised value of the land is 10 percent of the total appraised value, it is entered in the accounts at 10 percent of the cost, or $30,000. The building is entered at 90 percent of the cost, or $270,000. Note that it would *not* be correct to use the appraised value of one asset as the amount to be capitalized and capitalize the other asset at the difference. Thus, it would not be correct to record the land at $35,000 and the building at $265,000.

Acquisitions Recorded at Other than Cost

There are a few exceptions to the basic rule that acquisitions are recorded in the accounts at cost. If the company acquires an asset by donation or pays substantially less than the market value of the asset, the asset is recorded at its fair market value. This happens, for example, when a community donates land or a building in order to induce a company to locate there.

If the cost of an asset cannot be measured, then the asset is recorded at an amount determined by appraisal. This happens, for example, when the asset is acquired in exchange for stock which is not regularly traded and hence has no determinable market value. If property suddenly increases in value shortly after its acquisition, because, say, of the discovery of oil or of a mineral deposit, the amount originally recorded for this *fortunate acquisition* may be increased to reflect its current value.

Such exceptions to the general rule are relatively rare, and their rarity emphasizes the importance of the general rule: fixed assets are recorded at cost. Furthermore, as we shall see in the next section, changes in market value do not affect the accounting records for fixed assets. Competent investors acquire or build apartment houses or shopping centers with the expectation that part of the profit from this investment will be derived from the appreciation of the property. This appreciation may in fact occur, year after year, but it is not recorded in the accounts. The FASB states that "property, plant and equipment should not be written up by an entity to reflect appraisal, market or current values which are above cost to the entity."[3]

The reason for the supremacy of the cost concept over a system geared to changes in market value is the importance of the basic criterion of objectivity. We may know in a general way that the market value of an apartment house is increasing, but there is no objective way of measuring the amount of the increase until a sale takes place. When this happens, a new cost is established and recorded as such in the accounts of the new owner.

DEPRECIATION OF FIXED ASSETS

With the exception of land, most fixed assets have a limited useful life; that is, they will be of use to the company over a limited number of future accounting periods. A fraction of the cost of a fixed asset is properly chargeable as an expense in each of the accounting periods in which the asset is used by the company. The accounting process for this gradual conversion of fixed assets into expense is called *depreciation*.[4]

The question is sometimes asked: Why is depreciation an expense? The answer is that *all* goods and services consumed by a business during an accounting period are expenses. The cost of insurance protection provided in a year is an expense of that year even though the insurance premium was paid two or three years previously. Depreciation expense is conceptually just like insurance expense; the principal difference is that the fraction of total cost of a fixed asset that is an expense in a given year is difficult to estimate, whereas the fraction of the total cost of an insurance policy that is an expense in a given year can be easily calculated. This difference does not change the fundamental fact that both insurance policies and fixed assets provide service to the company over a

---

[3] APB *Opinion No. 6* (October 1965)

[4] If the asset is used in the manufacturing process, a fraction of its cost is properly chargeable as an item of product cost that is initially added to goods in process inventory, then flows through finished goods inventory, and becomes an expense (cost of goods sold) in the period in which the product is sold, as described in Chapter 6. In the interests of simplicity, in this chapter we shall not distinguish between the depreciation that is a product cost and the depreciation that is a period expense.

finite number of accounting periods and must therefore be charged as expenses of each of these periods.

The useful life of an asset is limited for one of two reasons: *deterioration,* which is the physical process of wearing out; and *obsolescence,* which refers to loss of usefulness because of the development of improved equipment or processes, changes in style, or other causes not related to the physical condition of the asset. No distinction need be made between the two since depreciation relates to both of them. Although the word "depreciation" is sometimes used as referring only to physical deterioration, this usage is incorrect. In many cases, a machine becomes obsolete, and consequently is no longer useful, even though it is in good physical condition.

Judgments Required

In order to determine the depreciation expense for an accounting period, three judgments or estimates must be made for each fixed asset:

1. The *service life* of the asset, that is, over how many accounting periods will it be useful to the company?

2. *Residual value* at the end of its life. The net cost of the asset to the company is its original cost less any amount eventually recovered through sale, trade-in, or salvage. It is this *net cost* that should be charged as an expense over the asset's life, *not* its original cost. In a great many situations, however, the estimated residual value is so small and uncertain that it is disregarded.

3. *The method of depreciation,* that is, the method that will be used to allocate a fraction of the net cost to each of the accounting periods in which the asset is expected to be used.

Managers, not being clairvoyant, cannot *know* in advance how long the asset will last or what its residual value will be, and they usually have no scientific or strictly logical way of deciding the best depreciation method. The amount of depreciation expense that results from these judgments is therefore an estimate, and often it is only a rough estimate.

Service Life

The service life of an asset is the period of time over which it is expected to provide service to the company that owns it. Service life may be shorter than the period of time that the asset will last physically for either of two reasons: (1) The asset may not provide service over its full physical life because it has become obsolete; or (2) the company may plan to dispose of the asset before its physical life ends. For example, although automobiles have an average physical life of about ten years, many companies trade in new automobiles every three years; in these companies, the service life is three years.

Estimating the service life of an asset is a difficult problem. Rather than making an independent estimate, many companies use the *asset guideline periods* that are allowed by the Internal Revenue Service for income tax purposes. Examples of these lives are as follows: [5]

	Asset Guideline Period (years)
Office furniture and equipment....................	10
Automobiles and taxis.........................	3
Buses.......................................	9
Light trucks.................................	4
Heavy trucks.................................	6
Horses......................................	10
Cattle......................................	7

For production machinery and equipment, the guideline period is generally between 6 and 15 years depending on the industry in which the assets are used. For buildings, the guideline period ranges from 30 to 50 years, depending on the type of building. [6]

It should be emphasized that these numbers are only *guidelines*. If a company has reason to believe that some other estimate is better, it should by all means use the better estimate.

Depreciation Methods

Consider a machine purchased for $1,000 with an estimated life of 10 years and estimated residual value of zero. The problem of depreciation accounting is to charge this $1,000 as an expense over the 10-year period. How much should be charged as an expense each year?

This question cannot be answered by observing the amount of asset value physically consumed in a given year, for physically the machine continues to be a machine; usually, there is no observable indication of its decline in usefulness. Nor can the question be answered in terms of changes in the machine's market value during the year, for accounting is concerned with the amortization of cost, not with changes in market values. An indirect approach must therefore be used. Three conceptual ways of looking at the depreciation process are described below, together with the methods that follow from each. The FASB permits any method that is "systematic and rational," and all the methods described here meet those criteria.

---

[5] For income tax purposes, a company may select a life within what is called the asset depreciation range (ADR), which is the range between 80 percent and 120 percent of the asset guideline period.

[6] Source: Internal Revenue Service Revenue Procedure 71–25

STRAIGHT-LINE METHOD.   One concept views a fixed asset as existing to provide service over its life, with its readiness to provide this service being equal in each year of life, just as a three-year insurance policy provides equal insurance protection in each of the three years. This concept leads to the *straight-line* method, which is to charge an equal fraction of the net cost of the asset each year. For a machine whose net cost is $1,000 with an estimated service life of 10 years, one tenth of $1,000 is the depreciation expense of the first year, another one tenth is the depreciation expense of the second year, and so on. Expressed another way, the machine is said to have a *depreciation rate* of 10 percent per year, the rate being the reciprocal of the estimated useful life.

ACCELERATED METHODS.   A second concept takes what is perhaps a broader view of the asset since it relates to the *amount* of service provided each year. Some fixed assets are more valuable in their youth than in their old age—because their mechanical efficiency tends to decline with age, because maintenance costs tend to increase with age, or because of the increasing likelihood that better equipment will become available and make them obsolete. It is argued, therefore, that when an asset was purchased the probability that the earlier periods would benefit more than the later periods was taken into account, and that the depreciation method should reflect this. Such a line of reasoning leads to a method which charges a larger fraction of the cost as an expense of the early years than of the later years. This is called an *accelerated* method.[7]

Accelerated methods have been widely adopted since their use was permitted for income tax purposes beginning in 1954. The two methods specifically mentioned in the 1954 tax law, the double declining-balance method and sum-of-years'-digits (or simply "years'-digits") method, are described below. The effect of either of these methods is to write off approximately two thirds of the cost in the first half of the asset's estimated life, as contrasted with the straight-line method under which, of course, half the cost is written off in each half of the asset's estimated life. Thus, if an accelerated method is used, depreciation expense is greater in the early years and less in the later years as compared with the straight-line method.

In the *double declining-balance method*, the depreciation for each year is found by applying a rate to the net book value of the asset at the beginning of that year rather than to the original cost of the asset. *Net book value* is cost less total depreciation accumulated up to that time. If the declining-balance method is used, the tax law permits the company to take *double* the rate allowed under the straight-line method, hence the

---

[7] An argument can also be made for an opposite approach, that is, charging a smaller fraction of the cost to the early years and a larger fraction to the later years. This leads to an *annuity method*. It is relatively uncommon.

name, double declining balance.[8] The double rate is applied to the original cost of the asset, rather than to the net cost (i.e., original cost minus residual value).

In the *years'-digits method*, the numbers 1, 2, 3 . . . *n* are added, where *n* is the estimated years of useful life. The depreciation rate each year is a fraction in which the denominator is the sum of these digits and

Illustration 7–1

COMPARISON OF DEPRECIATION METHODS

Year	Straight-Line (10% rate)		Declining-Balance (20% rate)		Years'-Digits		
	Annual Depre- ciation	*Net Book Value, 12/31*	*Annual Depre- ciation*	*Net Book Value, 12/31*	*Rate*	*Annual Depre- ciation*	*Net Book Value, 12/31*
0..........	$ ...	$1,000	$	$1,000.00	....	$	$1,000.00
First.......	100	900	200.00	800.00	10/55	181.82	818.18
Second.....	100	800	160.00	640.00	9/55	163.64	654.54
Third......	100	700	128.00	512.00	8/55	145.45	509.09
Fourth.....	100	600	102.40	409.60	7/55	127.27	381.82
Fifth.......	100	500	81.92	327.68	6/55	109.09	272.73
Sixth.......	100	400	65.54	262.14	5/55	90.91	181.82
Seventh.....	100	300	52.43	209.71	4/55	72.73	109.09
Eighth......	100	200	41.94	167.77	3/55	54.55	54.54
Ninth......	100	100	33.55	134.22	2/55	36.36	18.18
Tenth......	100	0	26.84	107.38	1/55	18.18	0
Eleventh....	...	....	21.48	85.90	....	....	....
Twelfth....	...	....	17.18	68.72*	....	....	....
	$1,000		$931.28*			$1,000.00	

* Under the strict declining-balance method, depreciation continues until the asset is disposed of or until the net book value declines to residual value. Many companies, however, switch from an accelerated method to the straight-line method in the later years of life, and thus write off the entire cost in a specified number of years. This practice is permitted for tax purposes.

the numerator is for the first year, *n*; for the second year, *n* − 1; for the third year, *n* − 2; and so on. Assume, for example, a machine with an estimated life of 10 years. The sum of the numbers 1, 2, 3 . . . 10 is 55. Depreciation in the first year would be $10/55$ of the net cost; in the second year, $9/55$; in the third year, $8/55$; and so on.

Illustration 7–1 is an example of the way these three methods work out for a machine costing $1,000 with an estimated life of 10 years and no residual value. Illustration 7–2 shows the same depreciation patterns graphically.

[8] Under the 1969 income tax law the rate applicable to certain assets was limited to 1.5 times the straight-line, rather than twice the straight-line rate.

As an incentive to modernize their plant and equipment, taxpayers are permitted to deduct in the year of acquisition 20 percent of the cost of certain assets, in addition to regular depreciation for that year. This deduction is limited to a total of $2,000 per year. It is allowed only for tangible personal property (not buildings) with an estimated useful life of at least six years. It does not increase the total amount of depreciation that can be taken over the life of the asset; this remains equal to the net cost of the asset; that is, regular depreciation is calculated on 80 percent of the cost, not 100 percent.

Illustration 7–2

PATTERNS OF ANNUAL DEPRECIATION

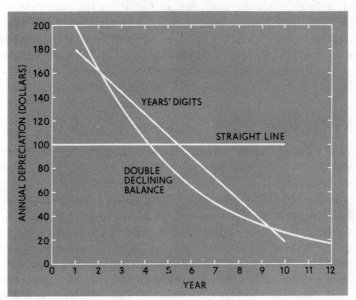

UNITS-OF-PRODUCTION METHOD.   A third concept of depreciation views the asset as consisting of a bundle of service units, the cost of each unit being the total cost of the asset divided by the number of such units, and the depreciation charge for a period therefore being related to the number of units consumed in the period. This leads to the units-of-production method. If a truck has an estimated net cost of $12,000 and is expected to give service for 300,000 miles, depreciation would be charged at a rate of $0.04 per mile, the depreciation expense in a year in which the truck traveled 50,000 miles being $2,000.[9]

---

[9] An alternative method is to charge a decreasing rate as the number of miles increases, as in the accelerated methods.

Choice of a Method

In deciding on the best depreciation method, tax considerations should be kept completely separate from financial accounting considerations. For tax purposes, the best method is that which minimizes the effect of taxes. Unless tax rates applicable to the business are expected to increase, this is usually one of the accelerated methods.

With respect to financial accounting, each of the concepts described above has its advocates. An essential requirement is that there *be* a method. The practice of charging "whatever the income statement can stand," which was widespread in the early part of this century, is indefensible. In the 1950s and 1960s, many companies used an accelerated method in financial accounting, but in the 1970s the majority of companies seem to have reverted to the straight-line method.[10] It follows that most companies use a different depreciation method for tax purposes than they use for financial accounting purposes.[11] This difference in treatment requires an adjustment in income tax expense which will be discussed in Chapter 8.

Accounting for Depreciation

Assume that on December 31, 1963, the Trantor Company purchased for $90,000 a building with an estimated useful life of 45 years and zero residual value, and that it has decided to depreciate this building on a straight-line basis, that is, $2,000 per year. Let us now consider how to record this depreciation on the accounting records.

It would be possible to reduce the asset value by $2,000 a year and to show on the balance sheet only the remaining amount, which at the end of 1964 would be $88,000; but this is *not* ordinarily done. Instead, a separate contra account is shown on the balance sheet for the accumulated amount of depreciation. This item is usually called *accumulated depreciation*, or it may have some other name such as "allowance for depreciation," "reserve for depreciation," and so on. (The last term is another example of a misleading use of the word "reserve"; the depreciation process does not "reserve" money or anything else.) Both the original

---

[10] *Accounting Trends and Techniques 1973* reports the following methods used by 600 companies for financial accounting (some companies used more than one method):

Straight-line	565
Accelerated	205
Units of production	38
Other	1
Total	809

[11] According to *Accounting Trends and Techniques 1973*, 84 percent of companies did this.

cost and the accumulated depreciation figures appear on the balance sheet. The figures as of December 31, 1964, would look like this:

```
Building........................................ $90,000
      Less: Accumulated depreciation..............   2,000
      Net.......................................  $88,000
```

As of December 31, 1965, another year's depreciation would be added, and the balance sheet would then show:

```
Building........................................ $90,000
      Less: Accumulated depreciation..............   4,000
      Net.......................................  $86,000
```

The foregoing figures can be interpreted as follows:

Original cost of the building... $90,000
That portion of the cost charged to operations for all periods to date...........   4,000
That portion of the cost remaining to be charged to operations of future
    periods... $86,000

On the income statement, the expense item is usually labeled *depreciation expense*. In the income statement for 1964, this item for the Trantor Company would be $2,000 (disregarding depreciation on assets other than the building we are considering), and $2,000 would also appear in the income statement for 1965, for 1966, and for following years until either the building was disposed of or it was fully depreciated. Usually, the depreciation expense account includes depreciation for all types of fixed assets, but there must be a separate accumulated depreciation account for each category of fixed assets (building, machinery, office equipment, and so forth) shown separately on the balance sheet, except for the category, land, since land does not depreciate.

The annual journal entry, which is one of the adjusting entries, would therefore be as follows:

```
Depreciation Expense..................... 2,000
      Accumulated Depreciation, Building.....        2,000
```

If the Trantor Company should use its building for more than 45 years, depreciation would cease to be accumulated at the end of the 45th year, since by then the total cost of the building would have been charged to expense. (If the fact that its life will be longer than 45 years becomes apparent earlier, the depreciation rate should be decreased so as to spread the remaining book value over the longer period.) Until the asset is disposed of, it is customary to continue to show the asset on the balance sheet. Thus, from December 31, 2008, onward, the balance sheet would show the following:

```
Building........................................ $90,000
      Less: Accumulated depreciation..............  90,000
      Net.......................................  $      0
```

Often, half a year's depreciation is recorded in the year of acquisition and half a year's depreciation in the year of disposal no matter what the actual date of acquisition or disposal is, on the grounds that depreciation is a rough estimate and there is no point in attempting to calculate it to exact fractions of a year. This practice, if followed consistently, is permitted for tax purposes. Similarly, if accounts are kept on a monthly basis, half a month's depreciation may be recorded in the month of acquisition.

Reporting in Financial Statements

The Financial Accounting Standards Board requires that the income statement show the amount of depreciation expense as a separate item, and that the balance sheet show the balances of major depreciable assets by nature or function, accumulated depreciation by classes or in total, and a general description of the method(s) of computing depreciation for major classes of depreciable assets.[12]

The Investment Credit

In order to encourage purchases of machinery and equipment, the income tax statute in certain years[13] permits a credit against income tax of a stated percentage of the cost of such assets, provided they are long-lived and meet certain other criteria. This is called the *investment credit*. The investment credit is a direct reduction in taxes; that is, if a company acquired $100,000 of equipment in 1974 when the investment credit was 7 percent, it could deduct $7,000 from the income tax it would otherwise pay for 1974. Furthermore, for tax purposes the company can depreciate the full cost of the asset (less residual value) over its useful life; it is not required to deduct the investment credit in calculating the amount to be depreciated.

The FASB approves either of two methods of handling the investment credit for accounting purposes. The first method, called the *cost-reduction*, or *deferral* method, is to spread the effect of the investment credit over the useful life of the asset. This can be done by reducing the depreciation expense of each year of the useful life. The second method, called the *flow-through* method, reduces income tax expense, and hence increases net income, in the year in which the credit is taken.

---

[12] APB *Opinion No. 12* (December 1967).

[13] The Congress enacts an investment credit law in years in which it desires to stimulate the purchase of fixed assets, and it repeals this law in years in which such a stimulus is believed to be unnecessary.

The accounting entries involved in both methods are shown in the following example:

EXAMPLE: Assume that in December 1974 a company purchased $100,000 of machinery that qualifies for the investment credit, that the service life of these assets is 10 years and that straight-line depreciation is used. The investment credit is $7,000, and this $7,000 is subtracted from the income tax liability in 1974.

Under the deferral method, the investment credit would be recorded, in effect, as:

```
Income Tax Liability................. 7,000
       Machinery.......................      7,000
```

Note that net income for 1974 is unaffected by this entry. In 1975 and subsequent years depreciation expense would be calculated on a net cost of $93,000, rather than $100,000, and would therefore be $9,300 per year. This has the effect of increasing net income $700 in each of the next 10 years, as compared with what the net income would have been had the depreciation expense been $10,000 per year.

Under the flow-through method, the investment credit would be recorded in 1974 as:

```
Income Tax Liability................. 7,000
       Income Tax Expense...............      7,000
```

This has the effect of decreasing income tax expense and hence increasing 1974 net income by $7,000.

DISPOSAL OF FIXED ASSETS

Suppose that at the end of 10 years the Trantor Company sells its building. At that time, $^{10}\!/_{45}$ of the original cost, or $20,000, will have been built up in the Accumulated Depreciation account, and the net book value of the building will be $70,000. If the building is sold for $70,000 cash, the accounts are changed, as follows: Cash is increased by $70,000; the Building account is decreased by $90,000, and Accumulated Depreciation is decreased by $20,000, which is the amount of depreciation accumulated up to that time. The entry is as follows:

```
Cash...................................... 70,000
Accumulated Depreciation................. 20,000
       Building..............................      90,000
```

This has the effect of eliminating from the accounts both the original cost of the building and the accumulated depreciation thereon.

If the building were sold for less than $70,000, say $60,000, the transaction would be recorded as follows: Cash is increased by $60,000, the

Building account is decreased by $90,000, Accumulated Depreciation is decreased by $20,000, and an account, Loss on Sale of Fixed Assets, or some similar title, is set up, as in the following entry:

```
Cash....................................... 60,000
Accumulated Depreciation.................. 20,000
Loss on Sale of Fixed Assets............. 10,000
    Building.............................          90,000
```

Note that the effect on the Building and Accumulated Depreciation accounts is identical with that in the previous illustration: the amounts relating to this building disappear. The loss is a decrease in owners' equity, reflecting the fact that the total depreciation expense recorded for the preceding 10 years was less than what we now know to have been the actual net cost of the building over that period of time. The actual net cost turns out to have been $30,000, whereas the total depreciation expense charged has amounted to only $20,000.

Since the depreciation expense as originally recorded turns out to have been incorrect, the Retained Earnings account which reflects the net of all revenue and expenses is also incorrect, and there is therefore some logic in closing the Loss on Sale of Fixed Assets account directly to Retained Earnings, thus correcting the error contained therein. Nevertheless, the matching concept requires that this loss be shown as an expense on the income statement of the current period. If a charge against revenue is discovered in a certain period, it is an expense of that period.

If an asset is sold for more than its book value, the entries correspond to those described above. The account, Gain on the Sale of Fixed Assets, is usually classified as nonoperating revenue on the income statement.

A trade-in involves the disposal of an asset, and the asset traded in is treated in the accounting records exactly like the sale of the building described above; that is, both its cost and its accumulated depreciation are removed from the books. As mentioned in the preceding section, the value of the trade-in depends on whether the new asset is similar or dissimilar to the asset traded. If the new asset is similar, the value of the trade-in is assumed to be its net book value; therefore, no gain or loss on the transaction can arise. If the new asset is dissimilar, the trade-in is valued at its market value, and a gain or loss can arise. This distinction between similar (or "like kind") and dissimilar assets is also made for income tax purposes.

Debits to Accumulated Depreciation

If a machine is given an unusual major overhaul which makes it "as good as new," the cost of this overhaul is sometimes debited to Accumulated Depreciation rather than to Maintenance Expense on the ground that the overhaul has actually canceled or offset some of the accumulated depreciation. Or, it can be argued that the overhaul has extended the useful life of the machine, and that the depreciation accumulated up to the time of overhaul is therefore excessive. In theory, if the estimated useful life has changed, the depreciation rate should be recalculated and the accounts changed to reflect the new estimate of useful life; but in practice, charging the overhaul to Accumulated Depreciation may have approximately the same effect.

GROUP AND COMPOSITE DEPRECIATION

The procedure described above related to a single fixed asset, one building. To find the total depreciation expense for a whole category of assets, this procedure could be repeated for each single asset, and the total depreciation for all the assets in the category would then be recorded by one journal entry. This is the procedure used in many businesses.

An alternative procedure is to treat several assets together rather than making the calculation for each one separately. If similar assets with approximately the same useful life, such as all typewriters or all general-purpose lathes, are treated together, the process is called *group* depreciation. If dissimilar assets are treated together, the process is called *composite* depreciation.

The depreciation rate in composite depreciation is a weighted-average rate, the weights being the dollar amounts of assets in each of the useful-life categories. All the production equipment in a plant, for example, might be included in a single composite account, even though the useful lives of the various items of equipment were not the same. The Internal Revenue Service Asset Guideline Periods referred to above give a single depreciation rate for all the machinery and equipment in most types of manufacturing plants (e.g., 11 years for the machinery and equipment in a chemical plant). These are composite rates.

Annual depreciation expense under group or composite depreciation is computed in a manner similar to that described above for an individual asset. If the straight-line method is used, for example, the depreciation rate is applied to the total cost of the whole group of assets.

The accumulation of depreciation does not stop when one item in the group reaches its estimated useful life, however, but continues indefinitely unless it becomes apparent that the accumulation is too large or too small for the whole group of assets. In this case, the depreciation rate is changed.

If a group or composite method is used, no gain or loss is recognized when an individual asset is sold or otherwise disposed of. The asset account is credited for the cost, and the difference between cost and the sales proceeds is simply debited to Accumulated Depreciation. This procedure assumes that gains on some sales are offset by losses on others.

SIGNIFICANCE OF DEPRECIATION

The amount shown as accumulated depreciation on the balance sheet does not represent the "accumulation" of any tangible thing; it is merely that portion of the assets' original cost that has been already charged off against revenue.

Occasionally a company does set aside money for the specific purpose of purchasing new assets, and this process is sometimes called "funding depreciation." This transaction is completely separate from the depreciation mechanism described above. If depreciation is funded, cash or securities are physically segregated; that is, they are set aside in such a way that they cannot be used in the regular operation of the business (for example, a special bank account may be created). This fact is reflected on the balance sheet by an asset titled "New Building Fund," or some similar name, the offsetting entry being a credit to Cash. This practice is not common and is mentioned here only to emphasize, by contrast, the point that the depreciation process itself is *not* a means of automatically creating a fund for the replacement of assets.

There is a widespread belief that, in some mysterious way, depreciation does represent money, specifically, money that can be used to purchase new assets. Depreciation is *not* money; the money that the business has is shown by the balance in its Cash account.

> EXAMPLE: This quotation is from a well-known publication: "Most large companies draw much of the cash flow they employ for expanding and modernizing their operations from their depreciation reserves." This statement is not true in anything remotely approaching a literal sense. Possibly the author intended some figurative, rather than literal, meaning, but it is difficult to imagine how the statement could be true in even a figurative sense.

There is also a widespread belief that the book value of assets is related to their real value, and this is equally erroneous.

> EXAMPLE: An auditor's report included the following statement: "Our inspection of insurance policies in force at the close of the year disclosed that the plant assets, on the basis of book values, were amply protected against fire." Such a statement has little if any significance. What the management wants to know is whether the insurance policies equal the *actual cash value* of the assets, and this is unlikely to correspond to their *book value*.

Concluding Comment

The key to a practical understanding of depreciation is a sentence from *Accounting Research Bulletin No. 43*:[14] *Depreciation is a process*

---

[14] *Accounting Research Bulletin No. 43*, Chapter 9, Section C, par. 5.

of allocation, not of valuation. Depreciation expense does *not* represent the shrinkage in real value during an accounting period; physically, the machine may be as useful and as valuable at the end of the period as it was at the beginning. Neither does the net book value represent the market value of the assets on hand. Depreciation expense is a write-off of a portion of the *cost* of the asset, and it follows that the net book value of fixed assets reported on the balance sheet represents only that portion of the original cost of the fixed asset which has *not yet* been charged to expense.

No one really knows how long an asset will last or what its residual value will be at the end of its life. Without this knowledge, the depreciation number is necessarily an estimate.

OTHER ASPECTS OF FIXED ASSETS

Depletion

Natural resources such as coal, oil, other minerals, and timber are called *wasting assets.* The process of writing off the cost of these fixed assets to expenses in the accounting periods benefited is called *depletion.* The objective is the same as that for depreciation: to amortize the cost in some systematic manner over the asset's useful life. The units-of-production method is ordinarily used. For example, if an oil property cost $500,000 and is estimated to contain one million barrels of oil, the depletion rate is 50 cents per barrel; the total depletion for a year in which 80,000 barrels of oil were produced would be $40,000.

For income tax purposes, however, the depletion allowance usually bears no relation to cost; rather, it is a percentage of revenue. The permitted percentage (as of 1974) varies from 5 percent on clay, gravel, and other common materials to 22 percent on oil and gas. This is perhaps the most clear-cut example of an income tax provision that is inconsistent with generally accepted accounting principles. Advocates of this provision in the tax law claim that it stimulates exploration for and development of new supplies of natural resources and is therefore in the national interest.

Accretion and Appreciation

Accretion is the increase in value of timberland, cattle, and other agricultural products that arises through the natural process of growth. Since accretion does not represent realized revenue, it is ordinarily not recognized in the accounts, although the *costs* incurred in the growing process may be added to the asset value, just as is done in the case of costs incurred in the manufacture of products.

Appreciation is also an increase of value and is therefore *not* the opposite of depreciation, which is a write-off of *cost*. Appreciation of either fixed assets or inventory is recognized in the accounts only under highly unusual circumstances; for example, if a new owner takes over a business and an appraisal discloses that the current market value of fixed assets was substantially above their book value, the asset values often are written up to their current value. Generally, however, increases in value are recognized in the accounts only when revenue is realized, whereas expiration of cost is recognized when it occurs.

INTANGIBLE ASSETS

Intangible long-lived assets, such as goodwill, organization cost (i.e., cost incurred to get a business started), trademarks, and patents are usually converted to expenses over a number of accounting periods. The periodic write-off is specifically called *amortization*, although the word "amortization" is also used in the broad sense of any write-off of a cost over a period of years. The amortization of intangible assets is essentially the same process as the depreciation of tangible assets.

Acquisition of Intangibles

As is the case with other long-lived assets, intangible assets are recorded at the cost of acquiring them. In many transactions involving the acquisition of a patent right, a copyright, or a franchise by the payment of cash or by a note or other definite obligation, the measurement of cost is straightforward.

In the case of goodwill, however, the problem is more complicated. Goodwill is rarely acquired by a separate purchase. Instead, it usually arises as part of a transaction in which one company acquires all the assets of another company. Some of the acquired assets are tangible and their value at the time of acquisition is their fair market value at that time. Usually, these values are determined by appraisal, but in some cases the book value of these assets is accepted as their market value. If there is evidence that the fair market value differs from book value, either higher or lower, the market value governs. Goodwill is the difference between the fair market value of the identifiable assets acquired and the total amount paid. If the purchase price is paid in something other than cash or some other asset whose value can be objectively measured, problems arise in determining what the purchase price actually was; these were discussed in an earlier section. In short, the amount of goodwill recorded as an asset is the difference between the purchase price, which may be an estimate, and the cost of the identifiable assets, which may also be arrived at by a series of estimates.

EXAMPLE: Company A acquires all the assets of Company B, giving Company B $500,000 cash and 50,000 shares of the common stock of Company A. Although there is no established market for this stock, it is estimated to have a value of $1,000,000. Company B has cash of $50,000, accounts receivable which are believed to have a realizable value of $60,000, and other tangible assets that are estimated to have a current market value of $1,100,000. The amount of goodwill is calculated as follows:

Total purchase price ($500,000 cash + $1,000,000 stock).		$1,500,000
Less:		
Cash acquired............................	$ 50,000	
Accounts receivable.......................	60,000	
Other tangible assets (estimated)..............	1,100,000	1,210,000
Goodwill.............................		$ 290,000

As can be seen from the above example, goodwill is a residual, and its amount is influenced by estimates both of the consideration given for the purchase and of the value of the tangible assets. This topic is discussed further in Chapter 10.

Amortization of Intangibles

The cost of an intangible asset is amortized over its service life. The FASB requires that amortization be on a straight-line basis. If the useful life is limited by laws or agreement (e.g., 17 years for a patent) the service life cannot be longer than this period, and it may be shorter if the company believes that because of obsolescence, technological advances or other reasons, the real service life will be shorter than the legal life.

Some intangibles, particularly goodwill, have no determinable service life. For these the company selects a period over which the cost must be written off. This period cannot exceed 40 years.[15] Some intangibles, such as the cost of organizing a company, are usually written off over a much shorter period, such as five years or ten years; or they may be charged as an expense of the first year in which revenue is earned since they are not usually material enough in amount to warrant taking the trouble to capitalize and then amortize them. For income tax purposes, however, goodwill and other intangible assets that do not have a determinable service life cannot be amortized at all.

The amount of annual amortization is ordinarily credited directly to the asset account, rather than being accumulated in a separate contra account as is the case with accumulated depreciation.

Leasehold improvements are the costs incurred by the lessee to im-

---

[15] See APB *Opinion No. 17* (August 1970) par. 29.

prove leased property. Since, as a matter of law, any remaining value of these improvements reverts to the owner when the leased property is given up, the benefits to the lessee automatically end when he gives up the leased property, and the cost must therefore be written off over the time he expects to have the use of the property.

Deferred Charges

In a broad sense, deferred charges are assets which will be charged against revenue in future accounting periods. In this sense, any asset subject to depreciation, depletion, or amortization is a deferred charge. By custom, however, the term deferred charge is usually restricted to long-lived, intangible assets. Goodwill is literally a deferred charge but is usually reported separately from other deferred charges if material in amount.

Intangible assets that will be charged against revenue in the next accounting period are called *prepaid expenses* and, if material in amount, are reported as current assets. The line between prepaid expenses and deferred charges is usually not drawn precisely. Some companies report "deferred charges and prepaid expenses" as a single item, which is a noncurrent asset.

Research and Development Costs

Research and development costs are costs incurred for the purpose of developing new or improved goods, processes, or services. The fruits of research and development efforts are increased revenues or lower costs. Since these fruits will not be picked until future periods, often five years or more after a research project is started, a good case can be made for capitalizing research and development costs and amortizing them over the periods benefited. This practice was common at one time, but the FASB no longer permits it. Instead, it requires that research and development costs be charged off as an expense of the current period.

The reason for the FASB standard is that by their very nature, the benefits to be derived in the future from research and development efforts are highly uncertain. One study concludes that "of all the dollars of new product expense, almost three-fourths go to unsuccessful products."[16] The efforts which are eventually unsuccessful cannot be identified in advance; otherwise, they would not have been undertaken. Although near the end of the development stage, the success of certain projects seems reasonably assured, the FASB has concluded that there is no objective way of distinguishing between these projects and the

[16] Booz-Allen & Hamilton, Inc. *Management of New Products* (Chicago: Booz-Allen & Hamilton, Inc., 1968) p. 12.

unsuccessful ones. The concept of conservatism therefore dictates that all research and development costs be expensed.

If one company does research and development work for another company and is paid for this work, these payments constitute revenue, and the related costs are held as an asset in Work in Process Inventory. They are matched against revenue and therefore are charged as expenses in the period in which the revenue is earned.

Investments

The stocks and bonds that a company owns are regarded as being in a separate category from the intangibles described above. They are initially recorded at cost. They are not amortized by charging a fraction of the cost as an expense of future periods, because their service potential presumably does not expire with the passage of time. Instead, they are held as an asset until they are sold. The accounting treatment of these investments will be discussed further in Chapter 10.

SUMMARY

Tangible fixed assets are recorded at their acquisition cost, which includes all elements of cost involved in making them ready to provide service. A portion of this cost (less residual value, if any) is charged as depreciation expense to each of the accounting periods in which the asset is expected to provide service. Any systematic and rational method may be used for this purpose. The straight-line or units-of-production method is ordinarily used for financial accounting purposes, but an accelerated method is ordinarily used for income tax purposes. A corresponding reduction is made each year in the net book value of the asset account.

When an asset is disposed of, its cost and accumulated depreciation are removed from the accounts, and any gain or loss appears on the income statement.

Intangible assets are also recorded at cost. In the case of goodwill, this cost is the difference between the price paid for a company and the fair market value of the tangible assets acquired; it is therefore derived from estimates of the value of other assets, rather than being estimated directly. If intangible assets have a determinable service life, their cost is amortized over that life. For assets with no determinable service life, the amortization period must not exceed 40 years.

CASES

CASE 7-1. PALMER CORPORATION (B)

After the controller of the Palmer Corporation had ascertained the changes in accounts receivable and the allowance for doubtful accounts in 1974, he made a similar analysis of fixed assets and accumulated depreciation. Again he examined the December 31, 1973, balance sheet [Exhibit 1 in Palmer Corporation (A), p. 142]. He also reviewed the following transactions which he found to be applicable to these accounts:

1. On January 2, 1974, one of the factory machines was sold for its book value, $1,964. This machine was recorded on the books at $15,865 with accumulated depreciation of $13,901.
2. Tools were carried on the books at cost, and at the end of each year a physical inventory was taken to determine what tools still remained. The account was written down to the extent of the decrease in tools as ascertained by the year-end inventory. At the end of 1974, it was determined that there had been a decrease in the tool inventory amounting to $3,988.
3. On March 1, 1974, the company sold for $831 cash an automobile which was recorded on the books at a cost of $2,970 and had an accumulated depreciation of $1,842 as of January 1, 1974. In this and other cases of sale of fixed assets during the year, the accumulated depreciation and depreciation expense items were both increased by an amount which reflected the depreciation chargeable for the months in 1974 in which the asset was held prior to the sale, at rates listed in Item 7 below.
4. The patent listed on the balance sheet had been purchased by the Palmer Corporation on December 31, 1967, for $50,000. This patent had been granted on December 31, 1965. The cost of the patent was to be written off as an expense over the remainder of its legal life. (The legal life of a patent is 17 years from the date granted.)
5. On July 1, 1974, a typewriter which had cost $457 and had been fully depreciated on December 31, 1973, was sold for $35.

216

6. On October 1, the company sold a desk for $40. This piece of furniture was recorded on the books at a cost of $239 with an accumulated depreciation of $194 as of January 1, 1974.

7. Depreciation on fixed assets was figured as follows:

Buildings... 2%
Factory machinery.................................... 10*
Furniture and fixtures................................ 10
Automotive equipment................................ 20
Office machines...................................... 10

* Included in the factory machinery cost of $1,826,979 was a machine costing $41,602 which had been fully depreciated on December 31, 1973, and which was still in use.

Questions

1. Analyze the effect of each of these transactions upon the fixed asset accounts, accumulated depreciation, and any other accounts which may be involved in a manner similar to that used in Palmer Corporation (A), and prepare journal entries.
2. Give the correct totals for the fixed assets and the amount of accumulated depreciation as of December 31, 1974, after the transactions affecting them had been recorded.

CASE 7–2. PROBLEMS IN CAPITALIZATION

The brief descriptions presented below are representative of types of problems in which it is necessary to determine whether given expenditures should be accounted for as assets (i.e., be capitalized) or as expenses:

1. The Bruce Manufacturing Company used its own maintenance crew to build an additional wing on its existing factory building. Questions arose as to the proper accounting treatment of the following items:

a. Architects' fees.
b. The cost of snow removal during construction.
c. Cash discounts earned for prompt payment on materials purchased for construction.
d. The cost of building a combined construction office and tool shed which would be torn down once the factory wing had been completed.
e. Interest on money borrowed to finance construction.
f. Local real estate taxes for the period of construction on the portion of land to be occupied by the new wing.
g. The cost of mistakes made during construction.

b. The overhead costs of the maintenance department which include: supervision; depreciation on buildings and equipment of maintenance department shops; heat, light, and power for these shops; and allocations of cost for such items as the cafeteria, medical office, and personnel department.

i. The cost of insurance during construction, and the cost of damages or losses on any injuries or losses not covered by insurance.

2. The Archer Company bought a large piece of land, including the buildings thereon, with the intent of razing the buildings and constructing a combined hotel and office building in their place. The existing buildings consisted of a theater and several stores and small apartment buildings, all in active use at the time of the purchase.

a. What accounting treatment should be accorded that portion of the purchase price considered to be the amount paid for the buildings which were subsequently razed?

b. How should the costs of demolishing the old buildings be treated?

c. Suppose that a single company had owned this large piece of land, including the buildings thereon, and instead of selling to the Archer Company had decided to have the buildings razed and to have a combined hotel and office building constructed on the site for its own benefit. In what respects, if any, should the accounting treatment of the old buildings and the cost of demolishing them differ from your recommendations with respect to (*a*) and (*b*) above?

3. The Midland Manufacturing Company purchased a new machine. It is clear that the invoice price of the new machine should be capitalized and it also seems reasonable to capitalize the transportation cost to bring the machine to the Midland plant. Questions have arisen, however, on the following items:

a. The new machine is heavier than the old machine it replaced; consequently the foundation under the machine has had to be strengthened by the installation of additional steel beams. Should this cost be charged to the building, added to the cost of the machine, or be expensed?

b. The installation of the machine took longer and was more costly than anticipated. In addition to time spent by the regular maintenance crew on installation, it became necessary to hire an outside engineer to assist in the installation and in "working out the bugs" to get the machine running properly. His costs included not only his fee but also his transportation, hotel expense, and meals. Moreover, the foreman of the department and the plant superintendent both spent a considerable amount of time assisting in the installation work.

Before the new machine was working properly a large amount of material had been spoiled during trial runs.

c. In addition to the invoice price and transportation, it was necessary to pay a state sales tax on purchasing the machine.

d. In connection with payment for the new machine the machine manufacturer was willing to accept the Midland Company's old machine as partial payment. The amount allowed as a trade-in was larger than the depreciated value at which the old machine was being carried in the books of the Midland Company. Should the difference have been treated as a reduction in the cost of the new machine or a gain on disposal of the old one?

CASE 7–3. MASSASOIT TRUST COMPANY

The Massasoit Trust Company conducted a commercial banking business in a city of approximately 100,000. The company did not own its banking quarters but operated under a lease which still had six years to run in 1968. While the lease contained no renewal provisions, the bank had occupied the building since 1905 under successive 10-year leases. Relations with the owner of the building, who was also the operator of a nearby department store, continued to be cordial. The lease provided, however, that the owner could cancel the lease on two years' notice if he required the property for his own business.

In the spring of 1968, the directors of the bank were considering a proposal to remodel and air condition the bank quarters. The bank had received firm bids from contractors on the work to be done, and these totaled approximately $63,000.

In the course of the discussion, a debate arose over the way in which the expenditure would be carried in the bank's books. One of the directors favored carrying the improvement as an asset and depreciating it over its physical life, which he estimated at about 25 years.

Several directors objected to this procedure. Under the so-called "rule of fixtures," which was a well-established legal principle, permanent improvements to leased property were generally considered to be the property of the owner of the real estate. Since the bank did not own the property, these directors did not think the improvements should be considered as an asset. They favored charging the entire cost of the improvements as an expense in the current year, which had been the procedure with minor renovation expenses in the past.

Other directors felt that capitalizing the expenditure would be acceptable, but they did not think it wise to adopt a depreciation period longer than the life of the lease. They also wondered what consideration should be given to the two-year cancellation provision.

The first director was not convinced by either of these approaches. He said he would not favor the remodeling project were he not convinced that the lease would be renewed as it had been in the past. He was also disturbed about the effect that a rapid write-off might have on the bank's earnings.

Section 178 (c) of the Internal Revenue Code provides that for income tax purposes, as a general rule, improvements made to leased assets should be amortized over either the remaining life of the lease or the life of the improvement, whichever is shorter. If, however, upon completion of the improvement, the remaining life of the lease is less than 60 percent of the useful life of the improvement, it is ordinarily presumed that the lease will be renewed, and this longer life will determine the amortization period.

Exhibit 1

MASSASOIT TRUST COMPANY

Statement of Condition, December 31, 1967
(thousands of dollars)

RESOURCES

Cash on hand and in banks	$ 2,464
U.S. government securities	6,886
Other securities	275
Loans and discounts	2,587
Other assets	42
	$12,254

LIABILITIES

Commercial deposits		$ 8,667
Savings deposits		2,402
Total deposits		$11,069
Reserve for taxes, etc.		61
Capital stock	$350	
Surplus	774	1,124
		$12,254

In 1967, the Massasoit Trust Company had a gross revenue of $285,000, including $205,000 in income from loans, discounts, and investments in securities. After operating expenses, but before income taxes, earnings were approximately $70,000. Federal income taxes amounted to about $20,000. The operating expenses were largely of a fixed nature.

The bank's statement of condition as of December 31, 1967, is given in Exhibit 1. According to the state banking law, trust companies could accept deposits of up to 10 times the amount of their capital and surplus. The law also required 15 percent of deposits to be maintained as a liquid reserve; the balance could be used for loans, discounts, and investments in United States government and other securities. The bank was not permitted to loan an amount greater than 20 percent of its capital stock and surplus to any one individual or firm.

Questions

1. Why should the directors be concerned about this problem?
2. What action do you recommend?

CASE 7–4. BRAZOS PRINTING COMPANY

The Brazos Printing Company was founded in 1950 as a one-man job printing firm in a small southwestern town. Shortly after its founding, the owner decided to concentrate on one specialty line of printing. Because of a high degree of technical proficiency, the company experienced a rapid growth.

Exhibit 1

BRAZOS PRINTING COMPANY

Condensed Balance Sheet as of March 31, 1972

ASSETS			EQUITIES	
Current Assets:				
Cash.................		$143.660	Current liabilities........	$ 56,022
Other current assets.....		88,038	Common stock...........	154,000
Total Current Assets		$231,698	Retained earnings.........	116,506
Fixed Assets:				
Land.................		11,900		
Buildings.............	$122,400			
Less: Accumulated depreciation.........	69,600	52,800		
Equipment.............	$ 92,690			
Less: Accumulated depreciation.........	62,560	30,130		
Total Assets...		$326,528	Total Equities.......	$326,528

However, the company suffered from a competitive disadvantage in that the major market for its specialized output was in a metropolitan area over 300 miles away from the company's plant. For this reason, the owner, in 1972, decided to move nearer his primary market. He also decided to expand and modernize his facilities at the time of the move. After some investigation, an attractive site was found in a suburb of his primary market, and the move was made.

A balance sheet prepared prior to the move is shown in Exhibit 1. The transactions that arose from this move are described in the following paragraphs:

1. The land at the old site together with the building thereon was sold for $52,400. The land had originally cost $11,900. The building appeared on the company's books at a cost of $122,400, and a depreciation allowance of $69,600 had been accumulated on it.

2. Certain equipment was sold for $7,000 cash. This equipment appeared on the books at a cost of $25,500 less accumulated depreciation of $14,300.

3. A new printing press was purchased. The invoice cost of this equipment was $28,000. A 2 percent cash discount was taken by the Brazos Company, so that only $27,440 was actually paid to the seller. The Brazos Company also paid $112 to a trucker to have this equipment delivered. Installation of this equipment was made by Brazos workmen who worked a total of 60 hours. These men received $3.50 per hour in wages, but their time was ordinarily charged to printing jobs at $7 per hour, the difference representing an allowance for overhead ($2.80) and profit ($0.70).

4. The city to which the company moved furnished the land on which the new plant was built as a gift. The land had an appraised value of $35,000. The appraisal had been made recently by a qualified appraiser. The company would pay property taxes on its assessed value, which was $22,400.

5. The Brazos Company paid $5,300 to have an old building on the gift plot of land torn down. (The value of this building was not included in the appraised or assessed values named above.) In addition, the company paid $3,400 to have permanent drainage facilities installed on the new land.

6. A new strip caster with an invoice cost of $7,000 was purchased. The company paid $4,500 cash and received a trade-in allowance of $2,500 on a used strip caster. The used strip caster could have been sold outright for not more than $2,100. It had cost $4,200 new, and accumulated depreciation on it was $1,800.

7. The company erected a building at the new site for $140,000. Of this amount, $105,000 was borrowed on a mortgage.

8. After the equipment had been moved to the new plant, but before operations began there, extensive repairs and replacements of parts were made on a large paper cutter. The cost of this work was $1,400. Prior to this time, no more than $140 had been spent in any one year on the maintenance of this paper cutter.

9. Trucking and other costs associated with moving equipment to the new location and installing it were $2,100. In addition, Brazos Company employees worked an estimated 125 hours on that part of the move that related to equipment.

10. During the moving operation, a piece of equipment costing $3,500 was dropped and damaged; $700 was spent to repair it. The management

believed, however, that the salvage value of this equipment had been reduced to $350. Up until that time, the equipment was being depreciated at $280 per year, representing a 10 percent rate after deduction of estimated salvage of $700. Accumulated depreciation was $1,120.

Question

Analyze the effect of these transactions on the items in the balance sheet and income statement. For transactions that affect owners' equity, distinguish between those that affect the net income of the current year and those that do not. In most cases, the results of your analysis can be set forth most clearly in the form of journal entries.

CASE 7–5.   UNITED STATES STEEL CORPORATION

United States Steel Corporation is the nation's largest steel producer. This case is concerned with U.S. Steel's depreciation accounting policies and treatment of the investment credit between 1946 and 1973.

The 1947 Change

For several years prior to 1947 the management of United States Steel Corporation had been concerned with the effects upon the company's asset replacement program of the steady rise in the general price level since the late 1930s. This concern arose chiefly from the realization that expenses for depreciation of plant and equipment were not sufficient to provide for the replacement of such facilities when they were worn out or became obsolete.

As a step toward stating depreciation in an amount which would reflect in current dollars of diminished buying power the same purchasing power represented by the original plant expenditure, the company deducted, in arriving at net income for 1947, an amount of $26.3 million over and above its regular depreciation charge (based on the straight-line method.) Although the federal tax authorities would not allow the extra depreciation as a deduction in arriving at taxable income, the company's executives considered it essential that they recognize this element of cost in arriving at a measure of income to be used in other matters of company management.

In its 1947 annual report the management stated that "while awaiting accounting and tax acceptance, U.S. Steel believed that it was prudent for it to give some recognition to increased replacement costs rather than to sit idly by and witness the unwitting liquidation of its business should inadequate recording of costs result in insufficient resources to supply the tools required for sustained production."

In its opinion on the 1947 financial statements, the company's independent auditors stated that the corporation had included in costs additional depreciation of $26.3 million "in excess of the amount determined in accordance with the generally accepted accounting principle heretofore followed of making provision for depreciation on the original cost of facilities."

Carman G. Blough, director of research of the American Institute of Certified Public Accountants, commented on this practice as follows:

> There can be no argument but that a going concern must be able to replace its productive assets as they are used up if it is to continue to do business. It is also important for management to understand that the difference between cost and estimated replacement value may be significant in determining production and pricing policies. It does not follow, however, that the excess of the cost of replacement over the cost of existing assets should be accounted for as current charges to income. All who have dealt with appraisal values know how very difficult it is just to determine current replacement costs, but the most striking difficulty in this respect is the impossibility of predicting what will be the eventual cost of replacing a productive asset. How many men are prepared to state what the price level will be two years from today, to say nothing of trying to guess what it will be five or ten years hence when many of those assets are to be replaced.[1]

Similarly, the AICPA stated in 1947 that it "disapproves immediate write-downs of plant costs by charges against current income in amounts believed to represent excessive or abnormal costs occasioned by current price levels."[2]

The 1948 Retreat

In its annual report for 1948, U.S. Steel announced that it was abandoning the policy adopted in 1947 and was substituting in its place a method of charging "accelerated depreciation on cost," which was explained as follows:

> The accelerated depreciation is applicable to the cost of postwar facilities in the first few years of their lives when economic usefulness is greatest. The amount thereof is related to the excess of current operating rates over U.S. Steel's long-term peacetime average rate of 70% of capacity. The annual accelerated amount is 10% of the cost of facilities in the year in which the expenditures are made and 10% in the succeeding year, except that this amount is reduced ratably as the operating rate may drop, no acceleration being made at 70% or lower operations. The accelerated depreciation is an

---

[1] "Replacement and Excess Construction Costs," *Journal of Accountancy*, Vol. 74 (October, 1947), p. 335.

[2] *Accounting Research Bulletin No. 43*, Chapter 9, paragraph 9.

addition to the normal depreciation on such facilities, but the total depreciation over their expected lives will not exceed the cost of the facilities.

This method was made retroactive to January 1, 1947, and there was included in the $55,335,444 deducted for accelerated wear and exhaustion of facilities for 1948 an amount of $2,675,094 to cover a deficiency in the $26,300,000 sum reported in 1947 as "depreciation added to cover replacement cost." In other words, the new method when applied to the 1947 situation resulted in a deduction that exceeded the figure actually reported in 1947. It was again pointed out at this time that the accelerated depreciation was not "presently deductible for federal income tax purposes." The company's independent auditors stated in their report to the shareholders for 1948 that they "approved" the new policy.

Management's convictions on the change in policy were clearly set forth by the chairman of the board of directors in the following quotation from the company's annual report for 1948:

U.S. Steel believes that the principle which it adopted in 1947 and continued in 1948 is a proper recording of the wear and exhaustion of its facilities in terms of current dollars as distinguished from the dollars which it originally expended for those facilities. However, in view of the disagreement existing among accountants, both public and private, and the stated position of the American Institute of Certified Public Accountants, which is supported by the Securities and Exchange Commission, that the only accepted accounting principle for determining depreciation is that which is related to the actual number of dollars spent for facilities, regardless of when or what buying power, U.S. Steel has adopted a method of accelerated depreciation based on cost instead of one based on purchasing power recovery.

The 1953 Change

United States Steel Corporation continued its policy of charging accelerated depreciation through 1952. Deductions for accelerated depreciation for 1947 through 1952 totaled slightly more than $201 million; none of this sum, however, had been allowed in computing taxable income during that period.

During and after the Korean War, U.S. Steel was granted Certificates of Necessity which permitted amortization of designated facilities over a 60-month period for tax purposes regardless of the facilities' probable economic life. Management decided to depreciate these facilities in the corporate accounts over the 60-month period.

In 1953, U.S. Steel changed its accelerated depreciation policy, as explained in this note to the 1953 financial statements:

Since 1946 U.S. Steel has followed the policy of reflecting accelerated depreciation on the cost of new facilities in the first few years of their lives when the economic usefulness is greatest. The amounts charged to income for accelerated depreciation have been related to U.S. Steel's rate of operations.

Under the Internal Revenue Code, that portion of the cost of facilities certified by the Defense Production Administration as essential to the defense effort is covered by a Certificate of Necessity and can be written off for tax purposes at the rate of 20% per year. The effect of amortization of these facilities is to charge to income a greater portion of their cost in the earlier years of life, and therefore, follows the principle of accelerated depreciation.

U.S. Steel has included in wear and exhaustion in 1953, as a measure of the accelerated depreciation for the year, $105,137,893, representing amortization on its facilities covered by Certificates of Necessity.

In commenting on the effect of accelerated amortization and the tax laws, management pointed out that it had to be regarded as a temporary expedient, since "for many companies the addition of amortization on new facilities to so-called regular depreciation on old facilities may approximate, temporarily, a truer total of wear and exhaustion on all facilities based on current dollar value. But it automatically guarantees something of a future crisis." As an example of this, management cited the recently constructed Fairless Works. A portion of this plant's cost was amortized over five years, thus partially offsetting "inadequate" depreciation charges for other facilities. It was stated that this situation would naturally change when the five-year amortization was completed.

Management noted in 1954 that the new methods of accelerated depreciation, first allowed for tax purposes in 1954, would ease the future crisis, but even these provisions, applicable to new assets only, would fall far short of providing adequate depreciation on the relatively more numerous and older existing facilities.

The 1956 Chart

In its 1956 report, U.S. Steel included a chart (see Exhibit 1) comparing "wear and exhaustion recorded" with "wear and exhaustion needed." To calculate "total wear and exhaustion needed," as shown in the chart, the following statistical procedure was followed: Excluding the amount of nontax-deductible accelerated depreciation from 1947 through 1952 (see Exhibit 1), and including only regular depreciation on emergency facilities, the amount of wear and exhaustion previously recorded for *each year* included in the chart was subdivided according to the acquisition years of the assets being depreciated. Each yearly subdivision was then adjusted to reflect the change in the *Engineering News-Record*'s index of construction cost from the various earlier acquisition years to any given year included in the chart. The sum of that year's adjusted depreciation amounts gave the "total wear and exhaustion needed" for that year. The process was repeated for every year in the chart. Notice that each year's deficiency is in dollars of the buying power that prevailed in *that* year.

Exhibit 1

WEAR AND EXHAUSTION RECORDED VERSUS WEAR AND EXHAUSTION NEEDED

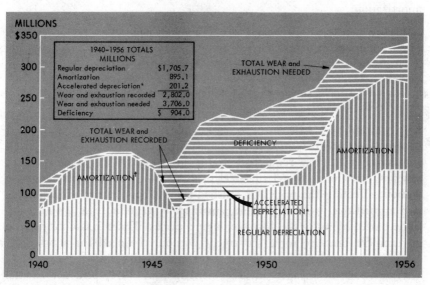

* Not deductible for tax purposes.
† Additional amortization due to ending of emergency period allocated to years 1941–1945.

INFLATION IN COST OF FACILITIES*

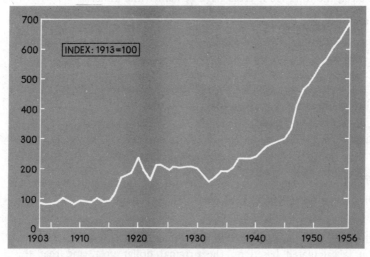

* From *Engineering News-Record* Construction Cost Index.

SOURCE: *United States Steel Corporation Annual Report*, 1956. Used by permission.

The 1959 Strike

In 1959, management noted the approaching exhaustion of emergency amortization:

This (depreciation) deficiency has been aggravated by the running out of 5-year amortization permitted on varying percentages of the total costs of certain defense and defense-supporting facilities covered by Certificates of Necessity. The need for revision of the tax laws as they relate to depreciation . . . continues to be most vital to the maintenance of existing and the addition of new productive capacity.

In the spring of 1959, the representatives of the United Steelworkers of America and the major steel companies met to negotiate a new wage contract. The union requested sizable increases in wages and fringe benefits, contending that large steel profits would permit these increases without affecting the prices of finished steel. The steel industry spokesmen argued this was not possible; any *sizable* wage increase would have to be passed along in the form of higher prices. There was considerable government pressure for a settlement without the need for a price increase in order to avoid the threat of further inflation.

A full-page newspaper advertisement in May 1959, paid for by the union, read in part:

STEELWORKERS SHARE OF
STEEL INDUSTRY'S INCOME HAS
NOT INCREASED SINCE 1952

True, there have been wage increases, but because fewer men are making more steel, the total labor costs have remained the same.

Please examine these LABOR COSTS:

1952 . . . . 42.1 ¢ of each sales dollar
1958 . . . . 42.8 ¢ of each sales dollar

(notice they are about the same)

Now examine the NET PROFITS:

1952 . . . . $143,678,740
1958   301,558,231

(profits have DOUBLED)

A nationwide steel strike lasted from July until mid-November.

On December 8, 1959, J. S. Seidman, president of the AICPA, released to the press a statement explaining the issues in the steel strike:

The industry's contention was that under conventional accounting, depreciation is calculated based on the original dollar cost, and that this is inadequate because it fails to give effect to the tremendous change that has taken place in the purchasing power of the dollar, as a result of which it would cost many more dollars today to replace the plant than were originally spent. The industry maintains that realistic profits should be figured by reference to replacement figures. On that basis, the industry's profits are one half of what the financial statements show.

The labor officials contend that original cost is all that should be recovered, and that anything in excess of that is profit. Furthermore, they say that the original cost should be spread over the expected period in which the plant will be used. However, the companies have been following the tax laws in the way they write off depreciation, and the tax laws have allowed a higher write-off to be bunched in early years and counterbalanced by a lower write-off in later years. The figures presented by the steel industry cover the earlier years where there is the higher write-off. The labor people say that the depreciation amounts should be reduced by this excess write-off in the early years. Reducing the depreciation would result in an increase in profits.

. . . All of this raises a question as to whether the conventional accounting use of historical dollars is meaningful in an inflationary period.

Investment Credit

By 1962, the inflationary pressures on the economy had diminished. Also in 1962, U.S. Steel benefited from two changes in the system of federal income taxation: adoption of the new guideline procedures for depreciation lives set forth in Revenue Ruling 62–21 added $44 million to the wear and exhaustion amounts previously determined; and the use of the investment tax credit resulted in a $8.2 million reduction in federal income taxes.

The investment tax credit provided by the Revenue Act of 1962 was intended to stimulate capital investment. It allowed a credit directly against the company's federal income tax liability of 7 percent of the cost of "qualified" depreciable property. However, rather than treating this in its published financial statements as a reduction in 1962 income tax expense ("flow through" method), U.S. Steel spread the reduced taxes over the lives of the assets which qualified for the 7 percent credit ("deferral" method).

1968 Changes

During 1968, economic pressure increased on companies within the steel industry. The contract with the United Steelworkers was due to terminate and there was a widespread expectation that a strike would be called on August 1. As a result, steel users stockpiled inventories heavily. The high volume of orders during the first half of the year resulted in capacity operations by steel mills, including the use of less efficient, marginal production equipment. In addition, foreign imports of steel had increased substantially during the first half of 1968. To meet the stiff price competition, many domestic producers engaged in price "discounting" to customers despite general acceptance of standard prices by the industry.

The labor dispute was settled without a strike on July 30. Production fell sharply as customers reduced excess inventories. It was anticipated that the normal ordering pattern would not be resumed until January 1969.

Under these conditions third quarter earnings were sharply reduced. U.S. Steel's 1968 third quarter profits fell 70 percent below those of the corresponding quarter of 1967. Bethlehem Steel Corporation reported a decline of 0.6 percent, Republic Steel 31 percent, National 21 percent, Jones and Laughlin 86 percent, and Youngstown Sheet and Tube 57 percent. Only Armco Steel and Inland reported profit increases over the previous year.

The effect of the profit decline would have been more severe, except that many of the companies switched from accelerated to straight-line depreciation in the third quarter. The exact method of change varied among the steelmakers: some applied the change only to equipment purchased after 1967, others applied it to all depreciable property on hand. Several companies also switched from deferring to flowing through their investment tax credits.

Despite these changes, U.S. Steel continued to follow its policies of accelerated depreciation and deferral of the investment tax credit through the first three quarters of 1968. However, when the 1968 annual report was issued, it contained this statement:

During 1968, a number of [steel] companies announced a change in their method of determining depreciation for financial reporting purposes whereby depreciation for the year is reported on a straight-line basis rather than on the accelerated basis previously used. . . . [In 1962] U.S. Steel adopted the accounting method by which it deferred this [investment tax] credit over the lives of the properties acquired. All other major steel companies now flow the full investment credit to income as realized.

U.S. Steel considered the procedures it previously followed in connection with depreciation and the investment credit to be preferable to other methods in the reporting of results of operations. However, to enhance the comparability of financial statements in the steel industry and to bring depreciation and investment credit accounting policies more in line with methods followed by U.S. businesses in general, U.S. Steel, for financial reporting purposes, revised the lives of certain properties and changed its methods of recording depreciation and investment credit for the year 1968 to a straight-line basis and a flow-through basis, respectively. The effect of these changes was to increase reported income for the year 1968 by $94.0 million or $1.74 per share of common stock.

U.S. Steel has continued with these policies through 1973. Certain financial data for 1946–73 are shown in Exhibit 2.

Exhibit 2

U.S. STEEL CORPORATION

Selected Financial Statistics 1946–1973
(millions of dollars, except earnings per share)

Year	Net Income	Earnings per Share*	Depreciation	Capital Expenditures	Investment Tax Credit Taken	Amortization of Emergency Facilities
1973	$325.8	$6.01	$358.0	$435.8	$30.3	—
1972	157.0	2.90	326.6	412.8	23.5	—
1971	154.5	2.85	290.1	452.0	23.5	—
1970	147.5	2.72	296.5	514.5	31.1	—
1969	217.2	4.01	289.6	601.8	35.3	—
1968	253.7	4.69	253.1	697.4	38.6	—
1967	172.5	3.19	354.7	574.7	33.4	—
1966	249.2	4.60	344.3	440.7	20.8	—
1965	275.5	4.62	324.5	353.6	13.7	—
1964	236.8	3.91	335.8	292.6	.6	—
1963	203.5	3.30	307.8	244.7	.6 (est.)	—
1962	163.7	2.56	265.9	200.6	.4 (est.)	—
1961	190.2	3.05	210.5	326.8	—	—
1960	304.2	5.16	208.4	492.4	—	$ 13.7
1959	254.5	4.25	189.9	366.1	—	22.2
1958	301.5	5.13	204.9	448.1	—	57.2
1957	419.4	7.33	276.0	514.9	—	115.8
1956	348.1	6.01	277.6	311.8	—	140.2
1955	370.1	6.44	285.2	239.8	—	147.7
1954	195.4	3.23	261.8	227.4	—	142.8
1953	222.1	3.77	236.6	361.4	—	105.1
1952	143.6	2.27	176.9	469.2	—	46.2
1951	184.3	3.05	162.1	352.4	—	12.8
1950	215.5	3.64	143.9	179.3	—	—
1949	165.9	2.69	119.7	179.1	—	—
1948	129.6	2.00	146.0	275.2	—	—
1947	127.1	1.95	114.0	206.6	—	—
1946	88.6	1.21	68.7	201.0	—	—

* As originally reported, adjusted to reflect 3 for 1 stock split in 1949 and 2 for 1 split in 1955.

Questions

1. Do you agree with U.S. Steel's handling of depreciation in its 1947 report? Should a company be prohibited from using such a method if in its own best judgment this is the best method?
2. Do you agree with the nature and timing of the subsequent changes in depreciation method?
3. Do you agree that in 1968 U.S. Steel should have changed from depreciation and investment tax credit accounting methods that it considered "preferable to other methods" in order to be comparable with their competitors' methods? Were any of the steel companies justified in making these changes in 1968?
4. Once having adopted an accounting practice, under what circumstances should a company be permitted to change it?

CHAPTER 8

OTHER EXPENSES AND NET INCOME

In the preceding chapters, we have discussed the accounting treatment of most of the items that affect net income. In this chapter we discuss the remaining items. Topics include personnel costs, income tax allocations, foreign currency adjustments, extraordinary items, and discontinued operations.

This chapter also describes price level adjustments and the method called direct costing. Although neither of these practices is currently used in the measurement of net income, an understanding of them helps in appraising the significance of the amount reported as net income under currently accepted accounting principles.

PERSONNEL COSTS

Personnel costs include wages and salaries earned by employees, and other costs that are related to the services furnished by employees. As a matter of custom, the word "wages" usually refers to the compensation of employees who are on a piece-rate, hourly, daily, or weekly basis; while the word "salaries" usually refers to compensation expressed in monthly, or longer, terms. Alternatively, the word "wages" may be related to employees who must be paid overtime when they work more than 40 hours in a week, as required by the Fair Labor Standards Act, and the word "salaries" may be related to employees who are exempt from this provision. (The latter are called *exempt* employees.)

Payroll Transactions

The effect on the accounting records of earning and paying wages and salaries is more complicated than merely debiting expenses and crediting cash, for when wages and salaries are earned or paid, certain other transactions occur almost automatically.

An employee is rarely paid the gross amount of wages or salary he earns, since from his gross earnings there must be deducted:

1. An amount representing his contribution under the Federal Insurance Contribution Act (F.I.C.A.), which in 1974 was 5.85 percent of the first $13,200 of wages or salary earned each year.
2. The withholding deduction, which is an account withheld from gross earnings to apply toward his income tax.
3. Deductions for pension contributions, savings plans, health insurance, union dues, and a variety of other items.

None of these deductions represents a cost to the business. In the case of the tax deductions, the business is acting as a collection agent for the government; the withholding of these amounts and their subsequent transfer to the government does not affect net income or owners' equity. Rather, the withholding creates a liability, and the subsequent transfer to the government pays off this liability. Similarly, the business is acting as a collection agent in the case of the other deductions. The employee is paid the net amount after these deductions have been taken.

When wages and salaries are earned, other costs are automatically created. The employer must pay a tax equal in amount to the employee's F.I.C.A. tax, and the employer must also pay an additional percentage of the employee's pay (the rate varies in different states) for the *unemployment insurance tax*. Collectively, F.I.C.A. and unemployment insurance are called *social security taxes*. The *employer's* share of these taxes *is* an element of cost.

Thus, if an employee with three dependents earns $150 for his work in a given week in 1974, there would be deducted from his pay $8.78 F.I.C.A. tax contribution and $15.60 for withholding tax, and he would receive the balance, $125.62. This is his "take-home pay." (Other possible deductions are omitted for purposes of simplification.) The *business* would incur an expense of $8.78 for F.I.C.A. and an additional expense of, say, $6.00 for the federal and state unemployment insurance taxes, or a total of $14.78 for the two social security taxes.

The journal entries for these transactions are as follows:

1. When wages are earned, wages expense:

```
Wages Expense.............................. 150.00
    Wages Payable..........................        150.00
```

2. When wages are earned; business tax expense:[1]

```
Social Security Tax Expense.................... 14.78
    F.I.C.A. Taxes Payable.....................        8.78
    Unemployment Taxes Payable.................        6.00
```

3. When the employee is paid:

```
Wages Payable.............................. 150.00
    Cash...................................        125.62
    F.I.C.A. Taxes Payable.................          8.78
    Withholding Taxes Payable..............         15.60
```

4. When the government is paid:

```
F.I.C.A. Taxes Payable........................ 17.56
Unemployment Taxes Payable....................  6.00
Withholding Taxes Payable.................... 15.60
    Cash......................................        39.16
```

In practice, the above entries would be made for all employees as a group rather than separately for each person. The government does require, however, that a record be kept of the amount of F.I.C.A. tax and withholding tax accumulated for each employee, and that the employee be furnished a copy of this record.

As emphasized in Chapter 6, any item of cost may be a product cost or a period cost depending on whether the item is or is not involved in the manufacturing process. This is the case with personnel costs. The costs of employees involved in the manufacturing process are product costs and are first charged to Goods in Process Inventory. The costs of other employees are period costs and are an expense of the period in which the employees work.

Pensions

The above transactions, although complicated, involve no new problem in the application of accounting principles. One matter related to wages does involve a very difficult problem. This is the liability and related expense for pensions.

About 30 million Americans work for companies that agree to pay them pensions when they retire. All or part of the cost of these pensions is borne by the company; the remainder, if any, comes from contributions made by employees. Accounting for the company's cost for pensions is a particularly difficult matter because the expense is incurred

---

[1] This entry matches the tax expense with wages *earned* in the period, which is in principle the correct treatment. Some businesses compute the tax as of the period in which the wages are *paid*, on the grounds that this involves a much simpler calculation and that there is no material difference between the results of the two methods.

during the years in which the employee works for the company, but the payments to him are made at some distant future time, and the total amount of the payment is uncertain, depending on how long he lives, on his final wage or salary, and possibly on other considerations.

The pension plans of many companies are *funded;* that is, an estimate is made of the amount that will be necessary to meet the future pension payments arising out of the employees' earnings in the current year, and this amount is either set aside in a trust fund or paid to an outside agency that guarantees to make the future pension payments. The amount paid into such a fund is a deductible expense for income tax purposes, provided certain other conditions are met, and is usually treated as an expense of the current year for financial accounting purposes. If the company retains the fund, the following entries are required each year:

```
Pension Expense.......................  100,000
    Pension Liability..................           100,000
    To establish the expense and related
    liability.

Pension Fund (a noncurrent asset)......  100,000
    Cash...............................           100,000
    To transfer cash to the fund.
```

When the pension is paid to the retired employee, the entry is as follows:

```
Pension Liability............................  500
    Pension Fund.............................        500
```

If the plan is not funded, only the amount actually paid to retired employees is deductible for income tax purposes. This is *not*, however, an acceptable basis for measuring pension expense in accordance with generally accepted accounting principles. The accrual concept requires that the amount of expense in a year be computed on the basis of the pension obligation that was created in the year, which is related to employee earnings in the year, not to the pensions paid in the year. The amount of pensions paid in a year is, of course, a function of the amount of employee earnings in prior years.

PAST SERVICE BENEFITS. When a pension plan is first adopted, an especially difficult problem arises: What shall be done about the liability created for employees who are entitled to benefits because of the years they have worked for the company up to the time of adoption of the plan? Although this liability arises as a result of work done in prior years, for income tax purposes the estimated amount thereof may be treated as a tax deduction over the next 10 or 12 *future* years. The FASB also requires that these *past-service benefits* be spread over the income of future years, not more than 40 years, nor less than 10 years.[2]

---

[2] APB *Opinion No. 8*, November, 1966.

Even a careful estimate of the future liability under a pension plan may turn out to be wrong, partly because such factors as whether the employee will stay with the company until retirement and his length of life after retirement are quite uncertain, and also because there is a tendency to liberalize benefits as time goes on. Consequently, the actual amount of expense attributable to the work done in a given year cannot be known for many years later.

INCOME TAX ALLOCATIONS

Permanent Differences and Timing Differences

For most revenue and expense transactions, the amount used in calculating taxable income for income tax purposes is the same as the amount reported on the income statement in accordance with generally accepted accounting principles. Thus, there is a likelihood that if a company reports an income of $1 million before taxes, and if the tax rate is approximately 51 percent[3] the Provision for Income Taxes (an expense) should be approximately $510,000.

There are two important classes of exceptions, however. First, the income tax regulations permit certain deductions from taxable income that will never be counted as expenses and they permit that certain revenue items be omitted from taxable income. A tax depletion allowance that exceeds depletion as calculated on a cost basis is an example of such a deduction, and revenue earned on products made in Puerto Rico is an example of a revenue exclusion. These create a *permanent* tax difference. In other situations, the income tax regulations permit revenue to be recognized in a later period, or expenses in an earlier period, than the method used in financial accounting. These create a *timing* tax difference.

No special accounting arises in the case of permanent tax differences. The amount reported as Provision for Income Taxes of the current period is simply lower than it would be if the preferential treatment did not exist.

Accounting for Timing Differences

In the case of timing differences, however, an adjustment in Provision for Income Taxes in the current period is required. This adjustment

---

[3] In 1974, federal income taxes on ordinary corporations were 22 percent of the first $25,000 of taxable income and 48 percent of income in excess of $25,000. Many states also impose corporate income taxes. For most calculations, it is safe to assume that income taxes (federal plus state) are approximately half of taxable income. In the illustrations in this book, however, we shall usually assume an effective tax rate of 51 percent simply because this makes it easier to distinguish the income tax from the income after tax.

makes the amount of Provision for Income Taxes reported for a period match the amount of income reported on the income statement for the period and is therefore consistent with the matching concept.

We shall illustrate the application of this principle by assuming a company that uses an accelerated method of depreciation in calculating its taxable income and the straight-line method for calculating its net income for financial accounting purposes, for this is the most common cause of timing differences in income taxes. For simplicity, we shall assume that the company acquired a single asset in Year 1 at a cost of $1,500,000, that the asset has negligible residual value, and that it is depreciated for tax purposes by the sum-of-the-years'-digits method over a period of five years.

Part A of Illustration 8–1 shows how the company would calculate its income taxes in each of these five years, assuming income before depreciation and taxes was $1,000,000 in each year.[4] For income tax purposes, depreciation expense in the first year is $500,000 so taxable income is $500,000, and the income tax is 51 percent of $500,000, or $255,000. Each year thereafter, the amount of depreciation decreases, so the amount of taxable income increases, and the income tax increases correspondingly.

Part B shows the calculations for financial accounting. Assuming that for its financial accounting the company used the straight-line method, depreciation expense is ⅕ of $1,500,000, or $300,000 per year, and its income before tax is $700,000 per year. Because the income tax paid, as calculated in Part A, increases from one year to the next, reported net income would decrease year after year *if* net income were calculated simply by subtracting each year's income tax from the pretax income for that year. This phenomenon occurs because the income tax was calculated on a different amount than the accounting income before tax; that is, the income tax was not matched to the pretax income.

Part C shows how the Provision for Income Taxes can be made to match the reported income. The income tax actually payable for each year is adjusted so that it equals what the tax amount *would have been* if it had been calculated on the basis of the income as reported for financial accounting purposes. Each year, the income before tax is $700,000 and at a tax rate of 51 percent, the income tax on this amount would be $357,000. Provision for Income Taxes is adjusted from the amount actually paid so that it equals $357,000 in each year. In Year 1, this requires an addition of $102,000 to the tax actually paid, and in Year 5 it requires a subtraction from actual taxes of $102,000.

---

[4] In the sum-of-the-years'-digits method, it will be recalled, the numbers of the years are first summed, in this case totalling 15, and each year's depreciation rate is a fraction in which the denominator is this sum and the numerator is, for the first year, n (the number of years), for the second year, $n - 1$, and so on. Thus depreciation in the first year is 5/15 of $1,500,000, or $500,000.

Illustration 8–1

CALCULATION OF TAX ALLOCATION, SINGLE ASSET
(000 omitted)

Part A. Calculation of Income Tax

Year	Income before Depreciation and Taxes	Years' Digits Depreciation	Taxable Income	Income Tax (at 51%)	Income After Tax
1	$1,000	$ 500	$ 500	$ 255	$ 245
2	1,000	400	600	306	294
3	1,000	300	700	357	343
4	1,000	200	800	408	392
5	1,000	100	900	459	441
Totals	$5,000	$1,500	$3,500	$1,785	$1,715

Part B. Accounting Income, Without Allocation

Year	Income before Depreciation and Taxes	Straight-Line Depreciation	Pretax Income	Income Tax (from above)	Net Income
1	$1,000	$ 300	$ 700	$ 255	$ 445
2	1,000	300	700	306	394
3	1,000	300	700	357	343
4	1,000	300	700	408	292
5	1,000	300	700	459	241
Totals	$5,000	$1,500	$3,500	$1,785	$1,715

Part C. Accounting Income, Income Tax Allocated

Year	Pretax Income	Income Tax Expense Paid (as in A)	Allocated	Net	Net Income	Deferred Income Tax
1	$ 700	$ 255 + $102 =		$ 357	$ 343	$102
2	700	306 +	51	357	343	153
3	700	357	0	357	343	153
4	700	408 −	51	357	343	102
5	700	459 −	102	357	343	0
Totals	$3,500	$1,785	0	$1,785	$1,715	

Note that these adjustments affect only the *timing* of the recognition of income tax expense. As shown by the totals of Parts A, B, and C, over the whole five-year period the total amount of tax and the total amount of net income are exactly the same, whether or not the adjustment is made.

Accounting Entries

The actual income tax due for a year is calculated as in Part A and is recorded in the following journal entry (for Year 1):

```
Provision for Income Taxes............. 255,000
    Income Tax Liability...............       255,000
```

This amount is then adjusted to reflect the income tax that should be matched with accounting income. For Year 1, this requires an addition of $102,000 to Provision for Income Taxes, so the entry is:

```
Provision for Income Taxes............. 102,000
        Deferred Income Taxes................        102,000
```

After this entry, Provision for Income Taxes totals $357,000, which is the amount reported on the income statement for Year 1.

In Year 5, the adjusting entry will have the opposite effect. It will reduce actual income taxes by $102,000, viz:

```
Deferred Income Taxes.................. 102,000
        Provision for Income Taxes........        102,000
```

Nature of Deferred Income Taxes Liability

Deferred Income Taxes, which is the account credited in these adjusting entries, is a liability account. It is shown separately from Income Tax Liability, which is the amount actually owed the government at the time. Deferred Income Taxes is not a liability in the sense that the amount is owed to the government as of the date of the balance sheet. It is a liability only in the sense of a deferred credit to income, that is, it is an amount that will reduce income tax expense in the years in which income tax actually paid exceeds the amount of income tax that matches the reported income. These are Years 4 and 5 in the example given above.

In the example given above, the amount by which income tax was reduced in the later years exactly equalled the amount by which it was increased in the early years, so that at the end of the life of the asset, the balance in the Deferred Income Tax account was zero. This is always the case with respect to a single asset. If, however, we drop the assumption that the company operates with only a single asset and make instead the more realistic assumption that a company acquires additional assets each year, a strange situation develops in the Deferred Income Taxes liability account. This is shown in Illustration 8–2.

In this illustrative situation, it is assumed that the company begins operations in Year 1, and that it acquires a $1,500,000 asset each year, each with a service life of five years. For the first five years, these acquisitions make the company grow in size; thereafter, they replace assets whose service life has ended. (The asset acquired in Year 6 replaces the asset acquired in Year 1.) In Year 1, the Deferred Income Tax account increases by the amount of income tax allocation, which is $102,000, the same amount shown in Illustration 8–1. In Year 2, it increases further by the additional adjustment of $51,000 for the asset

Illustration 8–2

BEHAVIOR OF DEFERRED INCOME TAX ACCOUNT

($000 omitted)

Changes in Deferred Income Tax Account

	Year 1	Year 2	Year 3	Year 4	Year 5	Year 6
Beginning Balance...............	0	102	255	408	510	510
For $1,500 Asset added in Year						
1............................	102	51	0	−51	−102	0
2............................		102	51	0	− 51	−102
3............................			102	51	0	− 51
4............................				102	51	0
5............................					102	51
6............................						102
Ending Balance..................	102	255	408	510	510	510

acquired in Year 1 and also by the $102,000 for the asset acquired in Year 2. In Year 3 it increases still further. In Year 4 the account is decreased by the debit adjustment for the Year 1 asset, but this is more than offset by the credits for Year 3 and Year 4 assets, so the balance continues to increase. In Year 5, the account stabilizes, with increases exactly being offset by decreases, and these offsetting entries continue in future years.

Note, however, that as long as the company grows in size, the balance in the liability account continues to increase, and that even if it stops growing in size, as is assumed in Year 6, a sizable balance remains in the liability account. This balance remains permanently; there will always be a balance in the Deferred Income Taxes account unless the company stops acquiring assets. For this reason, many companies report a large deferred income taxes liability on their balance sheet. This is not an obligation owed to some outside party, and it is unlikely that the balance in the account ever will be eliminated, or even that it will decrease. Rather, the balance represents, in effect, a permanent investment of capital by the government because of the government's willingness to allow assets to be depreciated more rapidly for income tax purposes than the company considers appropriate for financial accounting purposes.

It is possible for the Deferred Income Taxes account to have a debit balance. For example, prepaid rents are taxable income in the year received, even though accounting principles treat them as deferred revenue. If there were no other differences betwen its tax return and its income statement, a firm owning rental properties could have greater taxes payable than its reported income tax expense, giving rise to a debit balance in the deferred taxes account.

FOREIGN CURRENCY ADJUSTMENTS

If a U.S. firm engages in transactions with foreign firms, or has branch operations or subsidiaries in foreign countries, then these foreign transactions must be converted into dollars in preparing the U.S. firm's financial statements. *Exchange rates* are used to translate the foreign currency amounts into dollars. Such a rate expresses a unit of foreign currency in terms of its U.S. dollar equivalent. These rates fluctuate, often widely, depending on the relative strengths of the dollar and the foreign currency in international trade. In accounting, these rates are characterized either as the *current rate,* i.e., the rate in effect during the current period, or the *historial rate,* i.e., the rate that was in effect when a specific transaction or event occurred. Most revenue and expense items of foreign branches or subsidiaries are translated at the average rate of exchange prevailing during the accounting period. If the exchange rate has fluctuated widely during the period, the translations are made at the average rate applicable to each month in the period. Many companies, however, translate depreciation expense at historical rates, rather than at current rates. This is because they carry the fixed assets of their foreign branches and subsidiaries at historical cost, that is, at the exchange rates prevailing at the time the fixed assets were acquired. To be consistent, depreciation expense which writes off this cost is also stated at the historical rate.

If an American firm buys or sells goods abroad, or borrows from or grants credit to a foreign entity, the firm may experience a *currency gain or loss* as a result of exchange rate fluctuations between the date the transaction was entered into and the date cash is transmitted.[5]

EXAMPLE: The Payson Shoe Store received a shipment of shoes from an Italian manufacturer with an invoice for 1,000,000 lire. On the date the invoice was received and the transaction journalized, the exchange rate was $.001526 per lira, giving a $1,526 account payable for the shoes received. Thirty days later, when Payson paid its bill in lire, the exchange rate had increased to $.001535 per lira. Thus Payson had to pay $1,535 to buy the required lire, and a currency exchange loss of $9 was realized. This would be accounted for as follows:

```
Accounts Payable.............................. 1,526
Loss on Foreign Exchange......................     9
    Cash......................................       1,535
```

---

[5] Such a gain or loss will not occur, of course, if the transaction involves only dollars. For example, if a U.S. firm sells goods to a Japanese firm, with payment to be made in dollars, then the U.S. firm will realize no currency gain or loss.

Foreign currency gains and losses for the accounting period are combined into a net amount, and shown as an operating item on the income statement.

EXTRAORDINARY ITEMS

Until recently accountants tended to classify items in the income statement in such a way that the revenue and expenses involved in the normal operations of the business were separated from nonoperating items, such as interest expense (which was viewed as a financial cost rather than an operating expense) and unusual costs such as those of a strike, a fire, or the loss on the disposal of an asset. Their objective in making such a separation was to show the income that resulted from the normal operations of the business, and which would be likely to recur in future years, other things being equal.

In 1973 the publication of APB *Opinion No. 30* ended this practice in most circumstances. *Opinion No. 30* requires that, with two exceptions, *all* revenues and expenses be considered as relating to operations. The basic reason for this change was to correct an abuse that sometimes occurred under the former practice, whereby a company would charge certain nonrecurring costs directly to retained earnings, so that these costs would not appear on any income statement. In a few companies, the direct debits to retained earnings over a period of years almost equalled the sum of the net income amounts reported for these years. Other companies reported a variety of losses as "extraordinary," in the hope that readers would regard them as abnormal and not likely to recur in the future.

The first of the two exceptions, extraordinary items, will be described in this section, and the other, discontinued operations, in the next section.

Definition of Extraordinary Items

The definition of an extraordinary item is extremely narrow. It has two parts:[6]

1. The event must be *unusual;* that is, it should be highly abnormal and unrelated to, or only incidentally related to, the ordinary activities of the entity.

2. The event must occur *infrequently;* that is, it should be of a type that would not reasonably be expected to recur in the forseeable future.

The words of this definition do not convey its narrowness as clearly as do the illustrations that are used to explain it. The following gains and losses are specifically *not* extraordinary:[7]

---

[6] APB *Opinion No. 30* (June 1973), par. 20.

[7] *Ibid.,* par. 23.

1. Write-down or write-off of accounts receivable, inventory, or intangible assets.
2. Gains or losses from changes in the value of foreign currency.
3. Gains or losses on disposal of a segment of a business (discussed in the next section).
4. Gains or losses from the disposal of fixed assets.
5. Effects of a strike.
6. Adjustments of accruals on long-term contracts.

By contrast, the only items that are mentioned as possible examples of extraordinary items are major casualties (such as earthquakes), the loss when a foreign government expropriates assets, and a major loss resulting from the enactment of a new law, such as a pollution-control law.

Accounting Treatment

In those rare cases in which extraordinary gains or losses can be identified, they are reported separately near the bottom of the income statement. The amount reported is the net amount after the income tax effect of the item has been taken into account.

> EXAMPLE: If a company had an extraordinary loss of $100,000, its taxable income presumably would be reduced by $100,000. At an income tax rate of 51 percent, its income tax would be reduced by $51,000, and the ultimate effect on net income would therefore be only $49,000. The format used for this section of the income statement is:

Income before extraordinary items	$1,000,000
Extraordinary items (less applicable income taxes of $51,000)	49,000
Net income	$ 951,000

DISCONTINUED OPERATIONS

The other type of transaction which, if material, must be reported separately on the income statement is the gain or loss from the discontinuance of a division or other identifiable segment of the business. The transaction must involve a whole business unit, as contrasted with the disposition of an individual fixed asset or discontinuance of one product in a product line. Discontinuance may occur by abandoning the segment and selling off the remaining assets for whatever they will bring, or it may occur by selling the whole segment as a unit to some other company. In the former case a loss is likely, whereas in the latter case there may be either a gain or a loss, depending on how attractive the segment is to another company.

The effect of the decision to dispose of the segment is recorded on the income statement in the period in which the decision is made, which may well be earlier than the period in which the actual sales transaction is consummated. Unless a specific agreement has been implemented in the current period, the amount of gain or loss must be estimated. This estimate may be quite complicated, for it must take into account: the estimated revenues and the estimated expenses of the discontinued segment during the period in which it continues to be operated by the company, that is, until another company takes it over; the estimated proceeds of the sale; and the book value of the assets that will be written off when the segment is disposed of.

Accounting Treatment

As is the case with extraordinary items, the amounts related to discontinued operations are reported after their income tax effect has been taken into account. Two items are shown:

1. The income or loss attributable to the operations of the segment during the current year, and
2. The estimated net gain or loss after all aspects of the sale, the effect of operations until the disposal is consummated, the write-off of assets that are not sold, and any other effects are taken into account.

The required income statement format (slightly condensed) is:

Income from continuing operations, before income taxes		$2,000,000
Provision for income taxes		1,020,000
Income from continuing operations		$ 980,000
Discontinued operations:		
Income of discontinued Division X		
(less applicable income tax of $26,000)	$25,000	
Gain on disposal (less applicable income taxes		
of $75,000)	75,000	100,000
Net income		$1,080,000

NET INCOME

As is indicated in the examples of income statement format shown in the above sections, the last item on the income statement is always labelled "Net Income," without any qualifying phrase. The term "net income" never appears as a label for any other item on the income statement. Note that in the example above, the label is "income from continuing operations," not "*net* income from continuing operations."

"Net income" therefore means, unambiguously, the net addition to retained earnings during the accounting period, regardless of whether it arises from ordinary operations or from other events and regardless of whether the transactions entering into its determination are recurring or are highly unusual.

PRICE LEVEL ADJUSTMENTS

Nature of the Problem

The accountant measures the goods and services that enter into the calculation of net income essentially at their acquisition cost, that is, at the prices paid when these goods and services were originally acquired by the company. The economist, however, often measures cost not in terms of the price originally paid for the goods and services, but rather in terms of "real prices"; that is, he adjusts acquisition prices to allow for changes in purchasing power of the monetary unit. In periods when there are substantial changes in prices, such as the downward movement in the early 1930s or the inflationary movement which began in the 1940s, the difference between the accounting concept of income and the economist's concept of income can be substantial.

This difference arises because the purchasing power of the monetary unit of measurement is different at different times. Thus, the measuring stick used in accounting is unlike the yardstick used to make linear measurements. A yardstick is always 36 inches long, but a balance sheet contains some items, such as cash, that are stated at current purchasing power; other items, such as inventory, that are stated in monetary units that reflect purchasing power of the recent past; and still other items, such as plant and equipment, stated at amounts that reflect purchasing power of several years previous to the current date.

Supplementary Financial Statements

In some countries, especially those with a high rate of inflation, changes in the purchasing power of the monetary unit are explicitly incorporated in the basic financial statements. In the United States, however, this is not done. Since the 1930s, a number of accountants and accounting organizations have argued for such a change. In 1969, *Statement No. 3* of the Accounting Principles Board (predecessor of the FASB) recommended, but did not require, that companies prepare financial statements adjusted for price level changes. These statements were to be *in addition to*, but not instead of, the conventional financial statements.

Only a very few companies accepted this recommendation and prepared supplementary statements. The general feeling was that the confusion resulting from having two sets of financial statements for the same company offset the advantages. There is little support for the idea of doing away with the conventional statements, because the historical cost concept underlying these statements makes them more objective and easier to comprehend than the alternative.

With the continued inflation of the 1970s, interest in preparing supplementary statements grew, and in 1974 the Financial Accounting Standards Board was considering the possible requirement that all companies should prepare supplementary financial statements that reflected the effect of changes in the price level. Note that these supplement but do not replace the conventional statements.

General Approach

The amounts reported on the conventional balance sheet and income statement are on a "units of money" basis. The effect of price level changes is reported by restating each of these amounts on a "units of general purchasing power" (GPP) basis. In making this restatement, one type of adjustment is required for monetary items and quite a different type is required for nonmonetary items.

A *monetary item* is an asset that will be realized in the stated number of dollars, or a liability that will be paid in the stated number of dollars. Cash, accounts receivable, marketable securities, and most liabilities are examples. Balance sheet amounts for these items are not changed in constructing the GPP statement, since the conventional balance sheet shows the current purchasing power of a monetary asset and the amount currently required to discharge a monetary liability. By holding monetary assets in a period of inflation, a company has suffered a loss, however, since the purchasing power of these assets has declined. Conversely, a company gains by holding monetary liabilities since it can pay off these liabilities with dollars that have a lower purchasing power than the dollars which the creditor furnished the company at the time the liability was incurred. Thus, losses from holding monetary assets and gains from holding monetary liabilities affect the GPP net income for the period as reported on the income statement.

With *nonmonetary items*, the effect is the reverse. Balance sheet amounts are increased to reflect the increased purchasing power committed to these assets, but no holding loss or gain is reported in the income statement because none has occurred.

In making price level adjustments, an index of *general* price level changes is used. The objective is to take account of changes in the general purchasing power of the dollar, not changes in the prices of specific assets. For this purpose the best index is generally regarded to be the "Gross National Product Implicit Price Deflator" prepared by the U.S. Department of Commerce.

The first time that General Purchasing Power statements are prepared, the accountant must go back into history and adjust the fixed assets acquired in each year according to the price index in that year, and adjust the depreciation accumulated in each year according to the price index for each year in which depreciation was recorded. Thereafter, the GPP balance sheet at the beginning of the year is taken as a starting point, and the new adjustments take into account only the price level changes during the year. The longer an asset has been owned by a company, the larger is the adjustment. Thus if a building was acquired for $100,000 in 1958 when the GNP deflator index was 100, its cost would appear on a December 31, 1974 balance sheet at $170,000 since the index at the end of 1974 was about 170.

Illustration of the Calculation

The calculations required to make a set of price-level adjusted statements are quite lengthy. They are described in detail in the FASB document, *Financial Reporting in Units of General Purchasing Power*.[8] The essence of the process can be discerned from the highly simplified financial statements shown in Illustration 8–3. It is assumed that the company began operations January 1, 19X1, obtained capital from stockholders and from a creditor (i.e., a note payable) and used this capital to acquire land and depreciable fixed assets (plant). On January 1, 19X1, the price level index was 100 and by December 31, 19X1 it had risen to 110, an increase of 10 percent.

The monetary balance sheet items are not adjusted. The nonmonetary items are restated by multiplying them by the "index ratio," that is, the ratio as of the end of the period divided by the ratio as of the beginning of the period, or 110/100.

Accumulated depreciation is increased by the ratio 110/105 rather than 110/100 since it was assumed that depreciation expense was incurred evenly throughout the year, and the average price level during the year was $(110 + 100) \div 2 = 105$. (If the plant had been more than one year old, each year's addition to accumulated depreciation would have been adjusted by applying the index ratio applicable to that year.)

On a General Purchasing Power balance sheet, the capital stock and retained earnings amount are combined into a single item, stockholders' equity. The amount is the amount that makes the balance sheet balance. (In the simple example shown, the amount could be obtained by adjusting the appropriate stockholders' equity items separately, but in a real company with a complicated history of transactions affecting stockholders' equity, the separate adjustments would require much work.)

---

[8] The following description is based on the December 31, 1974, version of this document. It may be modified by subsequent action of the FASB.

Illustration 8–3

PROCESS OF MAKING PRICE LEVEL ADJUSTMENTS

	Units of Money	Type of Item	Adjustment	Restated to GPP
Balance Sheet, December 31, 19X1				
Assets:				
Cash and Receivables	$ 40,000	monetary	none	$ 40,000
Land	10,000	nonmonetary	110/100	11,000
Plant (at cost)	88,000	nonmonetary	110/100	96,800
Depreciation	(8,000)		110/105	(8,381)
Total	$130,000			$139,419
Equities:				
Note payable	$ 12,000	monetary	none	$ 12,000
Capital stock	109,000	nonmonetary	balancing	127,419
Retained earnings	9,000	nonmonetary		
Total	$130,000			$139,419
Income Statement for 19X1				
Revenues	$100,000	nonmonetary	110/105	$104,762
Depreciation	(8,000)	nonmonetary	110/105	(8,381)
Other expenses	(83,000)	nonmonetary	110/105	(86,952)
GPP loss			see below*	(1,108)
Net income	$ 9,000			$ 8,321

* Calculation of GPP loss:

Loss on cash and receivables: 40,000 − (40,000 × 110/104) .... $(2,308)

Gain on notes payable: (12,000 × 110/100) − 12,000 1,200

Net general purchasing power loss.. $(1,108)

Income statement items are nonmonetary items and are restated at the applicable index ratio. In the example, it is assumed that revenues and expenses are incurred evenly throughout the year; accordingly, the ratio 110/105 is used. If there were seasonal variations within the year, ratios reflecting these variations would have been used.

Note especially the calculation of the general purchasing power gain or loss (in the example it is a loss). This is the net effect of the gain from holding monetary liabilities and the loss from holding monetary assets. Since notes payable were held during the year, there was a holding gain of 110/100 or 10 percent. The monetary assets, cash and receivables had a corresponding loss, but it was calculated at the ratio of 110/104 because some of these assets were acquired during the year.

Note that the price level adjustment results in a significant decrease in reported net income.

DIRECT COSTING

In the final section of this chapter, we describe briefly an alternative approach to the measurement of net income, called *direct costing*, also called *variable costing*. As used in this context, direct costs are costs that vary with changes in production, and a direct cost system counts only such costs. This method is *not* in accordance with generally accepted accounting principles, and it *cannot* be used in calculating taxable income.[9] Nevertheless, many companies use it for internal purposes.

In the conventional system, the basic concept is *full costing;* that is, products should bear a fair share of all the costs involved in making them. In the direct cost system, only the direct costs are charged to products and thus pass through inventory accounts; other costs are charged off as expenses in the period in which they are incurred. Consequently, indirect costs affect net income more quickly in the direct cost system than in a full cost system. This effect can be seen in Illustration 8–4, in which

Illustration 8–4

COMPARISON OF FULL COSTING AND DIRECT COSTING

	Under Full Costing		Under Direct Costing	
	Period No. 1	*Period No. 2*	*Period No. 1*	*Period No. 2*
Activity:				
Units manufactured............	1	1	1	1
Units sold..................	0	2	0	2
Income Statement:				
Sales.......................	$ 0	$200	$ 0	$200
Cost of goods sold............	0	160	0	60
Manufacturing overhead........	0	0	50	50
Selling and administrative......	10	10	10	10
Net Income or Loss.............	$(10)	$ 30	$(60)	$ 80
Ending Inventory (Balance Sheet).....................	$ 80	$ 0	$ 30	$ 0

it is assumed that one unit is manufactured each period, but that the unit manufactured in the first period is not sold until the second period. The sales price is $100 per unit, direct costs are $30 per *unit*, and indirect costs are $50 per *period*. In the conventional full cost system, the entire

---

[9] *Accounting Research Bulletin No. 43* states: "As applied to inventories, cost means in principle the sum of the applicable expenditures and charges directly or indirectly incurred in bringing an article to its existing condition and location. . . . The exclusion of all overheads from inventory costs does not constitute an accepted accounting procedure." Internal Revenue Service Regulation 1.471.11, which becomes fully effective in 1976, requires full costs and spells out in some detail what items are to be included in full costs.

manufacturing cost of $80 is held in inventory at the end of Period No. 1, and is released as cost of goods sold in Period No. 2, along with the cost of the unit made and sold in that period. In direct costing, only the $30 of direct cost is held in inventory at the end of Period No. 1, and the $50 of indirect cost is charged as an expense of the period.

The conventional system is also called *absorption costing* because all manufacturing costs are absorbed by products, in contrast with direct costing, in which indirect costs are not absorbed by products.

With direct costing, indirect costs are viewed as being essentially the same as general and administrative costs; that is, these are costs associated with being in business rather than costs associated with the specific units of product manufactured. Proponents of direct costing assert that management can be misled by the income reported in a period if these costs are hidden away in inventory.

Since direct costing is not permitted under generally accepted accounting principles, companies that use it for internal purposes must recompute their inventory amounts for the balance sheet, and cost of goods sold for the income statement.

The significance of direct costing for our present purpose is that it illustrates the effect that differences between production volume and sales volume have on net income. Under conventional accounting, when production volume exceeds sales volume, some costs are held in inventory, rather than appearing on the income statement as expenses, and net income is therefore higher than would be reported if these costs appeared on the income statement.

SUMMARY

In analyzing transactions regarding wage and salary costs, a careful distinction must be made between the amount earned by the employee, the additional cost that the company incurs for payroll taxes, and the amount collected from employees which is to be transmitted to the government. Pension costs are a cost associated with work done in the current period although the actual pension payments may not begin until many years later.

The Provision for Income Taxes is calculated as if the income tax were computed on the amount of accounting income reported for the period. The entry required to adjust actual income tax payments liability to this basis creates another liability account, deferred income taxes. This account does not represent an amount due the government.

An extraordinary gain or loss and a gain or loss from a discontinued operation are reported separately on the income statement. The amount is adjusted for the applicable income tax.

Supplementary financial statements may be prepared in which items are restated in terms of current purchasing power. In a period of inflation, this restatement usually reduces reported net income.

In a direct cost system, products are carried in inventory at direct cost rather than at full factory cost. It is not permitted under generally accepted accounting principles.

CASES

CASE 8–1. UNIVERSITY COOPERATIVE*

The Board of Directors of University Cooperative were faced with the problem of trying to determine what the income for the fiscal year had been. University Cooperative was a membership group that operated a retail store which specialized in school supplies, books, and general merchandise similar to that found in middle-range department stores. The Cooperative distributed its annual earnings—the excess of revenues over expenses—to its 52,000 members. The membership was evenly divided between students who currently attended the University and older persons who either lived in the community or who had attended the University and chosen to maintain their memberships in the Cooperative. Thus, the Cooperative's membership could be characterized as having both a certain amount of continuity and a significant turnover.

"In past years we have never had much difficulty in determining what the income was, but this year there seems to be a great number of problems," remarked Marvin Brown, the President of the Cooperative.

"Well, I have always thought business was rather dull," observed Bill Simpkins, a young sociology instructor who was a member of the Board. "This problem should be easy to solve. After all, we are creative intellectuals who are not tied down by the imperialistic trappings of—."

"Hold on, Bill!" Marvin Brown interrupted. "This problem will require all of your creative talents; but before we start to discuss it, I want our controller, Frank Fox, to give us the facts."

"Thanks, Mr. Brown," replied Frank Fox. "As most of you are aware, the 1969–70 fiscal year, which ended September 30, was bad for business in general and for retail stores in particular. For the first time in 26 years our sales did not increase, but our expenses certainly have! Not only are our suppliers demanding higher prices, but the recent union agreement boosted labor costs significantly. To make matters worse, we are ex-

---

Accounting Problems

1. Inventory Writedown—general merchandise
A detailed physical inventory revealed that there was a shortage of $420,000, which contrasts sharply with the usual annual shortage of $20,000. Management estimates that this loss occurred over a ten-year period.

2. Inventory Valuation—women's dresses
The women's dress department in mid-1969, before the midi-dress had been extensively promoted, took advantage of an opportunity to buy a sizable inventory of mini-dresses. Then in early 1970, in anticipation of a swing in fashion preferences to the midi length, the department invested in a large inventory of midi-dresses. Now, the buyer was resigned to the fact that a substantial part of the inventory had little value. The original cost of the mini-dresses was $150,000 and of the midi-dresses, $190,000. When asked her opinion of sales prospects, the buyer speculated that if one of the two fashion extremes was clearly repudiated, the store could only hope to realize 10 percent of its investment in that style; but if the present indecisiveness continued, the store might recover one third of its investment in each style.

3. Change in Inventory Valuation Method
Whereas the Cooperative had historically relied on the Fifo method of valuing inventory, this year it changed to the Lifo method, and as a result, the inventory on the balance sheet was $175,000 lower while the cost of goods sold was that amount higher.

4. Sales of Assets
A building that had been owned for thirty-two years, now fully depreciated, was sold for a capital gain of $200,000. Management thought that the majority of this appreciation had occurred in the last fifteen years. The Cooperative sold a parcel of land for $36,000 more than it had paid for it in 1965.

5. Cancellation of Old Rebates
Each year the Cooperative issues rebate checks based on all sales, whether or not the members' addresses are known. Because the Cooperative's membership includes many transients, a significant number of these rebate checks are never claimed. Thus, while on the Cooperative's books the checks are recorded as paid, many in fact are never cashed, and consequently the cash balance per the bank exceeds the cash balance per the Cooperative's books. In 1970, the Cooperative's management decided to cancel $187,000 of these rebate checks, some dating back to 1954, because it was confident that they would never be claimed.

6. Write-Off of Accounts Receivable
In 1970 management reappraised its receivables, and after a thorough study, determined that, in addition to existing allowances for bad debts, some $93,000 should be written off as uncollectible. Some of these accounts were seven years old.

7. Revision of By-Laws
In 1970 the Cooperative revised the By-Laws pertaining to the management responsibilities and the election of the Board of Directors. In addition to the legal expenses, a considerable sum was expended in conducting a ballot among the membership for the purpose of approving these changes in the By-Laws. These costs were $79,000, and represented the first revision of the By-Laws in the Cooperative's 47-year history.

periencing high turnover and find that the sales people we can hire are just not as effective as they used to be. As if that were not enough, we have noticed that in the last year our inventory shortages—the difference between what our books say is in inventory and what actually is there when we take the physical count—are really getting out of hand. These shortages are directly traceable to shoplifting, which has become sort of a game among certain segments of the student population.

"While in past years we have generally averaged about $700,000 profit on $10,000,000 sales, for a 7% rebate, this year it is hard to say exactly what our profits are. I can say that I have identified $220,000 profit on sales of $8,800,000 before what the accountants describe as 'extraordinary' gains and losses. But here is the problem. There are a number of items that are quite subjective and a case can be made for assigning them retroactively to past periods, for lumping them into the current period, or spreading them out over future periods. The document I will now distribute (Exhibit 1) describes these problem items. The $220,000 profit does not include any of these items."

Frank Fox then explained the various accounting problems and answered questions. The complicated issues stimulated lively discussion but little agreement. Even Bill Simpkins, while boisterous throughout the session, seemed confused and unsure as to the best treatment. Finally, Marvin Brown indicated with an upraised hand that it was time to move on to the next item of the agenda.

"Gentlemen, you will agree, I am sure, that there are no easy answers to these accounting problems. It is important that we determine whether these items are properly related to the current operating period or to past or future periods. If the items should be allocated forwards or backwards, we must decide the relevant time frame. In approaching these decisions, we must keep in mind the interests of current members as well as those of past and future members. I have asked Arthur Young, who is studying business at the University, to summarize the arguments for various approaches to these problems and to propose a solution. He will be sending his recommendations in the very near future."

Questions

1. What accounting principles relate to the problems faced by University Cooperative?
2. What objective should be used as a guideline for decisions on these accounting problems? Are there any problems in allocating gains or losses to past periods?
3. How should each of these items be accounted for and why? If you allocate forwards or backwards, indicate the specific number of years and your supporting reasoning.

4. Assuming the Cooperative's By-Laws do not require that the rebate equal the net income as determined using generally accepted accounting principles, how large should the 1969–70 rebate be?

CASE 8–2. THE MILLION DOLLAR LATHE*

Thompson Products, for the 18th year, has continued its custom of furnishing its employees with a simple concise report of its financial operations, showing how much money the company took in and what happened to it. Revenues for 1956 totaled $306,508,120. Expenses, not including wages, salaries or dividends, were $175,535,061, leaving $130,973,059 to be divided among employees and shareholders. Of this, $117,960,454 went for payrolls, $4,183,904 was paid out in dividends, and $8,828,701 was plowed back into the business.

Why was it necessary to plow that much back into the business? The tale of the million-dollar turret lathe, included in the report, explains that. It seems that in 1942 the company bought a lathe for $12,000. Under federal tax laws, it was permitted to depreciate the cost of the lathe over a 14-year period. So, last year, when the lathe became obsolete, the company had $12,000 to buy a new one, plus $1,000, which was the resale value of the old one. But the replacement cost in 1956 was $35,000 for a lathe that would perform the same functions as the old model, or $67,000 for a new one with attachments to meet today's more exacting needs.

The company had only $13,000 to do a $67,000 job. The difference of $54,000 had to come out of profits, and in order to get that amount in 1956 the company had to earn a profit of more than $112,500 before taxes, because $54,000 was all there was left after the government took its corporate profit tax of 52 percent. And to earn that amount of profit, the company had to sell more than a million and a quarter dollars' worth of products to customers. It took more than $1,250,000 of sales to buy just one machine!

Thus, while $112,500 sounds like a lot of profit, in this case, the shareholders got none of it. The government took more than half, and the rest went to replace a machine. This story is duplicated hundreds of times each year throughout the company in the case of machines, large and small. This is why only a relatively small amount of profit is paid to shareholders in dividends, and why a large portion must be retained to finance expansion and replacement so the company can continue to operate and employees can continue working.

---

* This case consists of a quotation taken from a report prepared by the management of a company for the information of its employees.

Question

Comment on this statement. Is it the truth, the whole truth, and nothing but the truth?

CASE 8–3. R. L. BOGGS

According to the terms of his grandfather's will, R. L. Boggs received a bequest of $50,000. At the time of his grandfather's death, the general index of prices was 100. It rose rapidly while the estate was being settled, however, and had reached 120 when Boggs actually received the money. Since he felt that the inflationary rise in prices was likely to continue, he borrowed $30,000 for one year at 6 percent, with the intention of keeping most of the $80,000 fund invested in common stocks. His transactions during the ensuing year were as follows:

1. He bought common stocks for $75,000 when the price index was 125.
2. Later when the index was 133⅓, he sold for $30,000 stocks which had originally cost $25,000.
3. While the index was 133⅓, he received dividends of $6,000.
4. He bought additional common stocks for $40,000 when the price index was 150.
5. Near the end of the year the price index rose to 180 and remained steady for several weeks. Strong antiinflationary measures were being prepared by the government, and some steps to curb the rapidly rising price level had already been taken. Because of this, Boggs sold his entire portfolio of common stocks for $100,000, paid off the $30,000 note with interest, and invested the entire fund (except the amount required to pay the income tax) in tax-exempt state bonds purchased to yield 3 percent per annum.

Questions

1. Mr. Boggs asks you to analyze the results of his financial and investment policies in order to determine the net gains and losses in terms of purchasing power during the settlement of the estate and during the full year between the receipt of the cash and the purchase of the state bonds. Assume, for simplicity, that Mr. Boggs is subject to a flat 25 percent tax on all income and capital gains. He is particularly anxious to learn where and why the real gains and losses occurred. It is suggested that the end-of-year dollar (price index 180) be taken as the basic unit of measurement.
2. Mr. Boggs also asks you to show how the results of a second year will compare with those of the first in terms of purchasing power if the price index falls to 150 within six months and remains there for the rest of the

year. All this, of course, is entirely prospective, but he wants to know, nevertheless, how the book and real gains and losses on the state bonds under the assumed conditions would compare with the results obtained by investing in common stocks during the year just ended.

CASE 8–4. FOREVER STORES, INC.

Karl Stone, president and principal stockholder of Forever Stores, Inc., sat at his desk reflecting on the condition of his business in general,

Exhibit 1

FOREVER STORES, INC.

Comparative Balance Sheets at 12/31/73 and 12/31/72
(000,000 omitted)

	December 31	
ASSETS	*1973*	*1972*
Cash	$ 2.4	$ 2.3
Accounts Receivable	56.3	53.7
Inventories	34.3	32.7
Other Current Assets	0.6	0.6
Total Current Assets	93.6	89.3
Plant and Equipment	10.6	10.6
Less: Accumulated Depreciation	3.9	3.4
Net Plant and Equipment	6.7	7.2
Other Assets	3.4	3.5
Total Assets	$103.7	$100.0
LIABILITIES AND OWNERS' EQUITY		
Accounts Payable	$ 31.5	$ 29.9
Accruals	4.4	4.2
Other Current Liabilities	1.4	1.3
Total Current Liabilities	37.3	35.4
Long-term Debt	15.3	14.9
Other Liabilities	10.5	10.1
Common Stock	33.6	33.6
Retained Earnings	7.0	6.0
Total Owners' Equity	40.6	39.6
Total Liabilities and Owners' Equity	$103.7	$100.0

and on the 1973 results (see Exhibits 1 and 2) in particular. It hadn't been a great year, he mused, but it hadn't been a disaster either. At least he didn't have to worry about the energy crisis; his 94 jewelry stores were all located in high pedestrian-traffic areas of major metropolitan areas, and he had recently been assured by his regional managers that there had been no noticable slump in sales. Still, Stone feld mildly uncomfortable about another problem in the U.S. economy that didn't seem to want to go away: inflation. He felt that if he could only get some feel for the parameters of the situation as it affected Forever, he would be better able to deal with it. With this in mind he called his assistant, a recent business school graduate, into his office.

"Carole," he began, "I have the feeling that we're getting clobbered by rising prices, but these statements look as healthy as ever. Since it looks as

Exhibit 2

FOREVER STORES, INC.

Statement of Income and Retained Earnings
For Year Ended December 31, 1973
(000,000 omitted)

Sales		$100.0
Cost of Goods Sold		
Opening Inventory	$32.7	
Purchases	81.6	
Closing Inventory	(34.3)	80.0
Gross Margin		20.0
Depreciation		0.5
Other Expenses		13.8
Operating Profit		5.7
Interest Expense		1.7
Income Before Tax		4.0
Income Tax Expense		2.0
Net Income		$ 2.0
Retained Earnings, 12/31/72		$ 6.0
Add: 1973 Net Income		2.0
Less: Dividends paid, 1973		1.0
Retained Earnings, 12/31/73		$ 7.0

though inflation is here to stay, at least for a while, I think that this might be a good time to review some of our financial policies: capital structure, dividend policy, credit policies, things of that sort. But I have to be able to *see* what I'm fighting first; I need *information*. Do you see what I'm driving at?"

Carole Schultz shifted in her chair. "Yes, I believe I do," she replied. "What you're referring to are price-level adjusted financial statements; the techniques involved here have been part of GAAP for years, but have been largely ignored in practice. They relate a company's reported results to general price level changes in the economy."

Stone leaned back, looking slightly relieved. "Excellent. What do you need to construct these statements?"

"First, I'll need a table of the Gross National Product Implicit Price

Deflator (GNPI) going back to 1963, the year the company was formed," she responded, "but I can get that at the library (see Exhibit 3). Then, in addition to the basic financial statements, I'll need schedules that show the age of individual items in our 'non-monetary' accounts: Plant and Equip-

Exhibit 3

FOREVER STORES, INC.

Implicit Price Deflators For Gross National Product
For Years 1963–1973
(1958 = 100)

Year	GNPI	Adjustment Factor*
1963	107.2	1.477
1964	108.8	1.456
1965	110.9	1.428
1966	113.94	1.390
1967	117.59	1.347
1968	122.30	1.295
1969	128.20	1.235
1970	135.24	1.171
1971	141.60	1.118
1972	146.10	1.084
1973	153.94	1.029

Quarterly Averages

	1972		1973	
	GNPI	Adj. Factor	GNPI	Adj. Factor
I	144.85	1.093	149.81	1.057
II	145.42	1.089	152.46	1.039
III	146.42	1.082	155.06	1.021
IV	147.63	1.073	158.36	1.000

* These factors are the ratio of the fourth quarter 1973 GNPI (158.36) to the GNPI shown. Hence they can be used to adjust amounts for the year or quarter shown to December 31, 1973 price levels.
Source: U.S. Department of Commerce Bureau of Economic Analysis: *Survey of Current Business*, February 1974, for 1973 data; 1972 *Business Statistics* for all other data.

ment, Other Current Assets, Other Assets, Other Liabilities, and Common Stock and Surplus (Exhibit 4). I'll get on it right away."

"Fine," replied Stone. "While you're at it, I'd like you to think about the implications of the figures you come up with. I'd like to know what kinds of decisions the price-level adjusted data will help us make, and I'd also like to get your ideas on some of the weaknesses or pitfalls that we should watch out for. I have a meeting with another director later today, so I'd like to go over your results with you before then. I'll see you at three."

Exhibit 4

FOREVER STORES, INC.

Chronological Analysis of Selected Accounts
($000,000)

Plant and Equipment

Year Acquired	Gross Investment	Accumulated Depreciation* 12/31/72	Net Amount 12/31/72	Net Amount 12/31/73
1963.................	$ 3.6	$1.8	$1.8	$1.6
1965.................	1.5	0.6	0.9	0.8
1968.................	2.4	0.6	1.8	1.7
1970.................	2.1	0.3	1.8	1.7
1971.................	1.0	0.1	0.9	0.8
	$10.6	$3.4	$7.2	$6.7

Common Stock

Year Acquired	Amount
1963..........................	$16.8
1966..........................	8.4
1970..........................	8.4
	$33.6

* All Plant and Equipment depreciated straight-line over 20 years.

Questions

1. Identify the monetary assets and liabilities (those whose amounts are fixed by contract or otherwise, and will not change regardless of price level changes) and restate the December 31, 1972 amounts to December 31, 1973 using the adjustment factor of 1.073. Subtract the monetary liabilities from monetary assets to arrive at *net* monetary items. (In this and succeeding questions, round off the final result to the nearest $100,000.)

2. Restate the inventories for both years, assuming 35 percent of the ending inventories as of December 31 were acquired in the third quarter and the rest in the fourth quarter. Use the appropriate factors from Exhibit 3.

3. Adjust the cost and depreciation of fixed assets for the years 1963–72 to December 31, 1973 price levels for both years' balance sheets.

4. Adjust other current assets, other assets, and other liabilities on both years' balance sheets to December 31, 1973 levels, assuming these items were acquired in 1968.

5. Compute the 1973 price level gain or loss as follows: first add the 1972 year-end *historical* amounts of *net* monetary items (identified in Question 1) and 1973 historical monetary receipts (sales, increase in other liabilities, decrease in other assets); then subtract the 1973 historical monetary expenditures (purchases, other expenses, interest, taxes, and dividends paid). Then do the same thing for all these amounts adjusting to December 31, 1973 price levels. The difference between these unadjusted (historical) and adjusted totals is the price level gain or loss for 1973.

6. Prepare December 31, 1972 and 1973 balance sheets adjusted to December 31, 1973 price levels. (Stockholders' Equity is a "plug" figure, that is, the amount needed to make the statement balance.)
7. Prepare a 1973 statement of income restated in December 31, 1973 dollars.

CASE 8–5. OLIVER OPTICS COMPANY (A)

When John Oliver graduated from technical school he started making plans for a small business to grind special lenses and to make certain high-quality optical items for the scientific and military demand. At the time there was keen demand for a high-quality product and Oliver thought he could build a substantial business by stressing this quality element. He started his business January 1 and after a year of some very disturbing and revealing difficulties in meeting customers' high standards, Oliver thought he had things going well. By working hard and personally satisfying all complaints, he knew he had created much goodwill for his firm.

Oliver began his business with $10,000 of savings, including some money he had inherited. On March 31, he borrowed $4,000 on a one-year note (4%) from his uncle, who had intimated he would renew the note every year so long as Oliver needed the money. He had had large bills for materials, but had been able to keep from falling too far behind in his payments. Except for the accounts indicated below as unpaid, all bills had been paid in cash, including the interest on the note. On April 1, he had paid in advance the first 12 months' interest on the loan.

Mr. Oliver purchased some standard equipment at the first of the year "on time," agreeing to make a partial payment of $2,000 and to pay $500 every three months for four years. Since the payments were scheduled to start at once and since he had agreed to pay $120 interest every six months in advance, his initial payment was $2,620. A year having passed, the fifth payment of $500 would now have to be met, plus $120 interest. Previous installments had been paid in cash.

When the equipment was bought, the company insisted on Oliver's taking out four years' insurance which had cost a total of $400. The equipment presumably would be useful for at least 10 years, though Oliver contemplated that if all went according to his plans, he would have to get rid of the equipment in five years and buy some with a greater operating capacity. He estimated that the equipment could probably be sold for $2,000 at that time.

By the end of the first year Oliver had three people working for him. One was a young woman who took care of his office work as well as spending about one third of her time packing the delicate products as they were completed in the shop. The other two workers, hired in about the third month, spent all of their time in the shop. About 20 percent of Mr. Oliver's time was spent in office work and on selling trips, but the rest of the time he was to be found in the shop working with the other workers.

At the end of the year, Oliver's records included the following:

Salaries paid (through Dec. 31)	
Mary Schultz...	$ 2,400
John Bardell..	6,400
Peter Nutchell..	7,000
John Oliver...	12,000
Rent..	4,000
Unpaid bills from suppliers*..	10,260
Paid bills from suppliers (includes the initial payment and all subsequent interest and principal payments on the equipment loan)..............	24,240
Uncollected accounts	
U.S. Government..	10,300
Universities Scientific Supply Co...................................	8,260
Payment due Oliver for subcontract work, completed and shipped, Dec. 17—Pegasus Aircraft Co....................................	1,940
Spent on office supplies..	500
Inventory on hand, at estimated cost................................	6,400
Office supplies...	100
Various administrative and selling expenses (including travel, advertising and interest on uncle's loan)........................	5,460
Electricity, etc..	860
Cash on hand†..	1,460

* Does not include the balance due for the equipment referred to in the third paragraph.

† Does not include a check for $4,060 from Universities Scientific Supply Co. believed to be in the mail as their regular settlement of accounts as of the close of the previous month. December billings to Universities Scientific Supply Co. were $4,200.

Most of Oliver's sales were to two buyers, the U.S. Government and the Universities Scientific Supply Company. Oliver had sold some $620 worth of goods to one buyer earlier in the year when business was slow, and when the firm became bankrupt with no assets whatever and without having paid its bill, Oliver promised himself, "Never again." Other firms, he was told, protected themselves against such losses by use of a charge of 1% of year-ending accounts receivables as an allowance for bad debts.

In October, the Pegasus Aircraft Company had asked Oliver to do some work for them, altering special equipment which they sent on to Oliver's shop. The first lot had been completed before the year end, but the payment for the work, $1,940, had not been received. A second shipment, apparently valued at $6,000, had just come in (afternoon of December 31) from the Pegasus plant, but the alteration work (which would come to about $2,000) had not yet been started. Mr. Oliver ascertained that the $6,000 value of this incoming material had not been included in the totals for inventory listed above.

The inventory included 200 special items costing $1,600 which had been made for a government order, but had not as yet been shipped. Frankly, Mr. Oliver had wanted the situation to settle a little before making delivery, for a previous shipment of the same size (one half the original order) had not met the specifications of the government inspectors and 20 percent of the shipment was being returned as unsatisfactory. Fortunately the items carried a 30 percent markup over Oliver's cost, so he was not too badly off. Still Oliver was disturbed about the matter because he thought his inspection standards when the first batch had been made had been no different than those in force at any other time, and besides he was advertising high-quality products. He certainly had no idea as to why the 20 percent had been rejected. He intended to file an appeal to try to collect the full amount that he had billed the government (included in the $10,300 in the year-end listing given above), particularly since the rejected items could not be reworked and were not worth much to any other possible buyer.

Question

Prepare Mr. Oliver's income statement for the year and his ending balance sheet. You should show clearly how any figure not taken directly from the text has been determined.

CHAPTER 9

LIABILITIES AND OWNERS' EQUITY

This chapter describes the equities side of the balance sheet—liabilities and owners' equity. As mentioned in Chapter 2, liabilities and owners' equity represent the sources of the funds which have been used in acquiring the items on the asset side of the balance sheet. The process of identifying the needs for new funds and acquiring these funds is part of the function known as "financial management." The treasurer and other executives who are responsible for financial affairs in a company need a considerable store of technical knowledge regarding the various means of raising money, the legal and tax rules relating to financing, and so on. Other members of management should have some understanding of these matters, even though they scarcely can be expected to be conversant with all the details.

This chapter discusses the accounting aspects of these financial matters at a level that is intended to provide a general understanding to the nonfinancial manager. In the typical company, events of the type discussed in this chapter occur infrequently, but when they do occur they are likely to have a major impact on the financial statements.

NATURE OF LIABILITIES

In Chapter 2, a liability was defined as an obligation to an outside party. This definition is approximately correct; however, some legal obligations to outside parties are not liabilities in the accounting meaning of this word, and some accounting liabilities are not legally enforceable obligations.

As an example of an obligation that is not a liability, consider the case of an employee who has a written contract guaranteeing him employment at a stated salary for the next two years (e.g., professional athletes, coaches, executives). Such a contract is a legally enforceable claim against the business, but it is *not* a liability in the accounting sense, because according to generally accepted accounting principles this transaction is not recorded in the accounts until the person actually performs the work.

What distinguishes such a contract from those that do give rise to liabilities? Essentially, the distinction is determined by whether or not there is an asset or expense debit to offset the liability credit. When an employee works, the offsetting debit to the liability Accrued Wages Payable is Wages Expense. But when a contract is signed covering *future* employment, no expense account in the current period is affected, nor is an asset created. A liability is not created until the services have been performed. Similarly, the amount of interest on notes and bonds that is to accrue subsequent to the date of the balance sheet is not a liability.

An estimated allowance for future costs under a warranty agreement is an example of a liability that is not a definite obligation at the time it is set up. When a warranty agreement applies, the liability account is set up in the period in which the revenue is recognized, the offsetting debit being to an expense account such as Estimated Warranty Expense. Later on, when repairs or replacements under warranty are made, the liability account will be debited and other balance sheet accounts such as parts inventory will be credited.

Current Liabilities

As described in Chapter 2, current liabilities are those economic obligations which are payable in the near future, usually within the next twelve months, or during the next operating cycle if it is longer than twelve months (as with a whiskey distiller). Most firms' balance sheets will reflect these current liabilities: accounts payable (amounts due to suppliers in payment of materials sold to the firm); notes payable (amounts due to banks or other short-term lenders); taxes payable (owed to local, state, or federal governments); accrued expenses (most commonly, wages payable); and deferred revenue (such as prepaid rent or other advance payments such as for magazine subscriptions).

One noteworthy aspect of current liabilities is that in many cases they represent "free" sources of funds to the company. For example, many suppliers will give a company thirty days to pay for materials or supplies that have been sold to it. In effect, this credit policy by the supplier represents an interest-free thirty-day loan to the company.[1] Similarly,

---

[1] But if the supplier allows a "cash discount" for payment sooner than the 30 days (usually within 10 days), then in effect there *is* an interest charge to the firm if it does not pay during the period when the cash discount can be taken.

when a person prepays rent to a property owner this prepayment is, in effect, an interest-free loan from the renter to the owner. Interest-bearing notes payable are not free sources of funds.

Deferred Income Taxes

As discussed in Chapter 8, the amount of money payable by a corporation to the government in income taxes for the year will normally be a different amount than shown on the income statement as Provision for Income Taxes. This gives rise in most instances to a credit balance account called Deferred Income Tax. As the title suggests, the balance in the Deferred Income Tax account shows the cumulative total amount of tax payments the firm has postponed by using accounting methods on its *tax return* which result in lower taxable income than the "income before tax expense" figure shown on its *income statement*.

Deferred Income Taxes are not the same thing as *taxes payable*. The latter is an obligation to pay a specific amount of taxes by a specified date. Deferred income taxes, on the other hand, really arise as a result of applying the matching concept in the determination of the income statement tax expense of the period. Deferred income taxes are simply postponed taxes, and do not have the same formal characteristics of most other liabilities, such as a specified payment date or schedule. However, like other liabilities, deferred income taxes are classified as current and noncurrent. For example, deferred taxes arising from the tax effects of uncollected accounts receivable are a current item, whereas deferred taxes arising from fixed asset depreciation timing differences are noncurrent.[2]

Contingent Liabilities

A *contingent liability* exists when a current situation may result in a liability upon the occurrence of some future event, but the amount, if any, of the liability cannot reasonably be predicted as of the balance sheet date. The situation must exist currently; hence, possible future losses from fire, natural catastrophes, and war are not contingent liabilities. The amount must depend upon some future event, such as the settlement of a lawsuit; if the amount can be reasonably estimated now, it is not a contingent liability. Examples of contingent liabilities are possible penalties, fines, or damages from pending litigation; possible assessments of additional taxes; possible payments from default on debts which the company has guaranteed; possible refund resulting from renegotiation of contracts; and possible additional payments to employees for services they have already performed.

Contingent liabilities are *not* recorded in the financial statements them-

---

[2] APB *Opinion No. 11*, (December 1967), par. 57.

selves; however, they must be disclosed in a footnote if they are material in amount. By contrast, an obligation whose amount can be reasonably estimated *is* a liability, and is so recorded, even though the precise amount is not now known.

LONG-TERM LIABILITIES

The long-term debt instruments that a firm may employ to obtain capital include, among others, term loans, bonds, mortgage bonds, subordinated debentures, and convertible bonds. What these various instruments have in common is that the repayment obligation on the part of the corporation issuing the debt extends over a period of more than one year.

A *term loan* is a business loan with a maturity of more than one year, repayable according to a specified schedule. This schedule typically calls for equal periodic installments, although sometimes the final payment is larger than the others; this is called a *balloon payment*. Term loan maturities tend to run five years or less when the lender is a commercial bank; term loans from insurance companies typically run for five to fifteen years.

A *bond* is simply a certificate promising to pay its holder a specified sum of money (usually $1,000) plus interest at a stated rate. Although usually issued in units of $1,000, the price of a bond is usually quoted as a percentage of this face value; thus a price of 100 means $1,000. Bonds may be issued to the general public through the intermediary of an investment banker, or they may be "privately placed" with an insurance company or other financial institution. If the bond is not secured by specific assets of the issuing corporation, it is also referred to as a *debenture*.

A *mortgage bond* (or simply "mortgage") is a bond secured by designated "pledged" assets of the corporation, usually fixed assets. Should the firm default on the mortgage, the pledged assets are sold to repay the mortgage. If the proceeds from the sale of the pledged assets are less than the amount of the mortgage, then the mortgage holder becomes a general creditor for the shortfall.

A *subordinated debenture* has two features that differentiate it from a mortgage bond. First, the fact that it is a "debenture" means that it is not secured by the pledge of any specific asset. "Subordinated" means that in a liquidation the debt holder's claims on the firm's assets would be settled only if the claims of all unsubordinated creditors were settled in full. Subordinated debt holder's claims do, however, take precedence over those of preferred and common stockholders.

A *convertible bond* is one that may be converted at the option of the holder into a specified number of shares of the issuer's common stock.

Like other bonds, a convertible may be unsecured and subordinated, in which case it is called a "convertible subordinated debenture."

Recording a Bond Issue

To illustrate the entries typically made to record the proceeds from an issue of bonds, assume the Mason Corporation issues 100 bonds, each with a *par* value (also called *principal* or *face value*) of $1,000, with an interest rate (also called *nominal* or *coupon rate*) of 8 percent ($80 per year), payable in 20 years, and not secured by any specific Mason Corporation assets. (Such a bond would be called an "8 percent, 20-year debenture".) If the corporation receives $1,000 for each of these bonds, the following entry would be made:

```
Cash................................... 100,000
    Bonds Payable.....................         100,000
```

Frequently bonds are issued for less than their par value, that is, at a *discount*, or for more than their par value, at a *premium*. This happens when the prevailing interest rate at the time of issuance is different from the *coupon* rate, i.e., the rate printed on the bond.

> EXAMPLE: If the prevailing rate of interest or "yield" in the bond market is 9 percent for bonds with a risk similar to those issued by the Mason Corporation, potential investors will be unwilling to pay $1,000 for Mason Corporation 8 percent bonds. They would be willing to pay an amount such that the $80 annual interest on these bonds would be 9 percent of this amount. This amount (neglecting investment bankers' fees and other costs) works out to be approximately $889. The bond would therefore be sold at a discount of $111.[3]

The words "discount" and "premium" carry no connotation of "bad" or "good." They reflect simply a difference between the coupon interest rate for the issue and the going market rate of interest at the time of issuance. The stated rate may be made intentionally different from the going rate in the belief that this makes the bonds more attractive. The coupon rate also may differ from the going rate because of changed

---

[3] Although we speak of investors "paying" for a newly-issued bond, and commonly new issues of bonds are said to be "sold," it should be made clear that a bond is *not* an asset of the corporation which is sold, as are goods or services. Rather a bond represents a contribution of funds to the firm by an investor, who expects to be paid interest on his funds while the firm is using them, and to have his funds ultimately returned to him. To the investor, the bond *is* an asset, and if other parties desire to acquire it, the bond market provides the mechanism for him to convert his bond to cash. In this latter case, the investor *has* "sold" his bond, a sale which has no impact on the flow of funds into or out of the firm. (Similar comments apply to new issues of stock.)

market conditions between the time the coupon rate is established and the time the bond becomes available to investors. Usually, the coupon rate is quite close to the market rate as of the date of issue.

The offering of a bond issue to the public is usually undertaken by an investment banking firm which charges a fee for this service. In addition to this fee, the corporation also incurs printing, legal, and accounting costs in connection with the bond issue. These bond issue costs are set up as a deferred charge, which is an asset, and the asset is amortized over the life of the issue.[4] The premium or discount does not include the issue costs; rather it is based on the difference between the amount paid for the bond by the investor and the face value of the bond.

> EXAMPLE: Mason Corporation's bonds, which brought $889 each from investors, also had issue costs to Mason averaging $29 per bond, resulting in a net cash inflow to Mason of $860 per bond. The discount is $111 per bond, not $140.

If the conditions of the preceding examples are assumed, and the Mason Corporation received $86,000 from the issuance of $100,000 face amount of bonds, the following entry would be made:

```
Cash...................................  86,000
Bond Discount..........................  11,100
Deferred Charges.......................   2,900
    Bonds Payable......................          100,000
```

If the corporation received more than the face amount, say $110,000 (after issuance costs), the corresponding entry would be:

```
Cash................................... 110,000
Deferred Charges.......................   2,900
    Bond Premium.......................           12,900
    Bond Payable.......................          100,000
```

Balance Sheet Presentation

Bonds payable are shown in the long-term liabilities section of the balance sheet until one year before they mature, when ordinarily they become current liabilities. The description should give the principal facts about the issue, e.g., "8¾% Subordinated Debentures due 1994." When a bond issue is to be refunded with a new long-term liability, however, it is not shown as a current liability in the year of maturity since it will not require the use of current assets. If the bonds are to be retired in installments (as with *serial bonds*), that portion to be retired within a year is shown in the current liabilities section.

---

[4] APB *Opinion No. 21* (August 1971), par. 16.

Bond discount or premium is shown on the balance sheet as a direct deduction from or addition to the face amount of the bond, as illustrated:[5]

	Discount		*Premium*	
Bonds Payable:		Bonds Payable:		
Principal	$100,000	Principal		$100,000
Less unamortized		Add unamortized		
discount	11,100	premium		12,900
	$ 88,900			$112,900

The principal amount less unamortized discount or plus unamortized premium is sometimes referred to as the "book value" of the bond.

Bond Interest

An accounting entry is made to record the semiannual interest payments to bondholders and at the same time to amortize a portion of the bond premium or discount. The effect of this entry is that the *net* debit to Interest Expense reflects, not the stated amount of interest actually paid to bondholders (unless the holders paid par for the issue), but rather the effective rate of interest, which is larger or smaller than the stated rate, according to whether the bonds were sold at a discount or at a premium. The existence of bond discount in effect increases the interest expense, while the existence of bond premium decreases it.

Bond discount or premium may be amortized in one of two ways: by the straight-line method, in which the discount is debited (or the premium is credited) to Interest Expense in equal installments over the life of the issue; or by the compound interest method, in which the discount or premium is written off in such a way that the net interest expense bears a constant ratio to the book value of the bonds over the whole life of the issue. This ratio is the effective interest rate on the borrowed funds.

The following entry records the semiannual bond interest payment and amortization of discount on a straight-line basis for the 8 percent Mason Corporation bonds that were assumed to have been sold at $889 each:

```
Interest Expense.......................... 4,278
    Bond Discount.........................          278
    Cash..................................        4,000
```

The cash paid out as interest is $4,000, which is 8 percent × $100,000 × $\frac{1}{2}$ year. The $278 credit to Bond Discount is $\frac{1}{40}$ of the $11,100 that is to be amortized over 40 semiannual periods. The interest expense is the sum of these amounts.

---

[5] *Ibid.* APB *Opinion No. 21* also requires disclosure of the "effective" rate of interest on the bond (determined using techniques described in Chapter 19).

If the interest payment date does not coincide with the closing of the company's books, an adjusting entry is made to record accrued interest expense and the amortization of discount or premium. Assuming that the Mason Corporation bonds are sold at $889 each on September 30, that the interest dates are September 30 and March 31, and that the fiscal year ends on December 31, the following entries would be made:

1. Adjustment on December 31:

```
Bond Interest Expense........................  2,139
    Bond Discount................................        139
    Accrued Interest Payable.................      2,000
```

2. Payment of semiannual interest on March 31:

```
Bond Interest Expense........................  2,139
Accrued Interest Payable.....................  2,000
    Bond Discount................................        139
    Cash.........................................      4,000
```

3. Payment of semiannual interest on the following September 30:

```
Bond Interest Expense........................  4,278
    Bond Discount................................        278
    Cash.........................................      4,000
```

Bond issuance costs, which are treated as a deferred charge, are amortized in a manner completely analogous to bond discount.

Retirement of Bonds

Bonds may be retired in total, or they may be retired in installments over a period of years. In either case the retirement is recorded by a debit to Bonds Payable and a credit to Cash, or to a sinking fund which has been set up for this purpose. The bond discount or premium will have been completely amortized by the maturity date, so no additional entry is required for discount or premium at that time.

Bonds are sometimes retired at maturity out of a sinking fund which has been created in installments over the life of the issue to ensure sufficient funds are on hand at maturity to retire the bonds. Bond sinking funds may be controlled by the originating corporation, but they are usually controlled by a trustee, such as a bank. Prior to maturity, sinking funds are invested by the trustee so as to earn interest on the funds thus tied up. Sinking funds usually appear in the investment section of the assets side of the balance sheet.

Refunding a Bond Issue

Some bonds can be redeemed before their maturity dates by paying for them at a premium, that is, by paying more than the par value. Such bonds are said to be *callable* and contain a schedule of *call prices* as part of the terms of the issue. In periods when interest rates have declined, a company may consider it advantageous to *refund* a bond issue, that is, to call the old issue and float a new one with a lower rate of interest. At that point, the company must account for the *call premium* (the difference between the call price and par value), any other costs of the refunding, and any unamortized issue costs and discount (or premium) on the old bonds.

The bonds' face amount, adjusted for unamortized premium or discount and costs of issuance, is called the *net carrying amount* of the debt to be refunded. The price paid on refunding, including the call premium and miscellaneous costs of refunding, is called the *reacquisition price*. The difference between these two amounts must be reported as a separate loss or gain on the income statement for the period in which the refunding takes place.[6]

> EXAMPLE: If the 100 Mason Corporation bonds are called at the end of 10 years (half their scheduled life) by paying the call price to each bondholder, half the bond discount and issuance costs would not have been amortized. If the call price is $1,050 per bond and miscellaneous refunding costs are $1,000 in total, the loss is as follows:

$$\text{Reacquisition Price} = 105,000 + 1,000 \quad = 106,000$$
$$\text{Net Carrying Amount} = 100,000 - \tfrac{1}{2}(11,100)$$
$$- \tfrac{1}{2}\ (2,900) = \underline{93,000}$$
$$\text{Loss on Retirement of Bonds}: \quad \overline{13,000}$$

The accounting entries are:

```
Bonds Payable...............................  100,000
Loss on Retirement of Bonds.................   13,000
    Cash....................................             106,000
    Bond Discount...........................               5,550
    Deferred Charges (issue costs)..........               1,450
```

FORMS OF BUSINESS ORGANIZATION

Before discussing the other portion of the equities side of the balance sheet, owners' equity, the three principal legal forms of business ownership need to be described. These forms are: the sole proprietorship, the partnership, and the corporation.

Sole Proprietorship

A *sole proprietorship* is a business entity owned by a single person. Proprietorship is a simple form for the organization of a business: with

---

[6] APB *Opinion No. 26* (October 1972), par. 20.

the possible exception of necessary licenses or permits, all one does to form a proprietorship is to begin selling goods or one's services. There are no incorporation fees to pay; no restriction on the nature of the business; no special reports to file (except an additional schedule on the proprietor's personal income tax return); and no co-owners with whom to disagree, to share liability for their actions, or to share the profits of the business. Also, a proprietorship's profits (whether withdrawn by the proprietor or retained in the firm) are taxed at the proprietor's personal income tax rate, which may be lower than the corporate tax rate. (If the owner's personal tax rate exceeds the corporate rate, that is one incentive to incorporate.)

On the other hand, sole proprietorships have some disadvantages. Because they are small, because their owners have limited assets, and because they cannot issue stock or bonds, it is difficult for them to raise capital. Also disadvantageous is the liability of the proprietor for the firm's business debts. In the event of the firm's failure, the creditors have claims not only against the assets of the proprietorship (an accounting entity), but also against the personal assets of the proprietor, such as his home and car. Some one-owner firms are incorporated to protect the owner's personal assets from business claims.

Partnership

A *partnership* is a business with essentially the same features as a proprietorship, except that it is owned by two or more persons, called the partners. Like a proprietorship, a partnership is a relatively simple and inexpensive kind of organization to form. In a partnership each partner is personally liable for all debts incurred by the business, so in the event of the firm's failure, each partner's personal assets are jeopardized. Also, each partner is responsible for the business actions of the other partners. For example, in an architectural firm if one partner makes a mistake in a drawing for a structure that ultimately results in a lawsuit by the building's owner, the potential liability extends to all the partners, not just to the one who made the mistake.

Because several co-owners are involved in a partnership, there must be an agreement (perhaps implied or expressed only orally, but preferably and usually written) which includes the names of the partners, the partnership's purpose, the capital contributions of each partner, each partner's salary, the manner in which profits or losses will be shared, and the subdivision of the net assets if the partnership is dissolved. When the partnership's annual income is divided among the partners, each pays income tax on his share at his personal income tax rate, whether or not these profits are actually distributed to the partners in cash.

Corporations

The *corporation* is a legal entity with essentially perpetual existence, which comes into being under the aegis of the state, which grants it a *charter* to operate. The corporation is an "artificial person" in the sense that it is taxed on its net income as an entity, and legal liability accrues to the corporation rather than to its owners as individuals.

Compared with a proprietorship or a partnership, the corporate form of organization has these disadvantages: there may be significant legal and other fees involved in its formation; the corporation is limited in its activities to those specifically granted in its charter; it is subject to numerous regulations and requirements, including reporting of financial information; and it must secure permission from each state in which it wishes to operate. Moreover, its income is subject to *double taxation:* the corporation's net income is taxed, and distributions of any of this income to shareholders in the form of dividends is taxed again, this time at the shareholder's personal income tax rate.[7]

On the other hand, in addition to its limited liability and indefinite existence, a corporation has the advantage of being able to raise capital from a large number of investors through issuing bonds and stock. Moreover, a corporate shareholder can usually liquidate his ownership by selling his shares to someone else.

Most business firms in the United States do not operate as corporations. As of 1970, of the slightly more than 12 million U.S. business firms, 78 percent were proprietorships, 8 percent were partnerships, and 14 percent were corporations. However, the great bulk of *business activity* in the U.S. *is* performed by corporations. Using net sales figures as a measure of activity, in 1970 corporations accounted for 84 percent of total U.S. business sales of $2.1 trillion, whereas proprietorships accounted for 11 percent and partnerships for only 5 percent.[8]

ACCOUNTING FOR OWNERS' EQUITY

Proprietorship and Partnership Equity

Not much more need be said about the owner's equity accounts in a single proprietorship than the comments already made in Chapter 2. There may be a single account in which all entries affecting the owner's

---

[7] An exception is a "Subchapter S" corporation. These are corporations with ten or fewer stockholders which, if certain conditions are met, pay no corporate income tax. Instead, as in a partnership, the owners are taxed on their respective shares of taxable income at their personal tax rates.

[8] U.S. Bureau of the Census, *Statistical Abstract of the United States: 1973* (94th ed.). Washington, D.C., 1973.

equity are recorded, or a separate *drawing account* may be set up to handle periodic withdrawals made by the owner. If a drawing account is used, it may either be closed into the capital account at the end of the accounting period, or it may be kept separate so as to show the owner's original contribution of capital separate from the effect on his equity of subsequent events. As far as the ultimate effect is concerned, it is immaterial whether the owner regards his withdrawals as salary or as a return of profit; but if he wishes to compare his income statement with that of a corporation, he will undoubtedly treat a certain part of his withdrawals as salary (although in a corporation that is managed by its owners, the distinction between salary and dividends may also be quite fuzzy in practice).

A partnership has the problem of showing in the accounts the equity of the individual partners, and this varies depending on the terms of the partnership agreement. The accounts are set up to facilitate the computation of each partner's equity, in accordance with whatever the agreement may be. In the absence of a specific agreement, the law assumes that net income is to be divided equally among the partners, and this is also common in written partnership agreements. If such is the case, in a three-person partnership the capital account, or the drawing account, of each partner is credited with one third of net income. It is debited with the actual amount of the partner's withdrawals.

If the agreement is that profits are to be divided in proportion to the capital originally contributed by each partner, then the capital account is maintained to show the amount of that contribution, and other transactions affecting the partners' equity are debited or credited to separate drawings or personal accounts. If one of the partners made a temporary loan to the partnership, it would be shown in a liability account (but separate from loans made by outside parties) rather than in the partner's equity account.

Partnership agreements may also provide that the partners receive stated salaries and a stated share of residual profits after salaries, or a stated percentage of interest on the capital they invested and a stated share of residual profits, or a combination of salary and interest. The accounting required in connection with such arrangements depends on the specific terms of the agreement.

EXAMPLE: The partnership agreement of Paine and Webber provided that Paine (who worked half time) would receive a salary of $10,000 and Webber a salary of $20,000; that each would receive 6 percent interest on the capital they contributed; and that they would share equally in the remainder. In 1975 the average balance in Paine's capital account was $50,000 and in Webber's, $10,000. The partnership net income was $40,000.

The income of each partner would be computed as follows:

	Total	Paine	Webber
Salary	$30,000	$10,000	$20,000
Interest on Capital	3,600	3,000	600
Remainder	6,400	3,200	3,200
Total	$40,000	$16,200	$23,800

Whatever the partnership arrangement, the law does not regard salaries or interest payments to the partners as being different from any other type of withdrawal, since the partnership is not an entity legally separate from the individual partners.

Ownership in a Corporation

Ownership in a corporation is evidenced by a *stock* certificate. This capital stock may be either *common* or *preferred*. Each corporation is authorized in its charter to issue a maximum number of *shares* of each class of stock. The stock certificate shows how many shares of ownership it represents. Because a corporation's owners hold stock certificates which indicate their shares of ownership, owners' equity in a corporation is often called *shareholders' equity* or *stockholders' equity*.

The balance sheet amount for shareholders' equity consists of two parts: (1) the amount invested in the firm by its shareholders, called *contributed capital;* and (2) retained earnings. The amount of contributed capital, in turn, is the sum of two amounts: the par or stated value of the outstanding shares of capital stock; and the amount the shareholders have invested in the firm by paying more for their shares than this par or stated value. Before dealing in more detail with these owners' equity amounts, we should briefly describe preferred and common stock.

PREFERRED STOCK. Preferred stock pays a stated dividend, much like the interest payment on bonds. Preferred stock has preference, or priority, over common as to the receipt of dividends, as to assets in the event of liquidation, or as to other specified matters. Preferred stock may be *cumulative* or *noncumulative*. With cumulative preferred, if the corporation is unable to pay the regular dividend, the unpaid dividends add up or cumulate and are paid when the firm resumes payment of preferred dividends.

> EXAMPLE: In 1975 Cotting Corporation did not pay the $7 dividend on its 7% cumulative preferred stock. Hence, no dividend can be paid on the common stock in 1975. In 1976 holders of Cotting's common stock cannot be paid any dividend unless $14 is paid on the 7% cumulative preferred (the $7 1976 dividend plus the $7 from 1975).

Preferred stock is usually issued with a face or par value of $100 per share. The dividend rate (7% in the above example) is analogous to the coupon rate on a bond. Also like bonds, preferred stock may be convertible into a specified number of shares of common stock; this is called a *convertible preferred*. Unlike bonds, however, preferred stock does not have a maturity date; i.e., there is no provision for redemption of the preferred on a given date at its par value. (In liquidation, if sufficient assets exist after all liabilities have been settled, preferred stockholders are entitled to receive par for their shares.) Also, whereas bondholders can force the firm into bankruptcy if an interest payment on the bonds is missed, preferred stockholders have no such recourse. Interest on bonds is an expense, both for financial accounting purposes and for income tax purposes, whereas a dividend on stock, including preferred stock, is *not* an expense. Accounting treatment of preferred stock is substantially the same as for common stock, described below.

Compared with both common stock and bonds, preferred stock is a relatively small source of corporate funds. In 1972 corporations raised almost $42 billion using one of these three instruments: of this amount, 69 percent was raised by issuing bonds, 23 percent by common stock, and only 8 percent by preferred stock.[9]

COMMON STOCK. Common stock may be either par value or no-par value. *Par value stock*[10] appears in the accounts at a fixed amount per share (often $1, $10, or $100), which is specified in the corporation's charter or bylaws. Whereas par value on a bond or on preferred stock has meaning, on common stock this figure is arbitrary, essentially meaningless, and hence potentially misleading. Except by coincidence, the par value of the stock in a going concern has no relation either to the stock's market value or to its book value. *Book value* of common stock is the total common shareholders' equity as reported on the balance sheet, that is, the sum of common stock at par plus paid-in surplus attributable to the common plus retained earnings (or, stated another way, assets minus liabilities minus preferred stock), divided by the number of outstanding shares of common stock. Paid-in capital is the amount received from shareholders in excess of the par value.

No-par value stock has a *stated value*, which is fixed by the board of directors. The stated value governs the amounts to be entered in the Capital Stock account just as if it were a par value. The distinction between par value and no-par value stock is therefore of little practical significance.

Recording the Issue

To illustrate the issuance of stock, let us consider the Carroll Corporation, which received a charter from the state authorizing the is-

---

[9] U.S. Bureau of the Census, *Statistical Abstract: 1973.*

[10] Henceforth, the word "stock" unmodified by "common" or "preferred" will mean common stock.

suance of 20,000 shares of $10 par value common stock. If 1,000 shares of this stock are issued at par ($10) and immediately paid for, the following entry would be made:

```
Cash...................................... 10,000
     Common Stock.........................        10,000
```

Stock is almost always issued for more than its par or stated value; that is, it is issued at a *premium*. In such situations the Common Stock account still reflects the par or stated value, and the premium is shown separately, in an account variously called Paid-In Capital, Paid-In Surplus or Capital Surplus. (The Financial Accounting Standards Board suggests the more descriptive but cumbersome title "capital contributed in excess of the par or stated value of shares"). If 1,000 shares of Carroll Corporation $10 common stock were issued at $12 a share, the following entry would be made:

```
Cash...................................... 12,000
     Common Stock.........................        10,000
     Paid-In Capital......................         2,000
```

Unlike bonds, stock is rarely sold at a discount. In most states and under most circumstances, this is illegal. Even where sale at a discount is permitted, individual shareholders would be required to contribute the amount of the discount in cash if the company should go bankrupt, and such a possibility makes discount stock unattractive to investors. Corporations therefore set the par value or stated value low enough (usually $10, $1, or $0.10) so that in practice stock is almost always sold at a premium.

The offering of an issue of stock is often handled by an investment banking firm which receives a fee or "spread" for this service. Usually the corporation records only the net amount received from the investment banker, that is, the price paid by the public less the banker's spread, since this is the amount that the corporate entity receives.

In connection with the issuance of stock, the corporation itself incurs issue costs over and above the banker's spread. These amounts usually also are deducted from the amount received from the issue. Note that because of the spread and issue costs, the amount actually paid by the public is greater than the amount by which contributed capital (par value plus paid-in capital) increases on the balance sheet. Note also that these transactions are between the company and its shareholders. When one shareholder sells his stock to another shareholder, the amounts in the company's accounts are not affected in any way; the only change is in the company's detailed record of the identity of shareholders.

Treasury Stock

Treasury stock is a corporation's own stock that has been issued and subsequently reacquired by purchase. The firm may reacquire its shares for a number of reasons: to obtain shares which can be used in the future for acquisitions, bonus plans, exercise of warrants, and conversion of convertible bonds or preferred stocks; to increase the earnings per share; or to improve the market price of the stock. Such treasury stock while held by the corporation has no voting, dividend, or other shareholder rights.

Since treasury stock is clearly not a "valuable thing or property right owned by the business"—a corporation can't own a claim against itself— it is not shown as an asset. Rather, treasury stock is reported as a reduction in shareholders' equity, that is, as a reduction in the number and value of the shares outstanding.

In most companies, treasury stock purchased is debited to the Treasury Stock account at its reacquisition cost, regardless of its par or stated value. It continues to be shown at this cost until it is canceled or reissued, at which time adjustments are made in shareholders' equity to dispose of any differences between this cost, the paid-in value (i.e., the net proceeds at the time the stock was originally issued), and, in the event of reissuance, the amount then received.

If reissued, any excess of selling price above cost is credited to a contributed capital account (such as Capital Surplus from Treasury Stock Transactions), which may be shown as a separate item in the contributed capital section of the balance sheet. If treasury stock is sold at a price below cost, the loss may be deducted from the related contributed capital account if such an account already exists from prior transactions; otherwise the loss is debited to Retained Earnings. In no event is a gain or loss on the resale of treasury stock shown on the income statement or recognized for tax purposes.

Surplus Reserves

In an attempt to explain to shareholders why they do not receive dividends that are equal to the amount shown as retained earnings, a corporation may show on its balance sheet an appropriation, or *reserve*, as a separate item that is subtracted from retained earnings. Some of the terms used to describe the reasons for such an appropriation are as follows: *reserve for bond sinking fund*, which indicates a restriction on dividends in accordance with agreements made to bondholders; *reserve for contingencies*, indicating management's belief that funds may be required for an unusual purpose or to meet a possible obligation that does not yet have the status of a liability (such as settlement of a pending lawsuit, or a retroactive wage increase); *reserve for future inventory price decline*, indicating the possibility that inventory may be sold at a price less than the value reported on the balance sheet; and *reserve for expansion*, indicating an intention to use funds for the acquisition of new assets.

None of these reserves represents money, or anything tangible; the assets of a business are reported on the assets side of the balance sheet, not in the shareholders' equity section. The accounting entry creating the reserve involves a debit to Retained Earnings and a credit to the reserve. This entry simply moves an amount from one owners' equity account to another. It does not affect any asset account, nor does the reserve represent anything more than a segregated portion of retained earnings. Because the use of the word "reserve" tends to be misleading to unsophisticated readers of financial statements, it is fortunate that such usage is on the decline.

Retained Earnings

The remaining item of owners' equity is Retained Earnings. As pointed out in previous chapters, the amount of retained earnings represents the *cumulative* net income of the firm since its beginning, less the total dividends that have been paid to shareholders (or "drawings," in the case of unincorporated businesses). Stated slightly differently, retained earnings shows the amount of assets which have been financed by "plowing profits back into the business" rather than paying all of the company's net income out as dividends. The importance to owners (and others) of understanding in some detail *why* retained earnings have changed between two balance sheet dates as a result of the firm's operations is the essential underlying reason that the income statement is prepared.

Dividends

Dividends are ordinarily paid to shareholders in cash, but they sometimes are paid in other assets—the whiskey once distributed by a distillery corporation to its shareholders being a noteworthy example.

Dividends are debited to retained earnings in the period in which they are declared, that is, voted, by the board of directors, even though payment is made at a later date. For example, if the Carroll Corporation declared a $5,000 dividend on December 15 to be paid on January 15 to holders of record as of January 1, the entries would be as follows:

```
                           Dec. 15
Dividends (a temporary owners' equity
   contra account)......................... 5,000
     Dividends Payable (a liability account)        5,000
```

```
                        Dec. 31
Retained Earnings........................  5,000
    Dividends.............................              5,000
  A closing entry.

                        Jan. 15
Dividends Payable........................  5,000
    Cash..................................              5,000
```

Some shareholders, in the mistaken belief that the amount reported as retained earnings is "their money," put pressure on the directors to authorize cash dividends equal to, or almost equal to, that amount. Clearly, retained earnings are not money at all, and for any of a number of reasons, cash may not be available for dividend payments even though the balance sheet shows a large amount of retained earnings. These same shareholders may be quite satisfied with a *stock dividend*, which actually does not change their equity in the corporation, since it increases each shareholder's number of shares by the same percentage.

Although a stock dividend does not change either the corporation's earnings, assets or its shareholders' proportionate equity, it does increase the number of outstanding shares. In theory, therefore, such a dividend should reduce the per-share market price of the stock. However, in practice stock dividends are so small—usually 5 to 10 percent of the number of issued shares—that the market price of the shares may remain substantially unchanged. Hence the stock dividend may have some value to the shareholder as a dividend. To record a stock dividend the retained earnings account is debited with the fair value of the additional shares issued, with the credit being to the capital stock account.

EXAMPLE: The Bruce Corporation has 10,000 shares of common stock outstanding. Suppose that the directors voted a 5 percent stock dividend. Each shareholder would receive ½₀ of a share of new stock for every share he then held. If the stock currently had a market value of $12 a share, the common stock item on the balance sheet would increase by $6,000 (500 shares at $12 per share), and retained earnings would decrease by $6,000, but the *total* shareholders' equity would remain exactly as before, as would the *relative* holdings of the shareholders.

Since a stock dividend reduces retained earnings, and since the amount of cash dividends that can be legally declared is related to the amount of retained earnings, the declaration of a stock dividend reduces the maximum amount of dividends that henceforth can be paid. By declaring a stock dividend, therefore, the directors signal their intention that this amount will be invested permanently in the company. The converse does not apply, however, for failure to declare a stock dividend is by no means an indication that the directors do plan to distribute all the retained earnings.

An advantage of a stock dividend is that a shareholder may realize cash by selling his dividend stock while preserving the number of his owned shares intact; but if he does this, he should recognize that he is in fact selling a fraction of his equity in the business.

A *stock split-up* also merely increases the number of shares of stock outstanding, with no change in the total par or stated value of the stock and no change in contributed capital.[11] It has no effect on shareholders' equity; its effect is solely to repackage the evidence of ownership in smaller units. Hence, no transfer is made from retained earnings to capital stock when a stock split is effected.

A stock split automatically reduces the market price of a share of stock, thus allegedly making the stock appealing to a wider range of investors. Often, however, the price reduction is not quite proportional to the split since stock with a fairly low market price per share tends to be more attractive than stock with a high market price per share. Hence, if a stock selling at $150 is split "3-for-1," the new shares often will sell for somewhat more than $50 each, resulting in a gain in market value of each share owner's total holdings of the stock.

The stock referred to in the preceding paragraphs is the company's own stock. If the company distributes to its shareholders the shares of some other corporation's stock which it owns, this distribution is similar to a regular cash dividend, and is recorded in the same manner except that the credit is to the Investments asset account rather than to Cash. Such a transaction is called a *spin-off*.

Stock Options and Warrants

A *stock option* is the right to purchase shares of common stock at a stated price within a given time period. For example, an option could give its holder the right to buy 100 shares of Sterling Company common stock for $25 anytime between January 1, 1975 and December 31, 1979. If during this period the market price of Sterling's common stock rises to, say, $31, the holder of the option can *exercise* it by paying Sterling $25, and he will receive in return his share of stock, thus having a "paper gain" of $6. If the option is negotiable, it is generally called a *warrant*. Some companies have enough warrants outstanding that they are traded on stock exchanges, just as are other corporate securities. In this case,

---

[11] The technical difference between a stock dividend and a stock split-up is a matter of intent. The intent of a stock dividend is to give shareholders "ostensibly separate evidence" of their interests in the firm without having to distribute cash. The intent of a split-up is to drive down the market price of the shares to improve their marketability. The presumption is that any increase in shares smaller than 20–25 percent is not a stock split-up. (*Accounting Research Bulletin No. 43*, Ch. 7, sec. B, par. 1, 2 and 15.)

the warrant holder can sell the warrant and realize its value without actually exercising it.

Some corporations issue warrants in conjunction with the issuance of long-term debt, putting an exercise price on the warrants of about 15 to 20 percent above the current market price of the common. Often the warrants are "detachable" from the bonds, that is, they are in effect a separate security which can be transferred without necessarily transferring the bond. If the investor expects the firm to prosper, and expects this prosperity to be reflected in the market price of the common, then the warrant has value. The investor will then accept a lower interest rate on the bond than he would if no warrant were involved, reducing the cash interest cost of the bond to the issuer. Also, some small firms which investors regard as being very risky would not be able to attract investors to their bonds without using warrants as a "sweetener."

Many corporations also grant options to certain officers and employees, either to obtain widespread ownership among employees or as a form of compensation. Sometimes the number of shares purchasable by the option or the exercise price (or both) depend upon future events, such as the future market price of the stock or future earnings of the firm. If the options are intended as compensation, then their value should be debited to wages or salaries expense; otherwise the firm would be understating its personnel expense and overstating profits. The procedures for accounting for options issued to employees are complicated and are beyond the scope of this text.[12]

EARNINGS PER SHARE

In analyzing the financial statements of a corporation, investors pay particular attention to the ratio called "earnings per share." This is computed by dividing net income applicable to the common stock by the number of shares of common stock outstanding. The Financial Accounting Standards Board requires that earnings per share be reported on the income statement, and has provided detailed guidelines for making the calculation.[13]

If the corporation has a simple capital structure, with only one class of stock, the net income used in this ratio is the same as the net income shown on the income statement.

EXAMPLE: The 1975 income statement of McLean Corporation showed net income of $5 million. The corporation had one million shares of common stock outstanding in 1975. It therefore earned $5 per share.

---

[12] APB *Opinion No. 25* (October 1972).

[13] APB *Opinion No. 9* (December 1966), *No. 15* (May 1969), and *No. 30* (June 1973).

The various classes of stock that a corporation might issue can be divided into one of two categories: (1) *senior securities*, and (2) *common stock* and its equivalent. Senior securities, usually preferred stock, are those that have a claim on net income ahead of the claim of the common stockholders. The income figure used in the calculation of earnings per share is the amount that remains after the claims of the senior securities have been deducted from net income.

> EXAMPLE: The Nugent Corporation in 1975 had net income of $5 million. It had outstanding 100,000 shares of $6 preferred stock, and one million shares of common stock. Its earnings per share were therefore ($5,000,000 − $600,000) ÷ 1,000,000 shares = $4.40 per share.

If the number of shares of common stock outstanding fluctuates within a year, then a weighted average number of shares is computed.

> EXAMPLE: The Optel Corporation in 1975 had net income of $5 million. It had outstanding on January 1, one million shares of common stock, and on July 1 it issued an additional 500,000 shares, which were therefore outstanding for half of the year. Its average number of common shares outstanding was 1,000,000 + (500,000 × ½) = 1,250,000. Its earnings per share were $5,000,000 ÷ 1,250,000 = $4.

A *common stock equivalent* is a security which, although not in form a common stock, contains provisions that enable its holder to become a common stockholder and which, because of its terms and the circumstances under which it was issued, is in substance equivalent to a common stock. The value of a common stock equivalent is derived in large part from the value of the common stock to which it is related. Examples are convertible bonds, convertible preferreds, stock options, and warrants.

When a corporation has securities that are common stock equivalents, the Financial Accounting Standards Board requires that the amount of such securities be taken into account in calculating earnings per share. The detailed criteria for deciding whether a security is a common stock equivalent and if so how the equivalent number of shares should be calculated are much too lengthy to be given here. APB *Opinion No. 15* was the longest of the 31 Opinions of the Accounting Principles Board, and it was so complex that the AICPA has issued an "interpretation" that is over twice as long as the Opinion itself.

APB *Opinion No. 15* also states that if a corporation has securities that *may*, under certain circumstances, have a claim on common earnings—even though these securities are not equivalent common shares—then the corporation should report two numbers for earnings per share: (1) *primary earnings per share*, which is net income divided by the number of common and common equivalent shares, as above; and (2) *fully diluted earnings per share*, in which it is assumed that the maximum amount of potential conversion, exercise of warrants, and the like has taken place.

As pointed out in Chapter 8, gains or losses (net of applicable taxes) related to discontinued operations and extraordinary items must be shown separately in the income statement. This separate treatment also applies to earnings per share figures, as shown in Illustration 9–1.

Illustration 9–1

EXAMPLE OF REPORTING EARNINGS PER SHARE DATA

	Primary	Fully Diluted
Income from continuing operations	$4.08	$2.91
Income (loss) from discontinued operations	(.58)	(.41)
Income before extraordinary items	3.50	2.50
Extraordinary items	1.66	1.18
Net Income	$5.16	$3.68

BALANCE SHEET PRESENTATION

In the shareholders' equity section of the balance sheet (or in a separate statement or note if presentation of all the detail would make the balance sheet itself too long), the following detail is presented:

1. For *each* class of stock, the par or stated value, the number of shares authorized and issued and outstanding, rights and preferences as to dividends and as to amounts received in liquidation, amount of treasury stock, and number of outstanding options. The dollar amounts shown for each class of stock relate to the shares issued, not to the shares authorized.

2. The amount of paid-in capital.

3. The amount of retained earnings, in total, and a note as to any

Illustration 9–2

MERRILL LYNCH & CO., INC.

Shareholders' Equity Section of Balance Sheet

SHAREHOLDERS' EQUITY ($000)

Preferred stock, par value $25 per share—	
Authorized 1,000,000 shares;	
Outstanding 201,952 shares Series A, 4% cumulative	$ 5,049
Common stock, par value $1.33⅓ per share—	
Authorized 60,000,000 shares;	
Issued 32,449,188 shares	43,266
Paid-in capital	89,641
Retained earnings	321,908
Total	459,864
Less common stock in treasury, at cost—43,395 shares	696
Total shareholders' equity	$459,168

portion of this amount that cannot be distributed as dividends (such as a restriction arising under the terms of a bank loan).

Thus, the basic distinction is maintained between (1) the capital contributed by shareholders, and (2) the equity resulting from net income that has been retained in the business.

Illustration 9–2 (shown on page 285) shows the owners' equity section of an actual corporation's balance sheet.

SUMMARY

Equities consist of current liabilities, other liabilities (primarily long-term debt), and owners' equity. Current liabilities are distinguished from other liabilities by their time horizon (one year or less). Liabilities are distinguished from owners' equity by their nature as obligations to outside parties. Collectively the equities represent the sources of the funds which are invested in the firm's assets.

The liability arising from the sale of bonds is shown at its face amount and the difference between this amount and the amount paid by the investors for the bonds is recorded as bond premium or discount. Premium or discount is amortized over the life of the issue. This amortization is combined with the periodic interest payments to give the effective interest expense of each period.

In a corporation, shareholders' equity consists of two parts which should always be reported separately: (1) the contributed capital, which is the amount paid to the corporation by each class of shareholders, and which is further divided into (a) the par or stated value of stock, and (b) paid-in capital; and (2) retained earnings, representing the cumulative amount of net income that has not been paid out as dividends.

SUGGESTIONS FOR FURTHER READING

KELLEY, PEARCE C.; LAWYER, KENNETH; BAUMBACK, CLIFFORD M. *How to Organize and Operate a Small Business*, Ch. 10. Englewood Cliffs, N.J.: Prentice-Hall, Inc., 1968.

SYMONDS, CURTIS W. *Basic Financial Management.* American Management Association, Inc., 1969.

VAN HORNE, JAMES C. *Fundamentals of Financial Management.* Englewood Cliffs, N.J.: Prentice-Hall, Inc., 1971.

WELSCH, GLENN A.; ZLATKOVICH, CHARLES T.; and WHITE, JOHN ARCH. *Intermediate Accounting*, 3d ed., chaps. 15 and 16. Homewood, Ill.: Richard D. Irwin, Inc., 1972.

WESTON, J. FRED; BRIGHAM, EUGENE F. *Essentials of Managerial Finance*, 3d ed. Hinsdale, Ill.: The Dryden Press, 1974.

WIXON, RUFUS, ed. *Accountants' Handbook.* 5th ed. New York: Ronald Press Co., 1970.

CASES

CASE 9–1. PIQUA PRODUCTS

On December 31, 1969, Piqua Products issued 10-year bonds having a maturity value of $5,000,000. The bonds carried an 8% coupon, and the proceeds (ignoring issuance costs) were $4,444,444.

The Piqua bonds required semiannual interest payments and they were redeemable between June 30, 1975 and June 30, 1978 at 104; thereafter until maturity they were redeemable at 102. They were also convertible into Piqua's $10 par value common stock according to the following schedule:

Before June 30, 1975: 50 shares of common per $1,000 face value of bonds.

July 1, 1975 to June 30, 1978: 40 shares of common per $1,000 face value of bonds.

After June 30, 1978: 30 shares of common per $1,000 face value of bonds.

The following transactions occurred in connection with the bonds:

December 31, 1974: Bonds having a face value of $1,000,000 were converted into common stock.

December 31, 1975: Bonds having a face value of $1,000,000 were reacquired by Piqua on the open market at a price of 90. The reacquired bonds were cancelled immediately.

Questions

1. Show how the proceeds from the bond issue would be carried on the balance sheet as of December 31, 1969.
2. Determine the amount of interest expense to be deducted in arriving at net income for the year ended December 31, 1970.
3. Show the entries to record the conversion of the bonds in 1974.
4. Show the entries to record the retirement of the bonds in 1975.

CASE 9–2. KEMP FOODS CORPORATION

"Here's the entire mess," said Ed McCowan as papers of various sizes and colors fluttered from the large manila envelope and spread over the desk of Dan Conner, CPA. "I bought 40 shares of Kemp Foods common last year in May. Since then I've received proxy statements, notices of stock splits, stock certificates, quarterly financial statements and a few dividend checks. When this thick annual report came in yesterday's mail, I called you. I knew what to do with those little dividend checks, but to tell the truth I don't know what the rest of this means. I thought the annual report would explain things, but I don't see any relationship between my 40 shares and the big numbers and big words in the report."

"It appears that you saved everything, Ed," said Dan Conner. "Let's see if we can list things as they happened from the beginning." He made these notes on a desk pad as he selected papers from the assortment before him:

```
May   5, 1964—Bo't 40 common at 38 plus commission.............  $1,539.60
July  20        —Rec'd cash div.—40 at 25¢......................       10.00
Oct.  20        —   "    "    "    "  "  "......................       10.00
      25        —Rec'd 2 shares common stock div.
Jan.  20, 1965—Rec'd cash div.—42 at 25¢......................       10.50
Mar.  15        —Rec'd 21 shares—3 for 2 stock split
Apr.  20        —Rec'd cash div.—63 at 20¢......................       12.60
```

"Now, let's look at the quotations in today's *Wall Street Journal* and see how you've made out over the past year. Here it is on the Pacific Coast Exchange. The closing price yesterday (June 10, 1965) was 28½. Now we'll look at the April 30, 1965, annual report together and see what it tells us."

The Company

Kemp Foods Corporation was established in Illinois in 1927 to acquire and operate three small vegetable canning plants. Operations were expanded to include canning of fruits and frozen food processing. The growth of these newer activities in the late 1940s was responsible for transfer of company headquarters to California. In 1965 the company had 15 canning and processing plants throughout the Midwest and on the West Coast.

Kemp's operations had always been profitable. Earnings per share of common reached an historic high of $2.27 in the fiscal year ended April 30, 1965. Net income for the year was $1.3 million on sales of almost $59 millon. Shareholders' equity at April 30, 1965, exceeded $13 million. The company's comparative balance sheets at the close of the two most recent

Exhibit 1

KEMP FOODS CORPORATION

Comparative Balance Sheet

April 30, 1965 and 1964

ASSETS	1965	1964
Current Assets:		
Cash...	$ 996,020	$ 1,124,588
Receivables (net).................................	5,076,894	5,084,087
Inventories, at the lower of cost (first-in, first-out basis) or market..	10,440,509	8,708,578
Total Current Assets............................	$16,513,423	$14,917,253
Prepaid expenses...................................	$ 133,434	$ 230,002
Plant and Equipment:		
Land...	$ 290,349	$ 346,319
Buildings and leasehold improvements.................	4,200,760	4,719,515
Machinery and equipment..........................	3,916,508	4,275,927
Automotive equipment.............................	601,393	586,030
Construction in progress...........................	2,033,324	. . .
	$11,042,334	$ 9,927,791
Less: Accumulated depreciation and amortization........	5,038,251	4,532,968
Net Plant and Equipment.........................	$ 6,004,083	$ 5,394,823
Total Assets.................................	$22,650,940	$20,542,078
LIABILITIES		
Current Liabilities:		
Bank loans.......................................	$ 2,192,500	$ 1,350,000
Current maturities of long-term debt..................	170,790	163,478
Accounts payable and accrued liabilities...............	2,187,440	1,770,026
Income taxes.....................................	1,014,527	936,889
Dividends payable.................................	126,811	102,554
Total Current Liabilities.........................	$ 5,692,068	$ 4,322,947
Long-term debt, noncurrent portion....................	$ 3,660,223	$ 3,831,013
Deferred income taxes and other expenses...............	$ 273,850	$ 174,225
Stockholders' Equity:		
Cumulative 4% preferred stock, par value $100; authorized 15,000 shares, issued 8,995 shares, less 198 shares in treasury..	$ 879,700	
Common stock, par value $5; authorized 1,000,000 shares, issued 590,552 shares, (4,482 shares in treasury—see below)...	2,952,760	
Paid-in surplus (Exhibit 2).........................	2,853,702	
Retained earnings (Exhibit 2):		
Reserve for plant expansion.......................	1,466,676	
Unappropriated*.................................	4,997,457	
	$13,150,295	
Less: Treasury stock, common (4,482 shares at cost)....	125,496	
Total Stockholders' Equity.......................	$13,024,799	$12,213,893
Total Liabilities.............................	$22,650,940	$20,542,078

* Under terms of the long-term debt agreement $2,330,808 of retained earnings at April 30, 1965 is restricted against payment of cash dividends on or purchase of common stock.

Exhibit 2

KEMP FOODS CORPORATION

Common Stock, Paid-In Surplus, and Retained Earnings
For the Year Ended April 30, 1965

	Common Stock		Paid-In Surplus	Retained Earnings	
	Shares	Par Value		Reserve for Plant Exp.	Unappro-priated
Balance at May 1, 1964..........	375,130	$1,875,650	$3,197,277	$3,500,000	$2,742,831
Add:					
Net income for the year........					1,376,871
Gain on sale of 600 shares common treasury stock..........			17,716		
Discount on 245 shares of preferred stock purchased........			4,003		
Reduction in reserve for plant expansion..................				(2,033,324)	2,033,324
Total......................	375,130	$1,875,650	$3,218,996	$1,466,676	$6,153,026
Transfer to common stock in connection with 3 for 2 stock split.................	196,690	983,450	(983,450)		
Cash dividends:					
Preferred ($4.00 per share)...					(35,386)
Common ($0.95 per share)....					(408,367)
5% stock dividend, recorded at fair market value of $38 per share..................	18,732	93,660	618,156		(711,816)
Balance at April 30, 1965........	590,552	$2,952,760	$2,853,702	$1,466,676	$4,997,457

years are shown in Exhibit 1 (on page 289). An analysis of common stock, paid-in surplus, and retained earnings is in Exhibit 2.

Most of the funds needed to finance the company's growth had been provided internally. Modest cash dividends had been paid quarterly without interruption since 1946, when the common stock was split 3 for 1. In 1952, after a public offering of preferred and common stock, a policy of supplementing the regular cash dividends with stock dividends to common stockholders was adopted. Five percent stock dividends were declared in each year thereafter except for 1955 and 1956 when stock dividends were 20 and 10 percent respectively. The 4 percent preferred stock was gradually being retired as it became available in the market at an attractive price. Some funds had been obtained by the use of long-term debt and future expansion was to be financed more extensively in this way.

The price of Kemp Foods' common stock had risen steadily since the early 1950s. For example, the price had ranged from a low of 12¾ to a high of 18⅝ in the year 1969 and reached an all time high of 43½ early in 1964.

Questions

1. Evaluate Ed McCowan's investment at June 10, 1965.
2. Examine the stockholders' equity section of Kemp Foods' balance sheet to:
   (*a*) Determine how each item was originally created.
   (*b*) Explain changes during the year ended April 30, 1965.
3. Contrast Kemp's methods of reporting preferred treasury stock and common treasury stock.
4. What is the effect of Kemp's acquisition of treasury stock upon investor McCowan's holdings?
5. Suggest improvements Kemp might make in reporting stockholders' equity information on its balance sheet.

CASE 9–3.   TRELEASE INDUSTRIES, INC.*

Trelease Industries, Inc. was a manufacturing firm whose stock was traded on a regional stock exchange. Information related to the firm's capital structure and income is given below.

MARKET PRICE OF COMMON STOCK. The following table reflects the average market price of Trelease's common stock over a three-year period:

Average Price:	1972	1971	1970
First quarter	50	45	40
Second quarter	60	52	41
Third quarter	70	50	40
Fourth quarter	70	50	45
December 31 closing price	72	51	44

CASH DIVIDENDS. Cash dividends of $0.125 per common share were declared and paid for each quarter of 1970 and 1971. Cash dividends of $0.25 per common share were declared and paid for each quarter of 1972.

CONVERTIBLE DEBENTURES. 4% convertible debentures with a principal amount of $10,000,000 due 1990 were sold for cash at a price of 100 in the last quarter of 1970. Each $100 debenture was convertible into two shares of common stock. No debentures were converted during 1970 or 1971. The entire issue was converted at the beginning of the third quarter of 1972 because the issue was called by the company. These

---

* This case is based on the illustrative example given in APB *Opinion No. 15* (May 1969).

convertible debentures were *not* common stock equivalents under the terms of APB–15. The bank prime rate at the time the debentures were sold in the last quarter of 1970 was 6%. The debentures carried a coupon interest rate of 4% and had a market value of $100 at issuance. The cash yield of 4% was not less than 66⅔% of the bank prime rate. Cash yield is the same as the coupon interest rate in this case only because the market value at issuance was $100.

CONVERTIBLE PREFERRED STOCK.   600,000 shares of convertible preferred stock were issued for assets in a purchase transaction at the beginning of the second quarter of 1971. The annual dividend on each share of this convertible preferred stock is $0.20. Each share is convertible into one share of common stock. This convertible stock had a market value of $53 at the time of issuance and *was* therefore a common stock equivalent under the terms of APB–15 at the time of its issuance because the cash yield on market value was only 0.4% and the bank prime rate was 5.5%. Holders of 500,000 shares of this convertible preferred stock converted their preferred stock into common stock during 1972 because the cash dividend on the common stock exceeded the cash dividend on the preferred stock.

WARRANTS.   Warrants to buy 500,000 shares of common stock at $60 per share for a period of five years were issued along with the convertible preferred stock mentioned above. No warrants have been exercised.

The number of common shares represented by the warrants was 71,428 for each of the third and fourth quarters of 1972 ($60 exercise price × 500,000 warrants = $30,000,000; $30,000,000 ÷ $70 share market price = 428,572 shares; 500,000 shares − 428,572 shares = 71,428 shares). No shares were deemed to be represented by the warrants for the second quarter of 1972 or for any preceding quarter because the market price of the stock did not exceed the exercise price for substantially all of three consecutive months until the third quarter of 1972.

COMMON STOCK.   The number of shares of common stock outstanding was as follows:

	1972	1971
Beginning of year	3,300,000	3,300,000
Conversion of preferred stock	500,000	. . . .
Conversion of debentures	200,000	. . . .
End of year	4,000,000	3,300,000

WEIGHTED AVERAGE NUMBER OF SHARES.   The weighted average number of shares of common stock and common stock equivalents was determined as follows:

	1972	1971
Common stock:		
Shares outstanding from beginning of period.........	3,300,000	3,300,000
500,000 shares issued on conversion of preferred stock; assume issuance evenly during year..............	250,000	....
200,000 shares issued on conversion of convertible debentures at beginning of third quarter of 1972....	100,000	....
	3,650,000	3,300,000
Common stock equivalents:		
600,000 shares convertible preferred stock issued at the beginning of the second quarter of 1971, excluding 250,000 shares included under common stock in 1972..	350,000	450,000
Warrants: 71,428 common share equivalents outstanding for third and fourth quarters of 1972, i.e., one-half year..............................	35,714	....
	385,714	450,000
Weighted average number of shares...............	4,035,714	3,750,000

The weighted average number of shares would be adjusted to calculate fully diluted earnings per share as follows:

	1972	1971
Weighted average number of shares.................	4,035,714	3,750,000
Shares applicable to convertible debentures converted at the beginning of the third quarter of 1972, excluding 100,000 shares included under common stock for 1972.	100,000	200,000
Shares applicable to warrants included above..........	(35,714)	....
Shares applicable to warrants based on year-end price of $72..	83,333	....
	4,183,333	3,950,000

NET INCOME. Income before extraordinary item and net income would be adjusted for interest expense on the debentures in calculating fully diluted earnings per share. Taxes in 1972 were 52.8% and were 48.0% in 1971. Trelease's net income (before preferred stock dividends) was as follows:

1972:	Income before extraordinary item...............	$12,900,000
	Net income................................	13,800,000
1971:	Net income................................	10,300,000

Questions

1. Be prepared to explain the calculations shown above for arriving at the weighted average number of common shares, common stock equivalents, and fully diluted shares.

2. Compute Trelease's primary and fully diluted earnings per share for 1972 and 1971.

3. Starting with the item "income before extraordinary items," complete the remainder of the 1972 and 1971 income statements.

CASE 9–4. GULF & WESTERN INDUSTRIES

The following quote is taken from the fiscal year 1969 mid-year report of Gulf and Western Industries:

In utilizing G & W's assets in a manner to best serve its shareholders, management from time to time has invested in marketable securities and realized profits from such activities. On January 31, 1969, the marketable securities portfolio, at cost, and receivable from sale of marketable securities, amounted to $276 million. While management cannot assure that there will continue to be gains from its investment activities, it intends, when the opportunity is presented, to attempt to enhance our shareholders' value through prudent and timely investments in marketable securities.

In *Accounting Research Bulletin Number 43*, the AICPA adopted the following position (paraphrased):

Marketable securities represent the investment of cash available for current operations. . . . Marketable securities specifically exclude investments made for the purposes of control, affiliation, or other continuing business advantage. . . . It is important that the cost of temporary investments be supplemented by information which reveals their market value at the balance sheet date. . . . Only in the case of certain investment companies whose business is trading in securities is it generally accepted to take unrealized appreciation of securities into the accounts.

During 1968 G & W had acquired 505,000 shares of Sinclair Common Stock in the open market for cash at prices ranging upward from $72 a share. Pursuant to exchange offers in November and December 1968, G & W acquired an additional 186,000 shares of Sinclair Common. On January 8, 1969, G & W granted to Atlantic Richfield Refining an option to purchase 618,360 shares of Sinclair between August 1, 1969 and September 3, 1969 at a price of $130 per share. At that time, Sinclair was selling publicly for $116 per share. On the same date, Atlantic issued to G & W a warrant, exercisable between January 1, 1971 and December 31, 1976, to purchase 618,360 shares of Atlantic Common for $125 a share. Atlantic was selling publicly at that time for $108 per share. On March 4, 1969, Sinclair merged with Atlantic and each share of Sinclair held by G & W (including 177,400 additional shares purchased in the open market during 1969) was exchanged for 0.6 shares of Atlantic Common and one share of Atlantic's $2.80 Cumulative Convertible Preference Stock.

On August 28 the following announcement appeared in *Moody's Industrials News:*

Gulf and Western announced yesterday that it had sold on the New York Stock Exchange approximately 371,000 shares of Atlantic-Richfield Common at $110.75 a share and approximately 618,000 shares of Atlantic's $2.80 Preferred at $70.75 a share. The proceeds were approximately $84,500,000. Lehman Brothers acted as brokers for the sale, placing the shares with institutional buyers. . . . In consideration for Atlantic cancelling its option to buy the shares for approximately $80.5 million, G & W agreed to pay Atlantic approximately $2,000,000. . . . Gulf & Western still holds a considerable block of Atlantic-Richfield.

Gulf & Western's fiscal year ended on July 31, 1969. Its annual report will probably be released in October 1969.

Questions

1. Assuming that G & W's cost for the Sinclair stock averaged $90 a share, and that zero value was assigned to the warrant received on January 8, 1969, what was the gain on the shares sold on August 27, 1969? What is the unrealized gain on the shares still held by G & W?
2. Should the gain on the Atlantic stock sold in August 1969 be recognized in G & W's earnings statement for the year ended July 31, 1969 or in the next fiscal year? When should the unrealized gain on the remaining Atlantic shares be recognized? Do you believe G & W should carry marketable securities at cost or at market on its balance sheet?

CHAPTER 10

ACQUISITIONS AND CONSOLIDATED STATEMENTS

Many American business entities consist of several corporations, each with separate *legal* status. Despite this separate legal status, it is usually more meaningful to report on the results of these organizations in a way that treats them as a single *economic* entity. This chapter deals first with the accounting for newly acquired entities, and then with the accounting for these separate legal entities on a continuing consolidated basis.

ACQUISITIONS AND MERGERS

When two companies combine their operations to become a single firm, the act of combining is called an acquisition or a merger. In common usage, an *acquisition* is said to occur if one corporation buys either the assets, net assets (assets minus liabilities), or the stock of another corporation. If the firms are combined through an exchange of one corporation's stock for the other's, then a *merger* is said to have occurred. The FASB refers to both of these kinds of transactions as *business combinations*.

There are three types of combination: horizontal, vertical, and conglomerate. A *horizontal* combination occurs when the combining firms are in the same line of business; for example, the merger of two railroads. A *vertical* combination occurs when the two companies are involved in different stages of the production and marketing of the same end-use product; for example, the acquisition of a weaving mill by a manufacturer of clothing. A *conglomerate* combination occurs when the combining firms are in essentially unrelated lines of business; for example, the acquisition of a meat-packing firm by an electronics firm.

296

With the exception of the Depression and World War II years, there has been an average of over 750 mergers and acquisitions of large firms per year since 1920. In the period 1965–69, the *pace* of new business combinations accelerated, particularly in the area of conglomerate combinations. In 1968, the number of major conglomerate mergers was triple the number in either 1964 or 1971. The assets of the acquired firms in 1968 major conglomerate combinations totaled nearly $12 billion, almost ten times the assets of firms acquired in horizontal and vertical mergers that year.[1] Major acquirers included such "conglomerate" corporations as Litton Industries, Ling-Temco-Vought, Gulf and Western Industries, International Telephone and Telegraph, and Textron. Each of these firms offered a wide diversity of product lines and services.

> EXAMPLE: In 1963, Gulf and Western Industries was a manufacturer and distributor of automobile parts, with total assets of $48 million. By 1970, G & W had 11 "operating groups" which were involved in 37 separately identified product lines and services, ranging from cigars to movie production; 1970 assets totaled $2.2 billion. During the twelve months between July 31, 1967 and July 31, 1968, G & W's total assets grew from $749 million to $2.1 billion, almost entirely as a result of acquisitions.

Accounting for Business Combinations

If the acquiring corporation pays cash for the acquired firm, the accounting method used to record the acquisition is called the *purchase* method. However, if one firm in the combination issues its stock in exchange for the stock of the other firm, the acquisition is accounted for by use of either the purchase method or the *pooling of interests* method. Prior to the issuance of APB *Opinion No. 16* in August 1970, companies usually chose the pooling method when issuance of stock was involved

In accordance with APB *Opinion No. 16*, however, purchase and pooling are no longer viewed as equally acceptable alternative methods in accounting for a business combination when an exchange of stock is involved; rather, whether the proper treatment is pooling or purchase is determined according to detailed criteria set forth in that Opinion. These criteria are such that many combinations that formerly could have been recorded as poolings of interests henceforth must be accounted for as purchases.

The criteria are complicated, detailed, and subject to various interpretations. Only a summary of their general thrust is appropriate here. In general, to qualify for pooling treatment, the following conditions must be met:

---

[1] U.S. Bureau of the Census, *Statistical Abstract of the United States: 1973* (94th edition). Washington, D.C., 1973.

–Each combining company is autonomous and independent and has not been a subsidiary or division of another corporation within the previous two years.

–The combination is effected in a single transaction or is completed according to a specific plan within one year.

–One corporation issues only common stock with rights identical to the majority of its outstanding voting common stock in exchange for substantially all of the voting common stock of the other company.

–Neither of the combining companies has recently (usually, within two years) reacquired shares of voting common stock for purposes of using these shares for business combinations.

–The ratio of the interest of an individual common stockholder to those of other common stockholders in a combining company remains the same as a result of the exchange of stock.

–No provisions of the combination's plan relating to the issue of securities or other consideration are pending.

–The combined corporation does not agree to retire or reacquire any of the common stock issued to effect the combination.

–The combined corporation does not enter into other financial arrangements for the benefit of the former stockholders of one of the combining companies.

–The combined corporation does not intend to dispose of a significant part of the assets of the combining companies within two years after the combination, other than disposals in the ordinary course of business and to eliminate duplicate facilities or excess capacity.

To illustrate accounting for the pooling and purchase methods, we will use the balance sheets for two hypothetical corporations shown in Illustration 10–1. We assume that Corporation A is planning to acquire all of the stock of Corporation B; thus A will take over the assets and assume the liabilities of B. We also assume that the consideration that will be involved in the combination is Corporation A common stock having a market value of $6 million. Finally, we assume that Corporation A can arrange the transaction in such a way that it can qualify either as a pooling or as a purchase, at its discretion. One of the factors A's management will consider in deciding which way to arrange the combination is the impact on its post-acquisition consolidated financial statements of the pooling and purchase accounting treatments, respectively.

ACCOUNTING AS A POOLING. Assume that A plans to issue 100,000 shares of its stock, having a market value of $60 per share, in exchange for the 100,000 outstanding shares of B stock, and that accounting would be on a pooling basis.

Illustration 10–1

PRE-ACQUISITION BALANCE SHEETS
(thousands of dollars)

	Corporation A	Corporation B
ASSETS		
Cash and marketable securities.........................	$ 6,000	$1,000
Accounts receivable.................................	5,000	1,400
Inventories...	6,400	1,800
Total Current Assets.............................	$17,400	$4,200
Plant and equipment (net of accumulated depreciation)......	10,600	2,800
Total Assets....................................	$28,000	$7,000
LIABILITIES AND OWNERS' EQUITY		
Accounts payable..................................	$ 6,000	$1,700
Other current liabilities.............................	1,500	300
Total Current Liabilities..........................	$ 7,500	$2,000
Long-term debt....................................	8,200	1,600
Total Liabilities.................................	$15,700	$3,600
Common stock (par plus paid-in capital)*...............	$ 2,500	$ 700
Retained earnings..................................	9,800	2,700
Total Owners' Equity.............................	$12,300	$3,400
Total Liabilities and Owners' Equity..............	$28,000	$7,000
*Number of shares outstanding.......................	1,000,000	100,000

In qualifying for pooling treatment, the underlying premise is that there is a "marriage" of the two entities, with the two stockholder groups agreeing to a simple merging of the two firms' resources, talents, risks, and earnings streams. Accordingly, under pooling treatment, the balance sheets of A and B simply would be added together to arrive at the new consolidated balance sheet for A. If there were any intercorporate obligations involved—for example, a receivable on A's balance sheet which was due from B—these would be eliminated. With this exception, the new whole enterprise (the A–B combination) is accounted for as the sum of its parts, as shown in the first column of Illustration 10–2. In particular, it should be noted that the assets and liabilities of the combined firm are carried at the sum of their previous *book* values, and are not written up (or down) to their current values. Similarly, the common stock and retained earnings accounts of the combining firms are simply added to determine the combined firm's owners' equity. Notice also that when one compares A's pre-acquisition balance sheet in Illustration 10–1 with the pro-forma pooling one in 10–2, there is no evidence of the fact that A paid $6 million for B's net assets, which had a book value of only $3.4 million; this $2.6 million difference appears nowhere on the balance sheet.

ACCOUNTING AS A PURCHASE. Now, suppose that A arranges the combination so that purchase accounting is required. The underlying philosophy of this treatment is that instead of a "marriage" of A and B, A

Illustration 10–2

CORPORATION A
PRO-FORMA CONSOLIDATED BALANCE SHEETS
(thousands of dollars)

	"Pooling" Accounting	*"Purchase"* Accounting
ASSETS		
Cash and marketable securities............................	$ 7,000	$ 7,000
Accounts receivable......................................	6,400	6,400
Inventories..	8,200	8,200
Total Current Assets.................................	$21,600	$21,600
Goodwill..	—	1,500
Plant and equipment (net of accumulated depreciation)........	13,400	14,500
Total Assets..	$35,000	$37,600
LIABILITIES AND OWNERS' EQUITY		
Accounts payable..	$ 7,700	$ 7,700
Other current liabilities..................................	1,800	1,800
Total Current Liabilities.............................	$ 9,500	$ 9,500
Long-term debt..	9,800	9,800
Total Liabilities....................................	$19,300	$19,300
Common stock (par plus paid-in capital)*..................	$ 3,200	$ 8,500
Retained earnings.......................................	12,500	9,800
Total Owners' Equity.................................	$15,700	$18,300
Total Liabilities and Owners' Equity..................	$35,000	$37,600
*Number of shares outstanding.........................	1,100,000	1,100,000

is buying the net assets of B. In accordance with the cost concept, the net assets of B should go onto A's balance sheet at the amount paid for them, that is, $6 million.

This treatment involves two steps: first, B's tangible assets are revalued at their fair value. In Illustration 10–2 it is assumed that all of the assets on B's balance sheet reflected their current values except for plant and equipment; these had a book value of $2.8 million, but a market value of $3.9 million, an increase of $1.1 million. Hence, with purchase accounting the consolidated plant and equipment account shows $14.5 million ($10.6 million for A's pre-acquisition plant and equipment plus the acquired fixed assets of B, newly-valued at $3.9 million).

Second, after this revaluation of B's tangible assets, any excess of the purchase price over the total amount of B's revalued tangible net assets is shown on the consolidated balance sheet as an asset called "goodwill."[2]

---

[2] The preferred caption for this account is the more descriptive "excess of cost over net assets of acquired companies." However, "goodwill" is still frequently used. It should also be noted that APB *Opinion No. 16* rejects the concept of "negative goodwill" in most cases; i.e., it is assumed that if the purchase price of the acquired firm is less than the total market or appraised value of the tangible net assets, then

This amount is $1.5 million as shown in the second column of Illustration 10–2: the $6.0 million purchase price minus $3.4 million pre-acquisition book value minus the $1.1 increase in asset valuation. Hence of the $2.6 million excess of the $6 million purchase price over the $3.4 million book value of Corporation B (which appeared nowhere under pooling accounting), $1.1 million has been assigned to fixed assets, and the remainder, $1.5 million, is shown on the balance sheet as goodwill. This goodwill must be amortized over the time period that A will receive the benefits the "goodwill" represents (e.g., B's clientele, future earnings potential, and other valuable intangibles for which A has paid this $1.5 million excess over the revalued net assets), but in no case over longer than 40 years.[3]

Comparing the two balance sheets in Illustration 10–2, it can be seen that the pooling transaction will result in a more "attractive" balance sheet than will a purchase; the amount shown for plant and equipment is lower (though physically these assets are identical in either case), so future depreciation charges will be lower; no goodwill appears, meaning there will be no future goodwill amortization expense; and retained earnings is higher.

Earnings Impact

We have seen how the consolidated balance sheet of the new A–B Corporation would differ under purchase and pooling alternatives. To understand fully the financial reporting impacts of the alternatives, the effect on reported earnings must also be considered.

Assume that in the first year after the acquisition, there are no benefits from "synergism," and hence the projected combined A–B earnings are the same as the sum of the projected earnings of the two firms if they remained independent. Assume also that no intercorporate transactions are contemplated if the merger is not consummated (otherwise, the effects of such transactions would have to be eliminated when consolidating the income statements).

Illustration 10–3 shows that under *pooling* treatment of the combined

---

the fixed assets have been overvalued and should be reduced in valuation to the point where the revalued net assets and the purchase price are equal (zero goodwill). Only if the purchase price is still lower than the revalued net assets after the fixed asset values have been reduced to zero can a deferred credit, sometimes called "negative goodwill," be recorded.

[3] APB *Opinion No. 17* (August 1970), par. 29. Prior to this Opinion some firms did not amortize goodwill at all. Of 197 companies disclosing the time period for amortizing goodwill in their 1972 financial statements, 95 used the maximum 40-year amortization period. (*Accounting Trends and Techniques*, 1973).

Illustration 10–3

PRO-FORMA CONSOLIDATED INCOME RESULTS

If Independent Corporations:	*Corporation A*	*Corporation B*
Income before taxes..................................	$4,200,000	$1,050,000
Income tax expense.................................	2,100,000	525,000
Net income.......................................	$2,100,000	$ 525,000
Number of outstanding shares.........................	1,000,000	100,000
Net income per share..............................	$2.10	$5.25
Combined A–B, Pooling Treatment:		
Income before taxes.................................		$5,250,000
Income tax expense.................................		2,625,000
Net income.......................................		$2,625,000
Number of outstanding shares........................		1,100,000
Net income per share...............................		$2.39
Combined A–B, Purchase Treatment:		
Unadjusted pre-tax income...........................		$5,250,000
Adjustments:		
Additional depreciation expense.....................		(110,000)
Amortization of goodwill...........................		(50,000)
Adjusted income before taxes........................		$5,090,000
Income tax expense.................................		2,545,000
Net income.......................................		$2,545,000
Number of outstanding shares........................		1,100,000
Net income per share...............................		$2.31

firm's results, the net incomes of A and B are simply added to arrive at the consolidated figure. A's pre-acquisition stockholders would benefit from the combination, since net income per share would be $2.39 instead of $2.10.

Under *purchase* accounting, in order to arrive at a consolidated income figure, two adjustments must be made to the sum of the two firms' pre-tax incomes. First, after the acquisition the consolidated depreciation expense would be greater than the sum of the independent firms' depreciation because the B Corporation's plant and equipment amount was written up from $2.8 million to $3.9 million. Illustration 10–3 assumes that this will result in an additional $110,000 depreciation expense for each of the next 10 years. Secondly, the $1.5 million goodwill must be amortized; Illustration 10–3 assumes an amortization period of 30 years is being used, or $50,000 per year. Thus under the purchase assumption, net income is lower than with a pooling.

Illustration 10–3 illustrates why pooling would likely be preferred by Company A's management, and why prior to the issuance of APB Opinion No. 16 acquiring companies chose pooling treatment over purchase treatment for acquisitions made with stock. If the combination were accounted for as a purchase, the net income would be lower ($2.545

million vs. $2.625 million) but the number of outstanding shares would be the same; hence purchase treatment net income would be $2.31 per share instead of $2.39.

The accounting treatment when stock is exchanged in a combination is no longer a matter of management discretion. It is, however, a continuing matter of discussion among accountants, some of whom feel APB Opinion No. 16 is too restrictive, and others of whom feel pooling treatment should never be permitted.

CONSOLIDATED STATEMENTS

A "company," as it is thought of by its management, its employees, its competitors, and the general public, may actually consist of a number of different corporations, created for various legal, tax, and financial reasons. The existence of a family of corporations is by no means peculiar to "big business." A fairly small enterprise may consist of one corporation that owns the real estate and buildings, another that primarily handles production, another for marketing activities, and over them all a *parent* corporation which is the locus of management and control. Each of these corporations is a legal entity, and each therefore has its own financial statements. The "company" itself may not be a separate legal entity, but it is an important economic entity, and a set of financial statements for the whole business enterprise may be more useful than the statements of the separate corporations of which it consists.

Such statements are called *consolidated financial statements.* They are prepared by first adjusting and then combining the financial statements of the separate corporations; usually, no separate journals or ledgers are kept for the consolidated entity.

Basis for Consolidation

The legal tie that binds the other corporations, or *subsidiaries,* to the parent is the ownership of their stock. A firm usually is not consolidated unless more than 50 percent of its common stock is owned by the parent. Some companies use an even higher percentage as the criterion for consolidation of subsidiaries.

Even though it is 100-percent owned by the parent, a subsidiary may not be consolidated if its business is so different from that of the other companies in the family that including it in the consolidation would result in financial statements that do not well describe the family as a whole. General Motors Corporation does not consolidate the statements of General Motors Acceptance Corporation with those of its other corporations because GMAC is a huge financial corporation dealing principally in installment payments on automobiles, and its assets and liabilities are quite unlike those of an industrial company. Some companies do not consolidate their foreign subsidiaries.

Unconsolidated Investments

If a subsidiary is *not* consolidated, the amount of the parent's investment in it appears as an asset on the parent's balance sheet. APB *Opinion No. 18* (March 1971) requires that for both domestic and foreign subsidiaries the *equity method* be used to record this investment if the parent has 20% or greater ownership of the subsidiary. With the equity method, the amount of the asset is the acquisition cost of the subsidiary's stock, plus the parent's share each year after acquisition of any earnings (or minus the amount of losses). The corresponding annual entry is a credit (debit, if the subsidiary had a loss) to an income account, Revenue from Investments. If a dividend is paid by the subsidiary, the parent's cash account is debited and the asset investment account is reduced by the amount of the dividend. Note that this method is a departure from the basic concept that assets are reported at cost.

The equity method is used to record the asset amount of an investment in another firm where the portion of stock owned is at least 20 percent, unless the investing corporation can demonstrate that it does not "exercise significant influence" over the investee firm. Where such influence does not exist, or where the amount of stock owned is less than 20 percent, the *cost method* may be used to record the investment. With the cost method, the asset amount is shown simply at the acquisition cost of the stock; any dividends paid from earnings by the investee firm are shown as revenue to the company that owns the stock; they do not change the asset amount of the investment on the owning company's balance sheet.

In summary, three treatments of investment are possible depending, with some qualifications, on the amount of stock that a company owns, as follows:

Amount of ownership	Treatment
Over 50 percent..........	Consolidated statements
20–50 percent............	Equity method
less than 20 percent.......	Cost method

Consolidation Procedure

Illustration 10–4 shows the consolidation process in the simplest possible situation, consisting of the parent company and one subsidiary company, named "Parent" and "Subsidiary," respectively. Parent owns 100 percent of Subsidiary's stock; this is an asset which is shown on its balance sheet as Investment in Subsidiary. The investment is recorded at

Illustration 10–4

CONSOLIDATION WORK SHEET

| | Separate Statements | | Intercompany Eliminations | | Consolidated Balance Sheet |
	Parent	Subsidiary	Dr.	Cr.	
Assets					
Cash..................	45,000	12,000			57,000
Accounts receivable.......	40,000	11,000		(1)* 5,000	46,000
Inventory...............	30,000	15,000		(2) 2,000	43,000
Fixed assets, net..........	245,000	45,000			290,000
Investment in subsidiary....	55,000			(3) 55,000	
	415,000	83,000			436,000
Liabilities and Owners' Equity					
Accounts payable.........	20,000	13,000	(1) 5,000		28,000
Other current liabilities.....	25,000	9,000			34,000
Long-term liabilities.......	100,000	—			100,000
Capital stock............	100,000	40,000	(3) 40,000		100,000
Retained earnings.........	170,000	21,000	(2) 2,000		174,000
			(3) 15,000		
	415,000	83,000			436,000

* Parenthetical numbers correspond with text description.

cost, and it is assumed here that Parent purchased Subsidiary's stock at its book value (capital stock plus retained earnings) as of the time of acquisition.

In the illustration, the separate balance sheets of Parent and Subsidiary are given in the first two columns. If the two columns were added at this point, the sum of the balance sheet amounts would contain some items which, so far as the consolidated entity is concerned, would be counted twice. To preclude this double counting, adjustments are made in the next two columns; these are explained below. Essentially, these adjustments eliminate the effect of transactions that have occurred between the two corporations as separate legal entities. Since the consolidated financial statements should report only assets owned by the consolidated entity and the equities of parties *outside* the consolidated entity, these internal transactions must be eliminated. The consolidated balance sheet that results from these adjustments appears in the last column. The adjustments are as follows:

1. INTERCOMPANY FINANCIAL TRANSACTIONS. The consolidated balance sheet must show as accounts receivable and accounts payable only amounts owed by and owed to parties outside the consolidated business; therefore, amounts that the companies owe to one another must be elimi-

nated. Assuming that Parent owes Subsidiary $5,000, this amount is eliminated from their respective Accounts Payable and Accounts Receivable accounts. The effect is as in the following journal entry (although it should be remembered that no journal entries actually are made in the books of either corporation):

```
Accounts Payable (Parent)................... 5,000
     Accounts Receivable (Subsidiary).......        5,000
```

Interest on intercompany loans would also be eliminated in a similar manner.

The payment of dividends by the subsidiary to the parent is a financial transaction that has no effect on the consolidated entity. In the separate statements, this was recorded on Parent's books as a credit to Revenue from Investments (which was closed to Parent's Retained Earnings), and on Subsidiary's books as a debit to Dividends (which was closed to Subsidiary's Retained Earnings). Since this transaction ultimately affected only the two retained earnings accounts, adding to one the same amount that was subtracted from the other, the act of combining the two of them automatically eliminated its effect; therefore, no further adjustment is necessary.

2. INTERCOMPANY PROFIT. In accordance with the realization principle, the consolidated company does not earn revenue until sales are made to the outside world. The revenue, the related costs, and the resulting profit for sales made between companies in the consolidated entity must therefore be eliminated from the consolidated accounts.

The sales and cost of sales on intercompany transactions are subtracted from the total sales and cost of sales figures on the consolidated income statement; if this were not done, the figures would overstate the volume of business done by the consolidated entity with the outside world. In order to do this, records must be kept that show both the sales revenue and the cost of sales of shipments made within the family.

EXAMPLE: Subsidiary sold goods costing it $52,000 to Parent for $60,000. Parent then sold these goods to outside customers for $75,000. The total gross margin on these sales was $23,000 ($75,000 minus $52,000). Of this amount, $8,000 appeared on Subsidiary's income statement and $15,000 on Parent's; hence the consolidated income figure would not be overstated. However, the correct consolidated sales figure is $75,000, not $135,000 ($60,000 plus $75,000); similarly, the correct consolidated cost of goods sold amount is $52,000, not $112,000. Thus Subsidiary's sales and Parent's cost of goods sold must be reduced by the $60,000 intercompany transfer to avoid double counting:

```
Sales (Subsidiary)......................... 60,000
     Cost of Goods Sold (Parent)...........        60,000
```

If the goods have not been sold to the outside world, intercompany transactions will affect the Inventory account of the company receiving the goods and the Retained Earnings account of the company selling them, and adjustments to these accounts are required. Assume that in the preceding example, Parent sold to outside customers only three fourths of the products it acquired from Subsidiary, and the other one fourth remains in Parent's inventory at the end of the year at its cost to Parent of $15,000. The products sold to the outside world present no problem, since they have disappeared from inventory and the revenue has been realized. The $15,000 remaining in Parent's inventory, however, is regarded by Subsidiary as a sale, the $2,000 profit on which (one fourth of $60,000 minus $52,000) appears in Subsidiary's Retained Earnings. This portion of the profit must be eliminated from the consolidated balance sheet. This is done by reducing Subsidiary's Retained Earnings and Parent's Inventory by the amount of the profit, as in the following entry:

```
Retained Earnings (Subsidiary)............. 2,000
    Inventory (Parent)....................        2,000
```

3. ELIMINATION OF THE INVESTMENT. The Parent company's investment in the Subsidiary's stock is strictly an intrafamily matter and must therefore be eliminated from the consolidated balance sheet. Since it is assumed here that the stock was purchased at book value, the $55,000 cost shown on Parent's books must have equaled Subsidiary's Capital Stock plus Retained Earnings at the time of purchase. We know that Capital Stock is $40,000; the difference, $15,000, must therefore equal the balance of Retained Earnings at that time. The additional $6,000 of retained earnings now shown on Subsidiary's books has been created subsequent to the acquisition by Parent. To eliminate the investment, therefore, the entry in effect is as follows:

```
Capital Stock (Subsidiary)................. 40,000
Retained Earnings (Subsidiary)............. 15,000
    Investment in Subsidiary (Parent)......        55,000
```

The necessary eliminations having been recorded, the figures for the consolidated balance sheet can now be obtained by carrying each line across the work sheet.

In the preceding example, two of the most difficult problems in preparing consolidated statements did not arise because of simplifying assumptions that were made. These problems are described below.

Asset Valuation

In the example, it was assumed that Parent purchased Subsidiary's stock at its book value. Usually, a subsidiary's stock is purchased at a figure different than its book value. As explained earlier in this chapter, purchase accounting for an acquisition requires that the book value of the acquired assets be adjusted to show their fair value, and that any remaining excess of purchase price over the revalued net assets be shown as an asset called Goodwill.[4] In the above illustration, if Parent had paid $65,000, rather than $55,000, for Subsidiary's stock, and if Subsidiary's assets were found to be recorded at their fair value, there would be goodwill of $10,000, and the adjustment marked (3) above would have been:

```
Goodwill.....................................  10,000
Capital Stock (Subsidiary)..................  40,000
Retained Earnings (Subsidiary)..............  15,000
      Investment in Subsidiary..............          65,000
```

In future years this adjustment will be increasingly lower, ultimately reaching $55,000, reflecting the requirement that Parent amortize the goodwill over a period no longer than 40 years.

Minority Interest

If in the illustration above, Parent had owned less than 100 percent of Subsidiary's stock, then there would exist a *minority interest*, that is, the equity of Subsidiary's other owners. On the consolidated balance sheet, this minority interest appears as a separate equity item, just above owners' equity. For example, if Parent owned 80 percent of Subsidiary's stock, for which it had paid 80 percent of Subsidiary's book value, or $44,000, adjustment (3) above to eliminate the investment would have been as follows:

```
Capital Stock (Subsidiary)..................  32,000
Retained Earnings (Subsidiary)..............  12,000
      Investment in Subsidiary..............          44,000
```

As this elimination suggests, at the time Parent acquired 80 percent of Subsidiary's stock, the Minority Interest amount was $11,000, the sum of the remaining 20 percent of Subsidiary's Capital Stock and Retained Earnings.

After the acquisition, this minority interest would increase by 20 percent of the increase in Subsidiary's retained earnings, *after* elimination of Subsidiary's profit on sales to Parent. Thus this intercompany profit adjustment is in effect prorated between Parent and the minority holders in proportion to their respective ownership. Hence, if Parent owned 80

---

[4] As previously explained, if the merger were such that it required treatment as a pooling of interests, no goodwill would arise.

percent of Subsidiary, on the consolidated balance sheet the following amounts would appear:

Minority Interest...................................... 11,800
Owners' Equity:
    Capital Stock..................................... 100,000
    Retained Earnings................................ 173,200

The $11,800 figure for Minority Interest is the net sum of four amounts: $8,000, which is 20 percent of Subsidiary's Capital Stock; plus $3,000, which is 20 percent of Subsidiary's Retained Earnings at the time of the acquisition ($15,000); plus $1,200, which is 20 percent of the $6,000 increase in Subsidiary's Retained Earnings since acquisition ($21,000 minus $15,000); less $400, which is 20 percent of the eliminated $2,000 intercompany profit. Similarly, the consolidated Retained Earnings figure, which was $174,000 when we assumed Parent owned 100 percent of Subsidiary, is now $800 less, reflecting the 20 percent minority interest in the $6,000 post-acquisition increase in Subsidiary's Retained Earnings ($1,200) adjusted downward for the minority interest's share of the $2,000 intercompany profit elimination ($400).

Concluding Comment

The preceding brief discussion of consolidated statements is by no means adequate as a basis for actually preparing consolidated financial statements. A great many problems in addition to those discussed above arise in practice. The illustration given does, however, indicate the main types of problems and the principles applied in solving them, and thus should help the user, as distinguished from the preparer, in understanding how the figures on a consolidated statement were derived.

SUMMARY

A business may consist of more than one corporation, in which case it is often more meaningful to report the separate legal entities' financial information in a way that treats them as a consolidated economic entity.

When two companies combine their operations, an acquisition or merger takes place. These business combinations are accounted for either as purchases or as poolings of interests, according to the criteria of APB *Opinion No. 16*. Treatment as a purchase usually gives rise to an asset called Goodwill, which is the excess of the acquisition cost over the fair value of the net assets acquired, and which must be amortized over a period not to exceed 40 years.

In preparing consolidated statements, the effects of intercompany transactions must first be eliminated from the accounts of the separate corporations, and then the accounts are combined. Unconsolidated subsidiaries and investments in 20 to 50 percent of another firm's stock are accounted for using the equity method; smaller investments are recorded at cost.

CASES

CASE 10-1. PROBLEM IN ACCOUNTING FOR BUSINESS COMBINATIONS

The Able Company is considering acquiring the Baker Company. In exchange for Baker's 40,000 shares of stock, Able will distribute to Baker's shareholders 100,000 shares of Able common stock. This stock is authorized but not issued. In recent talks with Able's investment banker about a possible new public offering of 100,000 shares, the investment banker had expressed a willingness to offer the shares to the public at $8 per share.

Below are Able's and Baker's balance sheets, projected to the proposed

Condensed Balance Sheets
As of the Proposed Acquisition Date
($000)

ASSETS	Able	Baker
Current assets...........................	$ 400	$ 250
Fixed assets (net)........................	600	300
Total Assets.........................	$1,000	$ 550

EQUITIES		
Current liabilities........................	$ 250	$ 100
Long-term debt...........................	100	10
Common stock ($1 par)....................	100	40
Paid-in surplus..........................	300	100
Retained earnings........................	250	300
Total Equities.........................	$1,000	$ 550

Condensed Income Statements
For the First Year after Combination
($000)

Sales....................................	$2,000	$1,500
Expenses................................	1,600	1,200
Income..............................	$ 400	$ 300
Income Tax Expense......................	160	120
Net Income..........................	$ 240	$ 180

311

acquisition date. Also shown are pro-forma income statements for the two firms for a one-year period following the proposed acquisition date; these reflect the best estimates of results of operations if the two firms were *not* to merge, but were to continue to operate as separate companies. There are no intercompany receivables or payables, and no intercompany sales or other transactions are contemplated if the business combination is not consummated.

An appraiser has been retained by the two firms and has appraised Baker's net assets (assets less liabilities) at $600,000. The difference between this amount and Baker's book value is wholly attributable to the appraiser's valuation of Baker's fixed assets. Able's certified public accountant has not yet determined whether the combination would qualify for pooling of interests treatment under APB *Opinion No. 16.*

Questions

1. Prepare consolidated balance sheets as of the proposed acquisition date, assuming accounting treatment of the combination: (a) on a pooling of interests basis; and (b) on a purchase basis.
2. Assuming that in its first year of operations a combined Able-Baker company would achieve the same results of operations as the sum of the two firms' independent operations, what would be Able-Baker's net income that year on a pooling basis? What would net income be on a purchase basis, assuming a goodwill amortization period of forty years and average fixed asset life of ten years? (Use a 40% tax rate and straight-line depreciation.)
3. As Able's president, what would you hope the accountant will conclude regarding accounting treatment of the combination? Why?

CASE 10–2. ALBION INC.

Albion Inc. was a heavy-equipment manufacturing firm with annual sales in excess of $500 million. Among its products were large industrial turbines, overhead cranes, and numerically controlled metalworking equipment. Effective January 1, 1971, Albion had paid cash for 80 percent of the stock of the Steele Engineering Company, a full-service engineering firm which had been closely held by its founders and a few other long-time employees. Steele was one of the largest firms in its field, and had a consistent record of profitability. In the past, most of these profits had been paid out each year as dividends to the owners.

Albion had been hesitant about acquiring a professional service firm, since all of Albion's experience was manufacturing-related. Nevertheless, it had bought Steele for two reasons. First, it was thought that through its consulting engineering work for industrial firms, Steele could increase sales of Albion's various products. Second, Albion had not been satisfied with the performance of its own engineering section, and felt matters would improve if it purchased many of these services from Steele. As of the end of 1971, both of these reasons seemed valid, and during 1971, Albion had purchased $25 million of services from Steele. Steele's costs for these services had been $11 million. As of December 31, 1971, Albion owed Steele for the total $25 million.

In early January 1972, the accountant for Albion reminded the president that Accounting Principles Board *Opinion No. 18* would apply for financial statements for periods beginning after December 31, 1971. Accordingly, the accountant suggested that Albion might want voluntarily to follow APB–18 when issuing its 1971 statements. It was clear that APB–18 would not permit continued use of the cost method to record

Balance Sheets

As of December 31, 1971

(000 omitted)

	Albion	Steele
Assets		
Cash	$ 11,000	$ 5,000
Accounts receivable	65,000	113,000
Inventories	136,000	18,000
Fixed assets, net	200,000	50,000
Investment in subsidiary*	36,000	—
Total Assets	$448,000	$186,000
Liabilities and Owners' Equity		
Accounts payable	$ 81,000	$ 23,000
Other current liabilities	25,000	45,000
Long-term debt	52,000	50,000
Capital stock	100,000	20,000
Retained earnings	190,000	48,000
Total Liabilities and Owners' Equity	$448,000	$186,000

* At cost, which equalled the fair value of the net assets of the subsidiary at the time of acquisition.

Income Statements

For the Year Ended December 31, 1971

(000 omitted)

	Albion	Steele
Sales	$525,000	$279,000
Cost of goods sold	240,000	112,000
Gross margin	$285,000	$167,000
Other expenses†	170,000	92,000
Income before taxes	$115,000	$ 75,000
Income tax expense	55,000	36,000
Net Income	$ 60,000	$ 39,000
Dividends Declared and Paid	$ 30,000	$ 16,000

† Net of other revenues, including earnings on investments.

Albion's investment in Steele. The question was whether Steele should be left unconsolidated, with Albion's investment in Steele recorded using the equity method, or whether Steele should be consolidated. The president asked the accountant to recast Albion's 1971 statements on both of these bases.

Questions

1. Change Albion's 1971 financial statements to reflect the use of the equity method in accounting for Steele as an unconsolidated subsidiary.
2. Change Albion's 1971 financial statements so as to treat Steele as a consolidated subsidiary.
3. Which treatment should be used for the 1971 statements?
4. Assume that Albion paid $40 million for the 80 percent interest in Steele. Assume further that the difference of $4 million related solely to the fair value of patents held by Steele which had a remaining legal life of 15 years as of 1/1/71. How do your calculations in Questions 1 and 2 change? Would your answer to Question 3 change?

CHAPTER 11

THE STATEMENT OF CHANGES
IN FINANCIAL POSITION

APB *Opinion No. 19* (March 1971) requires that a company must publish a third financial report called the *statement of changes in financial position* (SCFP) in addition to the balance sheet and income statement. The SCFP is similar in many respects to the statements which many companies had published voluntarily under various titles such as "funds flow statement," "sources and applications of funds," and "cash flow statement." In this chapter both the concept underlying the SCFP and the basic analytical techniques for its preparation will be discussed.

THE CONCEPT OF FLOW STATEMENTS

The balance sheet gives a "snapshot" view at a point in time of the *sources* from which a firm has acquired its funds and the *uses* which the firm has made of these funds. The equities side of the balance sheet delineates these sources, and the asset side shows the uses. A flow statement explains the *changes* that took place in a balance sheet account or group of accounts during the period *between* the dates of two balance sheet "snapshots." The income statement is a flow statement; it explains changes that occurred in the retained earnings account by summarizing the increases (revenues) and decreases (expenses) in retained earnings during the accounting period. This explanation of changes in a single balance sheet account, retained earnings, is so useful to the managers, creditors, and owners of a company that it has long warranted its status as a separate financial statement, so long, in fact, that many people forget its intimate relationship with the company's balance sheet.

Another type of flow statement can be constructed simply by summarizing the debits and credits to the Cash account during the period. Such a statement shows the flow of cash into (i.e., receipts) and out of (i.e., disbursements) the business during the period. It therefore shows why the Cash balance changed during the period, just as the income statement shows why the Retained Earnings balance changed.

Illustration 11–1

CAMPUS PIZZERIA, INC.

Summary of Cash Receipts and Disbursements
For the Year 1975

Receipts:

Sales		$48,000
Advance on party		100
Total Receipts		$48,100
Disbursements:		
Ingredients	$23,000	
Wages	12,000	
Rentals	5,400	
Utilities	2,000	
Miscellaneous supplies	1,000	
Tax estimate payments	650	
Equipment down payment	1,000	
Loan to employee	500	
Total disbursements		45,550
Increase in Cash Balance		$ 2,550

Illustration 11–1 shows such a summary of cash receipts and disbursements. It is based on the following situation:

William Snelson started Campus Pizzeria, Inc. on January 1, 1975, at which time the firm had no receivables or payables. During the first year of operation, Campus had cash sales of $48,000. Cash expenses included $23,000 for pizza ingredients, $12,000 for wages, $600 for equipment rentals, $4,800 for store rental, $2,000 for utilities, $1,000 for miscellaneous supplies, and $650 in payment of estimated taxes. In early January, ovens, tables, and chairs were acquired, for which Campus paid $1,000 cash down payment, and signed a $2,000 mortgage note with the supplier, payable in full (plus accrued interest at 9%) in January 1977. Snelson's intent was to depreciate this equipment on a straight-line basis over five years. In addition, as of December 31 there was an unpaid December utilities bill of $200, and Campus owed $800 to its ingredients vendor. Because the vendor delivered frequently, Campus had essentially no inventory on hand at the end of December. Also, Campus had loaned an employee $500 which she was to repay in early 1976. Finally, a customer had paid Campus a $100 advance for a pizza party Campus was to cater on New Year's Day, and another customer owed Campus $150 for a Christmas Eve party.

The "receipts" section of Illustration 11–1 shows the sources from which cash was received, and the "disbursements" section shows the uses made of cash. The statement of changes in financial position gives similar information, but it differs from the summary of cash receipts and disbursements in some important respects, as will be described below. There are two versions of the statement of changes in financial position, one of which is called the cash basis, and the other, the working-capital basis. The cash-basis SCFP will be described first.

STATEMENT OF CHANGES IN FINANCIAL POSITION— CASH BASIS

The cash-basis SCFP differs from the summary of cash receipts and disbursements in three ways. First, it is prepared by a rearrangement of items on the income statement and balance sheets, rather than from entries made to the Cash account. Second, it highlights the amount of cash generated by the firm's operations; this amount can be calculated from Illustration 11–1, but it does not appear there explicitly. Third, the SCFP shows some items that do not go directly through the Cash account. Because of these differences, the cash-basis SCFP is more informative than the simple summary of cash receipts and disbursements.

The construction of a cash-basis SCFP for Campus Pizzeria, Inc. is described below. The basic data used to construct it are taken from the income statement and balance sheets shown in Illustration 11–2, and the Statement itself is shown in Illustration 11–3.

The first step is to determine the amount of cash that was generated by the operations of the business. This is done by adjusting the revenue and expense items on the income statement so as to show the cash receipts and cash disbursements associated with these items. Specifically:

1. The income statement revenue amount is adjusted to the amount of sales-related cash inflows. First, the $150 accounts receivable increase must be deducted, since an increase in accounts receivable during the year means that the year's revenues exceeded collections (cash inflows from sales). This first adjustment, then, gives us the $48,000 cash collected for 1975 sales. (If accounts receivable had *decreased* during the year, this means that the amount of cash collected exceeded the sales revenue for the period, and the amount of the decrease should therefore be *added* to sales revenue.)

Second, an adjustment must be made to reflect the 1975 cash inflow

Illustration 11–2

CAMPUS PIZZERIA, INC.

Income Statement
For the Year 1975

Revenues*......................................		$48,150
Cost of sales†.................................		35,800
Gross margin...............................		$12,350
Other expenses:		
Rentals..................................	$5,400	
Depreciation‡.............................	600	
Utilities§.................................	2,200	
Miscellaneous supplies......................	1,000	
Interest‖.................................	180	9,380
Income before taxes..........................		$ 2,970
Income tax expense..........................		650
Net income..................................		$ 2,320

* The revenues include the $48,000 cash sales plus the $150 owed Campus for the party it catered on Christmas Eve. The $100 advance payment for the New Year's party is not revenue of this period; it appears as $100 deferred revenue on the balance sheet.
† $23,000 ingredients paid + $800 ingredients used but not yet paid for + $12,000 wages.
‡ $3,000 equipment cost ÷ 5 years
§ $2,000 paid in cash + $200 payable.
‖ One year's accrued (but unpaid) interest at 9% on the $2,000 mortgage note.

Balance Sheets
As of January 1 and December 31, 1975

	January 1		December 31
Assets			
Cash...	$1,200		$3,750
Accounts receivable............................	0		150
Notes receivable...............................	0		500
Equipment at cost..............................	$0	$3,000	
Accumulated depreciation......................	0	600	
Equipment, net.............................	0		2,400
Total Assets.............................	$1,200		$6,800
Equities			
Accounts payable.............................	$ 0		$1,000
Deferred revenue.............................	0		100
Accrued interest..............................	0		180
Mortgage note payable.........................	0		2,000
Contributed capital...........................	1,200		1,200
Retained earnings.............................	0		2,320
Total Equities............................	$1,200		$6,800

of $100 from the advance payment, which is not included in 1975 revenues because the service (catering the New Year's Day party) will be performed in 1976. Together, these two adjustments to the revenue amount convert it to the amount of cash inflows from selling pizzas, $48,100. The reader can confirm the correctness of these adjustments by noting the $48,100 cash receipts (all from operations) in Illustration 11–1.

Illustration 11–3

CAMPUS PIZZERIA, INC.

Statement of Changes in Financial Position (Cash Basis)
For the Year 1975

Sources of Cash

From operations:

Revenues......................................	$48,150	
Adjustments to convert to cash basis:		
Increase in accounts receivable................	(150)	
Increase in deferred revenue...................	100	
Cash generated from revenues.................		$48,100
Expenses......................................	$45,830	
Adjustments to convert to cash basis:		
Depreciation expense........................	(600)	
Increase in accounts payable..................	(1,000)	
Increase in accrued interest...................	(180)	
Cash disbursed for expenses...................		44,050
Net cash generated by operations.................		$ 4,050
From other sources:		
Mortgage note..............................		2,000
Total sources of cash............................		$ 6,050

Uses of Cash

Loan to employee............................	$ 500	
Acquisition of equipment......................	3,000	
Total uses of cash..............................		$ 3,500
Net Increase in Cash...........................		$ 2,550

2. Income statement expenses are totaled, and this $45,830 total is then adjusted to convert it to cash outflows for expenses:

   a. The $45,830 overstates cash outflows because the $600 depreciation expense did not require a cash outflow (note that there is no $600 disbursement for depreciation in Illustration 11–1). Hence a $600 deduction is made to reflect this overstatement.

   b. The income statement included as expenses $800 of ingredients and $200 of utilities which have not yet been paid out of cash; thus again the expenses total overstates cash outflows, and this $1,000 overstatement, the increase in accounts payable, is deducted.

   c. The interest expense of $180 has not been paid; this $180 must also be deducted so as not to overstate cash outflows.

   d. If Campus had inventories whose beginning and ending balance sheet values were different, this inventory change also would have given rise to an adjustment of the expense figure to convert it to the cash basis, since purchases (cash outflows) and uses (expenses) of these items would have differed during the year. Such an adjustment is not necessary here.

3. The cash inflows and outflows associated with revenues and expenses are then combined into a net amount of cash generated by opera-

tions, $4,050. The reader can verify this figure by netting the cash receipts and the cash outflows for operations (all the outflows except the equipment down payment and loan) in Illustration 11–1. Note, however, that the receipts and disbursements statement did not highlight the net amount of cash generated by Campus' ongoing operations of making and selling pizzas. To most users of financial statements it is highly informative to show clearly how much cash the company's operations have generated (or required).

4. The sources of cash other than operations are identified. The treatment of the mortgage note that was given for the equipment illustrates an important feature of the Statement of Changes in Financial Position, namely, that this statement is prepared on what is called the *all financial resources* concept. This means that each significant change in financial resources is set forth separately on the statement, even though a given transaction may have no net effect on cash. In the case of the mortgage note, the $2,000 is shown as a source of cash, even though Campus did not actually receive the $2,000 in cash because the note holder and the equipment supplier were the same entity. In effect, the SCFP treats the mortgage note and the acquisition of equipment as if they were two separate transactions, one a source of cash (from the mortgage note holder), and the other a use of cash (the purchase of the equipment). The use of cash for the equipment is $3,000, of which $2,000 came from the mortgage note, and the other $1,000 from the Cash account directly. The reason for this treatment is simply to make the Statement more informative than it would be if only the net effect of the transaction were shown. The SCFP shows this transaction as if it were two separate transactions, that is, it is shown as it would have been shown had the noteholder and the equipment supplier been different parties.

5. The sources of cash are then totaled. Note that this amount is much smaller than the cash receipts in Illustration 11–1, because cash outflows for expenses are subtracted from inflows from revenues to arrive at a *net* source of cash from operations.

6. The uses of cash are identified. Because of netting expense outflows against revenue inflows, these uses of cash reflect *nonoperations* outflows, in this case the loan to an employee and the purchase of fixed assets. Note how the SCFP's "all financial resources" concept reflects the economic fact that $3,000 worth of equipment was purchased, whereas in Illustration 11–1 one really cannot tell what the cost of these assets was, since only the $1,000 down payment actually flowed through the Cash account.

7. Finally, the sources and uses of cash are netted to arrive at the $2,550 cash balance increase. Note how much more useful than the cash flow statement the SCFP is in understanding *why* Campus Pizzeria's cash balance changed.

Recapitulating, the procedure for constructing a cash-basis SCFP is as follows:

1. Find cash generated by sales by adjusting the revenue amount on the income statement:

   a. Add the increase in deferred revenues (or subtract a decrease); and

   b. Add the change in the Accounts Receivable balance if it decreased during the period, or subtract if the change was an increase.

2. Find cash disbursed for expenses by adjusting the total expenses on the income statement:

   a. Subtract from expenses the depreciation expense; similarly subtract amortization of patents or goodwill, which are expenses but are not cash outflows.

   b. Subtract from expenses the change in Accounts Payable if it was an increase, or add the change if it was a decrease. Do the same with accrued wages or any other liability that is related to current operations. (Do *not* adjust for changes in Notes Payable, which are usually caused by financial transactions rather than by operations.)

   c. Add to expenses the amount of a build-up in inventories, or subtract the decrease in inventories.[1]

3. Combine the adjusted amounts from Steps 1 and 2 to arrive at "net cash generated by operations."

4. Identify any non-operations sources of cash, e.g., loans and issuance of bonds, preferred stock, or common stock.

5. Combine the amounts from Steps 3 and 4 to arrive at "total sources of cash."

6. Identify any uses of cash *other than* cash used for expense items. This will include purchase of fixed assets, repayment of loans, refunding bond issues, purchase of treasury stock, and payment of cash dividends.

7. Net the sources and uses to determine the increase or decrease in cash. This amount can be verified by subtracting the beginning cash balance from the ending cash balance.

STATEMENT OF CHANGES IN FINANCIAL POSITION— WORKING-CAPITAL BASIS

In practice, most firms issuing an SCFP do not prepare it on the cash basis, but rather on the *working-capital basis*.[2] Working capital is defined as current assets minus current liabilities, and is a broader definition of funds than is cash. By using working capital as the definition of funds, in

---

[1] An alternative point of view is that a change in inventory levels is not a simple operations accrual-to-cash adjustment, but rather represents a conscious management decision to invest or disinvest in inventory. Advocates of this viewpoint would show an inventory increase as a "use" of cash, and a decrease as "cash from other sources," rather than showing the change as an adjustment to expenses.

[2] Over 95 percent of the firms surveyed in the AICPA's *Accounting Trends and Techniques* (1973 edition) used the working-capital basis for the SCFP in 1972.

essence transactions are "put through a less fine sieve" to filter them out for the SCFP. For example, paying an account payable affects cash, so this transaction would be reflected in a cash-basis SCFP. However, the transaction has no effect on working capital, since a current asset (cash) and a current liability (accounts payable) decrease by the same amount; hence the transaction would not be reflected as a source or use in a working-capital basis SCFP. Thus, when funds are defined as working capital, there is no need to show the details of the more or less continuous movement of resources between current liabilities and current assets which results from the manufacture and sale of goods and the collection of receivables from customers. Indeed, the focus is on the usually more significant flows affecting noncurrent assets (i.e., long-term investments) and *permanent capital,* the name given to the sum of long-term liabilities and owners' equity. With this single exception, the working-capital basis SCFP is prepared in exactly the same manner as the cash-basis SCFP.

Illustration 11–4 depicts resource flows, and gives examples of flows between various accounts. Any transaction which changes one account above the dotted line and another account below the dotted line will change working capital, and hence represents a working capital flow

Illustration 11–4

RESOURCE FLOWS AND THE WORKING-CAPITAL BASIS SCFP

Common examples of working capital flows, all shown on the SCFP:
·1.   A fixed asset is purchased for cash; a fixed asset is sold for cash.
2.   A bond is redeemed; new common stock is issued.
3.   A fixed asset is purchased using a one-year note.
4.   A long-term note's maturity date becomes less than one year hence; a six-month note is refinanced so as not to be due for two years.

Resource flows not affecting working capital, but shown on the SCFP:
5.   A fixed asset is purchased using a long-term mortgage note.
6.   A convertible bond is converted to common stock.

Resource flows not affecting working capital and not shown on the SCFP (working-capital basis):
7.   Raw materials are purchased on vendor 30-day credit; a 90-day note is repaid.
8.   Goods for inventory are purchased for cash; an account receivable is collected.

which is reflected in the SCFP. Any transaction changing two current asset accounts or two current liability accounts by offsetting amounts, or a transaction changing a current liability and a current asset by the same amount, has *no* effect on working capital, and is not depicted as a source or use of working capital in the SCFP. On the other hand, transactions such as those represented by arrows 5 and 6 in Illustration 11–4, which *do not* affect working capital but *do* constitute significant investment and/or financing activities of the firm, are included in an SCFP prepared on either the cash or working-capital basis, consistent with the SCFP's "all financial resources" concept.

The SCFP in Illustration 11–5 was prepared on the working-capital basis using the most commonly seen format for the SCFP. The top part shows the causes and net amount of the change in working capital, that is, the net effect of the firm's financing activities (sources of working capital) and investing activities (uses of working capital). The lower portion of the SCFP explains the internal content of the working capital change, i.e., how much the various current asset and current liability accounts changed during the period. Although these changes could be calculated from the firm's beginning and ending balance sheets, they are

Illustration 11–5

CAMPUS PIZZERIA, INC.

Statement of Changes in Financial Position (Working-Capital Basis)
For the Year 1975

Sources of Working Capital

From operations:
Net income....................................	$2,320	
Add expenses not using working capital:		
Depreciation.................................	600	
Total working capital generated by operations...........		$2,920
From other sources:		
Mortgage note................................		2,000
Total sources of working capital.....................		$4,920

Uses of Working Capital

Acquisition of equipment...........................	$3,000
Net Increase in Working Capital.....................	$1,920

Changes in Working Capital Accounts

Account	*Increase (decrease) in Working Capital*
Cash..	$2,550
Accounts receivable.............................	150
Notes receivable...............................	500
Accounts payable...............................	(1,000)
Deferred revenue...............................	(100)
Accrued interest...............................	(180)
Net Increase in Working Capital.................	$1,920

shown in the SCFP to present a complete picture of the changes in financial position.

In comparing this SCFP with the one prepared on the cash basis (Illustration 11–3), one notes five differences that arise from defining funds as working capital instead of as cash. First, there is no adjustment for accounts receivable. The $150 for the catered Christmas Eve party *is* a source of working capital in 1975, even though the cash has not been received, since a current asset account (accounts receivable) increased in 1975 without an offsetting entry in some other current account. (The $150 credit was to revenues—an increase in Retained Earnings.) Second, the $100 prepaid revenue was a source of cash in 1975 but was not a source of working capital, since it increased both a current asset, Cash, and a current liability, Deferred Revenue, by $100, leaving working capital unchanged. Since the 1975 income statement did not include this $100 as revenue, no adjustment to the net income figure is necessary in arriving at working capital from operations. Third, there similarly was no working capital flow resulting from the $500 short-term loan to an employee, so this was not a use of working capital even though it did use cash. On the other hand, the $200 utilities and $800 ingredients expenses, which have not yet used cash (because the bills are unpaid) *have* used working capital: expense accounts (temporary subdivisions of Retained Earnings) have been debited, and Accounts Payable has been credited, thus reducing working capital by $1,000. As can be seen in Illustration 11–2, the net income figure reflects this use of working capital, and no adjustment is necessary. Similarly, the $180 accrued interest has not used cash, but has decreased working capital during 1975. In combination, these five differences explain why working capital increased by $1,920, while cash went up by $2,550.

Misconceptions about Depreciation

Also noteworthy in the SCFP in Illustration 11–5 is the way in which working capital generated by operations was determined. Instead of calculating this figure by showing revenues (a source of working capital) and then subtracting the expenses which used working capital, the starting point was the net income figure, to which depreciation was added.[3] This add-back of depreciation was done because depreciation is the only expense in Campus' accrual-basis income statement which did not represent a use of working capital. All of Campus' other expenses either re-

---

[3] The reader should realize that *adding* depreciation to net income, as in Illustration 11–5, and *subtracting* depreciation from expenses, as in Illustration 11–3, are completely equivalent, since reducing an expense increases net income.

duced cash or increased accounts payable, both of which reduced working capital. However, the journal entry for depreciation expense shows clearly that neither current assets nor current liabilities is affected, and hence depreciation is neither a source nor a use of working capital:

```
Depreciation Expense............................ 600
   (equivalent to a direct debit to Retained
   Earnings)
      Accumulated Depreciation....................        600
```

(This entry also shows that depreciation does not use cash, as reflected in the expense adjustment in Illustration 11–3.)

Another way of calculating the working capital generated by Campus' operations would be to recast the income statement in a way that segregates expenses using working capital from those that do not:

Revenues.................................	$48,150	
Expenses using working capital..............	45,230	
Working capital generated by operations........	$ 2,920	(1)
Expenses not using working capital...........	600	(2)
Net income...............................	$ 2,320	(3)

The working capital from operations could then be read directly from line (1). However, because income statements do not use this format, what is usually done is to deduce line (1) by starting with line (3) and adding line (2), since the numbers for these two lines can be found in the standard-format income statement (or sometimes in a footnote, for depreciation). Either approach results in the same $2,920 amount.

Unfortunately, many people misunderstand this calculation in which expenses not requiring working capital (or cash) are adjusted to arrive at the working capital (or cash) generated by operations. These people have the misconception that depreciation is a source of funds (defined either as working capital or as cash), as exemplified by these quotations:[4]

"Most people pay too little attention to depreciation reserves as a contributor to corporate health. In some years depreciation actually exceeds net profit."

"Depreciation money is cash. In your bank account, depreciation dollars and profit dollars look alike."

"Company X shifted to accelerated depreciation last year, thus increasing its depreciation charge and its cash flow earnings by $6 million."

---

[4] Adapted from quotations collected by William J. Vatter and reported by him in "Operating Confusion in Accounting," *Journal of Business*, University of Chicago, July 1963, pp. 290–301.

These statements are fallacious. Depreciation is *not* a source of funds. For example, in the case of Company X, if on its income statement its depreciation expense increases by $6 million because it shifts from straight-line to accelerated depreciation, its income *before* taxes will decrease by this same $6 million. (Its net income *after* taxes will decrease by less than $6 million because of the lower provision for income taxes, but the adjustment in income tax expense merely reflects deferred taxes, and does not affect the flow of funds.)

Depreciation is a source of funds only in the tenuous sense that depreciation expense reduces taxable income, and hence reduces the cash outflow to the Internal Revenue Service in payment of taxes. For example, if Campus Pizzeria had used accelerated depreciation instead of straight-line in preparing its tax return, it could have reduced taxable income this year and hence reduced the cash outflow associated with its tax payments this year.[5] This does not mean however, that *depreciation* was a source of funds. The funds transaction was the income tax payment, and depreciation merely entered into the calculation of taxable income and hence reduced the tax payment. By the same token, Campus could have reduced its taxes this year by increasing *any* expense, such as by throwing a handful of mozzarella cheese on the floor for every one thrown on a pizza; would one then say that wasted cheese is a source of funds?

The point to remember, then, is this: depreciation is the accountant's way of *matching* costs of fixed assets with the benefits derived from those assets; *depreciation is not a source of funds.* The funds flow occurs when the assets are acquired; moreover at that time the flow is a *use* (investment) of funds, not a source. Depreciation simply spreads that outflow over the life of the assets for purposes of measuring results of operations.

PREPARATION OF THE SCFP

Unlike the balance sheet and income statement, which are prepared directly from the firm's accounts, the SCFP is derived *analytically* from those accounts, explaining changes in assets and equities between the beginning and ending balance sheets of the period. Therefore, a logical way to prepare an SCFP is to use a work sheet which contains the beginning and ending balances in these accounts. We then can analyze the funds flows by "reconstructing" in summary form the transactions that caused the balance sheet changes.

Illustration 11–6 contains beginning and ending balance sheets for the

---

[5] But recall that this only delays the tax payment until later years, when accelerated depreciation charges will be less than if straight-line were used.

Illustration 11–6

FAIRWAY CORPORATION

Balance Sheets
As of December 31, 1975 and 1974

	1975	*1974*
Current Assets:		
Cash....................................	$ 122,000	$ 230,000
Accounts receivable..........................	675,000	586,000
Inventories................................	655,000	610,000
Total Current Assets......................	$1,452,000	$1,426,000
Current Liabilities:		
Accounts payable...........................	$ 388,000	$ 332,000
Notes payable.............................	133,000	142,000
Long-term debt due within one year.............	35,000	—
Taxes payable.............................	108,000	144,000
Total Current Liabilities....................	$ 664,000	$ 618,000
Working capital...............................	$ 788,000	$ 808,000
Plant and equipment (net of accumulated depreciation).............................	1,217,000	1,000,000
Total Working Capital and Noncurrent Assets...	$2,005,000	$1,808,000
Long-Term Liabilities:		
Bank loans................................	$ 370,000	$ 322,000
Bonds payable.............................	233,000	243,000
Total Long-Term Liabilities..................	$ 603,000	$ 565,000
Shareholders' Equity:		
Common stock ($1 par).......................	$ 60,000	$ 50,000
Other paid-in capital.........................	167,000	133,000
Retained earnings...........................	1,175,000	1,060,000
Total Shareholders' Equity...................	$1,402,000	$1,243,000
Total Long-Term Liabilities and Shareholders' Equity...................................	$2,005,000	$1,808,000

Fairway Corporation, recast in a format which isolates working capital; this is done for use on the work sheet for an SCFP prepared on a working-capital basis.[6]

The SCFP Work Sheet

Illustration 11–7 is the work sheet for preparation of Fairway's 1975 SCFP. On it have been entered the balances from Illustration 11–6, and in the final column the net account changes have been calculated. The

---

[6] The work sheet for a cash-basis SCFP is similar to the one for working-capital basis. We have chosen to illustrate preparation of the working-capital basis SCFP since most SCFP's the reader will encounter in corporate annual reports are prepared on the working-capital basis.

Illustration 11–7

FAIRWAY CORPORATION

Work Sheet to Develop the Statement of Changes in Financial Position
(Working-Capital Basis) For the Year Ended December 31, 1975

| | Beginning Balances | Interim Entries | | Ending Balances | Net Change |
		Debit	Credit		
Debit-Balance Accounts					
Working capital	808,000	XXXX	XXXX	788,000	20,000 Cr
Plant and equipment (net of accumulated depreciation)	1,000,000			1,217,000	217,000 Dr
	1,808,000			2,005,000	197,000 Dr
Credit-Balance Accounts					
Bank loans	322,000			370,000	48,000 Cr
Bonds payable	243,000			233,000	10,000 Dr
Common stock ($1 par)	50,000			60,000	10,000 Cr
Other paid-in capital	133,000			167,000	34,000 Cr
Retained earnings	1,060,000			1,175,000	115,000 Cr
	1,808,000			2,005,000	197,000 Cr
Working Capital from Operations					
Working Capital from Other Sources					
Uses of Working Capital					

working capital line is entered so the debits and credits can be checked as balancing; it is the $20,000 decrease in working capital which we will be striving to explain. For each of the other accounts shown, we will try to "reconstruct" in summary form the journal entries that caused the changes. These entries which affect the amount of working capital will be classified either as one of two kinds of sources—Working Capital from Operations, or Working Capital from Other Sources—or as Uses of Working Capital. (These classifications correspond to the format of the SCFP, and will facilitate its final preparation.) The numbers in the entries that follow will correspond to those on the completed work sheet in Illustration 11–9. The reader may wish occasionally to refer back to Illustration 11–4 to recall which transactions affect working capital.

Work Sheet Entries

RETAINED EARNINGS. A relatively easy starting point for the analysis of interim changes is the change in Retained Earnings. Illustration 11–8 shows a condensed version of Fairway's income statement and a reconciliation of the beginning and ending balances of retained earnings. From these statements we can see that two things affected the level of retained earnings: net income, which is a source of working capital; and payment of cash dividends, which is a use. We thus can record these two entries on the work sheet:

```
(1)  Working Capital from Operations........... 170,000
          Retained Earnings....................            170,000
          (This reflects net income as a source.)
(2)  Retained Earnings........................  55,000
          Uses of Working Capital..............             55,000
          (This reflects the dividend payment
          as a use.)
```

At this point, note that the above two entries result in a net credit to Retained Earnings of $115,000. The last column of the work sheet shows that $115,000 Cr. was the amount of change we needed to explain. Thus the analysis of the change in Retained Earnings is complete, and another account change can now be analyzed.

PLANT AND EQUIPMENT (NET). The changes in this account would be caused by acquisition or disposal of fixed assets, and by changes in accumulated depreciation (a contra-asset account which has been netted

Illustration 11–8

FAIRWAY CORPORATION

Condensed Income Statement and Statement of Retained Earnings
For the Year Ended December 31, 1975

Sales..		$3,190,000
Cost of goods sold..........................		2,290,000
Gross margin...............................		$ 900,000
Less expenses:		
Depreciation.............................	$120,000	
Other expenses...........................	453,000	
Income taxes.............................	157,000	730,000
Net income.................................		$ 170,000
Retained earnings, Dec. 31, 1974..............		$1,060,000
Add: 1975 net income........................		170,000
		1,230,000
Less: Cash dividends paid....................		55,000
Retained earnings, Dec. 31, 1975..............		$1,175,000

against plant and equipment at cost in the illustrations). As explained at some length above, depreciation is an expense which is quite properly subtracted in arriving at net income, but which, unlike most expenses, does not affect working capital. Hence we must add back the depreciation expense to net income; otherwise, Working Capital from Operations would be understated. The $120,000 depreciation expense for the period is shown in the income statement in Illustration 11–8. The entry for the worksheet is:

```
(3)  Working Capital from Operations........... 120,000
         Accumulated Depreciation...............          120,000
         (This adds back to net income an expense
         which did not use working capital.)
```

Now we have reconstructed a $120,000 credit to net plant and equipment; but the net change to be explained is $217,000 Dr. Other company records indicate that $337,000 of new machinery was purchased during the year. Thus as another entry we have:

```
(4)  Plant and Equipment (at cost)............. 337,000
         Uses of Working Capital...............          337,000
         (To reflect the acquisition of new
         machinery.)
```

At this point, entries (3) and (4) explain the net increase of $217,000 in Plant and Equipment, so we can move on.

BANK LOANS. From internal records, we learn that Fairway did not pay off any of its bank loans, but did borrow $83,000 more from one bank. This is clearly a source of working capital other than from operations, giving this entry:

```
(5)  Working Capital from Other Sources......... 83,000
         Bank Loans.............................          83,000
         (This reflects the additional borrowing.)
```

Now since the net change in Bank Loans during the year was only $48,000 Cr., there must be one or more other entries with a net effect of $35,000 Dr. The records indicate that Fairway did *not* repay any bank loans in 1975, so we temporarily have a mystery. Investigation shows that of the $322,000 loans outstanding as of December 31, 1974, one has a payment of $35,000 due on March 1, 1976. Thus as of December 31, 1975, this $35,000 was a *current* liability—Long-Term Debt Due Within One Year. Because we have defined funds as working capital, on March 1, 1975, when this payment was reclassified as a current liability, a use of working capital occurred. (Note that on March 1, 1976, when the payment will be made, working capital will *not* be affected by the pay-

Illustration 11–9

FAIRWAY CORPORATION

Work Sheet to Develop the Statement of Changes in Financial Position (Working-Capital Basis)
For the Year Ended December 31, 1975

	Beginning Balances	Interim Entries Debit	Interim Entries Credit	Ending Balances	Net Change
Debit-Balance Accounts					
Working capital	808,000	XXXX	XXXX	788,000	20,000 Cr
Plant and equipment (net of accumulated depreciation)	1,000,000	(4) 337,000	(3) 120,000	1,217,000	217,000 Dr
	1,808,000			2,005,000	197,000 Dr
Credit-Balance Accounts					
Bank loans	322,000	(6) 35,000	(5) 83,000	370,000	48,000 Cr
Bonds payable	243,000	(7) 10,000		233,000	10,000 Dr
Common stock ($1 par)	50,000		(8) 10,000	60,000	10,000 Cr
Other paid-in capital	133,000		(8) 34,000	167,000	34,000 Cr
Retained earnings	1,060,000	(2) 55,000	(1) 170,000	1,175,000	115,000 Cr
	1,808,000			2,005,000	197,000 Cr
Working Capital from Operations					
Net income		(1) 170,000			
Add: depreciation expense, which did not use working capital		(3) 120,000			
Working Capital from Other Sources					
Additional bank loans		(5) 83,000			
Issuance of common stock		(8) 44,000			
Uses of Working Capital					
Payment of dividend			(2) 55,000		
Purchase of machinery			(4) 337,000		
Bank loan payment currently due			(6) 35,000		
Redemption of bonds			(7) 10,000		
Check:		417,000	437,000		20,000 Cr

ment since cash and this current liability will decrease by the same amount.) The entry is:

```
(6)  Bank Loans.................................  35,000
        Uses of Working Capital................           35,000
        (This reflects that a portion of the loan
        payable became a current liability.)
```

Now the net change in Bank Loans of $48,000 Cr. has been explained.

BONDS PAYABLE. During the year, Fairway Corporation called $10,000 face value worth of its bonds. This payment required cash, so working capital decreased:

```
(7)   Bonds Payable............................. 10,000
            Uses of Working Capital.................            10,000
            (This reflects calling of a portion of
            the bonds.)
```

No other explanation of the Bonds Payable work sheet line is necessary.

CONTRIBUTED CAPITAL. The remaining two account changes to be analyzed are those in common stock at par, and other paid-in capital; that is, contributed capital. The records of Fairway reveal that during the year 10,000 shares of $1 par common stock were issued, for which the firm received $44,000. This nonoperating source of working capital leads to this worksheet entry:

```
(8)   Working Capital from Other Sources.......... 44,000
            Common Stock ($1 par)...................            10,000
            Other Paid-In Capital...................            34,000
            (This reflects the issuance of 10,000
            shares of common stock.)
```

This entry completes the analysis of interim changes on the work sheet. The change of every nonworking-capital account has been explained, and the offsetting entries have been classified as sources or uses of working capital. As a check, the debits (sources) and credits (uses) below the double line are added and the net change compared with the top line of the work sheet: both changes are $20,000 Cr., showing the accuracy of the amounts of the interim changes.

Preparing the SCFP

The actual preparation of the SCFP is now straightforward; the SCFP is shown in Illustration 11–10. The upper portion of the SCFP was prepared directly from the lower part of the work sheet. Again, this reflects Fairway's major financing and investing activities during 1975. The lower portion explains the internal content of the $20,000 decrease in working capital; these changes are calculated directly from the balance sheet current asset and current liability accounts.

Summary of Preparation Procedures

To prepare a working-capital basis SCFP, the following steps are taken:

Illustration 11-10

FAIRWAY CORPORATION

Statement of Changes in Financial Position (Working-Capital Basis)
For the Year Ended December 31, 1975

Sources of Working Capital

From operations:

Net income..................................	$170,000	
Add: depreciation expense....................	120,000	
Total working capital generated by operations...		$290,000

From other sources:

Bank loans................................	$ 83,000	
Issuance of common stock......................	44,000	
Total working capital generated from other sources...........................		127,000
Total sources of working capital..........		$417,000

Uses of Working Capital

Payment of cash dividend.......................	55,000	
Purchase of machinery..........................	337,000	
Portion of bank loan currently due...............	35,000	
Redemption of bonds...........................	10,000	
Total uses of working capital............		$437,000
Net increase (decrease) in working capital..........		$ (20,000)

Changes in Working Capital Accounts

Account	Working Capital Increase (Decrease)
Cash..	$(108,000)
Accounts receivable................................	89,000
Inventories..	45,000
Accounts payable...................................	(56,000)
Notes payable......................................	9,000
Long-term debt due within one year.....................	(35,000)
Taxes payable......................................	36,000
Increase (decrease) in working capital..................	$ (20,000)

1. From the company's balance sheets, calculate the beginning and ending balances of working capital. Enter these amounts, together with balances of the noncurrent accounts, on a work sheet such as in Illustration 11-7. Calculate the difference between the beginning and ending balance for working capital and for each noncurrent account (last column of Illustration 11-7).[7]

2. For each noncurrent account, analyze the nature of the interim transactions causing the account change, and classify this change as either

[7] In some simple situations, the SCFP can be prepared from the balance sheet and income statement without use of a work sheet, just as the reader could probably have prepared Campus Pizzeria's income statement and ending balance sheet from the text without using journal entries or T-accounts. However, a person must have correctly "internalized" the concepts of the SCFP to be able to prepare one without using a work sheet.

working capital from operations, working capital from other sources, or uses of working capital. This analysis will require reference to the income statement (e.g., partially to explain the change in retained earnings), and to other financial records of the company.

3. After the noncurrent account changes have been analyzed and classified, the interim entry debits and credits are totaled, and then combined as a check to see that their net amount is equal to the amount of change in working capital.

4. The top portion of the SCFP is prepared directly from the bottom portion of the work sheet.

5. To complete the SCFP, the change in each current account is calculated from the balance sheet, and classified according to whether the change increased or decreased working capital. These current account changes are listed in the bottom portion of the SCFP so as to explain the change in the internal content of the working capital (i.e., current) accounts. This step also serves as a double check on the correctness of the working capital change calculation in the upper portion of the SCFP.

USES OF THE SCFP

The statement of changes in financial position, prepared on either basis, is used for two principal purposes: (1) as a means of analyzing what has happened in the past, and (2) as a means of planning what is going to happen in the future.

As a tool of historical analysis, the statement sheds light on the investing and financing policies that the company has pursued. Of particular interest is the policy with respect to the acquisition of new fixed assets. What kinds of new assets were required? To what extent were they financed by internally generated funds, and to what extent by borrowing or other external sources? How much of the company's need for funds was it able to meet by funds generated from operations? For financial resources obtained externally, what proportion was from debt and what from equity? Some companies deliberately limit their growth to an amount that can be financed from internally generated funds. Others do not hesitate to go to the capital market for funds. For these latter firms, the balance selected between risky, lower-cost debt and less risky, higher-cost equity is of considerable interest, as discussed in Chapter 12.

As a tool of planning, a projected SCFP is an essential device for planning the amount, timing, and character of new financing. Estimated uses of funds for new fixed assets, for working capital, for dividends, and for the repayment of debt are made for each of several future years, usually at least two or three years, but in some cases 10 years or more. Estimates are made of the funds to be provided by operations, and the difference, if it is positive, represents the funds that must be obtained by borrowing or the issuance of new equity securities. If the indicated amount of new funds required is greater than management thinks it is feasible to raise, then the plans for new fixed asset acquisitions and the dividend policies are reexamined so that the uses of funds can be brought into balance with anticipated sources of financing them.

For shorter-term financial planning, a cash budget is essential. The cash budget is a cash flow statement, similar to the cash-basis SCFP shown above except that amounts are estimates of the future rather than those recorded in the past. Projections are made for each of the next several months or several quarters. One way to prepare such a budget is to list all the estimated uses of cash and all the sources other than from additional financing. The difference between these totals is the amount of cash that must be obtained by borrowing or selling additional stock if the planned program is to be carried out. If it is believed that this amount cannot be raised, the indication is that the estimated uses of cash must be cut back.

In sum, the time horizon involved in a decision is the key factor in determining whether the more appropriate projected SCFP is one prepared on a cash basis or one prepared on the working-capital basis. For example, suppose a bus manufacturer receives an order to deliver fifty buses over the next two years. If this sale is profitable, both the cash and working capital figures will be increasing. To a bank being asked by the firm for a two-year loan, repayable in one "balloon" payment at the end of the second year, a projected flow of working capital will suffice as an indicator of the manufacturer's ability to repay the loan. On the other hand, if the loan is for a ninety-day period, the timing of the projected cash payments for the buses may be critical in determining the firm's ability to repay this short-term note. Because many firms make decisions having both short- and long-term horizons, in these businesses projections of both cash and working capital are usually made.

SUMMARY

The statement of changes in financial position (SCFP) explains the differences in account amounts between the beginning and ending balance sheets for an accounting period. Increases in asset amounts represent uses of funds; i.e., investments the firm has made during the period. Increases in liabilities and owners' equity reflect the sources of the funds which were used to make the investments.

The SCFP can be prepared on either a cash basis or on a working-capital basis. The latter way tends to focus attention on the major funds flows in the firm, and downplays the recurring flows among current asset and current liability accounts.

The net amount of funds generated by operations is not the same as net income: some expenses (notably, depreciation) that were subtracted in arriving at net income for the period, do not use either cash or working capital. In practice, the amount of funds generated by operations is derived from the net income figure by adding back depreciation and other expenses which did not use funds; however, one must not infer from this calculation that depreciation is itself a source of funds, for it definitely is not.

The SCFP reports some financing and investing activities that do not cause a change in cash or working capital, such as the purchase of fixed assets with a long-term mortgage note. These activities are reported so that the SCFP gives a complete picture of the resource flows of the firm.

CASES

CASE 11–1. ABC COMPANY*

Mr. Jones of the ABC Company started the year in fine shape. His company made widgets—just what the customer wanted. He made them for $0.75 each, sold them for $1. He kept an inventory equal to shipments of the past 30 days, paid his bills promptly, and billed his customers 30-days net. The sales manager predicted a steady increase of 500 widgets each month. It looked like his lucky year, and it began this way:

January 1.   Cash, $875; receivables, $1,000; inventory, $750.

JANUARY
In January, he sold 1,000 widgets; shipped them at a cost of $750; collected his receivables—winding up with a tidy $250 profit and books like this:

February 1.   Cash, $1,125; receivables, $1,000; inventory, $750.

FEBRUARY
This month's sales jumped, as predicted, to 1,500. With a corresponding step-up in production to maintain his 30-day inventory, he made 2,000 units at a cost of $1,500. All receivables from January sales were collected. Profit so far, $625. Now his books looked like this:

March 1.   Cash, $625; receivables, $1,500; inventory, $1,125.

MARCH
March sales were even better: 2,000 units. Collections: On time. Production, to adhere to his inventory policy: 2,500 units. Operating results for the month, $500 profit. Profit to date: $1,125. His books:

April 1.   Cash, $250; receivables, $2,000; inventory, $1,500.

APRIL
In April, sales jumped another 500 units to 2,500, and Jones patted his sales manager on the back. His customers were paying right on time. Production was pushed to 3,000 units,

---

* Adapted from an article in *Business Week*.

and the month's business netted him $625 for a profit to date of $1,750. He took off for Florida before he saw the accountant's report. Suddenly he got a phone call from his treasurer: "Come home! We need money!" His books had caught up with him:

May 1.   Cash, $000; receivables, $2,500; inventory, $1,875.

Questions

1. Why did the ABC Company need money?
2. Assume that business keeps growing at 500 widgets per month. How much cash will the company need, month by month, through December?

CASE 11–2.   JOHN BARTLETT (B)

Referring to Case 3–3, John Bartlett (A), prepare the following for the accounting period beginning when Bartlett first began to organize his firm (the $10,000 investment by the retired manufacturer) and ending with the last event (#11) of the case:

a.   A statement of cash receipts and cash expenditures.
b.   A cash-basis statement of changes in financial position.
c.   A working-capital basis statement of changes in financial position.

Compare and contrast (*a*) with (*b*) and (*b*) with (*c*). Which of the three would you find most useful as a shareholder? as a bank being asked by Bartlett for a ninety-day loan? as a manager of Bartlett Manufacturing?

CASE 11–3.   MARRETT MANUFACTURING COMPANY (B)

Refer to the situation in Marrett Manufacturing Company (A) (Case 6–2). Prepare a statement of changes in financial position for the year 1976 on both a cash and working-capital basis.

CASE 11–4.   OLIVER OPTICS COMPANY (B)

Referring to Case 8–5, Oliver Optics Company (A), prepare a working-capital basis statement of changes in financial position for the year ending December 31.

CASE 11–5. PAYSON MANUFACTURING COMPANY

In July, 1971, Eldon Carter, treasurer of the Payson Manufacturing Company, was reviewing his working capital position. It was his custom to calculate working capital needs for the next 6 months in January and July of each year, and to formulate plans for meeting such needs.

The Payson Manufacturing Company, which had been founded in 1959, operated a small machine shop in the suburbs. The company had originally manufactured lapping plates and made gauges and special tools on order. In 1966 a newly designed industrial stapling machine was added to its line.

Operating losses and poor financial management had kept the company in financial difficulty during the greater part of its early history. Matters were made worse by a conflict which developed between the common and preferred stockholders. Inability of these two groups to agree had prevented the taking of corrective measures.

In the spring of 1967 this situation came to the attention of Mr. Carter, a businessman who specialized in rehabilitating financially weak concerns. He analyzed the company and found that it had in its employ a number of skilled machinists and possessed good equipment suitable for precision work. Mr. Carter was also impressed by prospects for the company's stapling machine, which was far superior to competitive products. As a result of his analysis, Mr. Carter concluded that with competent management the company could be operated profitably. The two stock-holding groups were approached and an agreement worked out whereby Mr. Carter became, in effect, head of the company. For his efforts he was to receive a fixed salary plus a percentage of profits. Mr. Carter, who was an officer of a number of other concerns, was to devote only part of his time to the Payson Manufacturing Company.

During the next few years Mr. Carter concentrated on obtaining firm-fixed-price Army contracts for the manufacture of precision instruments. Because of rigid economies which he instituted these contracts proved highly profitable. These profits and Mr. Carter's skillful financial management soon rehabilitated the company. By the end of 1969 the deficit accumulated during many years of unprofitable operations had been eliminated.

The pull-out of American troops from Vietnam brought cancellation of the company's Army contracts. Mr. Carter immediately took steps to curtail overhead and administrative expenses, but he retained the company's skilled machinists.

Sales and production efforts were concentrated on the industrial stapling machine. Margins available on the company's traditional products were at a level that Mr. Carter considered too low. Until a better price could be obtained he did not intend to manufacture these items.

Demand for the stapling machines was good. Monthly shipments during the first half of 1971 averaged about 75 units priced at $600 each. More units could have been sold and shipped, but Mr. Carter did not wish to risk overextending the company while conditions were so unsettled.

Early in May an invitation was received to bid on an Army contract for the manufacture of 301 specialized field trailers. Mr. Carter thought that a good profit could be made on the trailers, so he decided to submit a bid. His first bid of $2,160 a unit was rejected but a second bid of $1,845 was accepted. One "prototype" trailer was to be produced during August for the purpose of testing design and production methods. It was to be retained at the plant, but invoiced on September 1 at $1,845. This experimental unit was to be manufactured from materials on hand. Direct labor for this unit was estimated at $1,500. The lessons learned during the making of the first unit were expected to enable the company to start trailer production at full scale about September 1. Production was expected to be maintained at a fairly constant rate until November 30. Delivery of the trailers was to start the first week in October and was to be made at the rate of 100 units a month during October, November and December.

Estimated per unit direct costs of producing the trailer were as follows: labor, $726; material, $384. In addition to the estimated direct labor cost of $726 per unit, Mr. Carter estimated that the build-up of the additional labor force needed for trailer production would require some $7,500 in extra wage expense during August. Similarly some $9,000 of additional wage expense was budgeted for December so as to permit less abrupt reduction of the work force upon completion of the contract. Virtually all of the $9,000 would be paid out in the first three weeks of December.

To insure against delays in delivery Mr. Carter intended to keep a minimum of one month's supply of raw material on hand at all times during the production period. Work-in-process inventory for trailer production was expected to average $60,000 during the period of full-scale production. The great majority of the company's purchases were made on terms of amount due in 30 days ("net/30"), and invoices were paid promptly when due. Wages were paid every Friday.[1] The production process from raw material to finished product was estimated to take a month. The Army would accept shipments in lots of 25 units and payment would be received about 60 days after shipment.

Estimated per unit direct costs of producing the stapling machine were as follows: materials, $120; labor, $108. A minimum inventory of a 3 months' supply of raw material was currently considered necessary be-

---

[1] There were 4 pay days in July, 5 in August, 4 each in September and October, 5 in November, and 4 in December.

cause of unsettled conditions. Work-in-process inventory for stapling machine production was expected to continue at the present level. All current inventory was usable. The length of the production process was 4 weeks. Units were shipped as soon as produced, and terms of sale were net/30. The company had a backlog of orders for 350 machines. Production and shipments, however, were expected to continue at the rate of about 75 units a month through the first quarter of 1972.

Monthly indirect expenses were currently running as follows: depreciation, $1,620; other factory overhead, $10,500; administration, $7,050. Tooling for the Army contract started in July. During July and August tooling expenses and experimental manufacture of the prototype were expected to increase factory overhead by about $3,600 a month. Starting in September, when full-scale production of the trailers was to

Exhibit 1

PAYSON MANUFACTURING COMPANY

Balance Sheets

Assets	Dec. 31 1969	Dec. 31 1970	June 30 1971
Current Assets:			
Cash...................................	$ 38,946	$ 48,198	$ 83,259
Accounts receivable, net....................	144,321	88,749	58,779
Inventory................................	136,542	102,048	
Raw material...........................			39,402
Work-in-process........................			19,908
Prepaid expenses.........................	2,175	3,537	975
Total Current Assets........................	$321,984	$242,532	$202,323
Fixed Assets:			
Plant and equipment, at cost..................	$139,521	$141,459	$143,328
Less: Accumulated depreciation..............	43,602	59,748	63,171
Plant and equipment, net....................	$ 95,919	$ 81,711	$ 80,157
Total Assets........................	$417,903	$324,243	$282,480
Liabilities and Shareholders' Equity			
Current Liabilities:			
Accounts payable.........................	$ 83,004	$ 52,014	$ 27,198
Accrued liabilities........................	28,776	5,508	14,331
Taxes payable............................	69,012	96,828	55,179*
Total Current Liabilities......................	$180,792	$154,350	$ 96,708
Long-term Liabilities:			
Due officers..............................	41,502		
Due U.S. government on contract advances......	65,988		
Shareholders' Equity:			
Preferred stock, 6%........................	$ 63,000	$ 63,000	$ 63,000
Common stock ($10 par)....................	51,000	51,000	51,000
Retained earnings.........................	15,621	55,893	71,772
Total Liabilities and Shareholders' Equity...	$417,903	$324,243	$282,480

* Payable as follows: $20,861 on September 15, 1971; $20,860, December 15, 1971; $3,365, March 15, 1972; $3,364, June 15, 1972; $3,365, September 15, 1972; $3,364, December 15, 1972.

Exhibit 2

PAYSON MANUFACTURING COMPANY

Income Statements

	12 months ending 12/31/69	12 months ending 12/31/70	6 months ending 6/30/71
Sales, net.....................................	$848,664	$994,725	$260,898
Cost of sales:			
Material...............................	$109,644	$291,195	$ 65,040
Direct labor.............................	349,098	257,274	45,837
Depreciation............................	19,545	16,146	9,726
Factory overhead........................	158,526	143,820	61,542
Total Cost of Sales....................	$636,813	$708,435	$182,145
Gross Margin........................	$211,851	$286,290	$ 78,753
Less: Operating expense			
Shipping expense........................	$ 28,683	$ 17,658	$ 705
Selling expense...........................	31,326	22,440	—
Administrative expense....................	94,599	129,900	44,325
Total operating expense................	$154,608	$169,998	$ 45,030
Net operating income..................	$ 57,243	$116,292	$ 33,723
Other charges............................	924	1,563	—
Income before taxes.....................	$ 56,319	$114,729	$ 33,723
Tax expense..............................	25,350	72,549	13,461
Net Income...........................	$ 30,969	$ 42,180	$ 20,262

begin, factory overhead was expected to become about $13,500 a month until the end of November. Administration expense was expected to increase to about $9,000 a month from September 1 to the end of December.

The Army contract had made necessary the purchase of $6,000 of special tools. Delivery of these tools was expected in August; it was to be paid for C.O.D. Upon completion of the contract these tools would be scrapped. An additional $15,000 would also have to be spent for the replacement of old machinery which appeared to be nearing the end of its useful life. There was no way of knowing, however, when this machinery would finally break down. Mr. Carter was confident that he could find replacements within a few days in the event of an emergency.

Mr. Carter worked out a tentative purchase schedule for the various material requirements. The schedule is reproduced as Exhibit 3. It shows the amounts of purchases in the months that they were expected to be booked.

The company maintained a small deposit account with a local bank and kept the remainder of its cash in an account with the Fourth National Bank. The company had originally banked with the Farmers and Merchants Bank, a small local institution from which it had borrowed

Exhibit 3

PAYSON MANUFACTURING COMPANY

Tentative Schedule of Purchases
July–December, 1971

	July	Aug.	Sept.	Oct.	Nov.	Dec.
Raw Material (staplers)........	—	$ 5,982	$ 9,000	$ 9,000	$9,000	$9,000
Raw Material (trailers)........	—	38,400	38,400	38,400	—	—
Special Tools (trailers)........	—	6,000	—	—	—	—
Total....................	—	$50,382	$47,400	$47,400	$9,000	$9,000

Replacement Machinery........ $15,000 (uncertain date)

from time to time to help finance production on government contracts. In recent years, however, Mr. Carter sensed that Mr. Applegate, the bank's president, was becoming apprehensive about lending money to the company. Mr. Carter attributed this reluctance to the fact that Mr. Applegate had had little experience in lending money to industrial concerns; the greater portion of the bank's commercial loans were to local storekeepers. Therefore Mr. Carter withdrew his account from the bank. A small account was opened at another local bank and the remainder of the company's funds were deposited with the Fourth National Bank, a medium-sized bank with a legal loan limit of $450,000. Mr. Carter had discussed the company's prospects in general terms with the bank's officers on a number of occasions, but he had never requested a loan.

Mr. Carter considered his current cash balance of almost $84,000 to be in excess of operating needs. He was willing to reduce cash to a minimum of $15,000. No dividend payments were scheduled for the remainder of 1971.

It was Mr. Carter's policy not to plan more than 6 months in advance, since he believed that it was impossible to predict with any accuracy what was going to happen for a longer period. The company's plans for the first half of 1972 would be made in the light of conditions as they developed and of the company's prospective financial condition at the end of 1971.

Questions

1. Set up a work sheet, with columns for each of the next six months (July–December, 1971), and develop a schedule of monthly cash inflows and outflows. In preparing this schedule, assume the following:
   a. All accounts receivable as of June 30, 1971 are collected in July, and all June 30, 1971 accounts payable are paid in July.
   b. Work-in-process inventories, prepaid expenses, and accrued liabilities will remain constant at their June 30, 1971 levels.
   c. The $15,000 machine will be purchased in July, 1971.

Remembering Payson's desire to have a minimum cash balance of $15,000, what does your schedule reveal about Payson's borrowing needs over the next six months?

2. Use the data from the case and from your cash flow work sheet to prepare: an income statement for the six months ending December 31, 1971; a balance sheet as of December 31, 1971; and a cash-basis statement of changes in financial position for the six months ending December 31, 1971. Assume a tax rate of 40 percent, and ignore interest on any new borrowings that will be needed during these six months. Assume the old machine replaced in July had originally cost $10,000, was fully depreciated, and had no residual value. For preparing these three statements, you will probably find it useful to draw up T-accounts for each balance sheet and income statement account, and post six-month totals from your cash flow work sheet (appropriately adjusted to the accrual basis) to these accounts.

CHAPTER 12

FINANCIAL STATEMENT
ANALYSIS

In previous chapters the focus has been on conveying an understanding of the information contained in the three basic financial statements—the balance sheet, the income statement, and the statement of changes in financial position. In this chapter we shall describe how this information is analyzed, both by parties outside the firm and by the company's own management. In keeping with the management focus of this book, the emphasis will be on management's uses of financial data.

BUSINESS OBJECTIVES

All analyses of accounting data involve comparisons. An absolute statement, such as "X Company earned $1 million profit" is, by itself, not useful. It becomes useful only when the $1 million is compared with something else. The comparison may be quite imprecise and intuitive. For example, if we know that X Company is an industrial giant with tens of thousands of employees, we know intuitively that $1 million profit is a poor showing because we have built up in our minds the impression that such companies should earn much more than that. Or, the comparison may be much more formal, explicit, and precise, as is the case when the $1 million profit this year is compared with last year's profit. In either case, it is the process of comparison that makes the figure meaningful.

In order to decide the types of comparisons that are useful, we need first to consider what a business is all about—what its objectives are—for the comparisons are essentially intended to shed light on how well a business is achieving its objectives. As a generalization, it may be said that *insofar as it can be measured quantitatively, the overall objective of a*

345

business is to earn a satisfactory return on the funds invested in it, consistent with maintaining a sound financial position.[1] It should be noted that this statement is limited to facts that can be expressed numerically. Personal satisfaction, social responsibility, ethical considerations, and other nonmeasurable objectives are also important and must be taken into account whenever possible in appraising the overall success of the enterprise.

The foregoing statement of objectives has two aspects: (1) earning a satisfactory return on investment, and (2) maintaining a sound financial position. Each aspect is discussed briefly below.

Return on Investment

Return on investment is defined to be net income divided by investment. The term "investment" is used in three different senses in financial analysis, thus giving three different return on investment figures: return on assets, return on owners' equity, and return on invested capital.

Return on assets (net income divided by total assets) reflects how much the firm has earned on the investment of *all* the financial resources committed to the firm. Thus, this measure is appropriate if one considers the "investment" in the firm to include current liabilities, long-term liabilities, and owners' equity, which are the total sources of funds invested in the assets. It is a useful measure if one wants to evaluate how well an enterprise has *used* its funds, without regard to the relative magnitudes of the sources of those funds (short-term creditors, long-term creditors, bondholders, and shareholders). In particular, the return on assets measure often is used by top management to evaluate individual operations *within* a multi-divisional firm (e.g., the calculator division of an electronics firm) where the division manager has significant influence over the assets used in the division, but has little control over the financing of those assets because his division does not pay its own bills (current liabilities), cannot arrange its own loans, and cannot issue its own bonds or capital stock.

Return on owners' equity reflects how much the firm has earned on the funds invested by the shareholders (either directly or through retained earnings). This figure is clearly of interest to a present or prospective shareholder, and is also of concern to management, which presumably operates the business in the owners' best interests. The figure is not generally of interest to lower-level managers, however, who properly concern themselves with the efficient use of assets, without con-

---

[1] This statement is not consistent with the *profit maximization* assumption often made in economics. The techniques in this chapter are equally applicable under a profit maximization assumption, however, so there is no point in arguing here whether the profit maximization assumption is valid and useful. Discussion of this point is deferred to Chapter 18.

Illustration 12–1

RETURNS OF LEADING CORPORATIONS

	Percent Return on Equity		Percent Return on Sales	
	1972	1973	1972	1973
Dairy products.................................	12.8	13.1	3.1	3.0
Meat packing..................................	9.2	13.1	1.0	1.2
Other food products............................	14.2	14.6	3.8	3.7
Soft drinks.....................................	22.1	22.1	7.3	7.2
Distilling.......................................	11.1	11.8	3.4	3.6
Tobacco products...............................	16.0	16.4	5.3	5.4
Textile products................................	7.4	8.9	2.8	3.1
Clothing and apparel............................	9.8	9.1	2.9	2.6
Shoes, leather, etc..............................	11.8	8.4	3.5	3.1
Rubber and allied products......................	11.6	11.7	4.3	4.0
Lumber and wood products.......................	12.6	20.6	5.4	7.4
Paper and allied products........................	8.8	14.2	4.3	6.1
Printing and publishing..........................	13.8	15.2	6.2	6.6
Chemical products...............................	11.3	15.0	5.9	6.9
Drugs and medicines............................	19.8	20.6	9.9	10.1
Soap, cosmetics.................................	20.2	20.2	7.0	7.0
Petroleum products and refining..................	10.8	15.6	6.5	8.0
Glass products..................................	12.5	13.0	6.1	5.6
Other stone and clay products....................	10.8	11.9	5.6	5.6
Iron and steel..................................	6.1	9.4	3.2	4.2
Nonferrous metals..............................	7.1	11.6	4.0	5.0
Other metal products............................	10.4	12.1	3.6	3.6
Farm, constr., material-handling equip.............	12.4	14.8	4.8	5.0
Office equip., computers.........................	13.8	16.7	7.7	9.0
Other machinery................................	10.6	12.0	4.2	4.5
Electrical equipment and electronics...............	13.6	15.1	4.5	4.6
Household appliances............................	15.4	15.6	4.8	4.6
Autos and trucks................................	17.2	17.7	5.2	5.0
Automotive parts................................	13.5	14.4	4.7	4.6
Aerospace......................................	8.9	11.7	2.5	3.1
Instruments, photo goods, etc.....................	17.0	17.3	8.6	8.4
Total Manufacturing...........................	12.1	14.8	5.1	5.6
Total Mining.................................	10.7	15.1	8.3	9.7
Total Trade..................................	11.8	12.4	2.2	2.2
Class I railroads................................	2.9	3.5	3.6	3.8
Common carrier trucking.........................	18.8	13.5	4.2	3.3
Air transport...................................	7.6	6.6	2.7	2.3
Total Transportation..........................	4.8	5.0	3.3	3.1
Total Public Utilities..........................	10.3	10.6	11.9	11.9
Total Services................................	12.1	12.3	4.1	4.2
Total Financial...............................	7.3	6.7	—	—
Grand Total..............................	10.6	12.0	—	—

Equity is stockholders' equity, i.e., the excess of total assets over total liabilities.
Source: Adapted and condensed from First National City Bank *Monthly Economic Letter*, April 1974. Data are for 4,640 companies.

cern for the relative roles of creditors and shareholders in financing those assets. Illustration 12–1 shows average return on equity for various industries; note that the 1973 range is from 3.5% to 22.1%.

The third return measure is *return on invested capital*. Invested capital (also called "permanent capital") is equal to noncurrent liabilities plus owners' equity, and hence represents the funds entrusted to the firm for long periods of time. Return on invested capital focuses on the use of this permanent capital of the firm, which excludes the current liabilities. It is presumed that the current liabilities will fluctuate more or less automatically with changes in current assets, and that both vary with the level of current operations. The more important question is how well the firm is using its permanent capital, which the firm has obtained in the expectation of earning a satisfactory return on it.

Invested capital is also equal to working capital (current assets minus current liabilities)[2] plus noncurrent assets. This equivalency points out that the owners and long-term creditors of the firm in effect must finance the plant and equipment and other long-term assets of the firm, and also the portion of current assets not financed by current liabilities.

Some firms also use return on invested capital to measure divisional performance. This is appropriate in those instances where a division has significant influence over all asset acquisition decisions, including purchasing and production scheduling (which determines inventory levels), credit policy (accounts receivable), and cash management, and where the division also controls the level of its current liabilities.

Because of its management orientation, we will use the return on invested capital measure in further discussions in this chapter of return on investment.

Sound Financial Position

In addition to desiring a satisfactory return, the investor expects that his capital will be protected from more than a normal amount of risk. The return on the *shareholders'* investment could be increased if incremental investments in the assets for new projects were financed solely by liabilities, provided the return on these incremental investments exceeds the interest cost of the added debt. This move, however, would increase the shareholders' risk of losing their investment, since the interest charges and principal repayments on the liabilities are fixed obligations, and failure to make these payments when due could throw the company into bankruptcy. The degree of risk in a situation can be

---

[2] Occasionally, "working capital" is taken to mean total current assets. This is of course confusing and is unnecessary since "total current assets" is a perfectly good term. In order to avoid any possibility of confusion, the term "net working capital" is sometimes used for the difference between current assets and current liabilities.

measured in part by the relative amounts of liabilities and owners' equity, and of the funds available to discharge the liabilities. This analysis also involves the use of ratios.

STRUCTURE OF THE ANALYSIS

Although in practice financial statement analysis might start anywhere, we shall assume here that management first looks at the firm's performance in the broadest terms, and then works down through various levels of detail in order to identify the significant factors which accounted for the overall results. In making this analysis, management uses ratios and percentages. If the values of these ratios are compared with their values for other time periods, this comparison is called a *horizontal* or *trend analysis*.

Illustration 12–2

FACTORS AFFECTING RETURN ON INVESTMENT

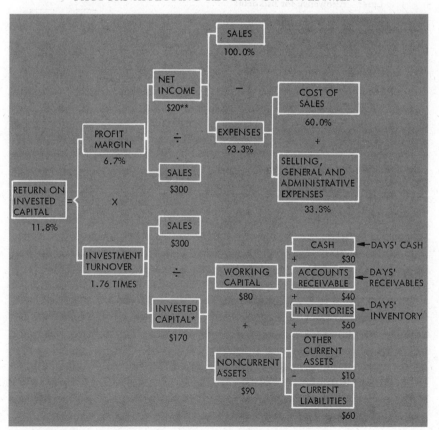

* As pointed out in the text, invested capital is also equal to long-term liabilities plus owners' equity.

† Dollar figures are millions of dollars, and correspond to amounts in the financial statements in Illustrations 12–3 and 12–4.

A *ratio* is simply one number expressed in terms of another. It is found by dividing one number, the base, into the other. A *percentage* is one kind of ratio, in which the base is taken as equaling 100 and the quotient is expressed as "per hundred" of the base.

Dozens of ratios can be computed from a single set of financial statements, but usually only a few are helpful in a given situation. Thus,

Illustration 12–3

ARLEN COMPANY

Balance Sheets
(in millions of dollars)

	December 31 1975	December 31 1974
ASSETS		
Current Assets:		
Cash...	$ 30	$ 30
Accounts receivable................................	42	32
Less: Allowance for bad debts.......................	2	2
Accounts receivable, net............................	40	30
Merchandise inventory..............................	60	50
Prepaid expenses..................................	10	10
Total Current Assets..............................	$140	$120
Fixed Assets:		
Land...	$ 30	$ 30
Buildings and equipment............................	120	120
Less: Accumulated depreciation......................	70	60
Net buildings and equipment.........................	50	60
Total Fixed Assets................................	$ 80	$ 90
Other Assets:		
Goodwill and patents...............................	$ 10	$ 0
Total Assets.....................................	$230	$210
LIABILITIES AND SHAREHOLDERS' EQUITY		
Current Liabilities:		
Accounts payable..................................	$ 30	$ 25
Accrued wages....................................	10	10
Estimated income taxes payable......................	20	15
Total Current Liabilities...........................	$ 60	$ 50
Long-term Liabilities:		
Mortgage bonds, 9 percent..........................	$ 40	$ 40
Total Liabilities..................................	$100	$ 90
Shareholders' Equity:		
Common stock (5,000,000 shares outstanding)*........	$ 60	$ 60
Retained earnings.................................	70	60
Total Shareholders' Equity.........................	$130	$120
Total Liabilities and Shareholders' Equity............	$230	$210

* The market prices as of Dec. 31, 1975 and 1974 were $38 and $32, respectively.

although many frequently used ratios are described below, the best analytical procedure is not to compute all of them mechanically but rather to decide first which ratios might be relevant in the particular type of investigation being made and then to compute these, and only these, ratios.

Illustration 12–2 shows some of the important ratios and other relationships that aid in the analysis of how satisfactory a company's performance was. These ratios can be grouped into four categories: overall measures, tests of profitability, tests of investment utilization, and tests of financial condition. The ratios calculated below are based on a hypothetical company's financial statements, which are shown in Illustrations 12–3 and 12–4.

Illustration 12–4
ARLEN COMPANY

Condensed Income Statement, 1975
(in millions of dollars, except for per share figure)

	Dollars	Percentage
Gross sales	$303	101.0
Less: Returns and allowances	3	1.0
Net sales	300	100.0
Less: Cost of sales	180	60.0
Gross Margin	120	40.0
Operating expenses*	78	26.0
Operating profit	42	14.0
Interest	4	1.3
Income before taxes	38	12.7
Provision for income taxes	18	6.0
Net Income	$ 20	6.7
Net income per common share	$4.00	

* Includes depreciation of $10 million.

Overall Measures

PRICE/EARNINGS RATIO.

$$\frac{\text{Price per share}}{\text{Earnings per share}} = \frac{\$38.00}{\$4.00} = 9.5 \text{ times}$$

The broadest and most widely used overall measure of performance is the price/earnings, or "P/E" ratio. This measure involves an amount not directly controlled by the company, the market price of its common stock; thus the P/E ratio is the best indicator of how *investors* judge the firm's performance.[3] Management, of course, is interested in this market

---

[3] Major newspapers such as *The Wall Street Journal* print firms' P/E ratios along with the daily stock quotations.

appraisal, and a decline in the company's P/E ratio not explainable by a general decline in stock market prices is cause for concern. Also, management compares its P/E ratio with those of similar companies to determine the marketplace's relative rankings of the firms.

Basically the P/E ratio reflects investors' expectations about the company's performance. As Illustration 12–5 indicates, P/E ratios for industries vary, reflecting differing expectations about the relative rate of

Illustration 12–5

PRICE/EARNINGS RATIOS FOR VARIOUS INDUSTRIES, 1974

Industry	P/E*
Aerospace	5
Airlines	12
Appliances	8
Automotive	6
Banks and bank holding companies	10
Beverages	15
Building materials	8
Chemicals	11
Conglomerates	6
Containers	7
Drugs	23
Electrical, electronics	11
Food processing	9
Food and lodging	11
General machinery	11
Instruments	14
Leisure time	13
Metals and mining	12
Miscellaneous manufacturing	9
Nonbank financial	10
Office equipment, computers	17
Oil	11
Oil service and supply	21
Paper	10
Personal care products	20
Publishing	9
Radio and TV broadcasting	8
Railroads	10
Real estate and housing	10
Retailing (food)	9
Retailing (nonfood)	9
Savings and loan	7
Service industries	10
Special machinery	10
Steel	6
Textiles and apparel	7
Tire and rubber	8
Tobacco	10
Trucking	9
Utilities	9
All Industries	11

* P/E's are based on Feb. 22, 1974 stock prices and previous 12-months' earnings per share.
  Source: *Business Week*, March 9, 1974.

growth in earnings in those industries. Thus, for example, because of the energy crisis in the winter of 1973, expectations for the automotive industry were not high (P/E = 6), whereas investors anticipated higher earnings in the oil service and supply industry (P/E = 21) because of increased oil exploration and drilling activities. At times, as in 1974, the P/E ratios for virtually all companies decline because predictions of general economic conditions suggest that corporate profit growth will slow down or even reverse.

RETURN ON INVESTMENT. As mentioned above, this overall measure can be looked at in three different ways, depending on whether one views "investment" as being total assets, invested capital, or shareholders' equity. These returns are calculated as follows:[4]

$$\text{Return on Assets} = \frac{\text{Net Income} + \text{Interest} (1 - \text{tax rate})}{\text{Total Assets}} = \frac{\$20 + \$2}{\$230} = 9.6\%$$

$$\text{Return on Invested Capital} = \frac{\text{Net Income} + \text{Interest} (1 - \text{tax rate})}{\text{Noncurrent Liabilities} + \text{Shareholders' Equity}}$$
$$= \frac{\$20 + \$2}{\$40 + \$130} = 12.9\%$$

$$\text{Return on Shareholders' Equity} = \frac{\text{Net Income}}{\text{Shareholders' Equity}} = \frac{\$20}{\$130} = 15.4\%$$

These formulas immediately raise the question, why is after-tax interest expense added back to net income when figuring return on assets or invested capital, but not when calculating return on shareholders' equity? The reason is that in calculating these returns the analyst is attempting to determine how well management has *used* a "pool" of capital, whether that pool is thought of as being all funds required to finance the assets, the funds invested by long-term creditors and shareholders, or only the capital invested by shareholders. The analyst can then compare these returns with the *cost* of using the pools of funds. However, in arriving at the net income figure, *part* of the cost of capital —the interest on the debt portion—is subtracted as an expense, resulting in a number (net income) which understates the earnings that have been generated by using either the total pool of capital or the invested capital pool. To arrive at the "real" returns on these two pools we must either: (1) prepare a special income statement which excludes interest as an expense; or (2) adjust the net income figure to reflect the exclusion of interest expense. As was the case with the depreciation adjustment we sought in the preceding chapter, it is easier to adjust the net income figure than it is to prepare a special statement. Note that the amount of the adjustment is the *net* interest expense of the firm: because interest expense

---

[4] As in Illustrations 12–2, 12–3, and 12–4, balance sheet and income statement amounts in these calculations are understood to be millions of dollars.

is tax deductible, this net expense is the interest expense multiplied by the complement of the tax rate.

On the other hand, in determining the return on the shareholders' investment, interest expense *should* be included in the earnings calculation, since the earnings accruing to the shareholders (i.e., net income) must reflect the fact that payments (in the form of interest) must be made to the creditors for the use of their funds.

In sum, the returns calculated using the above formulas reflect the earnings generated by using a pool of funds, *excluding* the cost of those funds. The returns on assets and on invested capital should be compared with the firm's *cost of capital* (both debt and equity portions), whereas the return on shareholders' equity should be compared with the cost of only the shareholders' equity portion of capital.

Generally accepted accounting principles treat the cost of the debt portion of capital, that is, interest, as an expense. However, the cost of shareholders' equity capital is ignored in calculating net income. Some people calculate return on assets and on invested capital as follows:

$$\text{Return on Assets} = \frac{\text{Net Income}}{\text{Total Assets}} = \frac{\$20}{\$230} = 8.7\%$$

$$\text{Return on Invested Capital} = \frac{\text{Net Income}}{\text{Invested Capital}} = \frac{\$20}{\$170} = 11.8\%$$

Calculating the two ratios in this manner is conceptually unsound, for they do not reflect either the pre-capital-cost returns or the returns net of capital costs; rather, they show the returns net of some, but not all, capital costs.

A more representative return figure is arrived at by using the average investment during the period, rather than the year-end investment. This would give these returns:

$$\frac{\$20 + \$2}{\frac{1}{2}(\$230 + \$210)} = \frac{\$22}{\$220} = 10.0\%$$

$$\text{Return on Invested Capital} = \frac{\$20 + \$2}{\frac{1}{2}(\$170 + \$160)} = \frac{\$22}{\$165} = 13.3\%$$

$$\text{Return on Shareholders' Equity} = \frac{\$20}{\frac{1}{2}(\$130 + \$120)} = \frac{\$20}{\$125} = 16.0\%$$

However, were a significant amount of new debt or equity funds raised, say, near the end of the year, using the beginning of the year figures rather than the simple average would be more meaningful.

Still another variation on return on investment calculations is to exclude from the investment base any intangible assets, such as Arlen's goodwill and patents. Using simple averages to determine investment, we would have these figures:

$$\text{Return on Tangible Assets} = \frac{\$20 + \$2}{\frac{1}{2}(\$220 + \$210)} = \frac{\$22}{\$215} = 10.2\%$$

$$\text{Return on Tangible Invested Capital} = \frac{\$20 + \$2}{\frac{1}{2}(\$160 + \$160)} = \frac{\$22}{\$160} = 13.8\%$$

$$\text{Return on Tangible Equity} = \frac{\$20}{\frac{1}{2}(\$120 + \$120)} = \frac{\$20}{\$120} = 16.7\%$$

Investment Turnover and Profit Margin

As Illustration 12–2 suggests, return on investment can be looked at as the combined effect of two factors. Algebraically, it is clear that the following is in fact an equality:

$$\frac{\text{Net Income}}{\text{Investment}} = \frac{\text{Net Income}}{\text{Sales}} \times \frac{\text{Sales}}{\text{Investment}}$$

The interesting result of this algebraic "trickery" is that each of the two factors on the right-hand side of the equation has meaning of its own. Net income divided by sales is called *profit margin* and sales divided by investment is called *investment turnover*.

These relationships suggest the two fundamental ways that the return on investment can be improved. First, it can be improved by improving the profit margin, that is, by earning more profit per dollar of sales. Second, it can be improved by increasing the investment turnover. In turn, the investment turnover can be increased in either of two ways: (1) by generating more sales volume with the same amount of investment, or (2) by reducing the amount of investment required for a given level of sales volume.

As one can see from Illustration 12–2, these two factors can be further decomposed into elements which can be looked at individually. The point of this decomposition is that no one manager can significantly influence the overall measure, return on investment, simply because it *is* an overall measure reflecting the combined effects of a number of factors. However, the items on the right-hand side of Illustration 12–2 (which could be subdivided still further) do correspond with the responsibilities of individual managers. For example, the manager who is responsible for the firm's credit policies and procedures has influence over the level of accounts receivable, whereas the amount of cash on hand is a management problem for the treasurer; the vice president of marketing has sales responsibility, whereas the vice president of production is responsible for controlling manufacturing costs, which in turn determine the cost of sales. Thus the outside analyst, as well as the firm's management, can use the return on investment chart to identify potential problem areas in the business. Some techniques are described below.

Tests of Profitability

Illustration 12–4 shows each of the items on the income statement expressed as a percentage of sales. (Examining relationships within a statement in this way is called a *vertical analysis*.) Usually, net sales is taken as 100 percent, as in the illustration. Of the percentages shown, gross margin (40 percent), the operating profit (14 percent), income before taxes (12.7 percent), and net income (6.7 percent) are perhaps the most important.

The *gross margin percentage* indicates the average mark-up or gross margin obtained on products sold. Since it is an average, it does not necessarily represent the mark-up on individual products, and these may differ widely from the average. Gross margin percentages vary widely among industries, but within an industry the percentages for individual companies tend to be similar.

PROFIT MARGIN.

$$\text{Profit Margin} = \frac{\text{Net Income}}{\text{Net Sales}} = \frac{\$20}{\$300} = 6.7\%$$

The profit margin is a measure of overall profitability. This measure is also referred to as the *net income percentage* or the *return on sales*. Some people, particularly critics of a given industry or company, treat this measure as if it were the most important single measure of performance. This is erroneous, because net income, considered by itself, does not take into account the investment employed to produce that income. As Illustration 12–1 indicates, public utilities have a high return on sales, but their return on equity is somewhat below average, reflecting the very large investment base that a utility must finance. The following example illustrates this point:

EXAMPLE: Company A operates a supermarket, and Company B operates a department store. Operating results of each are summarized below:

	A Super- market	B Department Store
Sales	$10,000,000	$10,000,000
Net income	200,000	1,000,000
Total investment	1,000,000	5,000,000
Profit margin	2%	10%
Return on investment	20%	20%

Supermarkets typically operate on a low gross margin, and therefore have a small profit on each dollar of sales, but they also have a much smaller investment per dollar of sales than do department stores. Thus an investor in Company A earns just as high a return on each dollar of his investment as an investor in Company B, even though Company A has a much smaller profit per dollar of sales.

Illustration 12–2 suggests the things top management needs to examine if the profit margin is unsatisfactory. Perhaps dollar sales volume has declined, either because fewer items are being sold, or they are being sold at lower prices, or both. Maybe expenses have gotten out of control: perhaps there is a growing inefficiency in the factory, or management has gotten careless about administrative expenses (expensive new headquarters, corporate jets, and so on). The second part of this book (particularly Chapters 16 and 22) deals with gaining visibility and control over expenses.

Tests of Investment Utilization

Ratios which deal with the lower "branch" of Illustration 12–2 represent tests of investment utilization. Whereas profitability tests focus on income statement figures, utilization tests involve both balance sheet and income statement amounts. We have already looked at the all-encompassing utilization ratio—return on investment. In this section less broad measures will be examined.

INVESTMENT TURNOVER.   As with other ratios involving investment, three turnover ratios can be calculated. Management generally thinks of investment turnover in terms of invested capital:

$$\text{Invested Capital Turnover} = \frac{\text{Sales}}{\text{Invested Capital}} = \frac{\$300}{\$165} = 1.82 \text{ times}^5$$

This ratio reflects how "capital intensive" a business is. For Arlen, this figure can be interpreted as follows: "Arlen Company generates $1.82 in sales for every dollar of invested capital." If the manager looking at this ratio has a financial orientation, he will be thinking of "invested capital" as equal to the sum of noncurrent liabilities and owners' equity. On the other hand, if he has an operations orientation, he may think of the arithmetically equivalent sum of working capital plus noncurrent assets as being the invested capital.

The other two investment turnover ratios are these:

$$\text{Asset Turnover} = \frac{\text{Sales}}{\text{Assets}} = \frac{\$300}{\$220} = 1.36 \text{ times}$$

$$\text{Equity Turnover} = \frac{\text{Sales}}{\text{Shareholders' Equity}} = \frac{\$300}{\$125} = 2.40 \text{ times}$$

These figures have interpretations analogous with that for invested capital turnover. One often sees asset turnover, rather than invested capital turnover, reported in the financial press.

---

[5] This figure differs from the 1.76 times investment turnover shown in Illustration 12–2 because ratios there are based on year-end balance sheet values rather than on averages of beginning and ending balance sheet amounts.

Because of industry disparities in investment turnover, one must be very careful in making judgments about the adequacy of a firm's turnover. In the preceding example, Company A's investment turnover is 10 times, whereas B's is only 2 times; yet both companies have the same overall financial performance, i.e., 20 percent return on investment. This reflects the relationship shown in Illustration 12–2: return on investment is profit margin multiplied by investment turnover. Thus if two firms have different turnover ratios, to achieve a given level of return on investment, the firm with the lower turnover will need to earn the higher profit margin, as is the case with Company B. Comparing the turnover ratios of two similar companies in the same industry is valid, of course, and may help explain why one achieves a higher return on investment than the other.

DAYS' CASH.   Cash is an asset which is necessary, but which does not earn a return, since firms' cash is kept in noninterest-bearing checking accounts. (We are excluding here marketable securities, which are short-term investments of excess cash.) Thus it is almost as important that a company not have too much cash on hand as it is that there not be too little.

One way to judge how well the firm is managing its cash is to calculate roughly how many days' bills the cash on hand would pay. The first step is to use the income statement to estimate cash expenses: a rough approximation would be to take total expenses and subtract noncash expenses such as depreciation. This total is then divided by 365 (some people use 260—52 weeks of 5 working days) to arrive at:

$$\text{Cash costs per day} = \frac{\$270}{365} = \$.74 \text{ per day}$$

This figure can then be divided into the cash balance to determine approximately the "days' cash" on hand:

$$\frac{\text{Cash Balance}}{\text{Cash costs per day}} = \frac{\$30}{\$.74 \text{ per day}} = 41 \text{ days}$$

Combining these two steps, the formula is:

$$\text{Days' Cash} = \frac{\text{Cash Balance}}{\text{Cash Expenses} \div 365}$$

It must be emphasized that this is a rough approximation. The calculation focuses on routine operating expenses; it does not take account of cash needed for major asset purchases. Thus a firm might appear to have too many days' cash on hand because it has just issued bonds to finance construction of a new plant. On the other hand, firms with good cash management procedures would not even let that cash sit idle, but would invest it in short-term securities for as long as possible, even if that is only two or three days. Hence, one should not take the hypothetical

Arlen Company's days' cash (41) as a guide: the figure will usually be two weeks or less in firms that manage their cash well.

DAYS' RECEIVABLES. A calculation similar to that used in days' cash can be used to see how many days' worth of sales the amount in accounts receivable represents. The formula is:

$$\text{Days' Receivables} = \frac{\text{Receivables}}{\text{Sales} \div 365}$$

The result is also called the average *collection period* for the receivables. If possible, the sales figure used should be just *credit* sales, which is more closely related to receivables than is total sales. Also, the receivables figure should be net of bad debt allowances, and the sales figure net of discounts. For Arlen we have:

$$\text{Days' Receivables} = \frac{\$40}{\$300 \div 365} = 49 \text{ days}$$

The collection period can be related roughly to the credit terms offered by the company. A rule of thumb is that the collection period should not exceed $1\frac{1}{3}$ times the regular payment period; that is, if the company's typical terms call for payment in 30 days, it is said that the average collection period should not exceed 40 days. Like all rules of thumb, this one has a great many exceptions. Changes in the ratio indicate changes in the company's credit policy or changes in its ability to collect its receivables.

As with the other ratios, comparisons should be made with the collection period of other firms in the same industry and with a firm's own ratio for previous years. For example, in industries with excess capacity, looser credit policies are sometimes used as a competitive marketing tool, thus increasing the days' receivables. What is of concern is a firm's collection period being significantly longer than its competitors', suggesting inadequate collection procedures.

DAYS' INVENTORY. Completely analogous with the above two ratios is the number of days' sales that could be made from existing inventory. One subtlety here is that sales figures and inventory figures are not comparable, since selling price includes the cost of sales plus the gross margin. Thus instead of using sales per day as the denominator, *cost* of sales per day should be used:[6]

$$\text{Days' Inventory} = \frac{\text{Inventory}}{\text{Cost of Sales} \div 365} = \frac{\$60}{\$180 \div 365} = 122 \text{ days}$$

---

[6] If a firm's gross profit margin has remained about constant, then sales per day could be used in calculating and comparing this ratio over several years. However, the ratio would understate days' inventory. Nevertheless, one frequently encounters inventory turnover figures based on sales values rather than cost of sales.

This ratio will of course vary with the nature of the business. The ratio should be low for a grocery store, where inventory spoilage is a problem. On the other hand, a jewelry store with a wide selection of expensive and unusual items may have many days' inventory on hand. One must also consider the seasonality of the business; for example, an outerwear manufacturer should have large inventories in the summer, but small ones by Christmastime, since most outerwear is sold by retailers between August and December.

Another common inventory ratio is *inventory turnover:*

$$\text{Inventory Turnover} = \frac{\text{Cost of Sales}}{\text{Average Inventory}} = \frac{\$180}{\$55} = 3.3 \text{ times}$$

This measure is indicative of the velocity with which merchandise moves through a business. Turnover may fall either because of an inventory build-up in anticipation of increased sales, or because sales volume has declined and excess goods are on hand. Thus, as is often the case with ratio analysis, it is not always possible to determine whether a movement in the ratio reflects a favorable or an unfavorable situation without knowing additional (usually qualitative) information.

In sum, each of these measures of asset utilization gives an indication of how well the firm is managing its assets. The investment turnover figures permit a comparison of similar firms' investment bases vis-a-vis the sales generated by the firms. The days' cash, receivables, and inventory figures help identify whether a firm is tieing up excessive amounts of funds in current assets. Excess levels of assets hurt performance because they require additional capital, and there is a cost associated with this capital. To the extent that debt could be reduced by cutting the level of assets, interest costs would fall, increasing net income, and the investment base would decrease, thus having a doubly favorable impact on return on investment.

Tests of Financial Condition

Whereas the previously discussed ratios deal with the firm's operations and asset management, tests of financial condition look at the company's liquidity and solvency. *Liquidity* refers to the company's ability to meet its current obligations. Thus liquidity tests focus on the size and relationships of current liabilities and of current assets, which presumably will be converted into cash in order to pay the current liabilities. *Solvency*, on the other hand, pertains to the company's ability to meet the interest costs and repayment schedules associated with its long-term obligations.

CURRENT RATIO. As a rough test of a firm's ability to meet its current obligations, one can see if its current assets exceed its current liabilities; if its current assets do not exceed its current liabilities by a comfortable margin, the firm may be unable to pay its current bills. It is difficult to compare working capital amounts for firms, however, because larger companies require more dollars of working capital. Thus one determines if current assets exceed current liabilities by division (rather than by subtraction) giving:

$$\text{Current Ratio} = \frac{\text{Current Assets}}{\text{Current Liabilities}} = \frac{\$140}{\$60} = 2.3$$

In other words, Arlen's current assets are 2.3 times its current liabilities.

The current ratio is the most commonly used of all balance sheet ratios. It is not only a measure of the company's liquidity but also is a measure of the margin of safety that management maintains in order to allow for the inevitable unevenness in the flow of funds through the current asset and liability accounts. If this flow were absolutely smooth and uniform each day (so that, for example, money coming in from customers exactly equaled maturing obligations), the requirements for such a safety margin would be small. Since a company rarely can count on such an even flow, it needs a supply of liquid funds to be assured of being able to pay its bills when they come due. The current ratio indicates the size of this buffer.

In interpreting the current ratio, consideration of the proportion of various types of current assets is important. A company with a high percentage of its current assets in the form of cash is more liquid than one with a high percentage in inventory, even though the companies have the same current ratio. Also, the nature of business must be considered. For example, a specialty store that sells high-fashion clothing needs a relatively high current ratio since there is high risk involved in both this firm's accounts receivable and inventory. On the other hand, a metals distributor with a lower current ratio than the clothing manufacturer's may be no more risky, since the primary current asset would be inventories of steel, copper, and aluminum shapes, which do not become obsolete and whose prices may be increasing.

ACID-TEST RATIO. Some current assets will not in fact be converted into cash, e.g., prepaid insurance. Also, inventories may not be able to be sold quickly. Therefore another liquidity measure exists which considers just the *quick assets*, i.e., current assets other than inventories and prepaid expenses. This measure is called the *quick ratio* or *acid-test ratio*, and measures the extent to which liquid resources are readily available to meet current obligations.

$$\text{Acid-Test Ratio} = \frac{\text{Quick Assets}}{\text{Current Liabilities}} = \frac{\$70}{\$60} = 1.2$$

Generally an analyst would expect to see a quick ratio of at least 1.0, unless the inventory of the firm was fast-moving and not subject to obsolescence.

DEBT/EQUITY RATIOS. These ratios deal with solvency. The division of equities among current liabilities, long-term liabilities, and owners' equity has an important bearing on solvency. These relationships are shown in the following condensed 1975 data of Arlen Company, derived from Illustration 12–3.

Liabilities and Shareholders' Equity

Current liabilities...............................	26%
Long-term liabilities............................	17
Shareholders' equity.............................	57
Total Liabilities and Shareholders' Equity.........	100%

Of the ratios apparent in the above tabulation, the most important are those showing the relationship between *debt capital* and *equity capital*. Debt capital is another name for noncurrent liabilities. From the point of view of the company, debt capital is risky because if bondholders and other creditors are not paid promptly, they can take legal action to obtain payment which can, in extreme cases, force the company into bankruptcy. Equity capital is much less risky to the company because stockholders receive dividends only at the discretion of the directors.[7] Because the stockholders have less certainty of receiving dividends than the bondholders have of receiving interest, stockholders usually are unwilling to invest in a company unless they see a reasonable expectation of making a higher return (dividends plus stock price appreciation) than they could obtain as bondholders; that is, they would be unwilling to give up the relatively certain prospect of receiving 7 percent or 8 percent interest on bonds, unless the probable, but less certain, return on an equity investment were considerably higher, say 12 percent or more.

From the company's standpoint, the greater the proportion of its invested capital that is obtained from stockholders, the less worry the company has in meeting its fixed obligations; but in return for this lessened worry, the company must expect to pay a higher overall cost of obtaining its capital. Conversely, the more funds that are obtained from bonds, the more the company can *trade on the equity;* that is, it can use funds obtained at relatively low interest rates in the hopes of earning more on these funds for the stockholders. A company with a high proportion of long-term debt is said to be highly *leveraged.* The debt/equity ratio shows the balance that the management of a particular company has struck between these forces.

Unfortunately, the debt/equity ratio (often called simply the *debt*

---

[7] Note that "risk" is here viewed from the standpoint of the company. From the standpoint of investors, the opposite situation prevails. Thus bondholders have a relatively low risk of not receiving their payments, and stockholders have a relatively high risk. From this latter standpoint, equity capital is called "risk capital."

ratio) is defined in two quite different ways; the user must always be careful to ascertain which meaning is intended in a given situation. One definition includes the current liabilities, and the other excludes them. Including current liabilities, the 1975 debt/equity ratio for Arlen Company is 43 to 57, or 0.75 to 1. Excluding current liabilities, the corresponding figures are 17 to 57, or 0.30 to 1. This difference in meaning is confusing in general, but in particular situations it is less so, because a company or an industry usually settles on one meaning or the other, and those who use the ratios then have a common basis of understanding.

A variation of the debt/equity ratio is the *debt/capitalization* ratio. Capitalization is usually defined to be invested capital, i.e., noncurrent liabilities plus owners' equity. For Arlen this ratio would be 17 to 74, or 0.23 to 1 (23%). Some analysts prefer the debt/capitalization ratio over debt/equity because the former shows the percentage of invested capital accounted for by debt. The two ratios give exactly the same information, however; for example, a debt/equity ratio (excluding current liabilities) of 0.50 is identical in meaning with a debt/capitalization ratio of 0.33.

TIMES INTEREST EARNED.

$$\frac{\text{Operating Profit}}{\text{Interest}} = \frac{\$42}{\$4} = 10.5 \text{ times}$$

The numerator of this ratio is the amount of earnings available to meet the fixed obligations of debt interest. In the example, interest requirements are said to be *covered* 10.5 times. This ratio is a measure of the level to which income can decline without impairing the company's ability to meet interest payments on its liabilities. Income is taken before income taxes because if income declined, income taxes would decline correspondingly. The ratio implies that income is equivalent to additional cash, which is not necessarily the case, of course.

If preferred stock is outstanding, a similar coverage ratio can be computed for the preferred stock dividends, but here the numerator is income after interest charges and after taxes ($20 million).

A company may have fixed obligations in addition to its interest payments, as, for example, when it has rental commitments on leased property. In such a case coverage is properly computed by adding these other obligations to the amount of interest, but excluding them from the earnings figure in the numerator, just as interest expense was not included when interest coverage was calculated. The ratio is then labeled "Times Fixed Charges Earned" or "Fixed Charges Coverage."

DIVIDEND YIELD. The dividend yield is based on the relationship between the amount of cash dividends declared during the year and the market price of the common stock. Assuming Arlen declared $2 per share in dividends in 1975, as of December 31, 1975, the yield was:

$$\frac{\text{Dividends per Share}}{\text{Price per Share}} = \frac{\$2}{\$38} = 5.3\%$$

The yield on stocks is often compared with the yield, or interest, on bonds, but such a comparison is not valid. This is because the earnings of bondholders consist entirely of their interest, whereas the earnings of stockholders consist not only of their dividends, but also of retained earnings. Although stockholders do not receive retained earnings, the fact that part of the net income has been retained in the business and presumably invested in income-producing assets should enhance earnings per share and thus increase the market value of the stockholders' investment.

Strictly speaking, dividend yield is not really a measure of a firm's financial condition. Some very healthy companies pay no dividends, because of the availability of new income-producing projects which the firm can finance in part by retaining earnings. Moreover, for a firm that does pay dividends, the yield will drop if the stock price increases at a faster rate than the dividends. Conversely, the yield will increase if a firm holds its dividend payments constant while its stock price is dropping. Nevertheless, many investors do think of the yield as telling them something about the financial condition of the company, and a drop in yield caused solely by a cut in dividends may in fact indicate financial problems for a company.

DIFFICULTIES IN MAKING COMPARISONS

Reasonably accurate reports of actual performance often can be obtained by outsiders (although the problems involved in obtaining them may be by no means trivial). Finding an adequate standard against which these actuals can be measured, however, is often a perplexing and difficult matter.

Some of the problems are described below. Financial statement analysis is used as an example, but the same problems arise in analyzing other types of quantitative data. When a person says that performance is "good" or "poor," "better" or "worse," he is, either implicitly or explicitly, comparing actual performance to some standard that he believes is relevant.

Deciding on the Proper Basis for Comparison

Subject only to minor qualifications, a youth who runs a mile in six minutes (or, expressed as a rate, 10 miles per hour) is a better miler than a youth who runs a mile in seven minutes. In business, there are many situations in which one cannot tell whether a higher number represents better performance than a lower number, or whether it represents poorer performance.

A high current ratio is by no means necessarily better than a low current ratio. For example, the current ratio for the Arlen Company on December 31, 1975, was 2.3 to 1. Suppose that $40 million of the current liabilities came due the very next day and that the company in fact paid these liabilities, using every dollar of its available cash and liquidating other current assets as well. A balance sheet prepared subsequent to this transaction would show $100 million of current assets and $20 million of current liabilities, and the current ratio would accordingly be 5 to 1, which is more than double the ratio of the previous day. Yet one could scarcely say that a company that had used up all its cash was in an improved financial condition. Or, conversely, consider what happens when a company expands, as illustrated by the Arlen Company balance sheet at the end of 1975 compared with its balance sheet for the end of 1974. Current assets have increased by $20 million, and current liabilities have increased by only $10 million; the current ratio has dropped from 2.4 : 1 to 2.3 : 1. The decrease may indicate no worsening of the company's liquid position at all; rather, it may reflect the result of a well carried-out expansion program.

In some comparisons the direction of change that represents "good" or "better" is reasonably apparent. Generally, a high net profit percentage is better than a low one, and a high return on investment is better than a low one. Even these statements have many qualifications, however.

Many standards can usefully be thought of as a *quality range* rather than as a single number. When actual performance is within this range, it may be regarded as being satisfactory. When it begins to go outside the range, *in either direction*, there is an indication of an unsatisfactory situation. For a certain company, the current ratio may be considered satisfactory if it is within the range 2 : 1 to 3 : 1. Below 2 : 1, there is the danger of being unable to meet maturing obligations. Above 3 : 1, there is an indication that funds are being left idle rather than being efficiently employed. As another example, a too-high profit ratio may indicate that the company is only "skimming the cream" off the market; a deeper penetration may increase sales and total return on investment even if the ratio of profit to sales is reduced.

Differences in the Situations Being Compared

No reasonable person would expect a 12-year-old youth to run as fast as a 19-year-old athlete; in judging the youth's performance, we attempt to compare his speed with that of others of the same age and sex and with similar training. Differences in the factors that affect one company's performance this year as compared with those that affect the same company's performance last year, or the performance of another company, are complex and difficult to evaluate. Nevertheless, some attempt must be made to allow for these differences. In general, this task is least difficult when all the figures being compared pertain to the same company (although even here changes in size, in the functions performed by the company, in outside influences, and so on, may make comparisons of tenuous validity). The task is more difficult when attempting to compare one company with another, even if they are both of the same size and in the same industry, and it becomes exceedingly difficult if the two companies are in different industries or if they are of substantially different size.

Changes in the Dollar Measuring Stick

Accounting figures are expressed in historical dollars. A change in the value of a dollar, that is, a change in price levels, may therefore seriously lessen the validity of comparisons of ratios computed for different time periods. Also, a ratio whose numerator and denominator are expressed in different kinds of dollars may have no useful meaning.

The fact that asset amounts are stated as unexpired historical dollar costs causes particular difficulty in making comparisons of ratios calculated from such amounts. Two companies, for example, might have facilities that are physically identical in all respects except age, and they might operate exactly the same way and earn exactly the same net income. If, however, the buildings and equipment of one company had been purchased at a time when prices were low or if they had been almost fully depreciated, and if the buildings and equipment of the other company had been purchased at a time of higher prices or if they were relatively new, then the return-on-investment ratio for the company that carried its assets at a low book value would be much higher than the ratio for the other company.

Differences in Definition

The terms "one mile" and "six minutes" used to measure the runner are precisely defined and easily measured, but the individual elements making up such terms as "current assets" and "current liabilities" are by no means precisely defined, and there is considerable diversity in practice as to how they should be measured. Similarly, "profit" may mean: net income as determined by using generally accepted accounting principles (which in turn can be a range of values, depending on the particular methods used for depreciation, inventory valuation, and so forth); income after taxes based on the firm's income tax return; profit as determined by procedures required by a regulatory agency; or profit as shown on a report intended only for the use of management, which may be a different profit figure than any of the above amounts.

Hidden Short-Run Changes

A balance sheet may not reflect the average or typical situation. A balance sheet is prepared as of one moment of time, and it tells nothing about short-term fluctuations in assets and equities that have occurred within the period bounded by the two balance sheet dates. Many department stores, for example, end their fiscal year and publish annual balance sheets as of January 31. By that date, Christmas inventories have been sold out and many of the Christmas receivables have been paid, but Easter merchandise has not started to arrive and payables for this merchandise have not yet been generated. Current assets (other than cash) and current liabilities as reported on the January 31 balance sheet are therefore likely to be lower than at other times of the year; as a result, ratios such as inventory turnover and the average collection period may be distorted, and other ratios may not be representative of the situation at other seasons. A company that is analyzing its own data can study the seasonal movements by using monthly, rather than annual, balance sheets, but these are ordinarily not available to the outsider.

The outside analyst should also recognize that companies have been known to take deliberate steps to "clean up" their balance sheets. They may, for example, pay off loans just before the end of the year, which usually increases the current ratio; they then borrow again early in the next year. Such transactions, which are called *window dressing*, may not be discernible on the balance sheet.

The Past as an Indication of the Future

Financial statements are historical documents, and financial ratios show relationships that have existed in the past. The manager or analyst is, of course, interested in what is happening now and what is likely to happen in the future rather than what did happen in the past. Often the outside analyst has no choice but to rely on past data as an indication of the current situation, but he should not be misled into believing that the historical ratios necessarily reflect current conditions, and much less that they reflect future conditions.

POSSIBLE BASES FOR COMPARISON

There are four types of standards against which an actual figure can be compared: (1) experience; (2) a goal; (3) an historical figure; and (4) an external figure, that is, a figure for performance in another company, or other companies.

Experience

The manager or analyst gradually builds up his own idea as to what constitutes "good" or "poor" performance. One of the important advantages that an experienced person has over inexperienced ones is that he possesses a feeling for what are "right" relationships in a given situation, developed on the basis of his knowledge about similar situations. (Of course, if he is not competent, his feeling may well be incorrect.) These subjective standards of a competent analyst or manager are more important than standards based on mechanical comparisons.

Goals

Many companies prepare *budgets*, which show *what performance is expected to be under the circumstances prevailing*. If actual performance corresponds with budgeted performance, there is a reasonable inference that the performance is good. There are two important qualifications that affect this inference, however. First, the budgeted figures may not have been set very carefully in the first instance, and the comparison can of course be no more valid than the goal figures themselves. Secondly, the goals were necessarily set on the basis of certain assumptions as to the conditions that would be prevailing during the period, and if these assumptions turn out to be incorrect, the goal figures are also incorrect as a measure of results "under the circumstances prevailing." If, because of a recession or other economic phenomenon outside the control of management, net income is lower than the amount budgeted, it cannot fairly be said that the difference between actual and budgeted income indicates "poor" performance. Nevertheless, the budget is a type of standard that has fewer inherent difficulties than either the historical standards or the external standards. Of course, outside analysts frequently do not have access to a company's budget figures.

Historical Standards

A comparison of current performance with past figures for the same company usually does not run into the problem of differences in accounting practice. If practices have changed, the change is presumably known to the analyst. Moreover, the analyst can also recollect, or find out from supplementary data, some of the circumstances that have changed between the two periods and thus allow for these changes in making his comparison. At best, however, a comparison between a current figure and an historical figure in the same company can show only that the current period is "better" or "worse" than the past. In many cases this does not provide a sound basis for judgment, for the historical figure may not have represented an acceptable standard. If a company increases its return on investment from 1 percent to 2 percent, it has improved, but it nevertheless is not doing very well.

External Standards

When one company is compared with another, the environmental and accounting differences affecting the two sets of figures may raise serious problems of comparability. If, however, the analyst is able to allow for these differences, even approximately, he obtains an outside check on performance that has the advantage, over a standard derived from internal sources, of being arrived at independently. Moreover, the two companies may well have been affected by the same set of economic conditions, so this important cause of noncomparability may not be operating.

Corporations whose stock is traded on organized security exchanges file annual reports with the U.S. Securities and Exchange Commission, and these "Form 10–K" reports are likely to be more useful for comparisons than the annual reports sent to shareholders, both because the SEC prescribes a uniform format and terminology and because the 10–K reports usually contain more detailed information than reports to shareholders.

Many sources contain *average ratios* for groups of companies in the same industry or of similar size. Perhaps the best known are those published by Dun & Bradstreet, Inc. For each of 125 industry groups, the following ratios are published (starred items have been described above; the derivation of the others should be apparent):

*Current ratio.
*Net profit margin.
*Return on tangible equity.
Net profit as a percentage of net working capital.
Net sales as a percentage of tangible equity.
Net sales as a percentage of net working capital.
*Collection period.
*Inventory turnover.
Fixed assets to tangible equity.
Current liabilities to tangible equity.
*Debt/equity ratio.
Inventory to net working capital.
Current liabilities to inventory.
Long-term debt to net working capital.

Ratios are also prepared by Robert Morris Associates for their members. A variety of ratios will also be found in *Moody's Manual of Investments, Standard and Poor's Corporation Records,* and other publications prepared for investors.

Standard and Poor's Corporation has available a COMPUSTAT service which consists of magnetic tapes containing pertinent financial and statistical information for several thousand industrial companies and utilities in the United States and Canada. The information is available on an annual basis for the past 20 years. The financial information consists of 19 balance sheet items, 22 income statement items, 19 additional statistical items including stock prices, dividends, and a variety of ratios computed from the above. All companies are grouped and coded by industry classifications.

Use of these industrywide ratios involves all the difficulties of using ratios derived from one other company plus the special problems that arise when the figures for several companies are thrown together into a single average. Nevertheless, they may give some worthwhile impressions about the average situation in an industry.

Many trade associations and other groups collect and publish figures for the companies in an industry. In some instances, the association prescribes in detail the accounting definitions and concepts to be used in reporting these figures, and the resulting figures are therefore much more comparable than those compiled by the sources mentioned above, which must use the basic data in whatever form the company chooses to report it.

USE OF COMPARISONS

The principal value of an analysis of financial statement information is that it suggests questions that need to be answered; such an analysis rarely provides the answers. An unfavorable difference between actual performance and whatever standard is used, if it is large, indicates that something *may be* wrong, and this leads to an investigation. Even when the analysis indicates strongly that something *is* wrong (as when one company's income has declined while incomes of comparable companies have increased), the analysis rarely shows what the *cause* of the difficulty is. Nevertheless, the ability to pick from the thousands of questions that *might* be asked those few that are really worth asking is an important one.

It is well to keep in mind the basic relationships shown in Illustration 12–2, or some variation of these that is applicable to the situation being analyzed. The only number that encompasses all these relationships is a return-on-investment ratio. A change in any less inclusive ratio may be misleading as an indication of better or worse performance unless possible compensating changes in factors not covered by the ratio are taken into account. An increase in dollars of net income indicates improved performance only if there was no offsetting increase in the investment required. An increase in the net profit margin indicates improved performance only if there was no offsetting decrease in sales volume or increase in investment. An increase in the gross margin percentage indicates improved performance only if there was no offsetting decrease in sales volume, increase in investment, or increase in expenses.

In short, the use of any ratio other than return on investment, taken by itself, implies that all other things are equal. This *ceteris paribus* condition ordinarily does not prevail, and the validity of comparisons is lessened to the extent that it does not. Yet the return-on-investment ratio is so broad that it does not give a clue as to which of the underlying factors may be responsible for changes in it. It is to find these factors, which if unfavorable indicate possible trouble areas, that the subsidiary ratios of profitability are used. Furthermore, the return-on-investment ratio tells nothing about the financial condition of the company; liquidity and solvency ratios are necessary for this purpose.

In addition to, or in place of, the simple ratio of one number to another, many business people develop a more complicated set of interrelationships that they find useful in isolating the key factors that affect good performance. An automobile dealer may say: "If the gross profit on service and parts sales is large enough to cover total general and administrative expenses, and if we break even on used car sales, then we will earn an adequate profit for the whole business from the gross margin less selling costs on new car sales." Usually, there is no way of demonstrating that these relationships are logically correct—there is no logical reason why gross profit on one part of the automobile dealer's business should just equal general and administrative costs for the whole business—but the fact is that they do work out.

SUMMARY

The numbers on financial statements are usually most useful for analytical purposes when they are expressed in relative terms in the form of ratios and percentages. Although a great many ratios can be calculated, only a few are ordinarily necessary in connection with a given problem.

The essential task is to find a standard or norm with which actual performance can be compared. In general, there are four types of standards: (1) subjective standards derived from the analyst's experience; (2) goals, or budgets, set in advance of the period under review; (3) historical figures, showing performance of the same company in the past; and (4) the performance of other companies, as shown by their financial statements, or by averages compiled from the financial statements of a number of companies. None of these is perfect, but a rough allowance for the factors that cause noncomparability often can be made.

The comparison may then suggest important questions that need to be investigated; it rarely indicates answers to the questions.

SUGGESTIONS FOR FURTHER READING

BERNSTEIN, LEOPOLD A. *Financial Statement Analysis: Theory, Application, and Interpretation.* Homewood, Ill.: Richard D. Irwin, Inc., 1974.

FOULKE, ROY A. *Practical Financial Statement Analysis,* 6th ed., New York: McGraw-Hill Book Co., Inc., 1968.

KENNEDY, RALPH DALE, and STEWART YARDWOOD MCMULLEN. *Financial Statements: Form, Analysis, and Interpretation,* 6th ed., Homewood, Ill.: Richard D. Irwin, Inc., 1973.

CASES

CASE 12–1. TEXACO INC.

Exhibits 1 and 2 show financial statements for Texaco Inc. Exhibit 3 gives financial ratios for Texaco and three other oil companies.

Exhibit 1

TEXACO INC.

Income Statements
Years Ended December 31
($ in millions)

	1973		1972	
Revenues	$11,835	100.0%	$8,972	100.0%
Cost of goods sold	7,875	66.5	5,892	65.7
Gross profit	$ 3,960	33.5%	$3,080	34.3%
Other expenses:				
Selling and administration	$ 869	7.3%	$ 789	8.8%
Dry hole costs	50	0.4	43	0.5
Depreciation, depletion, amortization	551	4.7	427	4.8
Interest	143	1.2	108	1.2
Taxes other than income taxes	305	2.6	254	2.8
	$ 1,918	16.2%	$1,621	18.1%
Income before taxes	$ 2,042	17.3%	$1,459	16.3%
Income tax expense	733	6.2	556	6.2
Income before minority interest	$ 1,309	11.1%	$ 903	10.1%
Minority interest	17	0.1	14	0.2
Net income	$ 1,292	10.9%	$ 889	9.9%

Additional Information for 1973

Average capital stock outstanding.............. 271,958,000 shares
Price range of stock.......................... 25–43⅛
Dividends per share........................... $1.73

Figures in this and succeeding exhibits may not add owing to rounding.

373

Exhibit 2: TEXACO INC.

Consolidated Balance Sheets
As of December 31

($ in millions)

	1973		1972	
ASSETS				
Current Assets:				
Cash	$ 277	2.0%	$ 266	2.2%
Marketable securities (at cost)	325	2.4	284	2.4
Accounts and notes receivable (net)	2,026	14.9	1,745	14.5
Inventories:*				
Crude oil, petroleum products	1,286	9.5	763	6.3
Materials and supplies	73	0.5	61	0.5
Total Current Assets	$ 3,987	29.3%	$ 3,119	25.9%
Investments and Advances	$ 1,117	8.2%	$ 1,025	8.5%
Property, plant, and equipment	$12,560	92.4%	$11,839	98.4%
Less: Depreciation, depletion and amortization	4,083	(30.0)	3,990	(33.2)
Net property, plant, and equipment	$ 8,477	62.4%	$ 7,849	65.2%
Deferred Charges	$ 15	0.1%	$ 39	0.3%
Total Assets	$13,595	100.0%	$12,032	100.0%
LIABILITIES AND SHAREHOLDERS' EQUITY				
Current Liabilities				
Notes payable	$ 215	1.6%	$ 700	5.8%
Long-term debt due within one year	49	0.4	43	0.4
Accounts payable and accrued liabilities	1,675	12.3	1,129	9.4
Estimated income taxes	325	2.4	291	2.4
Total Current Liabilities	$ 2,264	16.7%	$ 2,163	18.0%
Long-term Debt	$ 1,778	13.1%	$ 1,360	11.3%
Deferred Income Taxes	$ 1,360	10.0%	$ 1,171	9.7%
Reserves for Employee Benefit Plans	$ 97	0.7%	$ 71	0.6%
Minority Interest in Subsidiaries	$ 104	0.8%	$ 92	0.8%
Shareholders' Equity				
Capital stock	$ 2,313	17.0%	$ 2,312	19.2%
Retained earnings	5,757	42.3	4,935	41.0
Less: Treasury stock	77	(0.6)	72	(0.6)
Total Shareholders' Equity	$ 7,992	58.8%	$ 7,175	59.6%
Total Liabilities and Shareholders' Equity	$13,595	100.0%	$12,032	100.0%

* Inventories of crude oil and petroleum products are stated at cost on the Fifo method; materials and supplies are stated at average cost. This method was used throughout the 1970–1973 period.

Exhibit 3

COMPARATIVE RATIOS IN THE OIL INDUSTRY

	1970	1971	1972	1973
Earnings per share				
Texaco	$3.02	$3.32	$3.27	
Continental	$3.06	$2.16	$3.38	$ 4.81
Exxon	$5.91	$6.52	$6.83	$10.90
Mobil	$4.77	$5.33	$5.65	$ 8.34
*Price/earnings ratio**				
Texaco	9.9	10.4	10.5	
Continental	8.5	14.9	9.7	8.5
Exxon	10.4	11.5	11.5	8.6
Mobil	9.9	9.9	11.1	7.1
Return on assets†				
Texaco	8.7%	8.7%	7.8%	
Continental	6.2%	4.5%	6.1%	7.5%
Exxon	7.4%	7.8%	7.7%	10.3%
Mobil	6.6%	6.8%	6.7%	8.4%
Return on invested capital†				
Texaco	11.8%	11.8%	11.0%	
Continental	8.5%	6.1%	8.5%	11.0%
Exxon	10.7%	11.2%	11.2%	15.8%
Mobil	9.4%	9.7%	9.9%	13.2%
Gross profit margin				
Texaco	38.2%	36.1%	34.3%	
Continental‡	43.2%	42.9%	44.3%	43.8%
Exxon‡	56.5%	56.0%	59.8%	60.1%
Mobil‡	55.8%	55.8%	58.7%	57.7%
Return on sales				
Texaco	12.1%	11.2%	9.9%	
Continental‡	5.4%	3.3%	4.6%	5.4%
Exxon‡	7.0%	6.9%	6.8%	8.6%
Mobil‡	5.8%	5.8%	5.6%	6.7%
Asset turnover†				
Texaco	0.68	0.74	0.75	
Continental	0.99	1.09	1.14	1.22
Exxon	0.97	1.04	1.04	1.14
Mobil	1.05	1.10	1.12	1.19
Days' cash†				
Texaco	15	16	13	
Continental	20	14	9	12
Exxon	8	8	9	8
Mobil	7	6	6	7
Days' receivables†				
Texaco	78	70	71	
Continental	64	53	53	55
Exxon	60	54	54	52
Mobil	63	60	61	61
Days' inventories†				
Texaco	60	55	51	
Continental§	57	48	44	54
Exxon‖	70	66	71	71
Mobil#	77	75	75	64

Exhibit 3 (*continued*)
COMPARATIVE RATIOS IN THE OIL INDUSTRY

	1970	1971	1972	1973
Inventory turnover†				
Texaco................................	6.1	6.7	7.2	
Continental§........................	6.4	7.7	8.4	6.7
Exxon‖...............................	5.2	5.5	5.2	5.1
Mobil#...............................	4.7	4.8	4.9	5.7
Current ratio†				
Texaco................................	1.74	1.71	1.44	
Continental...........................	1.67	1.74	1.52	1.56
Exxon................................	1.54	1.57	1.51	1.55
Mobil................................	1.58	1.45	1.25	1.17
Acid-test ratio†				
Texaco................................	1.28	1.24	1.06	
Continental...........................	1.21	1.30	1.14	1.12
Exxon................................	1.09	1.10	1.07	1.13
Mobil................................	1.20	1.06	0.91	0.88
Debt/Capitalization ratio†				
Texaco................................	14%	16%	16%	
Continental...........................	31%	32%	30%	28%
Exxon................................	18%	19%	18%	16%
Mobil................................	18%	19%	17%	16%
Interest coverage				
Texaco................................	16.7	18.1	14.5	
Continental...........................	7.1	7.0	8.6	9.5
Exxon................................	11.5	12.9	15.6	22.3
Mobil................................	12.7	15.3	17.1	22.1
Yield*				
Texaco................................	5.4%	4.6%	4.8%	
Continental...........................	5.8%	4.7%	4.6%	3.7%
Exxon................................	6.1%	5.1%	4.8%	4.5%
Mobil................................	5.1%	4.8%	4.2%	4.8%

* Based on average of year's high and low stock prices.
† Based on year-end balance sheet amounts, rather than on average amounts.
‡ Revenue figures reported by Continental, Exxon, and Mobil include excise taxes collected from consumers by the company and remitted to the government. These excise taxes are reported as part of tax expenses by these three firms.
§ In 1970 and 1971, inventory cost was determined on a Lifo basis for 52 percent of the inventories, and the remainder under Fifo or average cost. In 1972 and 1973, cost for 59 percent of the inventories was determined on the Fifo basis, 38 percent on Lifo, and the remainder at average cost.
‖ In 1970 and 1971, approximately half of inventory cost was determined on a Lifo basis, and half on Fifo. In 1972 and 1973, approximately 60 percent of inventory cost was determined on the Fifo basis, the remainder on Lifo.
In 1970 and 1971 respectively, about 35 percent and 33 percent of inventories were valued under the Lifo method, the remainder at average cost. For 1972 and 1973 respectively, 30 percent and 35 percent of inventories were valued on the Lifo basis, the remainder at average cost.

Questions

1. Calculate and fill in the 1973 ratios for Texaco Inc.
2. What conclusions would you draw about Texaco from the (completed) data in Exhibit 3. What questions do those data raise for you?

CASE 12-2. MARRETT MANUFACTURING COMPANY (C)

Using the actual 1975 and projected 1976 financial statements based on Marrett Manufacturing Company (A) (Case 6-2), calculate the following ratios for 1975 and 1976. (Because we have no balance sheet as of December 31, 1974, use *year-end* balance sheet account amounts throughout.)

1. Return on assets.
2. Return on equity.
3. Gross margin percentage.
4. Return on sales.
5. Asset turnover.
6. Days' cash.
7. Days' receivables.
8. Days' inventories (finished goods only).
9. Inventory turnover (all inventories).
10. Current ratio.
11. Acid-test ratio.
12. Times interest earned.

As an outside analyst, what questions would you want to ask Marrett's management, based on these ratios?

CASE 12-3. NEWTON DESIGN GROUP

Newton Design Group (NDG) was a thirty-person architectural firm located in a large midwestern city. The firm had been founded ten years earlier by Chloe Sterling, who had left a position with a prominent Chicago architectural firm so she could "be her own boss." Under Ms. Sterling's direction, NDG had prospered, and had a reputation for being able to design attractive and functional buildings which could be built within the client's often-limited construction budget.

In March 1975, Ms. Sterling was contacted by Jack Baker, the vice president of Environmental Design Services, Inc. (EDS). EDS was a Texas-based firm which promoted its ability to take a "total systems approach" to any design problem. EDS had been formed four years earlier when its president, Charles Furey, had incorporated his architectural firm and changed its name from Furey Design Services, Inc. In the last two years, EDS had broadened its available services by acquiring small firms in the areas of planning, landscape architecture, interior design, graphics, and structural engineering. In all of these acquisitions, the owner-managers of the acquired firms had agreed to continue their involvement for a minimum of three years, and had accepted EDS com-

Exhibit 1

ENVIRONMENTAL DESIGN SERVICES, INC. AND SUBSIDIARIES

Consolidated Balance Sheet

	Dec. 31, 1973	Dec. 31, 1974
ASSETS		
Current Assets:		
Cash, including certificates of deposit of $200,000 (1974)......	$ 28,073	$ 372,964
Notes receivable–current installments (Note 2).............	—	152,500
Accounts receivable–less allowance for losses: $12,000 (1973), $41,000 (1974).............................	408,165	835,247
Inventories (Note 3)..................................	52,940	229,672
Prepaid expenses.....................................	11,604	22,324
Total Current Assets.............................	$500,782	$1,612,707
Equipment and Leasehold Improvements		
—at cost less accumulated depreciation of $5,250 (1973) and $14,127 (1974).................................	$ 33,456	$ 106,857
Other Assets:		
Notes receivable–less current installments (Note 2)...........	—	$ 397,500
Model homes and site (Note 4).........................	$ 56,000	—
Deferred research and development costs (Note 4)..........	183,019	272,248
Deferred cost of proposed public offering..................	36,166	—
Deposits and other assets..............................	9,867	32,894
Total Other Assets...............................	$285,052	$ 702,642
Total Assets..................................	$819,290	$2,422,206
LIABILITIES AND STOCKHOLDERS' EQUITY		
Current Liabilities:		
Notes payable (Note 3)................................	$ 75,000	$ 72,357
Accounts payable.....................................	119,410	133,086
Accrued salaries and payroll taxes.......................	36,792	46,962
Contracts payable....................................	24,317	18,656
Federal and state taxes on income (Note 5):		
Current..	79,725	20,057
Deferred.......................................	180,000	259,000
Total Current Liabilities.........................	$515,244	$ 550,118
Long-Term Debt–Subordinated Promissory Note..............	$ 43,887	—
Deferred Taxes on Income (Note 5).......................	—	$ 217,000
Minority Interests....................................	—	$ 36,889
Stockholders' Equity (Notes 6 and 7):		
Common stock–authorized 2,000,000 shares, $.20 par value per share, issued and outstanding 770,000 shares (1973) and 1,000,800 shares (1974)..........................	$154,000	$ 200,160
Additional paid-in capital.............................	—	1,009,258
Retained earnings....................................	106,159	408,781
Total Shareholders' Equity.........................	$260,159	$1,618,199
Total Liabilities and Shareholders' Equity............	$819,290	$2,422,206

mon stock as the consideration for selling their firms to EDS. In 1974, EDS made a public offering of 230,000 shares of its common stock.

EDS was now interested in expanding its market area northward, and was interested in acquiring NDG as a means of establishing a base for EDS in the midwest. Mr. Baker's visit to NDG was a very preliminary one, and no agreements were made. He told Ms. Sterling that if NDG were interested in "joining the EDS family," EDS would acquire the firm from her in exchange for shares of EDS stock, the number of which would be negotiated later. He left her a copy of EDS's annual report, which contained financial statements for 1973 and 1974.

After Mr. Baker's departure, Ms. Sterling looked through the annual report. She noticed that in the last year EDS had begun to expand into the areas of land development and modular housing, a further extension of the EDS "full-services" approach. The annual report spoke of EDS's ability "to create total living environments and to provide the broadest capability of services available to the shelter industry from a single source."

Exhibit 2

ENVIRONMENTAL DESIGN SERVICES, INC. AND SUBSIDIARIES

Consolidated Income Statements

	Year Ended Dec. 31	
	1973	1974
Revenues:		
Building design and related services..............	$1,368,061	$1,687,704
Sale of mobile/modular units....................	58,978	448,649
System sales and royalties (Note 4).............	—	270,315
Land sales......................................	—	571,893
Other..	—	37,186
Total Revenues.........................	$1,427,039	$3,015,747
Expenses:		
Cost of sales...................................	$ 646,603	$1,443,802
Selling, administrative and general expenses........	371,500	906,534
Total Expenses.........................	$1,018,103	$2,350,336
Income before Taxes on Income and Minority Interests.	$ 408,936	$ 665,411
Taxes on Income:		
State...	$ 31,860	$ 47,000
Federal:		
Current.....................................	35,000	
Deferred....................................	155,000	294,000
	$ 221,860	$ 341,000
	$ 187,076	$ 324,411
Minority Interests in Net Income of Subsidiaries.....	—	$ 21,789
Net Income....................................	$ 187,076	$ 302,622
Net Income per Common and Common Equivalent Share (Note 8)...............................	$.23	$.30

Exhibit 3

ENVIRONMENTAL DESIGN SERVICES, INC. AND SUBSIDIARIES

Consolidated Statement of Changes in Financial Position (Working-Capital Basis)

	Year Ended Dec. 31	
	1973	*1974*
Sources of Working Capital:		
Operations:		
Net income....................................	$187,076	$ 302,622
Add: Expenses not requiring working capital:		
Depreciation–straight line method....................	4,318	13,175
Provision for minority interests.....................	—	21,789
Provision for long-term deferred taxes on income.......	—	217,000
Total Working Capital Generated by Operations.....	$191,394	$ 554,586
Other Sources:		
Net proceeds of public stock offering.................	—	$1,053,818
Exercise of stock options...........................	—	1,600
Disposals of equipment.............................	—	27,708
Proceeds from sales of minority interests..............	—	15,100
Increase in long-term debt..........................	59,684	—
Decrease in other assets............................	—	13,139
Total Working Capital from Other Sources.........	$ 59,684	$1,362,443
Total Sources of Working Capital.............	$251,078	$1,665,951
Uses of Working Capital:		
Decrease in long-term debt............................	—	$ 43,887
Additions to equipment...............................	31,584	114,284
Increase in noncurrent notes receivable.................	—	397,500
Increase in deferred research and development		
costs (net)..	239,019	33,229
Increase in other assets..............................	45,139	—
Cash dividends paid..................................	10,000	—
Total Uses of Working Capital.................	$325,742	$ 588,900
Increase (Decrease) in Working Capital	($ 74,664)	$1,077,051
Changes in Working Capital–increase (decrease):		
Current assets:		
Cash..	($ 7,901)	$ 344,891
Notes receivable..................................	—	152,500
Accounts receivable...............................	294,202	427,082
Inventories.......................................	28,331	176,732
Prepaid expenses..................................	10,214	10,720
Current liabilities:		
Notes payable....................................	(75,000)	2,643
Accounts payable.................................	(107,060)	(13,676)
Accrued salaries and payroll taxes...................	(24,745)	(10,170)
Contracts payable.................................	(8,520)	5,661
Taxes on income..................................	(184,185)	(19,332)
	($ 74,664)	$1,077,051

Exhibit 4

ENVIRONMENTAL DESIGN SERVICES, INC. AND SUBSIDIARIES

Selected Notes to Consolidated Financial Statements

Note 2–Notes Receivable. The notes receivable originated primarily from land sales, and are due in installments through 1979.

Note 3–Inventories. Inventories consist of the following:

	Dec. 31, 1973	Dec. 31, 1974
Design services in progress at accumulated costs.......	$17,101	$ 38,510
Modular housing units (lower of cost–Fifo method, or market).....................................	27,029	57,000
Real estate projects at cost........................	8,810	134,162
	$52,940	$229,672

Note 4–Deferred Research and Development Costs. The $183,019 as of December 31, 1973 and the $56,000 model home and site (a total of $239,019) was planned to be amortized at $100 per unit sold for a period not to exceed five years. During 1974, the subsidiary involved changed its operation from manufacturing modular homes to the sale of systems and the management of a plant, as the agent of another company, the agreement with which provided EDS a fee as consideration for use of the technology EDS had developed. During 1974, deferred R & D was increased to $272,248 as a result of capitalization of the excess of actual cost of the units sold over 80 percent of the sales price thereof. A portion of the sales price of future units sold will continue to be applied as recovery of development costs, together with amortization over a period not to exceed five years.

Note 5–Taxes on Income. Deferred taxes on income (current and noncurrent) represent the tax effect of differences in reporting for financial statements from those used for the federal and state income tax returns. These differences result primarily from the use for income tax purposes of the cash basis of accounting by certain subsidiaries, the installment basis of reporting gross profit on certain real estate sales and the current deduction of research and development costs.

Note 8–Net Income per Common and Common Equivalent Share. Earnings per common and common equivalent share is based upon the weighted-average number of shares outstanding after giving retroactive effect to the 7,700 for 1 stock split in September 1973 plus the dilutive effect of the exercise of all of the stock options and warrants outstanding. The number of shares used in the calculation was 798,742 (1973) and 999,356 (1974).

When she examined the financial statements in the annual report, she had some difficulty in assessing EDS's financial condition. If she were to sell NDG for EDS stock, she wanted to have a clearer picture of EDS's "health." Accordingly, she called her younger sister, who was currently working on an M.B.A. degree, and asked her to see what could be gleaned from EDS's financial statements (Exhibits 1–4). Ms. Sterling also called her stockbroker, and learned that EDS stock, which was traded "over-the-counter," was currently quoted at $4 bid—$4½ asked.

Question

As Ms. Sterling, what questions concerning EDS's financial situation would you want to ask Mr. Baker?

CHAPTER 13

UNDERSTANDING FINANCIAL STATEMENTS

The first section of this chapter describes information contained in annual reports that is in addition to the financial statements information that has been discussed in preceding chapters. The next section reviews the criteria and concepts that were introduced in Chapters 1, 2, and 3, bringing together amplifications and qualifications to the concepts that have been developed in later chapters. Alternative treatments of accounting transactions that are possible within the framework of these concepts are described. Finally, the chapter discusses the meaning of information contained in financial statements, in view of all the above.

ADDITIONAL INFORMATION IN ANNUAL REPORTS

The annual report that a company prepares for the use of shareholders, financial analysts, and other outside parties contains important information in addition to the three financial statements that have been described in earlier chapters. At its option, a company may include in the report information about products, personnel, manufacturing facilities, or any other topics. A company is *required* to include three other types of information: the auditor's opinion, notes to the financial statements, and comparative data.

The Auditor's Opinion

All companies whose securities are listed on an organized stock exchange, nearly every company that sells its securities to the public, most other corporations, and a great many unincorporated businesses have

382

their financial statements and the accounting records from which they are produced examined by independent, outside public accountants called auditors. Usually, these are certified public accountants (CPAs), who meet prescribed professional standards and who have received a certificate or license to practice from the state in which they do business. The auditor's examination relates only to the financial statements, including notes, and not to other material that may appear in a company's annual report. The results of the auditor's examination are reported in a letter which ordinarily consists of two paragraphs, a scope paragraph and an opinion paragraph.

SCOPE PARAGRAPH. The paragraph describing the scope of the auditor's examination reads as follows:

We have examined the accompanying balance sheet of _____ Company as of (date) and the related statements of income and changes in financial position for the year then ended. Our examination was made in accordance with generally accepted auditing standards and accordingly included such tests of the accounting records and such auditing procedures as we considered necessary in the circumstances.

The key words in this paragraph are: *such tests . . . as we considered necessary*. They signify that the auditor, not the management, is responsible for deciding on how thorough a job is required. The management cannot ask the auditor, for example, to "make as much of an audit as you can for $10,000." If the auditor's freedom is abridged in any material way, he is required to indicate this fact by adding to the above paragraph, "except . . ." Such exceptions are rare.

In making their examination, auditors no longer rely primarily on a detailed rechecking of the analysis, journalizing, and posting of each transaction; rather, they satisfy themselves that the accounting system is designed to ensure that the data are processed properly. This reliance on the system is relatively new. Up until 1949, the U.S. General Accounting Office received a copy of every one of the millions of accounting documents generated annually in the federal government and, theoretically at least, checked each of them for propriety and accuracy. When the General Accounting Office changed its emphasis to a reliance on properly designed accounting systems, it not only was able to release several *thousand* employees but also was able to do a better auditing job by concentrating its efforts on checking the reliability of accounting systems and by examining the relatively few important or unusual transactions which previously had tended to be buried in the detail.

In addition to the examination of the adequacy of the accounting system, the auditors make test checks of how well it is working, they verify the existence of assets (for example, they usually are present at the taking of physical inventory, they ask a sample of customers to *confirm* or verify the accuracy of the accounts receivable shown for each of them, they check bank balances, and so on), and they make sure that especially important or nonroutine transactions are recorded in conformity with generally accepted accounting principles. The observation of inventories and the confirmation of receivables is regarded as being so important that the omission of either of these tests must be specifically mentioned in the "scope" paragraph of the opinion.

These checks provide reasonable assurance that errors have not been committed through oversight or carelessness and that there has been no fraudulent activity. They do not provide absolute assurance, however, for almost any system can be beaten. Although spectacular frauds receive much publicity, they occur in only a tiny fraction of companies.

OPINION PARAGRAPH. The other paragraph in the auditor's letter ordinarily reads as follows:

In our opinion, the accompanying financial statements present fairly the financial position of _____ Company at (date) and the results of its operations and changes in financial position for the year then ended, in conformity with generally accepted accounting principles applied on a basis consistent with that of the preceding year.

The three significant points in this opinion are indicated by the words: (1) *present fairly*, (2) *in conformity with generally accepted accounting principles*, and (3) *applied on a consistent basis*.

FAIRNESS. The word *fairly* should be contrasted with the word *accurately*. The auditor does not say that the reported net income is the only, or the most accurate, figure that could have been reported. He says, rather, that of the many alternative principles that could have been used, those actually selected by the management do give a fair picture in the circumstances relevant to the particular company. This contrast between "fairness" and "accuracy" is further emphasized by the fact that the auditor's report is called an "opinion" rather than a "certificate." The auditor does not certify the accuracy of the report; instead, he gives his professional opinion that it is fair.

Many people have the impression that the auditor is responsible for *preparing* the financial statements. This is not so. Preparation of the statements is the responsibility of the management, not of the auditor. When two or more alternative practices are permitted by generally accepted accounting principles, and either is "fair" (which is of course an ambiguous criterion), management, not the auditor, decides which one is to be used. In the opinion, the auditor does not state that management has necessarily made the *best* choice among alternative principles, but only that the choice made by management was an acceptable one.

PRINCIPLES. The second phrase means that each of the accounting principles used in preparing the statements is "generally accepted." As we have noted, for many transactions there are several generally accepted alternative treatments, and the auditor's opinion merely states that the management has selected one of these. If the Financial Accounting Standards Board (or its predecessor bodies) has issued a pronouncement on a certain point, this constitutes a "generally accepted accounting principle." Rule 203 of the AICPA Code of Professional Ethics states that no departures from such pronouncements can be regarded as a generally accepted accounting principle "unless the member can demonstrate that due to unusual circumstances the financial statements would otherwise have been misleading." Such circumstances are exceedingly rare. If they do exist, the report must describe the departure, give the reasons for making it, and show its approximate effect on the reported results. Thus, for all practical purposes, generally accepted accounting principles are what the FASB says they are.

CONSISTENCY. The third point, *consistency*, refers, it will be noted, to consistency with practices followed in *the preceding year*. It does not mean *internal* consistency, that is, it does not mean that the principle used to measure fixed assets is consistent with that used to measure inventory, or even that each corporation in a consolidated enterprise follows practices that are consistent with those of other corporations in the same enterprise. The consistency doctrine is nevertheless of great significance because it does mean that the figures for one year are comparable with those of the preceding year, and assurance of such comparability is essential if meaningful comparisons are to be made.

QUALIFIED OPINIONS. The paragraphs quoted above constitute a *clean* opinion. If the auditor cannot make these statements, he gives his reasons, and the opinion is then called a *qualified* opinion. There are two general types of qualified opinions. In one type, the auditor uses the phrase "subject to . . ." and then describes a circumstance that prevents him from giving a clean opinion. Such a circumstance may be uncertainty as to the outcome of some event, such as a pending lawsuit, which may have a material effect on the company's condition. In the other type, the auditor uses the phrase "except for . . ."; this qualification is used when a generally accepted principle is not adhered to. Before making a qualified opinion, the auditor will of course discuss the situation with the management of the company, and in many cases the management is willing to change the financial statements rather than having an exception reported.

Notes to Financial Statements

The balance sheet, income statement, and statement of changes in financial position are accompanied by a set of notes that amplify and clarify information given in the statements themselves. These notes are an integral part of the statements.

One of these notes, usually the first, summarizes the accounting policies that the company has followed in preparing the statements. Among other topics, this note usually describes the basis of consolidation if the statements are consolidated statements, depreciation methods, policies with respect to the amortization of intangible assets, inventory methods, and policies regarding the recognition of revenues.

Other notes give details on long-term debt, including the maturity date and interest rate of each bond issue; a description of stock option plans and other management incentive plans; and the total rental expense and the minimum amount of rent that must be paid in the future under current commitments.[1] Additional detail on the composition of inventories and of fixed assets, the amount of revenues and/or the amount of income earned by each of the main segments of the company may also be reported. Many annual reports have several pages of these notes.

Full Disclosure

A fundamental accounting principle is that the financial statements and the accompanying notes must contain a full disclosure of material financial information. This includes not only information known as of the balance sheet date but also information which may come to light after the end of the accounting period which may affect the information contained in the financial statements. For example, if in February 1975 one of the company's important plants were destroyed by fire, this fact should be disclosed, even though the fixed asset amount on the December 31, 1974, balance sheet was correct as of that time.

There is not general agreement as to what constitutes full disclosure. In general, if an item of economic information would cause an informed investor to appraise the company differently than he would appraise it without that item of information, it should be disclosed. Clearly, there is room for disagreement as to what such items are, but in recent court decisions an increasingly broad view has been taken of disclosure requirements, and these decisions have resulted in a corresponding increase in the amount of information disclosed in annual reports.

Comparative Statements

In addition to the financial statements for the current year, the annual report must also contain comparable information for at least the preceding year. Many companies also include summaries of important balance sheet and income statement items for a period of 5 to 10 years.

The information from prior years that is published in the current annual report is usually the same information as that originally published. There are some circumstances, however, in which information for prior

---

[1] This is required by APB *Opinion No. 31* (June 1973).

years is restated. If the accounting entity is changed, either by the acquisition of other companies or by the disposition of segments of the business, the numbers for prior years are restated so that they include data for the entity as it currently exists.

EXAMPLE: If the Cameron Company in 1975 acquired Subsidiary A and disposed of one of its own subsidiaries, B, the financial statements of 1974 and earlier years would be restated by adding the financial data for Subsidiary A and subtracting those of Subsidiary B.

The FASB also requires that certain changes in accounting principles be reflected by restating the financial statement information for prior years.[2] These include: (1) a change from the Lifo method of inventory to another method: (2) a change in the method of accounting for long-term contracts from the completed-contract method to the percentage-of-completion method, or vice versa; and (3) a change in certain accounting practices of extractive industries.

With these few exceptions, prior year statements are not restated. Instead, when a company makes a change in its accounting practices that affects the net income reported in prior periods, the *cumulative* effect of this change on the net income of all prior periods is calculated, and this amount is reported on the *current* year's income statement. When a company has reason to believe that estimates that influenced the reported net income in prior years were incorrect (such as when subsequent events show that the estimated service life of depreciable assets was too long or too short), it does not go back and correct the financial statements for the prior years. These rather strict restrictions on recasting the data in prior year financial statements exist because of the FASB's belief that public confidence in the financial statements would be lessened if they were subject to frequent restatement as time went on.

SEC Reports

In addition to the annual report to its shareholders, every company that is under the jurisdiction of the Securities and Exchange Commission must file an annual report with the SEC. This report is filed on SEC Form 10–K, and is therefore known as the 10–K report. In general, the financial data in this report are consistent with, but in somewhat more detail than, the data in the annual report. The SEC requires additional data on lease commitments, on revenues and earnings by business segments, on short-term borrowing transactions, and on other matters. If the company changes auditors, it must assure the SEC that this change was not made because the former auditors refused to give a "clean" opinion on a controversial matter.

---

[2] APB *Opinion No. 20* (July 1971).

The Securities and Exchange Commission has statutory authority to prescribe the accounting principles that are to be followed in reports filed with it. It has decided, however, to rely on the Financial Accounting Standards Board for pronouncements of accounting policies.

The SEC also requires that certain financial data be included in the notice of annual meeting sent to all shareholders. These include the compensation of each top executive, and the compensation of officers and directors as a group.

In addition to their annual reports, companies under the jurisdiction of the SEC publish an interim income statement each quarter. This statement is not audited. It is a brief summary of the principal revenue and expense items for the quarter, prepared in accordance with the same accounting principles that the company uses in its annual report.

REVIEW OF CRITERIA AND CONCEPTS

In Chapter 1 we listed three criteria that governed financial accounting concepts and principles, and in Chapters 2 and 3 we described 10 basic concepts. It is appropriate here that we consider these criteria and concepts again with the benefit of the additional material that has been discussed in the intervening chapters.

Criteria

There are three basic accounting criteria:

1. Accounting information should be *relevant*. Accounting reports should provide information that describes as accurately and completely as possible the status of assets and equities, the results of operations, and changes in financial position.

2. Accounting information should be *objective*. The amounts reported should not be biased by the subjective judgments of management.

3. Accounting information should be *feasible*. Its value should exceed the cost of collecting and reporting it.

There is an inevitable conflict between the criterion of *relevance* on the one hand and the criteria of *objectivity* and *feasibility* on the other. Accounting concepts and principles reflect a workable compromise between these opposing forces. Failure to appreciate this fact is behind the feeling of many of the uninitiated that "accounting doesn't make sense."

Of the many examples of this conflict, perhaps the most clear-cut is that relating to the measurement of fixed assets. In general, the most relevant rule for stating fixed assets, the rule that would provide readers of financial statements with what they really want to know, would be: state fixed assets at their market value, what they are really worth. But such a rule would be neither objective nor feasible in most situations.

The market value of assets in a going concern depends upon the future earnings that will be generated with these assets. In special circumstances, outside experts can be relied upon to make estimates of future earnings, but there are by no means enough qualified appraisers in the country to make such estimates annually for all companies. Even if there were enough of them, the appraisers would be forced to rely heavily on the judgment of the management, because management is in by far the best position to know about future earnings prospects. To rely on the opinions of management, however, would introduce a highly subjective element. Shareholders, prospective shareholders, banks, and others use financial statements, in part, to find out how well management has done. It would be highly unrealistic to expect that management would make unbiased estimates under these circumstances.

At the other extreme, the most objective and feasible rules for measuring fixed assets would be either (1) state fixed assets at acquisition cost and report them as an asset at cost until they are disposed of, or (2) write them off the books immediately. In most cases either rule would be perfectly simple to apply and would involve little, if any, subjective judgment. But such rules would prohibit accounting from reporting on the income statement the expense called depreciation, which represents an estimate of the amount of asset cost that is properly charged to the operations of each accounting period. A net income figure that includes such an estimate of fixed asset expiration is much more relevant for most purposes than one that omits depreciation altogether.

So accounting takes a middle ground. Assets are originally booked at cost, which is an objectively determined amount in most cases, and this cost is charged as an expense in each accounting period over the useful life of the asset. The annual depreciation charge is an estimate, and any of several ways of making this estimate is permitted, but the number of permitted alternatives is small, and freedom to tamper with the estimates is further restricted by the concept of consistency.

Concepts

Ten basic financial accounting concepts were stated in Chapters 2 and 3. Others would classify and describe the basic concepts somewhat differently. The FASB currently (1975) is developing a statement of concepts, but until this statement is published, concepts must be deduced from principles and practices. The 10 concepts are repeated below, and amplifications and qualifications are given for certain of them.

1. *Money measurement. Accounting records only those facts that can be expressed in monetary terms.*

In the accounts, there are no exceptions to this concept, although nonmonetary information is often provided in the annual report. Assets are recorded at the number of dollars (or dollar equivalents) paid to acquire them. Although the purchasing power of the monetary unit changes because of inflation, accounting does not reflect these changes in purchasing power, except in supplementary financial statements which only a few firms publish. Thus, the monetary unit used in accounting is *not* a unit of constant purchasing power.

2. *Entity. Accounts are kept for entities as distinguished from the persons associated with those entities.*

In small businesses, particularly unincorporated businesses, some problems arise in distinguishing between transactions affecting the entity and transactions affecting the owners. In parent companies that have subsidiaries, there may be important problems involved in defining the entity for which consolidated financial statements are prepared. In general, a subsidiary is considered to be part of the consolidated entity if the parent owns more than 50 percent of its common stock, but there are some exceptions, as described in Chapter 10.

3. *Going Concern. Accounting assumes that an entity will continue to exist indefinitely and that it is not about to be sold.*

There is one important qualification to this statement; namely, if there is strong evidence that the entity will *not* continue in existence, the financial statements are prepared on a different set of principles than those described here; that is, amounts are recorded at their estimated liquidation value. This concept is the essential explanation of the fact that for most assets accounting does not attempt to keep track of changes in market value.

4. *Cost. An asset is ordinarily entered in the accounts at the amount paid to acquire it, and this cost, rather than market value, is the basis for subsequent accounting for the asset.*

There are important qualifications to this concept. In some transactions, the amount paid for the asset cannot be measured, and a substitute, such as the market value of the asset itself, is used. If the amount paid is obviously less than the market value of the asset, as in the case of donated assets, the asset is recorded at fair market value. There are differences of opinion as to how the cost of products manufactured by the company should be measured, as noted in Chapter 6.

Also, market value does affect the subsequent accounting for certain types of assets. Inventory and marketable securities are reported at the lower of their cost or their current market value. Certain investments are reported at the book value of the company whose stock is owned (i.e., the equity method), rather than at cost. These are all exceptions to the general rule, however. Ordinarily, asset accounting deals with cost, and the accounts reflect the write-off of cost, rather than changes in market value.

5. *Dual Aspect.* *The total amount of assets equals the total amount of equities.*

There are absolutely no exceptions to this concept. It is important not only because, mechanically, it lessens the possibility of making errors in recording transactions, but also because, conceptually, it aids in understanding the effect of transactions on a business. The fact that "for every debit there must be a credit" helps one to recognize both aspects of a transaction.

6. *Conservatism.* *An asset is recorded at the lower of two reasonably possible amounts, or a transaction is recorded in such a way that the owners' equity is lower than it otherwise would be.*

This concept has a certain amount of vagueness, and its application varies from time to time and from company to company. It explains why certain assets are recorded at the lower of cost or market value. It also explains why the FASB decided in 1974 that most research and development costs should be expensed in the current period; the Board concluded that the future benefits to be derived from these expenditures were too uncertain to warrant capitalizing them. They arrived at this conclusion despite the admitted fact that certain research and development costs benefit future periods and therefore conceptually are assets.

7. *Realization.* *Revenues are generally recognized in the period in which they are realized, that is, in the period in which goods are shipped to customers or in which services are rendered, and in an amount that is reasonably certain to be collected.*

Many problems arise in deciding on both the period in which the revenue for a given transaction should be recognized and the amount of such revenue. In unusual circumstances, the amount of revenue recognized may reflect a considerable amount of optimism as to future earnings, but the auditors will ordinarily detect and call attention to revenues whose realization is not reasonably certain. Chapter 5 is suggested as a refresher for exceptions and clarifications of this concept.

8. *Matching.* *Costs become expenses in an accounting period (1) when there is a direct association between costs and revenues, (2) when costs are directly associated with activities of the period itself, or (3) when costs cannot be associated with revenues of any future period.*

Differences of opinion about the application of this concept and of the realization concept are at the heart of most accounting controversies. We shall discuss these further in connection with our discussion of the income statement.

9. *Consistency.* *Once a company has decided on a certain method of accounting for a given class of events, it will use the same method of accounting for all subsequent events of the same character unless it has a sound reason to do otherwise.*

This concept is always adhered to in theory, but the practical problem is to decide when a "sound reason" to make a change exists. Although the desire to increase the amount of net income reported in the current period is at the root of certain changes in method, this is definitely not an acceptable reason for making the change. Nevertheless, some companies make a change for this purpose, and devise other reasons to justify it.

10. *Materiality. A departure from other concepts is permitted, in the interest of simplicity, when the effect of such a departure is not material.*

To the original statement of this concept, we have now added another aspect of materiality; namely, that all material information must be disclosed. In both this and the original sense, the problem is to decide what is material. The Securities and Exchange Commission has given guides for certain types of transactions, and the Financial Accounting Standards Board is (1975) attempting to develop more specific guidelines for overall use. Considerable judgment is, and probably always will be, necessary in applying this concept, however.

Importance of the Concepts

The many practices and procedures described in earlier chapters were amplifications and applications of the basic concepts, rather than additions to them. As a matter of practice, for example, accumulated depreciation is shown in a separate account rather than being credited directly to the asset account, but the basic idea of depreciation accounting is nevertheless in accordance with the concepts that assets are recorded at cost and costs are matched against revenue.

Any conceivable transaction, provided that it is clearly described, can be analyzed in terms of its effect on the assets and equities of the business in accordance with the basic accounting concepts. For an extremely large fraction of the transactions in a typical business, the analysis is simple: for a cash sale, debit Cash and credit Sales; for receipts from a credit customer, credit Accounts Receivable and debit Cash.

In a relatively small number of transactions, the analysis is difficult. For some of these, a correct answer can be found. For example, a number of transactions involve a credit to Cash or Accounts Payable for the purchase of something. The question is whether the offsetting debit is to an asset account or to an expense account, and the answer to this question depends on whether the business has, or has not, acquired a property right that has material value beyond the end of the accounting period. In still other cases, there is no unique "right" answer: accounting principles permit any of several treatments. In these cases, accountants simply use their best judgment.

Many of these situations require judgment because of inevitable uncertainties about the future. How long will the building really last? Is a decline in the market value of inventory only temporary, or should the inventory be written down? There are no unequivocal answers to such questions, and hence no way of arriving at a result with which everyone would agree.

Misconceptions about Concepts

Some of the basic concepts are intuitively sensible: for example, the idea that accounting data are expressed in monetary terms. Certain concepts, however, are rather different from the impression that the typical layman has about them.

Undoubtedly the greatest misconception relates to the cost concept. To the layman, it seems only reasonable that the accountant should report the *value* of assets—what they are really worth—rather than merely to trace the flow of costs. If he has had a course in economics, he knows that the economist discusses resources in terms of their current values. The layman finds it difficult to believe that the balance sheet is not, even approximately, a statement showing what the business is worth, especially when he sees on many balance sheets an item labeled "net worth." And even if he eventually recognizes that the balance sheet does not in fact report current values, he criticizes accounting and accountants for not being able to devise a way of doing this.

A related misconception is the layman's failure to appreciate the significance of the going-concern concept. If one accepts the idea that the productive assets are held not for sale but rather for their future usefulness, then one sees that the current sales value of these assets is not of overriding significance.

The layman also finds the matching concept a difficult one to comprehend. In his personal life, he knows that when he makes an expenditure to the grocer, to the service station, and so on, he is that much "out of pocket." He has difficulty in understanding the fact that many business expenditures are merely the exchange of one asset for another, with the business getting as much as it gives up. Expenses occur in the time period when costs expire—when they are used up—and this time period is not necessarily the same as the time period in which the expenditure is made.

Those who do understand the basic concepts do not necessarily agree with all of them. The accounting profession is constantly involved in debates over one or another of the currently accepted principles. Since they are not laws of nature, they are subject to change, and occasionally they are changed. At the same time, the *user* of accounting information must do the best he can with the situation as it exists. He may wish that the principles were different, but as he reads an accounting report he needs to know how it *was* prepared, not how it might have been prepared.

ACCOUNTING ALTERNATIVES

Notwithstanding the basic concepts and generally accepted accounting principles, there are considerable differences in the way a given transaction may be recorded. In part, these differences result from requirements imposed by regulatory agencies in certain industries, but more importantly, they result from (1) the latitude that exists within generally accepted accounting principles, and (2) judgments that must be made in applying a given principle.

Regulatory requirements

Certain groups of companies are required to adhere to principles that are not necessarily consistent with those recommended by the FASB. Railroads and other common carriers follow rules prescribed by the Interstate Commerce Commission; public utilities, by the Federal Power Commission; banks and insurance companies, by state regulatory agencies. Government agencies, colleges and universities, hospitals, and other nonprofit organizations follow practices that in important respects are inconsistent with the principles described above. In approving the financial statements of such bodies, the auditor does not state that the statements are prepared in accordance with "generally accepted principles"; rather, he says they are "consistent with practice followed in the industry," or words to that effect.

> EXAMPLE: Railroads do not depreciate the cost of their tracks. The asset account shows original cost for as long as the track is used, except that original cost is increased if track of a better quality is installed. Replacements are charged as an expense in the year in which the replacement is made. Thus, net income can be significantly reduced in a year in which extensive track replacements are made. Correspondingly, net income can be made to look good by not replacing track.

INCOME TAX PRINCIPLES.   Principles governing the calculation of income for federal income tax purposes are basically the same as the principles of financial accounting; that is, in general, taxable income is the difference between realized revenue and expired cost. There are, however, important differences, some of which are as follows:

First, taxpayers may, if they wish, disregard the accrual concept and elect to be taxed on the difference between cash receipts and cash expenditures. Many small businesses do this.

Second, the depletion allowance computed for tax purposes bears no relation to the principles of financial accounting.

Third, in taxation, a distinction is made between ordinary income and capital gains, with the latter being taxed less heavily than the former. In financial accounting, the distinction, although present, is not so important since both ordinary income and capital gains usually enter into the measurement of net income.

Fourth, the accrual basis of accounting is not completely followed in income tax accounting. For example, prepaid rent is counted as revenue in income tax accounting, but not in financial accounting.

Finally, as already pointed out, although the principles are basically the same, a company usually applies them differently in its tax accounting and its financial accounting. It does this primarily by changing the *timing*, rather than the *amount*, of revenues and expenses. Thus, for tax purposes, a company usually reports costs as early as it legitimately can and defers revenue until as late as it legitimately can. For accounting purposes, it tends to report costs in later time periods and revenues in earlier time periods.

Latitude in the Principles

In his Inventory,[3] Grady lists some 35 topics on which alternative treatments are permitted within generally accepted accounting principles, and gives from two to eight alternatives for each. These topics range in importance from cash discounts on sales, which may be accounted for either at the time the sale is made or the time the receivable is collected, to the basic question of whether a merger is to be recorded as a purchase or a pooling of interests.

Examples that have been mentioned in earlier chapters are as follows: inventory can be recorded at Lifo, at Fifo, or at average cost, or some parts of inventory may be handled one way and some the other; inventory cost may or may not include inward transportation, storage costs, handling costs, or cash discounts on purchases. Assets may be depreciated by any systematic and rational method. Revenue on long-term contracts may be recognized either by the percentage-of-completion method or the completed-contract method. Revenue on installment sales may be recognized either on the installment basis or when the sale is made. These alternatives exist, regardless of the circumstances; that is, a company can choose whatever alternative it prefers.

EXAMPLES:

1. According to Stanley P. Porter, companies accounting for 13 percent of sales of all petroleum companies charge costs incurred for oil

---

[3] Paul Grady, *Inventory of Generally Accepted Accounting Principles* (AICPA Accounting Research Study No. 7, 1965), pp. 373–79.

and gas exploration to expense, and the other petroleum companies capitalize these costs. Since the total expenditure for exploration is about $15 billion per year, this difference in practice is highly significant.[4]

2. In its 1973 ending balance sheet, Western Union Corporation capitalized $2.2 million of cost as start-up costs for a new subsidiary, *Gift America*. It argued that these costs should be matched against revenues that were expected to be earned by *Gift America* in future years. Its auditors disagreed with this treatment, on the grounds that the future profitability of the operation was too uncertain. The amount of net income reported in 1973 was $28.1 million.

Judgment in the Application of Principles

Within generally accepted accounting principles, there is much room for judgment in analyzing specific transactions. In part, these matters reflect differences in personal opinion as to what is or is not *material* and as to the importance that should be attached to the *conservatism* concept. In attempting to describe a complex situation, such differences are inevitable. In part, the differences reflect customs that have grown up in particular companies or industries.

Implications of These Differences

The existence of diversity in accounting practice should not be considered as a reason for criticizing accountants or accounting. The fundamental fact is that a business is a complex organism. There is no conceivable way of prescribing a uniform set of rules by means of which the significant facts about that organism can be reduced to a few pages of numbers, any more than there is any way of formulating a standard set of rules for biographers. Standard procedures for listing physical characteristics, birth dates, marital status, and certain other information about a person can easily be specified, but these details do not really describe the person completely. The accuracy and usefulness of the "picture" of a person that emerges from a biography depends on the author's skill and judgment in the collection, analysis, and presentation of information about his subject. So it is with financial statements.

Nor should the existence of diversity lead to frustration on the part of the user. The *consistency* concept prevents diversity from becoming chaos. Although Company A may follow practices that differ from those of other companies, Company A ordinarily follows the same practices

---

[4] *The Wall Street Journal*, April 28, 1972.

year after year, or if it changes, the doctrine of consistency requires that it disclose the change. Thus its statements are likely to be comparable with one another from year to year. Also, although railroads use rules that are different from those used by industrial companies, railroad A is likely to use approximately the same rules as railroad B, and thus the two can be compared (with some notable exceptions).

Inherent Limitations

In addition to the points noted above, it is important to remember that accounting has inherent limitations. The two most important limitations—limitations which no foreseeable improvement in accounting practice can overcome—are (1) accounting reports are necessarily monetary, and (2) they are necessarily influenced by estimates of future events.

Accounting reports are limited to information that can be expressed in monetary terms. Nothing in the accounts explicitly describes the ability of the company's personnel, the effectiveness of its organization, the impact of outside forces, or other nonmonetary information that is vital to the complete understanding of a business.

Some accounting numbers are influenced by future events which cannot conceivably be foreseen; these numbers are necessarily estimates. The depreciation expense of the current period, for example, depends partly on how long the assets will be used in the future. The real significance of accounts receivable and the related item of sales revenue cannot be assessed until the number of credit customers who will not pay their bills is known. The actual value of inventory depends on what the merchandise can be sold for in the future. The possible impacts of contingent future events, such as the results of pending or threatened litigation, retroactive agreements on wage rates, and redetermination of profits on contracts, are not shown in the financial statements, although if material they should appear in a footnote.

In accounting, one refers to the *measurement* of income rather than to the *determination* of income. To determine is "to fix conclusively and authoritatively"; accounting cannot do this. A measurement, on the other hand, is an approximation, according to some agreed-upon measuring stick, and this is what accounting sets out to do.

MEANING OF THE FINANCIAL STATEMENTS

In preceding chapters we have discussed in detail the treatment of specific items that are reported on the financial statements. With this discussion as background, we shall now attempt to summarize the meaning of each statement as a whole.

The Income Statement

The income statement is the dominant financial statement in the sense that when it comes to a choice between a fair income statement presentation and a fair balance sheet presentation, the decision is usually made in favor of the former. For example, those who advocate the Lifo inventory method do so in the belief that it provides a better measure of income than does the Fifo method, although they know full well that it can result in unrealistically low inventory amounts on the balance sheet. Many balance sheet items are simply the offsetting debits or credits for entries that were designed to measure revenues or expenses properly on the income statement. The deferred income tax item is perhaps the most notable example; although recorded as a liability, it does not in fact represent an obligation.

The income statement measures the changes in retained earnings that have occurred during the accounting period for whatever reason, except for the payment of dividends and certain other owners' equity transactions. It does not necessarily reflect only the more or less recurring results of normal operations since it includes, in addition to the results of normal operations, extraordinary transactions, the effect of accounting changes, the loss or gain on the disposal of assets, and even the loss or gain on the disposal of a major division.

In the majority of companies the amount of revenues realized from the sale of goods and services can be measured within fairly close limits. Adjustments to gross revenue are necessary to provide for uncollectible accounts, warranty costs, and similar items, but the proper amount of such adjustments often can be estimated within a narrow range. In some companies, such as those which sell on an installment basis, the amount of revenue that should be recognized is more difficult to estimate.

Usually, the appropriate amounts of expenses that should be deducted from revenues are more difficult to measure than are the revenue items. Judgments about these matters can have an important influence on net income.

One important source of difficulty is the distinction between capital costs, product costs, and expenses. The effect on the income of the current period of expenditures made during that period depends significantly on how these expenditures are classified. The difference is diagrammed in Illustration 13–1. Consider, for example, the expenditure of $1,000 for labor services. If the labor cost is incurred for selling, general, or administrative activities it is an expense, and the entire $1,000 affects income of the current period. If the labor cost is incurred in manufacturing a product, it is a product cost, and the $1,000 affects income only in the period in which the product is sold. (The diagram assumes that 40 percent of the products are sold in the current year.) If the labor cost is

Illustration 13–1

EFFECT ON INCOME OF ALTERNATIVE COST PRACTICES

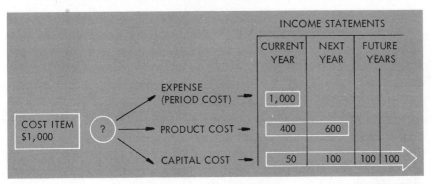

incurred in building a fixed asset, it is capitalized as part of the cost of the asset, and it affects net income over a succession of future periods, as the cost is depreciated. Wide latitude exists as to which expenditures are to be capitalized and which are to be expensed, and for those items that are capitalized, the amount to be charged as expense in a given period can vary widely depending on the estimate of service life and the method of depreciation, depletion, or amortization that is used.

EFFECT OF INFLATION. The expenses reported on the income statement are measured in terms of the acquisition cost of the resources used. In a period of inflation, acquisition cost is less than the current cost of the same resources, and the amount of net income reported may therefore overstate the success of the business as measured in terms of current costs. This is particularly so in the case of depreciation expense, which may greatly understate the current cost of fixed assets used during the period since it is derived from asset amounts that were booked when prices were much lower. For this reason, net income is not an amount that is available for distribution to the shareholders. Part of the reported net income must be thought of as an amount necessary to replace existing assets with higher cost assets.

EXAMPLE: Assume a company owns a single asset acquired in 1964 at a cost of $1,000,000, with a service life of ten years. For simplicity, assume no other costs. If the business earns revenue of $150,000 a year, its income will be $50,000 a year after $100,000 annual depreciation expense (disregarding income taxes). Over the 10-year period, its income will total $500,000. It might appear that the company could pay out this $500,000 in dividends, and replace the asset when necessary with the other $1,000,000 of revenue that was earned. If the cost of a replacement asset in 1974 has risen to $1,300,000, however, this policy won't work. The only way the company can continue to operate, short of raising additional capital, is to regard $300,000 of its retained earnings as an amount necessary to replace assets.

Statement of Changes in Financial Position

The statement of changes in financial position is a derived statement in the sense that it is prepared from data originally collected for reporting on the balance sheet or income statement. It shows the sources of additional working capital (or cash) that the business obtained during the period, and the purposes for which this additional working capital (or cash) was used. The information on this statement is not nearly so much affected by judgments about the capitalization of assets and the write-off of expenses as is the income statement. For example, the choices of depreciation method and service life can have a significant effect on net income, but they have no effect on the statement of changes in financial position because the amount of depreciation charged is neither a source nor a use of working capital (or cash). This is the principal reason that financial analysts like the statement of financial position. It is much more definite, much less subject to judgmental decisions and to manipulation. It does not, however, show how net income was earned, and since net income is the best overall measure of how well the business has performed during the period, the SCFP is not a substitute for the income statement.

The Balance Sheet

In a very broad sense, the balance sheet can be viewed as a statement of resources owned by a business and of the sources of the funds used to acquire these resources. Considering the individual balance sheet items, however, there is no single overall characterization that fits all of them. Rather, the balance sheet must be viewed as a collection of several types of items, with the amounts for each type being reported under different concepts than the amounts reported for the other types, and the whole being tied together only in the mechanical sense that the sum of the debit balances equals the sum of the credit balances. In terms of the method of measurement used, the principal types of balance sheet items are (1) monetary assets and liabilities, (2) inventories and marketable securities, (3) unexpired costs, and (4) other equities.

MONETARY ITEMS. These items include cash and other assets that represent a specific monetary claim against some external party and liabilities that represent a specific monetary obligation to some external party. Accounts Receivable is a monetary asset. The amount that each customer owes is definite, and it is usually possible to estimate the amount of uncollectible accounts within fairly close limits. Monetary assets are reported at essentially their current cash equivalent, and monetary liabilities (which include most liabilities) are reported at the current cash equivalent of the obligation.

INVENTORIES AND MARKETABLE SECURITIES. These items are reported at the lower of cost or market value. Except for the recognition of market value when it is below cost, inventories are similar to items in the next category, unexpired costs.

UNEXPIRED COSTS. Fixed assets, intangible assets, prepaid expenses and deferred charges are initially recorded at acquisition cost, and (except for land) are charged off as expenses in a succession of future accounting periods. Amounts reported on a given balance sheet, therefore, are amounts that have not yet been charged off. The balance sheet is their "temporary home" until the time comes for them to appear on an income statement.

OTHER EQUITIES. These include deferred income taxes, which is an item that arises as a consequence of the procedure that matches income tax expense with reported net income, and which definitely is not a claim by the government against the business. They also include the owners' equity section of the balance sheet. The amount shown in this section is strictly a residual. It arises from the net effect of the methods of measurement used for the other items. In particular, for reasons indicated above, the retained earnings amount does not indicate the amount that is available for payment of dividends.

For the balance sheet as a whole, it is approximately correct to state that, disregarding writedowns to market, the asset side shows the cash or cash equivalents of certain resources owned by the business and the unexpired cost of resources which the entity expects to use in future accounting periods. The equities side shows the sources from which the funds used to acquire these resources were obtained.

SUMMARY

In addition to the financial statements, the annual report contains the auditor's opinion, which shows that the underlying records have been examined and that the information is fair, consistent, and conforms to generally accepted accounting principles. The annual report contains explanatory notes, and may contain additional information about the company.

Although accounting principles are developed in accordance with three criteria and 10 basic concepts, they permit considerable latitude in the treatment of transactions. Also, accounting reports are necessarily influenced by judgments. A business is a complicated organism and no set of numbers can convey an accurate picture of its activities or its status.

The income statement reports revenues and expenses measured in accordance with accounting principles. It does not report the economic "well-offness" of the business, primarily because expenses are measured in terms of historical cost rather than current cost. The statement of changes in financial position is less affected by estimates and a company's practices with respect to the matching concept than is the income statement. Balance sheet items are reported under a variety of measurement concepts.

SUGGESTIONS FOR FURTHER READING

EDWARDS, EDGAR O., and PHILIP W. BELL. *The Theory and Measurement of Business Income.* Los Angeles: University of California Press, 1961.

MOONITZ, MAURICE. *The Basic Postulates of Accounting.* AICPA Accounting Research Study No. 1, 1961.

MORRISSEY, LEONARD E. *Contemporary Accounting Problems.* Englewood Cliffs, N.J.: Prentice-Hall, Inc., 1967.

SPROUSE, ROBERT T., and MAURICE MOONITZ. *A Tentative Set of Broad Accounting Principles for Business Enterprises.* AICPA Accounting Research Study No. 3, 1962.

CASES

CASE 13–1. DEMONSTRATION COMPANY

Mr. Hjalmar J. Thompson, Director of Thompson CPA Review Schools, was considering the use of a new practice set at the end of the two-week introductory portion of his class. The set was designed to meet two principal objectives. First, he hoped that it would serve as a screening device for identifying those students who had failed to grasp some of the more elementary concepts of financial accounting. Second, the set was designed to serve as a vehicle for introducing several new concepts which would be covered in more depth in the next section of his course.

The beginning of the year balance sheet for the Demonstration Company was as follows:

DEMONSTRATION COMPANY

Balance Sheet
As of January 1

Assets		Equities	
Cash	$ 5,000	Accounts payable	$10,000
Inventory	10,000		
Total Current Assets	$15,000	Total Current Liabilities	$10,000
Property, plant, and		Capital stock	$10,000
equipment	$15,000	Retained earnings	5,000
Less: Accum. deprec.	5,000		
Net Fixed Assets	$10,000	Total Owners' Equity	$15,000
Total Assets	$25,000	Total Equities	$25,000

In order to fulfill the objectives set out above, Mr. Thompson listed eleven items as having influenced the year's income statement, statement of changes in financial position, and year-end balance sheet of the Demonstration Company. He intended for these to be treated as the sole data available to a junior accountant preparing to update the books of the company in anticipation of issuing financial statements. The eleven items are described below.

403

1. A three-year insurance policy was purchased on January 1, for cash, at a cost of $300.
2. $10,000 worth of additional inventory was purchased on account during the year.
3. Accounts payable, in the amount of $8,000, were paid during the year.
4. During the course of the year, the following cash costs were incurred and paid:
   (a) Selling and Administrative–$3,000.
   (b) Cost of Preparing Inventory for Sale–$5,000.
5. Net sales for the year amounted to $25,000. Of this amount, $15,000 was collected in cash and $10,000 was outstanding at year end. The inventory sold had a book value of $13,000.
6. The firm borrowed $10,000 on July 1st. The debt was represented by renewable, 10%, 90-day notes. The entire amount was outstanding at year end, while interest of $250 was paid during the first week of October.
7. A customer deposit of $2,000–on merchandise not yet shipped–was received by the company in the fourth quarter.
8. Depreciation in the amount of $1,000 for book purposes and $2,000 for tax purposes was to be taken for the year.
9. An uninsured loss of $3,000 in inventory resulted from an early-morning fire.
10. The company received an out-of-court settlement of $3,000 (net of legal costs) as a result of legal action instituted four years earlier. This related to an anti-trust suit against one of the suppliers to the company. The auditor's opinion on the financial statements of the company four years earlier had been qualified as a result of this lawsuit.
11. The tax rate is, and forever will be, 50 percent on all taxable income.

Mr. Thompson has asked for your cooperation in field testing this practice set. Specifically, you are to complete the following assignment:

1. Prepare journal entries for the year.
2. Set up, and post, a set of T-accounts for use in collecting, summarizing, and rearranging the year's transactions.
3. Prepare a balance sheet for the Demonstration Company as of December 31.
4. Prepare an income statement for the year ending December 31. How will this differ from the income statement submitted with the firm's tax return?
5. Prepare a cash-basis statement of changes in financial position for the year ending December 31.

CASE 13–2. CLOVER LUNCH

Early in 1974, Mr. and Mrs. Robert Matthews decided to go into the restaurant business. Mr. Matthews was dissatisfied with his job as cook in a restaurant, where he earned $3.40 an hour. During July, 1974, the Matthews found a business which seemed to be what they wanted. This was the Clover Lunch, a lunch counter located in Fisher's Department Store, in a working-class section of town. The Clover Lunch was operated under a lease with the department store; only the equipment was actually the property of the operator of the lunchroom. The equipment was old, but Mr. Matthews thought that it was in fairly good condition.

The couple opened negotiations with the operator and quickly reached an agreement to take over the lease and equipment on September 1, and to pay the operator a price of $3,400. Of this price, Mr. Matthews estimated that $1,530 represented the fair value of the equipment. The lease expired on August 31, 1975, and was renewable for three years if Fisher's consented. Under the terms of the lease, Fisher's furnished space, heat, light, and water, and the operators (i.e., the Matthews) paid Fisher's 15 percent of gross receipts as rent.

The Matthews paid the $3,400 from their personal savings account and also transferred $1,700 to a checking account which they opened in the name of Clover Lunch.

Shortly after they started operations, the cooking range broke down. The Matthews thereupon sold the range for $136 (which was approximately its estimated value, as a part of the $1,530) and purchased a new range for $1,360. It was installed immediately, and they paid $204 for its installation. The coffee urn also broke down, but Mr. Matthews was able to repair it himself by working 16 hours one Sunday.

Early in 1975, the Matthews called in a firm which specialized in making out reports for small businesses, and requested financial statements for Clover Lunch for the period ended December 31, 1974. From their cash register and checkbook, they had the following figures:

Cash Receipts:

Cash receipts from customers	$10,914
Sale of cooking range	136
Total Cash Receipts	$11,050

Cash Disbursements:

Food and supplies	$ 4,697
City restaurant license, valid September 1, 1974, to September 1, 1975	75
15 percent rent paid to Fisher's for September, October and November	1,139
New cooking range	1,360
Installation of cooking range	204
Other operating expenses	30
Withdrawals for personal use	1,275
Total Cash Disbursements	$ 8,780

Before going home on December 31, the Matthews had estimated the value of food and supplies then on hand to be about $248 at cost.

Early in January, they paid two bills, the December meat bill of $294 and the bill for the December rent of $498.

The Matthews also explained to the accountant that the cash receipts of $10,914 included $1,240 received from the sale of 124 "coupon books" at $10 each. Each book contained coupons with a face value of $11, which could be used to pay for meals. As of December 31, coupons with a face value of $860 had been used to pay for meals; therefore coupons with a face value of $504 were still outstanding.

Questions

1. Prepare a balance sheet as of December 31, 1974, and an income statement and cash-basis statement of changes in financial position for the four-month period ending December 31, 1974. Explain briefly your treatment of the coupon books and of anything else you believe needs comment.
2. Comment briefly on the significant information revealed by your financial statements.

CASE 13–3.   FAIRMUIR INSTRUMENT CORPORATION

Fairmuir Instrument Corporation sold a line of high-temperature measuring instruments called pyrometers. The principal users of the equipment were steel mills and various metal extraction companies, and Fairmuir's small sales force had concentrated almost exclusively on establishing good relations with these customers. Occasional inquiries and orders came from other sources, such as scientific laboratories, but the company had never actively solicited these markets.

The device in its present form had been developed and put into production in the early 1960s. Essentially it utilized principles which had been known for almost a hundred years, but until the present development the accuracy attainable had fallen short of the requirements of modern industry. The company had introduced no new products until the last quarter of 1974. Effectively, the company had not faced any serious competition in its market area until 1970 and had maintained a stable sales level of around $3 million until that time.

During 1970 a competing product had been introduced to the market. Operating on completely different principles, this device performed substantially the same job as Fairmuir's product and gave similar levels of accuracy. The only major differences were in its useful life (five years) and its purchase price, each of which were about half of those of the Fairmuir product. The lower purchase price was an important sales advantage, and Fairmuir's sales had suffered accordingly. Exhibit 1 gives some of the financial data of Fairmuir Instrument Corporation from 1970 through 1974.

By 1971 the management of Fairmuir realized that without a new product to bolster its faltering sales volume, the company was facing a serious predicament. They therefore began a search for an additional product which would be suited to the capabilities of the company. In 1972 they approached an inventor who held patents for just such a product, with a view to buying the patents. After some negotiation a mutually satisfactory price was reached, and, as part of the agreement, the inventor agreed to join the company and lead the additional development work which was required before a commercial product was ready for marketing.

Exhibit 1

FAIRMUIR INSTRUMENT CORPORATION

Financial Data
As of December 31
(dollar figures in thousands)

	1970	1971	1972	1973	1974
Inventories related to pyrometers.......	$ 791	$ 806	$ 909	$ 805	$ 627
Working capital....................	933	1,021	1,165	1,155	819
Net assets.........................	1,889	1,965	1,995	1,926	1,549
Net sales of pyrometers..............	2,881	2,475	2,025	996	583
Other sales (net).....................	. . .	. . .	. . .	. . .	115
Net income (loss)....................	108	77	67	(91)	(376)

On top of the cost of the patents and the development expenses, the company was faced with substantial start-up costs and required an investment in inventories. The company's financial resources, already adversely affected by the lagging sales of pyrometers, were inadequate without an injection of fresh capital. The company's capital stock was closely held by members of top management and a few of their friends and family members. None of these people was willing to contribute any further capital.

Management believed that the recent poor operating results made it unwise to seek fresh equity capital at that time and they therefore decided that a bank loan was the only feasible recourse. It did not prove an easy matter to find a bank willing to make the required loan, but eventually this was done. In extending the loan the bank imposed several restrictions on the management of Fairmuir, one of these being that a minimum working capital[1] level of $800,000 should be maintained. By the end of

---

[1] Working capital was defined as the difference between current assets and current liabilities.

1974, with the sales of pyrometers still falling and the new product only just introduced to the market, the company was close to defaulting on the requirements of the working capital covenant.

In the 1974 audit, the public accountant was satisfied with all the accounts except for the valuation of the inventories related to pyrometers. Most of this inventory was in good condition, and had been carefully handled and stored. A few items of purchased parts had become obsolete and management had written them down. This represented an insignificant adjustment, however, and the bulk of the inventory was still reported on the company's books at cost. The auditor was not concerned about the physical condition of the inventory, but he had serious reservations as to the marketability of the product, and therefore the realization of the investment through profitable sales. In approaching management on this matter the auditor was aware that a large adjustment would throw the company into default on its loan covenant concerning working capital.

The auditor, Mr. Bill Adams, arranged a meeting with the president of Fairmuir Instrument Corporation, Mr. Tom Fairmuir, in order to discuss the 1974 financial statements. Part of the meeting is recorded below.

Mr. Adams: Everything seems to be in fine order except for your valuation of inventories relating to pyrometers, Tom. Now we discussed this matter briefly a few days ago, and you expressed the opinion that there would be no material loss of value in the inventories and that you would in fact be able to sell it all in the normal course of business. Since then I have examined your record of sales orders. At present you have only $58,000 worth of open orders on your books, compared with $65,000 worth at the beginning of the year. Your billings by quarters for the past year were fairly stable: $149,000, first quarter; $136,000, second quarter; $141,000, third quarter; and $157,000 in the final quarter.

I have also read several articles in trade publications, such as this one in *Steel Monthly,* which seem to indicate that your type of pyrometer is at a technical as well as an economic (in terms of purchase price) disadvantage.

Frankly, it appears to me that you are going to be left with a lot of inventory which will have to be marked down very significantly to sell it.

Mr. Fairmuir: Now hold it, Bill, things are not so bleak as that. In fact, we have plans for our pyrometers which will return the sales volume to its previous level, or close to it. Look at these letters, Bill. These are inquiries concerning substantial orders, and we have been receiving such inquiries at a greatly increased rate recently. If this continues, and I have no doubt that it will, and if even half of them become firm orders, we shall be selling pyrometers in 1975 at twice the 1974 level.

You know we hired a new sales manager this year? Well, he has reorganized our sales force and is beginning to get results. At the same time we have gone over our production process and reduced the manufacturing cost of our lines by some 10 percent. No doubt you noticed that our cost of goods figures were lower for the past two or three months. We expect to improve on that further in 1975. Of course this gives us some price flexibility when we are faced with a competitive situation. So you see, I have good reason to predict better results in the future.

Mr. ADAMS: What exactly has the new sales manager done?

Mr. FAIRMUIR: He reorganized the sales territories and reassigned the salesforce so that we should get greater market penetration. He released a couple of people who have clearly not been pulling their weight and hired a couple of bright young people to replace them. The main thing is that he has done wonders for the morale of the sales force. In addition he has identified, new markets and is helping the salespeople to break into these markets.

Mr. ADAMS: Why don't we look at the prospects market by market, Tom. You had sales of only $62,000 to steel mills in 1974. It seems as if the steel mills market is almost defunct, wouldn't you agree?

Mr. FAIRMUIR: It has certainly declined. However, some of our salespeople have built up a good relationship with their customers in the steel industry and we expect this to produce a certain loyalty. We should keep a small part of the business, say, billings of about $50,000 a year.

In the other metal extraction industries we know that our product has some distinct competitive advantages, such as its ruggedness and lower maintenance costs. With the new emphasis on selling we expect that our customers will be well aware of these advantages, and the downward sales trend should be reversed this year. On this basis we expect 1975's sales to this market to be at least $400,000 and to increase further in the future.

Mr. ADAMS: But look, Tom, that means an increase over this year's sales, bucking a strong downward trend. I can't base my opinion on your optimism, you know.

Mr. FAIRMUIR: Well, look at this market, which we think has great potential—scientific laboratories. We are going to place advertisements in some of the engineering journals and pay direct sales calls to many of the labs in our market areas, those which do a lot of high-temperature work. We anticipate a yearly volume of $200,000 to $300,000 in this market.

And, finally, we have set up a contract with a representative in Washington to handle our line in government sales. He has already gotten some orders for us and he seems certain that we can build up a stable volume of some $300,000 a year. Several government agencies are testing our product at the moment, including the Atomic Energy Commission. If we get our equipment specified for installation into government nuclear plants, we shall have a large continuing market.

Mr. ADAMS: So you expect sales of about $1 million this year, twice 1974's sales?

Mr. FAIRMUIR: No, not right away. But we are confident of substantially reversing the trend of recent years and eventually, say in two years or so, building our sales up to at least $1.5 million for pyrometers. For 1975 we predict sales of about $800,000.

Mr. ADAMS: Well, look at this from my point of view. I have a professional responsibility to give an opinion on your company's financial statements, and I cannot base my opinion on your predictions. I have to go on historic facts and reasonable expectations. The historic facts are that sales of pyrometers have been falling and you have only a small volume of open orders on your books.

You have a substantial inventory, the value of which can only be realized through the sale of pyrometers. Any other representation of these facts would mislead the reader of the statements.

Mr. FAIRMUIR: I agree with you on that, and in my opinion, we *will* realize the value of our inventory through normal sales. I could not contemplate a write-down in the value of the inventory. For one thing, it would not be right to do so since it would be misleading in valuing our assets. And for another, it could easily lead to a difficult situation with the bank and, at worst, lead to liquidation of the company. True, we have experienced a few bad years. But we are fighting back and I am confident we shall save our pyrometer line. And also our new line will start to contribute to profits this coming year.

The discussion continued for some time and became fairly heated. Finally, Mr. Adams terminated the discussion in order to consider the question further. He arranged a meeting with Mr. Fairmuir three days hence, at which time the two men agreed they would come to a decision as to whether or not the value of the inventory should be written down. Mr. Adams was concerned as to what opinion he should issue on Fairmuir's financial statements of 1974.

Questions

1. What further steps should Mr. Adams take in preparing for the coming meeting with Mr. Fairmuir?
2. Putting yourself in Mr. Fairmuir's position, what steps would you take in preparing for the meeting? If Mr. Adams insists that the value of the inventory be written down, what would you do?
3. Do you think that the value of the inventory should be written down? If so, how should the adjustment be made?
4. If it were not written down, how would you, as auditor, phrase your opinion?

PART II

Management
Accounting

CHAPTER 14

THE NATURE OF
MANAGEMENT ACCOUNTING

This chapter distinguishes management accounting from other types of information. It describes the three types of management accounting and their uses. It compares and contrasts management accounting information with information used for financial reporting. Finally, it makes some general observations regarding the use of accounting information by management.

MANAGEMENT ACCOUNTING AS ONE TYPE OF INFORMATION

In Part I our focus was on information reported in financial statements prepared for outside parties. In the remainder of the book we discuss accounting information intended for the use of management. Whereas financial accounting has been written about for over 400 years, little was written about management accounting until well into the 20th century. The actual practice of management accounting goes back much further, however. Many of the techniques to be described here were used by Josiah Wedgwood and Sons, Ltd., in the 18th century, for example. The need for a type of accounting that was not aimed primarily at the preparation of financial statements is set forth in this 1875 memorandum by Thomas Sutherland, a British business executive:[1]

The present system of bookkeeping in the Accountant's Department is admirably suited for the end it has in view, viz., that of ascertaining once a

---

[1] This memorandum was called to our attention by Professor Lyle E. Jacobsen, who saw it reprinted in the London *Economist* in 1960.

year or oftener the profits upon the company's transactions; but it is evident that in a business of this kind much detailed information is necessary regarding the working of the Company, and this information should be obtainable in such a practical form as to enable the Directors to see readily and clearly the causes at work in favor of or against the success of the Company's operations.

Information

The purpose of this section is to distinguish management accounting information from other types of information. *Information* is a fact, datum, observation, perception, or any other thing that adds to knowledge. The number 1,000 taken by itself is not information; it doesn't tell anyone anything. The statement that 1,000 students are enrolled in a certain school *is* information. Management accounting is one type of information. Its place in the whole picture is shown in Illustration 14–1.

Information can be either quantitative or nonquantitative. Impressions from the senses (hearing, vision, and so forth), conversations, television programs, and newspaper stories are examples of nonquantitative information. Management accounting is not, strictly speaking, concerned with nonquantitative information.

There are many types of quantitative information, of which accounting is one. Accounting information is distinguished from the other types in that it usually is expressed in monetary terms. Data on the age, ex-

Illustration 14–1

TYPES OF INFORMATION

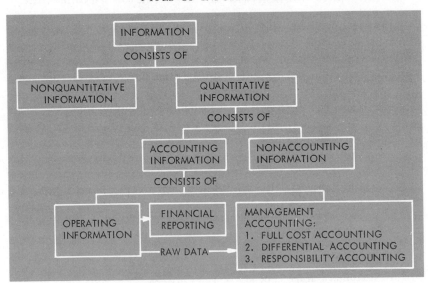

perience level, and other characteristics of an employee are quantitative, but they are not usually designated as accounting information. The line here is not sharply drawn, however; nonmonetary information is often included in accounting reports when it assists the reader in understanding what the report is intended to convey. For example, a management accounting report on sales for a retail automobile dealer would show, in addition to the monetary amount of sales revenue, the number of automobiles sold, which is nonmonetary information. There is no point in debating the question of whether this is or is not accounting. The important point is that the focus of accounting information is monetary, but that nonmonetary information is reported when it is helpful to do so.

It should be emphasized that managers want whatever type of information that helps them do their job, whether it be accounting or nonaccounting, quantitative or nonquantitative. A telephoned message, or even a rumor, that an important customer is so dissatisfied with a company's product that he is about to take his business elsewhere, is not accounting and not even quantitative, but it is certainly an important piece of information.

Operating Information

The bottom section of Illustration 14–1 indicates the general nature of accounting information. By far the largest quantity of such information consists of *operating information.* Operating information provides the raw data for (1) financial reporting and (2) management accounting.

In the course of its daily operations, a company generates a vast amount of accounting information. Viewed close up and in detail, the mass of this information is bewildering; but if one steps back a bit from the detail, one can see that most of it can be classified into a relatively few main streams. The principal streams are:

1. *Production.* These are records showing the detail on orders received from customers, instructions for manufacturing the goods to meet these orders, instructions for manufacturing goods that are to be held in inventory until orders are received, and corresponding detail on services rendered.

The nature of the production stream varies widely in different industries, but it tends to be similar for companies within a given industry. In some industries, such as banks and insurance companies, the majority of employees are engaged in processing production records; these employees process "paper" in essentially the same way that employees in a factory process raw materials.

2. *Purchasing and materials.* These are records having to do with material and services ordered, with their receipt, with keeping track of

material while it is in inventory, and with its issue to the production departments.

3. *Payroll.* These are records which show how much each employee has earned, the nature of the work that he did, and how much he has been paid. As described in Chapter 8, every company is required by law to furnish to its employees and to the government specified information on employee earnings, and because of this requirement there is a great deal of similarity in the payroll records of most companies.

4. *Plant and equipment.* These are records of the cost, location, and condition of each significant item of building, equipment, or other noncurrent asset used by the company, together with the related depreciation data.

5. *Sales and accounts receivable.* For every cash sale, there is a cash register record of some sort. For every credit sale there is an invoice giving detail of what was sold and to whom. For every customer there is a record of the amount he owes and the amount he has paid.

6. *Finance.* These are the checkbook and bank deposits that are familiar to everyone, and the less familiar but equally important records required to keep track of investments, the incurrence and payment of liabilities, and dividends and other transactions with shareholders.

7. *Cost.* These are records of costs incurred in manufacturing goods or rendering services.

8. *Responsibility accounting.* This is a record of the details of revenues, expenses, and investment classified by organization units.

These eight streams of data constitute the bulk of the information that exists in most companies. There are a wide variety of minor streams and variations of these main streams that need not concern us.

The relative importance and complexity of these streams varies greatly in different types of businesses. In a department store, the stream of data on sales and accounts receivable is relatively large because of the paperwork connected with charge purchases, while the payroll stream is relatively small because the number of employees per dollar of revenue is relatively small, and because the method of compensating employees is usually straightforward. In an automobile manufacturing company, the reverse would be the case. Its customers, who are automobile dealers, are no more numerous than those in a retail store that has sales one-tenth of one percent as great, yet it has tens of thousands of employees, and must keep records on what each of them earns and what work each does.

The eight streams of data, although separately identifiable, are interrelated. Thus, the accounts receivable stream is connected to the financial stream when cash payments are received from customers; and the purchases stream is connected to the financial stream when vendors are paid and to the production stream when material is used in the production process.

Management Accounting

In Part I we focused on the financial statements, namely, the balance sheet, the income statement, and the statement of changes in financial position. Most of the information used in the preparation of these financial statements is obtained from summaries of the streams of operating information that were listed above.

The financial statements obviously are also useful to management. They provide an overall picture of the financial condition of an entity and of the results of its activities. In Chapter 12, we described some management uses of this information. Management needs much more detailed financial information than that contained in the financial statements, however. In this Part II, we focus on this additional information.

The several streams of operating information provide much of the raw material of management accounting. Much of this information is not of direct interest to managers, however. In the normal course of events, a manager does not care about the amount of money that an individual customer owes, or the amount that an individual employee earned last week, or the amount that was deposited in the bank yesterday, or the placement of an individual purchase order for the replenishment of parts. Records must be kept of all these facts, but ordinarily these records are used by operating personnel rather than by managers. The manager is interested in summaries drawn from these records rather than in the records themselves.

In general, therefore, management accounting information is *summary* information. In order to understand it, we do need to know something about the source of raw material used for these summaries, but we need only enough of the detail to be able to understand the resulting summaries.

TYPES OF MANAGEMENT ACCOUNTING INFORMATION AND THEIR USES

Financial accounting is essentially a single process, governed by a single set of generally accepted accounting principles, and unified by the basic equation, Assets = Equities. By contrast, in management accounting there are *several* processes; there are *several* sets of principles that govern the compilation of the data; and there is no single unifying equation. Three different types of management accounting data exist, each of which is useful for certain purposes but invalid if applied to other purposes.

The three types of accounting constructions and their uses are summarized in Illustration 14–2. Each construction applies to revenues, to costs, and to assets, but for convenience in this brief introduction to them, we shall discuss them primarily in terms of cost. The three are: (1) full costs, (2) differential costs, and (3) responsibility costs. The remaining chapters of this book are arranged so that each type of accounting construction is discussed separately. Chapters 15 and 16 focus on full costs, Chapters 17, 18, and 19 on differential costs, and Chapters 20, 21, and 22 on responsibility costs.

Illustration 14–2

TYPES OF ACCOUNTING INFORMATION AND THEIR USES

Cost, Revenue, or Asset Construction	Uses	
	Historical Data	*Future Estimates*
1. Full	Financial reporting Reporting and analyzing performance Cost-type contracts	Long-range plans (programming) Normal pricing decisions
2. Differential	NONE	Alternative choice decisions (mostly short range, applicable to a specific operation)
3. Responsibility	Reporting and analyzing performance	Budgeting

These accounting constructions apply to two types of data, historical data and future estimates. The former is a record of what has happened, and the latter is an estimate of what is going to happen in the future. (It should be noted that in many situations an estimate of future costs is based on the record of historical costs.) In the useful characterization of Simon,[2] historical data tend to be *attention-directing* information and future estimates tend to be *problem-solving* information. The former alerts management to the existence of a problem; the latter helps management decide on the best way of solving the problem. We shall describe briefly below the uses of both the historical and the estimating types of these accounting constructions.

---

[2] Herbert A. Simon, *Administrative Behavior* (2d ed., New York: The Macmillan Co., 1957), p. 20.

Full Cost Accounting

The full cost of manufacturing goods is the sum of the direct costs of these goods plus a fair share of the indirect costs that are incurred for the manufacture of these and other goods. Full cost accounting measures these costs, not only for goods, but also for services, and for any other activity that is of interest to management.

Historical full costs are used in financial reporting, and we have already discussed their use for this purpose, particularly in Chapter 6 where we gave the journal entries that accumulated raw material costs, direct labor costs, and other manufacturing costs for goods as these goods moved through the manufacturing process. Historical full costs are also used in certain reports of performance that are prepared for the use of management and for the analysis of performance as revealed by these reports. This type of analysis was described in Chapter 12. In many contractual arrangements the buyer agrees to pay the seller the cost of the goods manufactured or the services rendered plus a profit margin, and "cost" in this context usually means full cost.

Estimates of what full costs are going to be in the future are used in some types of planning activities, particularly in the type of long-range planning that is called programming. In deciding what price to charge for its products, a company normally uses estimates of full costs plus a profit margin as a guide in arriving at the final selling price.

Differential Accounting

Differential accounting estimates how costs, revenues, and/or assets would be different if one course of action were adopted as compared with an alternative course of action.

> EXAMPLE: In a factory making desks, the differential cost of one additional desk is the sum of the direct material, direct labor, and other direct costs that will be incurred in making that one desk but that would not be incurred if that additional desk were not made. In this situation, the differential cost is less than the full costs of a desk, because the full cost includes a fair share of general manufacturing costs, which would be incurred whether or not one additional desk were manufactured.

By definition, differential costs are always estimates of future costs. As is the case with estimates of all types, they may be derived from historical cost records in some problems, but no management use is made of an historical record of differential costs as such.

As the above description suggests, differential costs are used in deciding on problems that involve a choice among alternative courses of actions; these types of problems are called alternative choice problems. Most such decisions involve short-run problems and involve a specific segment of the business, such as a specific manufacturing operation. For long-range, overall planning decisions, estimates of full costs are appropriate. Indeed, in the long run, all costs are differential, as we shall see in Chapter 18.

Responsibility Accounting

Responsibility accounting traces costs (and also revenues and/or assets) to individual organization units, which are called responsibility centers.

Estimates of future responsibility costs are used in the planning process, particularly in the annual planning process that is called budgeting. An historical record of the actual costs incurred in a responsibility center is used in reporting on the performance of that responsibility center and in analyzing this performance. Such reports are more useful for many management purposes than are financial accounting reports prepared in accordance with the full cost construction because they identify the manager who is responsible for performance. Corrective action can be taken only by individuals, so if performance is unsatisfactory, the person responsible must be identified before corrective action can be taken.

> EXAMPLE: A financial accounting report may indicate that the cost of goods sold in a certain period was too high. Such a report does not ordinarily identify the particular department that was responsible for this unsatisfactory situation. It might have been any one of several production departments, it might have been the purchasing department, or it might have been one of the general factory departments. Responsibility accounting seeks to identify the department responsible for the incurrence of each item of cost.

Relation to Planning and Control

In Chapter 1 we described briefly the management functions of planning, coordinating and control.

It should be emphasized that *there is not a one-to-one correspondence between the three types of management accounting construction and the three management functions*. The task of understanding management accounting would be much simpler if such a correspondence existed, but it does not. Overall planning uses primarily responsibility accounting, but to a certain extent it also uses full cost accounting and differential accounting. Some operating decisions use full cost information, while others use differential accounting information. Thus, the central scheme of this second part of the book is to discuss each of the three types of accounting constructions separately, first explaining what it is, and then discussing its use for various management purposes.

CONTRAST BETWEEN MANAGEMENT ACCOUNTING AND FINANCIAL REPORTING

We have mentioned some differences between management accounting and the financial reporting process which was the focus of Part I. It seems desirable to recapitulate these differences, add others, and also point out similarities.

Differences

In contrast with financial reporting, management accounting—

1. Has no single unifying concept.
2. Is not necessarily governed by generally accepted principles.
3. Is optional rather than mandatory.
4. Includes more nonmonetary information.
5. Has more emphasis on the future.
6. Focuses on segments as well as on the whole of business.
7. Has less emphasis on precision.
8. Is part of other processes rather than an end in itself.

1. LACK OF A UNIFYING CONCEPT. As already noted, financial accounting is built around the fundamental equation, Assets = Equities, whereas in management accounting there are three types of accounting, each with its own conceptual framework.

2. NOT GOVERNED BY GENERALLY ACCEPTED PRINCIPLES. The financial statements must be prepared in accordance with generally accepted accounting principles. Outsiders, who usually have no choice but to accept information just as the company provides it, need assurance that these statements are prepared in accordance with a mutually understood set of ground rules; otherwise, they could not make sense out of the figures. Generally accepted accounting principles provide these common ground rules. The management of a company, by contrast, can make and enforce whatever rules it finds most useful for its own purposes, without worrying about whether these conform to some outside standard. Thus, in management accounting there may well be information on sales orders received (i.e., the order "backlog") even though these are not financial accounting transactions, fixed assets may be stated at appraisal values, overhead costs may be omitted from inventories, or revenues may be recorded before they are realized, even though each of these concepts is inconsistent with generally accepted accounting principles. The basic question in management accounting is the pragmatic one: "Is the infor-

mation useful?" rather than, "Does it conform to generally accepted principles?"

EXAMPLE: A trade association of retail hardware stores collecting records of expenses from its member firms may specify that the report include as rent expense an amount equivalent to what rental costs would have been even though the building is owned and no rent as such was actually paid. This puts the reports of members who owned buildings on a basis comparable with those who rented buildings, and thus increases the comparability of the data. Such a practice would not be permitted in financial reporting; in accordance with the cost concept, only the actual costs incurred in occupying the building could be shown.

3. OPTIONAL.   Financial reporting *must* be done. Enough effort must be expended to collect data in acceptable form and with an acceptable degree of accuracy to meet the requirements of outside parties, whether or not the accountant regards this information as useful. The Financial Accounting Standards Board describes minimum standards of full disclosure. For most sizable corporations the Securities and Exchange Commission specifies detailed reporting requirements. All companies must keep records for income tax purposes, according to regulations of the taxing authorities. Management accounting, by contrast, is entirely optional. No outside agencies specify what must be done, or indeed that anything need be done. Being optional, there is no point in collecting a piece of information for management purposes unless its value, as an aid to management, is believed to exceed the cost of collecting it.

4. NONMONETARY INFORMATION.   The financial statements include primarily monetary information. Management accounting deals with nonmonetary as well as monetary information. Although the accounts themselves contain only money amounts, much of the information on management accounting reports is nonmonetary. They contain quantities of material, as well as the monetary cost of material; number of employees and number of hours worked, as well as labor costs; units of products sold, as well as dollar amounts of sales revenue; and so on.

5. FUTURE INFORMATION.   Financial accounting records the financial history of an enterprise. Entries are made in the accounts only after transactions have occurred. Financial accounting information is indeed used as a basis for making future plans, but the information itself is historical. Management accounting includes, in its formal structure, numbers that represent estimates and plans for the future, as well as information about the past. (Some financial accounting entries, such as those for depreciation, require that estimates of future conditions be made; the basic thrust of financial accounting is nevertheless historical.)

6. FOCUS ON SEGMENTS.   The financial statements describe the business as a whole. Some companies do subdivide total revenue according to the main lines of business in which they engage, and other companies sub-

divide certain costs in a similar fashion. The main focus, however, is on the entire business entity. In management accounting, by contrast, the main focus is on segments, that is, on products; or on individual activities; or on divisions, departments, and other responsibility centers. As we shall see, the necessity for dividing the total costs of the business among these individual segments creates important problems in management accounting that do not exist in financial accounting.

7. LESS EMPHASIS ON PRECISION. Management needs information rapidly, and is often willing to sacrifice some precision in order to gain speed in reporting. Thus, in management accounting, approximations are often as useful as, or even more useful than, numbers that are worked out to the last penny. Financial accounting cannot be absolutely precise either, so the difference is one of degree. The approximations used in management accounting are greater than those in financial accounting.

8. A MEANS RATHER THAN AN END. The purpose of financial accounting is to produce financial statements. When the statements have been produced, the purpose has been accomplished. (The accountant can, to be sure, play an important role in helping users to analyze and understand the statements, but this activity takes place after the completion of the financial accounting process.) Management accounting information is only a means to an end, the end being the planning, coordinating, and controlling functions of management. Management accountants assist management in using accounting data, but they should not adopt the attitude that the accounting numbers are an end in themselves.

Similarities

Although differences do exist, most elements of financial accounting are also found in management accounting. There are two reasons for this. First, the same considerations that make generally accepted accounting principles sensible for the purposes of financial accounting are likely to be present for purposes of management accounting. For example, management cannot base its internal reporting system on unverifiable, subjective estimates of profits submitted by lower echelons, which is the same reason that financial accounting adheres to the cost and realization concepts. Second, the operating accounting system must furnish the information used in preparing the financial statements. There is a presumption therefore, that the basic data will be collected in accordance with generally accepted financial accounting principles, for to do otherwise would require duplication of data collection activities.

Source Disciplines

Accounting is an applied science (or "art," as some prefer). All applied subjects were developed from foundations and concepts developed in a basic science or discipline. Management accounting has two such source disciplines. Part of management accounting is related to *economics,* which deals with the principles governing decisions on the use of scarce resources. Another part is related to *social psychology,*[3] which deals with the principles governing the behavior of people in organizations. The principles of these two disciplines are quite different from one another, and this fact causes problems in understanding the principles of management accounting that are derived from them. For example, for the purpose of deciding whether to purchase a new machine, we shall use accounting information developed according to principles that the economist specifies, but for the purpose of preparing a budget for the responsibility center in which that same machine is used we shall take account of the principles of social psychology; the latter may lead to quite different accounting constructions.

Some economists and some behavioral scientists criticize management accounting. Much of this criticism arises because each has the mistaken belief that management accounting relates solely to his discipline. One of the significant problems in the real world is to give the appropriate weight to each of these disciplines.

SOME GENERAL OBSERVATIONS

Before getting into the details, we here make some general observations about the nature and use of management accounting information. These usefully can be kept in mind throughout the study of the chapters that follow.

Different Numbers for Different Purposes

In mathematics, and in most of the physical sciences, there are definitions that are valid under a wide variety of circumstances. Such is not the case with most accounting definitions. Each of the several purposes described in the preceding section requires a different accounting construction. Since these different numbers may superficially resemble one another and since they may even be called by the same name, a person who is not familiar with them may easily become confused or frustrated. The most common source of confusion is the word "cost." As will be seen in later chapters, there are historical costs, standard costs, original costs, net costs, residual costs, variable costs, differential costs, incremental costs, marginal costs, opportunity costs, direct costs, estimated costs, full costs

---

[3] The boundaries of social psychology are not entirely clear. We mean to include those principles of psychology and of sociology that are intended to explain how individuals behave in situations ranging from two-person interactions to large groups.

and other kinds of costs. Some of these terms are synonymous; others are almost but not quite synonymous; still others, although not synonymous at all, are used by some people as if they were.

Accounting numbers should always be discussed in terms of the particular problem that they are intended to help solve, rather than in any abstract sense. A statement that "the cost of such-and-such is $100" literally has no meaning unless those who hear this statement understand clearly which of the several possible concepts of cost was intended. A useful procedure to follow in approaching a specific problem is to define, as carefully as possible, the purpose for which numbers are to be used in that problem and then to consider how the numbers should be assembled and used for that specific purpose.

Accounting Numbers Are Approximations

Accounting is a system for recording and summarizing measurements of business facts, and, as is the case with any measurement, an accounting number is an approximation rather than a precisely accurate statement. Most of the data used in the physical sciences are also measurements, and like scientists and engineers, users of accounting information must acquire an understanding of the degree of approximation that is present in the data.

Consider, for example, the concept of temperature. With the proper instruments, the temperature of the human body is easily measured to a tenth of a degree and that of a room to a degree or so, but the temperature of the sun is measurable only with an accuracy of a hundred degrees or so. Although these measurements differ widely in their degree of accuracy, each is useful for a particular purpose. Similarly, some accounting numbers, such as the amount of cash on hand, may be accurate within very narrow limits, while others are only rough approximations.

The degree of approximation is especially high in the case of the numbers used for planning purposes. Such numbers are always estimates of what will happen in the future. But businessmen are not clairvoyant; they do not *know* what will happen in the future, and the numbers used for planning purposes can be no better than their estimates of what the future holds.

Working with Incomplete Data

No one could ask a person to solve a problem in mathematics without furnishing him all the information he needs. In a business problem, on the other hand, one almost never has exactly the information he would like to have. In nearly every practical situation, the person who is struggling with the problem can think of additional information that would be helpful if it were available. Conversely, there are many business situations in which page after page of numbers are available, but only a small fraction of them are at all relevant to the problem at hand, and perhaps none of them is quite what one needs to solve the problem.

It is a fact of life, however, that problems must be solved, business decisions must be made, and often the decision cannot be delayed until all the pertinent information is available. One does the best he can with what he has, and then moves on to the next problem. John W. Gardner writes:

> Anyone who accomplishes anything of significance has more confidence than the facts would justify. It is something that outstanding executives have in common with gifted military commanders, brilliant political leaders, and great artists. It is true of societies as well as of individuals. Every great civilization has been characterized by confidence in itself.[4]

On the other hand, a decision should not be made if a vital, obtainable piece of evidence is missing. Deciding whether or not to act on the available evidence is one of the most difficult parts of the whole decision process. As the late Dean Wallace B. Donham put it: "The art of business is the art of making irrevocable decisions on the basis of inadequate information."

Accounting Evidence Is Only Partial Evidence

Few, if any, business problems can be solved solely by the collection and analysis of numbers. Usually, there are important factors that cannot be, or have not been, reduced to quantitative terms. For example, consider how the performance of a baseball player is judged. Every time a baseball player comes to bat, and almost every time he handles the ball in the field, a statistic is generated. Detailed records are published on his times at bat, walks, hits, slugging, singles, two-base hits, three-base hits, home runs, strikeouts, putouts, sacrifices, fielding chances, assists, errors, earned run average, and so on. Nevertheless, when the manager of the team must decide whether A is a better ball player than B, he knows better than to rely completely on the numerical information. Such factors as how well a player gets along with his colleagues, his ability to hit in the pinches, and other unmeasurable characteristics must also be taken into account. If the question of a ball player's ability could be answered solely by an analysis of statistics, there would be no reason for the millions of man-hours of discussion by the "hot-stove league" during the winter months.

Most business organizations are much more complicated than baseball teams; the "game" of business goes on all day, every day, rather than 162 discrete times a year, and business results are not expressed by the number

---

[4] *Annual Report 1965*, Carnegie Corporation.

of games won and lost. Business measurements are therefore much more difficult and less precise than baseball measurements.

Some people act as if problems could be completely solved by numerical analysis. They have the erroneous idea that solely from a knowledge of loads, stresses, and material strengths the engineer can figure just how a bridge should look, disregarding the element of judgment completely. At the other extreme, there are those who believe that intuition is the sure guide to a sound decision, and who therefore pay no attention to the numbers. Although the correct attitude is clearly somewhere between these extremes, there is no way of describing precisely where it is. The reader must reach his own conclusion on the relative importance of quantitative and nonquantitative data in the solution of management problems. The essential reason for these limitations has been well summed up by G. K. Chesterton:

> The real trouble with this world of ours is not that it is an unreasonable world, nor even that it is a reasonable one. The commonest kind of trouble is that it is nearly reasonable, but not quite. Life is not an illogicality; yet it is a trap for logicians. It looks just a little more mathematical and regular than it is; its exactitude is obvious, but its inexactitude is hidden; its wildness lies in wait.[5]

People, Not Numbers, Get Things Done

An obvious fact about business organizations is that they consist of human beings. Anything that the business accomplishes is the result of the actions of these people. Numbers can assist the people in the organization in various ways, but the numbers are nothing more than marks on pieces of paper; by themselves they accomplish nothing. But numbers don't talk back; they give the appearance of being definite and precise, and it is a comforting illusion to imagine that the construction of a set of numbers is synonymous with acting on a real problem.

An accounting system may be beautifully designed and carefully operated, but the system is of no use to management unless it results in action by human beings. For instance, three companies may use exactly the same system—the same chart of accounts, the same set of records and reports, the same procedure for collecting and disseminating information—with entirely different results. In one company, the system may be *useless* because management never acts on the information collected, and the organization has become aware of this fact. In the second company, the system may be *helpful* because management uses the information as a general guide for planning, coordinating, and control and has educated the organization to use it in the same spirit. In the third company, the

---

[5] *Orthodoxy* (London: Bodley Head, 1949 reprint), p. 131.

system may be *worse than useless* because management overemphasizes the importance of the numbers and therefore takes unwise actions.

SUMMARY

Accounting is one type of information. The total amount of information available to a manager includes nonquantitative as well as quantitative elements. The quantitative elements include both monetary and non-monetary amounts. Accounting is essentially monetary, but includes related nonmonetary data.

Most accounting information, in terms of quantity of data, is operating information. The mass of operating data flowing through a company consists of these streams: production, purchasing and materials, payroll, plant and equipment, sales and accounts receivable, finance, cost, and responsibility accounting. Data in these streams provide the raw material for financial statements. These statements are essentially summaries to meet the needs of investors and other outside parties and of managers inside the business.

There is no single, unified management accounting system. Rather, there are three different types of information, each used for different purposes. These are called: (1) full cost accounting, (2) differential accounting, and (3) responsibility accounting. The remainder of this book deals in turn with each of these three types.

As contrasted with financial reporting, management accounting: has several concepts rather than one; is not necessarily governed by generally accepted principles; includes more nonmonetary information; has more emphasis on the future; is optional rather than mandatory; focuses on segments of a business rather than on the whole; has less emphasis on precision; and is a means to an end rather than an end in itself. Nevertheless, the two subjects have much in common.

In solving management accounting problems it is well to keep in mind that terms, principally cost, are defined differently depending on the purpose; that accounting numbers are approximations; that they rarely provide exactly the information needed; that much more than accounting information is needed in the solution of a problem; and that human beings, not numbers, get things done.

SUGGESTIONS FOR FURTHER READING

ATKINSON, J. W. *An Introduction to Motivation.* Princeton, N.J.: D. Van Nostrand Company, 1964.

CAPLAN, EDWIN H. *Management Accounting and Behavioral Science.* Reading, Mass.: Addison-Wesley Publishing Company, 1971.

CYERT, R. M., and J. G. MARCH. *A Behavioral Theory of the Firm.* Englewood Cliffs, N.J.: Prentice-Hall, Inc. 1963.

HOMANS, G. C. *Social Behavior: Its Elementary Forms* 2d ed. New York: Harcourt, Brace & World, 1973.

LAWRENCE, P. R. and J. W. LORSCH. *Organization and Environment: Managing Differentiation and Integration.* Boston: Division of Research, Harvard Business School, 1967.

MCCLELLAND, D. C. *The Achieving Society.* New York: The Free Press, 1967.

CASES

CASE 14–1. BATES BOAT YARD

Upon returning to civilian life after several years in the Navy, Henry Bates sought a small business that he might buy. Being a thrifty fellow with no dependents, he had built up a fair amount of capital, the accumulation of which had been aided by the fact that he had seen considerable duty in areas where there had been nothing to buy.

Bates finally located a small boat yard for sale in a town on the coast of Maine where he had spent many summers. The proprietor was getting along in years and wished to retire. He was offering the yard for sale at what Bates believed to be a fair starting price that could probably be worked down to a very reasonable figure through negotiation.

It is not necessary here to go into the details of investigation and negotiation. Bates bought the yard. The business being somewhat larger than he could finance alone, he had borrowed the additional funds required from a friend, giving a mortgage on the property as security.

Bates realized the need of adequate accounting records if he was to manage the business successfully. The records on hand were for cash receipts and disbursements only. Actual balance sheets and profit and loss statements which had been prepared for the former owner for tax purposes were also available. A person who was a reasonably capable bookkeeper and general office factotum had been inherited with the business.

Having had a course in accounting in college, Bates felt that he could use cost and financial information with some intelligence but did not feel capable of initiating a suitable accounting system. Knowing that you, an old friend of his, have been studying such matters, he has asked you to tell him what kind of accounting records he should keep and what kind of financial and cost information he should develop in order to control operations and to make proper charges to customers for service rendered. In addition to the information above he has told you the following facts about his business.

One of the properties of the business was a large shed for the winter storage of boats. Being the most suitable building in the locality for such storage, there was great demand for space in it on the part of owners of expensive boats among the summer people.

There was plenty of empty land on the shore front for outdoor storage. In most cases where space was rented for this purpose, the yard was also hired to haul the boats in on equipment that it had for the purpose.

In the spring, and from time to time during other seasons, there was a goodly amount of business available in painting and repair work on boats.

There was a large-sized work shed containing woodworking tools and space in which to construct at one time about six boats up to 40 feet in length. Larger boats could be built outside when the weather was suitable, but Bates did not expect to get many, if any, orders for such craft. He did, however, expect to have from one to six boats up to 40 feet in length in construction at all times, some for local fishermen and some for summer people.

The property included a good-sized wharf and float, a store for the sale of marine hardware and supplies, and gasoline pumps. There being no yacht club in the town, the summer people who were boating-minded tended to gather around this wharf and store. Bates intended to encourage this and to add fishing tackle, sporting goods, and refreshments to the items handled by the store.

Question

What would you tell Bates concerning his accounting needs?

CASE 14–2. CROMPTON, LTD.

In ten years, Crompton, Ltd. had achieved noteworthy success in penetrating the highly competitive British abrasive products industry. Located in Sheffield, England, its factory employed more than 300 people, manufacturing grinding wheels for sale to steel converters and cutlery manufacturers in the Sheffield area.

From the time the company started in business, Mr. John Lucas, the factory manager, had controlled factory operations primarily by direct personal supervision. Because he had been so familiar with operations, he had known which departments were having difficulties and what they were doing to cope with them. He had worked very closely with the departmental foremen and they, in turn, had never been afraid to call on him for help and advice.

With the growth of the company, this arrangement became more and more difficult. Mr. Lucas had to rely more and more on the individual foremen to inform him of problems they were having, and he was quite sure that some of the foremen, particularly the newer ones, were not as effective as they should have been. Unfortunately, he had no evidence on which to decide which departments needed attention. With this in mind, he asked Mr. Hugh Field, a local accountant, to draw up a system of monthly reports that would supplement the knowledge that he would continue to gain by direct observation.

In the production of grinding wheels, abrasive grain was mixed with a bonding material according to the customer's requirements, molded in either a hot or a cold press, depending on the kind of bond, baked in a kiln, fitted with a bushing to take a motor spindle, "trued" to take off rough edges, shaped specially if needed, tested for balance and ability to withstand high speeds, and finally packed and shipped to the customer.

After several weeks of study and discussion with Crompton factory personnel, Mr. Field proposed that a report in the form illustrated in Exhibit 1 be prepared for each of the 18 production centers in the factory. One copy of the report would go to the foreman in charge of that production center; a second copy would go to Mr. Lucas.

Mr. Field explained that his objective had been to produce a simple report, with as few figures as possible. Accordingly he had limited the report to the following four items:

1. Gross production.
2. Rejection rate.
3. Net production per man-hour.
4. Direct labor cost.

Gross production was measured by the total "list price" of the products passing through the department. Mr. Field considered using some other indicator of production volume, such as the total number of units or total weight of the output, but rejected all these because the output varied so widely in size and complexity. The "list price" was a stabilized amount for each wheel, established a number of years earlier and unchanged since that time. Actual customer prices were set each year by multiplying the list price by a percentage (e.g., 115%) which management felt was "right" for the current market.

Rejections occurred in all production departments, although the majority were discovered in the testing department. At a weekly conference, the plant superintendent determined the source of the defect and allocated responsibility accordingly. Rejections were quoted as a percentage of gross production handled.

Net production per man-hour was gross production, minus rejects, all measured at list prices, divided by the number of direct labor hours.

Direct labor costs were the actual direct labor hours for the month multiplied by the actual wage rates paid individual workers during the

Exhibit 1

CROMPTON, LTD.

Hot Press Department Operating Report
November*

	November 4 weeks	October 4 weeks	September 5 weeks	August 2 weeks	July 4 weeks	January–June 26 weeks	Last Fiscal Year 52 weeks
Gross Production (£)†	14,091	8,984	13,120	3,382	8,590	60,119	83,064
Rejections (%)	6.35	10.48	10.78	9.10	13.41	8.90	11.14
Net production per man-hour (£/hr.)	10.5	9.3	11.6	7.6	9.1	8.4	6.1
Direct labor (£)	349	251	253	95	242	1,739	2,680

* Each "month" consists of either four or five full weeks, except August when the factory is closed for two weeks. A "year" consists of 52 weeks (50 working weeks plus two vacation weeks); approximately one year in every five, a calendar year includes 53 payroll dates, and that "year" consists of 53 weeks.

† £ = pounds, the British monetary unit.

month, including any premium payments for overtime hours. Departmental foremen were responsible for scheduling work in their departments and thus were expected to keep overtime premiums to the lowest level consistent with their delivery commitments.

Each report provided three sets of figures with which the most recent month's record could be compared: (1) the four immediately preceding months, separately for each month; (2) the six months prior to that, as semi-annual totals; and (3) the most recent complete fiscal year, as annual totals. Thus, the November figures could be compared with those for October, September, August and July; for January–June; and for the twelve months January–December of the preceding fiscal year.

Finally, Mr. Field suggested that the departments could be compared with each other to determine which were the most productive, which were showing the most improvement, and which seemed to need Mr. Lucas' attention the most.

Questions

1. In what ways does Exhibit 1 differ from the financial accounting reports you have studied?
2. What did Mr. Lucas mean by "control information"? Why did he need it?
3. What suggestions would you make for improving Exhibit 1 so as to be more useful to Mr. Lucas?

CHAPTER 15

ESSENTIALS OF
FULL COST ACCOUNTING

This is the first of two chapters describing the measurement and use of full cost information, which is one of the three types of constructions used in management accounting. This chapter defines the concept of full cost and describes how manufacturing costs are recorded and how they flow through a cost accounting system. Two types of cost accounting systems, job order and process costing, are described.

THE CONCEPT OF COST

"Cost" is one of the most slippery words used in accounting. It is used for a number of quite different notions. If someone says, without elaboration, "The cost of a widget is $1.80," it is practically impossible to understand exactly what is meant. The word "cost" becomes more meaningful when it is preceded by a modifier, making phrases such as "direct cost," "full cost," "opportunity cost," "differential cost," and so on; but even these phrases do not convey a clear meaning unless the context in which they are used is clearly understood.

General Definition

A generic definition is:
   Cost is a measurement, in monetary terms, of the amount of resources used for some purpose.
Three important ideas are included in this definition. First, and most basic, is the notion that cost measures the use of resources. The elements that constitute the cost of making something are physical quanti-

435

ties of material, hours of labor service, and quantities of other services. Cost measures how much of these resources was used. The second idea is that cost measurements are expressed in monetary terms. Money provides a common denominator that permits the amounts of individual resources, each measured according to its own scale, to be combined so that the total amount of all resources used can be determined. Third, cost measurement always relates to a stated purpose.

Cost Objective

Cost objective is the technical name for the purpose for which costs are measured. In each instance, the cost objective must be carefully stated and clearly understood. In a certain shoe factory, for example, the manufacture of one case (i.e., 12 or 24 pair) of Style 607 shoes may be one cost objective, the manufacture of one case of Style 608 shoes may be another cost objective, and the manufacture *and sale* of a case of Style 607 shoes may be still another cost objective.

In this chapter, we shall focus on cost objectives that are tangible goods, such as shoes, and only on the manufacturing cost of these goods, but it should be kept in mind that a cost objective is *any* purpose for which costs are measured. A cost objective can be a service, such as repairing a television set; it can be a fixed asset, such as a new building constructed by a company's own work force; it can be a current asset, such as material purchased for inventory.

Full Cost

Full cost means all the resources used for a cost objective. In some circumstances, full cost is easily measured. If Mr. X pays $20 for a pair of shoes at a shoe store, the full cost of the pair of shoes to Mr. X is $20; that is, he used $20 of his resources—in this case, money—to acquire the pair of shoes.

But suppose we ask: What was the full cost of *manufacturing* the pair of shoes? This is a much more difficult question. A shoe factory may make thousands of pairs of shoes a month. Some are plain while others have intricate patterns, some are made of leather while others are made of synthetic material, and some are large while some are small. Clearly, different amounts of resources are used for these different styles and sizes of shoes; that is, they have different costs.

In these circumstances, we need a more specific definition of full cost. It is: The *full cost* of a cost objective is the sum of (1) its direct costs, plus (2) a fair share of its indirect costs.

Direct costs are items of costs that are specifically traceable to or directly caused by a cost objective. Leather used in manufacturing a case of shoes is a direct cost of that case of shoes, and so are the wages earned by the employees who worked directly in making that case of shoes.

Indirect costs are elements of costs that are associated with or caused by two or more cost objectives jointly, but that are not directly traceable to each of them individually. The nature of an indirect cost is such that it is not possible, or at least not feasible, to measure directly how much of the cost is attributable to a single cost objective.

Although it is intuitively obvious that the cost elements directly traceable to a cost objective are a part of its cost, it is by no means obvious that some fraction of the elements of indirect cost are part of the cost. One can actually see the leather in a pair of shoes, and it is obvious that certain labor services were involved in fashioning this leather into shoes, so there is no doubt of the appropriateness of counting such material and labor as part of the cost of the shoes. But what is the connection between the salary of the factory superintendent and the cost of the shoes made in the factory? The superintendent did not work on the shoes; for most of the time he probably was not even in the same room where the shoes were being manufactured.

The basic rationale is that the indirect costs in the factory are incurred for the several cost objectives in the factory; to argue otherwise would be to assert that indirect costs are sheer waste. Consistent with this rationale, some fraction of the indirect costs must be part of the costs of each cost objective. The fact that indirect costs cannot be traced directly to *individual* cost objectives does not alter this conclusion. We shall defer until later the question of how the fraction, or fair share, of indirect costs applicable to each cost objective can be measured.

Applicable Accounting Principles

The measurement of the costs applicable to an accounting period and to the products manufactured in that period is in general governed by the cost concept and the matching concept introduced in Chapters 2 and 3 and discussed in more detail in Chapters 6, 7, and 8. These concepts and the principles related to them do not give much guidance as to how total product costs are to be assigned to individual products or groups of products, however. They permit any "systematic and rational" method of doing this.

In 1971 the Congress created the Cost Accounting Standards Board (CASB), and some cost accounting standards (which is a term synonymous with "principles") have now been published by that Board. Although the CASB's authority explicitly includes only the measurement of full costs on *government contracts*, its pronouncements have a considerable influence on other types of full cost measurement because in most respects problems involved in measuring the full cost of government contracts are the same as problems involved in measuring full costs in other situations.

Elements of Cost

Elements of cost are either material, labor, or services. In a full cost accounting system, these elements are customarily recorded in certain categories. These categories are shown in Illustration 15–1 and described below.

Illustration 15–1

ELEMENTS OF COST

DIRECT MATERIAL COST.   Direct materials (sometimes called "stores" or "raw materials") are those materials which actually enter into and become part of the specified finished product. They are to be distinguished from *supplies*, which are materials used in the operation of the business but not directly in the product itself, such as lubricating oil used in machinery.

DIRECT LABOR COST.   The direct labor costs of a product are those which can be specifically traced to or identified with the product or which vary so closely with the number of units produced that a direct relationship can be presumed to be present. The wages and related costs of workers who assemble parts into a finished product, or who operate machines in the process of production, or who work on the product with tools, are direct labor costs of the product.

PRIME COST.   Prime cost is the sum of direct labor cost and direct material cost.

SERVICES.   Services are distinguished from material in that they are intangible; they have no physical substance. Electricity, heat, and insurance protection are examples. Services are distinguished from labor in that they are performed by persons who are not employees. If a product is tested for quality by company personnel, the testing cost is a labor cost; but if the product is tested by an outside testing laboratory, the cost is a service cost.

Although, conceptually, services can be either direct or indirect, the amount of *direct* services in most manufacturing companies is relatively small. Thus, in most cost accounting systems for manufacturing operations, all services are classified as indirect cost. In these systems total direct cost is the sum of direct material and direct labor cost, that is, it is the prime cost.

FACTORY INDIRECT COST.   Factory indirect cost, often called "factory overhead," includes all manufacturing costs other than direct material and direct labor. One element of factory indirect cost is indirect labor, which represents wages and salaries earned by employees who do not work directly on a single product or other cost objective but whose services are related to the overall process of production; for example, janitors, forklift operators, toolroom personnel, inspectors, timekeepers, and foremen. Another element of factory indirect cost is indirect material cost, which is the cost of material used in the factory but not traced directly to individual products or other cost objectives; for example, lubricants for machines, supplies, and material items which, although a part of the final product, are too insignificant to be included in direct material cost (such as the glue, thread, and eyelets used in manufacturing shoes). Factory indirect cost also includes such elements of cost as heat, light, power, maintenance, depreciation, taxes, and insurance on assets used in the manufacturing process.

FULL FACTORY COST OR INVENTORY COST.   Full factory cost is the sum of direct and indirect factory costs. *This is the cost at which completed manufactured goods are carried as inventory, and the amount that is shown as cost of goods sold when the goods are sold.*[1] Note that the cost at which goods are carried in inventory does not include marketing costs, or those general and administrative costs that are unrelated to manufacturing operations. It includes only the costs that are incurred "up to the factory exit door."

MARKETING COST.   Marketing cost, also called "distribution costs" or "selling costs," can be classified as either *order-getting costs* or *logistics*

---

[1] As noted in Chapter 6, inventory is carried at cost unless (as is unusual) its market value is less than its cost.

costs. Order-getting costs, such as marketing management, advertising, sales promotion, and salespersons' compensation and expenses, are those incurred in the efforts to make sales. *Logistics costs* are those costs incurred "beyond the factory exit door" in storing the completed product, in transferring it to the customer, and in doing the associated record-keeping. They include warehousing costs, billing costs, and transportation costs. Logistics costs are also called *order-filling costs*.

GENERAL AND ADMINISTRATIVE COST. This is a catchall classification to cover items not included in the above categories. Examples of such items are: costs incurred in the general and executive offices; research, development, and engineering costs (which some companies include in factory indirect cost); public relations costs (which some companies include in marketing cost); donations; and miscellaneous items. General and administrative costs may include the cost of interest on borrowed capital, but in most companies interest is not counted as a cost at all for the purpose of measuring the full cost of cost objectives; instead, it is counted as an overall financial cost of the company.

SYSTEMS FOR COST ACCUMULATION

A *cost accounting system* is a particular method of collecting costs and assigning them to cost objectives. There are many types of such systems. At this point we shall describe the essentials of a common type of system that is used to assign factory costs to products in a manufacturing company. The measurement of full factory costs is necessary in order to obtain the proper amounts for the inventory items on the balance sheet and for the cost of goods sold item on the income statement. In Chapter 6 we described this measurement process in overall terms, giving the entries involved in tracing the flow of costs through the Raw Materials Inventory, Goods in Process Inventory, and Finished Goods Inventory accounts on the balance sheet and to the Cost of Goods Sold account on the income statement. The description that follows is not for a *different* process; it merely describes in more detail the flows discussed in Chapter 6.

The Account Flowchart

As an aid in understanding the flow of costs, the concept of the account flowchart is introduced here. Such a flowchart depicts the accounts used in a system, shown in T-account form, with lines indicating the flow of amounts from one account to another.

Most of the accounts on a cost accounting flowchart are either asset accounts or expense accounts. A characteristic of both asset and expense accounts is that increases are shown on the debit side and decreases are shown on the credit side. Since a line on a flowchart indicates a transfer "from" one account "to" another account, signifying that the first account is being decreased and the second account is being increased, it follows that the typical line on a cost accounting flowchart leads from the credit side of one account to the debit side of another. These flows represent events that happen during the manufacturing process. In addition to the lines designating "flow," other lines indicate entries for certain external transactions that are associated with the manufacturing process; an example is the transaction for the acquisition of raw material from an outside vendor, which is a debit to Raw Materials Inventory and a credit to Accounts Payable or Cash.

Flow of Costs

Illustration 15–2 illustrates the flowchart concept and shows the essential cost flows in a manufacturing company. This flowchart contains a hypothetical set of figures for a month's operation in a small company that manufactures and sells felt-tip pens, which are writing instruments similar to ballpoint pens.

The flowchart is divided into three sections: (1) *acquisition*, containing the accounts related to the acquisition of resources, which are asset and liability accounts; (2) *manufacture*, containing the accounts related to the manufacturing process; and (3) *sale*, the accounts related to the sale of products.

The cycle of operations depicted on the flowchart may be explained as follows:

1. During the month, $52,000 of raw materials were purchased on open account, $20,000 of various other assets were purchased for cash, and $60,000 of accounts payable were paid. The journal entries recording these transactions are as follows:

```
a.  Raw Materials Inventory................. 52,000
        Accounts Payable....................        52,000
b.  (Various asset accounts)................ 20,000
        Cash................................        20,000
c.  Accounts Payable........................ 60,000
        Cash................................        60,000
```

2. During the month, raw materials costing $49,000 (principally felt tips, plastic, ink, and wicks) were withdrawn from inventory and sent to the factory to be worked on. This decrease in Raw Materials Inventory and increase in Goods in Process Inventory is recorded in the following journal entry:

```
Goods in Process Inventory................. 49,000
    Raw Materials Inventory................        49,000
```

Illustration 15–2

ACCOUNTING FLOW CHART OF A PEN COMPANY

($000 omitted)

3. During the month, employees worked on this material and fashioned it into pens. The amount which they earned, $20,000, adds to the amount of Goods in Process Inventory, and the resulting liability increases Wages Payable, as recorded in the following journal entry:

```
Goods in Process Inventory.................. 20,000
     Wages Payable...........................        20,000
```

4. Factory indirect costs were incurred during the month amounting to $27,000. Of the total, $12,000 was ascertained from current invoices for such things as electricity and telephone bills, so the offsetting credits were to Accounts Payable. Indirect labor costs were $10,000, with the offsetting credit to Wages Payable. The remaining $5,000 represented depreciation, the charge-off of prepaid expenses, and other credits to asset accounts. All of these items are here summed up in the general account, Factory Indirect Costs, but in practice they are usually recorded in separate indirect cost accounts, one for each type of cost. The journal entry follows:

```
Factory Indirect Costs...................... 27,000
     Accounts Payable........................        12,000
     Wages Payable...........................        10,000
     (Various asset and liability accounts)..         5,000
```

5. Employees were paid $32,000 cash. This decreased the liability account, Wages Payable, and also decreases Cash. (The payment of wages also involves social security taxes, withholding taxes, and certain other complications; these matters have been omitted from this introductory diagram.) The journal entry follows:

```
Wages Payable............................... 32,000
     Cash....................................        32,000
```

6. Since the factory indirect cost is a part of the cost of the pens that were worked on during the month, the total cost incurred is transferred to Goods in Process Inventory, as in the following journal entry:

```
Goods in Process Inventory.................. 27,000
     Factory Indirect Costs.................        27,000
```

7. Pens whose total cost was $110,000 were completed during the month and were transferred to Finished Goods Inventory. This resulted in a decrease in Goods in Process Inventory, as recorded in the following journal entry:

```
Finished Goods Inventory.................... 110,000
     Goods in Process Inventory............        110,000
```

8. Pens with a cost of $115,000 were sold during the month. Physically, these pens were removed from inventory and shipped to the

customer. On the accounting records, this is reflected by a credit to Finished Goods Inventory and a debit to Cost of Goods Sold, as in the following journal entry:

```
Cost of Goods Sold...................... 115,000
     Finished Goods Inventory..............          115,000
```

9. For the same pens, sales revenue of $180,000 was earned, and this is recorded in the accounts as a credit to Sales and a debit to Accounts Receivable. Note that the Sales Revenue credit described here and the Cost of Goods Sold debit described in Entry No. 8 related to the same physical products, the same pens. The difference between the balances in the Sales Revenue and Cost of Goods Sold accounts, which is $65,000, therefore represents the gross margin earned on pens sold during the month. The journal entry for the sales transaction is as follows:

```
Accounts Receivable..................... 180,000
     Sales Revenue........................          180,000
```

10. Accounts receivable collected during the month amounted to $150,-000. Some of these collections were for sales made in the current month, but most were for sales made in previous months. The journal entry follows:

```
Cash.................................... 150,000
     Accounts Receivable..................          150,000
```

11. During the month $30,000 of selling and administrative expenses were incurred, $17,000 of which represented credits to Accounts Payable and $13,000 credits to various asset and liability accounts. These are recorded in the following journal entry:

```
Selling and Administrative Expense.......... 30,000
     Accounts Payable......................          17,000
     (Various asset and liability accounts)..          13,000
```

12. Since these expenses were applicable to the current period, the Selling and Administrative Expense account is closed to the Income Summary account, as in the following journal entry:

```
Income Summary............................. 30,000
     Selling and Administrative Expense......          30,000
```

13. The balances in the Sales and Cost of Goods Sold accounts are also closed to Income Summary. The balance in Income Summary then reflects the pretax income for the period. (To simplify the example, income taxes and certain nonoperating and financial items normally appearing on income statements have been excluded.) These closing journal entries follow:

```
Sales Revenue............................. 180,000
     Income Summary........................          180,000
```

```
Income Summary.......................... 115,000
     Cost of Goods Sold...................          115,000
```

Strictly speaking, the cost accounting system as such ends with Entry No. 8. The other entries are given in order to show the complete set of transactions for the company.

The income statement for the pen company is shown in Illustration 15–3.

Illustration 15–3

PEN COMPANY

Income Statement
For the Month of——

Sales......................................	$180,000
Cost of goods sold...........................	115,000
Gross margin...............................	$ 65,000
Selling and administrative expense...............	30,000
Income (before income taxes)...................	$ 35,000

JOB ORDER COSTING AND PROCESS COSTING

There are two principal systems for accumulating the costs of individual products. They are called, respectively, job order costing and process costing. Each is discussed below.

Essentially, a *job order* cost system collects cost for *each* physically identifiable job or batch of work as it moves through the factory, regardless of the accounting period in which the work is done. A *process* cost system collects costs for *all* the products worked on during an accounting period, and determines unit costs by dividing the total costs by the total number of units worked on.

Job Order Costing

The "job" in a job order cost system may consist of a single unit (e.g., a turbine or a house), or it may consist of all units of identical or similar products covered by a single job or production order (e.g., 1,000 printed books or 10 dozen Style 652 girdles). Usually each job is given an identification number, and its costs are collected on a separate record, called a *job cost record*, that is set up for that number. Anyone who has had an automobile repaired at a garage has seen such a record, except that the amounts that the customer sees have been converted from costs to retail prices. Costs are recorded as the job moves through the various departments in the factory. When the job is completed, these cost elements are totaled to find the total cost of that job. The sum of all the costs charged to all the jobs worked on in the factory during an accounting period is the basis for the entries debiting Goods in Process Inventory and crediting Raw Materials Inventory, Wages Payable, and Factory Indirect Costs accounts (i.e., Entries No. 2, 3, and 6 in Illustration 15–2). When each job is completed, the total cost recorded on the job cost record is the basis for the entry transferring the product from Goods in Process Inventory to Finished Goods Inventory (i.e., Entry No. 7), and this same cost is the basis for the entry transferring the product from Finished Goods Inventory to Cost of Goods Sold when the product is sold (Entry No. 8). The total cost recorded on all job cost records for products that are still in the factory as of the end of an accounting period equals the total of the Goods in Process Inventory account at that time.

In summary, in a job order cost system:

1. A separate job cost record is established for each job.
2. Costs chargeable to the job are entered on this record and are also debited to Goods in Process Inventory.
3. When the job is completed and transferred out of the factory, the total cost accumulated on the job cost record is the amount used to debit Finished Goods Inventory and to credit Goods in Process Inventory.
4. The balance in Goods in Process Inventory at the end of the accounting period is therefore the sum of the costs accumulated on all jobs still in the factory as reflected on the job cost records for uncompleted jobs.

Process Costing

In a process cost system, all manufacturing costs for an accounting period, such as a month, are collected in Goods in Process Inventory. These costs are *not* identified with specific units of product. A record of the number of units worked on is also maintained. By dividing total costs by total units, one derives a cost per unit; this cost per unit is used as the basis for calculating the dollar amount of the entries which records the transfer from Goods In Process Inventory, and the subsequent transfer from Finished Goods Inventory to Cost of Goods Sold.

EQUIVALENT PRODUCTION. A special problem that arises in a process cost system is that of taking into account the products that are only partially completed at the end of an accounting period. The units that were *worked on* in, say, September include the following: (1) units that were both started and completed during September; plus (2) units that were worked on but not completed by the end of September; plus (3) units that were started in August (or earlier) and completed in September.

Since 100 percent of the costs of the first type were incurred in September but only a portion of the costs of the second and third types was, production activity for September cannot be determined simply by adding up the number of units worked on during September. The three types of units must be converted to a common base, called *equivalent production,* that is, the equivalent of one completed unit. In order to convert the number of uncompleted products into their equivalence in terms of completed units, the assumption is often made that units still in process at the end of the period are 50 percent complete, and similarly that units in process at the beginning of the period were 50 percent complete at that time. Thus, in order to calculate the costs per unit worked on, each unit completed would be given a weight of one, each unit in process at the end of the period would be given a weight of one half, and each unit in process at the beginning of the period also would be given a weight of one half.[2]

> EXAMPLE: In a certain factory, costs incurred in September amounted to $22,000. During September, units were worked on as shown in Illustration 15–4, that is, 2,000 units were started and completed, another 300 units were started but not completed, and 100 units that had been started in August were completed. Thus, some work was done during September on a total of 2,400 units. The unit cost is *not* calculated by dividing $22,000 by the 2,400 units worked on, however, for to do so would be to neglect the costs incurred in the prior months for some units and the costs that will be incurred in the next month for still other units. Instead, it is assumed that in September one half of the work was done on partially completed units, so that each of them is equivalent to one half a unit that was begun and completed within the month. The number of equivalent units was therefore $2,000 + \frac{1}{2}(300) + \frac{1}{2}(100) = 2,200$ units. Since total factory costs for September were $22,000, the unit cost was $10.
>
> The 2,100 units transferred to Finished Goods Inventory would be costed at $10 per unit, a total of $21,000. The 300 partially completed units remaining in Goods in Process Inventory at the end of September would be costed at *one half* the unit cost, or $5 per unit, since it is assumed that they are only half completed.

The foregoing applies to direct labor costs and to factory indirect costs. Direct material costs may be treated differently, however, depending on when direct material enters the production process. If material is added evenly throughout the production process, it could reasonably be

---

[2] A more precise procedure would be to estimate the actual stage of completion, but this involves more effort. At the other extreme, some companies disregard the units in process and show no Goods in Process Inventory account. If the goods in process inventory is small, or if it remains relatively constant in size, no serious error is introduced. Another variation is to apply the 50 percent assumption separately to each department through which the product passes rather than to the factory as a whole.

Illustration 15–4

CALCULATION OF EQUIVALENT PRODUCTION

Period in Which Costs Were Incurred

Units		August	September	October
A.	2,000 all in current month		2,000	
B.	300 completed next month		½ of 300	½ of 300
C.	100 started in prior month	½ of 100	½ of 100	

Calculation of Equivalent Production

		Gross Units	Equivalent Production
A.		2,000	2,000
B.		300 (×½)	150
C.		100 (×½)	50
	Total	2,400	2,200

Unit cost: $22,000 ÷ 2,200 = $10

Goods in Process Inventory

Beginning balance (100 units)	500	To Finished Goods Inventory (2,100 units)	21,000
Costs incurred	22,000	Ending balance (300 units)	1,500
	22,500		22,500

costed by use of the 50 percent assumption described above. If, as is perhaps more common, all the raw material for a unit is issued at the beginning of the process, the direct material cost per unit would be obtained by dividing the total cost of material used by the number of units *started* during the period.

In any event, some reasonable assumption has to be made. In a process cost system, there is no precise way of determining the amount of costs attributable to partially completed units.

In summary, a process cost system works like this:

1. The costs of resources used in the manufacturing process during the accounting period are accumulated as debits to the Goods in Process Inventory account.
2. For cost elements, such as direct labor and factory indirect cost, that are incurred *throughout* the manufacturing process:
   a. Production is measured in terms of the number of equivalent units of production.
   b. A cost per unit is found by dividing total cost by the number of equivalent units.

3. For cost elements, such as direct material, that are incurred at the *beginning* of the manufacturing process, the cost per unit is found by dividing total cost by the number of units that started the production process.

4. Finished Goods Inventory is debited, and Goods in Process Inventory is credited, by an amount that is equal to the number of units completed in the period multiplied by these costs per unit.

5. Assuming that all direct material is issued at the beginning of the production process, the balance in Goods in Process Inventory at the end of an accounting period is the direct material cost of the units still in the factory plus an appropriate share (say, 50 percent) of the total direct labor and factory indirect cost of these units.

Choice of a System

Since a process cost system requires less recordkeeping than a job order system, there is a tendency to use it even though the products manufactured are not entirely alike. Thus, a manufacturer of canvas shoes may use a process cost system, even though there are some differences in cost among the various sizes, styles, and colors of shoes manufactured.

In a process cost system, the unit costs are *averages* derived from the total cost of the period. Differences in the costs of individual products are not revealed. Thus, if there are important reasons for keeping track of the differences between one product and another, or between one production lot of the same type of product and another, then a job cost system is more appropriate. For example, a job cost system would invariably be used if the customer paid for the specific item or production order on the basis of its cost (as is often the case in machine shops, print shops, and other "job shop" companies). Also, use of a job cost system makes it possible to examine actual costs on specific jobs, and this may help one to locate trouble spots; in a process cost system, costs cannot be traced to specific jobs.

For our purposes, there is no need to study differences in the detailed records required for the two types of systems. Both systems are essentially devices for collecting full factory costs. Either furnishes the information required for the accounting entries illustrated in Illustration 15–2. In practice, there are many cost accounting systems that use job costing in some departments and process costing in other departments.

Variations in Practice

The accounting system outlined in Illustration 15–2 will probably never be precisely duplicated in actual practice since it is a schematic representation of underlying structures. Companies build on the basic structure by adding accounts that collect the data in more detail so as to meet their particular needs for information. A company may, for example, set up several raw material inventory accounts, each one covering a different type of material, instead of a single account as shown in Illustration 15–2. Alternatively, the Raw Material Inventory account may be a controlling account, controlling dozens of individual subsidiary accounts. Another common variation is to have several goods in process accounts, one for each main department or "cost center" in the factory. Such a system is essentially like that shown in Illustration 15–2 except that work is transferred from one department to another. The finished goods of one department become, in effect, the raw material of the next department.

MEASUREMENT OF DIRECT COSTS

There are two general criteria for deciding whether or not a cost item is direct with respect to a specified cost objective. An item of cost is *direct:*

1. if the specified cost objective was intended to *benefit* from that item of costs; or
2. if the specified cost objective *caused* incurrence of the cost.[3]

If the benefit or the causal relationship for a single item of cost applies to two or more cost objectives, the item is indirect.

In this chapter, the cost objectives we are interested in are the manufacture of physical goods, such as pens or shoes. For these cost objectives, direct costs are those that directly benefit or are caused by the manufacture of the goods. For other types of cost objectives, the word "direct" could refer to quite different items of cost. Thus the salary of a department foreman is a direct cost of the department that he supervises, but it is an indirect cost of the goods made in that department because no beneficial or causal relationship exists between any single product and the foreman's salary.

> EXAMPLE: In a factory that manufactures shirts, the employees who operate the machines which are used to cut the cloth, sew the pieces together, make buttonholes, sew on buttons, attach the label, press the completed shirt, and inspect it, are direct workers. The employees who carry material from one work station to another and those who do production planning, timekeeping, and supervision are indirect workers.

---

[3] Cost Accounting Standards Board, *Statement of Operating Policies, Procedures, and Objectives*, March 1973, p. 17.

We shall now discuss in more detail the two principal types of direct product costs: direct labor costs and direct material cost. The discussion is in the context of a job cost system, but similar considerations are relevant in a process cost system.

Direct Labor Cost

There are essentially two problems in the measurement of direct labor cost: (1) measuring the *quantity* of labor time expended on the product, and (2) ascertaining the *price* per unit of labor time.

Measuring the quantity of labor time is relatively easy. A daily time-card, or comparable record, is usually kept for each direct worker, and on it a record is made of the time he spends on each job. Or, if direct workers are paid a piece rate, the record shows the number of pieces completed. These timecards are used both to measure labor costs and also as a basis for payroll computations. Problems do arise concerning the treatment of idle time, personal time, overtime, and so on, but these problems are beyond the scope of this introductory treatment.

Deciding on the best way to price these labor times is conceptually more difficult than measuring the quantity of time. The great majority of companies have a simple solution to this problem: they price direct labor at the amounts actually earned by the employees concerned (so much an hour if employees are paid on a day-rate or hourly rate basis; so much a piece if they are paid on a piece-rate basis). There may be either a separate labor rate for each employee or an average labor rate for all the direct labor employees in a department.

EXAMPLE: Assume that a certain job is worked on in four departments and that the time worked in each department (as shown by the timecards) and the labor rates are as indicated below. The direct labor cost of the job would be computed as follows:

Department	Direct Labor Hours on Job	Departmental Hourly Rate	Total Amount
A	20	$5.00	$100.00
B	3	4.50	13.50
C	6	3.80	22.80
D	40	3.00	120.00
Total direct labor cost of job			$256.30

Some companies add *labor-related costs* to the basic wage rate. They reason that each hour of labor effort costs the company not only the wages paid to the employee but also the social security taxes, pension contributions, and other fringe benefits paid by the employer.[4] The company must pay these labor-related benefits; they are caused by the fact that the employee works, and they are therefore part of the real cost of using the employee's services. A few companies even include a share of the costs of the personnel department and employee welfare programs as a part of direct labor cost. Using such a higher labor price gives a more accurate picture of direct labor costs. It also involves additional recordkeeping, however, and many companies do not believe the gain in accuracy is worthwhile.

Direct Material Cost

The measurement of direct material cost (or "raw materials cost") also has the two aspects of the *quantity* of material used and the *price* per unit of quantity. The quantity is usually determined from requisitions or similar documents that order material out of the storeroom and into production. The problem of pricing this material is similar to that for pricing direct labor. Material may be priced at solely its purchase or invoice cost, or there may be added some or all of the following *material-related costs:* inward freight, inspection costs, moving costs, purchasing department costs, and interest and space charges associated with holding material in inventory.

As was the case with labor costs, it is conceptually desirable to include these material-related items as part of material cost, but to do so may involve more recordkeeping than a company believes worthwhile.

The measurement of direct material costs is also affected by the assumption made about the flow of inventory costs, that is, Lifo, Fifo, or average cost. The effect of these alternative flow assumptions was discussed in Chapter 6.

ALLOCATION OF INDIRECT COSTS

Distinction between Direct and Indirect Costs

It is conceptually desirable that a given item of cost be classified as a direct cost rather than as an indirect cost. This is because an item of direct cost is assigned directly to a single cost objective, whereas, as will be discussed in a later section, the assignment of indirect costs to cost objectives is a more roundabout and usually less accurate process. Nevertheless, the category of indirect costs does, and must, exist.

Costs are not traced directly to a product for one of three reasons: (1) It is *impossible* to do so, as in the case of the factory superintendent's

---

[4] But *not* the *employee's* social security contribution. This is a deduction from the employee's earnings; it is therefore not a cost to the company. (See Chapter 8.)

salary already mentioned. (2) It is *not feasible* to do so; that is, the recordkeeping required for such a direct tracing would cost too much. (For example, the nails, the sewing thread, the eyelets, and the glue that are used on a pair of shoes cost only a few pennies, and it is not worthwhile to trace them to each case of shoes; they are therefore classified as indirect materials.) (3) Management *chooses* not to do so; that is, many companies classify certain items of costs as indirect simply because it has become customary in the industry to do so.

PROBLEMS OF DRAWING DISTINCTIONS. Problems arise in attempting to define the precise line between items of cost that are directly caused by or directly benefit a product, and other costs. For example, a cost may not be caused by a product even though it is incurred at the same time as the product is being manufactured.

> EXAMPLE: In a certain factory, Products A, B, and C were manufactured during regular working hours, and Product D was manufactured after regular hours. Overtime wages were paid to the employees who worked on Product D. These overtime wages might, or might not, be a direct cost of Product D. If the factory worked overtime because the general volume of orders was high, then the overtime is attributable to all the products worked on, and is an indirect cost. If, on the other hand, the overtime work on Product D was occasioned by a special request of the customer for Product D, then the overtime is a direct cost of Product D. It could also happen that the overtime was occasioned by a special need to make Product C quickly, and in order to meet this need, Product D was rescheduled from the regular work period to the overtime period; in this case, the overtime is truly a direct cost of Product C, even though overtime was not in fact paid during the hours in which Product C was being manufactured.

Moreover, there are differences of opinion as to how close the causal or beneficial relationship between the cost and cost objective must be in order to classify a cost item as direct. In many production operations, such as assembly lines of all types, refineries, and similar continuous process operations, a basic work force is required no matter what products are manufactured. Some would argue that the labor cost of this work force constitutes a cost that is required to operate the plant in general, much like depreciation on the machinery, and that it is therefore an indirect cost. Nevertheless, most companies consider such costs as direct labor.

Nature of Allocation

The cost of a cost objective includes, in addition to its direct costs, a *fair share* of the indirect costs that were incurred for several cost objectives, of which the cost objective in question is one. Thus, the factory cost of a case of shoes includes a fair share of all the indirect costs in the shoe factory. The idea of "fair share" sounds vague, and it is vague, but it is the only way of approaching the problem of measuring the indirect costs of a cost objective.

What is a fair share? Perhaps the best way to think about this question is from the viewpoint of the customer. Under ordinary circumstances, a customer should be willing to pay the cost of the product he buys plus a reasonable profit. Consider, for example, the customer of a job shop that offers printing services. A customer whose job requires the use of an expensive four-color printing press should expect to pay his share of the costs of operating that press, and he should expect to pay more per hour of press time than the customer whose job required only a small, inexpensive press. The customer whose job required a long time should expect to pay a relatively large share of the cost of plant facilities. Collectively, moreover, all the customers should expect to pay all the costs.

From the above line of reasoning, it follows that (1) all items of factory cost should be assigned to cost objectives, and (2) the amount assigned to an individual cost objective should depend on the benefits received or a causal incurrence, to the extent that a beneficial or causal relationship exists.

The process of assigning indirect costs to individual cost objectives is called *allocation*. The verb "to allocate" means "to assign indirect costs to individual cost objectives." Indirect costs are allocated to products by means of an overhead rate which is established prior to the beginning of the accounting period. Usually this rate is established annually. The method of calculating it is shown in Illustration 15–5. Before describing these calculations, we need to explain the term, cost center.

Cost Centers

A *cost center* is an accounting device for accumulating items of cost that have common characteristics. A cost center may correspond to an organization unit, such as a department, but there is no necessary correspondence between cost centers and organization units. There are two types of cost centers: production cost centers and service cost centers.

A *production cost center* is a cost center through which a product, or a product component, passes. Often a production cost center corresponds to a production department, but a group of similar machines (such as a bank of screw machines) may be a production cost center, and so may a single machine (such as each printing press in a printing shop).

A *service cost center* is a responsibility center or other unit that does not work directly on products or components. The maintenance department, the power plant, and general factory offices are examples. Service cost centers are often called indirect cost pools; the term "pool" conveys the notion of a container in which indirect costs are collected.

Calculation of Overhead Rate

Three steps are involved in the calculation of an overhead rate:

1. Estimates are made of the costs to be incurred in each cost center.
2. Estimated service center costs are reassigned, so that all costs are finally accumulated in production cost centers.
3. The total costs estimated for each production cost center are divided by a measure of activity, to give an overhead rate per unit of activity.

The calculations are shown in Illustration 15–5, using data for the pen company whose cost accounting system was shown in Illustration 15–2.[5]

Illustration 15–5

CALCULATION OF OVERHEAD RATE

Cost Item	Production Centers				Service Centers	
	Total	Barrel	Wick	Assembly	Occupancy	General
A. Initial Assignment to Cost Centers						
Indirect labor	$10,000	$1,700	$ 3,300	$ 0	$ 0	$5,000
Indirect supplies	5,000	500	1,500	900	600	1,500
Other	12,000	2,800	3,000	800	4,400	1,000
Subtotals	$27,000	$5,000	$ 7,800	$1,700	$5,000	$7,500
B. Re-assignment of Service Center Costs						
Occupancy		$1,500	$ 2,000	$1,000	$ (5,000)	$ 500
General		2,400	4,000	1,600		$ (8,000)
Indirect Cost	$27,000	$8,900	$13,800	$4,300		
C. Calculation of Overhead Rate						
Direct labor hours	7,000	2,100	3,500	1,400		
Overhead rate per direct labor hour		$4.24	$3.94	$3.07		

This company has three production cost centers, the barrel department, the wick department, and the assembly department. In addition, the

---

[5] These data are used so as to illustrate the relationship between the components of the overhead rate and the items of factory indirect cost. In actual practice, the overhead rate calculation in Illustration 15–5 is made at the beginning of the year, using *estimates* of the costs to be measured during the year, whereas the data in Illustration 15–2 are *actual* costs for a particular month. As explained later in this chapter, estimated costs are not likely to be the same as actual costs.

factory has two service cost centers, Occupancy and General. The Occupancy cost center is used to accumulate all costs associated with the factory building, such as building depreciation, building maintenance, heat, light, and property insurance. The General cost center is used to accumulate the cost of factory supervision and other general manufacturing costs that are not directly traceable to the other cost centers.

INDIRECT COST ACCUMULATION BY COST CENTERS. The first step in the allocation of indirect costs is to estimate what costs will be incurred and to assign all items of indirect factory costs for the period to some cost center (see Section A of Illustration 15–5). Indirect labor costs are assigned to the cost centers in which the employees will work. The costs of supplies and other indirect materials are assigned to the cost centers in which the materials will be used. Depreciation on machinery and power costs associated with the machine are assigned to cost centers in which the machines are located. In this step, each item of indirect cost is assigned to one, and only one, cost center, so that the sum of the costs for all the cost centers exactly equals the total indirect costs for the whole factory.

ASSIGNMENT OF SERVICE CENTER COSTS. The second step in the allocation of indirect costs is to assign the total estimated cost accumulated in each service cost center so that eventually all indirect costs are assigned to some production cost center (see Section B of Illustration 15–5). Some service center costs are assigned directly to the cost centers that receive the service. Maintenance department costs may be charged to operating departments on the basis of the maintenance service expected to be performed, for example. The costs of a power-generating plant may be assigned according to the metered usage of electricity in each cost center, just as if the electricity had been purchased from an outside company.

The costs of some service cost centers cannot be directly assigned to other cost centers. These costs must be allocated; that is, the costs must be assigned to other cost centers on some reasonable basis. The basis of allocation should correspond, as closely as is feasible, to one of the two criteria listed above; that is, it should have some connection with either benefits received or a causal relationship. The dozens of alternative bases of allocations that are used in practice can be grouped into the following principal categories:

1. *Payroll related.* Social security taxes paid by the employer, accident insurance, fringe benefits, and other costs associated with amounts earned by employees may be allocated on the basis of the total labor costs. Alternatively, as mentioned above, some or all of these costs may enter into the calculation of direct labor costs; if so, they will not appear as indirect costs at all. If certain indirect costs are ultimately charged to products by means of a direct labor rate (as will be described below), the

ultimate effect of treating these costs as indirect is approximately the same as if they were charged as part of direct labor costs.

2. *Personnel related.* Personnel department costs, and other costs that are associated with the number of employees rather than with the amount that they are paid, may be allocated on the basis of number of employees. (The distinction between "payroll related" and "personnel related" is a subtle one. Many companies do not attempt to make such a distinction; instead they allocate both types of costs together, usually on the basis of direct labor costs.)

3. *Material related.* This category of cost may be allocated on the basis of either the quantity or the cost of direct material used in production cost centers, or, alternatively, it may be excluded from indirect costs and charged to products as part of direct material cost, as already mentioned. The latter practice is conceptually preferable but it usually involves more recordkeeping.

4. *Space related.* Some items of cost are associated with the space that the cost center occupies, and they are allocated to cost centers on the basis of their relative area or cubic content. Occupancy cost in Illustration 15–5 is an example.

5. *Activity related.* Some costs are roughly related to the overall volume of activity in the cost center, or at least there is a presumption that the more work that a cost center does, the more costs are properly allocated to it. Electrical power costs and steam costs, if not directly assigned, fall into this category; and so do the costs of a variety of other service cost centers which, although not demonstrably a function of activity, are more realistically allocated in this way than in any other. The measure of activity may be an overall indication of the amount of work done by the cost center, such as its total labor cost, its total direct costs, or the total cost of its output. Alternatively, the measure of activity may be more closely related to the function of the service cost center whose costs are being allocated; for example, electric costs may be allocated on the basis of the total horsepower of motors installed in each cost center.

> EXAMPLE: The middle section of Illustration 15–5 illustrates the assignment of service center costs to production cost centers. Occupancy costs are allocated on the basis of the relative floor space in each cost center; the total cost of $5,000 is divided among the three production cost centers and the General service cost center using the percentages 30, 40, 20, and 10 because these represent each cost center's percentage of the total floor space.
>
> The costs of the General cost center are then allocated on the basis of the total direct costs (i.e., direct material + direct labor) charged to the three production cost centers. The total General cost is, after the addition of the allocated share of Occupancy cost, $8,000. Of this

amount 30 percent is allocated to Department 1, 50 percent to Department 2, and 20 percent to Department 3 because these are the percentages that each department's direct cost is to total direct cost.

STEP-DOWN ORDER.   Note that in Illustration 15–5 part of the cost of the Occupancy service cost center is charged to the General service cost center. It may well be that part of the cost of the General cost center should be charged to the Occupancy cost center, and this creates a problem. Whenever there are a number of service cost centers, the interrelationships among them could theoretically lead to a long series of distributions, redistributions, and re-redistributions. In practice, however, these redistributions are avoided by allocating the service center costs in a prescribed order, which is called the *step-down order*. In general, the least significant service centers are allocated first. In the illustration, the prescribed order is Occupancy first, and General second. No additional cost is allocated to a service cost center after its costs have been allocated. Since the step-down order is adhered to in all calculations, the results are always consistent.

CALCULATION OF OVERHEAD RATES.   The function of the overhead[6] rate is to assign an equitable amount of indirect cost to each product. In thinking about how this rate should be constructed, therefore, we need to address the question: Why, in all fairness, should one product have a higher indirect, or overhead, cost than another product? Depending on the circumstances, the following are among the plausible answers to this question:

1. Because more labor effort was expended on one product than on another, and indirect costs are presumed to vary with the amount of labor effort.
2. Because one product used more machine time than another, and indirect costs are presumed to vary with the amount of machine time.
3. Because one product had higher direct costs than another and was therefore able to "afford" a higher amount of indirect costs.

Each of these answers suggests a quantitative basis of activity that can be used to allocate indirect costs to products, viz:

1. The number of labor hours or labor dollars required for the product.
2. The number of machine-hours.
3. The total direct costs (i.e., direct material plus direct labor).

The machine-hours basis is common for production cost centers that consist primarily of one machine (such as a papermaking machine) or

---

[6] Since we have here referred to these costs as "indirect costs," it would be consistent to use the term "indirect cost rate." In practice, the term "overhead rate" is more widely used. "Burden rate" is also used.

a group of related machines. The direct labor cost basis is frequently used in other situations, since the direct labor cost is readily available on the job cost card. Direct labor hours are often used if a record of the number of hours worked on each job is readily available.

Having selected what appears to be the most appropriate measure of activity, the overhead rate for a production cost center is calculated by dividing the total indirect cost of the production cost center by the estimated total amount of activity for the period.

> EXAMPLE: Continuing with the example in Illustration 15–5, let us assume that the number of direct labor hours is the appropriate activity measure for the allocation of indirect costs to products. In the Barrel department, the number of direct labor hours for the period is estimated to be 2,100. This, divided into the estimated total indirect cost of $8,900, gives an overhead rate per direct labor hour of $4.24.

Usually, there is a single overhead rate for each production cost center. Thus, although service center costs are assigned to production cost centers by a variety of methods, with each method presumably the one that reflects most fairly the causal or beneficial relationship for the cost item, the total amount of indirect cost for the production cost center is allocated to products by one overhead rate.

Standard Volume

The most uncertain part of the process of establishing predetermined overhead rates is estimating what the level of activity will be. This amount is called the *standard volume* (or sometimes the *normal volume*). In many companies, standard volume is the volume anticipated for the next year. Some companies use instead the *average volume* expected over a *number of years* in the future. The overhead rate is lower if the estimated volume is high because the same amount of fixed cost is spread over a larger number of units. Therefore, the overhead rates resulting from the use of one of these concepts of standard volume can differ substantially from those calculated on the other concept.

The estimate of volume has a significant influence on overhead rates. In most companies, many important items of indirect cost do not vary with changes in volume; they are called *fixed costs*. To take the extreme case, if *all* indirect costs were fixed, the overhead rate would vary directly with the level of volume estimated for the forthcoming year. To the extent that not all costs are fixed, changes in overhead rates associated with changes in the estimate of volume are not as severe, but they are nevertheless significant in most situations. It is therefore important that careful attention be given to making the best possible estimate of volume as part of the procedure of calculating predetermined overhead rates.

EXAMPLE: A papermaking machine is a large, expensive machine that either runs at capacity or doesn't run at all. Its depreciation, the costs associated with the building in which it is housed, and most other items of indirect cost are unaffected by how many hours a year the machine operates. Assume that these indirect costs are estimated to be $1,000,000 a year, and that they are entirely fixed, that is, they are estimated to be $1,000,000 regardless of how many hours the machine operates during the year. If the measure of activity used in establishing the overhead rate is machine-hours, overhead rates will vary as shown below for various estimates of machine-hours to be operated during the year:

Indirect Cost	No. of Machine-Hours	Overhead Rate (per machine-hour)
$1,000,000	8,000	$125
1,000,000	6,000	167
1,000,000	4,000	250

The effect of the volume estimate on the amount of overhead cost assigned to products during the year is therefore great. Indeed, in a situation like this, in which indirect fixed costs are large relative to total costs, including direct labor and direct material, the accounted cost of the product may be affected more by the estimate of annual volume than by any other single factor.

The important point to remember is that the predetermined overhead rate will be relatively low if the estimated volume of activity is relatively high because the same amount of fixed cost will be spread over a larger number of units. This point will be discussed in more depth in Chapter 17.

Allocation to Products

The indirect cost for each product that passes through the production cost center is calculated by multiplying the cost center overhead rate by the number of activity units accumulated for that product.

EXAMPLE: Referring to the situation in Illustration 15–5, if in this factory a certain job, Job No. 307, required 30 direct labor hours in the barrel department, 20 direct labor hours in the wick department and 5 direct labor hours in the assembly department, its total indirect cost would be calculated as follows:

Production Cost Center	Direct Labor Hours	Overhead Rate	Indirect Cost
Barrel department	30	$4.24	$127.20
Wick department	20	3.94	78.80
Assembly department	5	3.07	15.35
Total indirect cost of Job No. 307			$221.35

Why Overhead Rates Are Predetermined

It would be possible to calculate overhead rates at the end of the period, rather than estimating them in advance, but this is rarely done. There are three advantages in using a predetermined overhead rate:

1. If overhead rates were calculated monthly, they would be unduly affected by conditions peculiar to that month. Heating costs in the winter, for example, are higher than heating costs in the summer, but no useful purpose would be served by reporting that shoes manufactured in the winter cost more than shoes manufactured in the summer.

2. The use of a predetermined overhead rate permits product costs to be calculated more promptly. Direct material and direct labor costs can be assigned to products as soon as the time records and material requisitions are available; but if overhead rates were calculated only at the end of each month, after all the information on indirect costs for the month had been assembled, indirect costs could not be assigned to products until after this calculation had been completed. With the use of a predetermined overhead rate, indirect costs can be allocated to products at the same time that direct costs are assigned to them.

3. The calculations of an overhead rate once a year requires less effort than going through the same calculations every month.

Unabsorbed and Overabsorbed Overhead

When a predetermined overhead rate is used, the amount of indirect costs allocated to products in a given month is likely to differ from the amount of indirect costs actually incurred in that month. This is because the actual indirect costs assigned to the cost center in the month, and/or the actual activity level for the month, are likely to be different from the estimates that were used when the predetermined overhead rate was calculated. If the amount of indirect cost allocated to products exceeds the amount actually assigned to the cost center, overhead is said to be *overabsorbed;* and if the amount is less, indirect costs are *underabsorbed* (or more commonly, *unabsorbed*). For management purposes, the amount of unabsorbed or overabsorbed overhead is useful information, as will be discussed in Chapter 22.

EXAMPLE: Assume in a certain production cost center, the predetermined overhead rate was calculated as follows:

	Average Month
Estimated indirect costs	$100,000
Estimated direct labor hours	25,000
Overhead rate, per direct labor hour	$4

In January, actual indirect costs were $110,000 and actual direct labor hours were 25,000. The amount of overhead allocated to products would be 25,000 × $4 = $100,000. The amount of unabsorbed cost would be $110,000 − $100,000 = $10,000.

In February, actual indirect costs were $150,000 and actual direct labor hours were 40,000. The amount of overhead allocated to products would be 40,000 × $4 = $160,000. The amount of overabsorbed cost would be $160,000 − $150,000 = $10,000.

The January numbers in the above example are typical of the situation that exists when costs get "out of control"; that is, costs were $10,-000 higher than they should have been. The February example typifies the situation when actual volume exceeds estimated volume.

For financial accounting purposes, the amount of unabsorbed or overabsorbed overhead in a given month is usually held in suspense as a temporary item on the balance sheet in the expectation that unabsorbed overhead in one month will be offset by overabsorbed overhead in another month. Any balance that exists at the end of the year theoretically should be divided among Goods in Process Inventory, Finished Goods Inventory, and Cost of Goods Sold in proportion to the relative size of these accounts, and many companies do this. Some companies, however, report the entire amount of the unabsorbed or overabsorbed overhead as an expense or adjustment to Cost of Goods Sold.

In the interest of simplicity, no account for overabsorbed or unabsorbed overhead was shown in the cost accounting flowchart given in Illustration 15–2. Such an account is often labeled an *Overhead Variance account*. The journal entry debits Goods in Process Inventory for the amount of costs absorbed, credits indirect cost accounts for the amount of indirect costs incurred, and debits or credits Overhead Variance for the difference.

EXAMPLE: If actual factory indirect costs were $28,000 and if only $27,000 were assigned to products on the basis of the overhead rates, the entry would be:

```
Goods in Process Inventory................. 27,000
Overhead Variance.......................... 1,000
     Factory Indirect Costs................         28,000
```

SUMMARY

Cost measures the amount of resources used for a cost objective.

A cost accounting system assigns to each product (1) its direct costs, that is, the costs that are directly traceable to it, and (2) a fair share of the indirect costs, that is, those costs incurred for several cost objectives. There are two main types of systems: (1) job order costing, in which costs are accumulated separately for each individual item or for a lot of similar items; and (2) process costing, in which costs are accumulated for all units together, and then are divided between completed units and partially completed units according to some reasonable assumption as to the stage of completion at the end of the period.

Items of cost are indirect because it is not possible to assign them directly, because it is not worthwhile to do so, or because the management chooses not to do so. Factory indirect costs are allocated to products by means of an overhead rate. This rate is calculated prior to the beginning of the period, usually once a year. The overhead rate is used to allocate indirect costs to the products that pass through the production cost center. The number of units of activity required for each product multiplied by the overhead rate gives the total amount of indirect cost allocated to that product.

SUGGESTIONS FOR FURTHER READING
(For Chapters 15 and 16)

Fremgen, James M. *Accounting for Managerial Analysis.* Rev. ed. Homewood, Ill.: Richard D. Irwin, Inc., 1972.

Horngren, Charles T. *Cost Accounting: A Managerial Emphasis.* 3d ed. Englewood Cliffs, N.J.: Prentice-Hall, Inc., 1972.

Matz, Adolph, and Currey, Othel J. *Cost Accounting Planning and Control.* 5th ed. Cincinnati: South-Western Publishing Co., 1972.

Neuner, John J. W. *Cost Accounting: Principles and Practice.* 8th ed. Homewood, Ill.: Richard D. Irwin, Inc., 1973.

Shillinglaw, Gordon. *Cost Accounting: Analysis and Control.* 3d ed. Homewood, Ill.: Richard D. Irwin, Inc., 1972.

Thomas, William E., ed. *Readings in Cost Accounting, Budgeting and Control,* 4th ed.; Cincinnati: South-Western Publishing Co., 1973.

CASES

CASE 15-1. LAREN MANUFACTURING COMPANY

Mr. James Laren, Jr., was asked to investigate the possibility of instituting new methods of cost control in the Laren Manufacturing Company, which was owned by his father. Mr. Laren, Sr., keenly felt the need for better cost control because his small plumbing and pipe fitting equipment firm competed on a price basis with large corporations that were firmly entrenched in the market.

James Laren, Jr., decided to start his investigation in the company's valve department, because this department produced almost one third of the company's total volume of sales. The valve department contained drilling and grinding machines, lathes, welding equipment, and assembly space. In this department all the operations necessary to produce and assemble valves were performed.

The valve department occupied almost one half the total floor space in the Laren Company's three-story plant. Section 1, the welding section, was located on the first floor of the plant and occupied about one sixth of the space on that floor. Sections 2, 3, and 4, as well as the office, toolroom and stock room were all located on the third floor. None of these sections occupied more than one fifth of the third floor's space. Section 5, the assembly section, occupied about one half of the second floor and one sixth of the third floor. Exhibit 1 describes the functions of these sections, each of which was under the supervision of a leadman.

Exhibit 2 indicates the flow of production through the various sections of the valve department. Valves in the standard line went through Sections 1, 2, 3, and 5. Special valves (i.e., valves not in the standard line) went through all five sections. Pieces produced for spare parts inventory did not go through Section 5 (assembly). In addition, any section of the valve department might perform some operations on products for other departments of the Laren Manufacturing Company.

Mr. Laren's investigation showed that all factory costing in the valve department (except material costs) was done on a departmentwide, direct-labor-hour basis; that is, each lot of products going through the

464

Exhibit 1

FUNCTIONS PERFORMED IN VALVE DEPARTMENT

Section 1 . . . . Welding	This section repairs casting defects, welds special fittings to valve bodies, and performs other welding operations required in fabrication of valve parts.
Section 2 . . . . Grinding	Grinding is done to prepare castings for further machining. Also, various parts which make up valves are ground for precision fit.
Section 3 . . . . Machining	All the necessary machining operations to produce various standard valves are done in this section.
Section 4 . . . . SpecialWork	Here, the layout, drilling, tapping, and special machining needed on valves other than the standard line are done.
Section 5 . . . . Assembly	This section is responsible for the assembly and testing of all valves produced in the department.

department was costed at a certain rate for each direct labor hour actually spent on the lot. Exhibit 3 shows the computation made to arrive at the cost figure of $8.64, which was the rate per labor hour in the whole department in August. Costs were accumulated and allocated to jobs each month.

Mr. Laren, Jr., did not feel that this method of obtaining and apportioning costs was accurate enough. He believed that problems could arise in trying to judge performance and in obtaining the true cost of different products by following this method. He proposed, therefore, that costs be collected monthly for each section of the department and that these costs

Exhibit 2

PRODUCTION FLOW THROUGH VALVE DEPARTMENT

Exhibit 3

CALCULATION OF MANUFACTURING COST PER DIRECT
LABOR HOUR IN THE VALVE DEPARTMENT*

(August)

Section	Labor Charge per Month	Burden	Total
1	$ 4,605		
2	2,790		
3	16,080		
4	6,150		
5	26,100		
Total	$55,725	$90,945	$146,670

Total number of hours worked: 16,970/month.
Average hourly charge: $146,670 ÷ 16,970 = $8.64

* Does not include materials.

be apportioned to jobs according to the amount of time spent in each section.

In order to study the effect of this proposal, Mr. Laren recomputed the costs for August so as to show the costs applicable to each section. Since direct labor charges were already being collected by sections, no change in procedures was necessary for the collection of labor costs. Some overhead items, such as the salary of a section chief, could be charged directly to the section in which they were incurred. Other overhead charges, such as heating and lighting, were allocated on bases that seemed to Mr. Laren to be reasonable. He divided the total overhead costs charged to each section by the number of labor hours worked in the section, and arrived at costing rates for each section. These are shown in Exhibit 4.

Mr. Laren made the following observations in support of his proposal for revising the costing rates.

Exhibit 4

PROPOSED COST PER DIRECT LABOR HOUR FOR EACH
SECTION OF THE VALVE DEPARTMENT*

(August)

Section	Total Hours	Labor Charge per Hour	Burden Charge per Hour	Total Cost per Hour
1	1,370	$3.36	$4.98	$ 8.34
2	1,000	2.79	4.65	7.44
3	4,000	4.02	9.84	13.86
4	1,800	3.42	6.30	9.72
5	8,800	2.97	3.27	6.24
Total	16,970			

* Does not include materials.

One of the items produced in largest volume by the department was Valve 301. A standard production run of Valve 301 required the following hours in the different sections of the department:

Section	Hours
1	15
2	10
3	65
5	40

Mr. Laren said that there obviously was a wide difference between the cost for this valve as figured under the present system and the cost as figured under his proposed system. His contention was that the present method led to false conclusions as to the profitability of a line.

Mr. Laren also saw problems in the valuation of the spare parts inventory produced by the valve department. The company produced a wide line of valves, and it was necessary to maintain an inventory of spare parts in order to be able promptly to supply repair parts to customers. The following amounts of time were usually spent on producing spare parts for inventory each month:

Section	Hours
1	160
2	145
3	560

When Mr. Laren's proposal was explained to the heads of the operating departments, it met with immediate and strong opposition. First to voice disapproval were the heads of other departments that had work totaling the following amounts done by the valve department each month:

	Hours
Welding (Section 1)	350
Grinding (Section 2)	250
Machining (Section 3)	1,100

These supervisors thought that it was unfair to change a sizable part of their department's costs, especially since they had no control over the costs incurred in the valve department.

Mr. Ahearn, foreman of the pipe fixture department, was very much against the proposal:

The valve department does the machining work on all the jobs that my department can't handle. If you raise my costs on this work, I'll never be able to stay within my budget, because the valve department is already charging me more than I could do the work for in my own department if I had the capacity.

The sales manager was also against the proposal:

If you start monkeying around with our cost system, we'll have to start changing our prices, and we're having enough trouble with price competition from the major companies as it is. After all, our complete valve line is showing a profit. You have to carry some items for sales reasons, regardless of their profitability, so why worry about the very small variation in cost between different items.

The foreman of the valve department also opposed the change:

I'm too busy to fool with more paper work. It takes all my time to get the production out without trying to keep up with this stuff, section by section. And my lead men in the sections don't have time for it either. The department is carrying all its costs now, so why put in an extra gimmick?

Mr. Laren, Sr., remained neutral on the question. He was most interested in whether or not the added cost and trouble of the proposed system would be justified by the benefits the system would give.

Questions

1. What is the difference in the cost of Valve 301 under the proposed method as compared with that under the present method? In value of spare parts added to inventory each month? In the cost of work done for other departments? Are these cost differences significant?
2. What causes the difference in costs given by the proposed method as compared with the present method?
3. Suppose that the company purchased a new $108,000 machine for Section 4 that both reduced machining time and resulted in higher quality special valves. As a result, the total time required for valves in Section 4 is reduced by 30 percent. The extra labor is transferred to other departments. About 10 percent of the overhead in Section 4 is variable with respect to machining time. The engineer's best estimate of the life of the machine is about five years. During August only special valves were worked on in Section 4.
   a. Calculate what the total cost per hour would be after the new machine is in operation if there were only one cost center in the valve department. Assume that operations are the same as actual operations in August in all other respects.
   b. Calculate what the total cost per hour would be if Section 4 were a separate cost center.
   c. What would happen to the computed costs per month of producing special valves with a single cost center, after purchase of the machine, as compared with the cost before purchase of the machine?
   d. What would happen to the computed costs per month of producing special valves with five cost centers, after purchase of the new machine, as compared with the cost before purchase of the machine?
   e. What do you conclude about the relative usefulness of the two methods (single cost center versus five cost centers)?

4. What management benefits, if any, would you expect from the proposed system, that is, the collection and allocation of costs by sections? Consider this question from the standpoint of (*a*) product pricing, (*b*) cost control, (*c*) inventory valuation, and (*d*) charges to other departments. Do you think these benefits would outweigh the costs of collection of the necessary data?

CASE 15–2. DAVIGO FOODS COMPANY

The Davigo Foods Company, located in a tomato-growing section, had for many years produced tomato specialties such as tomato juice cocktail, tomato paste, and ketchup. In 1973, it was able to extend its production season from four to nine months by the addition of various types of prepared spaghetti dinners and ravioli. In order to keep certain skilled personnel, the company had found a place for five workers in the shipping department during the three months when the remainder of the plant was closed.

These workers had been earning a wage of $3.90 an hour at their regular work, but they were willing to accept $2.91 an hour for the time they were in the shipping department. This meant that during the three months that they were in the shipping department the five had collectively received $2,580 less than they would have received at their regular rate of pay. However, the regular wage rate in the shipping department was $2.40 an hour, and the shipping department therefore had been charged with $1,320 more than it ordinarily would have paid for this type of work.

The head of the shipping department was indignant that his costs were increased by this amount and contended that he should be charged at a rate not higher than the regular $2.40 rate for his department and that a fairer rate would be the beginners' rate of $1.95, since these workers were not so efficient as his experienced work force.

Question

How would you account for the $2.91 an hour paid the five workers when they worked in the shipping department?

CASE 15–3. SYLVAN POOLS INC.

The idea behind Sylvan Pools was born in 1947, when the company's president, Herman Silverman, who at the time was operating a small landscaping business in Pennsylvania, was asked by a customer to convert a mudhole into a concrete pond. Silverman fulfilled the request by lining the mudhole with wire and hand cementing over the wire. As a result of this venture, Herman wondered why residential swimming pools could not be built as economically. That same year he experimented by building two such pools; the following year he built eight. Extending the simple methods used in the mudhole, Herman perfected the Unipour® method of swimming pool construction, which produced a pool with no seams or joints, and employed no forms in pouring the concrete. The result was a lifetime pool, impervious to all weather conditions, and even recommended for use in the winter as an ice skating rink.

In 1953, Herman was joined in the business by his brother Ira, who became Executive Vice President. The company continued to grow, building sixty pools in 1953 and eighty in 1954. The increased demand was kept manageable by keeping prices up, but in spite of the premium pricing policy the company reported losses regularly.

The reported results puzzled Herman and Ira. They knew that they were succeeding in producing a quality product, prices were at least in line with what the competition was charging, their employees seemed to be working efficiently, and yet their financial statements reported that they were losing money. Every manager in the company had his own explanation of the reasons, often based on his personal "back pocket slip" on costs. Everyone was sure that the company's problems were someone else's fault. In particular, interminable arguments resulted from the allocation procedures. No one could agree on whether labor hours, labor dollars, sales, or any other base was appropriate for allocating particular overhead items.

The U.S. Swimming Pool Industry

Formerly confined primarily to building large pools for institutions, the U.S. swimming pool industry was undergoing a major transformation in the late 1950s. Rising consumer affluence was permitting more individuals to own a private pool, resulting in an industry divided into two segments: commercial and residential. Almost all commercial pools were constructed by a few big companies. Residential pools, on the other hand, were marketed both by a few large companies, each putting in hundreds of pools per year, and by a large number of small companies, each putting in a few pools per year. There were few barriers to entry into the business—all that one needed was a bulldozer and a truck—resulting in many small firms being formed every year. Many of these firms were under-financed and run by people who did not have the expertise required; as a result, there was a high rate of turnover.

Residential pools were constructed of various materials. One of the advantages of gunnite or poured concrete was that every pool could be unique in size and shape. In the colder parts of the country, pool construction was necessarily a seasonal business. When winter came, installations stopped. Sales also dropped off in the winter, and peaked on the hottest summer days. Even though residential pools cost \$3,500–\$7,000, they were often purchased on impulse.

Company Background

In the early years of Sylvan Pools, Herman Silverman sold pools by night and worked with the construction crews by day. Sylvan gradually developed the consumer confidence so important in this business, and was able to develop strong relationships with several prominent architects and builders. These architects often required construction to Sylvan's specifications. As a result, Sylvan usually received the contract to build the pool since the Unipour® process was copyrighted. Sylvan's economical and dependable method of construction broke the barrier with the middle-to-upper income resident, and enabled the company to capture a large market share in Pennsylvania.

Sylvan's construction employees worked about nine months during the year although, due to bad weather, they did not always work a five-day week. However, they worked so hard and such long hours during the days that they did work, and Sylvan paid them such a high hourly rate, that employee turnover was practically nil and there was a very high sense of company loyalty. The office and sales staffs worked a twelve-month year.

During the slow winter season, the equipment and rolling stock were repaired and repainted in order to have them appear spanking new for the commencement of work in the Spring. Only repairs absolutely necessary to keep the equipment operating were made during the summer. Herman and Ira felt that a good-looking fleet of vehicles was important in enhancing Sylvan's quality image. Also, all of the construction workers wore uniforms in order to achieve this end.

The Construction of a Sylvan Pool

In addition to the pool shell itself, there were many subsidiary parts needed for a pool. Plumbing was required for filling and draining the pool. A filter was needed to clean the water, and often a heater was added to lengthen the swimming season. Lighting was usually installed, sometimes both underwater and above ground. A ladder and diving board were virtually standard equipment. While skimmers (water surface level outlets) were used to keep the water free of surface debris, an underwater vacuum cleaner was required to remove dirt which had settled on the bottom of the pool. A terrace was often installed around the pool and a fence was usually a legal requirement for safety reasons. Sometimes an alarm sensitive to waves in the pool was installed to detect uninvited swimmers. Some manufacturers offered covers for pools which could be locked above the water surface for safety. In inclement climates, pool enclosures, either rigid or supported by internal air pressure, were used to lengthen the swimming season.

Every pool Sylvan installed was unique in size, shape, the amount of materials required (ready-mix concrete was the predominant material), the amount of labor required, the distance from the main plant, and in the accessories desired by the owner. Every night, employees at the warehouse assembled on pallets the materials needed by each crew for the next day's work. Given the diversity in the pools, a different quantity and/or variety of material had to be "picked" for each pallet.

After plans had been approved by both Sylvan and the customer, a three-person excavation crew arrived with a bulldozer and trucks and made the excavation, adding finishing touches by hand, and laying down a crushed stone base to relieve hydrostatic pressure. Then a reinforcing crew of two workers arrived and assembled half-inch steel reinforcing rods into an electrically bonded mesh. Later, the pouring crew, which usually consisted of eight workers, using the Unipour® method poured the pool shell. The coping and tiling crew of three people installed the concrete coping and tiling around the edge of the pool. Terracing followed if required. Then the completion crew sanded and painted the pool, installed accessories, and cleaned up the site. Finally, fencing was installed if ordered.

Unexpected problems sometimes developed, especially in the excavation step. While items such as stumps could be observed and charged for accordingly, rocks or hardpan might appear after excavation had begun, blasting might be required, or the customer might exercise his privilege under the sales contract either to change the pool location, requiring new plans, or simply to have the hole refilled. In the contract, Sylvan protected itself by trying to assure that it would break even on the extra work required if unexpected problems occurred.

There were many crews of constant membership in each trade. Each step was completed in one day and it was important that excavation be followed promptly by reinforcing and pouring, lest rain cause wall collapse. Sylvan subscribed to a weather service and all trucks carried plastic tarpaulins to minimize rain damage. If rain was expected, the crews did not leave the home office, thus disrupting the schedule which had been established.

Actual Cost System

When a job was started, it received a code number, and all costs relevant to this job were identified by this number. When materials such as plumbing supplies, reinforcing rods, and accessories were requisitioned from the warehouse, a record of the quantity issued and the job code number was made on the requisition form. The quantity of material was multiplied by the purchase cost per unit (on a FIFO basis) to arrive at the actual cost of material used. Leftover materials returned to the warehouse were credited to the appropriate job. Invoices from ready-mix concrete companies were also recorded by code number. By summarizing all these items, it was easy to arrive at the total material cost for a given pool.

Similarly, labor costs were accumulated from employees' time cards which indicated how many hours had been spent at how much per hour on which pools. Finally, Sylvan's overhead costs which could not be directly identified with a particular pool were allocated among all pools on a basis proportional to the number of hours of labor devoted to each job. For example, if 5% of the hours worked during a calendar quarter were spent on pool A, then pool A would bear 5% of the allocated overhead incurred in that quarter.

Under this system, management knew toward the end of a quarter how much each pool built in the preceding quarter had cost. Income statements were prepared quarterly recognizing all costs recorded by the cost system and recognizing revenue for each pool as it was completed. Customer progress payments on pools were used as a much-needed source of cash, but were not recognized as revenue.

Salesmen, construction foremen, and management all had individual "back pocket slips" concerning costs. There were endless arguments about overhead allocations. According to Ira, "nobody really knew what the costs were" and the whole situation was "chaotic." The financial statements, which used a fiscal year end of March 31, appeared late and showed steady losses. Though their auditors urged them to file a petition in bankruptcy, the Silverman brothers pushed on, obtaining the cash they needed through good relations with their bankers. Sylvan just kept growing larger and larger.

Questions

1. What kind of information should a cost system provide to management?
2. How well does Sylan's system fulfill your idea of what a good system should be?
3. What recommendations for improvement would you make to Herman and Ira?

CASE 15–4. CRAIK VENEER COMPANY

The sales manager of the Craik Veneer Company received from the Groton Company an offer to buy one million feet per month of sound "backs" of $\frac{1}{24}$-inch birch veneer[1] at $8 per thousand surface feet. The sales manager wanted to accept the offer, but the production manager argued that it should not be accepted because the cost of production was at least $10 per thousand feet and probably more.

The Craik company manufactured rotary cut birch veneer from high-grade yellow birch logs bought in Vermont. Selected sections called "blocks" were cut out of those logs, the length of the block varying from 84 inches to 98 inches, depending on the length along the grain of the veneer being produced. These blocks, as cut for the lathe, cost an average of $200 per thousand board feet. A thousand board feet, log measure, was an amount of logs which, being sawed, would produce a thousand board feet of lumber. (A board foot is one square foot one inch thick.) After being cut, the blocks were put in vats filled with hot water and left there for 24 to 48 hours until the entire log was heated through.

Manufacturing Process

In the rotary veneer process, a block was put in a lathe in which a knife longer than the block, with a heavy frame, guide bars, and pressure bars, was brought against the side of the block so that it cut off a thin slice of wood the entire length of the block. The process was similar to unrolling a large roll of paper held on a horizontal shaft. The process could be controlled with skillful operation so it would produce veneer of uniform thickness. The Craik company produced principally $\frac{1}{24}$-inch veneer, and for the purposes of this case it may be assumed that all of its product was $\frac{1}{24}$-inch.

The sheet of veneer from the lathe, for instance from a 98-inch block, was brought onto a clipping table approximately 60 feet long. This table had rubber belts on its upper surface which moved the veneer along to the clipper. At this point the veneer was like a long sheet of paper moving along the table, the veneer being 98 inches along the grain. The clipper was a long knife extending entirely across the table. The clipper operator was one of the most highly skilled workers in the plant. Constantly inspecting the sheet of veneer, he first took one cut to get a straight edge. If the next section of the sheet was of high quality, he advanced the sheet not over 3 feet 8 inches, depending on customers' requirements. If the sheet showed a defect within 3 feet 8 inches, he made his cut just short of the defect. A worker called the "off bearer" piled these sheets on a hand truck reserved for high-grade or "face" veneer. If the defect was a knot, the clipper operator then advanced the sheet enough to clear the knot and took another cut, making a piece of waste possibly 3 inches wide. If he decided that a section of the sheet was not

---

[1] Veneer is a term applied to thin leaves or layers of wood. Generally veneer is made of valuable wood and is laid over a core of inferior wood.

of face quality, he cut it off for "backs," either 3 feet 8 inches or in lesser widths. Backs were put on another hand truck.

The clipper operator thus separated the whole sheet of veneer into faces, backs, and waste. The faces consisted of pieces of veneer 98 inches long along the grain and anywhere from 6 inches to 3 feet 8 inches wide. The sound backs were of the same size. The waste went to a chipper and was then burned. The term "faces" came from the fact that these veneer sheets were substantially perfect and could be used on the exposed parts of furniture or on the best face of plywood.[2] The backs had minor defects and were so called because they were used on the back of plywood panels. The quality required for faces was established by specifications and by the custom of the industry. The dividing line between sound backs and waste was similarly established. The Craik company had a reputation for using high-grade logs and for producing a high grade of veneer both on faces and backs.

Groton Company's Offer

The Groton Company's research and development department had developed two new lines of furniture, one in blond modern and one in colonial, in which the table tops, dresser tops and panels, drawer fronts, and other exposed parts were of birch veneer over lower-grade birch or poplar cores, with table legs, dresser frames, and so on, of solid birch. The Groton research people knew that while all sheets of backs contained defects, 50 to 60 percent of the area of backs as produced by Craik were of face quality. They had discovered that by buying backs 84 inches to 98 inches long they could cut clear face-quality veneer into lengths that would match their use requirements: enough 54 inches for their longest dresser tops and enough of other lengths down to 14-inch drawer fronts. The remainder of the veneer that was not of face quality could be used for such purposes as making plywood for drawer bottoms. The methods developed in the research department had been tested by cutting up several carloads of backs bought from Craik and by the manufacture and sale of the furniture.

On the basis of this experience the Groton Company offered Craik $8 per thousand feet for one million feet per month of sound backs in $\frac{1}{24}$-inch birch veneer for the next 12 months.

Cost Information

The Craik company cut an average of 12,000 board feet of logs a day in one eight-hour shift. With the high quality of logs it bought, it got

---

[2] Veneer is a single thin sheet of wood. Plywood consists of several sheets (three, five, or nine) glued together with the grain of alternate courses at right angles to add to the strength.

a yield of 18,000 surface feet of $\frac{1}{24}$-inch veneer per 1,000 board feet cut; this graded on the average 50 percent faces and 50 percent backs.

Labor and factory overhead costs together averaged $8 per thousand surface feet of veneer; selling costs averaged $1.50. Both the cost of the blocks and operating costs for the heating, lathe turning, and clipping operations were joint costs; backs had to be produced in order to get the faces. The remaining operations in drying, a slight amount of reclipping, storing, and shipping were in a sense separate costs as the operations were done on backs separately, although with the same equipment. The labor and factory overhead costs through clipping averaged $6.75 per 1,000 surface feet of veneer; those for drying and later operations, $1.25.

The selling price for $\frac{1}{24}$-inch birch faces 84 inches to 98 inches long was $40 per thousand surface feet. Face veneer 84 inches to 98 inches had a high price because it could be used on large surfaces, such as flush birch doors that require lengths up to eight feet. The veneer shorter in length along the grain, made from recutting backs, had a somewhat lower price because it could not be used for these purposes. Unlike faces, the price of backs fluctuated widely. Sometimes Craik could get $10 per thousand feet, but the insistence of the production manager on $10 had led to the accumulation of a heavy inventory of backs. Faces were easy to sell and were shipped substantially as fast as they were produced.

More effort was required to sell backs than to sell faces, although both were sold to the same customers by the same salesmen. Sometimes buyers of faces were required to take a percentage of backs in order to get a carload of faces. For these reasons the offer of the customer was attractive to the sales manager.

Discussion of Offer

When the production manager was first informed by the sales manager of the offer of $8 per thousand surface feet, the production manager contended that "Your salesmen are so lazy, they would give veneer away if nobody watched them." The production manager went on to say:

If a birch block cost $200 per thousand and we get 18,000 feet of $\frac{1}{24}$-inch-thick veneer from every thousand board feet of the block, the cost of the block to be allocated to a thousand feet of veneer, whether backs or faces, is $200 divided by 18,000 feet, or about $11.11 per thousand feet. Simple arithmetic proves that selling backs at $8 per thousand doesn't even pay for the material, let alone labor and overhead.

The sales manager countered that this argument was fallacious:

Allocating the cost of the block to the veneer in this manner implies that backs are as valuable as faces, which is not the case. The $11.11 material figure for a thousand feet of veneer that you get is merely an average of the value of faces and backs. The material for faces is worth considerably more per thousand feet than this figure; the material for backs is worth considerably less.

The sales manager suggested that the proper procedure was to allocate the cost of the block to faces and backs in proportion to the amounts for which the products were sold. Using this method, the ratio that the revenue of one of the two grades of veneer bore to the revenue received from both grades of veneer would be applied to the total cost of the block, the result representing the cost to be allocated to that particular grade. To illustrate this method, assume a block of a thousand board feet cost $200, and the selling prices and quantities of faces and backs are as shown in the following table:

Grade	$\frac{1}{24}$-Inch Veneer in Feet	Sales Revenue per 1,000 Feet	Net Value	Percent of Total	Cost Applicable to Each
Faces............	9,000	$40	$360	83.3%	$166.67
Backs...........	9,000	8	72	16.6	33.33
	18,000		$432	100.0%	$200.00

The material cost applicable to each product, then, per thousand feet of $\frac{1}{24}$-inch veneer would be $166.67/9,000 feet $\times$ 1,000 feet, or $18.52, for faces; and $33.33/9,000 feet $\times$ 1,000 feet, or $3.70, for backs.

The production manager again argued that this did not represent the true material cost, which was the same for both products, and added:

Under your method the material cost allocated to either faces or backs would be a function of their relative selling prices. If the selling price of faces fell from $40 per thousand to $20 per thousand and the price of backs remained the same, you would then charge much more material cost to backs, and much less to faces. Your method of allocating cost doesn't make sense.

The sales manager at this point said:

O.K., if you don't think that method is justified, then let's treat backs as a by-product. I think you'll agree that we would prefer to be making faces all the time, yet we can't. As long as we manufacture faces, we're going to produce backs as an undesirable consequence. Now if we consider backs as a by-product, we can charge all block costs to faces. The net proceeds from the sale of backs, after allowing for all conversion, selling and administrative expenses, can be credited to the raw material cost of faces. All profits and losses of the business would be borne by the main product.

The production manager, however, pointed out again that the cost of material allocated to faces would still be a function of the selling price of backs and, furthermore, there would be some difficulty in trying to value inventories at the end of an accounting period; and that any profits arising from the sale of backs would be hidden, since it would be included in the credit to faces. "It is important to determine the profit or loss being realized on the sale of backs so we can establish a firm sales policy," he said.

Because of their inability to resolve this question, the production manager and the sales manager consulted the president of the Craik Veneer Company, who, in turn, asked the controller to examine the cost situation to determine whether the $8 per thousand surface feet of $\frac{1}{24}$-inch backs would, or would not, result in a profit.

Questions

1. As controller, what method of allocating raw material costs would you recommend? What similarities and differences would be encountered in allocating labor and overhead costs as compared to material costs?
2. Should the sales manager accept the $8 per thousand feet offer that he received for the $\frac{1}{24}$-inch backs?
3. If a group of blocks containing 1,000 board feet costs $205, what would be the cost applicable to faces and backs under each of the methods of allocating costs described in the case, and other methods that you may devise, if the following conditions existed:
   a. The current market price of $\frac{1}{24}$-inch faces is $40 per thousand feet; $\frac{1}{24}$-inch backs are currently selling at $9 per thousand.
   b. 10,000 feet of $\frac{1}{24}$-inch faces and 8,000 feet of $\frac{1}{24}$-inch backs were produced from a group of blocks.
   c. Factory labor and overhead cost averaged $8 per thousand feet of veneer ($6.75 for operations through clipping and $1.25 for drying and later operations). Selling costs averaged $1.50 per thousand feet of veneer. If backs were not manufactured (i.e., if they were treated the same as waste), labor, overhead, and selling costs amounting to roughly $2 per thousand feet of backs might be saved.

CASE 15–5. BEALE COMPANY[1]

Early in November the new president of the Beale Company was eagerly awaiting the completion of the income statement for October. He knew that October sales had exceeded those for September by more than $50,000, and he was anxious to see how much of this increased sales volume was reflected as extra profit. But when the report came in, it showed

---

[1] Before studying this case, the student may wish to review the material on direct costing which appears at the end of Chapter 8.

an overall loss of $5,015. (See Exhibit 1.) In September, profit had been $3,509.

The president immediately thought some mistake had been made and called in the controller for an explanation. The controller said the figures were correct, but that in October the company had not produced anywhere near its normal volume and hence the charge for unabsorbed bur-

Exhibit 1

BEALE COMPANY

Condensed October Income Statement as Actually Prepared

Sales...	$336,903	
Cost of sales at standard............................	178,168	
Standard gross margin...............................		$158,735
Less: Manufacturing variances:		
Labor......................................	$ 4,321*	
Material.....................................	3,972	
Overhead:		
Volume..................................	26,870	
Spending................................	1,347	
Net manufacturing variances.................		27,868
Actual gross margin................................		$130,867
Selling expenses:		
Selling expenses..............................	$ 84,514	
Sales taxes...................................	3,236	
Freight allowed...............................	7,195	
Total selling expenses.........................		94,945
Operating income before administrative expenses.........		$ 35,922
Administrative expenses:		
General administrative expenses....................	$ 20,640	
Research expenses.............................	5,879	
Total administrative expenses....................		26,519
Operating income.................................		$ 9,403
Other revenues and expenses........................		(14,418)
Income (Loss)...................................		$ (5,015)

* Credit variance.

den had decreased the profit more than the added sales had increased it. He said that if the rate of sales were always the same as the rate of factory production, the kind of distortion that was bothering the president would not appear. When factory operations were out of phase with sales operations, however, such distortions were almost certain to result, so long as the company followed the commonly practiced accounting convention of charging or crediting periodic under- or overabsorbed factory overhead to the current profit and loss account.

The president reacted strongly to the controller's explanations: "I don't care a hoot for your accounting conventions. But I do know this: when our sales go up, with other things reasonably equal, I expect our profit to increase. If your reports can't show so simple a thing as that, why do we spend so much money on your department?"

As a matter of fact, the controller had been thinking about the problem that disturbed the president. He concluded that the solution was to take a radically different approach to the accounting treatment of overhead, namely, to charge all fixed overhead costs for the month to the current operating statement rather than to absorb them as a part of product costs. If this were done, there would be no problem of heavy over- or

Exhibit 2

BEALE COMPANY

Condensed October Income Statement, Proposed Style

Sales...		$336,903	
Standard "variable" cost of sales......................		123,133	
Standard gross margin above variable costs..............			$213,770
Selling expenses:			
Selling expenses.................................		$ 84,514	
Sales taxes.......................................		3,236	
Freight allowed..................................		7,195	
Total selling expenses...........................			94,945
Merchandising margin..............................			$118,825
Administrative expenses:			
General administrative expenses....................		$ 20,640	
Research expenses................................		5,879	
Total administrative expenses.....................			26,519
Additional factory expenses:			
Fixed factory overhead....................		$ 65,862	
Manufacturing variances:			
Labor variance........................	$4,321*		
Material variance.....................	3,972		
Overhead variance (spending)............	1,347	998	66,860
Operating income.........................			$ 25,446
Other revenues and expenses.................			(14,418)
Income (Loss)............................			$ 11,028

* Credit variance.

underabsorbed overhead as the volume of operations changed. Cost of goods sold would then reflect only the nonfixed factory costs, that is, variable costs, which the controller called "direct costs."

As an illustration of how his proposal would work out, the controller reworked the company's figures for October, with the startling result that instead of a loss of $5,015, the statement showed a profit of $11,028. (See Exhibit 2.) When this revised statement was shown to the president, he first exclaimed, "That's more like it." Then he hesitated and started to speculate: "But this means more taxes and more demands for wage increases and dividends and what-all. Maybe your idea isn't so good after all."

The controller was in favor of the new plan largely because of its simplified accounting procedures. For one thing there would be no fixed overhead costs in the standard cost figures for different products but only the three classes of direct costs: (a) raw materials, (b) direct labor, and (c) the portion of the outlay for other manufacturing expenses which varied directly with productive activity. Omission of fixed overhead costs from the individual product costs would mean that the vexing and expensive task of working out an acceptable allocation of overhead to each product would be unnecessary. Inasmuch as many of these prorations had in fact become out of date, the controller was further attracted to his plan by the possibility that the expense of the needed overhauling of the figures might be avoided.

The controller also believed the proposed system would greatly increase management's focus on the *controllable* portion of costs by spotlighting the variable elements. Since the fixed costs pertaining to factory operations tend to fall into quite a different category from that of the variable costs, he thought they should be segregated anyway. By way of analogy he suggested that, like a retail store, a manufacturing company "purchases" its product for a known "direct cost." Consequently the chief difference between the two kinds of business is that to make a profit the manufacturing company has to pay the fixed factory costs in addition to the selling salaries, administration costs, storage, and so forth. Furthermore, the fixed factory costs are like the occupancy costs (rent, maintenance, and so forth) of a retail store. On such a basis the factory's direct costs, that is, variable costs, are similar to the retail store's cost of purchases.

The controller argued that a further advantage of his proposal would be the provision of a more satisfactory basis for making the usual monthly comparison of margin figures in the company's product-by-product gross margin statement. When recast in the new form, with fixed costs excluded, the figures would be much more meaningful. The new margin figures would be much higher all down the line, but the controller was confident that once the management adjusted its thinking to the new basis, the value of knowing how much each product was contributing to fixed costs and profit would be greatly appreciated.

One of the sales executives supported the controller's argument on the usefulness of the new margin figures. He pointed out that if there were two products sold by one of his divisions, Products A and B, and if the situation were as described in the following example, Product B would clearly *appear to be* the more desirable item to sell:

Product	Total Factory Cost per Pound (Std.)	Selling Price	Margin	Percentage of Sales
A	$0.897	$1.55	$0.653	42.1
B	1.015	1.80	0.785	43.6

If, however, the new margin figures were to work out something as follows, then Product A was by all odds the product on which the company's selling effort really should be concentrated:

Product	Variable Factory Cost	Selling Price	New Margin	Percentage of Sales
A...........	$0.413	$1.55	$1.137	73.4
B...........	0.809	1.80	0.991	55.1

The controller's proposed method of keeping records, the sales executive reasoned, would thus reveal the true opportunities for profit. He cited one company he knew that had adopted a system similar to that proposed by the controller and had so redirected its selling effort that in less than eight months it had shifted from an operating loss to an operating profit and had maintained good profits ever since.

At this point in the discussion the treasurer entered the argument. He observed, cynically, that the first thing anyone knew, the sales department, in its efforts to get business, would be selling at its usual markup over the new standard cost figures (variable costs only). "When that time comes," he snorted, "how are we going to cover the fixed costs? Where do we get our capital replacements? We'll have to pay the piper sooner or later."

Turning to the controller, who had talked of the desired focus of the new system on variable costs, the treasurer gave his opinion, based on long experience, that it was the lack of control of the long-run costs that really wrecked a company. "You can make mistakes on the direct costs," he said, "but because things in this area are constantly changing and because one never makes much of a commitment anyway, the health of the company is really not seriously hurt. If necessary, a new management could quickly reverse the trend. But once a company lets the long-run costs get out of control, then the fat really is in the fire. I'm opposed to anything that leads us to take a shortsighted view of cost." To this argument the controller had little to say, except that it was a matter of emphasis, and that he still thought the variable costs the more important.[2]

All the group discussing the proposal were aware of the effect of the controller's scheme on the inventory item in the balance sheet. The treasurer, and the president too, were worried about this effect, and both wondered if the possible improvement to the operating statement was worth the price of distorting the balance sheet. The controller proposed that a footnote be carried in the balance sheet calling attention to the matter, and perhaps indicating the extent of the distortion.

When one of the officials asked about the income tax implications, the controller pointed out that the tax return was a special report, that it

---

[2] In the preceding year, variable costs had been about two thirds of total costs.

already differed from the company's operating reports in several respects, and that the reports he was suggesting were monthly profit estimates largely for internal use and not annual reports. Furthermore, if the company wished to do so, it could have the annual reports computed on the more orthodox basis. "But," he insisted, "let's make these monthly reports so that they help us, not handicap us."

Balance sheets for the company are shown in Exhibit 3, together with an indication of how the balance sheet figures would appear had the company used the direct cost method. Income statements for September, under both the present and proposed methods, are shown in Exhibit 4. In this exhibit, nomenclature and arrangement have been changed somewhat in order to facilitate comparison between the present and proposed systems.

Exhibit 3

BEALE COMPANY

Condensed Balance Sheets as Actually Prepared

	As of September 30	As of October 31
ASSETS		
Current Assets:		
Cash	$ 80,560	$ 95,553
Accounts receivable	150,428	178,610
Inventory	573,630	521,822
Total Current Assets	$ 804,618	$ 795,985
Plant and equipment (net)	2,120,450	2,108,788
Total Assets	$2,925,068	$2,904,773
LIABILITIES AND OWNERS' EQUITY		
Current liabilities	$ 397,480	$ 382,200
Mortgage payable	560,000	560,000
Total Liabilities	$ 957,480	$ 942,200
Owners' Equity:		
Capital stock	$1,000,000	$1,000,000
Retained earnings	967,588	962,573
Total Owners' Equity	$1,967,588	$1,962,573
Total Liabilities and Owners' Equity	$2,925,068	$2,904,773

Effect of "Direct Cost" Method

Had the Beale Company used the direct cost method, its balance sheets would appear as above except for the inventory and retained earnings items. These would appear as shown below:

	As of September 30	As of October 31
Inventory	$401,541	$365,776
Retained earnings	795,499	806,527

Note: In both present and proposed statements, the effect of income taxes is not shown. The Beale Company recorded estimated income tax expense only at the end of the calendar year.

Exhibit 4

BEALE COMPANY

Condensed Income Statement
September

	As Actually Prepared	Under Proposed Method
Sales..	$283,028	$283,028
Cost of sales at standard...........................	152,604	104,662
Standard gross margin..............................	$130,424	$178,366
Less: Manufacturing variances:		
Labor..	$ 5,426*	$ 5,426*
Material......................................	5,081	5,081
Overhead:		
Volume....................................	447*	....
Spending..................................	2,173	2,173
Fixed factory overhead.........................	....	65,862
Subtotal overhead and variances.................	$ 1,381	$ 67,690
Income before administrative and selling expenses......	$129,043	$110,676
Selling expenses (total)...........................	$ 85,482	$ 85,482
Administrative expenses (total)....................	26,026	26,026
Total administrative and selling expenses.........	$111,508	$111,508
Operating income.................................	$ 17,535	$ (832)
Other revenues and expenses.......................	(14,026)	(14,026)
Income (loss)....................................	$ 3,509	$(14,858)

* Credit variance.

Questions

1. What do you recommend?
2. Approximately how busy (relative to normal volume) was the factory in October?
3. Could the problem in the case ever arise with respect to annual statements of profit?

CHAPTER 16

ADDITIONAL ASPECTS OF
FULL COST ACCOUNTING

This chapter concludes the discussion of full cost accounting systems and the uses of full cost information. The topics discussed are: (1) accounting systems using standard costs, (2) joint product and by-product costs, (3) nonmanufacturing costs, (4) the validity of full costs, and (5) the uses of full cost information.

STANDARD COSTS

The basic objective of the system outlined in Chapter 15 was to charge units of product with a fair share of the *actual* costs incurred in making these products. Some cost accounting systems, in contrast, are based wholly or in part on the principle that the costs charged to individual products are the costs that *should have been incurred* on those products rather than the costs that *actually were incurred*. Such a system is called a standard cost system. The essential nature of standard costs, then, is that they represent costs that should have been incurred rather than costs that actually were incurred. Standard costs can be used either with a job order cost system or a process cost system.

In a standard cost system, each unit of product has a standard direct material cost, a standard direct labor cost, and a standard overhead cost for each production cost center. The total standard cost for the month is obtained by multiplying these standard unit costs by the number of units flowing through the cost center in that month. Because of the similar way in which overhead costs are treated in both a standard cost and an actual cost system, however, the term *standard cost* applies particularly to direct material cost and direct labor cost.

For direct material, the standard represents the amount of material that should be required to produce a unit of product priced at what the price of this material should be. The same principle applies to direct labor. Instead of charging each job for the number of hours that employees actually spend on that job times their actual hourly rate, the job is charged at a standard direct labor cost for a unit of the product, which is calculated by multiplying the standard number of hours that should be required to manufacture one unit by the standard labor cost per hour.

In an actual cost system, overhead is ordinarily assigned to products by means of a predetermined overhead rate. In a standard cost system, there would also be a predetermined overhead rate, but the overhead cost of a job would be calculated by multiplying this rate by a *standard* quantity, such as the standard direct labor hours. With this exception, the treatment of overhead costs is the same under the two systems.

Illustration 16–1 shows the system for the pen factory described in Chapter 15, shifted to a standard cost basis. It is the same as the actual cost system shown in Illustration 15–2 except that four *variance accounts* have been added. Standard costs are usually different from the costs actually incurred, and variance accounts are a repository for these differences. For example, if actual direct labor costs for the month were $20,000, the credit to the liability account Wages Payable must be $20,000. If the standard direct labor costs of the operations performed totaled only $17,000, Goods in Process would be debited for $17,000, and the $3,000 difference would be debited to the Labor Variance account. Entries to variance accounts are debits if actual costs are greater than standard costs, and they are credits if actual costs are less than standard costs.

Entries in Illustration 16–1 are for the same transactions, and are numbered the same, as the entries on Illustration 15–2. The four entries in which standard costs are introduced are:

Purchase of raw materials (Entry No. 1). A credit material price variance of $2,000 is created because the actual purchase price of the material was $52,000 whereas the standard cost of this material was $54,000.

Usage of raw material (Entry No. 2). The standard raw materials cost of pens processed was $49,000, but the material actually used during the month had a standard cost of only $48,000; therefore there was a credit material usage variance of $1,000.

Direct labor (Entry No. 3), explained above.

Overhead (Entry No. 6). Factory overhead costs applied to products by means of standard overhead rates were $26,000. Actual factory overhead costs incurred were $27,000. There was, therefore, a debit overhead variance of $1,000.

Illustration 16–1

A STANDARD COST SYSTEM

Note: Circled numbers refer to events described in Chapter 15.

In summary, the only mechanical difference between the accounts in a standard cost system and those in an actual cost system is that the former has variance accounts. Variance accounts are necessarily introduced whenever one part of a transaction is at standard cost and the other part is at actual cost.

Variations in the Standard Cost Idea

In the system shown in Illustration 16–1, standard costs were introduced when raw material entered inventory and when material, labor, and overhead were debited to Goods in Process Inventory. This is common practice, but standard costs can also be introduced at other points.

Instead of debiting Raw Materials Inventory at standard unit prices, some companies carry raw material at actual cost and make the conversion to standard cost when the raw material is issued for use in the production process. In such a system, there would be no material price variance account, and the material variance account would incorporate both the price and the usage components of the variance.

In another variation of the standard cost idea, the shift from actual to standard is made at a later point in the production process than that shown in Illustration 16–1. In such a system, elements of cost are charged into Goods in Process Inventory at actual cost, and the shift from actual to standard is made when the completed products are transferred from Goods in Process Inventory to Finished Goods Inventory. In this system, there would be only one variance account, and it would be generated as part of the entry recording this transfer.

Some companies do not use standard costs for all elements of cost. They may, for example, use standard direct labor costs, but actual direct material costs; or they may do the reverse. The choice depends on the advantages that are obtainable in the particular situation. Regardless of these variations, the essential points are: (1) in a standard cost system, some or all of the elements of cost are recorded at standard rather than at actual; and (2) at whatever point a shift from actual to standard is made, a variance account is generated.

Uses of Standard Costs

A standard cost system may be used for any or all of these reasons: (1) it provides a basis for controlling performance, (2) it provides cost information that is useful for certain types of decisions, (3) it may provide a more rational measurement of inventory amounts and of cost of goods sold, and (4) it may reduce the cost of recordkeeping.

USE IN CONTROL. A good starting point in the control of a manager's performance is to compare what the manager actually did with what he should have done. Standard costs provide a basis for such comparisons, as will be discussed in detail in Chapter 22.

EXAMPLE: If the standard direct material cost for all the shoes manufactured in a month was $243,107, and if the actual cost of the direct material used on those shoes was $268,539, there is an indication that direct material costs were $25,432 higher than they should have been. Without some standard, there is no starting point for examining the appropriateness of the $268,539 of direct material cost.

USE IN DECISION MAKING. Standard costs are often used as a basis for arriving at normal selling prices, especially when each job is different from other jobs because each is made according to an individual customer's specifications. In alternative choice decisions, of the type discussed in Chapters 18 and 19, standard costs are often the best available approximation of the differential costs that are relevant in making such decisions.

MORE RATIONAL COSTS. A standard cost system eliminates what otherwise might be an undesirable quirk in the accounting system. A standard cost system records the same costs for physically identical units of products, whereas, an actual cost system may record different costs for physically identical units. For example, the actual direct labor cost of each lot of a given style of shoes could be different, depending on such factors as whether the employees who worked on the shoes had a relatively high wage rate because of long seniority. The shoes themselves, however, are physically the same. Realistically, there is no good reason for carrying one pair of physically similar shoes in inventory at one cost and another pair at a different amount, or in charging cost of goods sold at different amounts. In a standard cost system, all shoes of the same style would be carried in inventory, and charged as cost of goods sold, at the same unit cost.

SAVING IN RECORDKEEPING. Because of the addition of standard costs to the system, it might appear that a standard cost accounting system requires more recordkeeping than an actual cost accounting system. In reality, when standard costs are used instead of actual costs, there may well be a *reduction* in the amount of effort required to operate the system. All the individual material requisitions for a month can be totaled and posted as a single credit to Raw Materials Inventory. Instead of making separate entries for direct material cost on each job cost sheet, one amount, the standard unit material cost, is all that is needed. Neither is there any need for direct workers to keep track of the time they spend on individual lots. One amount, the predetermined standard direct labor cost, is all that is needed.

There is furthermore a considerable reduction in the amount of recordkeeping required for finished goods inventory and cost of goods sold. Since all units of the same product have the same cost, the complications involved in keeping track of costs according to a Lifo, Fifo, or average cost assumption (as described in Chapter 6) disappear.

One aspect of a standard cost system, that of determining the individual standards, does involve additional effort. In many situations the effort required to do this is not great, but there can be no doubt that some effort is involved. The determination of standard unit costs is done only occasionally, however. Once a standard has been determined, it is used for months, or even years, without change.

ILLUSTRATION: BLACK METER COMPANY

As an illustration of some of the procedural details of a standard cost system, the system of the Black Meter Company (which is the disguised name for an actual company) is described below.

Description of Company

The Black Meter Company manufactures water meters in one standard design but in a wide range of sizes. The water meters installed in the basements of most homes are an example of its product. The meters consist basically of a hard rubber piston that is put in motion by the flow of water past it, a gear train that reduces this motion and registers it on a dial, and two heavy bronze castings which are bolted together around the measuring device.

The company has several production departments. The castings and many interior parts of meters are cast in the foundry and then are sent to one of the three machining departments, depending upon their size. Some of the mechanical parts are sent to a subassembly department where they are assembled into gear trains. Other parts go directly to the meter assembly department. There are also several departments that provide service to the production departments.

Overview of System

Since the company ships meters to customers as soon as they are completed, it does not have a Finished Goods Inventory account. It does have Raw Materials Inventory and Goods in Process Inventory accounts. It uses a standard cost system. Standard costs are established for each element of direct labor, direct material, and manufacturing overhead.

During the month, actual costs are accumulated: material is purchased, the earnings of workers are recorded, and manufacturing overhead items, such as water or electricity, are purchased and paid for. These entries are made at actual cost. Elements of cost are debited into inventory at predetermined *standard* costs, however. Since actual costs are different from standard costs, variance accounts are necessary.

Setting up Standard Costs

A standard unit cost is established for every type of material that is purchased. This is done annually by adjusting the current market price for any changes that are expected for the following year. For example, if the current price of copper is 30 cents a pound and no change is predicted, the standard cost for copper for the next year will be 30 cents a pound.

Standard rates for direct labor and manufacturing overhead are also determined annually. These rates are used to assign costs to products according to the number of standard direct labor hours incurred in the manufacture of each product. This is done on a departmental basis. For each production department, the accountants start with data on the actual direct labor payroll and the number of direct labor hours worked in each of the past few years. The departmental foreman gives his opinion as to adjustments that should be made to take account of future conditions. An amount for total labor cost and an amount for hours worked under normal conditions of activity is thus arrived at. By dividing the payroll amount by the normal number of hours, a standard direct labor rate per standard direct labor hour for each department is found.

Overhead costs for a production department include both the overhead costs incurred in that department plus an allocated portion of the costs of service departments. Estimates are made of these amounts for

Illustration 16–2

Department Number	Department Name	Labor	Overhead	Total Rate
	STANDARD LABOR AND OVERHEAD RATES EFFECTIVE JANUARY 1			
103	Carpenter and pattern shop	$4.06	$3.07	$7.13/hour
104	Toolroom	4.35	3.26	7.61/hour
108	Pattern storage	----	----	8.04/pound
120A	Foundry--molding	4.50	5.78	10.28/hour
120B	Foundry--grinding and snagging	3.50	2.90	6.40/hour
122	Small parts manufacture	3.72	3.38	7.10/hour
123	Interior parts manufacture	3.68	3.73	7.41/hour
124	Case manufacture	3.98	6.02	10.00/hour
125	Plating--rack	----	----	6.50/100 pcs.
130	Train, register, and interior assembly	3.70	3.97	7.67/hour
131	Small meter assembly	3.50	4.01	7.51/hour
132	Large meter assembly	3.90	5.98	9.88/hour
133	Meter testing	4.11	3.56	7.67/hour
134	Meter repair	3.50	3.66	6.16/hour

each production department under normal conditions. These estimated total overhead costs are divided by the standard number of direct labor hours for each producing department, the same amount that had been used in calculating the labor rate, to arrive at a manufacturing overhead rate per standard direct labor hour. These rates are given in Illustration 16–2.

Developing Standard Product Costs

The standard hourly rates (which include both direct labor and overhead) are used to develop a standard cost for each type of meter. Examples of these calculations are given in Illustrations 16–3, 16–4, 16–5, and 16–6. The examples show the development of the standard cost of a ⅝-inch HF Meter.

Illustration 16–3 shows the calculation for a ⅝-inch Chamber Ring which is manufactured in the foundry, and which is one component of the ⅝-inch HF Meter. As in the case with most parts, costs are calculated for a lot size of 100 units. The standard material cost is entered in the upper right-hand box. These parts are cast from bronze that has a standard cost of $0.3265 a pound. Since the standard weight of 100 pieces is 91 pounds, the standard material cost is $0.3265 × 91 = $29.712, as shown in the "Material Cost" box. The standard cost of the pattern used in the casting, $3.64, is also entered.

In order to apply the standard direct labor and manufacturing over-

Illustration 16–3

FOUNDRY STANDARD COST								
Drawing No. D-2408			Part 5/8" HF Chamber Rings		Material Cost			$29.712
					Pattern Cost			3.64
MATERIAL Gov't Bronze 100 Pcs. 91.0# at 0.3265/#								
Std. Man-Hrs. per 100 Pcs.	Prod. Center	Oper. No.	Operations and Tools	Machine	Std. Rate /Hr.	Total Cost	Total	
1.76	120 A	1	Mold	Match Plate	10.28	18.093		
0.45	120 B	2	Grind	Wheel	6.40	2.88		
0.68	120 B	3	Snag	Bench	6.40	4.35		
							58.675	

Illustration 16–4

RR-7			PARTS DEPARTMENT STANDARD COST				
Drawing No. X-2408			Part 5/8" HF Chamber Rings				Material Cost
Plating H.T. & E.T.			Material Gov't Bronze 100 pieces 89#				$58.675
Hours per 100 Pcs. St'd.	Prod. Center	Oper. No.	Operations and Tools	Machine	Std. Rate /Hr.		Total
0.75	122	1	Broach outlet #734	P.P.	7.10		5.325
0.55	123		Finish tap plate bore and face	Heald	7.41		4.076
0.93	123	2	Drill 6 holes	Drill	7.41		6.891
0.47	123		C-sink-3 holes tap plate side	Drill	7.41		3.483
0.17	123	3	Tap 3 holes tap plate side	Heskins	7.41		1.260
5.00	123		Rough & Finish inside & outside	Heald	7.41		37.050
0.20	123	4	C-sink 3 holes on bottom	Drill	7.41		1.482
0.30	123		Tap 3 holes on bottom	Drill	7.41		2.223
0.47	123	5	Spline inside	Spliner	7.41		3.483
0.50	123		Spline outside	Miller	7.41		3.705
5.80	123	6	Dress	Bench	7.41		42.978
			Total				170.631

head rates to any part, it is necessary to have the standard direct labor hours for the operations involved in making that part. These are obtained from time studies and are entered in the first column of the foundry form. The standard time to mold 100 chamber rings is 1.76 direct labor hours; to grind them, 0.45 hours, and to snag them, 0.68 hours. In the first column of numbers of the right-hand side of the foundry form, the combined standard direct labor and manufacturing overhead rate per standard direct labor hour for the operation is recorded. For example, Illustration 16–2 shows the labor and overhead rate for molding in Department 120A as $10.28 per standard direct labor hour, and this amount appears on Illustration 16–3 as the standard rate per hour for the molding operation. It is multiplied by the standard direct labor time of 1.76 hours to give a standard cost of labor and overhead of $18.093. The same procedure is followed for the other two foundry operations. The total standard foundry cost of 100 chamber rings is $58.675.

Illustration 16–4 accumulates additional standard costs for these 100

Illustration 16–5

ASSEMBLY DEPARTMENT STANDARD COST				

Drawing No. 2400	Assembly 5/8" Disc Interior			
Used on Assemblies of 5/8" HF & HD Meters				

Parts of Assembly	Cost	Parts of Assembly	Cost
K-2408 Chamber Ring	170.631		
K-2414 Chamber Top Plate	73.550		
K-2418 Chamber Bot. Plate	70.120		
K-2465 Disc Piston Assem.	142.010		
K-2422 Disc. Chbr. Diaphragm	7.660		
		K-4521 Chamber Screw (6)	7.000

Std. Man-Hrs. per 100 Pcs.	Prod. Center	Oper. No.	Operation and Tools	Machine	Std. Rate /Hr.	Total Cost	Total
2.6	130	1	Assemble Top Plate to Ring	Bench	7.67	19.942	
0.9	130	2	Fit Abutment for Interior	Bench	7.67	6.903	
1.1	130	3	Mill & Scrape Diahragm for Interior	Bench	7.67	8.437	
2.9	130	4	File Diaphragm Slots in Piston	Bench	7.67	22.243	
							528.496

chamber rings as they pass through the parts manufacture department. They enter the parts department at the standard cost of $58.675, the same cost at which they left the foundry. After the operations listed on Illustration 16–4 have been performed on them, they become finished chamber rings. These operations have increased the standard cost to $170.631. As shown in Illustrations 16–5 and 16–6, these parts are assembled into ⅝-inch HF disc interiors, and finally into ⅝-inch meters. In each of these assembly operations standard costs are added; the total standard cost of 100 meters is $1,760.596.

In the same manner, standard costs are calculated for all the meter sizes that the Black Meter Company manufactures.

Accounting Entries

All direct material, direct labor, and manufacturing overhead costs are debited to Goods in Process Inventory at standard costs. Actual costs are collected in total for the period, but no actual costs are collected for individual meters.

Illustration 16–6

ASSEMBLY DEPARTMENT STANDARD COST				

Drawing No. 2735		Assembly 5/8" HF ET FB		
Parts of Assembly		Cost	Parts of Assembly	Cost
2761 Top Case		270.60	K-5030 5/8" HF Dur. Bolt (6)	62.880
K-2776 Casting Gasket		13.25	K-4630 5/8" HF ac Nut (6)	35.440
X-2770 Bottom Case		100.14	K-5068 5/8" HF Washer (6)	20.140
2779 Casting Strainer		16.95	2782 Chamber Pin	3.966
3209 5/8" Closed Train		600.01	6172 Misc. Train Conn.	17.120
2400 5/8" HF Int. Assem.		528.496		
2412 5/8" HF Sand Plate		15.00		

Rate No.	Std. Man-Hrs. per 100 Pcs.	Prod. Prod. Center	Oper. No.	Operation and Tools	Machine	Std. Rate /Hr.	Total Cost	Total
	4.6	131	1	Assem. Train and Strainer to Case	Bench	7.51	34.546	
	5.6	131	2	Assem. Int. & Bottom to Meter	Bench	7.51	42.058	
								1760.596

MATERIAL. As soon as any material is purchased, the standard cost of that material is penciled on the vendor's invoice. Each purchase is journalized in an invoice and check register. This register contains columns in which to credit the actual cost of the material to Accounts Payable, to debit an inventory account for the standard cost, and to debit or credit the difference to a purchase price variance account. When material is issued for use in production, the quantity is the standard amount (e.g., 91 pounds in the example shown in Illustration 16–3), and the entry crediting Raw Materials Inventory and debiting Goods in Process Inventory is made at the standard cost (e.g., $29.712 in the example shown in Illustration 16–3).

LABOR. The basic document for recording direct labor costs is the job timecard. Each production employee fills out such a card for each order on which he or she works during a week. The timecard reproduced as Illustration 16–7 shows that B. Harris worked all week on one order. On the timecard Harris records the quantity finished, the actual hours worked, and the allowed hours. A payroll clerk enters each employee's daywork rate, the standard direct labor rate for that department, and extends the actual and standard direct labor cost of the work completed.

By totaling all the job timecards, the payroll clerk obtains the actual wages earned by each employee in each department, and also the total standard labor cost of the work done in each department. These amounts are the basis for an entry which credits Wages Payable for the actual amount and debits Goods in Process Inventory account for the standard amount of direct labor. The variance is recorded in a direct labor variance account.

MANUFACTURING OVERHEAD.   For each department, a cost clerk multi-

Illustration 16–7

Mach. No.	Prod. Center	Quantity Ordered		Order Number		
	130	*3,000*		*2I-86572*	*337*	Clock No.
	Part Name					
		⅝" Cl. Trains				
Prev. Quan. Fin.	Oper. No.	Operation Name				
0	*9*	*Finish Assem.*				
Quan. Finished	Std. Hours Per 100	Std. Hours	Std. Rate	Standard Labor		
2,300	*1.75*	*40. 25*	*3. 70*	*148.92*		
Quan. Finished						$ HALLIS
2,300			TIME CARD			Name
	Stop	Actual Hours	D.W. Rate	Earnings		
Sept. 20	*40. 0*	*40. 0*	*3. 65*	*146. 00*		
	Start			Gain or Loss		
Sept. 16	*00. 0*	Foreman		*2. 92*		

plies the standard direct labor hours worked by the manufacturing overhead rate for that department (as obtained from Illustration 16–2); this gives the amount of standard manufacturing overhead cost for the department for that month. This amount is debited to Goods in Process Inventory. During the month actual manufacturing overhead expenses have been accumulated in the invoice and check register and in various adjusting entries. The difference between the sum of the actual overhead costs and the standard manufacturing overhead cost is the manufacturing overhead variance, which is debited or credited to an overhead variance account.

When these transactions have been recorded, all material, direct labor, and manufacturing overhead have been charged into the Goods in Process Inventory account at standard cost, and variance accounts have been debited or credited for the difference between actual and standard.

Sales and Cost of Goods Sold

A duplicate copy of each sales invoice is sent to the office where a clerk enters in pencil the standard cost of the items sold (see Illustration 16–8). At the end of the month the cost clerk totals the figures on these

Illustration 16–8
CARBON COPY OF SALES INVOICE

Village of Vernon,
Attn: Village Clerk,
Vernon, N.Y.

Village of Vernon, Water Dept.,
Attn: E. J. Blackburn, Mayor
Vernon, N.Y.

STIBBS   Prepaid

10   5/8" x 3/4" Model HF Meters SG SH ET FB & 3/4"
                                                        248.00

1   Charge Gear #46X -- shipped 8-10-   .88   248.88
                                              Meters 176.06
                                              Parts   .48

                    Ship gear by P. Post

duplicate invoices to get amounts for sales revenue and for the standard cost of those sales. The standard cost is a credit to the Inventory account and a debit to the Cost of Goods Sold account. The total sales amount is a credit to Sales and a debit to Accounts Receivable. When this work is completed, the accounting department is in a position to obtain the monthly income statement (see Illustration 16–9). Note, incidentally, that although the net amount of the variance on this income statement is relatively small, there are sizable detailed variances that tend to offset one another. Management investigates these variances and takes action when warranted.

Illustration 16-9

BLACK METER COMPANY

Income Statement
June

Net sales...		$1,198,234
Less: Cost of goods sold at standard cost...........	$831,868	
Variances (detailed below)........................	5,357	826,511
Gross margin..		$ 371,723
Selling expense....................................	$ 92,107	
General and administrative expense................	177,362	269,469
Income before income taxes........................		$ 102,254
Income taxes.......................................		49,320
Net Income..		$ 52,934

Variances

	Debit	Credit
Favorable variances:		
Material price..............................		$ 62,608
Unfavorable variances:		
Material usage..............................	$ 22,457	
Direct labor................................	16,234	
Overhead...................................	18,560	57,251
Net Variance...............................		$ 5,357

JOINT PRODUCTS AND BY-PRODUCTS

Joint Products

Joint products are two or more dissimilar end products that are produced from a single batch of raw material or from a single production
process. The classic example is the variety of end products that are made
from a steer. The end products include hides, many different cuts of
meat, frozen meat dishes, pet food, fertilizers, and a variety of chemicals.
Up to a certain point in the production process, the raw material is
treated as a single unit. Beyond that point, which is called the *split-off
point*, separate end products are identified, and costs are accumulated
for each of these end products during subsequent stages of the manufacturing process. For example, up to the point at which the steer is
slaughtered and dressed, the costs of feed, grazing, transportation, and
other items are accumulated for the steer as a whole; beyond that point,
these costs must be divided among the many end products that are made
from the steer. The problem of joint costing is to find some reasonable
basis for allocating to each of the joint products the direct and indirect
costs that were incurred up to the split-off point.

This problem is essentially the same as that of allocating indirect costs
to cost centers. In both cases, the objective is to assign a fair share of the

joint or common costs to the separate end products, and in neither case can the results be an entirely accurate measure of the actual costs.

One common basis of allocating joint costs is in proportion to the *sales value* of the end products, minus the separate processing and marketing costs that are estimated to be incurred for each end product beyond the split-off point. If the selling price depends on cost, this method involves a certain amount of circular reasoning, but there may be no better alternative. If sirloin steak sells for twice the price of hamburger, it is reasonable that the steak should bear twice as much of the joint costs. Another basis of apportionment is *weight;* that is, the joint costs are divided in proportion to the weight of the joint material in the several end products. In the case of the steer, this method implicitly assumes that the hamburger is as valuable as the steak, which is unrealistic; but in other situations, the assumption that costs are related to weight might be reasonable. In any event, the amount of cost charged to each end product must be recognized as resulting from a judgmental decision, and hence not entirely accurate.

By-Products

By-products are a special kind of joint product. If management wishes to manufacture Products A and B in some predetermined proportion, or if it wishes to make as much of each end product as possible from a given quantity of raw material, then these products are ordinary joint products. On the other hand, if management's objective is to make Product A, but in so doing some quantity of Product B inevitably emerges from the production process, then Product A is a main product and Product B is a by-product. The intention is to make from a given amount of raw material as much of the main product and as little of the by-product as is possible. As management's intention changes, the classification changes.

> EXAMPLE: In the early part of the 20th century kerosene was the main product made from crude oil; subsequently, with the growth in consumption of gasoline, kerosene became a by-product; currently, kerosene has become a main product again because it is an important component of jet engine fuel.

A number of alternative procedures are used in measuring the cost of by-products. At one extreme, a by-product may be assigned zero cost, with all the costs being assigned to the main products. In such a case, the profit on the by-product is equal to its sales revenue. At the other extreme, by-products may be assigned a cost that is equal to their sales value, with the result that no profit or loss is attributed to the by-product and the entire profit of the process is attributed to the main product. The latter method sounds sloppy because there is no logical reason for asserting that the cost of a by-product actually is equal to its sales value. Since the by-product is, by its nature, of minor importance, no significant distortion usually rises from this assumption. Peculiar results sometimes occur, however. For example, animal feed is a by-product of the process of milling flour; at certain times the value of feed fluctuates widely, and these changes can have a significant effect on the cost assigned to the flour.

NONMANUFACTURING COSTS

Until the last two or three decades, most cost accounting systems dealt exclusively with the measurement of the manufacturing costs of tangible goods. This was probably because these were the only items of cost that needed to be assigned to goods in order to prepare the financial statements. Manufacturing costs of goods must be measured in order to obtain the amounts for Goods in Process Inventory and Finished Goods Inventory accounts on the balance sheet and the amount for Cost of Goods Sold on the income statement. Other costs were reported as expenses on the income statement in aggregate amounts. In recent years, cost accounting systems have been expanded to include the collection of information on other types of cost, that is, on costs not related to the manufacture of goods.

For nonmanufacturing costs, the guiding principles of cost measurement are the same as those already discussed in connection with manufacturing costs; namely, (1) that the full cost of a cost objective is the sum of its direct costs plus an equitable share of indirect costs, (2) that as many items of cost as are feasible should be treated as direct costs, and (3) that indirect costs should be allocated to individual cost objectives on the basis of intended benefits or a causal relationship.

These principles can be used to develop the full costs of goods, including the direct and indirect selling, general and administrative costs, as well as factory costs; they can be used to develop the full cost of divisions or other organization segments; they can be used to develop the full cost of services; and they can be used to develop the full cost of any function or activity, such as the cost of research and development.

Residual Expenses

Many full cost constructions require the allocation of general and administrative costs. To the extent feasible, these costs are allocated according to the basic criteria of causal relationship or benefits received. For example, the cost of the corporate personnel department might be allocated in proportion to the number of employees in the cost objective. Those items of general and administrative costs that cannot be related to activities on some rational basis are called *residual expenses*. The Cost

Accounting Standards Board requires[1] that residual costs be allocated to cost objectives by what is called, for historical reasons, the *Massachusetts Formula*. This formula provides that the percentage of residual expenses allocated to any cost center (i.e., department, division, or other segment) is the *arithmetical average* of the following three percentages:

a. The percentage of the cost center's payroll to the total payroll of all cost centers;

b. The percentage of the cost center's revenue to the total operating revenue of all cost centers; and

c. The percentage of the net book value of the cost center's tangible assets to the total net book value of the tangible assets of all cost centers.

The Massachusetts Formula is complicated, and it is therefore not now widely used except for measuring the costs applicable to those government contracts that are within the jurisdiction of the Cost Accounting Standards Board. Because of the increasing use of CASB standards for other purposes, its use seems likely to grow, however.

VALIDITY OF FULL COSTS

From the description given in this and the preceding chapter, it should be apparent that the full costs of a cost objective cannot be measured with complete precision if some items of cost are indirect, as is usually the case. Two equally well-informed and competent accountants can arrive at different costs for the same product or other cost objective. These differences arise from differences in judgment on the following matters, among others;

1. *Capital, product, and period costs.* In Chapter 13 we showed how the judgment as to whether a given item of cost should be classified as a capital cost, a product cost, or a period cost affects both the measurement of costs and the measurement of net income for a period.

2. *Measurement of direct costs.* If Company A classifies only the wages of direct workers as direct labor, but Company B includes labor-related costs, Company A's direct labor costs will be less than those in Company B. Since labor-related costs may amount to 20 percent or more of wages, this difference can be substantial.

3. *Distinction between direct and indirect costs.* In the above example, the labor-related costs that Company A excluded from direct costs were part of its indirect costs. Although a share of these indirect costs is allocated to products, the method of allocation is such that a different amount may be allocated to a given product than would be the case if the item were treated as a direct cost.

---

[1] Cost Accounting Standard 403.40 (7).

4. *Alternative allocation methods.* Many judgments must be made in deciding how the costs of service cost centers are assigned to production cost centers.

5. *Choice of an activity measure.* The amount of overhead allocated to a product is affected by the measure of activity used in the overhead rate. Measuring activity in terms of direct labor hours gives different results than measuring activity in terms of direct labor dollars, for example.

6. *Estimate of volume.* As illustrated in Chapter 15, the estimate of volume used in arriving at the overhead rate can have a significant influence on the unit overhead charge.

7. *Definition of cost center.* The amount of indirect cost allocated to a product can be significantly influenced by judgment as to how a cost center is defined. In some companies, each important machine is a cost center. At the other extreme, the entire plant may be a single cost center (giving rise to a *plantwide overhead rate*). There are a number of choices between these two extremes. In general, the more narrow the definition of a cost center, the more equitable is the resulting amount of indirect cost allocated to the product. On the other hand, it is also true that the more narrow the definition of the cost centers, the more cost centers there will be, and therefore more clerical work will be required to compute and apply separate overhead rates.

Tendencies toward Uniformity

Because of these and other factors, no one can measure precisely the "actual" amount of resources used in manufacturing a product. Nevertheless, there are forces tending toward uniformity of method. Most importantly, a given company usually uses the same practices for measuring full costs throughout the company; consequently, comparisons of the costs of various products can validly be made. Furthermore, within an industry, there tends to be a similarity of costing practices, and this facilitates cost comparisons within the industry.

USES OF FULL COST

Some of the uses that management makes of information on full costs are: (1) in financial reporting; (2) in analysis of profitability; (3) in answering the question: "What did it cost?"; (4) in arriving at regulated prices; and (5) in normal pricing.

Financial Reporting

We have already described how full factory cost is the basis for reporting goods in process inventory and finished goods inventory on the balance sheet and cost of goods sold on the income statement. When a company constructs a building, a machine, or some other fixed asset for its own use, the amount at which this asset is recorded in the accounts and reported on the balance sheet is its full cost.

Cost accounting information is also used to measure the income of the principal segments of the business. Government agencies require such information from certain companies.

Analysis of Segment Profitability

In Chapter 12 we discussed ratios and other techniques that are useful in analyzing the profitability of an entire business. Cost accounting makes it possible to make similar analyses of individual segments of a business. Such a segment might be an individual product, a product line (which is a family of related products), a plant, a division, a sales territory, or any other subdivision of the whole business that is of interest. Using the principles of cost accounting, the direct costs and an appropriate share of the indirect costs of the segment being reviewed can be determined. If the segment does not earn a reasonable profit, that is, if the revenue generated by this segment does not exceed these costs by an amount that represents a reasonable return on assets employed, there is an indication that something is wrong.

In the short run, a product, a division, or other segment of a business generally can be tolerated if its revenues at least exceed its out-of-pocket costs, but any part of the business which does not earn a satisfactory return on assets employed is not healthy, and consideration should be given to shifting the investment to a more attractive use.

What Did it Cost?

The problem of measuring the cost of something arises in a great many contexts: What did the Vietnam War cost? What did one bombing raid in that war cost? What did the last Presidential election cost? What was the cost of police protection in city X? What did it cost the U.S. Postal Service to send a letter from Chicago to San Francisco? What was the cost of operating a school cafeteria? What was the cost of a certain research project? These questions are usually answered by measuring the full cost of the cost objective.

COST-TYPE CONTRACTS. Full costs are used in contracts in which one party has agreed to buy products or services from another party at a price that is based on cost. There are tens of billions of dollars of such contracts annually. Because of the variations in methods of measuring cost, it is necessary that the method to be used in the particular contract be spelled out in some detail so as to avoid misunderstanding.

Setting Regulated Prices

Many prices are set not by the forces of the marketplace but rather by regulatory agencies. These include prices for electricity; gas and water; passenger and/or freight transportation by train, airplane, truck, bus, barge, and pipeline; telephone and telegraph; insurance premiums; services in buying and selling securities; and a long list of others. In each of these cases, the regulatory agency (Federal Communications Commission, Interstate Commerce Commission, state public utility and insurance commissions, and so on) allows a price that is equal to full cost plus an allowance for profit. In most cases, the regulatory agency provides a manual, which may contain several hundred pages, spelling out in great detail how costs are to be measured.

Normal Pricing

As we discussed in Chapter 12, a principal economic objective of a business is to earn a satisfactory return on its investment, that is, on the assets that it uses.

In order to earn a satisfactory return, revenues from the sale of goods and services must be large enough both to (1) recover all costs, and (2) earn a profit that is large enough to provide a satisfactory return on investment. The business will prosper if *for all the products combined,* total sales revenues exceed total costs by a sufficiently large amount. But selling prices must be set separately for *each product.* How can this be done for *each* product so that a satisfactory profit is earned for *all* products?

The general answer to this question is that each product should bear a *fair share* of the total costs of the business. We can expand this statement to say that in general the selling price of a product should be high enough (1) to recover its direct costs, (2) to recover a fair share of all applicable indirect costs, and (3) to yield a satisfactory profit. Such a price is a *normal price.*

It must be understood that the foregoing is a statement of general tendency rather than a prescription for setting the selling price for each and every product. For a number of reasons to be mentioned subsequently, the selling price of a given product usually is not set simply by ascertaining each of the cost and profit components and then adding them up. Nevertheless, the measurement of the cost of a product provides a starting point in an analysis of what the actual selling price should be.

THE PROFIT COMPONENT OF PRICE. The fact that an economic objective of a business is to earn a satisfactory return on assets employed suggests that logically the profit component of the selling price of a product should be related to assets employed in making the product. Nevertheless, it is common pricing practice to relate the profit component of the price to costs rather than to the amount of assets employed.

In some situations, it is easy to establish a profit margin expressed as a percentage of cost in such a way that the resulting selling price will give a satisfactory return on assets employed. In general, this is the case when all products have approximately the same unit cost and/or when the assets employed by products vary proportionately with their cost.

> EXAMPLE: A retail shoe store decides that a satisfactory profit is a 15 percent return (before income taxes) on its investment. If its total investment in inventory, accounts receivable, and other assets is estimated to be $200,000 then its profit must be $200,000 × 15 percent = $30,000 for the year. If its total operating costs, excluding the cost of the shoes, are estimated to be $70,000, then its selling prices must be such that the gross margin above the costs of the shoes comes out to $70,000 + $30,000 = $100,000. If the store expects to sell shoes that cost in total $300,000, then total sales revenue must be $400,000 in order to obtain this $100,000. The store can obtain the desired $100,000 by setting a selling price that is 33⅓ percent above the cost of the shoes ($400,000 ÷ $300,000 = 133⅓ percent). This pricing policy would generate revenue of $400,000 for the year if the expected sales volume were realized, of which $300,000 would go for the cost of the shoes, $70,000 for operating costs, and $30,000 for profit. Shoe store owners customarily describe such a set of numbers as demonstrating that they make a profit of 7.5 percent on sales (= $30,000 ÷ $400,000) but what is more important is that it is a return of 15 percent on assets employed (= $30,000 ÷ $200,000).

Although setting the profit margin as a percentage of costs or of selling price works satisfactorily if the assets employed for each product are proportionate to the costs of each product, it breaks down if this condition does not exist. Products, or companies, with a relatively low asset turnover require a relatively high profit margin, as a percentage of costs or of selling price, in order to earn a satisfactory return on assets employed. *Asset turnover* means revenues divided by assets employed. If sales revenues are $2,000,000 and assets employed are $1,000,000, then asset turnover is two times. Each dollar of assets employed is said to "generate" two dollars of sales revenue.

Assigning assets employed to products involves essentially the same techniques as assigning costs to products. These techniques are not described in detail here. Until fairly recently, it was widely believed that the accounting effort required to assign assets employed to products was so great and the results so unreliable that the effort was not worthwhile, but it is now recognized that practical ways of doing this are not so difficult as had been thought.

GROSS MARGIN PRICING. Retailers, wholesalers, distributors, and other companies that sell but do not manufacture products tend to set selling prices at a certain percentage above the cost of individual products. This percentage is called the *mark-on percentage*.[2] Although the mark-on percentage is applied to cost, there is a mathematical relationship between the mark-on percentage and the *gross margin percentage* which is the margin expressed as a percentage of sales revenue.[3] As indicated in the example of the shoe store given above, this mark-on is intended both to cover the operating costs of the business and also to provide a satisfactory return on assets employed. Operating costs and the amount of assets employed vary greatly in different types of trading companies, and there is a corresponding variation in their mark-ons. The higher the asset turnover and the lower the operating cost per dollar of sales, the smaller the mark-on needs to be in order to produce a satisfactory return on assets employed.

DIRECT COST PRICING. Some manufacturing businesses set selling prices at a certain percentage above the direct costs incurred in manufacturing their products; this is called *direct cost pricing*. Such a pricing policy is similar to the use of a uniform gross margin percentage by retailers and other merchandising companies. It is a sensible policy when the same general conditions exist as those in merchandising companies that use this policy, namely, when the amount of indirect costs that equitably should be borne by each product is substantially the same percentage of direct costs, and when the assets employed in each product are also substantially similar. When these conditions do not exist, the practice of setting selling prices as a certain percentage above direct cost can have unsatisfactory results. One reason why this practice is followed is that the allocation of indirect costs to products involves judgment, and some managers believe that the results are not sufficiently valid to be useful in making decisions on selling prices. They prefer to base pricing decisions on direct costs because these costs can be measured with a high degree of precision.

TIME AND MATERIAL PRICING. In this method one pricing rate is established for direct labor and a separate pricing rate for direct material. Each of these rates is constructed so that it includes allowances for indirect costs and for profit. This method of pricing is used in automobile garages, in job printing shops, in television repair shops, and in similar types of service establishments. It is also used by many professional per-

---

[2] The use of "mark-on" and "markup" in practice is confusing. Some people use "mark-on" and/or "markup" to mean the percentage of profit to *selling price*, rather than to cost, as defined above. In this text, *gross margin percentage* is used to refer to the percentage of profit to selling price.

[3] The gross margin percentage can be converted to a mark-on by dividing it by 100 minus the gross margin percentage. For example, if the gross margin percentage is 25, the mark-on percentage is $25 \div (100 - 25) = 33\frac{1}{3}$. The mark-on is always larger than the gross margin percentage.

sons and professional organizations, including physicians, lawyers, engineers, ski instructors, consultants of various types, and public accounting firms.

In time and material pricing the *time* component is expressed as a labor rate per hour, which is calculated as the sum of (1) direct salary and fringe benefit costs of the employee; (2) an equitable share of all indirect costs, except those related to material; and (3) an allowance for profit. The material component includes a *material loading* which is added to the invoice cost of parts and other material used on the job. This loading consists of an allowance for material handling costs and storage costs plus an allowance for profit. The loading might well be approximately 20 percent to 40 percent of the invoice cost of the materials.

ADJUSTING COSTS TO PRICES. Pricing, quite naturally, is usually thought of as the process of arriving at selling prices. However, there are some situations in which the process works in reverse: the selling price that must be charged in order to meet competition is taken as a given; the problem then is to determine how much cost the company can afford to incur if it is to earn a satisfactory profit at the given price. In the apparel business, for example, it is customary to use discrete price points— $19.75, $29.75, $39.75, and so on. The manufacturer designs individual garments to "fit" one of these price points. In order to insure that the company makes a satisfactory profit on a garment, the selling price is taken as a given, and the company calculates how much it can afford to spend on cloth, on labor, and on other elements of cost and still have a satisfactory profit margin.

PRICING STRATEGY. The foregoing discussion has emphasized the role of costs in arriving at selling prices. Actually, many companies have no pricing problem. A market price exists, customers will not pay more than this price, and there is no reason why the product should be sold at a lower price. Wheat and other products traded on commodity markets are the classic examples, but the situation also exists for companies in many other industries, such as small companies in industries where one or a few large companies exercise price leadership. Under such circumstances, a company makes no pricing calculations; it simply charges the market price.

If a company does have the problem of determining its selling prices, cost information at best provides a first approximation to the selling price. The price arrived at by the methods described above is often described as a *target price*. It is important information, but by no means is it the only information used in the final pricing decision. The selling price is one tactical device in the competitive game. It can be varied in either direction—lowered in an effort to take business away from competitors, or raised in the hope that additional profits will be generated without undue loss of volume. Marketing managers use many other tactical devices: advertising, sales promotion, displays, and so on. The selling price is one important tactic, and the manager needs information about the cost components of each product as a basis for making the pricing decision.

CONTRIBUTION PRICING. In the situations described above, the company makes pricing decisions with information on full costs as a first approximation. There are other situations in which individual products may be sold at a loss, that is, at a price that is below full costs. Even though these products are sold at a loss, under certain conditions they may increase the company's total profit. These are special situations, and they require special cost constructions. The approach is called contribution pricing, and it is described in Chapter 18.

SUMMARY

The essential idea of a standard cost accounting system is that costs and inventory amounts are recorded at what costs *should* have been rather than what they actually were. At some point in the flow of costs through the system there is a shift from actual costs to standard costs. Wherever this shift occurs, a variance develops. This can be as early in the process as the receipt of raw materials (in which case the variance is a Material Price Variance), or it can be as late as the movement of finished product from the factory to finished goods inventory.

When joint costs or by-product costs are involved, costs must be divided among the several cost objectives in some equitable fashion.

Nonmanufacturing costs can be assigned to cost objectives using the same principles as are used for assigning manufacturing costs.

Although it is impossible to measure full costs precisely whenever indirect costs are involved, such measures are useful if the costing practices are comparable within a company or an industry.

Information on the full cost of products and services is used: in financial reporting; in analyzing the profitability of a business segment; to answer the question, "What did X cost?"; as a basis for setting regulated prices; and as a first approximation in deciding on selling prices under normal circumstances.

CASES

CASE 16–1. BENNETT BODY COMPANY

Mr. Ralph Kern, the controller of the Bennett Body Company, received a memorandum from Mr. Paul Bennett, the company's president, suggesting that Mr. Kern review an attached magazine article and comment on it at the next executive committee meeting. The article described the Conley Automotive Corporation's cost accounting system. The Bennett Body Company was a custom manufacturer of truck bodies. Occasionally a customer would reorder an exact duplicate of an earlier body, but most of the time some modifications caused changes in design and hence in cost.

The Conley System

Mr. Kern learned from the article that Conley also manufactured truck bodies but that these were of standard design. Conley had 12 models that it produced in quantities based upon management's estimates of demand. In December of each year, a plan, or budget, for the following year's operations was agreed upon, which included estimates of costs and profits as well as of sales volume.

Included in this budget were estimated costs for each of the 12 models of truck bodies. These costs were determined by totaling estimated labor at an expected wage rate, estimated material at an expected cost per unit, and an allocation for overhead that was based on the proportion of estimated total overhead costs to estimated total direct labor dollars. This estimate for each model became the standard cost of the model.

No attempt was made in Conley's accounts to record the actual costs of each model. Costs were accumulated for each of the four direct producing departments and for several service departments. Labor costs were easily obtainable from payroll records, since all employees assigned to a producing department were classified as direct labor for that department. Material sent to the department was charged to it on the basis of signed issue slips. Overhead costs were charged to the department on the basis of the same percentage of direct labor as that used in determining the standard cost.

Since Conley's management also knew how many truck bodies of each model were handled by each department monthly, the total standard costs for each department could easily be calculated by multiplying the quantity of that model produced by its standard cost. Management watched closely the difference between the actual cost and the standard cost as the year progressed.

As each truck body was completed, its cost was added to Finished Goods Inventory at the standard cost figure. When the truck body was sold, the standard cost became the Cost of Goods Sold figure. This system of cost recording avoided the necessity of accumulating detailed actual costs on each specific body that was built; yet the company could estimate, reasonably well, the costs of its products. Moreover, management believed that the differences between actual and standard cost provided a revealing insight into cost fluctuations that eventually should lead to better cost control. An illustrative tabulation of the costs for Department 4 is shown in Exhibit 1. No incomplete work remained in this department either at the beginning or at the end of the month.

Exhibit 1

SUMMARY OF COSTS, DEPARTMENT 4, NOVEMBER

Standard	Num- ber of Bodies	Material		Labor		Overhead*	
		Per Unit	Total	Per Unit	Total	Per Unit	Total
Model 101.........	10	$150	$ 1,500	$220	$ 2,200	$220	$ 2,200
109.........	8	200	1,600	175	1,400	175	1,400
113.........	11	305	3,355	210	2,310	210	2,310
154.........	20	95	1,900	194	3,880	194	3,880
Total..............	49		$ 8,355		$ 9,790		$ 9,790
Actual costs........			9,120		10,030		10,030
Variances.........			$ − 765		$ − 240		$ − 240

*The overhead rate for Department 4 was 100 percent of direct labor cost.

The Bennett System

Because almost every truck body that Bennett built was in some respect unique, costs were accumulated by individual jobs.

When a job was started it received a code number, and costs for the job were collected weekly under that code number. When material (such as wood, metal tubing, steel forms or bars, canvas and paint) used for a particular job was issued to the workers, a record of the quantity issued was obtained on a requisition form. This quantity of material—so many units, board feet, linear feet, weight, and so on—was multiplied by the purchase cost per unit to arrive at the actual cost of material used. Maintenance of cumulative records of these withdrawals by code number made the total material cost of each job easy to determine.

Likewise, all labor costs of making a particular truck body were recorded. If a worker moved from job to job, a record was made of the worker's time spent on each job, and the worker's weekly wages were divided among these jobs in proportion to the amount of time spent on each. Throughout the shop, the time of any person working on anything directly related to an order—Job No. 1375J, for example—was ultimately converted to a dollar cost and charged to that job.

Finally, Bennett's overhead costs that could not be directly associated with a particular job were allocated among all jobs on the proportional basis of direct labor hours involved. Thus, if in some month 135 direct labor hours were spent on Job No. 1375J, and this was 5 percent of the 2,700 direct labor hours spent on all jobs at Bennett that month, then Job No. 1375J received 5 percent of all the overhead cost—supplies, salaries, depreciation, and so forth—for that month.

Under this system Bennett's management knew at the end of each month what each body job in process cost to date. They could also determine total factory cost and therefore gross profit at the completion of each job.

The note that Mr. Bennett attached to the magazine article read:

Ralph:

Please review the system of cost accounting described in this article with the view of possible applications to our company. Aside from the overall comparison, I am interested particularly in your opinion on—

1. Costs of paper work and recordkeeping, as compared with our system.
2. Possible reasons for cost differences between the actual and standard costs under Conley's system.
3. How you think Conley develops the standard cost of factory overhead for a particular model for the purpose of preparing the budget.
4. Whether you think that we should change our period for determining the overhead allocation rate from monthly to annually. If so, why?

These are just a few questions which might be helpful in your overall analysis. I would like to discuss this question at the next executive committee meeting.

Thank you.

Paul Bennett

Question

As Mr. Kern, what would you be prepared to say in response to Mr. Bennett's memorandum?

CASE 16–2. TREYNOR COMPANY

The Treynor Company had a standard cost system with separate accounts established to record factory variances. Variance accounts were closed at the end of the month to the Expense and Revenue Summary account. Two products were made, each with a standard cost as follows:

	Product A	Product B
Direct material cost (at standard cost of $2 per pound)	$ 10	$ 16
Direct labor cost (at standard rate of $4 per hour)	80	48
Overhead cost	20	40
Total	$110	$104

Raw material cost was debited to the Raw Materials Inventory account at the standard cost of $2 a pound upon delivery, any discrepancy between actual and standard price going to a variance account. All debits to Goods in Process were at standard.

Following are statements relating to operations in September:

1. On September 1, balances in the accounts were as follows:

	Dr.	Cr.
Raw Materials	$ 25,200	
Goods in Process	100,000	
Finished Goods	123,000	
Other Assets	400,000	
Accounts Payable		$ 40,000
Wages Payable		32,000
Other Liabilities		200,000
Stockholders' Equity		376,200
Total	$648,200	$648,200

Raw material on hand, Sept. 1, 12,000 lbs.

2. During September, the company bought and received 20,000 pounds of material, paying $24,000 cash of the total bill of $46,000, leaving $22,000 still payable as of September 30.

3. The materials warehouse issued 15,000 pounds of material to the production department during the month.

4. Production schedules for September called for 800 units of A and

1,200 units of B to be started through production during the month, and the 15,000 pounds of material was all used for this purpose.

5. Direct labor expense incurred during September was $120,000. Indirect labor expense was $30,000. Wages paid were $144,000 (disregard social security taxes).

6. Overhead expenses for September other than indirect labor were $40,000. Of this amount, $31,000 was credited to Other Assets and $9,000 to Accounts Payable.

7. Administrative and selling expenses were $40,000. The offsetting entry was to Accounts Payable.

8. Standard cost sheets showed that standard costs were charged to products, representing work done on those products during the month, as follows: labor, $121,600; overhead, $64,000.

9. During September, 1,100 units of A and 1,000 units of B were delivered to the warehouse as finished goods, although some of this production had in fact been started in August.

10. September sales were 1,000 units of A for $166,000 and 1,200 units of B for $170,000. The offsetting entry was to Other Assets.

Questions

1. Set up T accounts and record the above transactions. Adjust and close the accounts, carrying the process through to the transfer of September's net income to Retained Earnings.
2. Prepare an income statement for September. Ignore income taxes.
3. Prepare a balance sheet as of September 30.
4. Why is your figure for net income in September only a rough approximation at best?

CASE 16–3. BLACK METER COMPANY

Refer to the text description of Black Meter's cost accounting system, and consider the following:

1. Trace through the cost accounting procedures described so that you are able to show how the numbers in each illustration are derived from, and/or help derive, the other illustrations.

2. Try to imagine what an actual cost system for Black Meter would look like. How would it compare with the standard cost system in terms of:

a. Recordkeeping effort required?

b. Usefulness of cost information to Black Meter's management?

3. Develop a flowchart for Black Meter's system similar to the one in Illustration 16–1. In what respects, if any, do these two flowcharts differ?

4. Suppose that the direct labor rate for Department 120A was increased to $5.50 per hour, and that for Department 131 was increased to $4.50 per hour. What effect would these changes have on the succeeding illustrations and on the total standard cost of 100 ⅜-inch HF meters?

5. As a consultant to Black Meter Company's controller, what would be your evaluation of the present system?

CHAPTER 17

DIFFERENTIAL ACCOUNTING:
THE BEHAVIOR OF COSTS

In this chapter we introduce the concept of differential costs (and also differential revenues) and contrast this concept with the full cost concept. The chapter explains in an introductory way what the differential cost concept is and how differential costs aid the decision maker in the analysis of business problems. As a background for discussing the analysis of business problems, we describe how costs behave in certain situations, and particularly the effect that a change in volume has on costs.

THE DIFFERENTIAL CONCEPT

Cost Constructions for Various Purposes

In Chapters 15 and 16 we focused on the measurement of full costs, which is one type of cost construction. In the present chapter we introduce a second main type of cost construction, called *differential costs*. Some people have difficulty in accepting the idea that there is more than one type of cost construction. They say, "When I pay a company $180 for a desk, the desk surely cost me $180. How could the cost be anything else?" It is appropriate therefore that we establish the points that: (*a*) "cost" does have more than one meaning, (*b*)differences in cost constructions relate to the *purpose* for which the cost information is to be used, and (*c*) unless these differences are understood, serious mistakes can be made.

To explain these points, let us consider a furniture company that, among other things, manufactures and sells desks. According to its cost accounting records, maintained as described in Chapter 15, the full cost of manufacturing a certain desk is $200. Suppose that a customer offered to buy such a desk for $180. If the company considered that the only relevant cost for this desk was the $200 full cost, it would of course refuse the order. Its revenue would be only $180 and its costs would be $200; therefore the management would conclude that it would incur a loss of $20 on the order. But it might well be that the additional *out-of-pocket* costs of making this one desk—the lumber and other material and the wages paid to the cabinetmaker who worked on the desk—would be only $125. The other items making up the $200 of full cost as measured in the cost accounting system were items of cost which would not be affected by this one order. The management might therefore decide to accept this order at $180. If it did, the company's costs would increase by $125, its revenue would increase by $180, and its income would increase by the difference, or $55. Thus, the company would be $55 better off by accepting this order than by refusing it. Evidently, in this problem the wrong decision could be made if the company relied on the full cost information.

In this example, we used both $200 and $125 as measures of the "cost" of the desk. These numbers represent two types of cost constructions, each of which is used for a different purpose. The $200 measures the full cost of the desk, which is the cost used for the purposes described in Chapter 16. The $125 is another type of cost construction, and it is used for other purposes, one of which is to decide, under certain circumstances, whether an order for the desk should be accepted. We shall label this latter type of cost construction *differential cost*.

Differential Costs

Differential costs are costs that are different under one set of conditions than they would be under another set of conditions.[1] The term refers both to certain elements of cost and to amounts of cost. Thus, in many situations direct labor is an item of differential cost; also, if the amount of cost that differs in a certain problem is $1,000, the $1,000 is said to be the amount of differential cost.

Differential costs always relate to a specific situation. In the example described above, the differential cost of the desk in question was $125. Under another set of circumstances—for example, if a similar problem arose several days later—the differential costs might well be something other than $125. The differential cost to the *buyer* of the desk was $180. He paid $180 for the desk, which he would not have paid if he had not purchased the desk.

---

[1] Differential costs are also called *relevant* costs, but this term is not descriptive. All types of cost constructions are relevant for certain types of problems.

Differential Revenues

The differential concept also applies to revenues; that is, *differential revenues* are those that are different under one set of conditions than they would be under another set of conditions. In the example of the desk, the differential revenue of the furniture manufacturer was $180; his revenue would differ by $180 if he accepted the order for the desk from what it would be if he did not accept the order.

VARIABLE AND FIXED COSTS

In the example of the desk given above, the volume, or output, of the furniture manufacturer would be higher, by one desk, if it accepted the order compared with what it would have been if it did not accept the order. The proposal under consideration therefore had an effect on volume as well as on costs. This is the case with a great many problems involving differential costs, and we shall therefore discuss in some detail the relation of costs to volume. In order to do so, we introduce the concepts of variable costs and fixed costs.

In general usage, the word "variable" means simply "changeable," but in accounting, "variable" has a more restricted meaning. Variable refers not to changes in cost that take place over time, nor to changes associated with the seasons, but only to changes associated with the *level of activity*, that is, with the volume of output. If the total amount of a cost item increases as volume increases, the item is a variable cost; otherwise, it is not. There are three types of cost patterns: variable, fixed (nonvariable), and semivariable (partly variable).

Variable costs are items of cost that vary directly and proportionately with volume. For example, as volume increases by 10 percent, the total amount of cost also increases by 10 percent. Direct labor, direct material, lubricants, power costs, and supplies often are examples of variable costs.

Fixed costs do not vary at all with volume. Building depreciation, property taxes, supervisory salaries, and occupancy costs (heat and light) often behave in this fashion. These costs increase because of the passage of time, rather than because of the volume within a specified period of time. For example, the amount of a superintendent's salary for two months is double the amount for one month, but it is unaffected by changes in the level of activity within a month.

Although the term "fixed cost" may imply that the amount of cost is fixed and hence cannot be changed, such an implication is incorrect. The term refers only to items of cost that do not change with changes in *volume*. Fixed costs can be changed for other reasons, for example, a deliberate management decision to change them. The term "nonvariable" is therefore more appropriate than "fixed," but since "fixed cost" is in widespread business use, we use it here.

EXAMPLE: Plant protection costs, such as the wages of guards and watchmen, are ordinarily fixed costs since these costs do not vary with changes in volume. Plant protection costs will increase, however, if management decides that the current level of plant protection is inadequate. Alternatively, they will decrease if management decides that reductions in the current level are prudent.

Semivariable costs vary in the same direction as, but less than proportionately with, changes in volume. For example, if volume increases by 10 percent, the total amount of cost will increase, but by less than 10 percent. Semivariable costs are also called "semifixed" or "partly variable" costs. Examples may be indirect labor, maintenance, and clerical costs.

RELATION TO UNIT COSTS.   The foregoing description of the three types of cost was expressed in terms of *total* costs for a period. In terms of *unit* costs, the description of these types of cost is quite different. Variable cost per unit of volume is a *constant;* that is, it does not change as volume changes. Fixed cost per unit does change with changes in volume; as volume increases, fixed cost per unit decreases. Semivariable cost per unit also changes with changes in volume, but the amount of change is smaller than that for fixed cost.

EXAMPLE: Costs at three levels of volume are given below:

	Volume (Units)		
	100	*125*	*150*
Total cost:			
Variable cost..................	$400	$500	$600
Fixed cost......................	300	300	300
Semivariable cost...............	300	350	400
Unit cost:			
Variable cost..................	$4.00	$4.00	$4.00
Fixed cost.....................	3.00	2.40	2.00
Semivariable cost...............	3.00	2.80	2.67

Observe that as volume increases by 50 percent (i.e., from 100 to 150 units),

- Total variable cost increases by 50 percent.
- Total fixed cost remains unchanged.
- Total semivariable cost increases but by less than 50 percent.
- Variable cost per unit remains unchanged.
- Fixed cost per unit decreases.
- Semivariable cost per unit decreases, but not as much as fixed cost per unit.

VARIABLE COST VERSUS DIRECT COST.   We need to distinguish carefully between variable cost and direct cost. A *direct* cost is an element of cost that can be traced to a single cost objective, as contrasted with an indirect cost which applies to more than one cost objective. The labor cost for the time that a worker spends making Product X is a *direct* cost of Product X. Direct labor cost is also a *variable* cost for Product X because in normal circumstances it takes twice as much labor time to make two units as it takes to make one unit.

There are, however, many circumstances in which a direct cost is not a variable cost. If a certain machine is used exclusively for Product X and for no other products, then the depreciation on that machine is a *direct* cost of Product X; however, it is not normally a *variable* cost because the amount of depreciation is ordinarily accounted for as a function of the passage of time rather than of the quantity of items produced. The cost of electric power required to operate such a machine would be both a variable cost and a direct cost.

As a general rule, all items of variable cost are direct, but not all items of direct cost are variable.

CONTRIBUTION ANALYSIS

In this section we introduce a technique called *contribution analysis*. We do so both because contribution analysis is an important tool in analyzing differential costs and also because in explaining the technique we can clarify the relationships among, and differences between, variable costs, fixed costs, direct costs, indirect costs, full costs, and differential costs. Contribution analysis focuses on what is called the contribution margin.

The contribution margin for a business or for a product, service, or other segment of a business is the difference between its revenue and its variable costs. Illustration 17–1 contrasts the conventional income statement for a laundry and dry cleaning company with the same data rearranged so as to measure the contribution margin for each of its two services, dry cleaning and laundry. Analysis of the underlying records shows that of the $7,000 total revenue in June, $5,400 was earned on dry cleaning work and $1,600 on laundry. The expense items[2] on the income statement were analyzed to determine which amounts were variable, and of these, how much was attributable to dry cleaning and how much to laundry. Of the total amount of $3,300 for salaries and wages, $1,300 of wages was a variable expense of dry cleaning and $700 was a variable expense of laundry; the remaining $1,300 of salaries was a fixed expense, applicable to the business as a whole. The other variable expenses were

---

[2] Since this is an income statement, amounts deducted from revenues are called expenses. As pointed out in Chapter 3, expenses are one type of cost. Thus, although the description in this chapter uses the broader term, "costs," it applies equally well to that type of cost which is labeled "expense."

Illustration 17–1

CONTRAST BETWEEN CONVENTIONAL AND CONTRIBUTION MARGIN INCOME STATEMENTS

A. Income Statement—Conventional Basis
Month of June

Revenue...		$7,000
Expenses:		
Salaries and wages.................................	$3,300	
Supplies..	1,800	
Heat, light, and power.............................	400	
Advertising.......................................	200	
Rent...	700	
Depreciation on equipment.........................	800	
Other (telephone, insurance, etc.)..................	300	
Total expense................................		7,500
Net Loss...		$ (500)

B. Income Statement—Contribution Margin Basis
Month of June

	Dry Cleaning		Laundry	
Revenue...........................		$5,400		$1,600
Variable expenses:				
Wages...........................	$1,300		$700	
Supplies.........................	1,500		300	
Power...........................	250		50	
Total variable expenses..........		3,050		1,050
Contribution margin..................		$2,350		$ 550
Direct fixed expenses:				
Depreciation on equipment............		600		200
Contribution to indirect expenses........		$1,750		$ 350
Total contribution.................			$2,100	
Indirect fixed expenses:				
Salaries...........................	$1,300			
Heat and light......................	100			
Advertising........................	200			
Rent..............................	700			
Other.............................	300			
Total indirect fixed expenses.......			2,600	
Net Loss...........................			$ (500)	

found to be supplies and power. The total amount of variable expense was $3,050 for dry cleaning and $1,050 for laundry.

The contribution margin, which is the difference between revenue and total variable expenses, was therefore $2,350 for dry cleaning and $550 for laundry.

In addition to variable expenses, dry cleaning had $600 of direct fixed expense; this was the depreciation on the dry cleaning equipment. Laundry had $200 of direct fixed expenses. Subtracting these direct, but fixed, expenses from the contribution margin shows how much each service contributed to the indirect fixed costs of the business; the amounts were $1,750 for dry cleaning and $350 for laundry, a total of $2,100. Since the total of these indirect fixed costs was $2,600, this contribution was not large enough to produce net income for the month; the difference was the net loss of $500.

We shall use these numbers to illustrate the types of costs listed above:

• Variable costs (here expenses) are $3,050 for dry cleaning and $1,050 for laundry. They are variable because they vary with the volume of dry cleaning and laundry done.
• Fixed costs are the $800 of depreciation on equipment plus the $2,600 of indirect fixed expenses, a total of $3,400.
• Direct costs include not only the variable costs ($4,100) but also the depreciation of the dry cleaning equipment ($600) and of the laundry equipment ($200), a total of $4,900. These are direct because they are traceable directly to the separate services, but they are not all variable costs because the amount of depreciation does not change with the volume of work done.
• Indirect costs are those amounts (totaling $2,600) that are not traced directly either to dry cleaning or to laundry.
• Full costs are not shown on the analysis. In order to obtain full costs, it would be necessary to allocate the $2,600 of indirect costs to dry cleaning and to laundry, on some equitable basis.

In the above list, we omitted mention of differential costs. This is because we cannot identify differential costs in general; rather we must always relate them to a specific alternative choice problem.

EXAMPLES:
1. Suppose the management is considering certain actions that are intended to increase the volume of dry cleaning work and asks how increased volume will affect income. In this situation, the differential costs are the variable costs (and the revenue is, of course, differential revenue). Each additional dollar of dry cleaning business is expected to add 44 cents to profit, the percentage difference between dry cleaning revenue and variable costs.

2. Suppose the management is considering getting out of the laundry business. The analysis indicates that such a move would reduce costs by $1,250 (the sum of laundry variable expenses plus depreciation on the laundry equipment that will no longer be needed). The differential costs are therefore $1,250. However, $1,600 of laundry revenue also would be lost, so the move would result in a greater decrease in revenue than the saving in cost; the net loss would be increased by $350.

The message conveyed by the contribution analysis differs from the message conveyed by the conventional income statement. The income statement indicates that the business operated at a loss. Moreover, if the indirect expenses were allocated to the two services in proportion to their variable expenses, each of the two services would also show a loss, viz:

	Total	Dry Cleaning	Laundry
Contribution to indirect expenses	$2,100	$1,750	$ 350
Allocated indirect expenses	2,600	1,934	666
Net Loss	$ (500)	$ (184)	$(316)

From these numbers, someone might conclude that one or the other of these services should be discontinued in order to reduce losses. By contrast, the contribution analysis shows that each of the services made a contribution to indirect costs and that the total loss of the business would therefore not be reduced by discontinuing either of them.

Contrasts between Full Costs and Differential Costs

From the description given thus far in this chapter, we can identify three important differences between full costs and differential costs. One is in the nature of the costs, a second is in the source of data, and the third is in the relevant time perspective. Each is discussed below.

The full costs of a product or other cost objective are the sum of its direct costs plus an equitable share of applicable indirect costs. Differential costs include only those elements of cost that are different under a certain set of conditions. This is the most important difference between full costs and differential costs.

Information on full costs is taken directly from a company's cost accounting system. The system is designed to measure full costs on a regular basis, and to report these costs routinely. There is no comparable system for collecting differential costs. The appropriate items that constitute differential costs are assembled to meet the requirements of a specific problem. Each problem is different. Some of the data used to construct differential costs may come from the cost accounting system, but other data come from other sources.

Finally, the full cost accounting system collects costs on an historical basis, that is, it measures what the costs *were*. For certain purposes, such as setting selling prices, these historical costs are adjusted to reflect the estimated impact of future conditions; but for other purposes, such as financial reporting, the historical costs are used without change. *Differential costs always relate to the future;* they are intended to show what the costs *would be* if a certain course of action were adopted, rather than what the costs *were*. Historical costs are relevant only as a starting point for estimating what costs will be in the future. This point has not been emphasized adequately in the introductory examples given to this point. For example, in discussing differential costs in the laundry and dry cleaning situation shown in Illustration 17–1, we used data from the company's historical records, which was an oversimplification. Actually, the differential costs in this, and in any other problem in which differential costs are relevant, are estimates of what the costs *are going to be*, not what *they were*.

RELATION OF COSTS TO VOLUME

Since many differential cost problems involve changes in volume, that is, the level of activity, we need to consider carefully the effect that changes in volume have on costs. This section describes such cost-volume relationships and some of the tools that are helpful in analyzing these relationships.

Cost-Volume Diagrams

The relationship between costs and volume can be displayed on a cost-volume diagram, as in Illustration 17–2. In such diagrams, cost is always plotted on the vertical, or *y*, axis, and volume is plotted on the horizontal, or *x*, axis. This follows a conventional rule in geometry: the "dependent variable" is plotted on the *y* axis, and the "independent variable" is plotted on the *x* axis. In a cost-volume diagram, therefore, cost is implicitly assumed to be the "dependent variable" and volume the "independent variable"; that is, the amount of the cost *depends on* the volume or level of activity, rather than *vice versa*.

For the moment, think of volume as meaning the number of units of product manufactured or sold in a given time period, such as a month. Alternative methods of measuring volume will be discussed in a subsequent section.

Illustration 17–2 gives a generalized picture of the behavior of the three types of cost described earlier in this chapter. The fixed cost is $300 *for a period of time* regardless of the volume in that period. The variable cost is $0.80 *per unit of volume*, which means that the total variable cost in a period varies proportionately with volume. The semivariable cost starts at $200 and increases at a rate of $0.20 per unit of volume. Note that the semivariable cost can be decomposed into two elements, a fixed element of $200 per period of time and a variable element of $0.20 per unit of volume.

Illustration 17–2

FIXED, VARIABLE AND SEMI-VARIABLE COSTS

Behavior of Total Costs

If each separate cost element behaves according to one of the three patterns shown above, then the total cost, which is the sum of these separate elements, must vary with volume in the manner shown in Illustration 17–3, which was constructed simply by combining the three separate elements shown in Illustration 17–2.

Illustration 17–3

RELATION OF TOTAL COSTS TO VOLUME

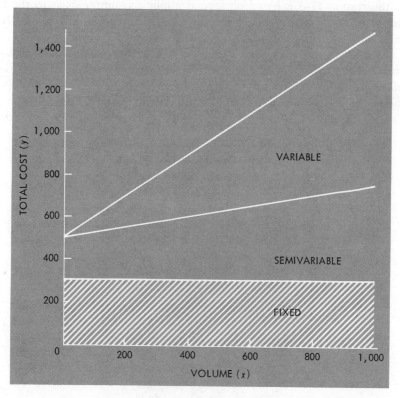

Since a semivariable cost can be split into fixed and variable components, the *behavior of total costs can be described in terms of only two components—a fixed component, which is a total amount per period, and a variable component, which is an amount per unit of volume.* In Illustration 17–3, the fixed amount is $500 per period (= $300 + $200) and the variable amount is $1 per unit of volume (= $0.80 + $0.20). The semivariable cost has disappeared as a separate entity, part of it being combined with the variable cost and the remainder being combined with the fixed cost. This combination can be made for any semivariable cost item that is expressed as a fixed dollar amount per period plus a rate per unit of volume, that is, any item for which there is a linear relationship between cost and volume. There is therefore no need to consider semivariable costs as a separate category. From this point on, we shall consider only the fixed and variable components of cost. Subsequently, we shall describe techniques for separating a semivariable cost into a variable rate per unit of volume and a fixed amount per time period.

Cost Assumptions

Illustration 17–3 is based on several implicit assumptions as to the behavior of costs, two of which are discussed below. The first is usually a reasonable one, but the second is actually quite unrealistic.

THE LINEAR ASSUMPTION. One cost behavior assumption is that all costs behave according to one of the three patterns described above, each of which is expressed by a straight line; that is, each relationship is *linear*. Actually, some items of costs may vary in steps, as in Illustration 17–4. This happens when the cost occurs in discrete "chunks," as when

Illustration 17–4

A COST ELEMENT WITH
A STEP FUNCTION

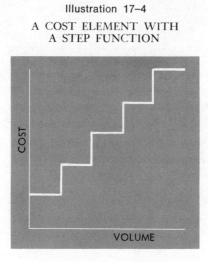

one indirect worker is added for every 500 additional hours of direct labor per month. Other items of cost may vary along a curve rather than a straight line; and in rare circumstances still others, such as the maintenance cost of idle machines, may actually decrease as volume increases.

In most situations, however, the effect of these discontinuities and nonlinear cost functions on total costs is minor, and the assumption that total costs vary in a linear relationship with volume is a satisfactory working approximation. This is a most fortunate fact. Many theoretical treatises discuss cost functions with various types of complicated curves. Such complicated curves are rarely used in practice, however, for it is usually found that the simple straight-line assumption, although perhaps not a perfect representation of cost-volume relationships, is close enough for practical purposes. In this book, therefore, we primarily describe linear relationships. If a real-life problem does involve nonlinear relationships, the general approach is similar to that described here; the only difference is that the arithmetic is more complicated.

FULL-RANGE ASSUMPTION. A second cost behavior assumption implicit in Illustration 17–3 is that costs move along a straight line throughout *the whole range* of volume, from zero to whatever number is at the far right of the diagram. This assumption is unrealistic. For example, at zero volume (i.e., when the factory is not operating at all), management decisions may cause costs to be considerably higher or considerably lower than the $500 shown in the diagram. Also, when production gets so high that a second shift is required, costs may behave quite differently from the way in which they behave under one-shift operations. Even within the limits of a single shift, it is to be expected that costs will behave differently when the factory is very busy, from the way they do when the factory is operating at a significantly lower volume. In short, the single straight line gives a good approximation of the behavior of costs *only within a certain range of volume.* This range is referred to as the *relevant range* because it is the range that is relevant for the situation being analyzed.

Illustration 17–5 shows the same cost pattern as Illustration 17–3, and

Illustration 17–5

DESIGNATION OF RELEVANT RANGE

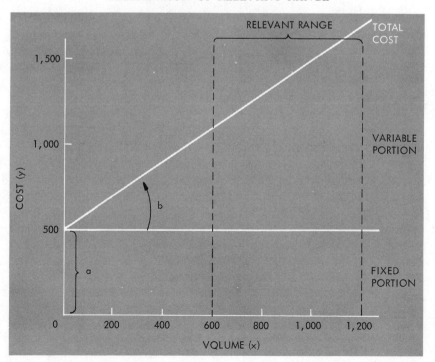

the relevant range is indicated by the dotted lines at 600 units and 1,200 units. Although the cost line extends back to zero, it does not imply that costs actually will behave in this fashion at volumes lower than 600 units; rather, it is drawn on the diagram solely as a means of identifying the fixed component of total costs. The fixed component (i.e., $500 per period) is the amount of costs indicated by the point where the cost line crosses the y axis, which is zero volume.

It is also important to note that the diagram shows the estimated relationship between costs and volume under a *certain set of conditions.* This is not an assumption; it is a fact. If any of these conditions should change—for example, if there is an increase in wage rates—the diagram is obsolete, and a new one must be drawn.

Equation for the Cost Line

As already pointed out, total costs at any volume are the sum of the fixed component ($500 per period in Illustration 17–5) and the variable component ($1 per unit). For example, at a volume of 1,000 units, cost is $500 + ($1 per unit times 1,000 units) = $1,500. Designating costs as y, volume as x, the fixed component as a, and the variable component as b, the cost at any volume can be found from the equation $y = a + bx$. This is simply the general equation for a straight line.[3]
Recapitulating:

Equation:	y	$=$	a	$+$	$(b$	$\cdot$	$x)$
Words:	Total Cost	$=$	Fixed per Period	$+$	(Variable per Unit	$\cdot$	Units)
Numbers:	$1,500	$=$	$500	$+$	($1	$\cdot$	1,000)

Unit Costs

It should be emphasized that the line we are studying represents *total* costs at various volumes. Such a line should not be confused with a line that represents *unit* costs. If total costs have a linear relationship with volume, then unit costs will be a curve that slopes downward to the right; this curve reflects the fact that unit costs decrease as volume increases. Illustration 17–6 is a unit cost curve derived from Illustration 17–5. Since unit cost is simply total cost divided by the number of units, Illustration 17–6 was obtained simply by dividing total cost at various volume levels by the amount of volume at those levels, plotting the results of each such calculation, and joining the dots.

---

[3] In some mathematics texts, the notation used is $y = mx + b$. In such a notation, m represents the *slope*, or cost per unit, and b represents the y-intercept or fixed cost per period. This difference in notation reflects the personal preference of mathematicians and has no other significance whatsoever.

Illustration 17–6

BEHAVIOR OF UNIT COSTS

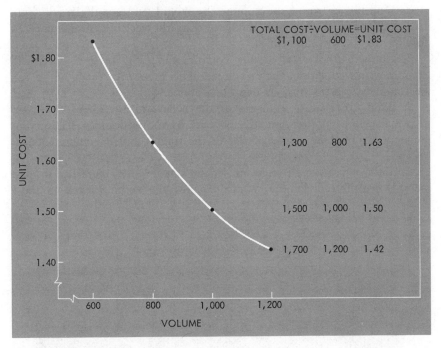

Estimating the Cost-Volume Relationship

In order to construct a cost-volume diagram, estimates must be made of what the amounts of costs are expected to be. These estimates often are made as part of the budgeting process, which is described in Chapter 21. In this process, estimates are made of all significant items of revenue and cost; these show what revenues and costs are expected to be at various volume levels in the following year.

Any of the following methods can be used to derive the *a* and *b* terms for the cost-volume formula:

1. Estimate total costs at each of two volume levels; this establishes two points on the line. (This is often called the *high-low method* because one of the volumes selected is likely to be quite high and the other is likely to be quite low; the upper and lower limits of the relevant range often are selected for this purpose.) Then proceed as follows:

a. Subtract total cost at the lower volume from total cost at the higher volume, and subtract the number of units for the lower volume from the number of units for the higher volume.

b. Divide the difference in cost by the difference in volume, which gives *b*, the amount by which total cost changes with a change of one unit of volume.

c. Multiply either of the volumes by *b* and subtract the result from the total cost at that volume, thus removing the variable component and leaving the fixed component *a*.

2. Estimate total costs at one volume, and estimate how costs will change with a given change in volume. This gives *b* directly, and *a* can be found by subtraction, as described above.

3. Build up separate estimates of the behavior of each of the items that make up total costs, identifying each item's fixed and variable components. From these estimates, derive the total *a* and *b* components directly.

4. Make a *scatter diagram* in which actual costs recorded in past periods are plotted (on the *y* axis) against the volume levels in those

Illustration 17–7

SCATTER DIAGRAM

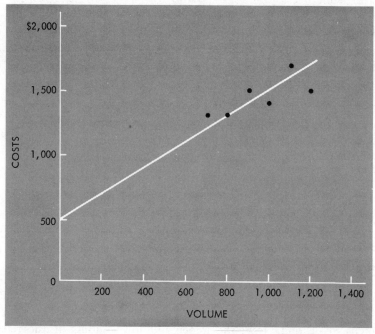

Months	Costs	Volume
July	$1,400	1,000
August	1,700	1,100
September	1,500	900
October	1,300	800
November	1,500	1,200
December	1,300	700

periods (on the *x* axis). Data on costs and volumes for each of the preceding several months might be used for this purpose. Draw a line that best fits these observations. Such a diagram is shown in Illustration 17–7. The line of best fit either can be drawn by visual inspection of the plotted points, or it can be fitted by a statistical technique called the *method of least squares* (see the Appendix, p. 544). In many cases a line drawn by visual inspection is better than a mathematically fitted line, because judgment can be used to adjust for unusual observations.

If the line is fitted visually, the *a* and *b* values can be determined by reading the values for any two points on the line and then using the high-low method described above. If the line is fitted statistically, the procedure gives the *a* and *b* values directly.

PROBLEMS WITH SCATTER DIAGRAMS. Estimating cost-volume relationships by means of a scatter diagram or by a least-squares calculation is a common practice, but the results can be misleading. In the first place, this technique shows, at best, what the relationship between costs and volumes *was in the past*, whereas we are interested in what the relationship *will be in the future*. The past is not necessarily a mirror of the future. Also, the relationship we seek is that obtaining under a *single set of operating conditions*, whereas each point on a scatter diagram may represent changes in factors other than the two being studied, namely, cost and volume.

Illustration 17–8 shows a common source of difficulty. In this scatter diagram, volume is represented by sales revenue, as is often the case.

Illustration 17–8

SCATTER DIAGRAM ILLUSTRATING DRIFT

* As measured by sales revenue.

Each dot is located by plotting the costs for one year on the y axis and the sales revenue for that year on the x axis. The dots lie along a well-defined path, which is indicated by the straight line, but this line may *not* indicate a relationship between costs and volume. It may, instead, indicate nothing more than the tendency for both revenues and costs to increase over the past six years because of inflationary factors. If this is the case, then the line shows the trend, or *drift*, of costs *through time*, not the relationship between cost and volume *at a given time*. Any scatter diagram in which volume is measured in *revenue* dollars (rather than in units, as in our previous diagrams), covering a period of years in which sales were generally increasing (or decreasing) each year, is likely to have this characteristic; and the longer the period covered, the more unreliable the diagram becomes.

Measures of Volume

Thus far, we have used "volume" as an abstract concept, but in a real-world situation volume must be measured in some concrete fashion. In Chapter 15 we described how indirect costs were allocated to products by means of an overhead rate. Such an overhead rate can be expressed as an amount per unit of product, per direct labor hour, per direct labor dollar, or in other ways. Each of these bases of overhead allocation is a measure of volume. Presumably, a certain measure is selected because it most closely reflects the conditions that cause costs to change. Essentially, two basic questions must be answered: (1) should the measure be based on *inputs*, or should it be based on *outputs?* and (2) should the measure be expressed in terms of *money amounts*, or should it be expressed in terms of *physical quantities?* Each of these questions is discussed below.

INPUT VERSUS OUTPUT MEASURES. *Input measures* relate to the resources that are used in a cost center. Examples for a production cost center are the number of direct labor hours worked, dollars of direct labor cost, number of machine-hours operated, or pounds of raw material used. *Output measures* relate to the work done by the cost center; in a production cost center, this is the amount of products produced, expressed either in terms of the number of units worked on or their dollar value. For cost-volume diagrams that show the relationship between overhead costs and volume, an input measure, such as direct labor costs, may be a good measure of volume since many elements of overhead cost tend to vary more closely with other input factors than with output. For example, it is reasonable to expect that indirect cost items associated with direct labor, such as fringe benefits, social security taxes, and payroll accounting, vary more closely with the amount of direct labor used than with the amount of products produced. Some indirect costs, such as inspection costs and plant transportation, might vary more closely with the quantity of products produced, however.

If the diagram represents total costs for a cost center, and if volume is measured in terms of direct labor, which is itself one element of cost, it can be argued that the same numbers affect both costs and volume. This is true, but the line nevertheless reflects changes in costs other than direct labor and is therefore useful.

MONETARY VERSUS NONMONETARY MEASURES. A volume measure expressed in physical quantities, such as direct labor hours, is often better than one expressed in dollars, such as direct labor cost, because the former is unaffected by changes in prices. A wage increase would cause direct labor costs to increase, even if there were no actual increase in the volume of activity. If volume is measured in terms of direct labor dollars, such a measure could be misleading. On the other hand, if price changes are likely to affect both labor and overhead to the same degree, the use of a monetary measure of volume may be a means of allowing implicitly for the effect of these price changes.

CHOICE OF A MEASURE. These considerations must be tempered by practicality. Total direct labor costs are often available in the cost accounting system without extra calculation, whereas the computation of total direct labor hours, or machine-hours, may require considerable additional work. Also, since the measure of volume for analytical purposes is often (but not always) the same as that used in allocating overhead costs to products for the purpose of financial accounting, the appropriateness of the measure for the latter purpose must also be taken into account.

THE PROFITGRAPH AND BREAK-EVEN ANALYSIS

The cost-volume diagram in Illustration 17–5 can be expanded into a useful device called the *profitgraph* (or "Profit-Volume graph," or "P/V graph") simply by the addition of a revenue line to it, for a *profitgraph is a diagram showing the expected relationship between total costs and revenue at various volumes.*[4] A profitgraph can be constructed either for the business as a whole, or for some segment of the business such as a product, a product line, or a division.

On a profitgraph, the measure of volume may be the number of units produced and sold, or it may be dollars of sales revenue. We have already stated the formula for the cost line: $y = a + bx$. Revenue is plotted on the profitgraph on the assumption of a constant selling price

---

[4] This device is also called a "break-even chart," but such a label has the unfortunate implication that the objective of a business is merely to break even.

per unit. Assuming that volume is to be measured as units of product sold and designating the unit selling price as p, the number of units of volume as x, and the total revenue as y, the total revenue (y) equals the unit selling price (p) times the number of units of volume (x); or $y = px$. For example, if the unit selling price is \$1.80, the total revenue from the sale of 1,000 units will be \$1,800.

A profitgraph showing these relationships is shown in Illustration 17–9. Although not shown explicitly on the diagram, it should be understood

Illustration 17–9

PROFITGRAPH

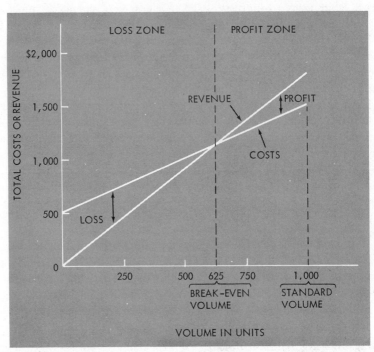

that the relationships are expected to hold only within the relevant volume range. Sometimes, several revenue lines are drawn on a profitgraph, each one showing what revenue would be at a specified unit selling price. This procedure helps to show how a change in selling price affects the profit at any given volume.

At the *break-even volume*, total costs equal total revenue. This is simply a geometric fact. The break-even point is of little practical interest in a profitable company, because attention is focused on the profit region which should be considerably above the break-even point. At lower volumes, a loss is expected; and at higher volumes, a profit is expected. The amount of loss or profit expected at any volume is the vertical distance between points on the total cost and revenue lines at that volume. The break-even volume is not the same as the "standard" volume used as a basis for determining overhead rates. In a profitable business, standard volume is considerably higher than the break-even volume.

Interpretation of the Profitgraph

The profitgraph is a useful device for analyzing the overall profit characteristics of a business. To illustrate such an analysis, assume the following situation, which is the same as that shown in previous diagrams:

Fixed costs.........................	$500 per period
Variable costs.......................	$1 per unit
Standard volume.....................	1,000 units
Selling price........................	$1.80 per unit

For simplicity, we shall assume that the company makes only one product. In this situation, total costs at *standard volume* will be $500 (fixed) plus $(1{,}000 \times \$1)$ (variable) = $1,500. Assuming that all costs are assigned to the product using an overhead rate that is based on standard volume, then the standard unit cost of the product will be $1,500 ÷ 1,000 units, or $1.50 per unit. At a selling price of $1.80 per unit, total revenue at standard volume will be $1,800, and income will be $300 (= $1,800 − $1,500). Income at standard volume will be $0.30 per unit (= $300 ÷ 1,000 units).

COMPUTATION OF BREAK-EVEN VOLUME. Recall that the break-even volume is the volume at which costs equal revenue.

Since revenue (y) at any volume (x) is
$$y = \quad px$$
And costs (y) at any volume (x) is
$$y = a + bx$$
And since at the break-even volume,
   costs = revenue:
Therefore the break-even volume is the
   volume at which
$$px = a + bx$$

If we let x equal the break-even volume, then for the above situation, we have:

$$\$1.80x = \$500 + \$1x$$
$$x = 625 \text{ units}$$

At the break-even volume of 625 units, revenue equals 625 units × $1.80 per unit, which is $1,125, and total costs equal $500 + (625 units × $1 per unit), which is also $1,125.

The equation for the break-even volume, x, can also be stated in the following form:

$$x = \frac{a}{p - b}$$

In words, this equation says that the break-even volume can be found by dividing the fixed costs (a) by the difference between selling price per unit (p) and variable cost per unit (b).

MARGINAL INCOME. From the relationships of costs and revenue at various volumes, an important conclusion can be drawn: although the profit at standard volume is $0.30 per unit, this unit profit will be earned *only* at the standard volume. At lower volumes the profit will be less than $0.30 per unit, and at higher volumes it will be more than $0.30 per unit.

Although profit per unit is different at each volume, there is another number that is constant for all volumes within the relevant range. This number is called the *unit contribution* or *marginal income. Marginal income is the difference between selling price and variable cost per unit.*

In our example, the marginal income is $0.80 per unit (= $1.80 − $1.00). Because it is a constant, it is an extremely useful way of expressing the relationship between revenue and cost at any volume. For each change of one unit of volume, profit will change by $0.80. Starting at the bottom of the relevant range, each additional unit of volume increases profit by the amount of marginal income.

We can use the above notation to express these relationships, adding the symbol i for total income or profit:

$$(p - b)x - a = i$$

In words, total income at any volume is marginal income ($p - b$) times volume minus fixed cost. In the above example, at standard volume of 1,000 units,

$$(p - b) \quad x \quad - \quad a \quad = \quad i$$
$$(\$1.80 - \$1) \, 1{,}000 - \$500 = \$300$$

That is, the marginal income of $0.80 per unit, times 1,000 units, minus the fixed cost of $500 gives total income of $300. Stated another way, if the marginal income is $0.80 per unit and fixed costs are $500, 625 units must be sold before enough revenue will be earned to cover fixed costs. After that, a profit of $0.80 per unit will be earned.

Improving Profit Performance

These cost-volume-profit relationships suggest that a useful way of studying the basic profit characteristics of a business is to focus not on the profit per unit (which is different at every volume), but rather on the total fixed costs and the marginal income per unit. In these terms, there are four basic ways in which the profit of a business that makes a single product can be increased:

1. Increase selling prices per unit (p).
2. Decrease variable costs per unit (b).
3. Decrease fixed costs (a).
4. Increase volume (x).

The separate effects of each of these possibilities are shown in the following calculations· and in Illustration 17–10. Each starts from a

Illustration 17–10

EFFECT OF 10 PERCENT CHANGE IN PROFIT FACTORS

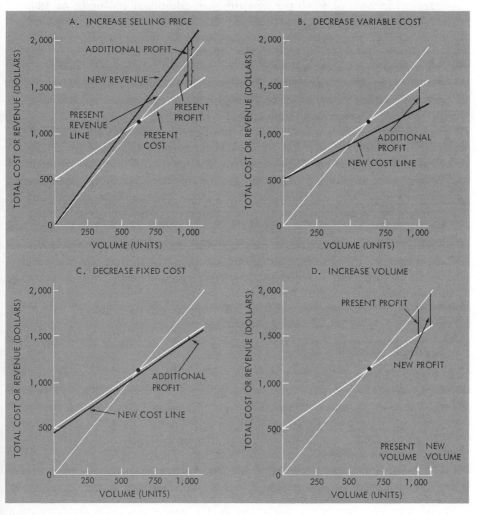

situation that is assumed to be "normal": selling price, $1.80; variable costs, $1 per unit; fixed costs, $500 per period; volume, 1,000 units; and hence profit, $300. The effect of a 10 percent change in each profit-determining factor is:

A. A 10 percent increase in selling price (ie., from $1.80 to $1.98) would add $180 to revenue and would have no effect on costs; therefore, profit would be increased by $180, or 60 percent.

B. A 10 percent decrease in variable costs would reduce variable costs by $100; profit would therefore increase by $100, or 33 percent.

C. A 10 percent decrease in fixed cost would amount to $50; profit would therefore increase by $50, or 17 percent.

D. A 10 percent increase in volume would increase profit by the marginal income of $0.80 per unit times an additional 100 units, or $80, which is an increase of 27 percent.

If, instead of varying each factor separately, we look at some of the interrelationships among them, we can calculate, for example, that a 20 percent (i.e., $100) increase in fixed costs could be offset either by a 6 percent increase in selling price, or a 12 percent increase in volume, or a 10 percent decrease in variable costs.

Another calculation made from a profitgraph is the *margin of safety. This is the amount or ratio by which the current volume exceeds the break-even volume.* Assuming current volume is the same as standard volume, which is 1,000 units, the margin of safety in our illustrative situation is 375 units, or 38 percent, of current volume. Sales volume can decrease by 38 percent before a loss is incurred, other factors remaining equal.

The foregoing calculations assume that each of the factors is independent of the others, a situation that is rarely the case in the real world. An increase in selling price often is accompanied by a decrease in volume, for example. Changes in the factors must therefore usually be studied simultaneously, rather than separately as was done above.

Several Products

The cost-volume-profit relationships described above apply in the situation in which the company makes only a single product. The relationship also holds in the company that makes several products if each product has substantially the same marginal income as a percentage of sales. A profitgraph could be constructed for such a company by using sales revenue, rather than units, as the measure of volume. In such a company each dollar of sales revenue produces the same marginal income as every other dollar of sales revenue. If, as is sometimes the case, the company is able to set selling prices so as to obtain the same marginal income on each of its products, such a profitgraph is a valid representation of its profit characteristics.

If, however, the company makes several products and they have *different* marginal incomes, the depiction of a valid cost-volume-profit relationship is more complicated. If the proportion of the sales of each product to the total remains relatively constant, then a single profitgraph is still valid. It shows the *average* marginal income for all products, rather than the individual marginal incomes of any product.

The proportion of sales of each product in a given period is called the *product mix* in that period. Changes in the product mix affect profits in a way that is not revealed by the type of profitgraph described above. For example, even if sales revenue does not change from one period to the next, profits will increase if in the latter period the proportion of products that have a high marginal income is greater than it was in the first period.

When products have different marginal incomes and when the product mix changes, the best approach to cost-volume-profit analysis usually is to treat each product as a separate entity, and to construct a profitgraph for that entity, just as we did for the business as a whole. This method requires that all costs of the business be allocated to individual products.

Other Influences on Costs

A cost-volume diagram, or a profitgraph, shows only what total costs are expected to be at various *levels* of volume. For example, the diagram shows that the variable cost of 200 units is double the variable cost of 100 units. There are many reasons, other than the level of volume, why the costs in one period are different from those in another period. Some of these are listed below.

1. *Changes in input prices.* One of the most important causes of changes in a cost-volume diagram is that the prices of input factors change. Inflation is a persistent, and probably permanent, phenomenon. Wage rates go up; salaries go up; material costs go up; costs of services go up. A cost-volume diagram can get seriously out of date, and hence be misleading, if it is not adjusted for the effect of these changes.

2. The *rate* at which volume changes. Rapid changes in the level of volume are more difficult for factory personnel to adjust to than are moderate changes in volume; therefore, the more rapid the change in volume, the more likely it is that costs will depart from the straight-line, cost-volume pattern.

3. The *direction* of change in volume. When volume is increasing, costs tend to lag behind the straight-line relationship either because the company is unable to hire the additional workers that are assumed in the

cost line or because supervisors try to "get by" without adding overhead costs. Similarly, when volume is decreasing, there is a reluctance to lay off workers and to shrink other elements of cost, and this also causes a lag.

4. The *duration* of change in volume. A temporary change of volume, in either direction, tends to affect costs less than a change that lasts a long time, for much the same reasons as were given in the preceding paragraph.

5. *Prior knowledge of the change.* If a production manager has adequate advance notice of a change in volume, he can plan for it, and actual costs therefore are more likely to remain close to the cost-volume line than is the case when the change in volume is unexpected.

6. *Productivity.* The cost-volume diagram assumes a certain level of productivity in the use of resources. As the level of productivity changes, the cost changes. Overall productivity in the United States tends to increase at a rate of about 3 percent a year, and labor costs are reduced correspondingly.

7. *Management discretion.* Some items of cost change because management has decided that they *should* change. Some companies, for example, have relatively large headquarters staffs, while others have small headquarters staffs. The size of these staffs, and hence the costs associated with their activities, can be varied within fairly wide limits, depending on management's judgment as to what the optimum size is. Such types of cost are called *discretionary costs.* They are discussed in more detail in Chapter 20.

8. *Measure of volume.* Volume is often measured by sales, either in units or in dollars. Costs are production costs. If the volume of sales does not correspond to the volume of production, the profitgraph may be misleading.

For these and other reasons, it is not possible to predict the total costs of a business in a certain period simply by predicting the volume for that period and then determining the costs at that volume by reading a cost-volume diagram. Nevertheless, the effect of volume on costs and profits is so important that the cost-volume diagram and the profitgraph are extremely useful tools in analysis. In using them, the interpretation of the relationships that they depict must be tempered by the influence of other factors, to the extent that they can be estimated.

Learning Curves

Studies have shown that the change in cost associated with a change in productivity has, in many situations, a characteristic curve that can be estimated with reasonable accuracy. This is called the *learning curve,* or the *experience curve.*

The phenomenon was first observed in the aircraft industry, where it was found that certain costs tend to decrease, per unit, in a predictable pattern as the workers and their supervisors become more familiar with the work; as the flow of work, tooling, and methods improve; as less scrap and rework result; as fewer skilled workers need to be used; and so on. The decreasing costs are a function of the learning process, which results in fewer and fewer man-hours being necessary to produce a unit of product as more units of the same product are completed. It should be

Illustration 17–11

EXAMPLES OF LEARNING CURVES

World Shipments of Integrated Circuits Learning Curve

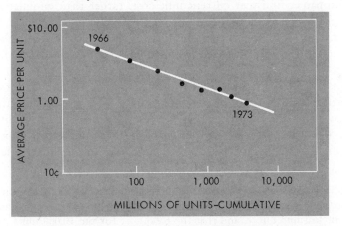

Direct Cost per Megawatt—Steam Turbine Generators
1946–1963

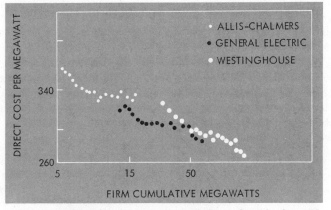

Source: From the publication *Perspectives*, by the Boston Consulting Group. The integrated circuits curve appeared originally in the First Quarter Report of Texas Instruments, Incorporated, April 18, 1973. The steam turbine generator curve was compiled from information furnished by General Electric, Westinghouse, and Allis Chalmers in connection with antitrust litigation.

noted, however, that not all costs decrease; for instance, material costs are not usually subject to the learning process, although they may decrease to the extent by which waste is eliminated.

Research in a number of industries has shown that there is a regular pattern to this cost reduction, and that this is likely to be a constant percentage reduction in unit cost when *cumulative* production doubles. For example, an 80 percent learning curve means that if the unit cost is $50 when production has reached 10,000 units, cumulative unit cost will decline to $40 per unit when production cumulates to 20,000 units. Cumulative unit cost is the total cost to date divided by the total number of units produced to date. (Such a relationship is a straight line when plotted on log-log graph paper.) In a variation of the learning curve phenomenon, some companies find that current unit cost, rather than cumulative unit cost, decreases in a constant proportion to volume increases.

Illustration 17–11 shows two examples of these relationships. Note the persistence of the approximately straight line relationship over a number of years.

Because of this phenomenon, historical unit costs tend to be higher than future costs, in terms of constant dollars. This is especially the case with new products, for the learning phenomenon has relatively little effect on the costs of products that have been manufactured for many years. Such products are said to be "near the bottom of the learning curve."

> EXAMPLE: Assume a company introduced Product A in 1963, made 10,000 units a year, that the costs of Product A were subject to an 80 percent learning curve, and that the total cost for the 10,000 units made in 1963 was $500,000. The unit cost in 1963 therefore was $50.
>
> In 1964 an additional 10,000 units were made. If the 80 percent learning curve held, cumulative unit cost of the 20,000 total units would be 80 percent of $50, or $40. The total cost of the 20,000 units would be $800,000 (= 20,000 × $40), the costs for 1964 would be $300,000 (= $800,000 − $500,000 costs of 1963), and the unit cost in 1964 would be $30 (= $300,000 ÷ 10,000), a $20 decrease from 1963.
>
> Carrying the example into later years gives a much less dramatic decline. For example by 1973, 100,000 units would have been produced. The 10,000 units produced in 1974 would represent only a 10 percent increase in the cumulative quantity, and the unit cost in that year would decrease by only about $0.50. In more detail:

Years since Intro- duction	Cumulative Quantity	Cumulative Unit Cost	Unit Cost for Increment	Average Annual Decrease
1	10,000	$50.00	$50.00	
2	20,000	40.00	30.00	$20.00
4	40,000	32.00	24.00	0.48
8	80,000	25.60	19.20	1.20
16	160,000	20.48	15.36	3.00

SOURCES OF DIFFERENTIAL COST DATA

Since the items of cost that are differential with respect to a given problem depend on the nature of that specific problem, it is not possible to identify items of differential cost in the accounting system and to collect these costs on a regular basis. Instead, the accounting system is designed so that it can furnish the raw data which are useful in estimating the differential costs for a specific problem. Differential costs are needed for a wide variety of problems, and it is rarely possible that all these needs can be foreseen. If feasible, an accounting system should be designed so that:

a. It identifies items of *variable costs* separately from items of fixed cost, and

b. It identifies the *direct costs* of various cost objectives.

In many companies, this can be done by the proper classification of accounts. Direct material costs and direct labor costs are variable costs, so no special identification is needed for them. For indirect factory costs and for selling, general, and administrative costs, items of cost that are variable are identified as such in the account structure. Similarly, items of cost that are direct with respect to the principal cost objectives are separately identified in the accounts. This is done, of course, only to the extent that such separate identification is believed to be worthwhile.

SUMMARY

Differential costs (or revenues) are those that are different under one set of conditions than they would be under another set of conditions. Differential costs are always constructed for a specified set of conditions. Variable costs are an important category of differential costs in situations in which changes in volume are involved, because total variable costs are different at each level of volume, in contrast with fixed costs which are unaffected by changes in volume.

The technique called contribution analysis finds the contribution margin, which is the difference between revenue and variable costs. Analysis of the relationships revealed by a contribution analysis is useful in making decisions on problems in which a proposed course of action affects the contribution margin of the business as a whole or of some segment thereof.

The level of volume has an important effect on costs. The effect can be depicted in a cost-volume diagram, or, if the relationship is approximately linear, by the equation $y = a + bx$. The diagram, and the equation, state that the total costs (y) at any volume are the sum of the fixed costs (a) plus the unit variable costs (b) times the number of units (x). These relationships hold only within a certain range of volume, the relevant range.

When a revenue line is superimposed on a cost-volume diagram, the diagram becomes a profitgraph. The profitgraph shows the relationship between revenue and costs (and hence the profit or loss) at any volume within the relevant range. It can be used to analyze the probable consequences of various proposals to change the basic relationships depicted therein. Since profit is affected by factors other than volume, however, the profitgraph does not tell the whole story.

APPENDIX

The Least-Squares Method

If the variable measured on the vertical axis is designated y and that on the horizontal axis x, then *any* straight line is described by the equation, $y = a + bx$. In order to describe a *specific* straight line, we must assign specific numerical values to the two constants (or "parameters") a and b.

The technique of fitting a straight line by the method of least squares makes use of this equation for a straight line. It fits a straight line through a series of observations of x, values such that the *sum of the squares of the distances of each observation from the line is at a minimum* (hence "least squares"). Distances from the points representing individual observations to the line of best fit are measured *vertically*, that is, parallel to the y axis.

To compute the parameters for the least-squares line, we write down in two adjacent columns every value of x and the corresponding value of y. In a third column we put the square of each value of x and in the fourth column, we put the product of each x times the corresponding y (i.e., xy). We then total each column and use the symbol Σx^2 to denote the sum of the squares of the x values, and Σxy to denote the sum of the products of x times the corresponding y. (Notice that Σx^2 does *not* denote the square of the sum of the x's, nor does Σxy denote the total of the x's times the total of y's; each pair of values is treated separately.) We then determine the parameters a and b in the equation for a straight line by solving the two simultaneous "normal equations":

$$Na + b(\Sigma x) = \Sigma y$$
$$a(\Sigma x) + b(\Sigma x^2) = \Sigma xy$$

N is the number of items, that is, the number of x, y pairs.

Suppose we have the following observations of cost and volume in four periods:

Volume (Units)	Cost
0	$10
1	12
2	13
3	15

We calculate:

$$\Sigma x, \ \Sigma y, \ \Sigma x^2 \text{ and } \Sigma xy:$$

(1) x	(2) y	(3) x^2	(4) xy
0	10	0	0
1	12	1	12
2	13	4	26
3	15	9	45
$\Sigma x = 6$	$\Sigma y = 50$	$\Sigma x^2 = 14$	$\Sigma xy = 83$

Therefore,

$$\Sigma x = 6, \ \Sigma y = 50, \ \Sigma x^2 = 14, \ \Sigma xy = 83, \ N = 4;$$

and the normal equations given above become

$$4a + 6b = 50$$
$$6a + 14b = 83$$

To solve for a and b, multiply the first equation by 3 and the second equation by 2 and get—

$$12a + 18b = 150$$
$$12a + 28b = 166$$

Subtract the first equation from the second and get—

$$10b = 16$$
$$b = 1.6$$

Therefore, $50 = 4a + 9.6$ (from the first normal equation with 9.6 written in place of $6b$):

$$4a = 40.4$$
$$a = 10.1$$

Therefore, the equation of the least-squares line is:

$$y = 10.1 + 1.6x$$

In terms of cost analysis

$$a = \text{Fixed cost per period} = \$10.1$$
$$b = \text{Variable cost per}$$
$$\text{unit of volume} \ \ \ \ = \$ \ 1.6$$

Most computers and some minicalculators have programs that will calculate a least-squares line automatically after the pairs of x, y values are entered.

CASES

CASE 17–1. HILL ASSOCIATES, INC.

Dr. Edgar Hill was introduced to the concept of the break-even chart while attending an executive training program during the fall of 1974. Dr. Hill was president and treasurer of Hill Associates, Inc. The company had been founded by Dr. Hill in 1959 to manufacture a product he had invented. Sales had grown to about $800,000 in 1974, and the company's plant had been expanded several times since it was first built to accommodate the growing demand.

When Dr. Hill returned to his office in January 1975, he called in his accountant, Paul O'Leary. Together they discussed the problem of constructing a break-even chart for Hill Associates. The critical problem seemed to be to determine the relationship between cost and volume. Mr. O'Leary agreed to see what he could do in this respect with data available in the company records.

As the first step, Mr. O'Leary consulted the records for the calendar year 1974 and assembled the information given in Exhibit 1. For each month of the year, this information consisted of: (a) the total amount of production during the month, valued at the selling price of the product;[1] and (b) the total amount of costs incurred during the month.

While he was assembling the data on 1974, it occurred to Mr. O'Leary that Hill Associates' cost-volume relationship might have changed over time. To check this possibility, he decided to look at data over the entire 10-year period from 1965 through 1974 inclusive. It was not possible to get monthly figures for this entire period, but Mr. O'Leary was able to obtain figures on *annual* production and *annual* costs. Mr. O'Leary recognized that the prices and wage rates paid by Hill Associates for goods and services had risen over the years and that Hill Associates had raised its own prices to customers in compensation. He felt that he ought to adjust for these price changes before trying to analyze the data and com-

---

[1] This amount was not necessarily equal to the amount of sales during the month, because sales were made from inventory; new production during the month was used to replenish inventory.

Exhibit 1

HILL ASSOCIATES, INC.

Production Volume and Cost
By Month, 1974

Month	Production (at sales value)	Costs
January	$51,000	$51,000
February	57,000	52,000
March	71,000	58,000
April	76,000	59,000
May	75,000	58,000
June	95,000	64,000
July	45,000	51,000
August	51,000	52,000
September	66,000	54,000
October	73,000	59,000
November	78,000	62,000
December	77,000	63,000

pare them with that given in Exhibit 1. Accordingly, for each year, he multiplied *both* production at sales value *and* costs by the ratio of Hill Associates' 1974 price to its price in the year in question. The adjusted figures, which Mr. O'Leary considered to be stated in 1974 dollars, are given in Exhibit 2.

Exhibit 2

HILL ASSOCIATES, INC.

Production Volume and Cost
By Year, 1965–1974
(in 1974 dollars)

Year	Production (at sales value)	Costs
1965	$289,000	$255,000
1966	391,000	381,000
1967	421,000	320,000
1968	489,000	436,000
1969	600,000	455,000
1970	573,000	491,000
1971	691,000	517,000
1972	687,000	551,000
1973	699,000	599,000
1974	815,000	683,000

Questions

1. Plot the data given in Exhibit 1 as points on graph paper and draw in a straight line which appears to give the "best fit" to the data. From this line, estimate the ratio of variable cost to production volume.
2. Repeat the above with the data of Exhibit 2.
3. Has Hill Associates' cost-volume relationship changed over time?

CASE 17-2. BILL FRENCH

Bill French picked up the phone and called his boss, Wes Davidson, controller of Duo-Products Corporation. "Say, Wes, I'm all set for the meeting this afternoon. I've put together a set of break-even statements that should really make the boys sit up and take notice—and I think they'll be able to understand them, too." After a brief conversation about other matters, the call was concluded and French turned to his charts for one last check-out before the meeting.

French had been hired six months earlier as a staff accountant. He was directly responsible to Davidson and, up to the time of this case, had been doing routine types of analysis work. French was an alumnus of a liberal arts undergraduate school and graduate business school, and was considered by his associates to be quite capable and unusually conscientious. It was this latter characteristic that had apparently caused him to "rub some of the working guys the wrong way," as one of his co-workers put it. French was well aware of his capabilities and took advantage of every opportunity that arose to try to educate those around him. Wes Davidson's invitation for French to attend an informal manager's meeting had come as some surprise to others in the accounting group. However, when French requested permission to make a presentation of some break-even data, Davidson acquiesced. The Duo-Products Corporation had not been making use of this type of analysis in its review or planning programs.

Basically, what French had done was to determine the level at which the company must operate in order to break even. As he phrased it,

The company must be able at least to sell a sufficient volume of goods so that it will cover all the variable costs of producing and selling the goods; further, it will not make a profit unless it covers the fixed, or nonvariable, costs as well. The level of operation at which total costs (that is, variable plus nonvariable) are just covered is the break-even volume. This should be the lower limit in all our planning.

The accounting records had provided the following information that French used in constructing his chart:

> Plant capacity—2 million units.
> Past year's level of operations—1.5 million units.
> Average unit selling price—$1.20.
> Total fixed costs—$520,000.
> Average variable unit cost—$0.75.

From this information, French observed that each unit contributed $0.45 to fixed overhead after covering the variable costs. Given total fixed costs of $520,000, he calculated that 1,155,556 units must be sold in order to break even. He verified this conclusion by calculating the dollar sales volume that was required to break even. Since the variable costs per unit were 62.5 percent of the selling price, French reasoned that 37.5 percent of every sales dollar was left available to cover fixed costs. Thus, fixed costs of $520,000 require sales of $1,386,667 in order to break even.

When he constructed a break-even chart to present the information graphically, his conclusions were further verified. The chart also made it clear that the firm was operating at a fair margin over the break-even requirements, and that the profits accruing (at the rate of 37.5 percent of every sales dollar over break-even) increased rapidly as volume increased (see Exhibit 1).

Exhibit 1

BREAK-EVEN CHART—TOTAL BUSINESS

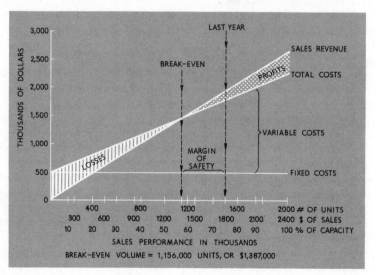

Shortly after lunch, French and Davidson left for the meeting. Several representatives of the manufacturing departments were present, as well as the general sales manager, two assistant sales managers, the purchasing officer, and two people from the product engineering office. Davidson introduced French to the few people whom he had not already met, and then the meeting got under way. French's presentation was the last item on Davidson's agenda, and in due time the controller introduced French, explaining his interest in cost control and analysis.

French had prepared enough copies of his chart and supporting calculations for everyone at the meeting. He described carefully what he had done and explained how the chart pointed to a profitable year, dependent on meeting the volume of sales activity that had been maintained in the past. It soon became apparent that some of the participants had known in advance what French planned to discuss; they had come prepared to challenge him and soon had taken control of the meeting. The following exchange ensued (see Exhibit 3 for a checklist of participants with their titles):

COOPER (production control): You know, Bill, I'm really concerned that you haven't allowed for our planned changes in volume next year. It seems to me that you should have allowed for the sales department's guess that we'll boost sales by 20 percent, unit-wise. We'll be pushing 90 percent of what we call capacity then. It sure seems that this would make quite a difference in your figuring.

FRENCH: That might be true, but as you can see, all you have to do is read the cost and profit relationship right off the chart for the new volume. Let's see—at a million-eight units we'd. . . .

WILLIAMS (manufacturing): Wait a minute, now! ! ! If you're going to talk in terms of 90 percent of capacity, and it looks like that's what it will be, you had better note that we'll be shelling out some more for the plant. We've already got okays on investment money that will boost your fixed costs by 10 thousand dollars a month, easy. And that may not be all. We may call it 90 percent of plant capacity, but there are a lot of places where we're just full up and we can't pull things up any tighter.

COOPER: See, Bill? Fred Williams is right, but I'm not finished on this bit about volume changes. According to the information that I've got here—and it came from your office—I'm not sure that your break-even chart can really be used even if there were to be no changes next year. Looks to me like you've got average figures that don't allow for the fact that we're dealing with three basic products. Your report here (see Exhibit 2) on costs, according to product lines, for last year makes it pretty clear that the "average" is way out of line. How would the break-even point look if we took this on an individual product basis?

FRENCH: Well, I'm not sure. Seems to me that there is only one break-even point for the firm. Whether we take it product by product or in total, we've got to hit that point. I'll be glad to check for you if you want, but. . . .

BRADSHAW (assistant sales manager): Guess I may as well get in on this one, Bill. If you're going to do anything with individual products, you ought to know that we're looking for a big swing in our product mix. Might even start before we get into the new season. The "A" line is really losing out and I imagine that we'll be lucky to hold two thirds of the volume there next year. Wouldn't you buy that Arnie? [Agreement from the general sales manager.] That's not too bad, though, because we expect that we should pick up the 200,000 that we lose, and about a quarter million units more, over in "C" production. We don't see anything that shows much of a change in "B." That's been solid for years and shouldn't change much now.

WINETKI (general sales manager): Bradshaw's called it about as we figure it, but there's something else here too. We've talked about our pricing on "C" enough, and now I'm really going to push our side of it. Ray's estimate of maybe half a million—450,000 I guess it was—up on "C" for next year is on the basis of doubling the price with no change in cost. We've been priced so low on this item that it's been a crime—we've got to raise, but good, for two reasons. First, for our reputation; the price is out of line class-wise and is completely inconsistent with our quality reputation. Second, if we don't raise the price, we'll be swamped and we can't handle it. You heard what Williams said about capacity. The way the whole "C" field is exploding, we'll have to answer to another half million units in unsatisfied orders if we don't jack the price up. We can't afford to expand that much for this product.

At this point, Anne Fraser (administrative assistant to the president) walked up toward the front of the room from where she had been standing near the rear door. The discussion broke for a minute, and she took advantage of the lull to interject a few comments.

FRASER: This has certainly been enlightening. Looks like you fellows are pretty well up on this whole operation. As long as you're going to try to get all the things together that you ought to pin down for next year, let's see what I can add to help you:

Number One: Let's remember that everything that shows in the profit area here on Bill's chart is divided just about evenly between the government and us. Now, for last year we can read a profit of about $150,000. Well, that's right. But we were left with half of that, and then paid our dividends of $50,000 to the stockholders. Since we've got an anniversary year coming up, we'd like to put out a special dividend of about 50 percent extra. We ought to hold $25,000 in for the business, too. This means that we'd like to hit $100,000 *after* the costs of being governed.

Number Two: From where I sit, it looks like we're going to have a talk with the union again, and this time it's liable to cost us. All the indications are—and this isn't public—that we may have to meet demands that will boost our production costs—what do you call them here, Bill—variable costs—by 10 percent across the board. This may kill the bonus-dividend plans, but we've got to hold the line on past profits. This means that we can give that much to the union only if we can make it in added revenues. I guess you'd say that that raises your break-even point, Bill—and for that one I'd consider the company's profit to be a fixed cost.

Number Three: Maybe this is the time to think about switching our product emphasis. Arnie Winetki may know better than I which of the products is more profitable. You check me out on this Arnie—and it might be a good idea for you and Bill French to get together on this one, too. These figures that I have (Exhibit 2) make it look like the percentage contribution on line "A" is the lowest of the bunch. If we're losing volume there as rapidly as you sales folks say, and if we're as hard pressed for space as Fred Williams has indicated, maybe we'd be better off grabbing some of that big demand for "C" by shifting some of the facilities over there from "A."

That's all I've got to say. Looks to me like you've all got plenty to think about.

DAVIDSON: Thanks, Anne. I sort of figured that we'd get wound up here as soon as Bill brought out his charts. This is an approach that we've barely touched, but, as you can see, you've all got ideas that have got to be made to

Exhibit 2

PRODUCT CLASS COST ANALYSIS

(normal year)

	Aggregate	"A"	"B"	"C"
Sales at full capacity (units)........	2,000,000			
Actual sales volume (units)........	1,500,000	600,000	400,000	500,000
Unit sales price..................	$ 1.20	$ 1.67	$ 1.50	$ 0.40
Total sales revenue..............	$1,800,000	$1,000,000	$600,000	$200,000
Variable cost per unit............	$ 0.75	$ 1.25	$ 0.625	$ 0.25
Total variable cost..............	$1,125,000	$ 750,000	$250,000	$125,000
Fixed costs....................	$ 520,000	$ 170,000	$275,000	$ 75,000
Profit	$ 155,000	$ 80,000	$ 75,000	......
Ratios:				
Variable cost to sales...........	0.63	0.75	0.42	0.63
Variable income to sales........	0.37	0.25	0.58	0.37
Utilization of capacity.........	75.0%	30.0%	20.0%	25.0%

fit here somewhere. I'll tell you what let's do. Bill, suppose you rework your chart and try to bring into it some of the points that were made here today. I'll see if I can summarize what everyone seems to be looking for.

First of all, I have the idea buzzing around in the back of my mind that your presentation is based on a rather important series of assumptions. Most of the questions that were raised were really about those assumptions; it might help us all if you try to set the assumptions down in black and white so that we can see just how they influence the analysis.

Then, I think that Cooper would like to see the unit sales increase taken up, and he'd also like to see whether there's any difference if you base the calculations on an analysis of individual product lines. Also, as Bradshaw suggested, since the product mix is bound to change, why not see how things look if the shift materializes as sales has forcast?

Arnie Winetki would like to see the influence of a price increase in the "C" line; Fred Williams looks toward an increase in fixed manufacturing costs of 10 thousand a month, and Anne Fraser has suggested that we should consider taxes, dividends, expected union demands, and the question of product emphasis.

I think that ties it all together. Let's hold off on our next meeting, fellows, until Bill has time to work this all into shape.

With that, the participants broke off into small groups and the meeting disbanded. French and Wes Davidson headed back to their offices

Exhibit 3

LIST OF PARTICIPANTS IN THE MEETING

Bill French....................	staff accountant
Wes Davidson................	controller
John Cooper..................	production control
Fred Williams................	manufacturing
Ray Bradshaw................	assistant sales manager
Arnie Winetki................	general sales manager
Anne Fraser..................	administrative assistant to president

and French, in a tone of concern asked Davidson, "Why didn't you warn me about the hornet's nest I was walking into?"

"Bill, you didn't ask!"

Questions

1. What are the assumptions implicit in Bill French's determination of his company's break-even point?
2. On the basis of French's revised information, what does next year look like:
    a. What is the break-even point?
    b. What level of operations must be achieved to pay the extra dividend, ignoring union demands?
    c. What level of operations must be achieved to meet the union demands, ignoring bonus dividends?
    d. What level of operations must be achieved to meet both dividends and expected union requirements?
3. Can the break-even analysis help the company decide whether to alter the existing product emphasis? What can the company afford to invest for additional "C" capacity?
4. Is this type of analysis of any value? For what can it be used?

CASE 17–3. AZIENDA VINICOLA ITALIANA

Azienda Vinicola Italiana produced and bottled wines. A large percentage of its sales were of special table wine. Most of its customers, located in the principal Italian cities, were served through local representatives. Its prices were in line with those of competitors.

In 1974 the firm sold 704,000 liters[1] of wine, in 871,850 bottles. In recent years demand had been increasing, and the firm had approached the limit of its productive capacity, which was estimated to be 900,000 bottles a year.

The production process was not complicated, since the firm did not buy grapes but rather bought either mosto[2] or bulk wine. This policy had the disadvantage that the firm could not assure itself of a consistently high-quality product. Moreover, it was estimated that if grapes were purchased, the price of raw material would be reduced by about Lit.[3] 55 per bottle. On the other hand, the purchase and installation of equipment needed for pressing grapes would require an additional investment of

---

[1] One liter is slightly more than one United States liquid quart.

[2] Mosto is the juice of grapes before the fermentation process takes place. The fermentation process takes about one month. During this process carbon dioxide develops, and the sugar is converted into alcohol. Therefore, mosto is an unstable product, and wine is a stable product.

[3] In 1974, 100 Italian lire (abbreviated "Lit.") equaled approximately U.S. $0.15.

about Lit. 275 million. No significant increase in labor costs was anticipated under such a practice.

In the production department there were 40 employees who worked a total of about 90,000 hours in 1974 and whose average wage per hour, including fringe benefits, was Lit. 2,000. The administrative manager was of the opinion that 40 percent of this labor expense should be considered as being fixed, while the remainder could be considered as varying proportionally with production volume.

In 1974, production had required 700,000 liters of mosto and bulk wine, purchased at a total cost of Lit. 301,136,000. The average cost incurred for auxiliary materials (bottles, stoppers, neckbands, labels, and so forth) was about Lit. 225 per bottle.

The income statement for 1974 is shown in Exhibit 1.

Exhibit 1

AZIENDA VINICOLA ITALIANA

Income Statement
For 1974 in Lire
(000 omitted)

Sales		960,685
Costs:		
Labor	178,568	
Raw materials	301,136	
Auxiliary materials	196,757	
General manufacturing expenses (including pay of two cellar foremen)	26,372	702,833
Gross margin		257,852
General administrative expenses (including the salary of a person skilled in the art of making and preserving wine)	92,098	
Depreciation	57,970	
Interest	41,250	
Advertising	43,450	234,768
Net Income		23,084

The administrative manager wished to reorganize the firm in order to exploit its productive capability to the utmost and, above all, to increase the net profit, which the owners did not consider satisfactory. They were of the opinion that a net profit of 8 or 9 percent of sales could be realized.

As a basis upon which to make decisions, the administrative manager intended to use charts of costs and revenues that he had seen other firms use and that he considered helpful. The first step in this graphic analysis was a study of costs, separating fixed costs from variable costs. For that purpose, he examined the income statements of preceding years and came to the conclusion that the figures for 1974 were representative. He also noticed that the different types of wine had been sold in more or less the same relative proportions each year, despite large fluctuations in the total volume of business, and this fact confirmed his belief that the figures for 1974 were representative. He therefore prepared the following analysis (in thousands of lire):

a. *Fixed Costs:*

40% of labor cost	71,427
Staff salaries	59,098
General manufacturing expenses	26,372
General administrative expenses	33,000
Advertising expenses	43,450
Interest	41,250
Depreciation	57,970
	332,567

b. *Variable Costs:*

60% of labor cost	107,141
Raw materials	301,136
Auxiliary materials	196,757
	605,034

The administrative manager assumed a maximum capacity of 900,000 bottles a year. At current prices he estimated this would produce sales revenue of Lit. 990 million.

With the present structure of costs and revenue, the profits resulting from an annual production of 900,000 bottles would be small. The administrative manager decided, therefore, to try to discover a way to change costs and revenue so as to obtain a profit of Lit. 88 million a year, which would be almost 9 percent of sales of Lit. 990 million.

Questions

1. Accepting the distribution between fixed and variable elements as estimated by the administrative manager, prepare a chart of costs and revenues. Determine the volume of production at which the firm reaches its break-even point and the profit at capacity operation.
2. Draw three other charts, each constructed so that a production of 900,000 bottles will produce a profit of Lit. 88 million, one in which selling price is assumed to increase, another in which fixed costs are assumed to decrease, and a third in which variable costs are assumed to decrease. What are the break-even points in each of these situations?
3. What are the most likely alternatives to consider so as to achieve a profit of Lit. 88 million?

CASE 17–4. HARCORD WHOLESALE GROCERS, INC.

Prior to 1972, Harcord Wholesale Grocers, Inc., had kept no departmental income statements. In order to control operations more effectively, the management decided at the beginning of that year to install departmental cost accounts. At the end of 1972, the new accounts showed that although the business as a whole had a gross margin of 13.1 percent and net income of 1.1 percent on net sales of $4,816,000, the fresh fruit and produce department had shown a substantial loss, with a gross margin of only 9.8 percent of its $832,032 net sales, against an expense rate of 14.2 percent. The income statement for this department is shown in Exhibit 1.

Exhibit 1

HARCORD WHOLESALE GROCERS, INC.

Fresh Fruit and Produce Department
Income Statement

		Percent
Net sales...	$832,032	100.0
Cost of sales...	750,492	90.2
Gross margin...	$ 81,540	9.8
Expenses:		
Payroll, direct labor, and supervision in the department.........	$ 41,280	
Salesmen's commissions (fruits sold by general salesmen selling for all departments on straight, uniform, commission basis)...	12,792	
Rent (charged to department on basis of yearly rental per square foot occupied; the company rented and occupied an entire building)...	32,880	
Taxes (assessed by state on average value of inventory)........	1,200	
Insurance (for protection of inventory).....................	960	
Depreciation (basis: 5 percent on departmental equipment).....	3,120	
Administration and general office (allocated on basis of departmental sales).......................................	25,648	
Interest on inventory (an accounting charge; actually there was no outside borrowing for working capital).................	470	
Total expenses.......................................	$118,350	14.2
Net Loss...	($ 36,810)	(4.4)

This loss led one executive to argue that the department should be discontinued. The executives agreed that, so far as the factor of customer satisfaction with the completeness of the company's line was concerned, it was not essential to continue selling fresh fruits and produce. Elimination of this department, in other words, was not expected to result in loss of sales by other departments.

After several protracted discussions of the proposal, one of the executives sought to end the controversy by saying that the company should discontinue either the department or the new accounting system.

Question

What action should be taken?

CASE 17–5. MORRIN AIRCRAFT COMPANY

On several occasions since late 1970 the Morrin Aircraft Company had received contracts from airlines for the manufacture of MA-900 passenger aircraft. In March 1973, Tom Scott, one of the buyers for Morrin, was trying to decide upon a fair price to offer the Pierce Company, a subcontractor, for the manufacture of metal containers used for passenger luggage and other cargo. These enclosed containers were loaded and unloaded in an airline's luggage or cargo area at an airport. They essentially eliminated manual handling of goods at the point where the airplane was parked. In addition to permitting quicker loading/unloading of the plane itself, the containers eliminated damage to goods caused by inclement weather, and resulted in more efficient usage of a plane's cargo hold.

The containers, made of a special lightweight alloy, required some difficult machining operations. Because the containers were put on or taken off aircraft by using special equipment, and since each airplane's cargo hold was equipped with special tracks to accommodate the containers, it was crucial that they be made exactly to Morrin's dimensions and other specifications.

The Pierce Company had been manufacturing the containers since December 1970, at which time its bid of $506 per container for the 120 containers then required was the lowest of the several bids considered. With each new order for the MA-900 that Morrin received, Mr. Scott successfully negotiated new contracts for the manufacture of the containers with Mr. White, the Pierce Company salesman. During this period Pierce continued to meet all quality standards and delivery schedules.

On each successive contract after the original one signed in December 1970, Mr. Scott had applied an 80 percent learning curve to the price of the previous order, excluding the cost of raw material and also excluding profit. Scott assumed that the tooling cost incurred by Pierce in manufacturing the containers was amortized over the cost of the original contract, and therefore he made no allowance for tooling cost in estimating the price of subsequent contracts. Although it appeared to Scott that White was not familiar with the use of learning curves in purchase contracting, White agreed to manufacture the containers at the prices quoted by Mr. Scott. As a result, the price paid per unit for the containers was lowered on each successive contract. The Pierce Company's production rate of containers was held essentially constant at eight a month. Application of the learning curve would not be valid if production was not reasonably steady.

In making his calculations of the price to offer Pierce after the first contract had been fulfilled, Mr. Scott had to rely on his own estimates of the raw material price, the tooling cost, and Pierce's profit. Scott knew from his previous experiences with Pierce that this company would refuse to reveal its cost and profit figures. Because of his past experience in purchasing and the use of the learning curve, however, Scott was confident that his estimates were fairly accurate. Morrin's own man-hour records showed that an 80 percent curve was appropriate for the production of similar containers for another airplane made in the 1960s, and this led Scott to conclude that the same 80 percent curve was applicable to the Pierce Company.

Breaking down the original bid of $506 per container, Mr. Scott estimated the profit was around $46, which was 10 percent of total cost, and the raw material was about $160 per unit. He estimated that Pierce's tooling cost was in the neighborhood of $7,200 and that this had probably been amortized over the 120 containers ordered under the first contract.

In order to set up his 80 percent curve to find the cumulative average price on which he could base his future price offers, Scott made the following calculations:

Original price per container.............................		$506
Less: Profit at 10 percent of cost.....................	$ 46	
Tooling cost on first order: $7,200 ÷ 120 units...	60	
Raw material cost per unit.....................	160	
Items not subject to learning curve.............		266
Costs subject to learning curve......................		$240

The adjusted costs of $240 per container for 120 units was plotted on log-log graph paper (see Exhibit 1). Scott then took double the quantity

Exhibit 1

EIGHTY PERCENT LEARNING CURVE

MA-900 Cargo Containers

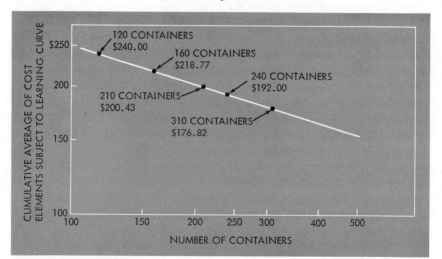

of the original order (or 240 units) and 80 percent of the unit cost ($192) and plotted his second point on the log-log graph paper. Through these two points he drew a straight line.

When Morrin required 40 more containers, Scott looked at his graph to find the new cumulative average of cost elements subject to the learning curve for the total quantity of the old and new orders, which amounted to 160 containers. The new cumulative average cost, as indicated by the graph, was $218.77 per container (see Exhibit 1). Using this information, Scott continued his calculations:

160 units at $218.77 per unit average for cost elements subject to learning curve	$35,003
Less: 120 units purchased at $240 per set average for cost elements subject to learning curve	28,800
Total price to be paid on new order for cost elements subject to learning curve	$ 6,203

The new average price per container to be paid on the new order for the cost elements subject to the learning curve was found to be $6,203 ÷ 40 new containers, or $155.08. To this new price of $155.08 per container Scott added back in the cost items not subject to the curve which previously had been subtracted:

Cost elements subject to learning curve	$155.08
Plus: Raw material	160.00
Average price per unit before profit	$315.08
Plus: Profit at 10 percent of cost	31.51
Total price per unit on the new order	$346.59

Scott believed that this figure of $346.59 per container was quite adequate, and he used it in his negotiations with Mr. White, who finally, but grudgingly, accepted this figure.

In subsequent negotiations, the prices Scott offered to the Pierce Company on successive contracts for the containers became lower and lower. White became more emphatic in his objections and warned Scott that "this learning curve business is going too far." However, each time Scott asked to see Pierce's cost data to justify some other price, White would give the same answer: "Our cost data are none of your business!"

On February 2, 1973, about one month before the final delivery of the latest order, which had been contracted for in November 1972, White complained that Pierce had recently experienced an increase in raw material cost which added $8 to the cost per container. Furthermore, White stated that modifications in the design of the containers since the original contract had increased the raw material cost per unit by another $12. These modifications in design, however, had not increased labor or overhead costs. White stated that because of these increased costs and the low $332 per unit price paid by Morrin for the currently produced containers, he was quite skeptical as to whether his company would take on any further contracts for containers, especially since at that time it could get all the business it wanted. He went on to say that his company was "sick and tired of producing containers at a loss for Morrin and having to make up these losses out of contracts with other companies." While Mr. Scott believed that the raw material cost increases mentioned by Mr. White were correct, he did not have any way of appraising the validity of White's statements about the Pierce Company's losing money on this contract with Morrin.

Two weeks after this conference between Scott and White, Morrin received aircraft orders which would require 100 more containers. Again Scott was confronted with the task of securing more containers. From December 1970 to March 1973, Pierce would have produced 210 containers. Over this period the price paid for the containers had decreased from $506 per unit on the first order to $332 per unit on the current order contracted for in November 1972 and scheduled for completion within the next two weeks. The total price of the 210 units *for the cost elements subject to the learning curve* was $42,090. This sum compared to $50,400 which would have been paid on 210 containers for these same cost elements if the learning curve had not been applied. A further saving to Morrin was realized because the profit which Pierce received per unit was a fixed percentage of cost. Thus with the lower calculated cost per unit based on the learning curve, the profit to Pierce was cut correspondingly.

Mr. Scott realized that it was important to continue dealing with Pierce for the additional 100 containers. Scott recalled that at 1970 price levels the Pierce Company's first bid of $506 per unit was the lowest of the several bids submitted; the next lowest bid at that time was $544. If Pierce refused to accept any more orders, dealing with a new subcontractor would probably result in a substantial increase in price. Scott estimated that the lowest price for which he could currently purchase containers from another subcontractor would be in the neighborhood of $560 per unit (including the amortized cost, over 100 units, of new tooling). Furthermore, Scott considered Pierce an excellent source of supply because it produced a satisfactory product and always met its delivery schedule.

On the other hand, Scott knew that the validity of the learning curve had been widely accepted in the aircraft industry and that it was especially applicable to the manufacture of items such as the containers, for which direct labor was a major cost component. Furthermore, it was his job as a purchasing agent for Morrin to get as low a price as possible commensurate with a satisfactory product.

Mr. Scott had an appointment with Mr. White the next day, at which time they would open negotiations for the 100 additional containers. Scott knew that White would suggest a substantial upward revision in the price.

Questions

1. If he used the 80 percent learning curve, what price would Mr. Scott calculate for the new order of 100 containers?
2. What is the highest price that the Morrin Aircraft Company should pay to the Pierce Company for the containers?
3. What price *should* Mr. Scott use as a basis for his negotiations?
4. What are the implications of the use of learning curves in purchase contracting to both the prime contractor and the subcontractor?
5. In what situations would the use of the learning curve in purchase contracting not be appropriate?

ALTERNATIVE CHOICE
DECISIONS

In Chapter 17 we introduced the concept of differential costs and differential revenues, and we described techniques for identifying these types of costs and revenues and for using them in the analysis of problems that involved changes in volume. In Chapter 18 we describe the use of differential costs in analyzing several other types of problems. Problems involving differential costs and revenues can be designated alternative choice problems, for in each case the manager seeks to choose the best one of several alternative courses of action.

NATURE OF ALTERNATIVE CHOICE PROBLEMS

In an *alternative choice problem* two or more alternative courses of action are specified and the manager chooses the one that he believes to be the best.[1] In many alternative choice problems, the choice is made on a strictly judgmental basis; that is, there is no systematic attempt to define, measure, and assess the advantages and disadvantages of each alternative. A person who makes a judgmental decision may do so simply because he is not aware of any other way of making up his mind, or he may do so, and with good reason, because the problem is one in which a systematic attempt to assess alternatives is too difficult, too expensive, or simply not possible. No mathematical formula will help solve a problem in which the attitudes or emotions of the individuals involved are dominant factors, nor is there any point in trying to make calculations if the

---

[1] In a broad sense, *all* business problems involve a choice among alternatives. The problems discussed here are those in which the alternatives are clearly specified.

available information is so sketchy or so inaccurate that the results would be completely unreliable.

In many other situations, however, it is useful to reduce at least some of the potential consequences of each alternative to a quantitative basis and to weigh these consequences in a systematic manner. In this and the next chapter, we discuss techniques for making such an analysis.

Business Objectives

In an alternative choice problem, the manager seeks the *best* alternative. "Best" refers to that alternative which is most likely to accomplish the objectives of the organization. Although it is safe to say that the dominant objective of a business is to earn a profit, such a statement is not specific enough for our present purpose.

When investors furnish funds to a business, they do so in the expectation of earning a return, that is, a profit, on these investments. Presumably the more profit that is earned on a given investment, the greater the satisfaction of the investors. This idea leads to the economists' statement that the objective of a business is to *maximize the return on its investment*. The maximization idea, however, is too difficult to apply in most practical situations. The manager does not know, out of all the very large number of alternative courses of action available to him, which one will produce the absolute maximum return on investment. Furthermore, return on investment is not the *only* objective of a business. Many actions which could increase return on investment are ethically unacceptable. Setting selling prices that charge all the traffic will bear is one example. For these reasons, the idea that an important objective of a business is to earn a *satisfactory* return on its investment is more realistic and more ethically sound than the idea that the sole objective is to maximize return on investment.

Satisfactory return on investment is an important objective, but it is by no means the only objective of a business. In many practical problems, personal satisfaction, friendship, patriotism, self-esteem, or other considerations may be much more important than return on investment. The company may have other measurable objectives, such as maintenance of its market position, stabilization of employment, avoidance of undue risk, or increasing its net income as reported on its income statement.[2] When these considerations are important or dominant, the solution to the problem cannot be reached by the techniques discussed here. The most these techniques can do is show the effect on return on investment of seeking

---

[2] For reasons described in Chapter 13, net income as measured by generally accepted accounting principles does not necessarily reflect the "well-offness" of a business.

some other objective. The problem then becomes one of deciding whether the attainment of the other objective is worth the cost.

Thus, the decision maker seeks *a* course of action which will produce a satisfactory return on investment. If there are two alternative solutions to a problem, he will choose the one which is likely to yield the *greater* return on investment, provided this is consistent with his other objectives.

STEPS IN ANALYSIS

The analysis of most alternative choice problems involves the following steps:

1. Define the problem.
2. Select possible alternative solutions.
3. Measure and weigh those consequences of each selected alternative that can be expressed in quantitative terms.
4. Identify those consequences that cannot be expressed in quantitative terms and weigh them against each other and against the measured consequences.
5. Reach a decision.

In this book, we focus primarily on information that can be expressed in quantitative terms. Thus, we are here interested primarily in Step 3 of the above list. Brief mention will be made of the other steps.

Steps 1 and 2.   Definition of the Problem and of Alternative Solutions

Unless the problem is clearly and precisely defined, quantitative amounts that are relevant to its solution cannot be determined. In many situations, the definition of the problem, or even the recognition that a problem exists, may be the most difficult part of the whole process. Moreover, even after the problem has been identified, the possible alternative solutions to it often are by no means clear at the outset.

> EXAMPLE: A factory manager is considering a machinery salesperson's proposal that a certain machine should be used to produce automatically a part that is now being produced by manual methods. At first glance, there may appear to be two alternatives: (*a*) continue to make the part by manual methods or (*b*) buy the new machine. Actually, however, several additional alternatives should perhaps be considered, such as these: (*c*) buy a machine other than the one recommended by the salesperson, (*d*) improve the present method of making the part, or even (*e*) eliminate the manufacturing operation altogether and buy the part from an outside source. Some thought should be given to these other possibilities before attention is focused too closely on the original proposal.

On the other hand, the more alternatives that are considered, the more complex the analysis becomes. For this reason, having identified all the possible alternatives, the analyst should eliminate on a judgmental basis those that are clearly unattractive, leaving only a few for detailed analysis.

In most problems, one of the alternatives is to continue what is now being done, that is, to reject a proposed change. This alternative is referred to as the *base case*.[3] It is used as a benchmark against which other alternatives are compared. Note that there must always be at least two alternatives. If only one course of action is open, the company literally has "no choice"; therefore, it has no decision to make and there is no need for analysis.

Step 3. Weighing and Measuring the Quantitative Factors

Usually, a number of advantages and a number of disadvantages are associated with each of the alternatives. The task of the decision maker is to evaluate each of the relevant factors and to decide, on balance, which alternative has the largest net advantage. If the factors, or variables, are expressed solely in words, such an evaluation is an exceedingly difficult task.

> EXAMPLE: Consider the statement: "A proposed manufacturing process will save labor, but it will result in increased power consumption and require additional insurance protection." Such a statement provides no way of weighing the relative importance of the saving in labor against the increased power and insurance costs. If, by contrast, the statement is: "The proposed process will save $1,000 in labor, but power costs will increase by $200 and insurance costs will increase by $100," the net effect of these three factors can easily be determined; that is, $1,000 - ($200 + $100) indicates a net advantage of $700 for the proposed process.

The reason why we try to express as many factors as possible in quantitative terms is demonstrated in the above illustration: once we have done this, it becomes easy to find the net effect of these factors by the simple arithmetic operations of addition and subtraction.

Step 4. Evaluating the Unmeasured Factors

For most problems, there are important factors that are not measurable; yet the final decision must take into account all differences between the alternatives being considered, both those that are measured and those not measured. The process of weighing the relative importance of these unmeasured factors, both as compared with one another and as compared

---

[3] For convenience, the base case may be identified as Case 1, and the other alternatives as Case 2, Case 3, and so on.

with the net advantage or disadvantage of the measured factors, is a judgmental process.

It is easy to underestimate the importance of these unmeasured factors. The numerical calculations for the measured factors often require hard work, and they result in a figure that has the appearance of being definite and precise; yet all the factors that influence the final number may be collectively less important than a single factor that cannot be measured. For example, many persons could meet their transportation needs less expensively by using public conveyances rather than by operating an automobile, but they nevertheless own an automobile for reasons of prestige, convenience, or other factors that cannot be measured quantitatively.

To the extent that calculations can be made, it is possible to express as a single number the net effect of many factors that bear on the decision. The calculations therefore reduce the number of factors that must be considered separately in the final judgment process that leads to the decision; that is, they narrow the area within which judgment must be exercised. Rarely, if ever, do they eliminate the necessity for this crucial judgment process.

Step 5.   Reaching a Decision

After his first attempt to identify, evaluate, and weigh the factors, the decision maker has two choices: (1) he can seek additional information or (2) he can make a decision and act on it. Many decisions could be improved by obtaining additional information, and it is usually possible to obtain such information. However, obtaining the additional information always involves effort (which means cost), and what is more important, it involves time. There comes a point, therefore, when the manager concludes that he is better off to act than to defer a decision until more data have been collected.

DIFFERENTIAL COSTS

In Chapter 17 we introduced the type of cost construction called differential costs. Since differential costs are normally used in analyzing alternative choice problems, we now discuss them in more depth.

If some alternative to the base case (i.e., the present method of operation or "status quo") is proposed, differential costs are those that will be different under the proposed alternative than they are in the base case. Items of cost that will be unaffected by the proposal are not differential. The term *out-of-pocket costs* is used generally to mean the same thing as differential cost. There is no general category of costs that can be labeled "differential." Direct labor costs are differential in many problems; but if in a specific situation people are going to be employed regardless of which alternative is adopted, labor costs are not differential.

EXAMPLE: A company is considering the possibility of buying Part No. 101 from an outside supplier instead of manufacturing the part as it is now doing. In this case the base case is to continue manufacturing Part No. 101, and the alternative (or Case 2) is to purchase Part No. 101 from the outside supplier. All revenue items, all selling and administrative expenses, and all production costs other than those directly associated with the manufacture of Part No. 101 will probably be unaffected by the decision. If so, there is no need to consider them. Items of differential cost could be as follows:

	If Part No. 101 Is Manufactured (Base Case)	*If Part No. 101 Is Purchased (Case 2)*	*Difference*	
			−	+
Direct material...............	$ 570	0	$ 570	
Purchased parts..............		$1,700		$1,700
Direct labor.................	600	0	600	
Power.......................	70	0	70	
Other costs..................	150	0	150	
Total..................	$1,390	$1,700	$1,390	$1,700
				−1,390
Net differential cost.........				$ 310

Since costs would be increased by $310 if Part No. 101 were purchased, the indication is that the proposal to purchase Part No. 101 should be rejected.

Mechanics of the Calculation

There is no prescribed format for making a comparison of the differential costs of the several alternatives. The arrangement should be that which is most convenient and which most clearly sets forth the facts to the decision maker.

EXAMPLE: For the problem described in the preceding example, the same result can be obtained, with somewhat less effort, by finding the net differences between the alternatives, viz:

	Costs if Part No. 101 Is Purchased
Purchase price of Part No. 101..........	$1,700
Costs saved by not manufacturing Part No. 101:	
Direct material..................... $570	
Direct labor....................... 600	
Power............................. 70	
Other costs........................ 150	
Total costs saved.................	−1,390
Net disadvantage in purchasing..........	$ 310

COSTS THAT ARE UNAFFECTED. Although items of cost that are unaffected by the decision are not differential and may be disregarded, a listing of some or all of these unaffected costs nevertheless may be useful so as to insure that all cost items have been considered. If this is done, it is essential that the unaffected costs be treated in exactly the same way under each of the alternatives. The net difference between the costs of the two alternatives, which is the result we seek, is not changed by adding equal amounts to the cost of each alternative.

EXAMPLE: Part No. 101 is one component of Product A. It may be convenient to list each of the items of cost, and the revenue of Product A for each of the alternatives, as in Illustration 18–1. The difference in

Illustration 18–1

CALCULATION OF DIFFERENTIAL PROFIT

Profit on Product A

	Base Case	*Purchase of Part No. 101*
Revenue............................	$10,000	$10,000
Costs:		
Direct material.....................	$1,570	$1,000
Purchased parts.....................	0	1,700
Direct labor.......................	3,000	2,400
Power............................	200	130
Other costs.......................	450	300
Occupancy costs....................	800	800
General and administrative...........	3,000	3,000
Total costs....................	9,020	9,330
Profit............................	$ 980	$ 670
	670 ←	
Differential profit....................	$ 310	

profit is the same $310 that was arrived at in the earlier examples. This is because the proposal to purchase Part No. 101 had no effect on the revenue of Product A, nor on the costs of Product A, other than those already listed.

The calculation in Illustration 18–1 requires somewhat more effort than those in the preceding examples, but it may be easier to understand, and the practice of listing each item of cost and revenue helps to insure that no items of differential cost are overlooked.

Danger of Using Full Cost

The full costs that are measured in a full cost accounting system may be misleading in alternative choice problems. In particular, when estimating differential costs, items of cost that are *allocated* to products should be viewed with skepticism. For example, a company may allocate overhead costs to products as 100 percent of direct labor cost; but this does not mean that if direct labor costs are decreased by $600 there will be a corresponding decrease of $600 in overhead costs. Overhead costs may not decrease at all; they may decrease, but by an amount less than $600; or they may even increase, as a result of an increased procurement and inspection work load resulting from the purchase of Part No. 101. In order to estimate what will actually happen to overhead costs, we must go behind the overhead rate and analyze what will happen to the various elements of overhead.

EXAMPLE: The full costs of Product A, as shown in Illustration 18–1, included an item of $800 for occupancy costs and an item of $3,000 for general and administrative costs. Occupancy cost is the cost of the building in which Product A is manufactured, and the $800 represents the share of total occupancy cost that is allocated to Product A. If Part No. 101, one part in Product A, is purchased, the floor space in which Part No. 101 is now manufactured no longer would be required. It does not necessarily follow, however, that occupancy costs would thereby be reduced. The costs of rent, heat, light, and other items comprising occupancy costs might not be changed at all by the decision to purchase Part No. 101. Unless the actual amount of occupancy cost were changed, this item of cost is not differential.

Similarly, general and administrative costs of the whole company probably would be unaffected by a decision to purchase Part No. 101; unless these costs would be affected, they are not differential.

Fringe Benefits

Labor costs are one of the important items of cost in many business decisions. The real cost of labor is significantly higher than the actual amount of wages earned. It includes such items as the employer's taxes for old-age and unemployment compensation; insurance, medical, and pension plans; vacation and holiday pay; and other fringe benefits. For business in general, these benefits average about 25 percent of wages earned, although there is a wide variation among different companies. In estimating differential labor costs, fringe benefits usually should be taken into account.

Opportunity Costs

Opportunity cost measures the value of the opportunity which is lost or sacrificed when the choice of one course of action requires that an alternative course of action be given up. Opportunity costs are not measured in accounting records, and they are not relevant in many alternative choice problems, but they are significant in certain situations. In general, if accepting an alternative requires that facilities or other resources must be devoted to that alternative that otherwise could be used for some other purpose, there is an opportunity cost, and it is measured by the profit that would have been earned had the resources been devoted to the other purpose.

> EXAMPLE: If the floor space required to make Part No. 101 can be used for some other revenue-producing purpose, then the sacrifice involved in using it for Part No. 101 is an opportunity cost of making that part. This cost is measured by the income that would be sacrificed if the floor space is used for Part No. 101; this is not necessarily the same as the allocated occupancy cost. If the floor space used for Part No. 101 could be used to manufacture another item that could be sold for a profit of $400, the $400 then becomes a cost of continuing to manufacture Part No. 101.

Opportunity costs are by their very nature "iffy." In most situations, it is extremely difficult to estimate what, if any, additional profit could be earned if the resources in question were devoted to some other use.

Other Terminology

The term "differential costs" does not have quite the same meaning as the term "variable costs." Variable costs are those that vary directly with changes in the volume of output. By contrast, differential costs are always related to specific alternatives that are being analyzed. If, in a specific problem, one of the alternatives involves a change in volume, then differential costs may well be the same as variable costs. Depending on the problem, however, the differential costs may include nonvariable items. A proposal to change the number of plant guards and their duties, for example, involves no elements of variable cost.

Marginal cost is a term used in economics for what accountants call variable costs. The marginal cost of a product is the cost of producing one additional unit of that product. Thus, marginal costs may be the same as differential costs in those problems in which an alternative under consideration involves changing the volume of output. *Incremental cost* and *relevant cost* are terms that usually mean the same thing as differential cost.

Estimates of Future Costs

Differential costs are estimates of what costs will be in the future. Nevertheless, in many instances our best information about future costs is derived from an analysis of historical costs. One can easily lose sight of the fact that historical costs, per se, are irrelevant. Historical costs may be a useful guide as to what costs are likely to be in the future, but using them as a guide is basically different from using them as if they were factual statements of what the future costs are going to be.

Except where future costs are determined by long-term contractual arrangements, differential costs are necessarily estimates, and they usually cannot be close estimates. An estimated labor saving of $1,000 a year for five years, for example, implies assumptions as to future wage rates, future fringe benefits, future labor efficiency, future production volume, and other factors that cannot be known with certainty at the time the estimate is prepared. Consequently, there is ordinarily no point in carrying computations of cost estimates to several decimal places; in fact, there is a considerable danger of being misled by the illusion of precision that such meticulous calculations give.

Book Value of Fixed Assets.   An element of historical cost that seems to cause considerable difficulty is the book value of fixed assets and the related depreciation expense. The book value of fixed assets is a *sunk cost*. A sunk cost exists because of actions taken in the past, not because of a decision made currently; therefore, a sunk cost is *not* a differential cost. No decision made today can change what has already happened. The past is history; decisions made now can affect only what *will* happen in the future.

It is sometimes suggested that when a proposed alternative involves the disposal of an existing machine, the depreciation on that machine will no longer be a cost, and that this saving in depreciation expense should therefore be taken into account as an advantage of the proposed alternative. This is not so. This argument overlooks the fact that the book value of the machine will, sooner or later, be recorded as a cost, regardless of whether the proposed alternative is adopted. If the alternative is not adopted, depreciation on the machine will continue, whereas if the alternative *is* adopted, the remaining book value will be written off when the machine is disposed of. In either case, the total amount of cost is the same, so the book value is not a differential cost.

EXAMPLE: A new production process is proposed as a substitute for operations now performed on a certain machine. The machine was purchased six years previously for $10,000, and depreciation on it has been recorded at $1,000 a year, a total of $6,000 to date. The machine therefore has a net book value of $4,000. The machine has zero market value, that is, the cost of removing it just equals its value as scrap metal. The new process is estimated to require $1,100 of additional direct labor costs annually, but operating costs of the machine, which are $500 a year, will be saved. The cost analysis of differential costs is shown in Part A of Illustration 18–2. The analysis indicates that the new process

Illustration 18–2

IRRELEVANCE OF SUNK COSTS

A. *Differential costs, one year*

	Base Case	*If New Process Is Adopted*
Additional direct labor costs.....	$ 0	$1,100
Machine operating costs........	500	0
Total.................	$500	$1,100
		−500
Net differential costs...........		$ 600
(Depreciation is not a differential cost)		

B. Net differential costs, four years ($600 × 4)............. ... $2,400

C. *Proof: Income Statements for four-year period*............

	Base Case	*If New Process Is Adopted*
Sales revenue................	$1,000,000	$1,000,000
Costs:		
Costs unaffected by the decision................	$700,000	$700,000
Process direct labor costs.....	0	4,400
Machine operating costs......	2,000	0
Depreciation on machine......	4,000	0
Loss on disposal of machine...	0	4,000
Total costs............	706,000	708,400
Profit.....................	$ 294,000	$ 291,600
	−291,600	
Decrease in profit if new process is adopted........	$ 2,400	

will have additional costs of $600 a year, and that it therefore should not be adopted.

It is sometimes argued, however, that this calculation neglects the $1,000 annual saving in depreciation costs that will occur if the machine is disposed of, and that the new process will actually save $400 a year (= $1,000 − $600), rather than incurring additional costs of $600 a year. This is a fallacious argument. The fact is that if the new process is accepted, the book value of the machine must be written off, and this amount exactly equals the total depreciation charge over the remaining life of the machine. Thus, there is no differential cost associated with the book value of the existing machine. If the new process is adopted, $4,000 of book value will be written off; whereas if the new process is not adopted, the same $4,000 will be recorded as depreciation expense over the next four years.

The irrelevance of sunk costs can be demonstrated by comparison of two income statements for the complete time periods of the remaining life of the machine, one showing the results of operations if the new process is adopted and the machine is scrapped, and the other showing the results if the process is continued on the present machine. Such a comparison is made in Section C of Illustration 18–2. This illustration demonstrates that there would be a loss of $2,400 over a four-year period, or $600 a year, if the new process were adopted.

The cost of an asset is supposed to be written off over its useful life. In the above example, we know by hindsight that this was not done, for if it had been done, the net book value of the machine would be zero at the time it was disposed of. This was an error, but it was an error made in the past, and no current decision can change it.

If the machine had a market value, this fact *would* be a relevant consideration, since its disposal would then bring in additional cash. If the income tax effect of writing off the loss on disposal were different from the tax effect of writing off depreciation over the four-year period, the effect of taxes is relevant. (The method of allowing for this tax effect will be discussed in Chapter 19.) The book value of the machine itself is not relevant. Ultimately, the book value is going to be charged against income, but whether this is done through the annual depreciation charge or through a lump-sum write-off makes no ultimate difference.

Importance of the Time Span

The question of what costs are differential depends to a considerable extent on the time span of the problem. If the proposal is to make only one additional unit of Part No. 101, only the direct material costs may be differential; the work could conceivably be done without any differential labor costs if workers were paid on a daily basis and had some idle time. At the other extreme, if the proposal involves a commitment to manufacture Part No. 101 over the foreseeable future, practically all items of manufacturing costs would be differential.

In general, the longer the time span of the proposal, the more items of cost are differential. In the very long run, all costs are differential. Thus, in very long-run problems, differential costs include the same elements as full costs, for in the long run one must consider even the replacement of buildings and equipment, which are sunk costs in the short run. In many short-run problems, relatively few cost items are subject to change by a management decision.

Example: Operating an Automobile

As an example of the fact that the cost elments that are differential in an alternative choice problem vary with the nature of the problem, consider the costs that are relevant for various decisions that may be made about owning and operating an automobile. A study made by Runzheimer and

Company and published by the American Automobile Association gives the national average cost in early 1973 of operating a 1973 eight-cylinder Chevrolet Impala four-door hardtop (equipped with standard accessories—radio, automatic transmission, and power steering) as follows:

	Average per Mile
Variable costs:	
Gasoline and oil	3.35 cents
Maintenance	0.78
Tires	0.62
Total variable costs	4.75 cents

	Amount per Year
Fixed costs:	
Fire and theft insurance	$ 45
Other insurance	322
License and registration	28
Depreciation	777
Total fixed costs	$1,172

The automobile is driven 10,000 miles a year. Assume that these costs are valid estimates of future costs (which actually is not the case because of inflation). What are the differential costs in each of these circumstances?

1. You own an automobile like that described above and have it registered. You are thinking about making a trip of 1,000 miles. What is the differential cost? Answer: The differential costs are 4.75 cents a mile times the estimated mileage of the trip; a trip of 1,000 miles therefore has a differential cost of $47.50. The fixed costs are not relevant since they will continue whether or not the trip is made. (Note that although no cash outlays may be made for maintenance or tires on this trip, these costs are nevertheless differential since the trip will cause these costs to be incurred sooner than if the trip were not made.)

2. You own an automobile but have not registered it. You are considering whether to register it for next year or to use alternative forms of transportation that you estimate will cost $1,000 for the 10,000 miles you expect to drive. Should you register it? Answer: The differential costs are the insurance and fees of $395 plus 4.75 cents a mile times the 10,000 miles you expect to travel by automobile, a total of $870. The $395 has become a cost because it is affected by the decision as to registration. If alternative transportation costs $1,000, you are well advised to register the automobile.

3. You do not own an automobile but are considering the purchase of the automobile described above. If your estimate is that you will drive 10,000 miles per year for five years and that alternative transportation

will cost $1,000 per year, should you do so? Answer: The differential costs are $1,172 a year plus 4.75 cents a mile times the 10,000 miles you expect to travel per year, or $1,172 + $475 = $1,647. If alternative transportation costs $1,000 a year, you are well advised to use alternative transportation.

Each of the above answers is, of course, an oversimplification because it omits nonquantitative factors and relies on averages. In an actual problem, the person would have data that more closely approximated the costs of his own automobile.

TYPES OF ALTERNATIVE CHOICE PROBLEMS

As noted earlier, a dominant objective of a business is to earn a satisfactory return on investment. The return on investment percentage is profit divided by investment. Profit is the difference between revenue and costs. Thus, three basic elements are involved in a company's return on investment: (1) costs, (2) revenue, and (3) investment, or

$$\frac{\text{Revenues} - \text{Costs}}{\text{Investment}}$$

Although the general approach to all alternative choice problems is similar, it is useful to discuss three subcategories separately. First, there are problems that involve only the cost element. In these problems, since revenue and investment elements are unaffected, the best alternative is normally the one with the lowest cost. Problems of this type are discussed in the next section. Second, there are problems in which both the revenue and cost elements are involved. Problems of this type are discussed in the latter part of this chapter. Third, there are problems that involve investment as well as revenues and costs. These are discussed in Chapter 19.

PROBLEMS INVOLVING COSTS

Alternative choice problems involving only costs have these general characteristics: The base case is the status quo, and an alternative to the base case is proposed. If the alternative is estimated to have lower differential costs than the base case, it is accepted (assuming nonquantitative factors do not offset this). If there are several alternatives, the one with the lowest differential cost is accepted. Problems of this type are often called *tradeoff problems* because one type of cost is traded off for another. Some examples are mentioned below.

METHODS CHANGE. The alternative being proposed is the adoption of some new method. If the differential costs of the proposed method are significantly lower than those of the present method, the method should be adopted (unless nonquantitative considerations are present).

PRODUCTION PLANNING.   In a factory that has a variety of machines, or in a chemical processing plant, several routes for scheduling products through the plant are possible. The route with the lowest differential cost is preferred. Other production decisions, such as whether to use overtime on one shift or to go to two-shift production, can be analyzed in terms of differential costs.

MAKE OR BUY.   Make-or-buy problems are among the most common type of alternative choice problems. At any given time, a business performs certain activities with its own employees, and it pays outside firms to perform certain other activities. It constantly seeks to improve the balance between these two types of activities by asking: Should we contract with some outside party to perform some function that we are now performing ourselves? Or, should we ourselves perform some activity that we now pay someone else to do?

As the example given above for Part No. 101 shows, the cost of the outside service (the "buy" alternative) usually is easy to estimate; the more difficult problem is to find the differential costs of the "make" alternative.

ORDER QUANTITY.   When the manufacture of a product involves setup costs that are incurred only once for each lot manufactured, the question arises of how many units should be made in one lot. If the demand is predictable and if sales are reasonably steady throughout the year, the optimum quantity to manufacture at one time, called the economic lot size or *economic order quantity*, is arrived at by considering two offsetting influences—setup costs (or ordering costs), and inventory carrying costs. The relevant costs are differential costs. A similar problem arises in deciding on the quantity of an item that should be purchased. A technique for analyzing this problem is given in a later section.

PROBLEMS INVOLVING BOTH REVENUES AND COSTS

In the second class of alternative choice problems, both costs and revenues are affected by the proposal being studied. Insofar as the quantitative factors are concerned, the best alternative is the one with the largest difference between differential revenue and differential cost, that is, the alternative with the most *differential income* or *differential profit*. Some problems of this type are described briefly below.

Supply/Demand/Price Analysis

In general, the lower the selling price of a product, the greater the quantity that will be sold. This relationship between a product's selling price and the quantity sold is called its *demand schedule,* or demand curve. As the quantity sold increases, the total cost of making the product increases by the variable cost of each additional unit. Since fixed costs do not change, total costs increase less than proportionately with increases in demand. This relationship is called the product's *supply schedule,* or supply curve.

The supply schedule usually can be estimated with a reasonable degree of accuracy, using the techniques described in Chapter 17. If the demand schedule also can be estimated, then the optimum selling price can be determined. This is the price at which marginal revenue (i.e., the revenue earned from selling one additional unit) equals marginal cost (i.e., the cost of making one additional unit, which is the variable cost). This optimum price can also be arrived at by estimating the total revenues and total costs, or total variable costs, for various quantities sold, and selecting the selling price that yields the greatest profit.

EXAMPLE: Assume that fixed costs for a product are $50,000 per month, and that variable costs are $100 per unit. The supply/demand analysis is given below:

Unit Selling Price	Estimated Quantity Sold	Total Revenue	Fixed Cost	Variable Cost (at $100 per unit)	Total Cost	Profit
$250........	500	$125,000	$50,000	$ 50,000	$100,000	$25,000
200........	1,000	200,000	50,000	100,000	150,000	50,000*
150........	1,500	225,000	50,000	150,000	200,000	25,000
125........	2,000	250,000	50,000	200,000	250,000	0

* Preferred alternative.

Column 1 shows various alternative selling prices, and Column 2 shows the estimated quantity that will be sold at each selling price. The next column shows the revenue earned at each selling price, which is the quantity sold at that price multiplied by the unit selling price. The next three columns show the costs estimated to be incurred for each quantity. The final column shows the profit, which is the difference between revenue and cost. Clearly, $200 is the best selling price, for at that price profit is $50,000, which is higher than the profit at either a higher or lower price. Since the fixed costs are a constant, they could be eliminated from the calculation without changing the result.

This type of analysis is feasible only if the demand schedule can be estimated. Since in most situations there is no reliable way of estimating how many units will be sold at various selling prices, this analysis cannot ordinarily be used. In the ordinary situation, the selling price is arrived at by adding a profit margin to the full cost of the product, as described in Chapter 16, or is set by competitive market forces.

Contribution Pricing

Although, as described in Chapter 16, full cost is the normal basis for pricing, and although a company must recover its full cost or eventually go out of business, there are some pricing situations where differential costs and revenues are appropriately used. In normal times, a company may refuse to take orders at prices that will not yield a satisfactory profit; but if times are bad, such orders may be accepted if the differential revenue obtained from them exceeds the differential costs involved. Differential costs are the costs that will be incurred if the order is accepted and that will not be incurred if it is not accepted. Differential revenue is the revenue that will be earned if the order is accepted and that will not be earned if it is not accepted. The company is better off to receive some revenue above its differential costs than to receive nothing at all. Such orders make some contribution to fixed costs and profit, and such a selling price is therefore called a *contribution price*, to distinguish it from a normal price.

Dumping, which is the practice of selling surplus quantities of a product in a selected marketing area at a price that is below full costs, is another version of the contribution idea. However, dumping may violate the Robinson-Patman Amendment in domestic markets, and is in general prohibited by trade agreements in foreign markets.

It is difficult to generalize on the circumstances that determine whether full costs or differential costs are appropriate. Even in normal times, an opportunity may be accepted to make some contribution to profit by using temporarily idle facilities. Conversely, even when current sales volume is low, the contribution concept may be rejected on the grounds that the low price may "spoil the market," or that orders can in fact be obtained at normal profit margins if the sales organization works hard enough.

Other Product Decisions

DISCONTINUING A PRODUCT.   If the selling price of a product is below its full cost, then conventional accounting reports will indicate that the product is being sold at a loss, and this fact may lead some people to recommend that the product be discontinued. Actually, such an action may make the company worse off rather than better off. It is better to have a product that makes some contribution to fixed overhead and profit than not to have the product at all. An analysis of differential revenues and differential costs is the proper approach to problems of this type. The contribution margin analysis for the laundry and dry cleaning business described in Chapter 17 illustrates such an approach.

ADDING SERVICES. A company can add to its net income if it can find additional ways of using its facilities such that the differential revenue from these uses exceeds the differential costs of providing them. For this reason, a gasoline service station may add a machine for vending soft drinks, a grocery store may decide to remain open in the evenings and on weekends, an airline may lease idle aircraft for charter flights, and a ski resort may offer special package deals on days when volume is low. In all these situations differential costs, rather than full costs, are relevant. In analyzing such problems, care must be taken to insure that the differential revenue is truly differential and that it does not represent a diversion from normal revenue. For example, a grocery store will not earn additional income by staying open nights if the revenue earned at night comes from customers who would otherwise have shopped at that store in the daytime.

SALE VERSUS FURTHER PROCESSING. Many companies, particularly those that manufacture a variety of finished products from basic raw materials, must address the problem of whether to sell a product that has reached a certain stage in the production process or whether to do additional work on it. Meat packers, for example, can sell an entire carcass of beef, or they can continue to process the carcass into hamburger and various cuts, or they can go even further and make frozen dinners out of the hamburger. The decision requires an analysis of the differential revenues and differential costs.

Let us designate the alternative of selling the product at a certain stage as the base case and that of processing it further as Case 2. For the base case, the relevant numbers are the sales revenue less any differential costs that are required to market the product at that stage. For Case 2, the numbers are the (presumably higher) sales revenue for the processed product, less the differential costs of the additional processing. If the differential income (i.e., revenue minus costs) of further processing exceeds that of the base case, then Case 2 is preferred. The important point to note about this analysis is that all costs incurred up to the point in the production process where this decision takes place may be disregarded. These costs are incurred whether or not additional processing takes place, and they are therefore not differential.

OTHER MARKETING TACTICS. The same analytical approach can be used for a number of other marketing problems, such as deciding which customers are worth soliciting by sales personnel and how often the salesperson should call on each customer; deciding whether to open additional warehouses or, conversely, whether to consolidate existing warehouses; deciding whether to improve the durability of a product in order to reduce the number of maintenance calls; and deciding on the minimum size of order that will be accepted.

Benefit/Cost Analysis

Revenue is a measure of the output of a profit-oriented organization. Nonprofit organizations also have outputs, but many of these organizations cannot measure their outputs in monetary terms. Similarly, the outputs of many organization units within a profit-oriented company cannot be expressed as revenue. In these situations a comparison of differential costs and differential revenues is not possible. Nevertheless, it is sometimes possible to use a similar approach by comparing differential costs, not with differential revenues but with some measure of the benefits that are expected as a consequence of incurring the additional costs. This approach is called a *benefit/cost analysis.*

Benefit/cost analysis is widely used in nonprofit organizations. It is also used in profit-oriented companies for analyzing such proposals as spending more money to improve safety conditions, or to reduce pollution, or to improve the company's reputation with the public, or to provide better information to management.

In a benefit/cost analysis, the cost calculations are usually straight-forward; the difficult part of the analysis is the estimate of the value of the benefits. In many situations, no meaningful estimate of the quantitative amount of benefits can be made. In such situations, the anticipated benefits are carefully described in words, and then the decision maker must answer the question: Are the perceived benefits worth *at least* the estimated cost? For example, "If we add $25,000 to the costs of the market research department, will the increased output of the department be worth at least $25,000?" The answer to this question is necessarily judgmental, but the judgment can be aided by a careful estimate of the differential costs and a careful assessment of the probable benefits.

SOME PRACTICAL POINTERS

The following points may be helpful in attacking specific problems:

1. Use imagination in choosing the possible alternatives to be considered, but don't select so many alternatives that you bog down before you begin. There is only a fine line between the alternative that is a "stroke of genius" and the alternative that is a "harebrained idea," but it is a crucial one.

2. Don't yield to the natural temptation to give too much weight to the factors that can be reduced to figures, even though the figures have the appearance of being definite and precise.

3. On the other hand, don't slight the figures because they are "merely" approximations. A reasonable approximation is much better than nothing at all.

4. Often, it is easier to work with total costs rather than with unit

costs. Unit cost is a fraction in which total cost is the numerator and number of units the denominator, that is,

$$\frac{\text{Total Cost}}{\text{Number of Units}} = \text{Unit Cost.}$$

Changes in either the numerator or the denominator result in changes in unit costs. An error is made if one of these changes is taken into account and the other is overlooked.

5. There is a tendency to underestimate the cost of doing something new because all the consequences may not be foreseen.

6. The *number* of arguments is irrelevant in an alternative choice problem. A dozen reasons may be, and often are, advanced against trying out something new, but all these reasons put together may not be so strong as a single argument in favor of the proposal.

7. Be realistic about the margin of error in any calculation involving the future. Fancy figures cannot be made out of rough estimates, nor is an answer necessarily precise or valid just because you spent a long time calculating it.

8. Despite uncertainties, a decision should be made if as much information is available as you can obtain at reasonable cost and within a reasonable time. Postponing action is the same as deciding to perpetuate the existing situation, which may be the worst possible decision.

9. Show clearly the assumptions you made and the effect of these on your estimates so that someone going over your analysis can substitute his own judgments if he wishes.

10. Do not expect that everyone will agree with your conclusion simply because it is supported with carefully worked-out figures. Think about how you can sell your conclusion to those who must act on it.

USEFUL DECISION MODELS

A model is a statement, usually in mathematical terms, of the relationships among variables in a specified set of circumstances. The contribution basis income statement for the laundry and dry cleaning business illustrated in Chapter 17 is a model. The relationships shown therein were: (Laundry revenues − laundry direct costs) + (dry cleaning revenues − dry cleaning direct costs) − indirect costs = income. More complicated models are useful in certain types of alternative choice problems. Some of these and related mathematical techniques are described below.

Economic Order Quantity

As already noted, under certain circumstances the economic order quantity to purchase, or the economic lot size in a manufacturing proc-

Illustration 18–3

DIFFERENT PRACTICES REGARDING SIZE OF ORDERS

A. Manufacture One Lot a Year

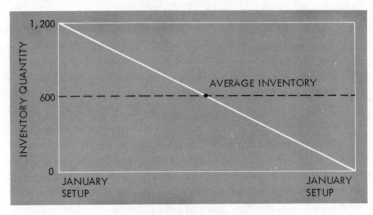

B. Manufacture Four Lots a Year

ess, can be estimated by considering the relationship between ordering costs (or setup costs) and inventory ordering costs. The nature of the problem is indicated in Illustration 18–3. This shows how two alternative policies for an item with annual sales of 1,200 units, occurring at an even rate of 100 per month, affect inventory levels and the number of setups. Part A shows that if the whole 1,200 units were manufactured in one lot, only one setup a year would be necessary, but inventory carrying costs would be high since the inventory would start with 1,200 units and would average 600 units over the year.[4] By contrast, as shown in Part B,

---

[4] Inventory is 1,200 units immediately after the lot has been manufactured and declines to zero a year later. Assuming that the decline is at a roughly even rate throughout the year, the average inventory for the year is one half the sum of the beginning plus ending inventories; thus: ½ (1,200 + 0) = 600.

the manufacture of four lots of 300 units each (i.e., one lot each quarter) would involve four times as much setup cost but a relatively low inventory carrying cost since there would be an average of only 150 units in inventory at any one time.

Total cost will be at a minimum when the increase in inventory carrying cost resulting from adding one more unit to a lot is equal to the corresponding decrease in setup costs per unit. A model has been developed that determines the optimum balance between setup costs on the one hand and inventory carrying costs on the other hand. The amount is called the economic order quantity. The equation is:

$$Q = \sqrt{\frac{2SR}{CK}}$$

In this equation:

Q = Economic order quantity (number of units in one lot).
S = Setup costs for one setup.
R = Annual requirements in units.
K = Inventory carrying charge, expressed as a percentage of average inventory value.
C = Factory cost per unit.

EXAMPLE: Estimates for a certain item are:

S (setup cost)	$300
R (annual requirements)	1,200 units
K (carrying charge)	20%
C (factory cost)	$10 per unit

$$\text{Economic order quantity} = \sqrt{\frac{2 \times \$300 \times 1,200}{\$10 \times 0.2}}$$
$$= \sqrt{360,000}$$
$$= 600 \text{ units}$$

Since 1,200 units are required per year, there must be $1,200 \div 600 = 2$ lots manufactured per year.

The costs used in this equation are differential costs. The differential setup costs include the extra labor costs involved in making the setup, plus fringe benefits on this labor, plus any differential overhead costs associated with making a setup. The differential inventory carrying charge includes an estimate of interest costs, and of the costs associated with the occupancy of warehouse space.

The above example had to do with manufacturing an item. The same approach can be used to determine the economic order quantity for *purchasing* an item from an outside vendor. Instead of "setup costs," the differential purchasing costs are incorporated in the formula. These include the costs of placing the order, receiving the goods, and paying the invoice. Factory cost per unit (C) becomes the unit purchase price of the item.

Expected Value

All the numbers used in alternative choice problems are estimates of what will happen in the future. In the foregoing examples, we used *single value* estimates; that is, each estimate was a single number representing someone's best estimate as to what differential costs or revenues would be. Some companies are experimenting with estimates made in the form of probability distributions rather than as single numbers. Instead of stating, "I think sales of Item X will be $100,000 if the proposed alternative is adopted," the estimator develops a range of possibilities, together with his estimate of the probability that each will occur. These separate possibilities are weighted by the probabilities. The sum of these weighted amounts is called the *expected value* of the probability distribution. It is computed as in the following example:

Possibilities: Sales Volume	*Estimated Probability*	*Weighted Amount*
(*a*)	(*b*)	(*a* × *b*)
$ 60,000	0.1	$ 6,000
80,000	0.1	8,000
100,000	0.4	40,000
120,000	0.2	24,000
140,000	0.2	28,000
	1.0 Expected value.............	$106,000

The probability 0.1 opposite $60,000 means that there is 1 chance in 10 that sales will be $60,000. The sum of the probabilities must always add to 1.0, because the estimates must include all possible outcomes. Although sales conceivably could be any amount between zero and an extremely high number, the estimator clearly cannot assign probabilities to each of a long list of possibilities. Therefore, he works only with a few numbers that are intended to be representative of the complete distribution. Rarely would there be more than 7 such possibilities; 5, as in the example above, is common, and the use of only three possibilities is also common.

The expected value of $106,000 would be used as the best estimate of differential revenue. If a single value estimate rather than an expected value were used, it would be $100,000 because this is the number with the highest probability. The $106,000 expected value is a better estimate of sales because it incorporates the whole probability distribution.

People in business do not find it easy to develop estimates in the form of probability distributions; but if they can do so, the validity of the estimates can be greatly increased.

Measuring Uncertainty

If two alternatives are expected to have approximately the same differential income, but the income is more certain to be earned in one case than in the other, the manager ordinarily would decide to accept the more certain alternative. For example, if he can earn $8,000 by buying $100,000 U.S. Treasury bonds and estimates $8,000 of earnings from an investment in a new product, he would prefer to buy Treasury bonds. The probability distribution illustrated in the preceding section can be used to derive a measure of uncertainty. It is called the *standard deviation*.

The standard deviation (symbol σ) is more precisely the root mean squared deviation, and this suggests how it is calculated: The deviation of each value from the mean is found (the expected value of a probability distribution is its mean), these deviations are squared, the squares are weighted by their probabilities, and the square root of the sum of these squared deviations is extracted.

EXAMPLE: The standard deviation of the sales value distribution given above, whose expected value is $106,000, is computed as follows:

Sales Value ($x10^3$)	Deviation ($x10^3$)	Squared Deviation ($x10^6$)	Weight	Weighted Amount ($x10^6$)
$ 60	$ −46	$2,116	0.1	$211.6
80	−26	676	0.1	67.6
100	− 6	36	0.4	14.4
120	14	196	0.2	39.2
140	34	1,156	0.2	231.2

Sum of Squared Deviations = $564.0 ($x10^6$) = 564,000,000

Standard Deviation = $24,000

The sales volume estimate therefore has a standard deviation of $24,-000. If two distributions have equal expected values, the one with the higher standard deviation is the more uncertain. The probability of earning the specified interest on Treasury bonds is almost 1.0.[5] The standard deviation from the expected value in the case of Treasury bonds is infinitesimally small.

If the expected values of two or more estimates are of substantially different amounts, the *relative* amount of uncertainty in each can be expressed by the *coefficient of variation*, which is simply the standard deviation divided by the expected value. Expected values and standard deviations can be calculated easily on a computer and on some mini-calculators.

If there are probability distributions for several variables involved in a problem, and some are interdependent, the problem of measuring the overall uncertainty of the alternative is more complicated. This problem can be solved on a computer using the *Monte Carlo method*. Essentially, the computer finds the differential income for the alternative under one

---

[5] It is not quite 1.0 as holders of Treasury gold certificates in 1934 learned to their sorrow. Few estimates of the future have a probability of 1.0; that is, the future is almost always uncertain.

set of revenues and costs, which it arrives at by selecting one possible value for each variable. It repeats this process hundreds of times, or thousands of times, each time using a set of values selected randomly from the probability distribution for each variable. From the results of all these trials, it computes an expected value, and a measure of uncertainty.

Decision Trees

A characteristic of the problems described in this chapter was that a single decision had to be made, and as a consequence of that decision estimated revenues would be earned and estimated costs would be incurred. There is another class of problems in which a series of decisions has to be made, at various time intervals, with each decision influenced by the information that is available at the time it is made. An analytical tool that is useful for such problems is the *decision tree.*

In its simplest form, a decision tree is a diagram that shows the several decisions or *acts* and the possible consequences of each act; these consequences are called *events.* In a more elaborate form, the probabilities and the revenues or costs of each event's outcomes are estimated, and these are combined to give an *expected value* for the event.

Since a decision tree is particularly useful in depicting a complicated series of decisions, any brief illustration is highly artificial. Nevertheless, the decision tree shown in Illustration 18–4 will suffice to show how the technique works.

Illustration 18–4

SIMPLE DECISION TREE

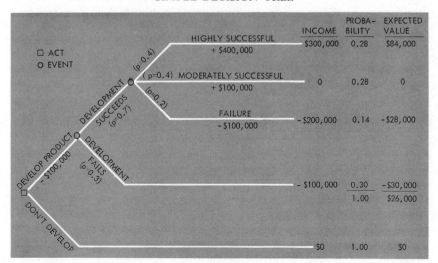

The assumed situation is this. A company is considering whether to develop and market a new product. Development costs are estimated to be $100,000, and there is a 0.7 probability that the development effort will be successful. If the development is successful, the product will be marketed, and it is estimated that:

a. if the product is highly successful, it will produce differential income of $400,000 (or a net $300,000 after subtracting the development cost);
b. if the product is moderately successful, it will break even, that is, its income of $100,000 will just offset the development cost;
c. if the product is a failure, it will lose $100,000 (or a total loss of $200,000 after taking account of the development cost).

The estimated probability of high success is 0.4; of moderate success, 0.4; and of failure, 0.2.

The expected value of each outcome is the monetary income or loss times the probability of that outcome's occurrence. Thus,

1. If development fails, the expected value is the development cost times the probability of failure: $-\$100,000 \times 0.3 = -\$30,000$, i.e., a $30,000 loss.
2. If development succeeds, but the product is a failure, the loss is $100,000 development cost plus $100,000 marketing costs, a total loss of $200,000. The total probability of development success *and* product failure is $0.7 \times 0.2 = 0.14$. The expected value of this outcome is $0.14 \times -\$200,000 = -\$28,000$.
3. If development succeeds and the product is moderately successful, the probability is 0.28 (0.7×0.4) and the differential net income is zero; hence the expected value is $0.28 \times \$0 = \$0$.
4. If development succeeds and the product is highly successful, the net income is $400,000 — $100,000 development costs, or $300,000, and the probability is again 0.28; hence the expected value of this outcome is $0.28 \times \$300,000 = \$84,000$.

The *total* expected value of the act "Develop Product" is the algebraic sum of the expected values of all possible outcomes on the "Develop Product" branch of the tree, that is, $26,000. This amount is then compared with the expected value of the other alternative act, "Don't Develop" (which is the base case). If the development is not undertaken there is a 100% chance (1.0 probability) that the incremental income will be $0; hence the expected value of "Don't Develop" is zero. Because the act "Develop Product" has the larger expected value, the decision would be to proceed with the development effort. This does not mean, of course, that the ultimate outcome is "guaranteed" to be differential income of $26,000; rather it means that based on the estimates that have been made in considering this decision, management should "gamble" and go ahead with the development, because the *expected* payoff from this gamble is positive, whereas if the gamble is not taken there will be zero payoff.

Linear Programming

In the situations described thus far, it has been assumed implicitly that the available resources are adequate to carry out whichever alternative is selected. However, in some situations this assumption is not valid. For example, a machine has only a certain amount of capacity, and if that capacity is used by one product it cannot be used for another. Similarly, a factory building has room for only so many machines. In these situations, there are *constraints* on the uses of resources. Linear programming is a model for solving problems with several constraints.

In linear programming, a series of mathematical statements is developed. The first, called the *objective function*, is the quantity to be optimized; this is usually a formula for differential costs which the model will minimize, or one for differential income, which is to be maximized. The other statements express mathematically the constraints of the situation.

> EXAMPLE: A company makes two products, each of which is worked on in two departments. Department 1 has a capacity of 500 labor hours per week; Department 2, 600 labor hours. The labor requirements of each product in each department are as follows:

Labor Hours per Unit:	Product A	Product B
Department 1	5	2.5
Department 2	3	5

As many units of B as can be made can also be sold, but a maximum of 90 units of A can be sold per week. The unit contribution (i.e., unit price minus unit variable costs) is $2 for A, and $2.50 for B. How many units of each should be made in order to maximize total contribution?

The problem can be expressed mathematically as follows:

$$\text{Maximize} \quad P = 2A + 2.5B \quad \text{(maximize profit, the objective function)}$$

Subject to	$5A + 2.5B \leq 500$	(Dept. 1 capacity constraint)
	$3A + 5B \leq 600$	(Dept. 2 capacity constraint)
	$A \leq 90$	(Product A sales constraint)
	$A \geq 0, B \geq 0$	(A negative number of units cannot be made)

In words, the above says find the number of units of A and B that should be made each week so as to maximize profit at $2 per unit for A and $2.50 per unit for B, subject to the constraint that a unit of A requires 5 hours in Department 1 and a unit of B requires 2.5 hours there, and only 500 hours per week are available in Department 1; and so forth.

This situation can be illustrated graphically as in Illustration 18–5. One can see from the table above that Department 2 could make 200 units of A if it worked only on A, or 120 units of B if it worked only on B; in Illustration 18–5 the line between these two extremes, labeled "Dept. 2 Capacity Constraint," shows all of the possible A–B product combinations that would utilize all of Department 2's available capacity of 600 hours. The other lines are drawn in the same manner.

The shaded area in Illustration 18–5, bounded by the axes and the three constraint lines, is called the "feasible set," because any A–B combination in that area can be produced and sold, whereas combinations outside that area are infeasible. A moment's reflection will reveal that the optimum A–B combination must lie on the "northeast" boundary of the feasible set because any point inside that boundary does not use up all the available manufacturing capacity and/or A sales "capacity," and hence does not maximize contribution since more units could be made and sold. What is also true, but is not intuitively obvious, is the fact that the optimum A–B combination lies at a *vertex* of that boundary; i.e., at either point w, x, y, or z.

What a linear programming computer program does, in effect, is calculate the profit, P, at each vertex of the feasible set boundary and

Illustration 18–5

LINEAR PROGRAMMING GRAPHICAL SOLUTION

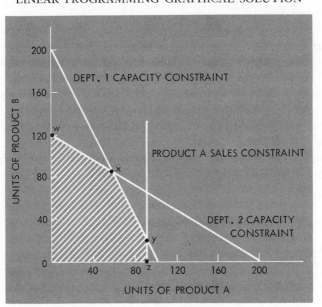

identify that point which gives the highest profit. Of course, for more realistic problems, such as determining the least costly delivery routes for a fleet of trucks or determining the most profitable mix of petroleum products to be refined from a quantity of crude oil, tens or even hundreds of mathematical statements are involved, and the problem cannot be solved manually. Computers can, and do, solve such problems rapidly.

SHADOW PRICES.   As part of the solution to a linear programming problem, the computer program also calculates a *shadow price* for each constrained resource; i.e., for each resource that is completely utilized at the optimum solution. For example, if the optimum solution involves using all of Department 2's capacity, the shadow price for this capacity would indicate the amount by which profit would increase if the capacity could be increased by one hour (to 601 hours); this shadow price would be the maximum amount the company should be willing to spend to add a unit of capacity (i.e., one labor hour) in Department 2.

SUMMARY

When an alternative choice problem involves changes in costs but not changes in revenue or investment, the best solution is the one with the lowest differential costs, insofar as cost information bears on the solution. Although historical costs may provide a useful guide to what costs will be in the future, we are always interested in future costs, and never in historical costs for their own sake. In particular, sunk costs are irrelevant. The longer the time span involved, the more costs that are differential.

When the problem involves both cost and revenue considerations, differential revenues, as well as differential costs, must be estimated. When revenue cannot be estimated, benefit/cost analysis is helpful in certain types of problems.

Differential costs and revenues rarely provide the answer to any business problem, but they facilitate comparisons and narrow the area within which judgment must be applied in order to reach a sound decision.

Mathematical models are useful in analyzing certain alternative choice problems.

SUGGESTIONS FOR FURTHER READING

BIERMAN, H.; BONINI, C. P.; FOURAKER, L. E.; and JAEDICKE, R.   *Quantitative Analysis for Business Decisions.* 4th ed.; Homewood, Ill.: Richard D. Irwin, Inc., 1973.

CHRISTENSON, C. J.; VANCIL, R. F.; and MARSHALL, P. W. *Managerial Economics: Text and Cases*. Rev. ed.; Homewood, Ill.: Richard D. Irwin, Inc., 1973.

NATIONAL ASSOCIATION OF ACCOUNTANTS. *Criteria for Make-or-Buy Decisions*, New York: NAA, 1973.

RAIFFA, HOWARD. *Decision Analysis*. Reading, Mass.: Addison-Wesley, 1968.

CASES

CASE 18–1. BOB MOGIELNICKI

In June 1974, Bob Mogielnicki went to work for the Brandywine Corporation, a medium-sized manufacturer of electrical controls and electronic devices. What particularly attracted Bob to the job offer from Brandywine was the fact that it presented an opportunity to assume line responsibilities after a brief training period. The position in question was that of supervisor of the parts fabrication shop at the company's San Jose plant.

At that time, the staff of the parts fabrication shop consisted of ten machine operators and two clerks in addition to the supervisor. The shop was producing five parts which were used by other departments of the San Jose plant in the assembly of final products. A statement of costs incurred by the parts fabrication shop during the first week of Bob's supervision is shown in Exhibit 1.

When he took over the parts fabrication shop, Bob was told by the plant manager, Mr. Wallis, that it was Bob's responsibility to see that the five parts being produced by the shop were acquired at the lowest possible cost to the company. For this reason, he had the authority to buy all or any of these parts from outside sources if he found this to be more advantageous to the company.

Exhibit 1

COST STATEMENT FOR WEEK OF SEPTEMBER 16, 1974

Prime Cost	
Labor	$1,397.56
Materials	3,116.80
Total Prime Cost	$4,514.36
Departmental Overhead	
Departmental supervision and services	$1,002.16
Depreciation	1,200.00
Total Departmental Overhead	$2,202.16
General Overhead	$1,500.00
Total Costs	$8,216.52

592

In order to carry out his responsibility for "make-or-buy" decisions, Bob felt he needed more cost information than was supplied by the weekly cost statement (Exhibit 1). He discussed his needs with the plant accountant, Mr. Dreyfus, and together they agreed on a format for a second weekly report, which would show the actual cost of producing 100 of each of the parts during the week in question. The first such report, corresponding to the cost statement of Exhibit 1, is shown in Exhibit 2.

Exhibit 2

PRODUCT COST REPORT FOR WEEK OF SEPTEMBER 16, 1974

Cost per 100 Units of Part No.

Cost Element	101	102	103	104	105
Labor.....................	$ 8.48	$13.30	$ 5.25	$ 7.33	$ 4.31
Materials.................	18.40	24.00	14.80	17.20	13.60
Total Prime Cost...........	$26.88	$37.30	$20.05	$24.53	$17.91
Overhead.................	22.42	35.15	13.88	19.38	11.39
Total Cost................	$49.30	$72.45	$33.93	$43.91	$29.30
Production (100 units).........	33	40	32	42	26

The figures in Exhibit 2 were obtained as follows:

1. *Direct labor/hundred.* Each machine operator kept a time sheet indicating the time (in hours and tenths of an hour) spent on each part. These times were accumulated for each part and costed at the direct labor rate of $3.50/hour. The total cost for each part was then divided by the amount of production.
2. *Direct materials/hundred.* When materials were drawn from the storeroom, an issue slip was prepared indicating the amount drawn and the part on which the materials were to be used. The amounts were totalled for each part and the totals divided by the amount of production.
3. *Overhead/hundred.* The total of all departmental and general overhead costs was divided by the number of direct labor hours to produce a cost per hour. This figure was multiplied by the number of direct labor hours charged to each part and the result was then divided by the amount of production.

After receiving the information in Exhibit 2 from Mr. Dreyfus, Bob Mogielnicki solicited bids on each of the five parts from several small shops in the San Jose area. The lowest bid received on each part was as follows:

Part No.	Lowest Bid
101	$65.00
102	90.00
103	37.50
104	60.00
105	34.50

After studying these bids, Bob concluded that the company should continue to make each part in its own shop.

In the spring of 1975, demand for Brandywine's products fell sharply because of a business recession. This decline was reflected in the workload in the parts fabrication shop. Because of the reduced workload, Bob Mogielnicki had laid off one machine operator and had transferred another to performing maintenance of equipment which had been deferred during the period of higher production.

When Bob received his product cost report for the week of April 14, 1975, shown in Exhibit 3, he discovered that costs were up on all five

Exhibit 3

PRODUCT COST REPORT FOR WEEK OF APRIL 14, 1975

	Cost per 100 Units of Part No.				
Cost Element	101	102	103	104	105
Labor	$ 9.02	$14.00	$ 5.60	$ 7.82	$ 4.33
Material	18.43	24.01	14.78	17.20	13.59
Total Prime Cost	$27.45	$38.01	$20.38	$25.02	$17.92
Overhead	30.92	48.00	19.20	26.80	14.86
Total Cost	$58.37	$86.01	$39.58	$51.82	$32.78
Production (100 units)	26	32	20	30	21

parts, and that part 103, in particular, now cost more to make than the bid of $37.50 per hundred he had received in the fall. Bob called up the owner of the shop who had made that bid and asked him for an updated bid. The owner responded with a bid of $36.00 per hundred, saying that his business was off and so he was willing to shave his earlier price a bit if it would help to keep his shop busy. Bob promptly accepted the reduced offer and asked the purchasing agent of the San Jose plant to issue a purchase order to the outside source for 4,000 units (about a two-week supply at the current usage rate). Bob estimated that his decision would save Brandywine about $140.

The cost reports for the week of April 28, 1975 (Exhibit 4) showed a further rise. Once again Bob checked with the sources of earlier bids, this time on parts 102 and 105, and learned that in both cases the bidders were sticking by their earlier quotes.

Exhibit 4

PRODUCT COST REPORT FOR WEEK OF APRIL 28, 1975

Cost per 100 Units of Part No.

Cost Element	*101*	*102*	*103*	*104*	*105*
Labor......................	$ 8.68	$13.33	—	$ 7.50	$ 4.50
Material....................	18.43	24.00	—	17.20	13.55
Total Prime Cost..............	$27.11	$37.33	—	$24.70	$18.05
Overhead....................	37.60	58.00	—	32.14	18.00
Total Cost...................	$64.71	$95.33	—	$56.84	$36.05
Production (100 units)............	25	30	—	28	20

Questions

1. What was the total overhead expense in Bob Mogielnicki's department for the week of April 14, 1975? What reasons can you give for the change from the week of September 16, 1974?
2. What should Bob Mogielnicki do with regard to parts 102 and 105?

CASE 18–2. HANSON MANUFACTURING COMPANY

In February 1974, Mr. Herbert Wessling was appointed general manager by Mr. Paul Hanson, president of the Hanson Manufacturing Company. Mr. Wessling, age fifty-six, had wide executive experience in manufacturing products similar to those of the Hanson company. The appointment of Mr. Wessling resulted from management problems arising from the death of Mr. Richard Hanson, founder and, until his death in early 1973, president of the Hanson company. Mr. Paul Hanson had only four years' experience with the company, and in early 1974 was thirty-four years old. His father had hoped to train him over a ten-year period, but his untimely death had cut this seasoning period short. The younger Hanson became president when his father died and had exercised full control until he hired Mr. Wessling.

Mr. Paul Hanson knew that during 1973 he had made several poor decisions and noted that the morale of the organization had suffered, apparently through lack of confidence in him. When he received the income statement for 1973 (Exhibit 1), the net loss of over $100,000 during a good business year convinced him that he needed help. He attracted Mr. Wessling from a competitor by offering a stock option incentive in addition to salary, knowing that Mr. Wessling wanted to acquire financial security for his retirement. The two men came to a clear understanding that Mr. Wessling, as general manager, had full authority to execute any changes he desired. In addition, Mr. Wessling

Exhibit 1

HANSON MANUFACTURING COMPANY

Income Statement
For Year Ending December 31, 1973

Gross sales......................................		$21,178,810
Cash discounts.............................		313,156
Net sales.......................................		$20,865,654
Cost of goods sold...........................		13,022,076
Gross Margin................................		$ 7,843,578
Less: Selling expense........................	$3,676,476	
General administration..................	1,306,040	
Depreciation.........................	2,716,880	7,699,396
Operating income.............................		$ 144,182
Other income................................		42,130
Income before interest........................		$ 186,312
Less: Interest expense.......................		290,166
Net Income (Loss)...........................		($ 103,854)

would explain the reasons for his decisions to Mr. Hanson and thereby train him for successful leadership upon Mr. Wessling's retirement.

The Hanson Manufacturing Company made only three industrial products, 101, 102, and 103. These were sold by the company sales force for use in the processes of other manufacturers. All of the sales force, on a salary basis, sold the three products but in varying proportions. The Hanson Company sold throughout New England and was one of eight companies with similar products. Several of its competitors were larger and manufactured a larger variety of products than did the Hanson Company. The dominant company was the Samra Company, which operated a branch plant in the Hanson Company's market area. Customarily, the Samra Company announced prices annually, and the other producers followed suit.

Price cutting was rare, and the only variance from quoted selling prices took the form of cash discounts. In the past, attempts at price cutting had followed a consistent pattern: all competitors met the price reduction, and the industry as a whole sold about the same quantity but at the lower prices. This continued until the Samra Company, with its strong financial position, again stabilized the situation following a general recognition of the failure of price cutting. Furthermore, because sales were to industrial buyers and because the products of different manufacturers were very similar, the Hanson Company was convinced it could not individually raise prices without suffering volume declines.

During 1973 the Hanson Company's share of industry sales was 12 percent for type 101, 8 percent for 102, and 10 percent for 103. The industry-wide quoted selling prices were $4.90, $5.16 and $5.50, respectively.

Exhibit 2

HANSON MANUFACTURING COMPANY

Analysis of Profit and Loss by Departments—Year Ended December 31, 1973

	Product 101		Product 102		Product 103		Total	
	Thousands	$ per cwt.	Thousands	$ per cwt.	Thousands	$ per cwt.	Thousands	Thousands
Rent	376	.1762	314	.3050	374	.3788	1064	
Property taxes	125	.0586	100	.0970	80	.0810	305	
Property insurance	104	.0490	80	.0774	105	.1066	289	
Compensation insurance	165	.0774	87	.0844	90	.0910	342	
Direct labor	2585	1.2126	1220	1.1844	1375	1.3930	5180	
Indirect labor	882	.4136	424	.4116	460	.4660	1766	
Power	45	.0210	50	.0484	60	.0610	155	
Light and heat	30	.0140	25	.0246	20	.0204	75	
Building service	20	.0094	15	.0150	15	.0150	50	
Materials	1529	.7170	942	.9152	970	.9824	3441	
Supplies	104	.0490	95	.0924	70	.0710	269	
Repairs	35	.0166	30	.0290	20	.0206	85	
Total	6001	2.8144	3382	3.2844	3639	3.6868	13022	
Selling expense	1821	.8540	915	.8890	940	.9524	3676	
General administrative	690	.3234	260	.2526	355	.3596	1306	
Depreciation	1130	.5298	856	.8310	731	.7408	2717	
Interest	104	.0490	80	.0776	105	.1064	290	
Total Cost	9745	4.5706	5493	5.3346	5770	5.8460	21011	
Less Other Income	20	.0096	10	.0100	10	.0100	42	
	9725	4.5610	5482	5.3246	5760	5.8360	20969	
Sales (net)	10335	4.8470	5195	5.0456	5335	5.4054	20866	
Profit (Loss)	610	.2860	(287)	(.2790)	(425)	(.4306)	(103)	
Unit sales (cwt.)	2132191		1029654		986974			
Quoted selling price	$4.90		$5.16		$5.50			
Cash discounts taken, percent of selling price	1.08%		2.22%		1.72%			

Note: Figures may not add exactly because of rounding.

Mr. Wessling upon taking office in February 1974, decided against immediate major changes. Rather he chose to analyze 1973 operations and to wait for results of the first half of 1974. He instructed the accounting department to provide detailed expenses and earnings statements by products for 1973 (see Exhibit 2). In addition he requested an explanation of the nature of the costs including their expected future behavior (see Exhibit 3).

Exhibit 3

HANSON MANUFACTURING COMPANY

Accounting Department's Commentary on Costs

Direct Labor: Variable. Union shop at going community rates of $3.20/hr. (including social security taxes). No abnormal demands foreseen. It may be assumed that direct labor dollars is an adequate measure of capacity utilization.

Compensation Insurance: Variable. Five per cent of direct and indirect labor is an accurate estimate.

Materials: Variable. Exhibit 2 figures are accurate. Includes waste allowances. Purchases are at market prices.

Power: Variable. Rates are fixed. Use varies with activity. Averages per Exhibit 2 are accurate.

Supplies: Variable. Exhibit 2 figures are accurate. Supplies bought at market prices.

Repairs: Variable. Varies as volume changes within normal operation range. Lower and upper limits are fixed.

General Administrative, Selling Expense, Indirect Labor, Interest, and Other Income: These items are almost nonvariable. They can be changed, of course, by management decision.

Cash Discount: Almost nonvariable. Average cash discounts taken are consistent from year to year. Percentages in Exhibit 2 are accurate.

Light and Heat: Almost nonvariable. Heat varies slightly with fuel cost changes. Light a fixed item regardless of level of production.

Property Taxes: Almost nonvariable. Under the lease terms Hanson Company pays the taxes; assessed valuation has been constant; the rate has risen slowly. Any change in the near future will be small and independent of production volume.

Rent: Nonvariable. Lease has twelve years to run.

Building Service: Nonvariable. At normal business level variances are small.

Property Insurance: Nonvariable. Three-year policy with fixed premium.

Depreciation: Nonvariable. Fixed dollar total.

To familiarize Mr. Paul Hanson with his methods, Mr. Wessling sent copies of these exhibits to Mr. Hanson, and they discussed them. Mr. Hanson stated that he thought Product 103 should be dropped immediately as it would be impossible to lower expenses on Product 103 as much as 43 cents per cwt. In addition he stressed the need for economies on Product 102.

Mr. Wessling relied on the authority arrangement Mr. Hanson had agreed to earlier and continued production of the three products. For control purposes he had the accounting department prepare monthly statements using as standard costs the costs per cwt. from the analytical profit and loss statement for 1973 (Exhibit 2). These monthly statements were his basis for making minor sales or production changes during the

Exhibit 4

HANSON MANUFACTURING COMPANY

Profit and Loss by Department, at Standard, Showing Variations from January 1 to June 30, 1974

Item	Product 101 Standard per cwt.	Product 101 Total at Standard	Product 102 Standard per cwt.	Product 102 Total at Standard	Product 103 Standard per cwt.	Product 103 Total at Standard	Total Standard (thousands)	Total Actual (thousands)	Variations + = Favorable − = Unfavorable
Rent........................	.1762	176	.3050	217	.3788	190	583	522	+ 61
Property tax................	.0586	58	.0970	69	.0810	41	168	154	+ 14
Property insurance..........	.0490	49	.0774	55	.1066	53	157	146	+ 11
Compensation insurance......	.0774	77	.0844	60	.0910	46	183	184	− 1
Direct labor................	1.2126	1209	1.1844	843	1.3930	698	2750	2764	− 14
Indirect labor..............	.4136	412	.4116	293	.4660	234	939	896	+ 43
Power.......................	.0210	21	.0484	34	.0610	31	86	84	+ 2
Light and heat..............	.0140	14	.0246	18	.0204	10	42	40	+ 2
Building service............	.0094	9	.0150	11	.0150	8	28	20	+ 8
Materials...................	.7170	715	.9152	652	.9824	492	1859	1856	+ 3
Supplies....................	.0490	49	.0924	66	.0710	36	151	150	+ 1
Repairs.....................	.0166	17	.0290	21	.0206	10	48	50	− 2
Total....................	2.8144	2806	3.2844	2339	3.6868	1848	6993	6866	+127
Selling expense.............	.8540	851	.8890	633	.9524	477	1961	1966	− 5
General administrative......	.3234	322	.2526	180	.3596	180	682	656	+ 26
Depreciation................	.5298	528	.8310	592	.7408	371	1491	1362	+129
Interest....................	.0490	49	.0776	55	.1064	53	157	146	+ 11
Total Cost...............	4.5706	4556	5.3346	3799	5.8460	2925	11280	10996	+284
Less Other Income...........	.0096	10	.0100	7	.0100	5	22	22	—
	4.5610	4547	5.3246	3792	5.8360	2920	11258	10974	+284
Actual sales................	4.8470	4832	5.0456	3593	5.4054	2710	11135	11134	− 1
Profit or Loss..............	.2860	285	(.2790)	(199)	(.4306)	(210)	(123)	160	+283
Unit sales (cwt.)...........		996859		712102		501276			

spring of 1974. Late in July 1974, Mr. Wessling received from the accounting department the six months' statement of cumulative standard costs including variances of actual costs from standard (see Exhibit 4). They showed that the first half of 1974 was a successful period.

During the latter half of 1974 the sales of the entire industry weakened. Even though the Hanson Company retained its share of the market, its profit for the last six months was small. In January 1975, the Samra Company announced a price reduction on Product 101 from $4.90 to $4.50 per cwt. This created an immediate pricing problem for all its competitors. Mr. Wessling forecast that if the Hanson Company held to the $4.90 price during the first six months of 1975, their unit sales would be 750,000 cwt. He felt that if they dropped their price to $4.50 per cwt. the six months' volume would be 1,000,000 cwt. Mr. Wessling knew that competing managements anticipated a further decline in activity. He thought a general decline in prices was quite probable.

The accounting department reported that the standard costs in use would probably apply during 1975, with two exceptions: materials and supplies would be about 5 percent below standard; and light and heat would decline about one third of 1 percent.

Mr. Wessling and Mr. Hanson discussed the pricing problem. Mr. Hanson observed that even with the anticipated decline in material and supply costs, a sales price of $4.50 would be below cost. Mr. Hanson therefore wanted the $4.90 to be continued since he felt the company could not be profitable while selling a key product below cost.

Questions

1. If the company had dropped Product 103 as of January 1, 1974, what effect would that action have had on the $160,000 profit for the first six months of 1974?
2. In January 1975, should the company reduce the price of Product 101 from $4.90 to $4.50?
3. What is Hanson's most profitable product?

CASE 18–3. ATHERTON COMPANY

Early in January, 1975, the sales manager and the controller of the Atherton Company met for the purpose of preparing a joint pricing recommendation for Item 345. After the president approved their recommendation, the price would be announced in letters to retail customers. In accordance with company and industry practice, announced prices were adhered to for the year unless radical changes in market conditions occurred.

The Atherton Company was the largest company in its segment of the textile industry; its 1974 sales had exceeded $12 million. Company salespersons were on a straight salary basis, and each salesperson sold the full line. Most of Atherton's competitors were small. Usually they waited for the Atherton Company to announce prices before mailing out their own price lists.

Item 345, an expensive yet competitive fabric, was the sole product of a department whose facilities could not be utilized on other items in the product line. In January 1973, the Atherton Company had raised its price from $3 to $4 a yard. This had been done to bring the profit per yard on Item 345 up to that of other products in the line. Although the company was in a strong position financially, it would require considerable capital in the next few years to finance a recently approved long-term

Exhibit 1

ITEM 345, PRICES AND PRODUCTION, 1969–74

| | Volume of Production (yards) | | Price | |
Year	Industry Total	Atherton	Charged by Most Competitors	Atherton Company
1969	610,000	213,000	$4.00	$4.00
1970	575,000	200,000	4.00	4.00
1971	430,000	150,000	3.00	3.00
1972	475,000	165,000	3.00	3.00
1973	500,000	150,000	3.00	4.00
1974	625,000	125,000	3.00	4.00

modernization and expansion program. The 1973 pricing decision had been one of several changes advocated by the directors in an attempt to strengthen the company's working capital position so as to insure that adequate funds would be available for this program.

Competitors of the Atherton Company had held their prices on products similar to Item 345 at $3 during 1973 and 1974. The industry and Atherton Company volume for Item 345 for the years 1969–74, as estimated by the sales manager, is shown in Exhibit 1. As shown by this exhibit, the Atherton Company had lost a significant portion of its former market position. In the sales manager's opinion, a reasonable forecast of industry volume for 1975 was 700,000 yards. He was certain that the company could sell 25 percent of the 1975 industry total if it adopted the $3 price. He feared a further volume decline if it did not meet the competitive price. As many consumers were convinced of the superiority of the Atherton product, the sales manager reasoned that sales of Item 345 would probably not fall below 75,000 yards, even at a $4 price.

During the pricing discussions, the controller and sales manager had considered two other aspects of the problem. The controller was concerned about the possibility that competitors would reduce their prices below $3 if the Atherton Company announced a $3 price for Item 345. The sales manager was confident that competitors would not go below $3 because they all had higher costs and several of them were in tight financial straits. He believed that action taken on Item 345 would not have any substantial repercussions on other items in the line.

The controller prepared estimated costs of Item 345 at various volumes of production (Exhibit 2). These estimated costs reflected current labor

Exhibit 2

ESTIMATED COST PER YARD OF ITEM 345 AT VARIOUS VOLUMES
OF PRODUCTION

	75,000	100,000	125,000	150,000	175,000	200,000
Direct labor	$ .800	$ .780	$ .760	$ .740	$ .760	$ .800
Material	.400	.400	.400	.400	.400	.400
Material spoilage	.040	.040	.038	.038	.038	.040
Department expense:						
Direct*	.120	.112	.100	.100	.100	.100
Indirect†	.800	.600	.480	.400	.343	.300
General overhead‡	.240	.234	.228	.222	.228	.240
Factory cost	$2.400	$2.166	$2.006	$1.900	$1.869	$1.880
Selling and administrative						
expense§	1.560	1.408	1.304	1.236	1.215	1.222
Total Cost	$3.960	$3.574	$3.310	$3.136	$3.084	$3.102

* Indirect labor, supplies, repairs, power, etc.
† Depreciation, supervision, etc.
‡ 30 percent of direct labor.
§ 65 percent of factory cost.

and material costs. They were based on past experience except for the estimates of 75,000 and 100,000 yards. The company had produced more than 100,000 yards in each of the last ten years, and earlier experience was not applicable because of equipment changes and increases in labor productivity.

Questions

1. How, if at all, did the company's financial condition relate to the pricing decision?
2. Should $3 or $4 have been recommended? (Assume no intermediate prices are being considered.)
3. What information not in the case would you like to have in making this pricing decision? (Do not let the lack of information prevent your answering Question 2!)

CASE 18–4. LIQUID CHEMICAL COMPANY

The Liquid Chemical Company manufactured and sold a range of high-grade products throughout Great Britain. Many of these products required careful packing, and the company had always made a feature of the special properties of the containers used. They had a special patented lining, made from a material known as GHL, and the firm operated a department especially to maintain its containers in good condition and to make new ones to replace those that were past repair.

Mr. Walsh, the general manager, had for some time suspected that the firm might save money, and get equally good service, by buying its containers from an outside source. After careful inquiries, he approached a firm specializing in container production, Packages, Ltd., and asked for a quotation from it. At the same time he asked Mr. Dyer, his chief accountant, to let him have an up-to-date statement of the cost of operating the container department.

Within a few days, the quotation from Packages, Ltd., came in. The firm was prepared to supply all the new containers required—at that time running at the rate of 3,000 a year—for £12,500[1] a year, the contract to run for a guaranteed term of five years and thereafter to be renewable from year to year. If the required number of containers increased, the contract price would be increased proportionally. Additionally, and irrespective of whether the above contract was concluded or not, Packages, Ltd., undertook to carry out purely maintenance work on containers, short of replacement, for a sum of £3,750 a year, on the same contract terms.

Mr. Walsh compared these figures with the cost figures prepared by Mr. Dyer, covering a year's operations of the container department of the Liquid Chemical Company, which were as follows:

	£	£
Materials.		7,000
Labour.		5,000
Department overheads:		
Manager's salary.	800 ✓	
Rent.	450	
Depreciation of machinery.	1,500	
Maintenance of machinery.	360 ✓	
Other expenses.	1,575 ✓	
		4,685
		16,685
Proportion of general administrative overheads.		2,250
Total Cost of Department for Year.		18,935

---

[1] At the time of this case, one British pound (£) was worth about $2.35.

Walsh's conclusion was that no time should be lost in closing the department and in entering into the contracts offered by Packages, Ltd. However, he felt bound to give the manager of the department, Mr. Duffy, an opportunity to question this conclusion before he acted on it. He therefore called him in and put the facts before him, at the same time making it clear that Duffy's own position was not in jeopardy; for even if his department were closed, there was another managerial position shortly becoming vacant to which he could be moved without loss of pay or prospects.

Mr. Duffy looked thoughtful and asked for time to think the matter over. The next morning, he asked to speak to Mr. Walsh again, and said he thought there were a number of considerations that ought to be borne in mind before his department was closed. "For instance," he said, "what will you do with the machinery? It cost £12,000 four years ago, but you'd be lucky if you got £2,000 for it now, even though it's good for another four years at least. And then there's the stock of GHL (a special chemical) we bought a year ago. That cost us £10,000, and at the rate we're using it now, it'll last us another four years or so. We used up about one fifth of it last year. Dyer's figure of £7,000 for materials probably includes about £2,000 for GHL. But it'll be tricky stuff to handle if we don't use it up. We bought it for £50 a ton, and you couldn't buy it today for less than £60. But you wouldn't have more than £40 a ton left if you sold it, after you'd covered all the handling expenses."

Walsh thought that Dyer ought to be present during this discussion. He called him in and put Duffy's points to him. "I don't much like all this conjecture," Dyer said. "I think my figures are pretty conclusive. Besides, if we are going to have all this talk about 'what will happen if,' don't forget the problem of space we're faced with. We're paying £850 a year in rent for a warehouse a couple of miles away. If we closed Duffy's department, we'd have all the warehouse space we need without renting."

"That's a good point," said Walsh. "Though I must say, I'm a bit worried about the workers if we close the department. I don't think we can find room for any of them elsewhere in the firm. I could see whether Packages can take any of them. But some of them are getting on. There's Walters and Hines, for example. They've been with us since they left school 40 years ago. I'd feel bound to give them a small pension—£150 a year each, say."

Duffy showed some relief at this. "But I still don't like Dyer's figures," he said. "What about this £2,250 for general administrative overheads? You surely don't expect to sack anyone in the general office if I'm closed, do you?" "Probably not," said Dyer, "but someone has to pay for these costs. We can't ignore them when we look at an individual department, because if we do that with each department in turn, we shall finish up by convincing ourselves that directors, accountants, typists, stationery, and the like don't have to be paid for. And they do, believe me."

"Well, I think we've thrashed this out pretty fully," said Walsh, "but I've been turning over in my mind the possibility of perhaps keeping on the maintenance work ourselves. What are your views on that, Duffy?"

"I don't know," said Duffy, "but it's worth looking into. We shouldn't need any machinery for that, and I could hand the supervision over to a foreman. You'd save £300 a year there, say. You'd only need about one fifth of the workers, but you could keep on the oldest. You wouldn't save any space, so I suppose the rent would be the same. I shouldn't think the other expenses would be more than £650 a year." "What about materials?" asked Walsh. "We use about 10 percent of the total on maintenance," Duffy replied.

"Well, I've told Packages, Ltd., that I'd let them know my decision within a week," said Walsh. "I'll let you know what I decide to do before I write to them."

Questions

1. Assuming no additional information can be readily obtained, what action should be taken?
2. What, if any, additional information do you think is necessary for a sound decision?

CASE 18–5. MARTALL BLANKET COMPANY

In the spring of 1971, the Martall Blanket Company was negotiating a large contract for blankets with the U.S. Navy. A question arose as to the method that the company should use in estimating the price that it would ask for these blankets.

In January 1971, the production manager prepared an estimate of production for the 1971–72 season. This estimate, shown in Exhibit 1, was

Exhibit 1

PRODUCTION ESTIMATE 1971–72

Style	Size	Quantity
Ashmont	72 × 90	12,000
Velona	72 × 90	26,000
Fairfax	72 × 90	22,000
Total domestic		60,000
Army	66 × 84	75,000
Navy	66 × 90	25,000
Total		160,000

made on the assumption that the mill would be operated at three-shift capacity. There was general agreement in the company that demand was strong enough to warrant capacity operations for the foreseeable future. Production facilities could be used to make any of the blankets shown on Exhibit 1 interchangeably.

The production estimate was sent to the cost department, which prepared cost and selling price estimates for each blanket appearing thereon. Raw material prices were obtained by averaging the prices of material on hand and the prices of expected purchases for the period of the budget. Standard costs for labor, factory expense, and processing materials were added to raw material costs so as to arrive at a total manufacturing cost per blanket. These standard costs had been estimated in 1968 but had been corrected subsequently for actual cost experience through ratios applied to labor, factory expense, and processing materials. Selling, advertising, administrative, and interest charges were added at $24 per loom.[1] (At $24 a loom it was possible to absorb these charges at 85 percent of three-shift capacity.)

Profit was also computed on a similar loom basis at $60 a loom. This $60 rate was set so as to return to the blanket division $162,000 profit for the year at three-shift operations. This was considered a "reasonable return" on investment. Thus the cost and pricing sheet submitted by the cost department, Exhibit 2, furnished the prices at which the various types of blankets would have to be sold in order to realize the budgeted total profit.

The Units per Loom column in Exhibit 2 showed the number of blankets that could be produced on one loom running for 40 hours (one shift per week).

The vice president in charge of government contracts questioned the selling price that the cost department had calculated for Navy blankets. He pointed out that at this price, profit on Navy blankets would be 13.5 percent of cost, whereas the profit on Army blankets would amount to only 12.3 percent of cost. Furthermore, the profit margin on Navy blankets was higher, both in absolute terms and as a percentage of cost, than the profit on any of the domestic blankets. The Army contract had already been negotiated at $7.83 per blanket, and the vice president knew that the Navy would be most reluctant to pay a price that was out of line with the price the Army paid. The company gave the government negotiators full access to all its cost information.

The vice president realized that the difference in profit margins arose because of the manner in which selling and administrative cost and profit were allocated. He asked the controller either to provide an adequate

---

[1] As a measure of output, a "loom" meant the number of blankets that could be produced on one loom running for 40 hours.

Exhibit 2

COMPUTATIONS OF COSTS AND SELLING PRICES FOR 1971-72

| Style | Size (inches) | Weight (pounds) | Raw Material | Labor | Expense | Processing Materials | Total Mfg. Cost | Units per Loom | Selling Admin. Interest, Adv. | | Total Cost Sold | Profit per Loom | Profit per Blanket | Net Selling Price | Invoice Selling Price | Retail Price 40% |
									Per Loom	Per Blanket						
Ashmont	72 × 90	3.75	$4.12	$0.93	$0.66	$0.58	$6.29	64	$24.00	$0.38	$6.67	$60.00	$0.94	$7.61	$7.76	$12.94
Velona	72 × 90	4.00	4.39	0.94	0.66	0.58	6.57	60	24.00	0.40	6.97	60.00	1.00	7.97	8.13	13.55
Fairfax	72 × 90	5.00	5.43	1.03	0.74	0.59	7.79	56	24.00	0.43	8.22	60.00	1.07	9.29	9.48	15.80
Army	66 × 84	3.75	4.83	0.99	0.63	0.18	6.63	70	24.00	0.34	6.97	60.00	0.86	7.83		
Navy	66 × 90	4.25	5.85	1.08	0.64	0.19	7.76	54	24.00	0.44	8.20	60.00	1.11	9.31		

justification of the price computed in Exhibit 2 or to recalculate the price. The controller replied with a memorandum, which included the following:

The problem of overhead (used hereafter to include selling, administrative, advertising, and interest charges) and profit distribution is probably the most important source of possible error. While the loom basis of allocation of these items is arbitrary in certain respects and may therefore be misleading, it is certainly not without logical foundation.

The fair basis of allocating profit and overhead apparently depends upon the market conditions existing at the time. If the division can produce more than can be sold, profit and overhead may well be distributed on a per-blanket basis; that is, we could add a certain percent to each type of blanket for overhead and profit, as you suggested. On the other hand, if the mill is operating at capacity in the sense that total capacity can be sold, the distribution on some measure of capacity, such as loom hours, will provide the fair answer, for such a method takes into account the time required to produce each blanket.

In allocating overhead and profit on a loom basis we have assumed that total blanket division capacity would be completely sold out for the coming fiscal year. For this reason I feel that the blanket prices previously submitted to you are justified.

Questions

1. Assume that Martall was considering the possibility of making Blanket X, on which the following information was available. (Items correspond to column headings in Exhibit 2.)

Size............	72 × 90 inches	Expense................	$0.59
Weight.........	3.75 lbs.	Processing materials.......	$0.57
Raw material.....	$4.38	Total manufacturing cost...	$6.37
Labor...........	$0.83	Units per loom..........	84

    Complete the columns in Exhibit 2 for Blanket X, including the retail price necessary to give the desired markup.
2. At what price should Navy blankets be sold?
3. How should the vice president explain this price in his contract negotiations?

CASE 18–6.　SHERMAN MOTOR COMPANY[1]

The Sherman Motor Company manufactured two specialized models of lightweight trucks in a single plant. Manufacturing operations were grouped into four departments: metal stamping, engine assembly, model

---

[1] Adapted from an example used by Robert Dorfman in "Mathematical or 'Linear' Programming: A Nonmathematical Exposition," *American Economic Review*, December, 1953.

101 assembly, and model 102 assembly. Monthly production capacity in each department was limited as follows, assuming that each department devoted full time to the model in question:

Department	—Monthly Capacity—	
	Model 101	Model 102
Metal stamping......................	2,500	3,500
Engine assembly.....................	3,333	1,667
Model 101 assembly..................	2,250	...
Model 102 assembly..................	...	1,500

That is, the capacity of the metal stamping department was sufficient to produce stampings for either 2,500 model 101 trucks or 3,500 model 102 trucks per month if it devoted full time to either model. It could also produce stampings for both models with a corresponding reduction in the potential output of each. Since each model 102 truck required five-sevenths as much of the capacity of the department as one model 101 truck, for every seven model 102 trucks produced it would be necessary to subtract five from the capacity remaining for model 101.

Exhibit 1

SHERMAN MOTOR COMPANY

Diagram Showing Production Possibilities

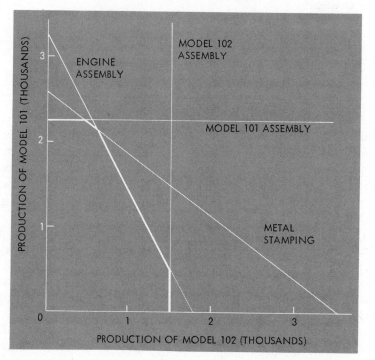

If, for example, 1,400 model 102 trucks were produced, there would be sufficient stamping capacity available for $2,500 - (\frac{5}{7}) \ (1,400) = 1,500$ model 101 trucks. Thus, the capacity restrictions in the four departments could be represented by the straight lines shown in Exhibit 1. Any production combination within the area bounded by the heavy portion of the lines was feasible from a capacity standpoint.

The prices to dealers of the two models, F.O.B. the Sherman plant, were $2,100 for model 101 and $2,000 for model 102. Sherman followed the price leadership of one of the larger manufacturers in the industry.

As a result of a sellers' market, Sherman currently was able to sell as many trucks as it could produce. The production schedules it had followed during the first six months of the year resulted in a monthly out-

Exhibit 2

SHERMAN MOTOR COMPANY

Standard Costs of Two Truck Models

	Model 101		Model 102	
Direct materials................		$1,200		$1,000
Direct labor:				
Metal stamping..............	$ 40		$ 30	
Engine assembly.............	60		120	
Final assembly..............	100	200	75	225
Overhead*				
Metal stamping..............	$216		$169	
Engine assembly.............	130		251	
Final assembly..............	445	791	175	595
Total....................		$2,191		$1,820

* See Exhibit 3.

put of 333 model 101 trucks and 1,500 model 102 trucks. At this level of production, both the model 102 assembly and the engine assembly departments were operating at capacity, but the metal stamping department was operating at only 56.2% of capacity and the model 101 assembly department was at only 14.8%. Standard costs at this level of production are given in Exhibit 2, and further details on overhead costs are given in Exhibit 3.

At a monthly planning session of the company's executives in July, dissatisfaction was expressed with the company's profit performance as reported in the six-month income statement just prepared (see Exhibit 4). The sales manager pointed out that it was impossible to sell the model 101 truck to yield a profit and suggested that it be dropped from the line in order to improve over-all profitability.

The controller objected to this suggestion. "The real trouble, Dick, is that we are trying to absorb the entire fixed overhead of the model

Exhibit 3

SHERMAN MOTOR COMPANY

Overhead Budget

Department	Total Overhead per Month*	Fixed Overhead per Month†	Variable Overhead per Unit Model 101	Variable Overhead per Unit Model 102
Metal stamping...............	$ 325,000	$135,000	$120	$100
Engine assembly..............	420,000	85,000	105	200
Model 101 assembly..........	148,000	90,000	175	. . .
Model 102 assembly..........	262,000	75,000	. . .	125
	$1,155,000	$385,000	$400	$425

* Based on planned production rate of 333 model 101 trucks and 1,500 model 102 trucks per month.
† Fixed overhead was distributed to models in proportion to degree of capacity utilization.

101 assembly department with only a small number of units of production. Actually these units are making a contribution to overhead, even though it's not adequate to cover fixed costs, and we'd be worse off without them. In fact, it seems to me quite possible that we'd be better off by *increasing* production of model 101 trucks, cutting back if necessary on model 102 production."

The production manager pointed out that there was another way in which output of model 101 trucks could be stepped up, which would not require a cutback in model 102 production. This would be through purchase of engines from an outside supplier, thus relieving the present capacity problem in the engine assembly department. If this course of action were followed, Sherman would probably furnish the supplier with the necessary materials but would reimburse him for his labor and overhead.

At this point the president entered the discussion. He asked the controller, the sales manager, and the production manager to get together to consider the two questions raised by their comments and to report their recommendations to him the next day. The two questions were:

Exhibit 4

SHERMAN MOTOR COMPANY

Income Statement
For Six Months Ending June 30

(dollar figures in thousands)

Net sales..	$21,950
Cost of goods sold..............................	20,683
Gross margin....................................	$ 1,267
Selling, administrative, and general expense.............	1,051
Income before taxes.............................	$ 216
Taxes on income................................	115
Net Income....................................	$ 101

(1) Assuming no change in present capacity and demand, what would be the most profitable product mix? (2) What was the maximum labor and overhead charge Sherman could afford to pay for engines if it purchased them from an outside supplier?

Question

What would be your reply to the questions raised by the president?

CHAPTER 19

CAPITAL INVESTMENT DECISIONS

In Chapter 18 we discussed those types of alternative choice problems which involved the use of differential costs and differential revenues. In Chapter 19 we extend the discussion to problems that involve differential *investments*. These are problems in which the proposal is to invest funds, that is, capital, at the present time in the expectation of earning a return on this money over some future period. Such problems are called *capital investment problems*. They are also called *capital budgeting problems* because a company's capital budget is a list of the investment projects which it has decided to carry out. In these problems, the only new element is the consideration of the differential investment; cost and/or revenues are treated in the same manner as already discussed in Chapter 18.

The analysis of capital investment problems is complicated. It is important that these problems be solved correctly because they often involve large sums of money and because they may commit or "lock in" the business to a certain course of action over a considerable period in the future.

WHAT IS PRESENT VALUE?

The analysis in this chapter is built around a concept called *present value*, which we shall define shortly. Many people have great difficulty in understanding this concept. The reason for this difficulty may stem from a failure to appreciate that there is a fundamental difference between the operation of a business and the conduct of one's personal affairs.

Children are taught that it is a good thing to put money into a piggybank; their parents congratulate them when the bank is finally opened and the accumulated coins are counted out. Thus, parents teach children that it is better to have money in the future than to spend it today. Stated more formally, parents teach that the value of money today is *less than* its value at some future time.

People in business think differently, however. They expect that money that they invest today will increase in amount as time passes because they expect to earn a profit on that investment. It follows that an amount of money that is available for investment today is more valuable to the manager than an equal amount of money that will not be available until some time in the future. This is because the money available today can be invested to earn still more money, whereas money that has not yet been received obviously cannot be invested today. To the manager, therefore, the value of money today is *more than* its value at some future time.

To make this idea more concrete, consider the Able Company. Its management expects that the company can earn a return of 10 percent per year on funds that are invested in the company's assets. (Incidentally, the rate of return is invariably expressed on a *per annum* basis; that is, the statement "return of 10 percent" is invariably taken to mean "10 percent per year.") If Able Company invested $100 today for a year, at an anticipated return of 10 percent, it would expect to have $110 at the end of the year. Thus $100 invested today is expected to have a *future value* of $110 a year from today. Conversely, it can be said that the expectation of having $110 a year from today has a *present value* of $100 if funds are expected to earn 10 percent; that is, the value of $110 to be received a year from today is equal to the value of $100 today.

Suppose Able Company expects to receive $100 a year from today. What is the present value of that amount? In a following section, the technique for answering this question is described, but for now, the answer simply is stated: the present value of $100 to be received a year from now is $90.91 if the business expects to earn 10 percent on its investments. That this *is* the correct answer can easily be demonstrated. If $90.91 is invested today for a year at 10 percent, it will earn 10 percent of $90.91, or $9.09, which added to the $90.91 makes $100. This exercise leads to a definition of present value:

> *The present value of an amount that is expected to be received at a specified time in the future is the amount which, if invested today at a designated rate of return, would cumulate to the specified amount.*

Finding Present Values

It is easy to demonstrate, as was done above, that the present value of $100 to be received one year from now at a rate of return of 10 percent is $90.91. For periods that are longer than a year, the arithmetic is more complicated because of the force of compound interest. Thus, we can demonstrate that at a 10 percent rate of return, $100 expected to be received two years from today has a present value of $82.64 because in the first year 10 percent of this amount, or $8.26, will be earned, bringing the total to $90.90, and in the second year 10 percent of $90.90, or $9.09, will be earned, bringing the total to $100. (The amount does not come exactly to $100 because the calculations were not carried to enough decimal places.)

The formula for calculating the present value of a payment of $1 to be received n years hence at an interest rate i is:

$$\frac{1}{(1 + i)^n}$$

We shall not use the formula directly, however, because it is more convenient to use a table of present values computed from it.[1] Such a table, for the present value of $1, is Table A, which appears on page 815. The present value amounts used in the above examples were taken from Table A. The number opposite Year 1 in the 10 percent column is $0.909. Since this is the present value of $1, to be received a year from now, the present value of $100 is 100 times this, or $90.90.

Inspection of Table A will reveal two fundamental points about present value:

1. Present value decreases as the number of years in the future in which the payment is to be received increases.
2. Present value decreases as the rate of return increases.

Application to Investment Decisions

When a company purchases a machine, it makes an *investment*; that is, it commits funds today in the expectation of earning a return on those funds over some future period. Such an investment is similar to that made by a bank when it loans money. The essential characteristic of both types of transactions is that funds are committed today in the expectation of earning a return in the future. In the case of the bank loan, the future return is in the form of interest plus repayment of the principal. In the case of the machine, the future return is in the form of earnings generated by profitable operation of the machine. We shall designate such earnings as the *cash inflows*. An investment is thus the purchase of a future stream of expected cash inflows.

When a company is considering whether or not to purchase a new machine, the essential question that it seeks to answer is whether the

---

[1] Also, computer programs and minicalculators are available that handle the calculations automatically.

future cash inflows are likely to be large enough to warrant making the investment. The problems discussed in this chapter all involve this general question: It is proposed that a certain amount be invested now in the expectation that a return will be earned on the investment in future years. Is the amount of anticipated future cash inflows large enough to justify investing these funds in the proposal? Illustrative of these problems are the following:

1. *Replacement.* Shall we replace existing equipment with more efficient equipment? The future expected cash inflows on this investment are the cost savings resulting from lower operating costs, or the profits from additional volume produced by the new equipment, or both.
2. *Expansion.* Shall we build or otherwise acquire a new plant? The future expected cash inflows on this investment are the profits from the products produced in the new plant.
3. *Cost reduction.* Shall we buy equipment to perform an operation now done manually, that is, shall we spend money in order to save money? The expected future cash inflows on this investment are savings resulting from lower operating costs.
4. *Choice of equipment.* Which of several proposed items of equipment shall we purchase for a given purpose? The choice often turns on which item is expected to give the largest return on the investment made in it.
5. *Buy or lease.* Having decided that we need a building or a piece of equipment, should we lease it or should we buy it? The choice turns on whether or not the investment required to purchase the asset will earn an adequate return because of the savings that will result from avoiding the lease payments.
6. *New product.* Should a new product be added to the line? The choice turns on whether the expected cash inflows from the sale of the new product are large enough to warrant the investment in equipment, working capital, and the costs required to make and introduce the product.

Note that all these problems involve two quite dissimilar types of amounts. First, there is the investment, which is usually made in a lump sum at the beginning of the project. Although not literally made "today," it is made at a specific point in time which for analytical purposes is called "today," or *Time Zero.* Second, there is a stream of cash inflows, which it is anticipated will result from this investment, usually over a period of years.

These two types of amounts cannot be compared directly with one another because they occur at different points in time. In order to make a valid comparison, we must bring the amounts involved to equivalent values at the same point in time.

The most convenient point is to calculate the values at Time Zero. In order to do this, we need not adjust the amount of the investment since it is already stated at its Time Zero or present value. We need only to convert the stream of future cash inflows to their present-value equivalents, and we can then compare them directly with the amount of the investment. To do this, we multiply the cash inflow for each year by the present value of $1 for that year at the appropriate rate of return. This process is called *discounting* the cash inflows. The rate at which the cash inflows are discounted is called the *required rate of return*.

The difference between the present value of the cash inflows and the amount of investment is called the net present value.

EXAMPLE: A proposed investment of $1,000 is expected to produce a cash inflow of $600 per year for each of the next two years. The assumed rate of return is 10 percent. The present value of the cash inflows can be compared with the present value of the investment as follows:

	Year	Amount	Present Value of $1 @ 10%	Total Present Value
Investment.............	0	$1,000	1.000	$1,000
Cash inflow............	1	600	0.909	$ 545
	2	600	0.826	496
		Present value of cash inflows		$1,041
		Net present value		$ 41

After the amount of cash inflow has been made comparable with the amount of investment, the basic decision rule is:

A proposed investment is acceptable if the present value of its future expected net cash inflows equals or exceeds the amount of investment; i.e., if its net present value is equal to or greater than zero.

This is a general rule, and some qualifications to it will be discussed in a later section. To apply it, the approach is as follows:

1. Estimate the amount of investment.
2. Estimate the amount of cash inflow in each future year.
3. Find the present value of these cash inflows. This is done by discounting the cash inflow amounts at the required rate of return.
4. Subtract the amount of investment from the present value of the inflows to determine the net present value.

Return on Investment

So far, we have shown how the present value of amounts to be received in the future can be calculated if cash inflows and the rate of return are given. It is useful to look at the situation from another viewpoint: How can the rate of return be calculated when the investment and the cash inflows are given?

Consider the familiar situation of a bank loan. When a bank lends $1,000 and receives interest payments of $80 at the end of each year for five years, with the $1,000 loan being repaid at the end of the fifth year, the bank correctly is said to earn a return of 8 percent on its investment of $1,000. Note that the return percentage is always expressed on an annual basis and that it is found by dividing the annual return by the amount of the investment outstanding during the year. In this case, the amount of loan outstanding each year was $1,000 and the return was $80 in each year, so the rate of return was $80 ÷ $1,000, or 8 percent.

Illustration 19–1

DEMONSTRATION OF MEANING OF RETURN ON INVESTMENT

Year	Cash Inflow (a)	Return at 8% on Investment Outstanding (b)	Balance, to Apply against Investment (c) = (a − b)	Investment Outstanding End of Year (d)
0	$...	$...	$...	$1,000
1	250	80	170	830
2	250	66	184	646
3	250	52	198	448
4	250	36	214	234
5	250	19	231	3*

* Arises from rounding.

If, however, a bank lends $1,000 and is repaid $250 at the end of each year for five years, the problem of finding the return becomes more complicated. In this situation, only part of the $250 annual cash inflow represents the return, and the remainder is a repayment of the principal. It turns out that this loan also has a return of 8 percent, in the same sense as the loan described in the preceding paragraph: namely, the $250 annual payments will repay the loan itself and in addition will provide a return of 8 percent of the *amount of principal still outstanding each year*. The fact that the return is 8 percent is demonstrated in Illustration 19–1. Of the $250 repaid in the first year, $80, or 8 percent of the $1,000 then outstanding, is the return, and the remainder, or $170, reduces the investment, or principal, making it $830. In the second year, $66 is a return of 8 percent on the $830 of investment then outstanding, and the remainder, $184, reduces the investment to $646; and so on. (The residual of $3, rather than $0, at the end of the fifth year arises from the fact that the true return is slightly less than 8.000 percent.)

It can be seen from the above examples that when an investment involves annual interest payments with the full amount of the investment being repaid at its termination date, the computation of the return is simple and direct; but when the annual payments combine both principal and interest, the computation is more complicated. Some business problems are of the simple type. For example, if a business buys land for $1,000, rents it for $80 a year for five years, and then sells it for $1,000 at the end of five years, the return is 8 percent. Many business investment decisions, on the other hand, relate to depreciable assets, whose characteristic is that they have no, or very little, resale value at the end of their useful life. The cash inflows from these investments must therefore be large enough for the investor both to recoup the investment itself during its life and also to permit him to earn a satisfactory return on the amount not yet recouped, just as in the situation shown in Illustration 19–1.

Stream of Cash Inflows

The cash inflows on most business investments are a series of amounts received over several future years. The present value of the stream of cash inflows can be found by discounting each year's cash inflow by the appropriate factor from Table A.

EXAMPLE: Is a proposed investment of $1,000 with expected cash inflow of $250 a year for five years acceptable if the required rate of return is 8 percent? The present value of the cash inflows can be computed as follows:

Year	Cash Inflow (a)	Present Value of $1 at 8% (from Table A) (b)	Present Value (a × b)
First..............................	$250	0.926	$232
Second..........................	250	0.857	214
Third.............................	250	0.794	198
Fourth...........................	250	0.735	184
Fifth..............................	250	0.681	170
Total Present Value............			$998[2]

The total present value of the cash inflows is slightly less than $1,000, which means that the rate of return on the proposed investment would be slightly less than 8 percent; therefore, the proposal is not acceptable.

---

[2] In order to illustrate certain points, the numbers given in this and certain other examples have been structured so that the amount of investment is almost the same as the present value of cash inflows. Since the numbers are estimates, with an inevitable margin of error, the decision in a real-world problem would not be as clearcut as the examples indicate. This point is discussed in a subsequent section.

The above computation using Table A was laborious. Table B (page 816) has, for many problems, a more convenient set of present value amounts than those in Table A. It shows the present value of $1 to be received annually for *each* of the next *n* years in the future. Each number on Table B was obtained simply by cumulating, that is, adding together, the amounts for the corresponding year and all preceding years in the same column on Table A.[3] Table B can be used directly to find the present value of a stream of *equal* cash inflows received annually for any given number of years; therefore it reduces considerably the arithmetic required in problems of the type illustrated in the preceding example. Note that in order to use Table B, the amount of cash inflows must be the same for each year.

> EXAMPLE: Assume the same facts and question as in the preceding example. Table B shows the present value of $1 received *each year* for five years at 8 percent to be $3.993; therefore, the present value of $250 a year for five years is $250 \times \$3.993 = \$998$, which is the same result as that computed in the preceding example.

Although the values in Table B are cumulative from year 1, they can also be used to find the present value of a stream of cash inflows between any two points in time. The procedure is to subtract the value for the year *preceding* the first year of the cash inflow from the value for the last year of the cash inflow.

> EXAMPLE: What is the present value of $1,000 a year to be received in years 6 through 10 if the required rate of return is 8 percent?
> *Solution:*

Time Period	Present Value of $1 per Year at 8%
For 10 years	$6.710
For years 1–5	3.993
Difference (= years 6–10)	$2.717

For $1,000 a year: $1,000 \times 2.717 = \$2,717$

Other Present Value Tables

Tables A and B are constructed on the assumption that cash inflows are received once a year and on the last day of the year. For many problems this is not a realistic assumption because cash in the form of increased revenues or lower costs is likely to flow in throughout the year. Nevertheless, annual tables are customarily used in business investment problems, on the grounds that they are easier to understand

---

[3] Table B is technically known as a table of "Present Value of an Annuity of $1."

than tables constructed on other assumptions, such as monthly or continuous compounding, and that they are good enough considering the inevitable margin of error in the basic estimates.

Annual tables *understate* the present value of earnings if earnings are in fact received throughout the year rather than entirely on the last day of the year. The amount of the understatement can be seen in Illustration 19–2. Tables are available showing the present values of earnings flows

Illustration 19–2

EFFECT OF RAPID RECEIPTS

Approximate Ratio of Present Value of Faster Receipts to Present Value of Annual Receipts at Various Discount Rates

Frequency of Receipt	Discount Rates			
	6%	10%	15%	25%
Semiannually....................	1.01	1.03	1.04	1.06
Monthly.......................	1.03	1.05	1.07	1.11
Continuously...................	1.03	1.05	1.08	1.12

that occur quarterly, monthly, or even continuously, but they are not commonly used. Close results often can be obtained from a table that is based on the assumption that the amount is received at the *middle* of the year rather than at the *end* of the year.

Table A and Table B are often used in combination, as illustrated in the next example, which also relates the computation discussed here to the concept of return on investment discussed at the beginning of this section.

EXAMPLE: Is a proposed investment of $1,000 with annual cash inflows of $80 a year for the next five years with the $1,000 to be repaid at the end of five years acceptable if the required rate of return is 8 percent? *Solution:* As shown by the following calculation, the cash inflows have a present value of $1,000, so the proposal is acceptable:

Year	Payment	8% Discount Factor	Present Value
1–5....................	$80/year	3.993 (Table B)	$ 319
End of 5...............	$1,000	0.681 (Table A)	681
Total present value....			$1,000

ESTIMATING THE VARIABLES

We now turn to a discussion of how to estimate each of the four elements involved in capital investment calculations. These are:

1. The required rate of return;
2. The amount of cash inflow in each year;
3. The economic life, which is the number of years for which cash inflows are anticipated; and
4. The amount of investment.

Required Rate of Return

Two alternative ways of arriving at the required rate of return will be described: (1) trial and error, and (2) cost of capital.

TRIAL AND ERROR. Recall that the higher the required rate of return, the lower the present value of the cash inflows. It follows that the higher the required rate of return, the fewer the investment proposals which will have cash inflows whose present value exceeds the amount of the investment. Thus, if a given rate results in the rejection of many proposed investments that management intuitively feels are acceptable, there is an indication that this rate is too high, and a lower rate is selected. Conversely, if a given rate results in the acceptance of a flood of projects, there is an indication that it is too low. As a starting point in this trial-and-error process, companies often select a rate of return that other companies in the same industry use.

COST OF CAPITAL. In economic theory, the required rate of return should be equal to the company's *cost of capital*, which is the cost of debt capital plus the cost of equity capital, weighted by the relative amount of each in the company's capital structure.

EXAMPLE: Assume a company in which the cost of debt capital (e.g., bonds) is 4 percent and the cost of equity capital (e.g., common stock) is 15 percent, and in which 40 percent of the total capital is debt and 60 percent is equity.[4] The cost of capital is calculated as follows:

Type	Capital Cost	Weight	Weighted
Debt (bonds)	4%	0.4	1.6%
Equity (stock)	15	0.6	9.0
Total		1.0	10.6%

Thus, the cost of capital is 10.6 percent or, rounded, 11 percent.

In the above example, the 4 percent used as the cost of debt capital may appear to be low. It is low because it has been adjusted for the income tax effect of debt financing. Since interest on debt is a tax deductible

---

[4] For a more complete description of debt capital and equity capital, see Chapter 9.

expense, each additional dollar of interest expense ultimately costs the company only $0.49 (assuming a tax rate of 51 percent); income taxes are reduced by $0.51 for each additional interest dollar. For reasons to be explained, capital investment calculations should be made on an after-tax basis, so the rate of return should be an aftertax rate.

The difficulty with the cost-of-capital approach is that, although the cost of debt capital is usually known within narrow limits, the cost of equity capital is difficult to estimate realistically.[5] Presumably, the rate of return that investors expect, which is the cost of equity capital, is reflected in the market price of the company's stock, but the market price is also influenced by such other factors as general conditions of the economy, investors' estimate of the company's future earnings, and dividend policy. Techniques for isolating the cost of equity capital from these other factors are complicated; moreover, they do not usually give accurate results. For this reason, the cost-of-capital approach is not widely used in practice.

SELECTION OF A RATE. Most companies use a judgmental approach in establishing the required rate of return. Either they experiment with various rates, by the trial-and-error method described above, or they judgmentally settle upon a rate of 10 percent, 15 percent, or 20 percent because they feel that elaborate calculations are likely to be fruitless. In the examples in this book, a required rate of return of 10 percent is usually used. This seems to be a widely used rate in industrial companies, and it is the rate prescribed by the federal government for use in the analysis of proposed government investments. Few industrial companies would use a lower rate than 10 percent. Higher rates are used in certain industries in which profit opportunities are unusually good, and also by most firms in periods when future inflation rates are expected to be high.

ALLOWANCE FOR RISK. The required rate of return is higher than the general level of interest rates, that is, the rates at which banks and other financial institutions are willing to loan money.[6] The reason is that capital investments made by a business have a higher degree of risk and uncertainty than do bank loans. When a bank loans money, it has a high expectation of receiving a series of cash inflows that will equal the principal plus the stated amount of interest. The return from most business capital investment projects is much less certain because both the

---

[5] For methods of deriving such estimates, see Hunt, Williams, and Donaldson, *Basic Business Finance: Text and Cases* (4th ed.; Homewood, Ill.: Richard D. Irwin, Inc., 1970), or J. Fred Weston and Eugene F. Brigham, *Managerial Finance* (Fourth edition); Hillsdale, Ill., Holt, Rinehart and Winston, 1972, Chapters 10 and 11.

[6] Under unusual economic conditions, bank interest rates do exceed the required rate of return, but such situations are temporary.

economic life of the project and the cash inflow in each year of its life can be, at best, only roughly estimated.

The required rate of return that a company selects by the techniques described above applies to investment proposals of *average* risk. For essentially the same reason that the required rate of return for capital investment projects in general is higher than interest rates on bank loans, the return expected on an individual investment project of greater-than-average risk and uncertainty should be higher than the average rate of return on all projects in the company. Conceptually, it would be possible to use a higher-than-average required rate of return in the calculation of the net present value of projects of higher-than-average risk and uncertainty, but in practice many companies do not do this. Instead, they either introduce an element of conservatism into the calculations by deliberately shortening the estimate of economic life or by lowering the estimate of cash inflows, or they take the risk characteristics into account as a judgmental matter when the final decision on the project is made. A few companies use mathematical techniques that are designed to incorporate an allowance for uncertainty.[7]

Cash Inflow

The earnings from an investment are essentially the additional *cash* that is estimated to flow in as a consequence of making the investment as compared with what the company's cash inflow would be if it did not make the investment. The *differential* concept emphasized in Chapters 17 and 18 is therefore equally applicable here, and the discussion in those chapters should carefully be kept in mind in estimating cash inflows for the type of problem now being considered. In particular, recall that the focus is on cash inflows; accounting numbers derived from the accrual concept or including the allocation of overhead costs are not necessarily relevant.

Consider, for example, a proposal to replace an existing machine with a better machine. What are the cash inflows associated with this proposed investment? We note first that the existing machine must still be usable, for if it can no longer perform its function, there is no alternative and hence no analytical problem; it *must* be replaced. The comparison, therefore, is between (1) continuing to use the existing machine (the base

---

[7] These include (a) sensitivity analysis, which shows the change in the present value of cash inflows that results from systematically varying each of the main elements of the earnings calculations, and (b) calculation of a large number of cash inflow estimates, each based on different estimates of the main elements determining the cash inflows, and study of the resulting frequency distribution (i.e., the Monte Carlo technique described in Chapter 18). These techniques are not difficult if a computer is available.

case) and (2) operating the proposed machine (Case 2). The existing machine has certain labor, material, power, repair, maintenance, and other costs associated with its future operation. If the alternative machine is proposed as a means of reducing costs, there will be different, lower costs associated with its use. The difference between these two amounts of cost is the cash inflow anticipated if the new machine is acquired. These cash inflows usually are estimated on an annual basis. (Note that in this example, the differential cash inflow is really a reduction in cash outflows.)

If the proposed machine is not a replacement, but instead increases the company's productive capacity, and if the increased output can be sold, the differential income on this increased volume is a cash inflow anticipated from the use of the proposed machine. This differential income is the difference between the added sales revenue and the incremental costs required to produce that sales revenue; these costs usually include direct material, direct labor, direct selling costs, and any other costs that would not be incurred if the increased volume were not manufactured and sold.

If the proposed machine *both* is a replacement *and also* has greater saleable output than the machine it replaces, then the relevant flows are the *sum* of those discussed in the preceding two paragraphs.

Depreciation. *Depreciation on the proposed equipment is not an item of differential cost.* Depreciation is omitted from the calculation of net present value because the procedure itself allows for the recovery of the investment, and to count depreciation as a cost would be taking it into account twice. When we say that an investment of $1,000 which produces a cash inflow of $400 a year for five years has a net present value of $516 at a required rate of return of 10 percent, we mean that the cash inflow is large enough to (1) recover the investment of $1,000, (2) earn 10 percent on the amount of investment outstanding, and (3) earn $516 in addition. The recovery of investment is equivalent to the sum of the annual depreciation charges that are made in the accounting records; therefore it would be incorrect to include a separate item for depreciation in calculating cash inflow.

Depreciation on the existing equipment is likewise not relevant because the book value of existing equipment represents a sunk cost. For the reason explained in Chapter 18, sunk costs should be disregarded.

Income Tax Impact. For alternative choice problems in which no investment is involved, aftertax income is 49 percent of pretax income, assuming a tax rate of 51 percent. Thus, if a proposed cost reduction method is estimated to save $10,000 a year pretax, it will save $4,900 a year aftertax. Although $4,900 is obviously not as welcome to the shareholders as $10,000 would be, the proposed cost reduction method would increase income, and, in the absence of arguments to the contrary, the decision should be made to adopt it. This is the case with *all* the alternative choice problems discussed in Chapter 18.

When depreciable assets are involved in a proposal, however, the situation is quite different. In proposals of this type, *there is no simple relationship between pretax cash inflow and aftertax cash inflow* primarily because depreciation is not a factor in estimates of operating cash flows, whereas depreciation *is* an expense that is taken into account in calculating taxable income. Depreciation offsets part of what would otherwise be additional taxable income and is therefore called a *tax shield* in investment calculations. It shields the pretax cash inflow from the full impact of income taxes.

In order to calculate the aftertax cash inflow, therefore, we must take account of the depreciation tax shield. At the same time, we must be careful not to permit the amount of depreciation itself to enter the calculation of cash flows because this would lead to the same double counting that was referred to above.

Since most companies use accelerated depreciation in calculating taxable income, and since accelerated depreciation results in increasing amounts of taxable income, Table B cannot be used in calculating present values because it assumes a level flow each year. It would be possible to compute the aftertax income each year and to find the present value of each annual amount by using Table A. This is a cumbersome process, and to avoid it, Table C (page 817) has been devised. This table shows the present value of a stream of depreciation charges spread over n years assuming use of the sum-of-the-years'-digits method.

The procedure for finding the present value of the aftertax cash inflow is as follows:

1. Multiply the annual cash inflow by the complement of the tax rate (i.e., 1-tax rate) to find the aftertax cash inflow, neglecting depreciation.
2. Multiply this aftertax cash inflow by the appropriate discount amount from Table B, to find its present value.
3. Multiply the depreciable investment by the appropriate amount from Table C to find the present value of the stream of depreciation charges.
4. Multiply this present value by the tax rate to find the present value of the depreciation tax shield.
5. Add the amounts in steps 2 and 4 to find the aftertax present value of the cash inflow.

EXAMPLE: A proposed machine costs $1,000 and has estimated pretax inflows of $320 a year for five years. The required rate of return is 10 percent and the tax rate is 51 percent.

1. Annual aftertax cash inflow = pretax cash inflow ($320) × tax rate complement (49%) = $157
2. Present value of aftertax cash inflows =
   $157 × 3.791 (Table B)   = $595
3. Present value of depreciation =
   $1,000 × 0.806 (Table C) = $806
4. Present value of depreciation tax
   tax shield = $806 × .51   =   411
5. Total present value of aftertax
   cash inflows $1,006

The net present value is $1,006 − $1,000, or $6, and the proposal is therefore acceptable.

If the proposed machine is to replace a machine that has not been fully depreciated for tax purposes, then the tax shield is only the *differential* depreciation, that is, the difference between depreciation on the present machine and that on the new machine, because if the new machine is purchased, the old machine will presumably be disposed of, so its depreciation will no longer provide a tax shield to the operating cash flows. In this case, the present value of the tax shield of the remaining depreciation on the old machine must be calculated (usually year by year), and this amount must be subtracted from the present value of the depreciation tax shield on the proposed machine.

TAX EFFECT OF INTEREST. Interest actually paid (as distinguished from imputed interest) is an allowable expense for income tax purposes; therefore, if interest costs will be increased as a result of the investment, it could be argued that interest provides a tax shield similar to depreciation and that its impact should be estimated by the same method as that shown for depreciation, above. Customarily, however, interest is *not* included anywhere in the calculations either of cash inflows or of taxes. This is because the calculation of the required rate of return included an allowance for the tax effect of interest; that is, the estimate of the cost of debt was the aftertax cost of debt, which is approximately ½ of its pretax cost.

In problems where the method of financing is an important part of the proposal, the tax shield provided by interest may appropriately be considered. In these problems, the rate of return that results from the calculation is a return on that part of the investment which was financed by the shareholders' equity, not a return on the total funds committed to the investment.

EXAMPLE: Suppose a company is considering an investment in a parcel of real estate, and intends to finance 70 percent of the investment by a mortgage loan on the property. It may wish to focus attention on the return on its own funds, namely, the remaining 30 percent. In this case, it would be appropriate to include in the calculation both the interest on the mortgage loan and the effect of this interest on taxable income.

Economic Life

The economic life of an investment is the number of years over which cash inflows are expected as a consequence of making the investment. Even though cash inflows may be expected for an indefinitely long period, the economic life is usually set at a specified maximum number of years, such as 10, 15, or 20. This maximum is often shorter than the life that is actually anticipated both because of the uncertainty of cash inflow estimates for distant years and because the present value of cash inflows for distant years is so low that the amount of these cash inflows has no significant effect on the calculation. For example, at a discount rate of 10 percent, a $1 cash inflow in Year 21 has a present value of only 15 cents, and the *total* present value of a $1 cash inflow in *each* of the 30 years from Year 21 through Year 50 is only $1.40.

The end of the period selected for the economic life of a proposed investment is called the *investment horizon*. The term suggests that beyond this time cash inflows are not visible. Economic life can rarely be estimated exactly; nevertheless, it is important that the best possible estimate be made, for the economic life has a significant effect on the calculations.

When a proposed project involves the purchase of equipment, the economic life of the investment corresponds to the estimated service life of the equipment to the user. There is a tendency, when thinking about the life of a machine, to consider primarily its *physical life;* that is, the number of years the machine will provide service before it wears out. The physical life of an automobile, for example, is about 10 years, and that of a brick building, 50 years or more. Although the physical life is an upper limit, in most cases the economic life of an asset is considerably shorter than its physical life. There are several reasons for this. Technological progress makes machinery obsolete. Improvements will almost certainly be made sometime in all machines now in existence, but the question of *which* machines will be improved and *how soon* the improved machines will be on the market is a most difficult one to answer. Unless special information is available, the answer can be little more than an educated guess. Yet it is a guess that must be made, for the investment in a machine will cease to earn a return when it is replaced by an improved machine.

The economic life also ends when the company ceases to make profitable use of the machine. This can happen because the particular operation performed by the machine is made unnecessary by a change in style or a change in process, or because the market for the product itself has vanished, or because the company decides, for whatever reason, to discontinue the product, or even because the company goes out of business.

The key question is: Over what period of time is the investment likely to generate cash inflows for *this* company? For whatever reason, when the investment no longer produces cash inflows, its economic life has ended. In view of the uncertainties associated with the operation of a business, most companies are conservative in estimating what the economic life of a proposed investment will be.

UNEVEN LIVES. For many types of equipment, it is reasonable to assume that the present machine can be used, physically, for a period of time that is at least as long as the economic life of the proposed machine. In situations in which this assumption is not valid, however, differential cash flows on a proposed machine purchased now will not in fact occur each year of the period being considered, for a new machine must be purchased anyway when the physical life of the present machine ends. Thereafter, there may be no difference in the annual cost of the two alternatives (purchase the machine now versus don't purchase it now), since the same machine will be involved in both of them.

If the expected physical life of the present machine is significantly shorter than the expected economic life of the proposed machine, some way must be found of making an equivalence between the time periods covered by the two alternatives. For example, if the proposed machine has an economic life of 10 years but the present machine has a remaining physical life of only 6 years, the differential cash flows will occur for only 6 years. This fact raises the difficult question of treating the situation that will exist at the end of the sixth year.

One approach is to estimate the remaining value of the new machine at the end of the sixth year of its life. The analysis would then cover only the six-year period, with this remaining value being treated as a residual value, or implicit cash inflow at the end of the sixth year. Such an estimate is extremely difficult to make, however.

Investment

The investment is the amount of funds that a company risks if it accepts an investment proposal. The relevant investment costs are the differential costs. These are the outlays that will be made if the project is undertaken and that would not be made if it is not undertaken. The cost of the machine itself, its shipping costs, cost of installation, and the cost of training operators are examples of differential investment costs. These outlays are part of the investment, even though some of them may not be capitalized in the accounting records.

EXISTING EQUIPMENT. If the purchase of new equipment results in the sale of existing equipment, the net proceeds from the sale reduces the amount of the differential investment. In other words, the differential investment represents the total amount of *additional* funds that must be committed to the investment project. The net proceeds from existing equipment are its selling price less any costs incurred in making the sale and in dismantling and removing the equipment.

RESIDUAL VALUE. A machine may have a *residual value* (i.e., salvage or resale value) at the end of its economic life. In a great many cases, the estimated residual value is so small and occurs so far in the future that it has no significant effect on the decision. Moreover, any salvage or resale value that is realized may be approximately offset by removal and dismantling costs. In situations where the estimated residual value is significant, the net residual value (after removal costs) is viewed as a future cash inflow in the year of disposal and is discounted along with the other cash inflows. Other assets, such as repair parts or inventory, may also be released at the end of the project, and these are treated in the same fashion.

INVESTMENTS IN WORKING CAPITAL. An investment is the commitment, or locking up, of funds in any type of asset. Although up to this point depreciable assets have been used as examples, investments also include commitments of funds to additional inventory and to other current assets. In particular, if new equipment is acquired to produce a new product, additional funds will probably be required for inventories, accounts receivable, and increased cash needs. Part of this increase in current assets may be supplied from increased accounts payable and accrued expenses; the remainder must come from permanent capital. This additional working capital is as much a part of the differential investment as the equipment itself.

Often it is reasonable to assume that the *residual value* of investments in working capital is approximately the same as the amount of the initial investment; that is, that at the end of the project, these items can be liquidated at their cost. Under these circumstances, the amount of working capital is treated as a cash inflow in the last year of the project, and its present value is found by discounting that amount at the required rate of return.

SEVERAL ALTERNATIVES. Some proposals involve a choice among several alternatives, each involving a different amount of investment. For example, one alternative way of manufacturing a proposed new product may involve semiautomatic equipment, while another way may involve more expensive, fully automatic equipment. A useful way of approaching such problems is to start with the alternative that requires the smallest investment and to analyze the next most expensive alternative in terms of its differential investment and its differential earnings above those of the least expensive alternative. This question is asked: Is the *additional* investment in the second alternative justified by the *additional* cash inflows that are expected from it, over and above the cash inflows expected from the less expensive alternative? If it is not, the proposal with the smaller investment should be accepted.

DEFERRED INVESTMENTS. Many projects involve a single commitment of funds at one moment of time, which we have called Time Zero. For some projects, on the other hand, the commitments are spread over a considerable period of time. The construction of a new plant may require disbursements over several years, or a proposal may involve the construction of one unit of plant now and a second unit five years later. In order to make the present value calculations, these investments must be brought to a common point in time, and this is done by the application of discount rates to the amounts involved. In general, the appropriate rate depends on the uncertainty that the investment will be made; the lower the uncertainty, the lower the rate. Thus, if the commitment is an extremely definite one, the discount rate may be equivalent to the interest rate on high-grade bonds (which also represent a definite commitment) whereas if the future investments will be made only if earnings materialize, then the rate can be the required rate of return. In effect, in the latter case, the future investment is treated as a cash outflow.

INVESTMENT CREDIT. Income tax regulations permit a company under certain specified conditions to take an *investment credit* when it purchases new machinery, equipment, and certain other types of depreciable assets. As explained in Chapter 8, if a company buys a new machine for $10,000, it can subtract up to 7 percent of that amount, or $700, from its current tax obligation. This is a direct reduction of $700 in the net investment. In other words, the cost of the machine can be taken as 93 percent of the invoice amount.[8]

CAPITAL GAINS AND LOSSES. When an existing machine is replaced by a new machine, the transaction may give rise either to a gain or to a loss, depending on whether the amount realized from the sale of the existing machine is greater than or less than its net book value, and depending on whether the new machine is or is not of "like kind." The income tax treatment of this gain or loss may well differ from the accounting treatment. Depending on the circumstances, (1) the gain or loss may be included in the calculation of taxable income and thus subject to the regular income tax rate of, say, 51 percent, or (2) it may be subject only to a 30 percent tax rate, which is applicable to capital gains. Expert tax advice is needed on problems involving gains and losses on the sale of

---

[8] Note that the treatment of the tax credit for our purposes here is independent of whether the company intends to use the flow-through method or the deferral method of accounting for the credit in its financial statements (Chapter 8).

depreciable assets, for it is difficult to know which of these alternatives is applicable in a given case. In any event, when existing assets are disposed of, the relevant amount by which the new investment is reduced is the proceeds of the sale, adjusted for taxes.

Nonmonetary Considerations

We have described the quantitative analysis involved in a capital investment proposal. It should be emphasized that this analysis does not provide the complete solution to the problem because it encompasses only those elements that can be reduced to numbers. A full consideration of the problem involves nonmonetary factors. Many investments are undertaken without a calculation of net present value. They may be necessary for the safety of employees; they may be undertaken for the convenience or comfort of employees (such as a new cafeteria or a new recreation room); they may be undertaken to enhance community relations, or because they are required in order to meet pollution control or other legal requirements, or because they increase plant protection safeguards. For some proposals of this type, no economic analysis is necessary; if an unsafe condition is found, it must be corrected regardless of the cost. For other proposals, these nonmonetary factors must be considered along with the numbers that are included in the economic analysis. For all proposals, the decision maker must take into account the fact that all the numbers are estimates, and that he must apply his own judgment as to the validity of these estimates in arriving at a decision.

Based on a survey of 177 industrial companies, Fremgen reports that only 27 percent believed that the economic analysis was the most critical part of the capital investment decision process and only 12 percent believed it was the most difficult.[9] The others said that the proper definition of the proposal, the estimation of cash inflows, and the implementation of a decision after it had been made were more important. Thus, the techniques described in this chapter are by no means the whole story. They are, however, the only part of the story that can be described as a definite procedure; the remainder must be learned through experience.

Nonuse of Discounting

Not every business uses discounting techniques in analyzing investment proposals. In some cases, this is because the manager is not familiar

---

[9] James M. Fremgen, "Capital Budgeting Practices; A Survey," *Management Accounting*, May 1973, p. 19.

with the techniques. But there is a much better reason in many instances. Some managers, having studied the approach carefully, have concluded that it is like "trying to make a silk purse out of a sow's ear"; that is, in their opinion the underlying estimates of cash flows and economic life are so rough that the refinement of using discounting techniques is more work than it is worth. Therefore they prefer the simple payback method or the unadjusted return, which are described later in this chapter.

Those managers who do use one of the discounting methods argue that the extra work involved is small, and that the results, although admittedly rough, are nevertheless better than the results of calculations that do not take into account the time value of money.

The Overall Analytical Process

The technique described above is called the *net present value* method. Following is a summary of the steps involved in using this method in analyzing a proposed investment:

1. Select a required rate of return. Presumably, once selected, this rate will be used generally; it need not be considered anew for each proposal.
2. Find the net investment, which includes the additional outlays made at Time Zero, less the proceeds from disposal of existing equipment.
3. Estimate the economic life of the proposed project.
4. Estimate the differential cash inflows for each year or sequence of years during the economic life.
5. Estimate the residual values at the end of the economic life, which consist of the disposal value of equipment plus working capital that is to be released.
6. Find the present value of all the inflows identified in Steps 4 and 5 by discounting them at the required rate of return, using Table A or Table B.
7. Find the net present value by subtracting the net investment from the present value of the inflows. If the net present value is zero or positive, decide that the proposal is acceptable, insofar as the monetary factors are concerned.
8. Taking into account the nonmonetary factors, reach a final decision. (This part of the process is at least as important as all the other parts put together.)

As an aid to visualizing the relationships in a proposed investment, it is often useful to use a diagram of the flows similar to that shown in Illustration 19–3.

Illustration 19–3

CASH FLOW DIAGRAM

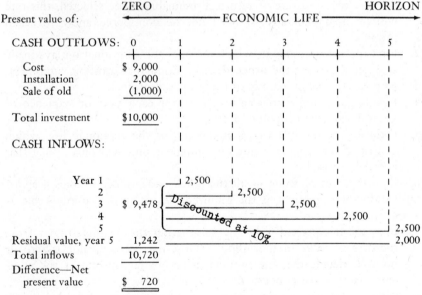

Present value of:	TIME ZERO	1	2	3	4	HORIZON 5
CASH OUTFLOWS:	0	1	2	3	4	5
Cost	$ 9,000					
Installation	2,000					
Sale of old	(1,000)					
Total investment	$10,000					
CASH INFLOWS:						
Year 1		2,500				
2			2,500			
3	$ 9,478			2,500		
4					2,500	
5						2,500
Residual value, year 5	1,242					2,000
Total inflows	10,720					
Difference—Net present value	$ 720					

Discounted at 10%

OTHER METHODS OF ANALYSIS

So far, we have limited the discussion of techniques for analyzing capital investment proposals to one method, the net present value method. We shall now describe three alternative ways of analyzing a proposed capital investment: (1) the discounted cash-flow method, (2) the payback method, and (3) the unadjusted return on investment method.

Discounted Cash-Flow Method

When the net present value method is used, the required rate of return must be selected in advance of making the calculations, for this rate is used to discount the cash inflows in each year, so as to find their present value. As already pointed out, the choice of an appropriate rate of return is a difficult matter. The *discounted cash-flow method* avoids this difficulty. It computes the rate of return which equates the present value of the cash inflows with the amount of the investment; that is, that rate which makes the net present value equal zero. This rate is called the *internal rate of return,* or the *project rate of return.*

If the management is satisfied with the internal rate of return, then the project is acceptable; if the internal rate of return is not high enough, then the project is unacceptable. In deciding what rate of return is "high enough," the same considerations as those involved in selecting a required rate of return apply.

The term "discounted cash flow" is not a descriptive name for this method, for the net present value method also involves the discounting of cash flows. The name is widely used, however. This method is also called the *time-adjusted-return method* or the *investor's method.*

Level Inflows. If the cash inflows are level—that is, the same amount each year—the computation is simple. It will be illustrated by a proposed investment of $1,000 with estimated cash inflow of $250 a year for five years. The procedure is as follows:

1. Divide the investment, $1,000, by the annual inflow, $250. The result, 4.0, is called the *investment/inflow ratio.*
2. Look across the five-year row of Table B. The column in which the figure closest to 4.0 appears shows the rate of return. Since the closest figure is 3.993 in the 8 percent column, the return is slightly less than 8 percent (just as it was in Illustration 19–1).
3. If management is satisfied with a return of slightly less than 8 percent, then it should accept this project (aside from nonquantitative considerations). If it requires a higher return, then it should reject the project.

The number 4.0 in the above example is simply the ratio of the investment to the annual cash inflows. Each number in Table B shows the ratio of the present value of a stream of cash inflows to an investment of $1 made today, for various combinations of rates of return and numbers of years. The number 4.0 opposite any combination of year and rate of return means that the present value of a stream of inflows of $1 a year for that number of years discounted at that rate is $4. The present value of a stream of inflows of $250 a year is in the same ratio; therefore it is $250 times 4, or $1,000. If the number is less than 4.0, as is the case with 3.993 in the example above, then the return is correspondingly less than 8 percent.

In using Table B, in this method it is usually necessary to interpolate, that is, to estimate the location of a number that lies between two numbers appearing in the table. There is no need to be precise about these interpolations because the final result can be no better than the basic data, and the basic data are ordinarily only rough estimates. A quick interpolation, made visually, is usually as good as the accuracy of the data warrants. Computation of a fraction of a percent is rarely warranted.

UNEVEN INFLOWS. If cash inflows are not the same in each year, the internal rate of return must be found by trial and error. The cash inflows for each year are listed, and various discount rates are applied to these amounts until a rate is found that makes their total present value equal to the amount of the investment. This rate is the internal rate of return. This trial-and-error process can be quite tedious if the computations are made manually; however, computer programs are available that perform the calculations automatically.

Payback Method

The number referred to above as the investment/inflow ratio is also called the *payback* because it is the number of years over which the investment outlay will be recovered or paid back from the cash inflow *if* the estimates turn out to be correct; that is, the project will "pay for itself" in this number of years. If a machine costs $1,000 and generates cash inflow of $250 a year, it has a payback of four years.

Payback is often used as a quick, but crude, method for appraising proposed investments. If the payback period is equal to or only slightly less than the economic life of the project, then the proposal is clearly unacceptable. If the payback period is considerably less than the economic life, then the project begins to look attractive.

If several investment proposals have the same general characteristics, then the payback period can be used as a valid way of screening out the acceptable proposals. For example, if a company finds that production equipment ordinarily has a life of 10 years and if it requires a return of at least 15 percent, then the company may specify that new equipment will be considered for purchase only if it has a payback period of 5 years or less; for Table B shows that a payback period of 5 years is equivalent to a return of approximately 15 percent if the life is 10 years. Stating the criterion in this fashion avoids the necessity of explaining the present value concept to supervisors in the operating organizations.

The danger of using payback as a criterion is that it gives no consideration to differences in the length of the estimated economic lives of various projects. There may be a tendency to conclude that the shorter the payback period, the better the project; whereas a project with a long payback may actually be better than a project with a short payback if it will produce cash inflows for a much longer period of time.

Discounted Payback Method

A more useful and more valid form of the payback method, but one that is not yet widely used, is the *discounted payback*. In this method the present value of each year's cash inflows is found, and these are cumulated year by year until they equal or exceed the amount of investment. The year in which this happens is the discounted payback period. A discounted payback of 5 years means that over a five year period the total cash inflows will be large enough to recoup the investment *and also* to provide the required return on investment.

Unadjusted Return on Investment Method

The *unadjusted return* method computes the net income expected to be earned from the project each year, in accordance with the principles of financial accounting, including a provision for depreciation expense. The unadjusted return on investment is found by dividing the annual net income by either the amount of the investment or by one half the amount of investment. (The use of one half the investment is on the premise that over the whole life of the project, an average of one half the initial investment is outstanding because the investment is at its full amount at Time Zero and shrinks gradually to nothing, or substantially nothing, by its terminal year.)

Since normal depreciation accounting provides, in a sense, for the recovery of the cost of a depreciable asset, one might suppose that the return on an investment could be found by relating the investment to its income after depreciation, but such is *not* the case. We described earlier the calculations for an investment of $1,000, with cash inflow of $250 a year for five years. These calculations showed that the present value of the cash inflows equaled $1,000 when discounted at a required rate of return of 8 percent. In other words, such an investment has a return of 8 percent. In the unadjusted return method, the calculation would be as follows:

Gross earnings	$250
Less depreciation (⅕ of $1,000)	200
Net Income	$ 50

Dividing net income by the investment ($50 ÷ $1,000) gives an indicated return of 5 percent. But we know that this result is incorrect; the true return is 8 percent. If we divide the $50 net income by one half the investment, that is, $500, the result is 10 percent, which is also incorrect.

This method is called the unadjusted return method because it makes no adjustment for the differences in present values of the inflows of the various years; that is, it treats each year's inflows as if they were as valuable as those of every other year, whereas actually the prospect of an inflow of $250 next year is more attractive than the prospect of an inflow of $250 two years from now, and that $250 is more attractive than the prospect of an inflow of $250 three years from now, and so on.

The unadjusted return method, based on the gross amount of the investment, will always *understate* the true return. The shorter the time period involved, the more serious is the understatement. For investments involving very long time periods, the understatement is insignificant. If the return is computed by using one half the investment, the result is always an *overstatement* of the true return. No method which does not consider the time value of money can product an accurate result.

Until fairly recently, the unadjusted return method was widely used, and it is still used in companies whose managers are unaware of the importance of the present value concept. Despite its conceptual weakness, the unadjusted return method does have a place in capital investment analysis, for it shows the effect of a proposal on the company's income statement. This effect, which is not shown in present value computations, may be significant in certain situations because of the importance that investors attach to the amount of net income reported on the income statement.

PREFERENCE PROBLEMS

There are two classes of investment problems, called, respectively, screening problems and preference problems. In a *screening problem* the question is whether or not to accept a proposed investment. The discussion so far has been limited to this class of problem. A great number of individual proposals come to management's attention, and by the techniques described above, those that are worthwhile can be screened out from the others.

In *preference problems* (also called ranking or rationing problems), a more difficult question is asked: Of a number of proposals, each of which has an adequate return, how do they rank in terms of preference? If not all the proposals can be accepted, which ones do we prefer? The decision may merely involve a choice between two competing proposals, or it may require that a series of proposals be ranked in order of their attractiveness. Such a ranking of projects is necessary when there are more worthwhile proposals than there are funds available to finance them, which is often the case.

Criteria for Preference Problems

Both the discounted cash-flow and the net present value methods are used for preference problems.

If the *discounted cash-flow method* is used, the preference rule is as follows: the higher the internal rate of return, the better the project. A project with a return of 20 percent is said to be preferable to a project with a return of 19 percent.

If the *net present value method* is used, the present value of the cash inflows of one project cannot be compared directly with the present value of the cash inflows of another unless the investments are of the same size. Most people would agree that a $1,000 investment that produces cash inflows with a present value of $2,000 is better than a $1,000,000 investment that produces cash inflows with a present value of $1,001,000, even though they each have a net present value of $1,000. In order to compare two proposals under the net present value method, therefore, we must relate the size of the discounted cash inflows to the amount of money that is risked. This is done simply by dividing the present value of the cash inflows by the amount of investment, to give a ratio that is generally called the *profitability index*. The preference rule then is as follows: the higher the profitability index, the better the project.

Comparison of Preference Rules

Conceptually, the profitability index is superior to the internal rate of return as a device for deciding on preference. This is because the discounted cash-flow method will not always give the correct preference as between two projects with different lives or with different patterns of earnings.

EXAMPLE: Proposal A involves an investment of $1,000 and a cash inflow of $1,200 received at the end of one year; its internal rate of return is 20 percent. Proposal B involves an investment of $1,000 and cash inflows of $300 a year for five years; its internal rate of return is only 15 percent. But Proposal A is *not* necessarily preferable to Proposal B. It is preferable only if the company can expect to earn a high return during the following four years on some other project in which the funds released at the end of the first year are reinvested. Otherwise, Proposal B, which earns 15 percent over the whole five-year period, is preferable.[10]

The incorrect signal illustrated in the above example is not present in the profitability index method. Assuming a required rate of return of 10 percent, the two proposals described above would be analyzed as follows:

Proposal (a)	Cash Inflow (b)	Discount Factor (c)	Present Value $(d = b \times c)$	Investment (e)	Index $(f = d \div e)$
A	$1,200 − 1 yr.	0.909	$1,091	$1,000	1.09
B	$ 300 − 5 yr.	3.791	1,137	1,000	1.14

The profitability index signals that Proposal B is better than Proposal A, which is in fact the case if the company can expect to reinvest the money released from Proposal A so as to earn only 10 percent on it.

Although the profitability index method is conceptually superior to the discounted cash-flow method, and although the former is also easier to calculate since there is no trial-and-error computation, the discounted cash-flow method is widely used in practice. There seem to be two reasons for this. First, the profitability index method requires that the required rate of return be established before the calculations are made, whereas many analysts prefer to work from the other direction; that is, to find the internal rate of return and then see how it compares with their idea of the rate of return that is appropriate in view of the risks involved. Second, the profitability index, like any index, is an abstract number that is difficult to explain; whereas the internal rate of return is similar to interest rates and earnings rates with which every manager is familiar.

SUMMARY

A capital investment problem is essentially one of determining whether the anticipated cash inflows from a proposed project are sufficiently attractive to warrant risking the investment of funds in the project.

In the net present value method, the basic decision rule is that a proposal is acceptable if the present value of the cash inflows expected to be derived from it equals or exceeds the amount of the investment. In order to use this rule, one must estimate: (1) the required rate of return,

---

[10] Note that this problem arises when a choice must be made between two competing proposals, only one of which can be adopted. If the proposals are noncompeting and the required rate of return is less than 15 percent, then both of them are acceptable.

(2) the amount of cash inflow in each year, (3) the economic life, and (4) the amount of investment. The required rate of return is the minimum rate that a company expects to earn on its investments. The cash inflows are discounted at the required rate of return. Cash inflows are those that are anticipated as a consequence of the investment. They are differential inflows.

Depreciation on the proposed assets is disregarded, but the effect of depreciation on income taxes must be taken into account.

Economic life is the number of years that the investment is expected to generate cash inflows. It is usually shorter than the physical life.

The amount of investment is the differential amount of funds that will be committed to the project. It includes working capital required for the project. The gross amount of investment is reduced by the net proceeds from the sale of assets that are disposed of if the project is undertaken. The present value of the residual value of assets that are sold or released at the end of the economic life may be either subtracted from the investment or added to operating cash inflows.

The discounted cash-flow method finds the rate of return that equates the present value of cash inflows to the amount of investment; it is a valid method. The simple payback method finds the number of years of cash inflows that are required to equal the amount of investment. The unadjusted return on investment method computes net income according to the principles of accounting and expresses this as a percentage of either the initial investment or the average investment. The simple payback and unadjusted return methods have conceptual weaknesses.

Preference problems are those in which the task is to rank two or more investment proposals in order of their desirability. The profitability index, which is the ratio of the present value of cash inflows to the investment, is the most valid way of making such a ranking. The discounted cash-flow method is also valid in most, but not all, preference problems. Other methods are generally not as useful for ranking purposes.

The foregoing are monetary considerations that can be incorporated in an economic analysis. Nonmonetary considerations are also important in making the actual decision; they are often as important as the monetary considerations and are in some cases so important that no economic analysis is worthwhile.

SUGGESTIONS FOR FURTHER READING

GRANT, EUGENE L., and IRESON, WILLIAM G. *Principles of Engineering Economy.* 5th ed. New York: Ronald Press Co., 1970.

HUNT, PEARSON; WILLIAMS, CHARLES M.; and DONALDSON, GORDON. *Basic Business Finance: Text and Cases.* 4th ed. Homewood, Ill.: Richard D. Irwin, Inc., 1970.

QUIRIN, G. DAVID. *The Capital Expenditure Decision.* Homewood, Ill.: Richard D. Irwin, Inc., 1967.

SOLOMON, EZRA, ed. *The Management of Corporate Capital.* Glencoe, Ill.: Free Press, 1959.

WESTON, J. FRED, and BRIGHAM, EUGENE F. *Managerial Finance,* 4th ed. Hillsdale, Ill.: Holt, Rinehart and Winston, 1972.

CASES

CASE 19–1. CAPITAL INVESTMENT PROBLEMS

A. Equipment Replacement

The Parsons Company is considering the purchase of new equipment to perform operations currently being performed on different, less efficient equipment. The purchase price is $10,000, delivered and installed.

A Parsons production engineer estimates that the new equipment will produce savings of $2,000 in labor and other direct costs annually, as compared with the present equipment. He estimates the proposed equipment's economic life at 10 years, with zero salvage value. The present equipment is in good working order and will last, physically, for at least 20 more years.

The company can borrow money at 8 percent, although it would not plan to negotiate a loan specifically for the purchase of this equipment. The company requires a return of at least 20 percent before taxes on an investment of this type. Taxes are to be disregarded.

Questions

1. Assuming the present equipment has zero book value and zero salvage value, should the company buy the proposed equipment?
2. Assuming the present equipment is being depreciated at a straight-line rate of 10 percent, that it has a book value of $4,800 (cost, $8,000; accumulated depreciation, $3,200), and has zero net salvage value today, should the company buy the proposed equipment?
3. Assuming the present equipment has a book value of $4,800 and a salvage value today of $3,000, and that if retained for 10 more years its salvage value will be zero, should the company buy the proposed equipment?
4. Assume the new equipment will save only $1,000 a year, but that its economic life is expected to be 20 years. If other conditions are as described in (1) above, should the company buy the proposed equipment?

643

B. Replacement Following Earlier Replacement

The Parsons Company decided to purchase the equipment described in Part A (hereafter called "Model A" equipment). Two years later, even better equipment (called "Model B") comes on the market and makes the other equipment completely obsolete, with no resale value. The Model B equipment costs $20,000 delivered and installed, but it is expected to result in annual savings of $5,000 over the cost of operating the Model A equipment. The economic life of Model B is estimated to be 10 years. Taxes are to be disregarded.

Questions

1. What action should the company take?
2. If the company decides to purchase the Model B equipment, a mistake has been made somewhere, because good equipment, bought only two years previously, is being scrapped. How did this mistake come about?

C. Effect of Income Taxes

Assume that the Parsons Company expects to pay income taxes of 50 percent and that a loss on the sale or disposal of equipment is treated as an ordinary deduction, resulting in a tax saving of 50 percent. The Parsons Company expects to earn 10 percent on its investment after taxes. Depreciation for tax purposes is computed on the sum-of-years' digits basis.

Questions

1. Should the company buy the equipment if the facts are otherwise as described in Part A (1)?
2. If the facts are otherwise as described in Part A (2)?
3. If the facts are otherwise as described in Part B?

D. Change in Earnings Pattern

Assume that the savings are expected to be $2,500 in each of the first five years and $1,500 in each of the next five years, other conditions remaining as described in Part A (1).

Questions

1. What action should the company take?
2. Why is the result here different from that in Part A (1)?
3. What effect would the inclusion of income taxes, as in Part C, have on your recommendation?

CASE 19–2.   RIVERBEND TELEPHONE COMPANY

The Riverbend Telephone Company was independently owned, and operated in the area between the west bank of the Short River and the state line. The company provided local telephone service to customers in several adjacent communities, and its lines joined with those of other companies to provide long distance telephone service. Operating as a public utility, the Riverbend Telephone Company was subject to regulation by the State Public Service Commission which periodically reviewed service and approved all changes in rates.

In recent years, the population of the area served by the company had grown rapidly as a result of a new bridge which facilitated daily commuting over the Short River to a nearby city. As a result of this growth, company personnel and equipment had been hard pressed to meet all demands for installation of new telephones and maintenance. For a time the company had used an outside contractor to handle overload work, but several poor experiences had caused abandonment of that practice. By late 1969 it was obvious that the company needed at least one new maintenance truck and crew.

The need to obtain a new truck arose at a critical period for the company. Earlier, Riverbend had made heavy commitments to purchase telephone equipment needed to improve service. Recent payments for new equipment had strained the net working capital position of the firm. Stockholders were unable to provide additional resources and hoped the company could avoid selling additional shares which would dilute their ownership. Interest rates were quoted at 9% on short-term notes and above 10% on long-term loans. Since the company had been earning only about 8% on net assets, the firm hoped to avoid unnecessary borrowing until interest rates dropped somewhat.

In November 1969, Mr. Warren Freeman, general manager of Riverbend, requested bids for the new truck from four truck dealers. The lowest bid received was from the Reliable Motors Company who quoted a cash price of $3,800 including all taxes and delivery charges. As an alternative, Reliable would lease the truck to Riverbend Telephone for five years at an annual rate of $900.

The truck which Riverbend Telephone Company needed was similar to several others which they already owned. At Mr. Freeman's request, the company accountant used records to estimate the cost of operating the new truck. His estimates are shown in Exhibit 1. The truck was expected to last for five years, at which time it could probably be sold for about $300. If the truck were purchased it would be depreciated by the straight-line method because that was the only method allowed by the State Public Service Commission.

If the truck were leased, Riverbend Telephone would have to pay the

Exhibit 1

ESTIMATED OPERATING EXPENSE OF MAINTENANCE TRUCK

Type of expense	Year of operation				
	1	2	3	4	5
Gasoline...	$ 450	$ 450	$ 450	$ 450	$ 450
Repairs and maintenance..........	100	116	131	145	158
Tires.........................	—	95	95	95	95
Insurance......................	300	300	300	300	300
Registration and taxes............	106	90	75	61	48
Depreciation (straight-line method)*.	700	700	700	700	700
Total expenses..............	$1,656	$1,751	$1,751	$1,751	$1,751

* Assumes original cost of $3,800, life of 5 years, and salvage value of $300.

annual lease charge on or before the first day of each year. In addition, they would be responsible for all costs of operation and maintenance of the truck except for tires, which Reliable Motors would supply. The proposed agreement also made Riverbend responsible for all risks to the truck and property damage, collision, personal injury, fire, and theft. Finally, Riverbend would reimburse Reliable for all costs of vehicle registration and taxes.

Mr. Freeman was unsure how he should view the alternatives presented by Reliable Motors. Leasing the truck would reduce the immediate demands on Riverbend Telephone's financial resources. Still, the prospect of paying $4,500 over five years when the truck could be purchased new for $3,800 raised questions about how well he would be serving company stockholders if he leased rather than purchased the truck. On the other hand, the operating expenses and lease payments would be allowable expense deductions in calculating income for tax purposes. Since the company had been paying and expected to continue paying income taxes of 40%, an increase in expenses of $900 per year would not really cost that much.

The effect of his choice on Riverbend's rate of return earned on net assets was also important to Mr. Freeman. In 1969 the State Public Service Commission had allowed another telephone company to raise its rates to provide revenues to increase its after-tax rate of return to just above 9% on investment. In an attempt to raise Riverbend's return without requesting higher rates, Mr. Freeman had not approved any new investments that would provide a rate of return on investment below 10% unless they were absolutely necessary. Since the truck had to be acquired and the choice was only whether it should be leased or purchased, Mr. Freeman was unsure whether his 10% return minimum made any difference in this case.

Mr. Freeman also wanted to consider how the State Public Service Commission might view leased assets in evaluating rates of return earned by utilities. Purchased assets were always included in total investment net of accumulated depreciation, and all operating expenses including depreciation were allowable deductions in determining annual income. While he was not able to ascertain exactly what the Commission might want, he reasoned that Riverbend could probably include all operating expenses and the lease payments among annual expenses in reports to the Commission, but he was unsure whether investment should be increased by the "fair value" of the leased asset before calculating return on investment.

Questions

1. Should the company buy or lease the new truck? (Assume that Riverbend Telephone uses the straight-line method of depreciation for tax purposes as well as for reports to shareholders and the State Public Service Commission).

2. If Riverbend Telephone purchased the truck and chose to depreciate it for income tax purposes only using the double-declining balance method, would this affect your decision to buy or lease? Assume that the annual depreciation expense would be:

Year	Depreciation
1970	$1,520
1971	912
1972	546
1973	328
1974	194

3. If the truck is leased, how should Mr. Freeman report investment and annual income for the Riverbend Telephone Company to the State Public Service Commission?

CASE 19–3. WILSON COMPANY

In March, 1975, the Wilson Company was considering a proposal to replace four hand-loaded transmission case milling machines with one automatic machine. The company operated a large machine shop that did machining work on a subcontract basis for local industries in the Detroit area. One of the contracts was to machine transmission cases for truck engines for the Maynard Automobile Company. The Wilson Company had negotiated such a contract with the Maynard Automobile Company for each of the previous 14 years. For the last few years, the contract had been for 60,000 transmission cases annually.

The unfinished cases were supplied by Maynard. With a hand-loaded machine, all the faces could not be machined at the same time. Each machine required the constant attention of one skilled machine operator.

The machines used by Wilson were only three years old. Each had an annual output of approximately 15,000 cases on a two-shift, five-day week basis; therefore, four machines had been purchased at a total cost of $295,000.

The useful life of a hand-loaded machine on a two-shift, five-day week basis was estimated to be 15 years. Its salvage value at the end of its useful life was estimated to be $2,000. Depreciation of $59,000 had been built up for the four machines, representing three years' accumulation. The purchase of the machines had been financed by a 10 percent bank loan, and $90,000 of this loan had not yet been repaid. It was estimated that the four machines could be sold in their present condition for a total of $120,000 net, after dismantling and removal costs. The book loss resulting from the sale would be a deductible expense for income tax purposes and would therefore result in a tax saving of 52 percent of the loss.

The machine being considered in 1975 was a fully automatic transfer-type milling machine, equipped with four machining stations. Automatic transfer equipment on this machine moved the part progressively from one station to the next and indexed at each station, finishing a complete case with each cycle of the machine. One skilled machine operator was required to observe the functioning of the machine and make any necessary adjustments.

An automatic transfer-type machine with an annual output of 60,000 transmission cases on a two-shift basis would be specially built by a machine tool manufacturer at an estimated cost of $340,000, delivered and installed. The useful life of this machine was estimated to be 15 years. No reliable estimate of scrap value could be made; a rough estimate was that it would approximate the removal costs.

The Wilson Company's engineering department was asked to prepare a study for the executives to use in deciding what action to take. Its findings were as follows: The direct labor rate for milling machine operators was $5.00 an hour, including provision for social security taxes and fringe benefits, which varied with the payroll. There would be a saving in floor space amounting to $800 annually on the basis of the charge made in 1975 for each square foot of floor space used. However, the factory layout was such that it would be difficult to use this freed space for some other purpose, and no other use was planned. Out-of-pocket savings of $10,000 a year for other cost items were estimated if the automatic machine was purchased.

The Wilson Company planned to finance any new equipment purchase with a bank loan at a rate of 10 percent.

Selected financial data for the company are shown in Exhibit 1. The

Exhibit 1

WILSON COMPANY

Condensed Income Statement, 1974

Net sales..................................	$5,364,213
Less: All costs and expenses...............	4,138,647
Income before taxes.......................	$1,225,566
Provision for income taxes..................	622,715
Net Income..............................	$ 602,851

Condensed Balance Sheet, December 31, 1974

Current assets.............	$3,051,349	Current liabilities..........	$ 930,327
Fixed assets (net)..........	4,239,210	8% mortgage bonds........	500,000
Other assets..............	151,491	Capital stock..............	1,000,000
		Retained earnings..........	5,011,723
Total Assets.........	$7,442,050	Total Liabilities.......	$7,442,050

company considered the picture given by these statistics to be normal and expected the same general pattern to prevail in the foreseeable future.

Question

What action, if any, would you recommend? Why?

CASE 19–4. PHILLIPS LAUNDRY

In January 1974, the Phillips Laundry installed a new shirt-pressing unit. The results obtained from operation of this unit were so satisfactory that early in 1975 Mr. Howard Phillips, president of the laundry, was considering the purchase of a second new shirt-pressing unit.

For the preceding several years Phillips' sales had amounted to roughly $350,000 each year. Mr. Phillips thought that sales probably would not change much during 1975, but he hoped eventually to increase sales volume. The business was subject to slight seasonal fluctuations, which necessitated employment of part-time labor during parts of the year.

The laundry had always operated profitably, although in recent years the shirt-laundering section had done no better than break even. Inasmuch as shirts made up an important part of the laundry's business, Mr. Phillips was extremely anxious to make this operation profitable. He had considered the possibility of raising shirt-laundering prices to the customer but had rejected this alternative because of the intense competitive conditions that existed in the area.

In order to determine where costs might be reduced, Mr. Phillips in 1973 had made a careful analysis of the operations performed on shirts. He concluded that high costs in the pressing department were his principal problem. At that time the shirt-pressing department included three separate but similar pressing units, called here Units A, B, and C. Each unit consisted of four presses. In each of Units A and B, a cuff and collar press and a front press were operated by one operator, a back press and a sleeve press were operated by a second operator, and two other workers did touch-up ironing and the folding of the finished shirts. Each of these two pressing units had a capacity of 90 shirts an hour. Unit C had four basically similar presses, but it was operated only when there were more shirts to be pressed than the other two units could handle. Two people employed on a part-time basis operated Unit C and turned out 40 shirts an hour.

Both the full-time and part-time employees were paid $2.25 an hour; social security taxes and fringe benefits increased this expense to $2.65 an hour. The company did not have a piecework incentive plan, but the workers were free to leave the plant when they finished a day's work. Full-time operators were guaranteed and paid for a 40-hour week. In practice, however, they averaged only 27.5 hours of actual work in a week; they had one hour off for lunch and two 15-minute rest periods daily. The remaining five hours a week was accounted for by their practice of leaving early. Part-time help was employed to operate the third unit rather than work the full-time operators over 27.5 hours.

In order to reduce shirt-pressing costs, Mr. Phillips made a major change in the shirt-pressing department in January 1974. At that time, he replaced Unit A with a new pressing unit, the Beager Model 70.

Each of the old units had cost $3,200 when purchased, and installation charges for all three units had amounted to $530. They were 18 years old, however, and had been fully depreciated on the laundry's books. With periodic replacement of parts and routine maintenance, they probably could have been kept in operating condition indefinitely, but Mr. Phillips thought that the new type of press had made them obsolete. The old presses had no resale value.

The new Beager pressing unit consisted of only three presses. It occupied only about half the space of one of the old four-press units. Building depreciation, light, and other space costs allocated to each press unit were approximately $2,600 a year. Thus, this saving in space was worth $1,300 a year.

On the Beager pressing unit, one worker operated both a collar and cuff press and also another machine that pressed the body of the shirt in one operation. This worker was able to operate these two presses simultaneously because of automatic timers that made it unnecessary to watch one press while inserting or removing a shirt from another press. A second person operated the sleeve press and did all the folding for the unit. The touch-up, hand-ironing operation was completely eliminated. Even without this touch-up operation, there was a marked improvement in the appearance of shirts turned out by the new Beager unit as compared with those turned out on the old units. The capacity of the Beager unit operated by two workers was 70 shirts an hour.

Under the revised setup, then, the shirt-pressing department consisted of (*a*) the new Beager unit, which was operated by two people on a full-time basis and which had a capacity of 70 shirts an hour; (*b*) one old unit, which was operated by four people on a full-time basis and had a capacity of 90 shirts an hour; and (*c*) a second old unit, which was operated only when needed by two workers on a part-time basis, with a capacity, when operated in this manner, of 40 shirts an hour. Mr. Phillips continued his policy of using Unit C on a part-time basis rather than have his employees work over 27.5 hours a week. Exhibit 1 shows the number

Exhibit 1

SELECTED DATA FROM THE PRESSING DEPARTMENT FOR 1974

Type of Unit	Capacity in Shirts per Hour	No. of Hours in Operation in 1974	No. of Shirts Pressed in 1974	No. of Hours for which Each Operator Was Paid
A. 2-worker unit (full-time basis)........	70	1,375*	96,250	2,080
B. 4-worker unit (full-time basis)........	90	1,375*	123,750	2,080
C. 2-worker unit (part-time basis).......	40	900	36,000	1,350†

* There were 250 working days in 1974. The presses were actually in operation about 5.5 hours a day.
† Part-time employees were paid for their lunch hours and rest periods.

of hours the presses of each unit were in operation in 1974, the number of shirts each unit pressed, and the number of hours for which the operators of each unit were paid.

The cost of the three new presses of the Beager unit was $21,700 f.o.b. the factory. Freight to the Phillips Laundry was $600, and installation charges were $275. There was no disruption of work while the presses were being installed over a weekend, but there was some slowdown while the operators became accustomed to the new methods and procedures used. The slowdown resulted in an increase in labor cost for the period of about $250. Power costs were increased by the cost of electricity for a five-horsepower motor that powered the body press. The motor used one kilowatt of electricity an hour at a cost of 12 cents a kilowatt-hour. Also, it was estimated that costs of operating the boiler and air compressor used to produce steam would increase about $15 a month.

During 1974 the Beager unit performed much as expected. Mr. Phillips was pleased with the results and therefore was led to consider a second change in February 1975. At about that time, the manufacturer of Beager machines brought out a new model, Model 85, which was equipped with an automatic folding table. The capacity of this unit, which also was operated by two workers, promised to be 85 shirts an hour. In the new setup, as Mr. Phillips conceived it, a Model 85 unit would replace Unit B, the pressing unit then being operated by four people. The two Beager units would then be operated on a full-time basis, 1,375 hours each a year, and the remaining old unit, Unit C, would be operated only when necessary by two workers on a part-time basis. This arrangement would give Mr. Phillips one Beager unit with a potential capacity of 85 shirts an hour, one Beager unit with a capacity of 70 shirts an hour, and one old unit with a capacity of 40 shirts an hour when operated by two people or 80 shirts an hour when operated by four.

The Beager Model 85 would cost $24,720 f.o.b. the factory; freight would be $700; and the installation cost would be $320. The body press of the second Beager unit would have its own five-horsepower motor. Costs of operating the boiler and air compressor would be increased about $15 a month by use of the Beager Model 85 in place of the old equipment in Unit B.

A year-end balance sheet and an income statement for 1974 are shown in Exhibits 2 and 3.

Exhibit 2

PHILLIPS LAUNDRY

Balance Sheet
December 31, 1974
(figures rounded to hundreds of dollars)

ASSETS

Current Assets:

Cash	$ 10,900
Accounts receivable	14,600
Prepaid expenses	7,200
Total current assets	$ 32,700

Fixed Assets:

Machinery and equipment (net)	160,700
Building (net)	121,800
Total Assets	$315,200

LIABILITIES AND OWNERS' EQUITY

Current Liabilities:

Accounts payable	$ 8,500
Accrued expenses	2,900
Total current liabilities	$ 11,400

Long-Term Liabilities:

Mortgage loan	83,500
Total Liabilities	$ 94,900

Owners' Equity:

Capital stock	106,000
Retained earnings	114,300
Total Liabilities and Owners' Equity	$315,200

Exhibit 3

PHILLIPS LAUNDRY

Income Statement,
Year Ending December 31, 1974
(figures rounded to hundreds of dollars)

Net sales.................................			$348,500
Laundry operating costs:			
Productive labor.......................	$123,700		
Productive supplies....................	33,000		
Power..............................	11,200		
Plant overhead.........................	45,500		
Total operating costs.................		$213,400	
Collection and delivery...................		48,400	
Sales promotion...........................		12,000	
Executive salaries.......................		18,900	
Office and administrative..................		22,300	
Total costs........................			315,000
Income before taxes.....................			$ 33,500
Federal income tax......................			10,100
Net income.............................			$ 23,400

Question

Should the Phillips Laundry buy a Beager Model 85 for use in Unit B?

CASE 19–5. ORKNEY BISCUIT COMPANY, LTD.

Mr. Percy Jones, managing director of Orkney Biscuit Company, Ltd., was trying to decide whether to expand the company by adding an entirely new and different product line. The proposal seemed likely to be profitable, and adequate funds could be obtained from outside investors to finance the new venture.

Orkney Biscuit had long been regarded as a well-managed company. It had succeeded in keeping its present product lines up to date and had maintained a small but profitable position in a highly competitive industry.

The amount of capital employed by the company in support of its present operations was approximately £4,000,000, and was expected to remain at this level whether the proposal for the new product line was accepted or rejected. Net income from these existing operations amounted to about £400,000 a year, and Mr. Jones's best forecast of the future was that this would continue to be the income from present operations, regardless of whether the new product line was introduced or rejected.

Introduction of the new product line would require an immediate investment of £400,000 in equipment and £250,000 in additional work-

Exhibit 1

INCOME FORECAST FOR NEW PRODUCT LINE

Year	(1) Forecasted Incremental Cash Flow from Operations	(2) Depreciation on New Equipment	(3) Forecasted Incremental Income before Tax (1) − (2)	(4) Income Tax at 40%*	(5) Forecasted Incremental Net Income after Tax (3) − (4)
1	− £ 350,000	£50,000	− £400,000	− £160,000	− £240,000
2	− 100,000	50,000	− 150,000	− 60,000	− 90,000
3	0	50,000	− 50,000	− 20,000	− 30,000
4	+ 200,000	50,000	+ 150,000	60,000	90,000
5	+ 500,000	50,000	+ 450,000	180,000	270,000
6	+ 1,000,000	50,000	+ 950,000	380,000	570,000
7	+ 900,000	50,000	+ 850,000	340,000	510,000
8	+ 650,000	50,000	+ 600,000	240,000	360,000

* When income before taxes was negative, the company was entitled to a tax rebate at 40 percent, either from taxes paid previous years or from taxes currently due on other company operations.

ing capital. A further £100,000 in working capital would be required a year later.

Sales of the new product line would be relatively low during the first year, but would increase steadily until the sixth year. After that, changing tastes and increased competition would probably begin to reduce annual sales. After eight years, the product line would probably be withdrawn from the market. At that time, the company would sell the equipment for its scrap value and liquidate the working capital. The cash value of the equipment and working capital at that time would be about £350,000.

The low initial sales volume, combined with heavy promotional outlays, would lead to heavy losses in the first two years, and no net income would be reported until the fourth year. The profit forecasts for the new product line are summarized in Exhibit 1.

Mr. Jones was concerned about the effect this project would have on Orkney's overall reported return on investment in the next three years. In response to this concern, his accountant provided him with the following figures (in thousands):

Year	Total Investment Start of Year	Net Income after Tax	Reported Return on Investment
1	£4,000	£160	4.0%
2	4,600	310	6.7
3	4,650	370	8.0
4	4,600	490	10.7
5	4,550	670	14.7
6	4,500	970	21.6
7	4,450	910	20.4
8	4,400	760	17.3

On the other hand, "eyeballing" the figures in Exhibit 1 led Mr. Jones to guess that if the proposal were analyzed using after-tax cash flows discounted at 10%, it might well show a positive net present value, and hence would be a worthwhile investment opportunity.

Questions

1. Find the net present value of the proposal, discounting after-tax cash flows at 10%.
2. To what extent, if any, would the low anticipated rate of return on investment in the first three years be likely to affect the decision to launch the new product line:
   a. If the Orkney Biscuit Company were a private company, owned entirely by Mr. Jones?
   b. If the Orkney Biscuit Company were a publicly owned company, with shares owned by a larged number of small investors, and Mr. Jones purely a salaried administrator?
   c. If the Orkney Biscuit Company were a wholly owned subsidiary of a much larger company and Mr. Jones expected to be a candidate to succeed one of the parent company's top executives who will retire from the company about two years from now?
3. Do you think that your analysis of these figures indicates that accountants should consider making major changes in their approach to income measurement?

CASE 19–6. CLIMAX SHIPPING COMPANY

The controller of the Climax Shipping Company, located near Pittsburgh, was preparing a report for the executive committee regarding the feasibility of repairing one of the company's steam riverboats or of replacing the steamboat with a new diesel-powered boat.

The Climax Shipping Company was engaged mainly in the transportation of coal from the nearby mines to the steel mills, public utilities, and other industries in the Pittsburgh area. The company's several steamboats also, on occasion, carried cargoes to places as far away as New Orleans. The boats owned by Climax were all steam-powered. All were at least 10 years old, and the majority were between 15 and 30 years old.

The steamboat the controller was concerned about, the Cynthia, was 23 years old and required immediate rehabilitation or replacement. It was estimated that the Cynthia had a useful life of another 20 years provided that adequate repairs and maintenance were made. Whereas the book value of the Cynthia was $39,500, it was believed that she would bring somewhat less than this amount, possibly around $25,000, if she were to be sold. The total of immediate rehabilitation costs for the Cynthia was estimated to be $115,000. It was estimated that these general rehabilitation expenditures would extend the useful life of the Cynthia for about 20 years.

New spare parts from another boat, which had been retired recently, were available for use in the rehabilitation of the Cynthia. An estimate of their fair value, if used on the Cynthia, was $43,500, which was their book value. Use of these parts would, in effect, decrease the immediate rehabilitation costs from $115,000 to $71,500. It was believed that if these parts were sold on the market they would bring only around $30,000. They could not be used on any of the other Climax steamboats.

Currently, the Cynthia was operated by a 20-member crew. Annual operating costs for this crew would be approximately as follows:

Wages...	$110,200
Vacation and sickness benefits..........................	1,880
Social security payments...............................	2,400
Life insurance..	1,800
Commissary supplies..................................	15,420
Repairs and maintenance..............................	24,400
Fuel..	34,500
Lubricants...	550
Miscellaneous service and supplies......................	12,000
Total...	$203,150

It was estimated that the cost of dismantling and scrapping the Cynthia at the end of her useful life after the overhaul would be offset by the value of the scrap and used parts taken off the boat.

An alternative to rehabilitating the steamboat was the purchase of a diesel-powered boat. The Quapelle Company, a local boat manufacturer, quoted the price of $325,000 for a diesel boat. An additional $75,000 for a basic parts inventory would be necessary to service a diesel boat, and such an inventory would be sufficient to service up to three diesel boats. If four or more diesels were purchased, however, it was estimated that additional spare parts inventory would be necessary.

The useful life of a diesel-powered boat was estimated to be 25 years, at the end of which time the boat would be scrapped or completely rehabilitated at a cost approximating that of a new boat. The possibility of diesel engine replacement during the 25-year life was not contemplated by the controller, since information from other companies having limited experience with diesel-powered riverboats did not indicate that such costs needed to be anticipated; but a general overhaul of the engines, costing at current prices $60,000, would be expected every 10 years.

One of the features the Quapelle Company pointed out was the 12 percent increase in average speed of diesel-powered boats over the steamboats. The controller discounted this feature, however, because the short runs and lock-to-lock operations involved in local river shipping would prohibit the diesel boats from taking advantage of their greater speed since there was little opportunity for passing and they would have to wait in turn at each lock for the slower steamboats. Presently only two diesel boats, out of about 40 boats, were operating on the river. The controller felt it would be many years, if at all, before diesel boats displaced the slower steamboats.

After consulting the Quapelle Company and other companies operating diesel-powered boats, the controller estimated that the annual operating costs of a diesel-powered boat would total $156,640, broken down as follows:

Wages for a 13-member crew	$ 77,300
Vacation and sickness benefits	1,320
Social security payments	1,680
Life insurance	1,170
Commissary supplies	10,020
Repairs and maintenance*	21,700
Fuel	28,800
Extra stern repairs	2,000
Miscellaneous service and supplies	12,650
Total	$156,640

* Excluding possible major overhaul of diesel engines.

Although the Climax controller had not considered the matter, the reader of this case may assume that at the end of the 20th year the diesel boat would have a realizable value of $32,500 and the inventory of parts of $37,500.

The controller was also concerned at this time with a city smoke ordinance which would take effect in two years. To comply with the regulations of the ordinance, all hand-fired steamboats had to be converted to stoker firing. Several of the Climax steamboats were already stoker-fired; the Cynthia, however, was hand-fired. The additional cost of converting the Cynthia to stoker firing was estimated to be $40,000, provided it was done at the same time as the general rehabilitation. This $40,000 included the cost of stokers and extra hull conversion and was not included in the $115,000 rehabilitation figure. The controller also knew that if $115,000 were spent presently in rehabilitating the Cynthia and it was found out later that no relief, or only temporary relief for one or two years, was to be granted under the smoke ordinance, the cost of converting to stoker firing would no longer be $40,000, but around $70,000. The higher cost would be due to rebuilding, which would not be necessary if the Cynthia was converted to stoker firing at the time of her general rehabilitation.

Conversion would reduce the crew from 20 to 18, with the following details:

Wages...	$100,650
Vacation and sickness benefits........................	1,650
Social security payments.............................	2,200
Life insurance......................................	1,620
Commissary supplies................................	13,880
Repairs and maintenance*...........................	24,400
Fuel*..	34,500
Lubricants*..	550
Miscellaneous service and supplies*..................	12,000
Total..	$191,450

* These costs would remain the same, whether the crew was 20 or 18.

All operating data the controller had collected pertaining to crew expenses were based on a two-shift, 12-hour working day, which was standard on local riverboats. He had been informed, however, that the union representing crew members wanted a change to a three-shift, eight-hour day. If the union insisted on an eight-hour day, accommodations on board the steamers or the diesels would have to be enlarged. The controller was perturbed by this fact, because he knew the diesels could readily be converted to accommodate three crews whereas steamers could not. How strongly the union would insist on the change and when it would be put into effect, if ever, were questions for which the controller could get no satisfactory answers. He believed that the union might have a difficult time in getting acceptance of its demands for three eight-hour shifts on steamers, since it would be very difficult, if not impossible, to convert the steamers to hold a larger crew, because of space limitations. The controller thought that the union might succeed in getting its demands accepted, however, in the case of diesel-powered boats. One of the diesel boats currently operating in the Pittsburgh area had accommodations for three crews, although it was still operating on a two-shift basis. The diesel boats that the Quapelle Company offered to build for Climax could be fitted to accommodate three crews at no additional cost.

Another factor the controller was considering at this time was alternative uses of funds. Climax had sufficient funds to buy four diesel-powered boats; however, there were alternative uses for these funds. The other projects which the management was considering at this time had an estimated return of at least 10 percent after taxes. The income tax rate at the time was 50 percent.

The company was conservatively managed and had no long-term debt outstanding. Its net worth exceeded $2 million. The company occasionally used unsecured bank loans to provide working capital during seasonal periods of peak need. Presently the company's liability for bank loans amounted to $150,000, which had been borrowed at 10 percent interest. The "prime" loan rate in New York City currently was 8 percent.

As a further inducement to have a contract to build a diesel boat, the Quapelle Company offered to lease a diesel boat to Climax. The lease terms offered by the Quapelle Company called for annual payments of $21,700 for 15 years plus $5,700 per year for an interest charge. At the end of 15 years, when the Quapelle Company had in effect recovered the value of the boat, it would charge a nominal rental of $2,850 a year. Title to the boat would continue to remain in the hands of the Quapelle Company. Climax would incur all costs of operating and maintaining the boat, including general overhaul every 10 years, and would still need to invest $75,000 in a basic spare parts inventory.

Questions

1. *If* management chooses to rehabilitate the Cynthia, should the stoker conversion be done immediately or delayed for two years?
2. *If* Climax acquires the diesel-powered boat, should they buy it or lease it?
3. Which alternative would you recommend?

CHAPTER 20

RESPONSIBILITY ACCOUNTING: THE MANAGEMENT CONTROL PROCESS

This chapter introduces the third type of management accounting information, which is called responsibility accounting. (The other two types are full-cost accounting and differential accounting.) As background for explaining the nature and use of management accounting, we first discuss the nature of organizations and the management control process that is an important management function in organizations. We also discuss three types of responsibility centers: expense centers, profit centers, and investment centers.

CHARACTERISTICS OF ORGANIZATIONS

An organization is a group of persons who work together for one or more purposes. These purposes are its *goals*, or its *objectives*. We have described the goals of business organizations in Chapter 18, noting that one dominant goal is earning a satisfactory return on investment.

An organization consists of human beings. A factory with its machines is not an organization; rather, it is the persons who work in the factory that constitute the organization. In an organization the human beings work together. A crowd walking down a street is not an organization, nor are the spectators at a football game when they are behaving as individual spectators. But the cheering section at a game is an organization; its members work together under the direction of the cheerleaders.

Management

An organization has one or more leaders. Except in extremely rare circumstances, a group of persons can work together to accomplish the

660

organization's goals only if they are led. In a business organization, the leaders are called managers, or, collectively, the management. An organization's managers decide what the goals of the organization should be; they communicate these goals to members of the organization; they decide the tasks that are to be performed in order to achieve these goals and on the resources that are to be used in carrying out these tasks; they see to it that the activities of the various parts of the organization are coordinated; they match individuals to tasks for which they are suited; they motivate these individuals to carry out their tasks; they observe how well these individuals are performing their tasks; and they take corrective action when the need arises. The leader of a cheering section performs these functions; so does the president of General Motors Corporation.

Organization Hierarchy

A manager can supervise only a limited number of subordinates. Old Testament writers put this number at 10. Although there can be considerable variation in this number, depending on the nature of the job to be done and on the personality and skill of the manager, clearly there is an upper limit to the number of persons that one manager can supervise directly, and it is a small number. It follows that in a company of any substantial size there must be several layers of managers in the organization structure. Authority runs from the top unit down through the successive layers. Such an arrangement is called an organization hierarchy.

The formal relationships among the various managers can be diagrammed in an *organization chart*. A partial organization chart is shown in Illustration 20–1. At the top is the board of directors which is responsible to the shareholders for the overall conduct of the company's affairs. Reporting to the board of directors is the president, who is the chief executive officer. A number of organization units report to the president. Some of these are *line* units; that is, their activities are directly associated with achieving the goals of the organization. They manufacture products, and they market products. Others are *staff* units; that is, they exist to provide services to other units and to the president.

The principal line units are here called divisions. Within each division there are a number of departments, and within each department there are a number of sections. Other names are used for these organization units in different companies.

All the units in Illustration 20–1 are organization units. Thus, Section A of Department 1 of Division A is an organization unit. Division A itself, including all of its departments and sections, also is an organization unit. Each of these organization units is headed by a manager who is responsible for the work done by the unit. These organization units are called responsibility centers. A *responsibility center* is simply an organi-

Illustration 20–1

PARTIAL ORGANIZATION CHART

zation unit headed by a responsible manager. The manager is responsible in the sense that he is held accountable for the work done by his organization unit.

Environment

Any organization is a part of a larger society. The world outside the organization itself is called its *environment*. For a business organization, the environment includes customers, suppliers, competitors, investors, creditors, labor organizations, government agencies, and other forces. The organization is continually reacting with its environment. This is a two-way interaction: the organization affects the outside world, and it is affected by forces originating in the outside world. Management is responsible for managing the organization, but since the organization is part of society, management also must see to it that the organization acts as a respectable member of that society.

BEHAVIORAL ASPECTS OF MANAGEMENT CONTROL

An important management function is that of assuring that activities of members of the organization help to accomplish the organization's goals. The process used for this purpose is called *management control*. It is defined as follows: *Management control is the process by which managers assure that resources are obtained and used effectively and efficiently in the accomplishment of the organization's goals.*

This process has a behavioral aspect and a technical aspect. The behavioral aspect is discussed at length in books on organizational behavior or social psychology. Although we shall provide here only a brief discussion, it is an essential one because the technical aspects are meaningful only if one understands that they are intended to influence behavior. The management control process in part consists of inducing the human beings in an organization to take those actions that will help attain the company's goals and to refrain from taking actions that are inconsistent with these goals. Although for some purposes an accumulation of the costs of manufacturing a product is useful, management cannot literally "control" a product, or the costs of making a product. What management does—or at least what it attempts to do—is control the actions of the people who are responsible for incurring these costs.

Behavior of Participants

Each person in an organization is called a *participant*. A person becomes a participant—that is, he[1] joins an organization—because he believes that by doing so he can achieve his *personal* goals. His decision to contribute to the productive work of the organization once he has become a member of it is also based on his perception that this will help achieve his personal goals.

An individual's personal goals can be expressed as *needs*. Some of these needs are *material* and can be satisfied by the money that he earns on the job; that is, he needs enough money to provide for himself and for his family. Other needs are *psychological*. People need to have their abilities and achievements recognized; they need social acceptance as members of a group; they need to feel a sense of personal worth; they need to feel secure; they need the freedom to exercise discretion; they may need a feeling of power and achievement.

The relative importance of these needs varies with different persons, and their importance also varies with the same person at different times. For some people, earning a great deal of money is a dominant need; for others, monetary considerations are much less important. Only a relatively few people attach much importance to the need to exercise discretion or the need for achievement, but these few persons tend to be the leaders of the organization.[2] The relative importance that persons attach to their

---

[1] Although the male pronoun is used in place of the awkward "he or she," it should be understood that these observations apply equally to both men and women.

[2] McClelland argues that there is a relationship between the strength of the achievement motivation of the leaders of an organization and the success of that organization and that a similar relationship helps explain why certain countries

own needs is heavily influenced by the attitude of their colleagues and of their superiors.

Incentives

Individuals are influenced both by positive incentives and negative incentives. A *positive incentive*, also called a reward, is the satisfaction of a need, or the expectation that a need will be satisfied. A *negative incentive*, also called a punishment, is the deprivation of satisfaction of a need, or the fear of such deprivation. Research on incentives tends to support the following:

• Individuals are more strongly motivated by positive incentives than by negative incentives.

• Monetary compensation is an important incentive, but beyond the subsistence level the amount of compensation is not necessarily as important as nonmonetary rewards. Nevertheless, the amount of a person's earnings is often important indirectly as an indication of how his achievement and ability are regarded. (A person earning $50,000 a year may be disgruntled if a colleague whom he believes has only equal ability receives $51,000 a year.)

• The effectiveness of incentives diminishes rapidly as the time elapses between an action and the reward or punishment administered for it. This is why it is important that reports on performance be made available and acted on quickly. Management control cannot wait for the annual financial statements that appear three months or so after the year has ended.

• Needs may be unconscious, or they may be expressed as aspirations or goals. Motivation is weakest when the person perceives a goal as being either unattainable or too easily attainable. Motivation is strong when the goal can be attained with some effort and when the individual regards its attainment as important in relation to his needs.

• A person tends to accept reports of his performance more willingly and to use them more constructively when they are presented to him in a manner that he regards as objective; that is, without personal bias.

• Persons are receptive to learning better ways of doing things only when they personally recognize the inadequacies of their present behavior.

• Beyond a certain point, pressure for improved performance accomplishes nothing. This optimum point is far below the maximum amount of

---

have a rapid economic growth at certain times while others do not. See David McClelland, *The Achieving Society* (1971); and David C. McClelland and David G. Winter, *Motivating Economic Achievement* (New York: The Free Press, 1969).

pressure that conceivably could be exerted. (When the coach says, "Don't press; don't try too hard," he is applying this principle.)

TYPES OF INCENTIVES. Incentives take many forms. In some situations a quite simple signal can be effective.

EXAMPLE: In the New York City government there was a project to sort out and discard files on those Medicaid cases that had been closed. These files occupied 1,200 file cabinets. When the job started, each clerk was examining an average of 150 files a day, which was unsatisfactory. The supervisor then made the following change: instead of discarding files in a common container, each clerk was asked to pile them in front of his or her work station. As the piles mounted, it became apparent to everyone how much work each clerk was doing. Production immediately increased to 300 files a day.[3]

At the other extreme, the reward can be that the manager's compensation is related to his performance, that is, managers are paid a performance bonus. In view of the importance which many people attach to monetary compensation, this is a strong motivation indeed. In some cases it is too strong, for unless the basis for the bonus payment is very carefully worked out, incessant arguments will go on about the justice and equity of the bonus system. If, however, rewards are in the form of oral praise for good performance or criticism for poor performance, inequities in the numerical reports can be allowed for when interpreting the results.

Individuals differ in their needs and in their reactions to incentives of various types. An important function of the manager at each level is to adapt his application of the management control system to the personalities and attitudes of the individuals whom he supervises. Thus an impersonal system can never be a substitute for interpersonal actions; rather, the system is a framework that should be adapted by the manager to fit individual situations.

Goal Congruence

Since an organization does not have a mind of its own, the organization itself literally cannot have goals. The "organizational goals" that we have referred to are actually the goals of top management. Top management wants these organizational goals to be attained, but other participants have their own personal goals that *they* want to achieve. These personal goals are the satisfaction of their needs. In other words, participants act in their own self-interest.

The difference between organizational goals and personal goals suggests the central purpose of a management control system: the system

---

[3] From *Management Accounting*, December 1972, p. 63.

should be designed so that actions that it leads people to take in accordance with their perceived self-interest are actions that are also in the best interests of the company. In the language of social psychology, the management control system should encourage *goal congruence;* that is, it should be structured so that the goals of participants so far as feasible are consistent with the goals of the organization as a whole.

Perfect congruence between individual goals and organizational goals does not exist. For example, the individual participant wants as much salary as he can get, whereas from the viewpoint of the organization, there is an upper limit to salaries, beyond which profits will be adversely affected. As a minimum, however, the system should not encourage the individual to act against the best interests of the company. For example, if the management control system signals that the emphasis should be only on reducing costs, and if a manager responds by reducing costs at the expense of adequate quality or if he responds by reducing costs in his own responsibility center by measures that cause a more than offsetting increase in costs in some other responsibility center, he has been motivated, but in the wrong direction. It is therefore important to ask two separate questions about any practice used in a management control system:

1.   What action does it motivate people to take in their own perceived self-interest, and
2.   Is this action in the best interests of the company?

Cooperation and Conflict

The appearance of an organization chart implies that the way in which organizational goals are attained is that the top manager makes a decision, he communicates that decision down through the organizational hierarchy, and managers at lower levels of the organization proceed to implement it. It should now be apparent that this is *not* the way in which an organization actually functions.

What actually happens is that each subordinate reacts to the instructions of top management in accordance with how those instructions affect the subordinate's personal needs. Since usually more than one responsibility center is involved in carrying out a given plan, the interactions between their managers also affect what actually happens. For example, although the manager of the maintenance department is supposed to see to it that the maintenance needs of the operating departments are satisfied, if there is friction between the maintenance manager and an operating manager, the needs of that operating manager's department may, in fact, be slighted. For these and many other reasons, conflict exists within organizations.

At the same time, the work of the organization will not get done unless its participants work together with a certain amount of harmony. Thus, there is also cooperation in organizations. Participants realize that unless there is a reasonable amount of cooperation, the organization will dissolve, and the participants will then be unable to satisfy *any* of the needs which motivated them to join the organization in the first place.

An organization attempts to maintain an appropriate balance between the forces that create conflict and those that create cooperation. Some conflict is not only inevitable, it is desirable. Conflict results in part from the competition among participants for promotion or other forms of need satisfaction; and such competition is, within limits, healthy. A certain amount of cooperation is also obviously essential, but if undue emphasis is placed on engendering cooperative attitudes, the most able participants will be denied the opportunity of demonstrating their full potentialities.

Top Management Sponsorship

A management control system will probably be ineffective unless subordinate managers are convinced that top management considers the system to be important. Some systems are installed with no more management backing than the directive, "Let's have a good control system," and with no subsequent interest or action by top management. Such a system, instead of being a part of the management process, becomes a paper shuffling routine whose principal virtue is that it provides employment for a great many clerks.

Action is a sure signal, probably the only effective signal, that top management is interested in the control system. Basically, this action involves praise or other reward for good performance, criticism of or removal of the causes for poor performance, or questions leading to these actions. If, in contrast, reports on performance disappear into executive offices and are never heard about again, the organization has reason to assume that management is not paying attention to them. And if management does not pay attention to them, why should anyone else?

Participation and Understanding

Control is exercised in part by establishing standards of expected performance and comparing actual performance with these standards. Whatever standard of good performance is adopted, it is likely to be effective as a means of control only if the person being judged agrees that it is an equitable standard. If he does not agree, he is likely to pay no attention to comparisons between his performance and the standard; and he is likely to resent, and if possible reject, an attempt by anyone else to make such a comparison.

The best way to assure this agreement is to ask the person whose performance is to be measured to participate in the process of setting the standard. In order to participate intelligently, the manager needs to understand clearly what the control system is, what he is expected to do, what basis he is going to be judged on, and so on. Such an understanding probably cannot be achieved by written communication alone. Frequent meetings of supervisors for discussion and explanation are required.

The process of educating the individuals involved in the system is necessarily a continuous one. Not uncommonly, a system is introduced with a loud fanfare, works well for a time, and then gradually withers away in effectiveness as the initial stimulus disappears.

Focus on Line Managers

Since subordinates are responsible to their superiors, they should receive praise, criticism, and other incentives from their superiors. Staff people should not be directly involved in these motivation activities (except with respect to control of the staff organizations themselves). Line managers are the focal points in management control. Staff people collect, summarize, and present information that is useful in the management control process, and they make calculations that translate management judgments into the format of the control system. There may be many such staff people; indeed, the control department is often the largest staff department in a company. However, the significant decisions and control actions are the responsibility of the line managers, not of the staff.

THE MANAGEMENT CONTROL PROCESS

The management control process involves two separate but closely related activities: planning and control. *Planning* is deciding what should be done and how it should be done. It is an activity that goes on at all levels in an organization. When a salesperson decides what customers to call on tomorrow, the salesperson is engaged in planning. When the president decides to carry out a five-year expansion program, the president also is engaged in planning. *Control* is assuring that desired[4] results are attained. It is also an activity that is carried on throughout the organization. When a supervisor observes how diligently the employees are working, the supervisor is engaged in control, and so is the president

---

[4] "Desired" results are not necessarily the same as "planned" results. Changes in circumstances that occur after a plan has been prepared may make it desirable to depart from the plan.

when discussing the latest report on performance with one of the vice presidents. Although the word "planning" is not included in the name of the management control process, it should be understood that planning activities are fully as important as control activities in this process.

The management control process takes place within a framework of organizational goals and broad strategies for attaining these goals. The process of arriving at these goals and broad strategies is called *strategic planning*.

In a small organization, the implementation of strategic plans may involve primarily the development of an informal plan by the manager, his explanation to other members of the organization of what he wants done, and his subsequent observations to ascertain how well the members carry out the tasks assigned to them. This face-to-face control is feasible only in the tiniest of organizations, however. In a company with many separate organization units, each with its own specialized job to do, the strategies must be communicated to the managers of all these units, a formal implementation plan must be developed, and the efforts of each manager must be brought into harmony with one another. This is the management control process.

Management control should be distinguished from another planning and control process called *operational control*. This is the process of assuring that specific tasks are carried out effectively and efficiently. Operational control involves little management judgment and relatively little interaction among managers. The control system for inventories based on economic order quantity, described in Chapter 18, is an example of an operational control technique.

Thus there are three planning and control processes: strategic planning, management control, and operational control. We focus on the middle one.

Steps in the Management Control Process

Much of the management control process involves informal communication and interactions. Informal communication occurs by means of memoranda, meetings, conversations, and even by such signals as facial expressions. Although these informal activities are of great importance, they are not amenable to a systematic description. In addition to these informal activities, most companies also have a *formal* management control system. It consists of some or all of the following phases:

1. Programming.
2. Budgeting.
3. Operating and accounting.
4. Reporting and analysis.

As indicated in Illustration 20–2, each of these activities leads to the next. They recur in a regular cycle, and together they constitute a "closed loop." These four phases are described briefly below. Programming and Budgeting are discussed in detail in Chapter 21, and the other two steps in Chapter 22.

PROGRAMMING. *Programming is the process of deciding on the programs that the company will undertake and the approximate amount of resources that are to be allocated to each program.* Programs are the principal activities that the organization has decided to undertake in order to implement the strategies that it has decided upon. In a profit-oriented

Illustration 20–2

PHASES OF MANAGEMENT CONTROL

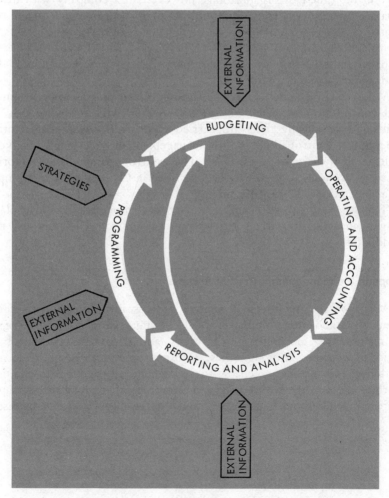

company, each principal product or product line is a program. If several product lines are manufactured in the same plant, the plant itself and additions or modifications to it may be identified as a program. There are also various research and development programs, some aimed at improving existing products or processes, others searching for marketable new products.

BUDGETING. *A budget is a plan expressed in quantitative, usually monetary, terms that covers a specified period of time, usually one year.* In the budgeting process each program is translated into terms that correspond to the responsibility of those managers who have been charged with executing the program or some part of it. Thus, although the plans are originally made in terms of individual programs, in the budgeting process the plans are translated into terms of responsibility centers. The process of developing a budget is essentially one of negotiation between the manager of a responsibility center and his superior. The end product of these negotiations is an approved statement of the revenues that are expected during the budget year, and the resources that are to be used in achieving the company's goals for each responsibility center and for the company as a whole.

OPERATING AND ACCOUNTING. During the period of actual operations, records are kept of resources actually consumed (i.e., costs) and the revenues actually earned. These records are structured so that costs and revenue data are classified both by programs and by responsibility centers. Data classified according to programs are used as a basis for future programming, and data classified by responsibility centers are used to measure the performance of responsibility center managers. For the latter purpose, data on actual results are reported in such a way that they can be readily compared with the plan as set forth in the budget.

REPORTING AND ANALYSIS. The management control system serves as a communication device. The information that is communicated consists of both accounting and nonaccounting data, and of both data generated within the organization and data about what is happening in the environment outside the organization. This information keeps managers informed as to what is going on and helps to insure that the work done by the separate responsibility centers is coordinated.

Reports are also used as a basis for control. Essentially, such reports are derived from an analysis that compares actual performance with planned performance and attempts to explain the difference. Based on these formal reports, and also on information received through informal communication channels, managers decide what, if any, action should be taken. They may, for example, decide to change the plan as set forth in the budget, and this leads to a new planning process. It is for this reason that the phases shown in Illustration 20–2 are depicted as a closed loop, with one leading to the next.

Management Control System Characteristics

Following is a list of the principal characteristics of a management control system:

1. A management control system focuses on *programs* and *responsibility centers.*

2. The information in a management control system is of two general types: (1) *planned data,* that is, programs, budgets, and standards; and (2) *actual data,* that is, information on what is actually happening, both inside the organization and in the environment.

3. Ordinarily, a management control system is a *total* system in the sense that it embraces all aspects of a company's operation. It needs to be a total system because an important management function is to assure that all parts of the operation are in balance with one another; and in order to examine balance, management needs information about each of the parts.

4. The management control system is usually *built around a financial structure;* that is, resources and revenues are expressed in monetary units. Money is the only common denominator which can be used to combine and compare the heterogeneous elements of resources (e.g., hours of labor, type of labor, quantity and quality of material, amount and kind of products produced). Although the financial structure is usually the central focus, nonmonetary measures such as minutes per operation, number of employees, and reject and spoilage rates are also important parts of the system.

5. The management control process tends to be *rhythmic;* it follows a definite pattern and timetable, month after month and year after year. In budget preparation, which is an important activity in the management control process, certain steps are taken in a prescribed sequence and at certain dates each year: dissemination of guidelines, preparation of original estimates, transmission of these estimates up through the several echelons in the organization, review of these estimates, final approval by top management, and dissemination back through the organization. The procedure to be followed at each step in this process, the dates when the steps are to be completed, and even the forms to be used can be, and often are, set forth in a policies and procedures manual.

6. A management control system is, or should be, a *coordinated, integrated system;* that is, although data collected for one purpose may differ from those collected for another purpose, these data should be reconcilable with one another. In particular, it is essential that data on actual performance be structured in the same way—that is, have the same definitions and the same account content—as data on planned performance. If this is not done, valid comparisons of actual and planned performance cannot be made. In a sense, the management control system

is a *single* system, but it is perhaps more accurate to think of it as a set of interlocking subsystems, one for programming, another for budgeting, another for accounting, and another for reporting and analysis.

RESPONSIBILITY CENTERS

We have used the term "responsibility center" to denote any organization unit that is headed by a responsible manager. As a basis for studying the management control process, we now go more deeply into the nature of responsibility centers. Illustration 20–3 provides a basis for doing this. The top section depicts a machine, which in some important respects is analogous to a responsibility center. A machine, in this case a gasoline engine, (1) uses inputs, (2) to do work, (3) which results in output. In the case of an engine, the inputs are fuel and air, and the output is mechanical energy. A responsibility center is like an engine in that it has inputs, which are physical quantities of material, hours of various

Illustration 20–3

NATURE OF A RESPONSIBILITY CENTER

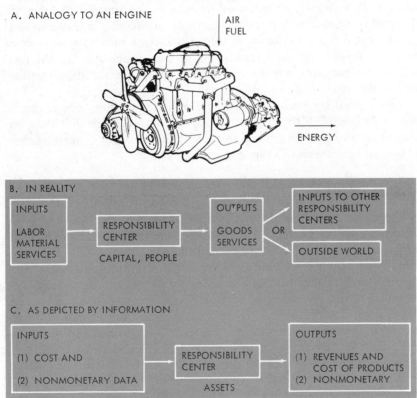

types of labor, and a variety of services; it *works* with these resources. Usually, working capital and fixed assets are also required. As a result of this work, it produces *outputs*, which are classified either as goods, if they are tangible, or as services, if they are intangible. These goods or services go either to other responsibility centers within the company or to customers in the outside world.

Responsibility accounting provides information about these inputs and outputs. Accounting measures inputs in terms of cost. Although the resources themselves are physical things such as pounds of material and hours of labor, for the purposes of a management control system it is necessary to measure these physical things with some common denominator so that the physically unlike elements of resources can be combined. That common denominator is money. The monetary measure of the resources used in a responsibility center is *cost*. In addition to cost information, nonaccounting information on such matters as the physical quantity of material used, its quality, the skill level of the work force, and so on, is also useful.

If the outputs of a responsibility center are goods or services sold to an outside customer, accounting measures these outputs in terms of revenue. If, however, products or services are transferred to other responsibility centers within the company, an accounting measure of output is more difficult to obtain. In some situations a monetary measure of output is feasible for such transfers. Alternative measures are the total cost of the goods or services transferred, or a nonaccounting measure, such as the number of units of output.

This general statement of the nature of a responsibility center can be used to help explain three types of responsibility centers which are important in management control systems. These are: (1) expense centers, (2) profit centers, and (3) investment centers.

Expense Centers

If the control system measures the expenses (i.e., the costs) incurred by a responsibility center but does not measure the monetary value of its output, the responsibility center is called an *expense center*. Every responsibility center has outputs; that is, it does something. In many cases, however, it is neither feasible nor necessary to measure these outputs in monetary terms. For example, it would be extremely difficult to measure the monetary value of the accounting department's contribution to the company. Although generally it is relatively easy to measure the monetary value of the outputs of an individual production department, there is no reason for doing so if the responsibility of the department manager is to produce a stated *quantity* of outputs at the lowest feasible cost. For these reasons, most individual production departments, and most staff units are expense centers. For an expense center, the accounting system records the cost incurred, but not the revenues earned.

Expense centers are not quite the same as cost centers. Recall from Chapter 15 that a *cost center* is a device used in a full cost accounting system to collect costs that are subsequently to be charged to cost objectives. In a given company, many, but not all, expense centers are also cost centers.

In the interests of completeness, we mention here the *revenue center*, which is a responsibility center in which revenues are recorded. Certain branch sales offices are examples of revenue centers. The following discussion omits further mention of revenue centers as such, since the general concepts applicable to them are a mirror image of those applicable to expense centers.

Profit Centers

Revenue is a monetary measure of outputs, and expense (or cost) is a monetary measure of inputs, or resources consumed. Profit is the difference between revenue and expense. If performance in a responsibility center is measured in terms of both (1) the revenue it earns and (2) the expense it incurs, the responsibility center is a *profit center*.

Although in financial accounting, revenue is recognized only when it is realized, in responsibility accounting revenue is defined as a monetary measure of the output of a responsibility center in a given accounting period, *whether or not the company realizes the revenue in that period*. Thus, a factory is a profit center if it "sells" its output to the sales department and records the revenue from such sales. Likewise, a service department, such as the maintenance department, may "sell" its services to the responsibility centers that receive these services. These "sales" generate revenues for the service department, and in these circumstances, the service department is a profit center.

Revenues that arise when one responsibility center "sells" its outputs to other responsibility centers within the company differ from revenues that arise from sales to customers, in that outside sales increase the company's assets (either accounts receivable or cash), while internal sales do not. These internal transfers are therefore called by some people "mere bookkeeping entries." As we shall see, they nevertheless can be important in the management control process.

A given responsibility center is a profit center only if management *decides* to measure its outputs in monetary terms. Revenues for a whole company are automatically generated when the company makes sales to the outside world. By contrast, revenues for an internal organization unit are recognized only if management decides that it is a good idea to do so. No accounting principle *requires* that revenues be measured for individual responsibility centers within a company. With some ingenuity, practically any expense center could be turned into a profit center because some way of putting a selling price on the output of most responsibility centers can be found. The question is whether there are sufficient positive benefits in doing so.

ADVANTAGES OF PROFIT CENTERS. A profit center resembles a business in miniature. Like a separate company, it has an income statement that shows revenue, expense, and the difference between them, which is profit. Most of the decisions made by the manager of a profit center affect the numbers on this income statement. The income statement for a profit center therefore is a basic management control document. Because his performance is measured by profit, the manager of a profit center is motivated to make decisions about inputs and outputs that will increase the profit that is reported for his profit center. Since he acts somewhat as he would act if he were running his own business, the profit center is a good training ground for general management responsibility. The use of the profit center idea is one of the important tools that has made possible the recent tendency of large companies to decentralize.

CRITERIA FOR PROFIT CENTERS. In deciding on whether to set up a given responsibility center as a profit center, the following points should be kept in mind:

1. Extra recordkeeping is involved if the profit center idea is used. In the profit center itself, there is the extra work of measuring output in monetary terms, and in the responsibility centers that receive its outputs there is the work of recording the cost of goods or services received.

2. If the manager of a responsibility center has little authority to decide on the quantity and quality of its outputs or on the relation of output to costs, then a profit center is usually of little use as a control device. This does not imply that the manager of a profit center must have *complete* control over outputs and inputs, for few, if any, managers have such complete authority.

3. When top management *requires* responsibility centers to use a certain service furnished by another responsibility center within the company, the service probably should be furnished at no charge, and the service unit therefore should not be a profit center. For example, if top management requires that internal audits be made, the responsibility centers probably should not be asked to pay for the cost of the internal auditing service, and the internal auditing unit should therefore not be a profit center.

4. If output is fairly homogeneous (e.g., cement), a nonmonetary measure of output (e.g., hundredweight of cement produced) may be adequate, and there may be no substantial advantage to be gained in converting this output to a monetary measure of revenue.

5. To the extent that a profit center puts a manager in business for himself, it promotes a spirit of competition. In many situations, competition provides a powerful incentive for good management. In other situations, however, organization units should cooperate closely with one another. In these situations, the profit center device may generate excessive friction between profit centers, to the detriment of the whole company's welfare. Also, it may generate too much interest in short-run profits to the detriment of long-run results. These difficulties are likely to arise when managers have an inadequate understanding of the management job, and the problems often can be overcome by education. If, however, they cannot be overcome, the profit center technique should not be used.

Transfer Prices

A *transfer price* is a price used to measure the value of products or services furnished by a profit center to other responsibility centers within a company. It is to be contrasted with a market price, which measures exchanges between a company and the outside world. Internal exchanges that are measured by transfer prices result in *revenue* for the responsibility center furnishing the goods or services and in *cost* for the responsibility center receiving the goods or services. Whenever profit centers are established, transfer prices must also be established. There are two general types of transfer prices: the market-based price and the cost-based price.

If a market price for the goods or services exists, a *market-based price* is usually preferable to a cost-based price. The "buying" responsibility center should ordinarily not be expected to pay more internally than it would have to pay if it purchased from the outside world, nor should the "selling" center ordinarily be entitled to more revenue than it could obtain by selling to the outside world. If the market price is abnormal, as for example when an outside vendor sets a low "distress" price in order to use temporarily idle capacity, then such temporary aberrations are ordinarily disregarded in arriving at transfer prices. The market price may be adjusted for cash discounts and for certain selling costs that are not involved in an internal exchange.

In a great many situations, there is no reliable market price that can be used as a basis for the transfer price, and in these situations, a *cost-based transfer price* is used. Two general types of cost-based price are discussed in the literature: (1) marginal cost and (2) full cost plus profit. Marginal cost, as explained in Chapter 18, has approximately the same meaning as variable cost. The marginal cost approach is consistent with the economic model of the firm that assumes the managers make decisions on the basis of complete knowledge of all supply and demand factors affecting the firm, but it is not much used in practice because few firms have such knowledge, particularly of their demand curve.[5]

If the *full cost approach* is used, the method of computing cost and the amount of profit to be included is set by top management in order to lessen arguments that would otherwise occur between the buying and the selling responsibility centers. If feasible, the cost should be a standard cost, for if it is an actual cost, the selling responsibility center can pass along its inefficiencies to the buying responsibility center; these inefficiencies will be included in the transfer price. In some situations, the costs are neither the standard nor the actual costs incurred in the selling responsibility center; they may instead be an estimate of the costs that *would be* incurred by the most efficient producer, if such costs can be estimated. A transfer price based on such estimates of cost may be a better measure of the output of the selling responsibility center than a price based on the manufacturing practices and equipment actually being employed.

Whatever the approach to setting the transfer price, there is usually a mechanism for negotiating the price of actual transactions between the buying and the selling responsibility centers. For example, the selling responsibility center may be willing to sell below the normal market price rather than lose the business, which could happen if the buying responsibility center took advantage of a temporarily low outside price. In such circumstances, the two parties negotiate a "deal." Unless both responsibility center managers have complete freedom to act, these negotiations will not always lead to an equitable result because the parties may have unequal bargaining powers; that is, the prospective buyer may not have the power of threatening to take its business elsewhere, and the prospective seller may not have the power of refusing to do the work. Thus, there usually needs to be an arbitration mechanism to settle disputes concerning transfer prices.

Investment Centers

An *investment center* is a responsibility center in which the manager is held responsible for the use of assets, as well as for revenues and expenses. It is therefore the ultimate extension of the responsibility idea. In an investment center the manager is expected to earn a satisfactory return on the assets employed in his responsibility center.

Measurement of assets employed, or the *investment base*, poses many difficult problems, and the idea of the investment center is so new that

---

[5] For the argument for the marginal cost approach, see: Jack Hirshleifer, "On the Economics of Transfer Pricing in the Divisionalized Firm," *Journal of Business*, April 1957, pp. 96–108.

there is considerable disagreement as to the best solution of these problems. For example, consider cash. The cash balance of the company is a
safety valve, or shock absorber, protecting the company against short-run
fluctuations in funds requirements. Compared with an independent company, an investment center needs relatively little cash, however, because
it can obtain funds from its headquarters on short notice. Part of the
headquarters cash balance therefore exists for the financial protection of
the investment centers, and headquarters cash can therefore logically be
allocated to the investment centers as part of their capital employed.
There are several ways of allocating this cash to investment centers just
as there are several ways of allocating general overhead costs.

Similar problems arise with respect to each type of asset that the investment center uses. A discussion of these problems is outside the
scope of this introductory treatment. For our present purpose, we need
only state that many problems exist and that there is much disagreement as
to the best solution, but despite the difficulties a growing number of
companies do find it useful to create investment centers.

Investment centers are normally used only for relatively large units,
such as a division that both manufactures and markets a line of products.
It has the effect of "putting the manager into business for himself" to
an even greater extent than does the profit center. Reports on performance show not only the amount of profit that the investment center
manager has earned, which is the case with reports for a profit center,
but also the amount of assets that he used in earning that profit. This
is obviously a more encompassing report on performance than a report
which does not relate profits to assets employed. On the other hand, the
possible disadvantages mentioned above for profit centers exist in a
magnified form in investment centers. Recordkeeping costs increase, and
there is the possibility that the manager will be motivated to act in ways
that are not consistent with the long-run best interests of the company
as a whole.

RESPONSIBILITY ACCOUNTING

The types of management accounting information discussed in earlier
chapters—full cost accounting and differential accounting—are both used
in the management control process. Full cost accounting is used to make
decisions of the type described in Chapter 16, particularly those relating
to selling prices and changes in product specifications. Differential accounting data are the principal type of accounting data used in the
programming phase of the management control cycle. These data assist
managers in deciding what capital investments to make, and what the
make-or-buy policy should be.

In addition to these two types, there is a third type of management accounting information that is specifically designed for the management control process. It is called responsibility accounting. Unlike the construction of differential costs and revenues, which is tailor-made for each problem, responsibility accounting involves a continuous flow of information throughout the organization. This information is intended to be helpful both for planning and for control. A formal definition is:

> *Responsibility accounting* is that type of management accounting that collects and reports both planned and actual accounting information in terms of responsibility centers.

An essential characteristic of responsibility accounting is that it focuses on responsibility centers. This is necessarily the case, for, as we noted above, the management control process is carried on by managers who head responsibility centers, and accounting information useful in this process must therefore relate to their sphere of responsibility. This difference in focus is what distinguishes responsibility accounting from full cost accounting. Full cost accounting focuses on goods or services rather than on responsibility centers. Although full cost accounting does make use of cost centers, some of which are also responsibility centers, cost centers are used merely as a means to an end. The emphasis is always on the cost of the goods or services, and the cost center is used as a means of assembling items of cost so that they can be assigned to goods and services. In making this distinction, we do not mean to imply that full cost accounting and responsibility accounting are two separate accounting systems; they are closely related and are more accurately described as two parts of the management accounting system.

> EXAMPLE: Company X makes two products, No. 1 and No. 2. It has two production departments, A and B, each of which is a production cost center. It also has two other departments, C and D, which are general and administrative service centers.
> The full costs of its products for a month are assembled and reported as shown in Part A of Illustration 20–4. Note that from this information, it is impossible to identify what costs the manager of any department was responsible for. In particular, the costs of Departments C and D are lumped together and are allocated first to production cost centers and then to products by means of an overhead rate. The full cost data show the total costs of Departments C and D to be $6,000 + $3,000 = $9,000, but they do not indicate how much of the $9,000 is the responsibility of the manager of Department C and how much is the responsibility of the manager of Department D.
> By contrast, responsibility accounting does identify the amount of costs that each of the four departmental managers is responsible for, as shown in Part B of the exhibit.
> Note that Part B, however, does not show the costs of the two products. Both types of information are needed. Note also that the total full

Illustration 20–4

CONTRAST BETWEEN FULL COSTS AND RESPONSIBILITY COSTS

A. Full Costs

	Product No. 1		Product No. 2	
	Total	*Per Unit*	*Total*	*Per Unit*
Volume (units)...................	2,000		1,000	
Cost item:				
Direct material...................	$14,000	$ 7.00	$ 6,000	$ 6.00
Direct labor....................	8,000	4.00	5,000	5.00
Factory indirect................	3,000	1.50	2,000	2.00
General and administrative........	6,000	3.00	3,000	3.00
Total costs................	$31,000	$15.50	$16,000	$16.00

B. Responsibility Costs

	Departments (Responsibility Centers)			
	A	*B*	*C*	*D*
Cost item:				
Direct material....................	$18,000	$ 2,000		
Direct labor.....................	4,000	9,000		
Supervision......................	700	900	$ 800	$1,400
Other labor costs.................	600	800	2,100	3,100
Supplies.........................	500	400	100	200
Other costs......................	300	800	500	800
Total costs................	$24,100	$13,900	$3,500	$5,500

costs is the same amount as the total responsibility costs. The two parts are different arrangements of the same underlying data.

Another important characteristic of responsibility accounting is implicit in the description of organizations given earlier in this chapter. Since the management control process influences the behavior of managers, in considering what type of accounting information is useful we must consider how accounting information affects human behavior. By contrast, our description of the use of differential accounting information was strictly impersonal; we made no mention of the behavior of the human beings who used this information in analyzing alternative choice problems. There was no need to bring these behavioral characteristics into the discussion because the process was essentially an economic analysis, and economics does not deal, except peripherally, with the behavior of individuals.

An Example: Computer Costs

As an illustration of how responsibility accounting information is structured so as to motivate managers, let us consider the problem of computer costs in a company that has a centralized computer department providing computer services to other responsibility centers. These services may be in the form of recurring reports, or they may involve the use of the computer in solving alternative choice problems or in other analyses. There are a great many ways of charging computer costs to the responsibility centers that use computer services, and each conveys a different message to the operating managers and to the computer center manager.

At one extreme, no charge at all might be made. If the computer is offered as a free service, operating managers are encouraged to explore the possibility of using the computer for work that was formerly done manually or for special analyses that otherwise would not be undertaken at all. This practice is often used when a company has just acquired a computer and wants to promote its use. This method also signals that the computer service manager is responsible for decisions regarding computer usage. If the demand for computer work is greater than the computer capacity, the computer service manager rations the available capacity among the uses that he considers to be most important.

Another possibility is to make no charge for recurring reports prepared by the computer but to charge for special analyses. This provides an incentive for shifting recurring data processing to the computer, but motivates the operating manager to consider whether elaborate studies of special problems are worth their cost.

As still another alternative, the total computer service costs might be allocated to all operating responsibility centers as a part of allocated overhead costs, the amount allocated to a responsibility center being based on its relative size. Since the cost is allocated, operating managers cannot make decisions that directly affect the amount charged to their responsibility centers. This method would. however, make operating managers aware of the magnitude of computer costs and could lead them to raise questions about the overall size of the computer operation.

Another possibility is to use a transfer price that is either related to prices charged by outside computer service organizations or is built up from full cost plus a profit margin. This motivates operating managers to decide whether each computer application is worth its cost. If a manager decides that a certain report is not sufficiently useful to warrant the cost, it would be discontinued. The operating manager might also be permitted to use an outside computer service if the outside service charged a lower price than the company computer unit charged. This would motivate the computer service manager to operate his responsibility center efficiently so that its prices would be equal to or less than outside prices.

As a variation on the transfer price, computer work done at night might be charged for at a lower rate than computer work done in the daytime. This would motivate users to decide whether the unattractiveness of using the computer after regular working hours is offset by the lower price and thus tends to spread the workload over the whole 24-hour period.

Each of these methods of handling the cost of computer services motivates the managers involved—both the managers of operating responsibility centers and the manager of the computer service—to act differently. The best method is the one that motivates them to act as top management wants them to act, and any of those described, or any of a number of others, can be best under a certain set of circumstances.

The above example indicates the considerations that are important in structuring responsibility accounting information. These considerations are basically different from those involved in full cost accounting, where the purpose is to measure the amount of resources used for goods or services, or from those involved in differential accounting, where the purpose is to estimate the amounts that are differential for a proposed course of action. Neither full cost accounting nor differential accounting is influenced by behavioral considerations; in responsibility accounting, behavioral considerations are dominant.

CONTROLLABLE COSTS

An item of cost is *controllable* if the amount of cost incurred in (or assigned to) a responsibility center is significantly influenced by the actions of the manager of the responsibility center. Otherwise, it is noncontrollable. There are two important aspects of this definition: (1) it refers to a specific responsibility center, and (2) it suggests that controllability results from a *significant* influence rather than from a *complete* influence. Each of these aspects is discussed below.

The word "controllable" must be used in the context of a specific responsibility center rather than as an innate characteristic of a given cost item. When the organization is viewed as a complete entity, *all costs are controllable*. For any item of cost, there is someone, somewhere in the company, who can take actions that influence it. In the extreme case, costs for any segment of the business can be reduced to zero by closing down that segment; costs incurred in manufacturing a component within the company can be changed by purchasing that component from an outside vendor; and so on. Thus, the important question is not what costs are controllable in general but rather what costs are controllable in a *specific responsibility center*, for it is these costs on which the management control system must focus.

The definition of "controllable" refers to a *significant* influence rather than to *complete* influence because only in rare cases does one individual have complete control over *all* the factors that influence any item of cost. The influence that the manager of a production department has over its direct labor costs may actually be quite limited: wage rates may be established by the personnel department or by union negotiations; the amount of direct labor required for a unit of product may be largely determined by the engineers who designed the product and who specified how it was to be manufactured; and the number of units produced, and hence total direct labor costs, may be influenced by the action of some earlier department in the production process, by the ability of the purchasing department to obtain materials, or by a variety of other factors. Nevertheless, the manager of a production department usually has a significant influence on the amount of direct labor cost incurred in his department. He has some control over the amount of idle time in his department, the speed and efficiency with which work is done, and other factors which to some extent affect labor costs.

Direct material costs and direct labor costs in a given responsibility center are usually controllable. With respect to the items of overhead cost, some elements are controllable by the responsibility center to which the costs are assigned, but others are not controllable. Indirect labor, supplies, and electricity are usually controllable. So are those charges from service centers that are based on services actually rendered by the service center. However, an allocated cost is *not* controllable by the responsibility center to which the allocation is made. The amount of cost allocated to a responsibility center depends on the formula used to make the allocation rather than on the actions of the responsibility center manager. This is so unless the cost is actually a direct cost that is allocated only for convenience, as in the case of social security taxes on direct labor.

Contrast with Direct Costs

The cost items in a responsibility center may be classified as either direct or indirect. Indirect costs are allocated to the responsibility center and are therefore not controllable by it, as explained above. All controllable costs are therefore direct costs. Not all direct costs are controllable, however.

EXAMPLE: Depreciation on departmental equipment is a direct cost of the department, but the depreciation charge is often noncontrollable by the departmental supervisor since he may have no authority to acquire or dispose of equipment. The rental charge for rented premises is another example of a direct but noncontrollable cost.

Contrast with Variable Costs

Neither are controllable costs necessarily the same as variable costs, that is, costs that vary with the volume of output. Some costs, such as indirect labor, heat, light, and magazine subscriptions, may be un-affected by volume, but they are nevertheless controllable. Conversely, although most variable costs are controllable, that is not always the case. In some situations, the cost of raw material and parts, whose consumption varies directly with volume, may be entirely outside the influence of the departmental manager.

> EXAMPLE: In an automobile assembly department, one automobile requires an engine, a body, five wheels, and so on, and there is nothing the supervisor can do about it. He is responsible for waste and spoilage of material, but not for the main flow of material itself.

Direct labor, which is usually thought of as the obvious example of a controllable cost item, may be noncontrollable in certain types of re-sponsibility centers. Situations of this type must be examined very carefully, however, in order to insure that the noncontrollability is real. Supervisors tend to argue that more costs are noncontrollable than actually is the case, in order to avoid being held responsible for them.

> EXAMPLE: If an assembly line has 20 work stations and cannot be operated unless it is manned by 20 persons of specified skills and hence specified wage rates, direct labor cost on that assembly line may be non-controllable. Nevertheless, the assumption that such costs are noncon-trollable may be open to challenge, for it may be possible to find ways to do the job with 19 persons, or with 20 persons who have a lower average skill classification and hence lower wage rates.

Converting Noncontrollable Costs to Controllable Costs

A noncontrollable item of cost can be converted to a controllable item of cost in either of two related ways: (1) by changing the basis of cost assignment; and/or (2) by changing the locus of responsibility for decisions.

CONVERTING ALLOCATED COSTS TO DIRECT COSTS. As noted above, allo-cated costs are noncontrollable by the responsibility center to which they are allocated. Many items of cost that are allocated to responsi-bility centers could be converted to controllable costs simply by as-signing the cost in such a way that the amount of costs assigned is influenced by actions taken by the manager of the responsibility center.

> EXAMPLE: If all electricity coming into a plant is measured by a single meter, there is no way of measuring the actual electrical consumption of each department in the plant, and the electrical cost is therefore nec-essarily allocated to each department and is noncontrollable. Electricity cost can be changed to a controllable cost for the several departments in the plant simply by installing meters in each department so that each de-partment's actual consumption of electricity is measured.

Services that a responsibility center receives from service units can be converted from allocated to controllable costs by assigning the cost of services to the benefiting responsibility centers on some basis that measures the amount of services actually rendered.

> EXAMPLE: If maintenance department costs are charged to production responsibility centers as a part of an overhead rate, they are noncontrollable; but if responsibility centers are charged on the basis of an hourly rate for each hour that a maintenance employee works there, and if the head of the responsibility center can influence the requests for maintenance work, then maintenance is a controllable element of the cost of the production responsibility center.

Practically any item of indirect cost could conceivably be converted to a direct and controllable cost, but for some (such as charging the president's salary on the basis of the time he spends on the problems of various parts of the business), the effort involved in doing so clearly is not worthwhile. There are nevertheless a great many unexploited opportunities in many companies to convert noncontrollable costs to controllable costs.

The same principle applies to costs that, although actually incurred in a responsibility center, are not assigned to the responsibility center at all, even on an allocated basis. Under these circumstances, the materials or services are "free" insofar as the head of the responsibility center is concerned, and since he does not have to "pay" for them (as part of the costs for which he is held responsible), he is unlikely to be concerned about careful use of these materials or services.

> EXAMPLE: Until relatively recently, the city of New York did not charge residents for the amount of water that they used. When water meters were installed and residents were required to pay for their own use of water, the total quantity of water used in the city decreased by a sizable amount.

CHANGING RESPONSIBILITY FOR COST INCURRENCE.   The most important decisions affecting costs are made at or near the top of an organization, both because top management presumably has more ability and because it has a broader viewpoint than lower level managers. On the other hand, the further removed these decisions are from the "firing line," the place where resources are actually used, the less responsive they can be to conditions currently existing at that place. Although there is no way of making a precise distinction, an organization in which a relatively high proportion of decisions are made at the top is said to be *centralized*, and one in which lower level managers make relatively more decisions is said to be *decentralized*.

In the context of our present discussion, a decentralized organization is one in which a relatively large fraction of total costs are controllable in the lower levels of responsibility centers. Many companies have found that if they have a good system for controlling performance, top management can safely delegate responsibility for many decisions, and thus use the knowledge and judgment of the person who is intimately familiar with current conditions at lower levels.

> EXAMPLE: Perhaps the most dramatic example of a shift from centralized to decentralized management is the change that has taken place in Communist countries. Beginning with Yugoslavia in the 1950s, and later extending to the USSR, there has been a recognition that the highly centralized planning and control process envisioned by Lenin simply does not work well in practice. Consequently, individual plant managers have been given much more authority to make decisions affecting the costs of their plants. This shift to decentralization required the installation of a more effective management control system.

Reporting Noncontrollable Costs

In the performance reports for responsibility centers, it is obviously essential that controllable costs be clearly separated from noncontrollable costs. Some people argue that the *separation* of controllable from noncontrollable costs is not enough; they insist that noncontrollable costs should not even be reported. Actually, there may be good reasons for reporting all, or certain types of, the noncontrollable costs assigned to a responsibility center. One reason is that top management may want the manager of the responsibility center to be concerned about such costs, the expectation being that his concern may indirectly lead to better cost control.

> EXAMPLE: The control report of a production department may list an allocated portion of the cost of the personnel department, even though the foreman of the production department has no direct responsibility for costs of the personnel department. Such a practice can be justified either on the ground that the foreman will refrain from making unnecessary requests of the personnel department if he is made to feel some responsibility for personnel department costs, or on the ground that the foreman may in various ways put pressure on the manager of the personnel department to exercise good cost control in his own department.

Another reason for reporting noncontrollable costs in responsibility centers is that if managers are made aware of the total amount of costs that are incurred in operating their responsibility centers, they may have a better understanding of how much other parts of the company contribute to their activities. Such a practice may boomerang, however, for managers may conclude that their controllable costs are so small, relative to the costs that they cannot control, that the controllable costs are not worth worrying about.

SUMMARY

An organization consists of responsibility centers. An important function of management is to plan and control the activities of the managers of these responsibility centers so that these activities help achieve the goals of the whole organization. This is the management control process. It is to be distinguished from the strategic planning process which sets goals and broad strategies, and from the operational control process which is concerned with the performance of routine tasks.

In the management control process, behavioral considerations are as important as economic considerations. In particular the motivational impact of various practices needs to be considered.

The steps in the management control process are programming, budgeting, operating and accounting, and reporting and analysis.

In addition to full cost accounting and differential accounting, a third type of accounting information is used in the management control process. It is called responsibility accounting and it reports both planned and actual accounting information in terms of responsibility centers. There are three types of responsibility centers: expense centers, in which inputs are measured in monetary terms; profit centers, in which both inputs and outputs are measured in monetary terms; and investment centers, in which assets employed are also measured. In profit centers and investment centers, a transfer price is used to measure products furnished to other responsibility centers.

Controllable costs are items of cost whose amount can be significantly influenced by actions of the manager of a responsibility center.

SUGGESTIONS FOR FURTHER READING

(Also see references at the end of Chapter 14.)

ANTHONY, ROBERT N. *Planning and Control Systems: A Framework for Analysis.* Boston: Harvard Graduate School of Business Administration, 1965.

ANTHONY, ROBERT N., DEARDEN, JOHN, and VANCIL, RICHARD F. *Management Control Systems: Cases and Readings.* Rev. ed. Homewood, Ill.: Richard D. Irwin, Inc., 1972.

BARNARD, CHESTER I. *The Functions of the Executive.* Cambridge, Mass.: Harvard University Press, 1968.

BEYER, ROBERT and TRAWICKI, DONALD J. *Profitability Accounting for Planning and Control.* 2d ed. New York: Ronald Press, Co., 1972.

Lewis, Ralph F.   *Management Uses of Accounting.* Rev. ed. New York: Harper & Row, 1970.

Powers, William T.   *Behavior. The Control of Perception.* Chicago: Aldine, 1973.

Solomons, David.   *Divisional Performance: Measurement and Control.* Homewood, Ill.: Richard D. Irwin. Inc., 1965.

CASES

CASE 20–1. GILLETTE SAFETY RAZOR COMPANY

On the morning of March 5, Miss Ruth Fillipetti, an employee of the Gillette Safety Razor Company, reported for work in the buffing room of the South Boston plant. At the stock cage she picked up a tray containing handles for one of the current models of the Gillette safety razor. These stamped copper handles had been sent to the buffing department for smoothing and polishing. After being polished, the handles went to the plating department for the final stage in their manufacture.

Miss Fillipetti's job was to smooth and polish the end of the razor handle. In this work she used a power-driven buffer wheel, against which she held the handle. The operation was not a difficult one, but it was not automatic; that is, she was required to place the end of the handle against the buffer wheel manually. For certain models, an automatic machine could be used that required only that the handles be placed on a moving belt of spindles. This belt carried the handles automatically across a buffer wheel. Miss Fillipetti spent the full day of March 5 buffing razor handle ends and by 5 o'clock had completed the smoothing and polishing of 2,100 pieces.

A close check was kept on the amount of work given to Miss Fillipetti and also on the amount of time she spent doing it. Although none of the employees of the Gillette Safety Razor Company was paid on a piece-rate basis, a daily comparison was made of the actual and standard times required to do the work assigned. On the morning of March 6 the timecard for Miss Fillipetti, together with timecards of other employees in the buffing room, was sent upstairs to the accounting department, where work and time requirements were posted and compared with previously established standard times. By 4 o'clock that afternoon—that is, the afternoon of March 6—the complete record of gains and losses with reference to standard times for work done on March 5 was reported back to the foreman in the buffing room. A procedure similar to that used for the buffing department was followed for each of the production departments of the razor division. In some departments the reports were referred to by the foreman when talking privately with operators, but in other departments the reports were posted daily. A portion of the March 5 report for the buffing department is reproduced as Exhibit 1.

The time standard set up for the operation of buffing the ends of the razor handles was 375 handles an hour.[1] The normal time to produce 2,100 units at the rate of 375 an hour was 5 hours and 36 minutes. The time records were kept in 5-minute units; and, therefore, the expected time for the work done by Miss Fillipetti on March 5 was listed on the report as $5\frac{7}{12}$ hours. Her day's work actually took $7\frac{10}{12}$ hours, so that a loss of $2\frac{3}{12}$ hours in standard time was indicated. When actual time exceeded standard allowable time, the amount lost was reported on the daily record sheet in red pencil; when actual time was under standard time, the gain was shown in black. A summary for the whole department was shown at the top of each report form.

Once a week the daily summary reports were combined into a weekly report that was furnished each of the foremen and the plant superintendent. From these weekly reports a continuous tabulation was maintained by the plant superintendent. The departmental labor control record for the buffing room shown in Exhibit 2 contains data for the three-month period beginning with the week ending December 23, through and including the week ending March 16.

The first column of the departmental labor control record (Exhibit 2) gives the normal or standard allowable hours for the volume of work done. Normal hours were the daily average of the "expected" hours shown on the daily report. Columns 2 and 3 of Exhibit 2 show the average daily hours lost and gained. Column 4 gives the daily average of actual hours required to do the same work for which the normal operating time is given in column 1. It will be noted that column 1 plus column 2 minus column 3 equals column 4. The entries in column 5, "General Ledger," refer to hours spent on special work ordered by the general office and therefore not part of the normal production flow. Column 6 gives the number of hours' work that was not measured and for which no normal times were available for comparison. Columns 7 and 8 relate to nonproductive time devoted to the work of maintenance and similar work not directly resulting in produced goods. The final column gives the total number of hours worked in the department.

A report similar to that shown in Exhibit 2 was prepared weekly for each of the departments engaged in manufacturing razors. Exhibit 3 shows for the weeks ending March 9 and March 16 the hours lost in each of six

---

[1] This operation was coded as 195 D 20; the "195" refers to the model, the "D" to the handle of the razor, and the "20" to the operation. A similar code number was given every other operation. The letter "B" was used to refer to the cap of the razor, "C" to the guard, and "A" to the complete razor. The operation on which Miss Fillipetti was engaged, 195 D 20, was known as "cut down and color."

Exhibit 1

DAILY REPORT OF PRODUCTION BY OPERATORS

GILLETTE SAFETY RAZOR COMPANY
DAILY REPORT OF PRODUCTION BY OPERATORS

DATE March 5   490 BUFFING DEPARTMENT

	Name	Operation Number	Acct.	Production Total Actual	Expected per Hour	Hours Expected	Actual	Diff. Red-Loss R	Bl.-Gain B
4126	MOORE, STELLA	195 D 20	502	2800	375	7 6/—	8		6/—
4126	MOORE, STELLA								
4127	MACCAREY, ELEANOR	1001 DG 25	502	2800			7		
4127	MACCAREY, ELEANOR	195 DG 25	502	400	400	1	1		
4128	MURPHY, ELLEN	1005 R 200	502	200			1	9/—	
4128	MURPHY, ELLEN	1005 RG 26	502	100				6/—	
4129	LEIGH, VIRGINIA	139 B 204	502	20000	2250	8 11/—	8		11
4129	LEIGH, VIRGINIA								
4130	FILLIPETTI, RUTH	195 D 20	502	2100	375	5 7/—	7 10/—		2 3/—
4130	FILLIPETTI, RUTH								
4131	LURRELLO, HELEN	139 B 24	502	14000	1750	8	8		
4131	LURRELLO, HELEN								

		Production		Hours		Diff. Red-Loss R	Bl.-Gain B
Operation Number	Acct.	Total Actual	Expected per Hour	Expected	Actual		
195 D 20	502	450	375	1	2 1/—	6/—	4/—
194 H 20	522	600	300	2	3 3/—		1 3/—

Total Expected Hours	181 9/—
" Productive Hours Not Measured	48 6/—
Lost Hours	13 3/—
Gained Hours	5
Nonproductive Hours Charged to This Dept.	50 4/—
" " Not Charged to This Dept.	2
Loaned Hours	48
Total Actual Hours Worked Incl. Loaned	343 10/—

No.	Name	Location	Acct	Amt 1	Amt 2					
4132	CONRAD, HORTENSE	Loaned								
4132	CONRAD, HORTENSE							8		
4133	O'LEARY, KATHARINE	1005 AG 210	502	76			3 —	9 —		
4133	O'LEARY, KATHARINE	195 D 20	502	2275	375	6	1 —	7	8	1 8—
4134	WOODROW, ESTHER	139 B 206	502	20000	2250	8	11 —		8	11
4134	WOODROW, ESTHER									
4135	ROVETA, MILDRED	195 C 24	502	12000	1750	6	10 —	8		1 2—
4135	ROVETA, MILDRED									
4136	CAPRA, JOSEPHINE	1004 A 20	522	500				5 —	3	
4136	CAPRA, JOSEPHINE	195 D 20	502	1600	375	4	3 —	7 —	4	4 —
4137	CASSIDY, ELINOR	195 D 20	502	2400	375	6	5 —	8		1 7—
4137	CASSIDY, ELINOR									
4138	LOVITT, MARION	Group								
4138	LOVITT, MARION									
4139	LESLIE, ALTHEA	1004 A 20	522	1100					8	
4139	LESLIE, ALTHEA									
4140	SMITH, MARY	139 B 29	502	14000	1750	8			8	
4140	SMITH, MARY									
4141	GRADY, ANNE	Loaned								
4141	GRADY, ANNE									
4142	LAMB, ELIZABETH	1001 D 211	502	23000	3500	6	7 —	8		1 5—
4142	LAMB, ELIZABETH									

Exhibit 2

DEPARTMENTAL LABOR CONTROL

Department 490—Buffing
(average daily hours)

Week Ending	Normal Hours (1)	Hours Lost (2)	Hours Gained (3)	Actual Measured Hours (4)	General Ledger (5)	Productive Hours Not Measured (6)	Nonproductive Hours (7)	Nonproductive Ratio to Normal Hours (8)	Total Hours (9)
December 9..	212.9	8.0	8.1	212.8	6.4	30.1	50.8	23.86	300.1
16..	183.8	10.5	5.6	188.7	12.7	23.4	51.3	27.91	276.1
23..	192.0	5.5	5.2	192.3	11.9	22.7	51.4	26.77	278.3
January 6..	174.7	9.2	5.0	178.9	2.0	39.8	57.6	32.97	278.3
13..	196.4	24.4	4.9	215.9	1.5	28.2	54.2	27.60	299.8
20..	194.9	14.6	6.1	203.4	4.0	54.5	50.3	25.80	312.2
27..	194.7	11.3	7.5	198.5	8.0	63.0	54.8	28.15	324.3
February 3..	160.8	10.5	4.5	166.8	6.0	106.9	56.7	35.26	336.4
10..	153.8	14.5	3.4	164.9	5.8	86.1	41.7	27.11	298.5
17..	168.4	19.7	5.4	182.7	3.6	72.7	50.9	30.23	309.9
24..	177.1	13.2	3.7	186.6	2.5	72.7	57.5	32.47	319.3
March 2..	192.5	10.6	3.5	199.6	1.8	68.3	54.8	28.47	324.5
9..	201.1	13.2	3.2	211.1	0.4	46.7	54.1	26.90	312.3
16..	169.6	5.4	4.8	170.2	. . .	17.7	56.3	33.20	244.2

Exhibit 3

EXCERPTS FROM PRODUCTION CONTROL REPORT

Selected Departments
(average daily hours)

Department	Hours Lost Week Ending March 9	Hours Lost Week Ending March 16	Measured Hours Week Ending March 9	Measured Hours Week Ending March 16	Total Hours Week Ending March 9	Total Hours Week Ending March 16
Cap and guard.......	0.3	0.7	167.9	208.5	297.2	279.2
Buffing.............	13.2	5.4	211.1	170.2	312.3	244.2
Handle inspection....	6.0	2.8	143.2	135.7	157.4	146.2
Wire and plating.....	0.1	. . .	79.3	86.3	181.7	188.1
Handle packing......	34.5	50.9	440.2	546.5	535.9	683.4
Auto-strop and probak department........	13.2	7.9	64.4	60.4	186.4	156.1

departments. The exhibit also shows the total number of hours reported for the departments and the number of measured hours for which losses were computed.

The daily report comparing actual and normal times by operators was prepared for the department foremen. The personnel department did not receive copies of the daily report and, therefore, could not make the operator's performance a formal part of his personnel record. It was estimated that the time of two clerks was required to prepare the daily and weekly reports for the entire razor division.

Questions

1. What is the source, so far as you can judge, of the entries in each of the columns of Exhibit 1? If you were handed this report, what would you look for first? Should the plant superintendent request that the daily production report be put on his desk?
2. If Miss Fillipetti's record on operation 195 D 20 continued to be poor, should the department manager refer the matter to the personnel department? Before taking such action, what should the department manager consider?
3. Rank, from best to poorest, the performance of Stella Moore, Ellen Murphy, Ruth Fillipetti, and Esther Woodrow.
4. What purpose could be served by the operating report illustrated in Exhibit 1? Is it worth the cost? Should the cost be shared by other reports, perhaps not shown in the case?
5. What is Exhibit 2? Why is this type of report called a comparative report? Why are the figures in Exhibit 2 in terms of daily averages instead of weekly totals?
6. Look at Exhibit 2, *not Exhibit 3,* and decide what items you would select to be included in a summary report comparing performance in various departments in the factory.
7. What do Exhibits 2 and 3 tell other than the number of hours put in by employees? Doesn't management really want to know whether any work was done during those hours?
8. If you were receiving these control reports, what standards would you develop?

CASE 20–2. BIRCH PAPER COMPANY

"If I were to price these boxes any lower than $480 a thousand," said Mr. Brunner, manager of Birch Paper Company's Thompson division, "I'd be countermanding my order of last month for our salesmen to stop shaving their bids and to bid full cost quotations. I've been trying for weeks to improve the quality of our business, and if I turn around now and accept this job at $430 or $450 or something less than $480, I'll be tearing down this program I've been working so hard to build up. The division can't very well show a profit by putting in bids which don't even cover a fair share of overhead costs, let alone give us a profit."

Birch Paper Company was a medium-sized, partly integrated paper company, producing white and kraft papers and paperboard. A portion of its paperboard output was converted into corrugated boxes by the Thompson division, which also printed and colored the outside surface of the boxes. Including Thompson, the company had four producing divisions and a timberland division, which supplied part of the company's pulp requirements.

For several years each division had been judged independently on the basis of its profit and return on investment. Top management had been working to gain effective results from a policy of decentralizing responsibility and authority for all decisions except those relating to overall company policy. The company's top officials felt that in the past few years the concept of decentralization had been successfully applied and that the company's profits and competitive position had definitely improved.

Early in 1975 the Northern division designed a special display box for one of its papers in conjunction with the Thompson division, which was equipped to make the box. Thompson's package design and development staff spent several months perfecting the design, production methods, and materials that were to be used; because of the unusual color and shape, these were far from standard. According to an agreement between the two divisions, the Thompson division was reimbursed by the Northern division for the cost of its design and development work.

When the specifications were all prepared, the Northern division asked for bids on the box from the Thompson division and from two outside companies, West Paper Company and Erie Papers, Ltd. Each division manager normally was free to buy from whichever supplier he wished, and even on sales within the company, divisions were expected to meet the going market price if they wanted the business.

Early in 1975 the profit margins of converters such as the Thompson division were being squeezed. Thompson, as did many other similar converters, bought its board, liner or paper; and its function was to print, cut, and shape it into boxes. Though it bought most of its materials from other Birch divisions, most of Thompson's sales were to outside customers. If Thompson got the order from Northern, it probably would buy its linerboard and corrugating medium from the Southern division of Birch. The walls of a corrugated box consist of outside and inside sheets of linerboard sandwiching the corrugating medium.

About 70 percent of Thompson's out-of-pocket cost of $400 a thousand for the order represented the cost of linerboard and corrugating medium. Though Southern division had been running below capacity and had excess inventory, it quoted the market price, which had not noticeably weakened as a result of the oversupply. Its out-of-pocket costs on both liner and corrugating medium were about 60 percent of the selling price.

The Northern division received bids on the boxes of $480 a thousand from the Thompson division, $430 a thousand from West Paper Company, and $432 a thousand from Erie Papers, Ltd. Erie Papers offered to buy from Birch the outside linerboard with the special printing already on it, but would supply its own inside liner and corrugating medium. The outside liner would be supplied by the Southern division at a price equivalent to $90 a thousand boxes, and would be printed for $30 a thousand by the Thompson division. Of the $30, about $25 would be out-of-pocket costs.

Since this situation appeared to be a little unusual, Mr. Kenton, manager of the Northern division, discussed the wide discrepancy of bids with Birch's commercial vice president. He told the commercial vice president, "We sell in a very competitive market, where higher costs cannot be passed on. How can we be expected to show a decent profit and return on investment if we have to buy our supplies at more than 10 percent over the going market?"

Knowing that Mr. Brunner had on occasion in the past few months been unable to operate the Thompson division at capacity, the commercial vice president thought it odd that Mr. Brunner would add the full 20 percent overhead and profit charge to his out-of-pocket costs. When he asked Mr. Brunner about this over the telephone, his answer was the statement that appears at the beginning of the case. Mr. Brunner went on to say that having done the developmental work on the box, and having received no profit on that, he felt entitled to a good markup on the production of the box itself.

The vice president explored further the cost structures of the various divisions. He remembered a comment the controller had made at a meeting the week before to the effect that costs that for one division were variable could be largely fixed for the company as a whole. He knew that in the absence of specific orders from top management, Mr. Kenton would accept the lowest bid, namely, that of the West Paper Company for $430. However, it would be possible for top management to order the acceptance of another bid if the situation warranted such action. And though the volume represented by the transactions in question was less than 5 percent of the volume of any of the divisions involved, other transactions could conceivably raise similar problems later.

Questions

1. Does the system motivate Mr. Brunner in such a way that actions he takes in the best interests of the Thompson division are also in the best interests of the Birch Paper Company? If your answer is "no," give some specific

instances related as closely as possible to the type of situation described in the case. Would the managers of *other* divisions be correctly motivated?
2. What should the vice president do?

CASE 20–3. SOUTH AMERICAN COFFEE COMPANY

The South American Coffee Company sold its own brands of coffee throughout the Middle West. Stock of the company, which was founded in 1903, was closely held by members of the family of the founder. The president and secretary-treasurer were members of the stock-owning family and other management personnel had no stock interest.

Sales policies and direction of the company were handled from the home office in Cincinnati, and all salespersons reported to the sales manager through two assistants. The sales manager and the president assumed responsibility for advertising and promotion work. Roasting, grinding, and packaging of coffee was under the direction of the vice president of manufacturing, whose office was in Cincinnati.

The company operated three roasting plants throughout the Midwest. Each plant had profit and loss responsibility and the plant manager was paid a bonus on the basis of a percent of his plant's gross margin. Monthly gross margin statements were prepared for each plant by the home office (see Exhibit 1). Exhibit 2 shows gross margin for the entire company. Each month the plant manager was given a production schedule for the current month and a tentative schedule for the next succeeding month. Deliveries were made as directed by the home office.

Exhibit 1

SOUTH AMERICAN COFFEE COMPANY

Operating Statement
Plant No. 1
April

Net sales (shipments at billing prices)		$744,620
Less: Cost of sales		
Green coffee—at contract cost.		$373,660
Roasting and grinding:		
Labor.	$38,220	
Fuel.	24,780	
Manufacturing expenses	33,620	96,620
Packaging:		
Container.	$84,620	
Packing carton.	9,140	
Labor.	12,260	
Manufacturing expenses	25,440	131,460
Total manufacturing cost		$601,740
Gross Margin on Sales.		$142,880

Exhibit 2

SOUTH AMERICAN COFFEE COMPANY

Income Statement
April

	Plants*			Green Coffee	Total
	1	2	3		
Net sales.........................	$744,620			$123,740	$2,856,400
Cost of sales					
Green coffee....................	373,660			111,270	1,421,680
Roasting and grinding............	96,620				299,440
Packaging......................	131,460				600,410
Purchasing department............					78,400
	$601,740				$2,399,930
Gross Margin....................	$142,880			$ 12,470	$ 456,470

* Detailed amounts for Plants 2 and 3 omitted here; total amounts include all three plants plus green coffee

All financial statements were prepared in the home office and billing, credit, and collection were done there. Each plant had a small accounting office at which all manufacturing costs were recorded. Plant payrolls were prepared at the plant. Green coffee costs were supplied each plant on a lot basis, as described below.

The procurement of green coffee for the roasting operations of the South American Coffee Company was handled by a separate purchasing unit of the company, which reported to the secretary-treasurer. Because of the specialized problems and the need for constant contact with coffee brokers, the unit was located in the section of New York City where the green coffee business was concentrated. The purchasing unit operated on an autonomous basis, keeping all records and handling all financial transactions pertaining to purchasing, sales to outsiders, and transfer to three company-operated roasting plants.

The primary function of the purchasing unit was to have available for the roasting plants the variety of green coffees necessary to produce the blends which were to be roasted, packed, and sold to customers. This necessitated dealing in 40 types and grades of coffee, which came from tropical countries all over the world.

Based on estimated sales budgets, purchase commitments were made which would provide for delivery in from three to fifteen months from the date that contracts for purchase were made. While it was possible to purchase from local brokers for immediate delivery, such purchases usually were more costly than purchases made for delivery in the country of origin and hence these "spot" purchases were kept to a minimum. A most important factor in the situation was the market "know-how" of the purchasing executives, who must judge whether the market trend was apt to be up or down and must make their commitments accordingly.

The result was that the green coffee purchasing unit was buying a range of coffees for advance delivery at various dates. At the time of actual delivery, the sales of the company's coffees might not be going as anticipated when the purchase commitment was made. The difference between actual deliveries and current requirements was handled through "spot" sales or purchase transactions in green coffee with outside brokers or other coffee roasters.

As an example, the commitments of the company for Santos No. 4 (a grade of Brazilian coffee) might call for deliveries in the month of May of 20,000 bags (of 132 pounds each). These deliveries would be made under 50 contracts which were executed at varying prices from three to twelve months before the month of delivery. An unseasonal hot spell at the end of April had brought a slump in coffee sales, and it developed that the company plants required only 16,000 bags in May. The green coffee purchasing unit therefore had to decide whether to store the surplus in outside storage facilities (which would increase the cost) or to sell it on the open market. This example was typical of the normal operation.

Generally speaking, the large volume of the company permitted it to buy favorably and to realize a normal brokerage and trading profit when selling in smaller lots to small roasting companies. Hence, the usual policy was to make purchase commitments on a basis of maximum requirements —and the usual result was that there was a surplus to be sold on a "spot" basis.

In accounting for coffee purchases, a separate cost record was maintained for each purchase contract. This record was charged with payments for coffee purchased, with shipping charges, import expenses and similar items, with the result that net cost per bag was developed for each purchase. Thus, the 50 deliveries of Santos 4 coffee cited in the example would come into inventory at 50 separate costs. The established policy was to treat each contract on an individual basis. When green coffee was shipped to a plant, a charge was made for the cost represented by the contracts which covered that particular shipment of coffee, with no element of profit or loss. When green coffee was sold to outsiders, the sales were likewise costed on a specific contract basis with a resulting profit or loss on these transactions.

The operating cost of running the purchasing unit was transferred in total to the central office, where it was recorded as an element in the general cost of coffee sales.

For the past several years there had been some dissatisfaction on the part of plant managers with the method of computing gross margin subject to bonuses. This had finally led to a request from the president to the controller to study the whole method of reporting on results of plant operations and the purchasing operation.

Question

What changes, if any, would you propose in the present reporting and control system? Explain.

CASE 20–4. EMPIRE GLASS COMPANY

Organization

Empire Glass Company was a diversified company organized into several major product divisions, one of which was the glass products division. This division was responsible for manufacturing and selling glass food and beverage bottles. Each division was headed by a divisional vice-president who reported directly to the company's executive vice-president, Landon McGregor.

Mr. McGregor's corporate staff included three men in the financial area—the controller, the chief accountant and the treasurer. The controller's department consisted of only two men—Mr. Walker and the assistant controller, Allen Newell. The market research and labor relations departments also reported in a staff capacity to Mr. McGregor.

All the product divisions were organized along similar lines. Reporting

Exhibit 1

TOP MANAGEMENT AND GLASS PRODUCTS MANAGEMENT

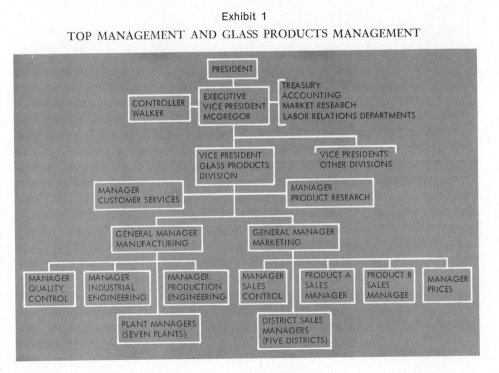

to each product division vice-president were several staff members in the customer service and product research areas. Reporting in a line capacity to each individual vice-president were also a general manager of manufacturing and a general manager of marketing. The general manager of manufacturing was responsible for all the division's manufacturing activities. Similarly, the general manager of marketing was responsible for all the division's marketing activities. Both of these executives were assisted by a small staff of specialists. There was also a controller and supporting staff in each division. Exhibit 1 presents an organization chart of top management and of the glass product division's management group. All the corporate and divisional management group were located in British City, Canada. Exhibit 2 shows the typical organization structure of a plant within the glass products division.

Exhibit 2

TYPICAL PLANT ORGANIZATION—GLASS PRODUCTS DIVISION

Products and Technology

The glass products division operated a number of plants in Canada producing glass food and beverage bottles. Of these products, food jars constituted the largest group, including jars for products like tomato catsup, mayonnaise, jams and jellies, honey, and soluble coffee. Milk bottles and beer and soft drink bottles were also produced in large quantities. A great variety of shapes and sizes of containers for wines, liquors, drugs, cosmetics, and chemicals were produced in smaller quantities.

Most of the thousands of different products, varying in size, shape, color, and decoration, were produced to order. According to British City executives, during 1963 the typical lead time between the customer's order and shipment from the plant was between two and three weeks.

The principal raw materials for container glass were sand, soda ash, and lime. The first step in the manufacturing process was to melt batches of these materials in furnaces or "tanks." The molten mass was then passed into automatic or semiautomatic machines, which filled molds with the molten glass and blew the glass into the desired shape. The ware then went through an automatic annealing oven or lehr, where it was cooled slowly under carefully controlled conditions. If the glass was to be coated on the exterior to increase its resistance to abrasion and scratches, this coating—often a silicone film—was applied at the lehr. Any decorating (such as a trademark or other design) was then added, the product inspected again, and the finished goods packed in corrugated containers (or wooden cases for some bottles).

Quality inspection was critical in the manufacturing process. If the melt in the furnace was not completely free from bubbles and stones (unmelted ingredients or pieces of refinery material), or if the fabricating machinery was slightly out of adjustment, or molds were worn, the rejection rate was very high. Although a number of machines were used in the inspection process, including electric eyes, much of the inspection was still visual.

Although glassmaking was one of the oldest arts, and bottles and jars had been machine molded at relatively high speed for over half a century, the glass products division had spent substantial sums each year to modernize its equipment. These improvements had greatly increased the speed of operations and had substantially reduced the visual inspection and manual handling of glassware.

Most of the jobs were relatively unskilled, highly repetitive, and gave the worker little control over work methods or pace. The moldmakers who made and repaired the molds, the machine repairmen, and those who made the equipment setup changes between different products were considered to be the highest classes of skilled workers. Wages were relatively high in the glass industry. Production employees belonged to two national unions, and for many years bargaining had been conducted on a national basis. Output standards were established for all jobs, but no bonus was paid to hourly plant workers for exceeding standard.

Marketing

Over the years, the sales of the glass products division had grown at a slightly faster rate than had the total market for glass containers. Until the late 1950s, the division had charged a premium for most of its products, primarily because they were of better quality than competitive products. In recent years, however, the quality of the competitive products had improved to the point where they now matched the division's quality level. In the meantime, the division's competitors had retained their former price structure. Consequently, the glass products division had been forced to lower its prices to meet its competitor's lower market prices. According to one division executive:

Currently, price competition is not severe, particularly among the two or three larger companies that dominate the glass bottle industry. Most of our competition is with respect to product quality and customer service. . . . In fact, our biggest competitive threat is from containers other than glass. . . .

Each of the division's various plants shipped their products throughout Canada to some extent, although transportation costs limited each plant's market primarily to its immediate vicinity. While some of the customers were large and bought in huge quantities, many were relatively small.

BUDGETARY CONTROL SYSTEM

In the fall of 1963, James Walker, Empire Glass Company controller, described the company's budgetary control system to a casewriter. Mr. Walker had been controller for some fifteen years. Excerpts from that interview are reproduced below.

"To understand the role of the budgetary control system, you must first understand our management philosophy. Fundamentally, we have a divisional organization based on broad product categories. These divisional activities are coordinated by the company's executive vice-president, while the head office group provides a policy and review function for him. Within the broad policy limits, we operate on a decentralized basis; each of the decentralized divisions performs the full management job that normally would be inherent in any independent company. The only exceptions to this philosophy are the head office group's sole responsibilities for sources of funds and labor relations with those bargaining units that cross division lines.

"Given this form of organization, the budget is the principal management tool used by head office to direct the efforts of the various segments of the company toward a common goal. Certainly, in our case, the budget is much more than a narrow statistical accounting device."

Sales Budget

"As early as May 15 of the year preceding the budget year, top management of the company asks the various product division vice-presidents to submit preliminary reports stating what they think their division's capital requirements and outlook in terms of sales and income will be during the next budget year. In addition, corporate top management also wants an expression of the division vice-president's general feelings toward the trends in these particular items over the two years following the upcoming budget year. At this stage, head office is not interested in too much detail. Since all divisions plan their capital requirements five years in advance and had made predictions of the forthcoming budget year's market when the budget estimates were prepared last year, these rough estimates of next year's conditions and requirements are far from wild guesses.

"After the opinions of the divisional vice-presidents are in, the market research staff goes to work. They develop a formal statement of the marketing climate in detail for the forthcoming budget year and in general terms for the subsequent two years. Once these general factors have been assessed, a sales forecast is constructed for the company and for each division. Consideration is given to the relationship of the general economic climate to our customers' needs and Empire's share of each market. Explicitly stated are basic assumptions as to price, weather conditions, introduction of new products, gains or losses in particular accounts, forward buying, new manufacturing plants, industry growth trends, packaging trends, inventory carry-overs, and the development of alternative packages to or from glass. This review of all the relevant factors is followed for each of our product lines, regardless of its size and importance. The completed forecasts of the market research group are then forwarded to the appropriate divisions for review, criticism, and adjustments.

"The primary goal of the head office group in developing these sales forecasts is to assure uniformity among the divisions with respect to the basic assumptions on business conditions, pricing, and the treatment of possible emergencies. Also, we provide a yardstick so as to assure us that the company's overall sales forecast will be reasonable and obtainable.

"The product division top management then asks each district manager what he expects to do in the way of sales during the budget year. Head office and the divisional staffs will give the district sales managers as much guidance as they request, but it is the sole responsibility of each district sales manager to come up with his particular forecast.

"After the district sales managers' forecasts are received by the divisional top management, the forecasts are consolidated and reviewed by the division's general manager of marketing. Let me emphasize, however, that nothing is changed in the district sales manager's budget unless the district manager agrees. Then, once the budget is approved, nobody is relieved of his responsibility without top management approval. Also, no arbitrary changes are made in the approved budgets without the concurrence of all the people responsible for the budget.

"Next, we go through the same process at the division and headquarters levels. We continue to repeat the process until everyone agrees that the sales budgets are sound. Then, each level of management takes responsibility for its particular portion of the budget. These sales budgets then become fixed objectives.

"I would say we have four general objectives in mind in reviewing the sales forecast:

1. A review of the division's competitive position, including plans for improving that position.
2. An evaluation of its efforts to gain either a larger share of the market or offset competitors' activities.
3. A consideration of the need to expand facilities to improve the division's products or introduce new products.
4. A review and development of plans to improve product quality, delivery methods and service."

Manufacturing Budgets

"Once the vice-presidents, executive vice-president, and company president have given final approval to the sales budgets, we make a sales budget for each plant by breaking down the division sales budgets according to the plants from which the finished goods will be shipped. These plant sales budgets are then further broken down on a monthly basis by price, volume, and end use. With this information available, the plants then budget their gross profit, fixed expenses, and income before taxes. Gross profit is the difference between gross sales, less discounts, and variable manufacturing costs—such as direct labor, direct material and variable manufacturing overheads. Income is the difference between the gross profit and the fixed costs.

"The plant manager's primary responsibility extends to profits. The budgeted plant profit is the difference between the fixed sales dollar budget and the sum of the budgeted variable costs at standard and the fixed overhead budget. It is the plant manager's responsibility to meet this budget profit figure, even if actual dollar sales drop below the budgeted level.

"Given his sales budget, it is up to the plant manager to determine the fixed overhead and variable costs—at standard—that he will need to incur so as to meet the demands of the sales budget. In my opinion, requiring the plant managers to make their own plans is one of the most valuable things associated with the budget system. Each plant manager divides the preparation of the overall plant budget among his plant's various departments. First, the departments spell out the program in terms of the physical requirements, such as tons of raw material, and then the plans are priced at standard cost.

"The plant industrial engineering department is assigned responsibility for developing engineered cost standards and reduced costs. Consequently, the phase of budget preparation covered by the industrial engineers includes budget standards of performance for each operation, cost center, and department within the plant. This phase of the budget also includes budgeted cost reductions, budgeted unfavorable variances from standards, and certain budgeted programmed fixed costs in the manufacturing area, such as service labor. The industrial engineer prepares this phase of the budget in conjunction with departmental line supervision.

"Before each plant sends its budget into British City, a group of us from head office goes out to visit each plant. For example, in the case of the glass products division, Allen Newell, assistant controller, and I, along with representatives of the glass products division manufacturing staffs, visit each of the division's plants. Let me stress this point: We do not go on these trips to pass judgment on the plant's proposed budget. Rather, we go with two purposes in mind. First, we wish to acquaint ourselves with the thinking behind the figures that each plant manager will send in to British City. This is helpful, because when we come to review these budgets with the top management—that is, management above our level —we will have to answer questions about the budgets, and we will know the answers. Second, the review is a way of giving guidance to the plant managers in determining whether or not they are in line with what the company needs to make in the way of profits.

"Of course, when we make our field reviews we do not know about what each of the other plants is doing. Therefore, we explain to the plant managers that while their budget may look good now, when we put all the plants together in a consolidated budget the plant managers may have to make some changes because the projected profit is not high enough. When this happens, we must tell the plant managers that it is not their programs that are unsound. The problem is that the company cannot afford the programs. I think it is very important that each plant manager has a chance to tell his story. Also, it gives them the feeling that we at headquarters are not living in an ivory tower.

"These plant visits are spread over a three-week period, and we spend an average of half a day at each plant. The plant manager is free to bring to these meetings any of his supervisors he wishes. We ask him not to bring in anybody below the supervisory level. Then, of course, you get into organized labor. During the half day we spend at each plant we discuss the budget primarily. However, if I have time I like to wander through the plant and see how things are going. Also, I go over in great detail the property replacement and maintenance budget with the plant manager.

"About September 1, the plant budgets come into British City, and the accounting department consolidates them. Then, the product division vice-presidents review their respective divisional budgets to see if the division budget is reasonable in terms of what the vice-president thinks the corporate management wants. If he is not satisfied with the consolidated plant budgets, he will ask the various plants within the division to trim their budget figures.

"When the division vice-presidents and the executive vice-president are happy, they will send their budgets to the company president. He may accept the division budgets at this point. If he doesn't, he will specify the areas to be reexamined by division and, if necessary, by plant management. The final budget is approved at our December board of directors meeting."

Comparison of Actual and Standard Performance

"At the end of the sixth business day after the close of the month, each plant wires to the head office certain operating variances, which we put together on what we call the variance analysis sheet. Within a half-hour after the last plant report comes through, variance analysis sheets for the divisions and plants are compiled. On the morning of the seventh business day after the end of the month, these reports are usually on the desks of the interested top management. The variance analysis sheet highlights the variances in what we consider to be critical areas. Receiving this report as soon as we do helps us at head office to take timely action. Let me emphasize, however, we do not accept the excuse that the plant manager has to go to the end of the month to know what happened during the month. He has to be on top of these particular items daily.

"When the actual results come into the head office, we go over them on the basis of exception; that is, we only look at those figures that are in excess of the budgeted amounts. We believe this has a good effect on morale. The plant managers don't have to explain everything they do. They have to explain only where they go off base. In particular, we pay close attention to the net sales, gross margin, and the plant's ability to meet its standard manufacturing cost. Incidentally, when analyzing the gross sales, we look closely at the price and mix changes.

"All this information is summarized on a form known as the Profit Planning and Control Report No. 1 (see Exhibit 3). This document is backed up by a number of supporting documents (see Exhibit 4). The plant PPCR No. 1 and the month-end trial balance showing both actual and budget figures are received in British City at the close of the eighth business day after the end of the month. These two very important reports, along with the supporting reports (PPCR No. 2—PPCR No. 11) are then consolidated by the accounting department on PPCR-type forms to show the results of operations by division and company. The consolidated reports are distributed the next day.

Exhibit 3

PROFIT PLANNING AND CONTROL REPORT NO. 1

Income Gain (+) or Loss (−) From		Actual	Ref.		Actual	Income Gain (+) or Loss (−) From	
MONTH					**YEAR TO DATE**		
Prev. Year	Budget					Budget	Prev. Year
			1	Gross Sales to Customers			
			2	Discounts & Allowances			
			3	Net Sales to Customers			
%	%	/////	4	% Gain (+)/Loss (−)	/////	%	%
				DOLLAR VOLUME GAIN (+)/ LOSS (−) DUE TO:			
		/////	5	Sales Price	/////		
		/////	6	Sales Volume	/////		
			6(a)	Trade Mix	/////		
			7	Variable Cost of Sales			
			8	Profit Margin			
				PROFIT MARGIN GAIN (+)/ LOSS (−) DUE TO:			
		/////	9	Profit Volume Ratio (P/V)	/////		
		/////	10	Dollar Volume	/////		
%	%	%	11	Profit Volume Ratio (P/V)	%	%	%
		Income Addition (+)			Income Addition (+)		
			12	Total Fixed Manufacturing Cost			
			13	Fixed Manufacturing Cost–Transfers			
			14	Plant Income (Standard)			
%	%	%	15	% of Net Sales	%	%	%
		Income Addition (+) Income Reduction (−)			Income Addition (+) Income Reduction (−)		
%	%	%	16	% Performance	%	%	%
			17	Manufacturing Efficiency			
		Income Addition (+)			Income Addition (+)		
			18	Methods Improvements			
			19	Other Revisions of Standards			
			20	Material Price Changes			
			21	Division Special Projects			
			22	Company Special Projects			
			23	New Plant Expense			
			24	Other Plant Expenses			
			25	Income on Seconds			
			26				
			27				
			28	Plant Income (Actual)			
%	%	/////	29	% Gain (+)/Loss (−)	/////	%	%
%	%	%	30	% of Net Sales	%	%	%
			36A				
Increase (+) or Decrease (−)				EMPLOYED CAPITAL	Increase (+) or Decrease (−)		
			37	Total Employed Capital			
%	%	%	38	% Return	%	%	%
			39	Turnover Rate			

_____   _____   _____19____

     Plant   Division   Month

Exhibit 4

BRIEF DESCRIPTION OF PPCR NO. 2—PPCR NO. 11

Individual Plant Reports	
Report	Description
PPCR No. 2	Manufacturing expense: Plant materials, labor, and variable overhead consumed. Detail of actual figures compared with budget and previous year's figures for year to date and current month.
PPCR No. 3	Plant expense: Plant fixed expenses incurred. Details of actual figures compared with budget and previous year's figures for year to date and current month.
PPCR No. 4	Analysis of sales and income: Plant operating gains and losses due to changes in sales revenue, profit margins and other sources of income. Details of actual figures compared with budget and previous year's figures for year to date and current month.
PPCR No. 5	Plant control statement: Analysis of plant raw material gains and losses, spoilage costs, and cost reductions programs. Actual figures compared with budget figures for current month and year to date.
PPCR No. 6	Comparison of sales by principal and product groups: Plant sales dollars, profit margin and P/V ratios broken down by end product use (i.e., soft drinks, beer). Compares actual figures with budgeted figures for year to date and current month.

Division Summary Reports	
Report	Description
PPCR No. 7	Comparative plant performance, sales and income: Gross sales and income figures by plants. Actual figures compared with budget figures for year to date and current month.
PPCR No. 8	Comparative plant performance, total plant expenses: Profit margin, total fixed costs, manufacturing efficiency, other plant expenses and P/V ratios by plants. Actual figures compared with budgeted and previous year's figures for current month and year to date.
PPCR No. 9	Manufacturing efficiency: Analysis of gains and losses by plant in areas of materials, spoilage, supplies and labor. Current month and year to date actuals reported in total dollars and as a percentage of budget.
PPCR No. 10	Inventory: Comparison of actual and budget inventory figures by major inventory accounts and plants.
PPCR No. 11	Status of capital expenditures: Analysis of the status of capital expenditures by plants, months and relative to budget.

"In connection with the fixed cost items, we want to know whether or not the plants carried out the programs they said they would carry out. If they have not, we want to know why they have not. Here, we are looking for sound reasons. Also, we want to know if they have carried out their projected programs at the cost they said they would.

"In addition to these reports, at the beginning of each month the plant managers prepare current estimates for the upcoming month and quarter on forms similar to the variance analysis sheets. Since our budget is based on known programs, the value of this current estimate is that it gets the plant people to look at their programs. Hopefully, they will realize that they cannot run their plants just on a day-to-day basis.

"If we see a sore spot coming up, or if the plant manager draws our attention to a potential trouble area, we may ask that daily reports concerning this item be sent to the particular division top management involved. In addition, the division top management may send a division staff specialist—say, a quality control expert if it is a quality problem—to the plant concerned. The division staff members can make recommendations, but it is up to the plant manager to accept or reject these recommendations. Of course, it is well know throughout the company that we expect the plant managers to accept gracefully the help of the head office and division staffs."

Sales-Manufacturing Relations

"If a sales decline occurs during the early part of the year, and if the plant managers can convince us that the change is permanent, we may revise the plant budgets to reflect these new circumstances. However, if toward the end of the year the actual sales volume suddenly drops below the predicted sales volume, we don't have much time to change the budget plans. What we do is ask the plant managers to go back over their budgets with their staffs and see where reduction of expense programs will do the least harm. Specifically, we ask them to consider what they may be able to eliminate this year or delay until next year.

"I believe it was Confucius who said: 'We make plans so we have plans to discard.' Nevertheless, I think it is wise to make plans, even if you have to discard them. Having plans makes it a lot easier to figure out what to do when sales fall off from the budgeted level. The understanding of operations that comes from preparing the budget removes a lot of the potential chaos and confusion that might arise if we were under pressure to meet a stated profit goal and sales declined quickly and unexpectedly at year-end, just as they did last year. In these circumstances, we don't try to ram anything down the plant managers' throats. We ask them to tell us where they can reasonably expect to cut costs below the budgeted level.

"Whenever a problem arises at a plant between sales and production, the local people are supposed to solve the problem themselves. For example, a customer's purchasing agent may insist he wants an immediate delivery, and this delivery will disrupt the production department's plans. The production group can make recommendations as to alternative ways to take care of the problem, but it's the sales manager's responsibility to get the product to the customer. The sales force are supposed to know their customers well enough to judge whether or not the customer really needs the product. If the sales manager says the customer needs the product, that ends the matter. As far as we are concerned, the customer's wants are primary; our company is a case where sales wags the rest of the dog.

"Of course, if the change in the sales program involves a major plant expense which is out of line with the budget, then the matter is passed up to division for decision.

"As I said earlier, the sales department has the sole responsibility for the product price, sales mix, and delivery schedules. They do not have direct responsibility for plant operations or profit. That's the plant management's responsibility. However, it is understood that the sales group will cooperate with the plant people whenever possible."

Motivation

"There are various ways in which we motivate the plant managers to meet their profit goals. First of all, we only promote capable people. Also, a monetary incentive program has been established that stimulates their efforts to achieve their profit goals. In addition, each month we put together a bar chart which shows, by division and plant, the ranking of the various manufacturing units with respect to manufacturing efficiency.[1] We feel the plant managers are one hundred percent responsible for variable manufacturing costs. I believe this is true, since all manufacturing standards have to be approved by plant managers. Most of the plant managers give wide publicity to these bar charts. The efficiency bar chart and efficiency measure itself is perhaps a little unfair in some respects when you are comparing one plant with another. Different kinds of products are run through different plants. These require different setups, and so forth, which have an important impact on a position of the plant. However, in general, the efficiency rating is a good indication of the quality of the plant manager and his supervisory staff.

"Also, a number of plants run competitions within the plants which reward department heads, or foremen, based on their relative standing

---

[1] $\text{Manufacturing efficiency} = \dfrac{\text{total standard variable manufacturing costs}}{\text{total actual variable manufacturing costs}} \times 100\%$

with respect to a certain cost item. The plant managers, their staffs, and employees have great pride in their plants.

"The number one item now stressed at the plant level is *quality*. The market situation is such that in order to make sales you have to meet the market price and exceed the market quality. By quality I mean not only the physical characteristics of the product but also such things as delivery schedules. As I read the company employee publications, their message is that if the company is to be profitable it must produce high-quality items at a reasonable cost. This is necessary so that the plants can meet their obligation to produce the maximum profits for the company in the prevailing circumstances."

The Future

"An essential part of the budgetary control system is planning. We have developed a philosophy that we must begin our plans where the work is done—in the line organization and out in the field. Perhaps, in the future, we can avoid or cut back some of the budget preparation steps and start putting together our sales budget later than May 15. However, I doubt if we will change the basic philosophy.

"Frankly, I doubt if the line operators would want any major change in the system; they are very jealous of the management prerogatives the system gives to them.

"It is very important that we manage the budget. We have to be continually on guard against its managing us. Sometimes, the plants lose sight of this fact. We have to be made conscious daily of the necessity of having the sales volume to make a profit. And when sales fall off and their plant programs are reduced, they do not always appear to see the justification for budget cuts. Although I do suspect that they see more of the justification for these cuts than they will admit. It is this human side of the budget to which we have to pay more attention in the future."

Question

Comment on the strong points and the weak points in the management control system of Empire Glass Company. What changes, if any, would you suggest?

CHAPTER 21

PROGRAMMING AND BUDGETING

This chapter describes the two principal formal types of planning processes. One, called programming, is the process of making decisions on major programs to be undertaken. The other, called budgeting, is the process for planning overall activities of the company for the next year. As background for this description, three types of cost used in responsibility accounting are discussed: engineered costs, discretionary costs, and committed costs.

Engineered Costs

Engineered costs are items of cost for which the right or proper amount of costs that should be incurred can be estimated. Direct labor cost is an example. Given the specifications for a product, engineers can determine the necessary production operations and they can estimate, within reasonably close limits, the time that should be spent on each operation. The total amount of direct labor costs that should be incurred can then be estimated by translation of these times into money by means of a standard wage rate, to arrive at a standard labor cost per unit. The standard unit cost multiplied by the the number of units of product gives what the total amount of direct labor cost should be. Since production engineering is not an exact science, this amount is not necessarily the exact amount that should be spent, but the estimates can usually be made close enough so that there is relatively little reason for disagreement. In particular, there can be no reasonable ground for denying that there is a direct relationship between volume (i.e., output) and costs; two units require approximately double the amount of direct labor that one unit

714

requires. Similarly, in most situations, direct material costs are engineered costs.

Discretionary Costs

Discretionary costs are items of costs whose amount can be varied at the discretion of the manager of the responsibility center. These costs are also called *programmed* or *managed* costs. The amount of a discretionary cost can be whatever management wants it to be, within wide limits. Unlike engineered costs, there is no scientific way of deciding what the "right" amount of cost should be, or at least there is no scientific basis that the management of the particular company is willing to rely on. How much should be spent for research and development? For public relations? For employees' parties and outings? For donations? For the accounting department? No one knows. In most companies, the discretionary cost category includes all general and administrative activities, all order-getting activities, and many items of factory indirect cost. In the absence of an engineering standard, the amount to be spent for a given item of cost must be a matter of judgment.

Although there is no "right" level for the total amount of a discretionary cost item, there may be usable standards for controlling some of the detail within it.

> EXAMPLE: Although no one knows the optimum amount that should be spent for the accounting function as a whole, it is nevertheless possible to measure the performance of individual clerks in the accounting department in terms of number of postings or number of invoices typed per hour. And although we cannot know the "right" amount of total travel expense, we can set standards for the amount that should be spent per day or per mile.

Furthermore, new developments in management accounting result in a gradual shift of items from the discretionary cost category to the engineered cost category. Several companies have recently started to use what they believe to be valid techniques for determining the "right" amount that they should spend on advertising in order to achieve their sales objectives, or the "right" number of sales personnel.

SPURIOUS RELATIONSHIPS. The decision as to how much should be spent for a discretionary cost item may take several forms, such as "spend the same amount as we spent last year," or "spend *b* percent of sales," or "spend *a* dollars plus *b* percent of sales." These decision rules result in historical spending patterns which, when plotted against volume, have the same superficial appearance as the patterns of engineered cost. The first type of decision gives a fixed cost line, the second a variable cost line, and the third a semivariable cost line.

These relationships are fundamentally different from those observed for engineered costs, however. For engineered costs, the pattern is inevitable; as volume increases, the amount of cost *must* increase. For discretionary costs, the relationship exists only because of a management decision, and it can be changed simply by making a different management decision.

> EXAMPLE: A company may have decided that research and development costs should be 3 percent of sales revenue. There can be no scientific reason for such a decision, for no one knows the optimum amount that should be spent for research and development. In all probability, such a rule exists primarily because management thinks that this is what the company can afford to spend. In this company there will be a linear relationship between sales volume and research and development costs. This is not a cause-and-effect relationship, however; and there is no inherent reason why research and development costs in the future should conform to the historical pattern.

ORDER-GETTING COSTS.   Costs of products that are incurred outside of the manufacturing facilities are collectively known as *marketing costs* or *distribution costs*. These costs can be divided into two main categories: logistics costs and order-getting costs. *Logistics costs* are the costs of storing finished products, moving them to customers, and doing the associated recordkeeping. They have essentially the same characteristics as manufacturing cost; that is, many items of logistics cost are engineered costs.

Order-getting costs are the costs of seeking orders, and include the costs of the sales organization, advertising, sales promotion and the like. These costs have fundamentally different characteristics from logistics costs. They may vary with sales volume, but the relationship is the reverse of that for factory costs: order-getting cost is the independent variable, and sales volume is the dependent variable. Order-getting costs vary not in response to *actual* sales volume but rather *in anticipation of* sales volume, according to decisions made by management.[1] They are therefore discretionary costs.

If management has a policy of spending more for order-getting activities when sales volume is high, then a scatter diagram of the relationship between order-getting costs and sales volume will have the same appearance as the diagrams for the relationship between production costs and production volume. The two diagrams should be interpreted quite differently, however. The production cost diagram indicates that production cost *necessarily* increases as volume increases, while the selling cost diagram shows either that selling cost has been *permitted* to increase with

---

[1] Exceptions are salespersons' commissions and other payments related to sales revenue. These items of course vary directly with sales revenue.

increases in volume, or that the higher costs have resulted in the higher volume. Further, subject to some qualifications, it may be said that for total factory indirect costs, the lower they are, the better; whereas low order-getting costs may reflect inadequate selling effort. The "right" level of order-getting costs is a judgment made by management.

Committed Costs

Committed costs are those that are the inevitable consequences of commitments previously made. Depreciation is an example; once a company has purchased a building or a piece of equipment, there is an inevitable depreciation charge so long as the building continues to be owned. When the manager of a baseball team has a five-year contract, his salary is a committed cost.

In the short run, committed costs are noncontrollable. They can be changed only by changing the commitment, for example, by disposing of the building or equipment whose depreciation is being recorded, or by buying up the baseball manager's contract.

PROGRAMMING

Programming is the process of deciding on the programs that the company will undertake and the approximate amount of resources that are to be allocated to each major program. Product lines, plants, and research and development are examples of programs. Program decisions must be made in all companies, but the procedures used in making them vary greatly among companies. Some companies, probably the majority, make program decisions when the need for them arises. If an opportunity to add a new product arises, it is considered at that time. These companies also make some program decisions as part of the budgeting process to be described in the next section. Other companies treat programming as a separate, formal process. On a regular basis, they prepare a *long-range plan* which shows the programs that the company plans to carry on for a number of years ahead—usually 5 years, but possibly as few as 3 years or (in the case of certain public utilities) as many as 20 years. The companies that do not have a formal long-range plan rely for program information on reports or understandings as to specific, important facets of their programs, particularly the amounts to be invested in capital assets and the means of financing these assets.

In those companies that do develop a formal long-range plan, programming is usually kept separate from budgeting. Assuming that the company's fiscal year begins January 1, the programming process would begin the preceding spring. At that time top management discusses and decides on changes in its basic goals and strategies, and disseminates these to divisional managers and other line executives. Managers of individual divisions prepare their programs, following the guidelines set forth by top management. These programs cover proposed actions for a number of years in the future. In the summer or early fall, these proposed programs are discussed at length with top management, and out of these discussions emerges a program for the whole company. This approved program forms the basis of the budgeting process, which begins in the fall.

Zero-Base Review

In addition to making decisions about proposed new programs, a company should also reconsider, from time to time, the appropriateness of its ongoing programs. Often such studies focus on responsibility centers, particularly those responsibility centers in which the amount of discretionary costs is relatively large. One device for making such a reevaluation of responsibility center activities is called the zero-base review.

As the term suggests, a *zero-base review* examines a certain program, function or responsibility center "from scratch." The reviewer judges what activities should be undertaken, and then estimates the proper level of those activities.[2] This approach of starting from a zero base is in sharp contrast with that used in budgeting, in which the starting point usually is the current level of spending.

In making a zero-base review, basic questions are raised about the activity, such as:

1. Should the activity be performed at all?
2. What should the quality level be? Are we doing too much?
3. Should it be performed in this way?
4. How much should it cost?

One way to examine the costs of a function is to make a comparison with the costs of performing similar functions in other parts of the company or in other companies. In some cases information can be obtained from trade associations and similar sources about the average cost of performing certain functions in other companies. Although there are problems of comparability; although, by definition, there is no way of finding a "correct" relationship between cost and output in a discretionary cost situation; although there is a danger in taking an average of other companies' costs as a standard; and although many other criticisms can be raised about such comparisons, they nevertheless can be useful. For example, they often lead to the following interesting question: If other companies can get the job done for $X, why can't we?

---

[2] This practice is sometimes, but erroneously, called *zero-base budgeting*. It is not a part of the annual budgeting process, however, because a zero-base review requires more time than is available in the normal budgeting process.

A good zero-base review is time consuming, and it is also likely to be a traumatic experience for the managers of responsibility centers. Such a review therefore cannot be made every year; rather reviews are scheduled so that all responsibility centers are covered once every four or five years. Alternatively, a form of zero-base review or *cost reduction program* may be made for the whole company when the need to reduce cost is urgent because of some crisis situation. A zero-base review establishes a new base for the budget, and the annual budget review attempts to keep costs reasonably in line with this base until the next zero-base review is made.

USES OF THE BUDGET

A budget is a plan expressed in quantitative, usually monetary terms, that covers a specified period of time, usually one year. Practically all large companies, and most other companies except the smallest, prepare budgets.[3] A budget is a tool for planning. It is equally useful for communicating plans, in motivating managers, and as a standard with which actual performance subsequently can be compared. Each of these uses is described below.

PLANNING. Although basic planning decisions are usually made in the programming process that occurs prior to the beginning of the budget cycle, the process of formulating the budget leads to a refinement of these plans; and when it discloses imbalances or unsatisfactory overall results, the budgeting process may lead to a change in plans.

COMMUNICATION. Management's plans will not be carried out (except by accident) unless the organization understands what the plans are. Adequate understanding includes not only a knowledge of specific plans (e.g., how many units are to be manufactured, what methods and machines are to be used, how much material is to be purchased, what selling prices are to be), but also a knowledge about policies and constraints to which the organization is expected to adhere. Examples of these kinds of information follow: the maximum amounts that may be spent for such items as advertising, maintenance, administrative costs; wage rates and hours of work; and desired quality levels. A most useful device for communicating quantitative information concerning these plans and limitations is the approved budget. Moreover, much vital information is communicated during the process of preparing the budget.

MOTIVATION. If the atmosphere is right, the budget process can be a powerful force in motivating managers to work toward the goals of the overall organization. Such an atmosphere is created when the manager

---

[3] In a study of 338 member companies of the Financial Executives Institute, 99 percent of the respondents reported that they prepared budgets. *Public Disclosure of Business Forecasts*, Financial Executives Research Foundation. (New York, 1972), p. 68.

of each responsibility center understands that top management regards the process as important, and when he participates in the formulation of his own budget in the manner to be described later in this chapter.

STANDARD FOR PERFORMANCE MEASUREMENT. A carefully prepared budget is the best possible standard against which to compare actual performance because it incorporates the estimated effect of all variables that were foreseen when the budget was being prepared. Until fairly recently, the general practice was to compare current results with results for last month or with results for the same period a year ago; this is still the basic means of comparison in many companies. Such a historical standard has the fundamental weakness that it does not take account of either changes in the underlying forces at work or in the planned program for the current year. During the period, a comparison of estimated actual performance with budgeted performance provides a "red flag," that is, it directs attention to areas where corrective action is needed.

TYPES OF BUDGETS

Although we have referred to "the" budget, the complete "budget package" in a company includes several items, each of which is also re-

Illustration 21–1

TYPES OF BUDGETS

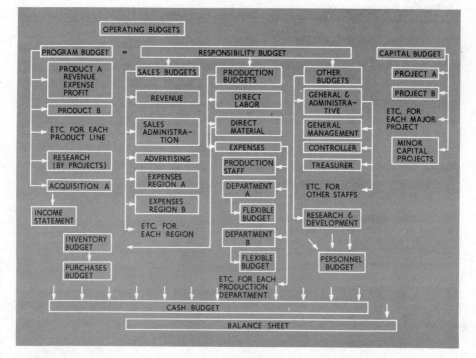

ferred to as a budget. We shall therefore refer to the total package as the *master budget*. Illustration 21–1 shows the components of this package in a typical company. The three principal parts of the master budget are:

1. An *operating budget*, showing planned operations for the forthcoming year, including revenues, expenses, and related changes in inventory;
2. A *cash budget*, showing the anticipated sources and uses of cash in that year; and
3. A *capital expenditure budget*, showing planned changes in fixed assets.

We shall first describe the nature of the operating budget and the steps involved in its preparation. We shall then describe the cash budget and the capital expenditure budget. Another document, the *budgeted balance sheet* is derived directly from the other budgets and is therefore not described separately.

THE OPERATING BUDGET

Program Budgets and Responsibility Budgets

The operating budget usually consists of two parts, a program budget and a responsibility budget. These represent two ways of depicting the overall operating plan for the business, two different methods of slicing the pie; therefore, both arrive at the same final figure for budgeted net income.

The *program budget* consists of the estimated revenues and costs of the major programs that the company plans to undertake during the year. Such a budget might be arranged, for example, by product lines and show the anticipated revenue and costs associated with each product line. This type of budget is useful to a manager when he is analyzing overall balance among the various programs of the business. It helps to answer such questions as these: Is the profit margin on each product line satisfactory? Is production capacity in balance with the size and capability of the sales organization? Can we afford to spend so much for research? Are adequate funds available? And so on. A negative answer to any of these questions indicates the necessity for revising the plan.

The *responsibility budget* sets forth plans in terms of the persons responsible for carrying them out. It is an excellent control device since it is a statement of the performance that is expected for each responsibility center manager against which his actual performance can later be compared. Each manager is responsible for preparing those parts of the operating budget that correspond to his sphere of responsibility.

In the factory, for example, there should be a responsibility budget for each department, showing the costs that are controllable by the foreman of the department. There may also be a program budget showing planned costs for each product, including both direct costs and allocated costs. The numbers of each set of budgets add up to total factory costs; but if several products were made in a factory in which there are several responsibility centers, the program budget would not be useful for control purposes, since the costs shown on it could not ordinarily be related to the responsibility of specific managers.

In some situations individual responsibility can be related to specific programs, and in these situations the program budget does serve as a means of control. The producer of a motion picture or a television "special," for example, has a budget for his particular program, and control is exercised in terms of that budget. This is also the case in the construction of major capital assets: buildings, dams, roads, bridges, ships, weapons systems, and the like.

Variable Budgets

If the total costs in a responsibility center are expected to vary with changes in volume, as is the case with most production and logistics responsibility centers, the responsibility budget may be in the form of a *variable budget* or *flexible budget*. Such a budget shows the planned behavior of costs at various volume levels. The variable budget is usually expressed in terms of the cost-volume equation described in Chapter 17, that is, a fixed amount for a specified time period plus a variable amount per unit of volume. (Recall from Chapter 17 the basic equation for determining the costs $[y]$ at any volume $[x]$; it is $y = a + bx$, in which a is the fixed amount and b is the variable amount per unit of volume x.) A variable budget may also be expressed as the costs that are planned at discrete levels of volume; that is, the costs planned at 60 percent of standard volume may be listed in one column, and costs planned at 70, 80, 90, 100, 110, 120, 130, and 140 percent of standard volume may be listed in other columns. When discrete volume levels are shown, a comparison of actual costs with budgeted costs requires an interpolation whenever the actual volume is between two of the specified volume levels.

When there is a variable budget, the costs at *one* volume level are used as part of the master budget. That volume level is the volume at which the company plans to operate during the budget period.

Nonfinancial Objectives

In addition to planned revenues and costs, various nonfinancial objectives may be developed during the budgeting process. These are especially useful in expense centers, and are a substitute for the planned revenue which is a measure of planned output in a profit center. In the market research department, for example, there may be a statement of the specific research activities that are planned for the period.

In both expense centers and profit centers, there may be a planned list of specific activities to be undertaken, such as the number of persons to be sent to training programs, a revision of some part of the control system, the preparation of a new operating manual, and so on.

In the control process, actual performance will be compared with these stated objectives. This practice is called *management by objectives*, although the term is not especially descriptive since the whole control apparatus, including the financial budget, is presumably related to the organization's objectives.

PREPARING THE OPERATING BUDGET

The preparation of a budget can be studied both as an accounting process and also as a management process. From an accounting standpoint, one studies the mechanics of the system, the procedures for assembling data, and budget formats. The procedures are similar to those described in Part I for recording actual transactions, and the end result of the calculation and summarizing operations is a set of financial statements—a balance sheet, income statement, and statement of changes in financial position—identical in format with those resulting from the accounting process that records historical events. The principal difference is that the budget amounts reflect planned future activities rather than data on what has happened in the past. We shall focus here on the preparation of an operating budget as a *management* process.

Organization for Preparation of Budgets

A *budget committee*, consisting of several members of the top management group, usually guides the work of preparing the budget. This committee recommends to the chief executive officer the general guidelines that the organization is to follow, disseminates these guidelines after his approval, coordinates the separate budgets prepared by the various organizational units, resolves differences among them, and submits the final budget to the president and to the board of directors for approval. In a small company, this work is done by the president himself, or by his immediate line subordinate. Instructions go down through the regular chain of command, and the budget comes back up for successive reviews and approvals through the same channels. Decisions about the budget are made by the line organization, and the final approval is given by the chief executive officer, subject to ratification by the board of directors.

The line organization usually is assisted in its preparation of the budget by a staff unit headed by the *budget director*. As a staff person, the budget director's functions are to disseminate instructions about the mechanics of budget preparation (the forms and how to fill them out), to provide data on past performance that are useful in preparation of the budget, to make computations on the basis of decisions reached by the line organization, to assemble the budget numbers, and to see to it that everyone submits his portion of the budget on time. The budget staff may do a very large fraction of the budget work. It is not the crucial part, however, for the significant decisions are always made by the line organization. Once the members of the line organization have reached an agreement on such matters as labor productivity and wage rates, for example, the budget staff can calculate the detailed amounts for labor costs by products and by responsibility centers; this is a considerable job of computation, but it is based entirely on the decisions of the line supervisors.

The budget staff is usually a unit of the controller's department. The budget staff is like a telephone company. It operates an important communication system; it is responsible for the speed, accuracy, and clarity with which messages flow through the system, but it does not decide on the content of the messages themselves.

Budget Timetable

Most companies prepare budgets once a year, and the budget covers a year. Separate budget estimates are usually made for each month or each quarter within the year. In some companies, data are initially estimated by months only for the next three months or the next six months, with the balance of the year being shown by quarters. When this is done a detailed budget by months is prepared shortly before the beginning of each new quarter.

Some companies follow the practice of preparing a new budget every quarter, but for a full year ahead. Every three months the budget amounts for the quarter just completed are dropped, the amounts for the succeeding three quarters are revised if necessary, and budget amounts for the fourth succeeding quarter are added. This is called a *rolling budget*.

Most components of the operating budget (see Illustration 21–1) are affected by decisions or estimates made in constructing other components. Nearly all components are affected by the planned sales volume and decisions as to inventory levels; the purchases budget is affected by planned production volume and decisions as to raw material inventory levels; and so on. Thus, there has to be a carefully worked out timetable specifying the order in which the several parts of the operating budget are developed and the time when each must be completed. In general, the steps covered by this timetable are as follows:

1. Setting budget guidelines.
2. Making the sales budget.
3. Initial preparation of other budget components.
4. Negotiation to evolve final plans for each component.
5. Coordination and review of the components.
6. Final approval.
7. Distribution of the approved budget.

In a company of average complexity, the elapsed time for the whole budget preparation process is approximately three months, with the most hectic part (steps 4, 5, and 6 above) requiring approximately one month. In highly complex organizations, the elapsed time may be somewhat longer. At the other extreme, a small business may go through the whole process in one afternoon.

Setting Budget Guidelines

The budget preparation process is *not* the mechanism through which most major program decisions are made, but rather is a means of implementing these decisions. When budget preparation begins, a great many decisions affecting the budget year already have been made. The maximum level of manufacturing operations has been set by the amount and character of available production facilities. (If an expansion of facilities is to take place during the budget year, the decision would ordinarily have been made a year or more previously because of the time required to build buildings and to acquire and install machinery.) If a new product is to go into volume production, considerable time would have already been spent prior to the budget year on product development, testing, design, and initial promotional work. Thus, the budget is not a *de novo* creation; it is built within the context of the ongoing business.

If the company has a formal program or long-range plan, this plan provides a starting point in preparing the budget. Alternatively, or in addition, top management establishes policies and guidelines that are to govern budget preparation. These guidelines vary greatly in content in different companies. At one extreme, there may be only a brief general statement, such as, "Assume that industry volume next year will be 5 percent higher than the current year." More commonly, detailed information and guidance are given on such matters as projected economic conditions, allowance to be made for price increases and wage increases, changes in the product line, changes in the scale of operations, allowable number of personnel promotions, and anticipated productivity gains. In addition, detailed instructions are issued as to what information is required from each responsibility center and how this information is to be recorded on the budget documents. In the absence of statements to the contrary, the organization customarily assumes that the factors affecting operations in the budget year will be similar to those in the current year.

EXAMPLE: The following guideline statement was developed by the budget committee of a large bank; it is relatively general and brief:

It is customary for the committee to summarize for your general guidance current thinking regarding deposits, loans, and loan rates. The expectations outlined below are for the overall bank. Therefore, it is important that the head of each department analyze the impact of expected general economic trends on the conditions peculiar to his own area of activity in order to project specific goals which he may reasonably expect to attain.

There is every indication that money market conditions will be such that demand deposit levels in our area will expand. In our judgment, we anticipate at least a 5 percent growth in demand deposits for all banks. Our overall goal, however, should be set somewhat higher to reflect an improvement in our relative position. Savings deposits will continue to climb moderately. Current rates for time and savings deposits should be used to project interest costs.

In all probability, loan demand will slacken seasonally in the early months of next year; in fact, many economists believe that the decline may continue through the second quarter of the year. We firmly believe that sometime between April and July loan demand should strengthen.

For the most part, the recent decline in the prime rate is reflected in the loan rate structure at this time. Accordingly, except where necessary rate adjustments are still anticipated, the existing rate structure should prevail.

Before preparing the budget, it is imperative that each supervisor closely evaluate discretionary expenses in his area and consider all means of economizing and reducing costs, particularly in such areas as personnel staffing, overtime, entertainment, stationery, etc. The salary administration policies explained in the Budget Instructions should be strictly followed.

In order to complete the budget for the entire bank by year-end, your full cooperation is necessary in meeting the deadlines which appear in the attached General Instructions.

Budget Committee

Making the Sales Budget

The amount of sales and the sales mix (i.e., the proportion represented by each product or product line) govern the level and general character of the company's operations. Thus, a sales plan must be made early in the budget process, for it affects most of the other plans. *The sales budget is different from a sales forecast.* A forecast is merely passive, while a budget should reflect the results of positive actions that management plans to take in order to influence future events. For example, this may be the sales *forecast:* "With the present amount of sales effort, we expect sales to run at about the same level as currently." By contrast, the sales *budget* may show a substantial planned increase in sales, reflecting management's intention to add sales personnel, to increase advertising and sales promotion, or to add or redesign products.

It follows that at the same time the sales budget is prepared, a selling expense budget should also be prepared because the size and nature of the order-getting efforts that are intended to influence sales revenue are given in the selling expense budget. However, in this early stage, it may suffice to show the main elements of selling expense, with such details as the expenses of operating field selling offices left until the next step.

In almost all companies the sales budget is the most difficult plan to make. This is because a company's sales revenue depends on the actions of its customers, which are not subject to the direct control of management. In contrast, the amounts of cost incurred are determined primarily by actions of the company itself (except for the prices of certain cost factors), and therefore can be planned with more confidence.

Basically, there are two ways of making estimates as a basis for the sales budget:

1. Make a *statistical forecast* on the basis of an analysis of general business conditions, market conditions, product growth curves, and the like; or
2. Make an *internal estimate* by collecting the opinions of executives and salespersons. In some companies sales personnel are asked to estimate the sales of each product to each of their customers; in others, regional managers estimate total sales in their regions; in still others, the field organization does not participate in the estimating process.

There are advantages and weaknesses in both the statistical and the internal methods. Both are often used together, but neither can be guaranteed to yield an even reasonably close estimate in view of the inevitable uncertainties of the future. Statistical techniques rest on the assumption that the future is likely to resemble the past. Such an assumption is reasonable in many situations. Thus, if sales have been increasing at the rate of 5 percent a year, and if there is no evidence that new factors will change this rate of increase, it is reasonable to predict that next year's sales will be 5 percent above this year's. This is the simplest type of forecast since it depends only on an extrapolation of past performance. A more complicated, and usually more reliable, procedure is to analyze the several factors that affect sales revenue and then predict the future behavior of each of these factors. Techniques for this purpose are described in the Appendix.

Initial Preparation of Other Budget Components

The budget guidelines prepared by top management, together with the sales plan, are disseminated down through the successive levels in the organization. Managers at each level may add other, more detailed information for the guidance of their subordinates. When the guidelines arrive at the lowest responsibility centers, the managers of these responsibility centers prepare proposed budgets for the items within their sphere of responsibility, working within the constraints specified in the guidelines.

Whenever feasible, estimates for physical quantities and for unit prices should be shown separately in order to facilitate the subsequent analysis of performance; that is, material cost is preferably shown as number of pounds times cents per pound, labor costs as number of hours times the hourly wage rate, and so on. The basic reason for such a separation is that different factors, and often different managers, are responsible for changes in the quantity component and the price component, respectively. For example, the purchasing officer is responsible for the cost per pound of raw material purchased, but the factory foreman is responsible for the quantity of raw material used. For similar reasons, the estimates are broken down by product lines, by significant items of cost, and in other ways that will facilitate subsequent analysis of actual performance as compared with the budgeted amounts.

Usually, the most recent data on actual costs are used as a starting point in making the expense estimates. The guidelines may provide specific instructions as to the permitted changes that can be made from current expenses, such as, "Assume a 5 percent price increase for purchased materials and services." In addition to following these instructions, the manager who prepares the budget, that is, the *budgetee*, expresses his judgment as to the behavior of costs not covered by the instructions.

Negotiation

Now comes the crucial stage in the process from a control standpoint, the negotiation between the budgetee and his superior.[4] The value of the budget as a plan of what is to happen, as a motivating device, and as a standard against which actual performance will be measured, depends

---

[4] In a perceptive study, Dr. G. Hofstede describes this process as a "game"; see *The Game of Budget Control* (Assen, The Netherlands: Van Gorcum & Co., N.V., 1967). A negotiation is a game, in the formal sense, as the reader who has participated in budget negotiations can appreciate.

largely on how skillfully this negotiation is conducted. Several recent studies have shown that the budget is more effective as a motivating device when it represents a "tight," but attainable, goal. If it is too tight, it leads to frustration; if it is too loose, it leads to complacency. The budgetee and his superior therefore seek to arrive at this desirable middle ground.[5]

The negotiating process applies principally to items of discretionary cost. If engineered costs have been properly analyzed, there is little room for differences of opinion about them. Committed costs, by definition, are not subject to negotiation so long as the commitment remains in force.

SLACK. Few machines and no organizations operate at 100 percent efficiency. Human beings will not exert maximum effort, hour after hour and day after day, and no reasonable manager expects them to do so. There is a great deal of waste motion, miscommunication and duplication of effort in any organization. The operation of Parkinson's Law ("costs tend to increase regardless of the amount of work done") causes costs to drift upward over a period of time. For all these reasons there is *slack* in an organization, that is, a difference between maximum efficiency and actual efficiency. The actual amount of slack cannot be measured. A certain amount of it is desirable; otherwise, the organization would not be an attractive place in which to work. The problem is to keep it within reasonable bounds. This a main objective of the negotiating process.

NEGOTIATING TACTICS. As did the budgetee, the superior usually must take the current level of expense as his starting point in the negotiations, modifying this according to his perception of how satisfactory the current level is. He simply does not have enough time during the budget review to reexamine each of the elements of expense so as to insure that the budgetee's estimates are optimum. One way of addressing the problem of slack is to make an arbitrary cut, say 10 percent,[6] in the budget estimates, but this has the weakness of any arbitrary action; it affects the efficient and the inefficient managers alike. Furthermore, if budgetees know that an arbitrary cut is going to be made, they can counter it by padding their original estimates by a corresponding amount.[7]

---

[5] The policy of some companies is to set the responsibility budget slightly tighter than the performance that reasonably can be expected. When this is done, a "budget reserve" is added to the responsibility budget so as to reduce the total company profit to the amount that reasonably can be expected. Individual managers are, of course, not told what the amount of this reserve is. If no such reserve were provided, the responsibility budget would not match the program budget.

[6] In a study of more than 30 companies, it was found that when the need for "belt tightening" arose, 80 percent routinely chose to cut discretionary costs by 10 percent. See Earl R. Gomersall, "The Ten Percent Syndrome," *Management Review*, August 1971.

[7] A tactic used by the chief executive officer in one major corporation is to choose at random a few budget items and ask the budgetee to explain them in detail.

There are more reasonable tactics for keeping costs in line during the negotiating process. The superior should require a full explanation of any proposed cost increases. He attempts to find reasons why costs may be expected to decrease, such as a decrease in the work load of the responsibility center or an increase in productivity resulting from the installation of new equipment or a new method, recognizing that these prospective decreases may ,not be voluntarily disclosed by the budgetee. Some managements, knowing that overall productivity in America increases by approximately 3 percent per year, expect similar productivity gains within their companies.

For his part, the budgetee defends his estimates. He justifies proposed cost increases by explaining their underlying causes, such as additional work that he is expected to do, the effect of inflation, the need for better quality output, and so on.

THE COMMITMENT.   The end product of the negotiation process is an agreement which represents an implicit *commitment* by each party, the budgetee and his superior. By the act of agreeing to the budget estimates, the budgetee says to his superior, in effect: "I can and will operate my responsibility center in accordance with the plan described in this budget." By approving the budget estimates, the superior says to the budgetee, in effect: "If you operate your responsibility center in accordance with this plan, you will do what we consider to be a good job." Both of these statements contain the implicit qualification of "subject to adjustment for unanticipated changes in circumstances" since both parties recognize that actual events, such as changes in price levels and in general business conditions, may not correspond to those assumed when the budget was prepared and that these changes may affect the plans set forth in the budget. In judging whether the commitment is in fact being accomplished as the year progresses, management must take these changes into account.

The nature of the commitment, both as to individual elements of expense and as to the total expense of the responsibility center, may be one of three types: (1) it may represent a *ceiling* (e.g., "not more than $X should be spent for books and periodicals"); (2) it may represent a *floor* (e.g., "at least $Y should be spent for employee training"); or (3) it may represent a *guide* (e.g., "approximately $Z should be spent for overtime"). Often, the individual items are not explicitly identified as to which of these three categories they belong in, but it is obviously important that the two parties have a clear understanding as to which item belongs in which category.

This top manager feels that, because the budgetee does not know in advance what he will have to defend in detail, he will be "on top of" all items in his budget during the budgeting process, and as a result will be more intimately familiar with the activities of his responsibility center.

Coordination and Review

The negotiation process is repeated at successively higher levels of responsibility centers in the organizational hierarchy, up to the very top. Negotiations at higher levels may, of course, result in changes in the detailed budgets that have been agreed to at lower levels. If these changes are significant, the budget should be recycled back down the organizational hierarchy for revision. If, however, the guidelines are carefully described, and if the budget process is well understood and well conducted by those who participate in it, such recycling ordinarily is not necessary. In the successive stages of negotiation, the person who has the role of superior at one level becomes the budgetee at the next higher level. Since he is well aware of this fact, he is strongly motivated to negotiate budgets with his budgetees that he can then defend successfully with his superiors. If his superior demonstrates that the proposed budget is too loose, this is a reflection on the budgetee's ability as a manager and as a negotiator.

As the individual budgets move up the organizational hierarchy in the negotiation and review process, they are also examined in relationship to one another, and this examination may reveal aspects of the plan that are out of balance. If so, certain of the underlying budgets may need to be changed. Major unresolved problems are submitted to the budget committee for resolution. The individual responsibility center budgets may also reveal the need to change planned amounts in the program budget, and these changes may in turn disclose that parts of the program appear to be out of balance. Various summary documents, especially the budgeted income statement, the budgeted balance sheet, and the cash-flow budget, are also prepared during this step.

Final Approval and Distribution

Just prior to the beginning of the budget year, the proposed budget is submitted to top management for approval. If the guidelines have been properly set and adhered to, and if significant issues that arise during the budgeting process are brought to top management for resolution, the proposed budget should contain no great surprises. Approval is by no means perfunctory, however, for it signifies the official agreement of top management to the proposed plans for the year. The chief executive officer therefore usually spends considerable time discussing the budget with each of the managers who reports to him. After top management approves the budget, it is submitted to the board of directors for final ratification.

The approved budget is then transmitted down through the organization. It constitutes authority to carry out the plans specified therein.

Variations in Practice

The preceding is a generalized description of the budget process. Not all companies prepare a budget for each responsibility center, and some companies that do develop a comprehensive budget treat the process more casually than is implied in the above description. Some companies formulate their budgets in a process that is essentially the reverse of that described; that is, instead of having budget estimates originate at the lowest responsibility centers, the budget is prepared by a high-level staff, blessed by top management, and then transmitted down to the organization. This *imposed budget* or "top down" budget is an unsatisfactory motivating device, and it is therefore not widely used.

Revisions

The budget is formulated in accordance with certain assumptions as to conditions that will prevail during the budget year. Actual conditions during the year will never be exactly the same as those assumed, and the differences may be significant. The question then arises as to whether or not the budget should be revised so that it will reflect what is now known about current conditions. There is considerable difference of opinion on this question.

Those who favor revising the budget point out that the budget is supposed to reflect the plan in accordance with which the company is operating, and that when the plan has to be changed because of changing conditions, the budget should reflect these changes. If the budget is not revised, it is no longer a statement of plans, they maintain.

The opponents of revising the budget argue that the process of revision not only is time consuming but also may obscure the goals that the company originally intended to achieve and the reasons for departures from these goals, especially since a revision may reflect the budgetee's skill in negotiating a change, rather than reflecting an actual change in the underlying assumed conditions. Since revisions for spurious reasons stretch the credibility of the budget, critics refer to such a revised budget as a "rubber standard." Many companies therefore do not revise their budgets during the year, and take account of changes in conditions when they analyze the difference between actual and budgeted performance.

Other companies solve this problem by having two budgets: a *baseline* budget set at the beginning of the year, and a *current budget* reflecting the best current estimate of revenue and expenses. A comparison of actual performance with the baseline performance shows the extent of deviation from the original plan, and a comparison of the current budget with the baseline budget shows how much of this deviation is attributable to changes in current conditions from those originally assumed.

Some managers use current budgets in lieu of reports of actual performance. Such a manager says: "I am not interested in actual costs because I literally can't do anything to control them; they have already happened. What I am interested in is how we now think we are going to come out, compared with how we originally planned to come out, as expressed in the baseline budget. If this comparison is not satisfactory, I can at least investigate what can be done to bring the situation back into line."

THE CASH BUDGET

The operating budget is usually prepared in terms of revenues and expenses. For financial planning purposes, it must be translated into terms of cash inflows and cash outflows. This translation results in the cash budget. The financial manager uses the cash budget to make plans to insure that the company has enough, but not too much, cash on hand during the year ahead.

There are two approaches to the preparation of a cash budget:

1. Start with the budgeted balance sheet and income statements, and adjust the amounts thereon to reflect the planned sources and uses of cash. This procedure is substantially the same as that described for the statement of changes in financial position in Chapter 11, except that the data are estimates of the future rather than historical. Its preparation is therefore not described again here.

2. Analyze those plans having cash-flow implications to estimate each of the sources and uses of cash. An example of this approach is shown in Illustration 21–2. Some points about this technique are briefly described below.

Collection of accounts receivable is estimated by applying a "lag" factor to estimated sales or shipments. This factor may be based simply on the assumption that the cash from this month's sales will be collected next month; or there may be a more elaborate assumption, for example, that 10 percent of this month's sales will be collected this month, 60 percent next month, 20 percent in the second month, 9 percent in the third month, and the remaining 1 percent will never be collected.

The estimated amount and timing of *raw materials purchases* is obtained from the materials purchases budget, and is translated into cash disbursements by applying a lag factor for the time interval that ordinarily elapses between the receipt of the material and the payment of the invoice.

Other operating expenses are often taken directly from the expense

Illustration 21-2

CASH BUDGET
(in thousands)

	January	February	March	April	May	Totals for Year
Gross shipments	1,200	1,987	2,063	1,387	2,363	21,000
Cash balance beginning of month	375	396	152	150	257	375
Add: Cash receipts:						
Collections of accounts receivable	1,380	1,350	1,605	1,635	1,680	19,305
Miscellaneous receipts	66	81	70	105	105	1,050
Total receipts	1,446	1,431	1,675	1,740	1,785	20,355
Total cash available	1,821	1,827	1,827	1,890	2,042	20,730
Less: Cash disbursements:						
Operating expenses	810	915	1,035	885	975	10,730
Raw materials purchases	503	570	1,050	600	607	7,140
Taxes		60	412	13		1,310
Equipment purchases					100	100
Dividends	112			135		517
Pension contribution		210				247
Total disbursements	1,425	1,755	2,497	1,633	1,682	20,044
Cash balance or (deficiency) end of month before bank loans or (repayments)	396	72	(670)	257	360	686
Bank loans or (repayments)		80	820		(200)	0
Cash Balance End of Month	396	152	150	257	160	686

budget, since the timing of cash disbursements is likely to correspond closely to the incurrence of the expense. Depreciation and other items of expense not requiring cash disbursements are excluded. Capital expenditures are also shown as an outlay, with amounts taken from the capital budget.

The bottom section of Illustration 21–2 shows how cash plans are made. The company desires a minimum cash balance of $150,000 as a cushion against unforeseen needs. From the budgeted cash receipts and cash disbursements, a calculation is made of whether the budgeted cash balance exceeds or falls below this minimum. In January the budgeted cash balance exceeds the minimum. In this company no action is planned, but in other situations, the company might well decide to invest the extra cash in marketable securities. In February, the budget indicates a balance of only $72,000; consequently, plans are made to borrow $80,000 to bring the balance to the desired level. The lower portion of the cash budget therefore shows the company's short-term financing plans.

THE CAPITAL EXPENDITURE BUDGET

The capital expenditure budget is essentially a list of what management believes to be worthwhile projects for the acquisition of new plant and equipment together with the estimated cost of each such capital investment project, and the timing of the related expenditures.

Proposals for capital investment projects may originate anywhere in the organization. The capital expenditure budget is usually prepared separately from the operating budget, and in many companies it is prepared at a different time and cleared through a capital appropriations committee that is separate from the budget committee.

In the capital expenditure budget, individual projects are often classified by purposes, such as the following:

1. Cost reduction and replacement.
2. Expansion and improvement of existing product lines.
3. New products.
4. Health and safety.
5. Other.

Proposals in the first two categories usually are susceptible to an economic analysis of the type described in Chapter 19. Some proposals for the addition of new products can also be substantiated by an economic analysis, although in a great many situations the estimate of sales of the new product is pretty much a guess. Proposals in the other categories usually cannot be sufficiently quantified so that an economic analysis is feasible.

Each proposed capital investment, except those for minor amounts, is accompanied by a justification. For some projects, the net present value or other measure of desirability can be estimated by methods described in Chapter 19. Other projects, such as the construction of a new office building or remodeling of employee recreation rooms, are justified on the basis of improved morale, safety, appearance, convenience, or other subjective grounds. A lump sum usually is included in the capital budget to provide for capital expenditure projects that are not large enough to warrant individual consideration by top management.

As proposals for capital expenditures come up through the organization, they are screened at various levels, and only the sufficiently attractive ones flow up to the top and appear in the final capital expenditure budget. On this document, they are often arranged in what is believed to be the order of desirability. Estimated expenditures are shown by years, or by quarters, so that the cash required in each time period can be determined. At the final review meeting, which is usually at the board-of-director level, not only are the individual projects discussed but also the total amount requested on the budget is compared with estimated funds available. Many apparently worthwhile projects may not be approved, simply because the funds are not available.

Approval of the capital budget usually means approval of the projects *in principle*, but does not constitute final authority to proceed with them. For this authority, a specific *authorization request* is prepared for the project, spelling out the proposal in more detail, perhaps with firm bids or price quotations on the new assets. These authorization requests are approved at various levels in the organization, depending on their size and character. For example, each foreman may be authorized to buy production tools or similar items costing not more than $100 each, provided his total for the year does not exceed $1,000; and at the other extreme, all projects costing more than $100,000 and all projects for new products, whatever their cost, may require approval of the board of directors. In between, there is a scale of amounts that various echelons in the organization may authorize without the approval of their superiors.

Some companies use *post-completion audits* to follow up on capital expenditures. These include both checks on the spending itself and also an appraisal, perhaps a year or more after the project has been completed, as to how well the estimates of cost and revenue actually turned out. In a few companies, there is very tight "linkage" between the cost savings estimated in a capital expenditure request and operating budget figures for the periods of projected savings. Such linkage, like post-completion audits, is aimed at motivating managers to make realistic savings estimates in their capital budgeting requests.

SUMMARY

In making plans and in exercising control, a distinction must be made between engineered costs, discretionary costs and committed costs.

Companies make two main types of plans: (1) program plans, which usually cover several future years and are focused on major programs, and (2) budgets, which are usually annual plans structured by responsibility centers. Budgets are used as a device for making and coordinating plans, for communicating these plans to those who are responsible for carrying them out, for motivating managers at all levels, and as a standard with which actual performance subsequently can be compared.

The operating budget is prepared within the context of basic policies and plans that have already been decided upon in the programming process. The principal steps are as follows: (1) dissemination of guidelines stating the overall plans and policies and other assumptions and constraints that are to be observed in the preparation of budget estimates; (2) preparation of the sales plan; (3) preparation of other estimates by the managers of responsibility centers, assisted by, but not dominated by, the budget staff; (4) negotiation of an agreed budget between the budgetee and his superior, which gives rise to a bilateral commitment by these parties; (5) coordination and review as these initial plans move up the organizational chain of command; (6) approval by top management and the board of directors; and (7) dissemination of the approved budget back down through the organization.

The *cash budget* translates revenues and expenses into cash receipts (inflows) and disbursements (outflows) and thus facilitates financial planning.

The *capital expenditure budget* is a price list of presumably worthwhile projects for the acquisition of new capital assets. Often it is prepared separately from the operating budget. Approval of the capital expenditure budget constitutes only approval in principle, for a subsequent authorization is usually required before work on the project can begin.

APPENDIX: SOME FORECASTING TECHNIQUES

Regression Analysis

In the appendix to Chapter 17 we described a technique for estimating the relationship between costs and volume by use of simultaneous equations to find the least squares line of "best fit." This technique is called *correlation analysis* or *regression analysis*. The same technique can be used to estimate the relationship between any two variables in which a cause-and-effect relationship is believed to exist.

A similar, but more complicated, technique, called *multiple regression analysis*, can be used to estimate the effect of several independent variables which together affect a single dependent variable, such as sales revenue. For example, if sales of a product are affected by the amount spent on advertising, the location of the product on the growth curve, the level of national income, the price level, and the activity level in certain specified industries, the separate effect of each of these factors can be isolated by this technique. Computer programs are available that perform the calculations automatically.

External Forecasts

Few companies, except the very largest, prepare their own forecasts of business conditions. Instead they rely on forecasts prepared by professional economists, either employed by the government, in universities, or in private practice. These professionals have larger data bases and more sophisticated computer analysis programs than most companies can afford to acquire and maintain. Data Resources, Inc., for example, forecasts by quarters for two years ahead not only for the economy as a whole, but also for individual states and for about 90 different industry groups. Companies use these data as a basis for their own forecasts by searching for series that seem to correlate well with their own sales.

Some professional economists forecast by preparing what are called *input-output tables*. Such a table shows, as of a given time, how the output of each industry in the economy requires inputs from other industries; for example, for a given output of the automobile industry, what inputs are required from the steel, aluminum, coal, electrical energy, textile, transportation, and other industries. Having constructed such a table, they can investigate the effect throughout the economy of varying the quantity of one of the outputs, and can use the results as a basis for forecasting. Although most companies cannot afford to construct such tables, they can obtain the results from professional economists.

Pilot Plants

Before starting full scale production of a new product or before starting up a new process, a company often tries out the idea on a small scale, called a *pilot plant*. The pilot plant not only helps to get the bugs out of the product or process, but it also provides a basis for estimating what costs will be incurred in full production. Because a scale-up to full production usually involves more than simply enlarging each element of the pilot plant by a constant factor, cost estimates derived from pilot plant operations must be used with care, but they nevertheless are the best available basis for estimating production costs.

Test Markets

Test markets are analogous to pilot plants. A company with a new product or a proposed new marketing technique tests it in one or a few markets to find out what happens to sales. It can use the results of the test market effort to estimate revenues and marketing costs when the product is marketed nationally, again with the caution that test market results may not be completely applicable on a national basis. Several mathematical models are available for use in such extrapolations of test market results.[8]

SUGGESTIONS FOR FURTHER READING

HOFSTEDE, G. H. *The Game of Budget Control*. Assen, The Netherlands: Van Gorcum & Co., N.V., 1967.

STEINER, GEORGE A. ed., *Top Management Planning*. New York: The Mac-Millan Co., 1969.

WELSCH, GLENN A. *Budgeting: Profit Planning and Control*. 3d ed. Englewood Cliffs, N.J.: Prentice-Hall, Inc., 1971.

---

[8] See, for example, David B. Montgomery and Glen L. Urban, *Management Science in Marketing* (Englewood Cliffs, N.J.: Prentice-Hall, Inc., 1969).

CASES

CASE 21–1. SOCIETÀ RIGAZIO

Società Rigazio manufactured a wide variety of metal products for industrial users in Italy and other European countries. Its head office was located in Milan and its mills in northern Italy provided about 80 percent of the company's production volume. The remaining 20 percent was produced in two factories, one in Lyon, France, and the other in Linz, Austria, both serving local markets exclusively through their own sales organizations.

Until recently the methods used by the Milan headquarters to review subsidiary operations were highly informal. The managing director of each subsidiary visited Milan twice a year, in October and in April, to review his subsidiary's performance and discuss his plans for the future. At other times the managing director would call or visit Milan to report on current developments or to request funds for specified purposes. These latter requests were usually submitted as a group, however, as part of the October meeting in Milan. By and large, if sales showed an increase over those of the previous year and if local profit margins did not decline, the directors in Milan were satisfied and did nothing to interfere with the subsidiary manager's freedom to manage his business as he saw fit.

Last year Società Rigazio found itself for the first time in twelve years with falling sales volume, excess production capacity, rising costs, and a shortage of funds to finance new investments. In analyzing this situation, the Milan top management decided that one thing that was needed was a more detailed system of cost control in its mills, including flexible budgets for the overhead costs of each factory.

The Lyon mill was selected as a "pilot plant" for the development of the new system. Because the Lyon mill produced a wide variety of products in many production departments, it was not possible to prepare a single flexible budget for the entire mill. In fact, Mr. Spreafico, the company's controller, found that the work done in most of the production departments was so varied that useful cost/volume relationships

740

could not even be developed on a departmental basis. He began, therefore, by dividing many of the departments into cost centers so that a valid single measure of work performed could be found for each one. Thus a department with both automatic and hand-fed cutting machines might be divided into two cost centers, each with a group of highly similar machines doing approximately the same kind of work.

The establishment of the cost centers did not change the responsibility pattern in the factory. Each department had a foreman who reported to one of two production supervisors; the latter were responsible directly to Mr. Forclas, the plant manager. Each foreman continued to be responsible for the operations of all the cost centers in his department. In some cases a cost center embraced an entire department, but most departments contained between two and five cost centers.

Once he had completed this task, Mr. Spreafico turned to the development of flexible budgets. For each cost center he selected the measure or measures of volume that seemed most closely related to cost (e.g., machine-hours) and decided what volume was normal for that cost center (e.g., 1,000 machine-hours per month). The budget allowance at the normal level of operations was to be used later as an element of standard product costs, but the budget allowance against which the foremen's performance was to be judged each month was to be the allowance for the volume actually achieved during that particular month.

Under the new system, a detailed report of overhead cost variances would be prepared in Lyon for the foreman in charge of a particular cost center and for his immediate superior, the production supervisor; a summary report, giving the total overhead variance for each cost center, would be sent to the plant manager and to Mr. Duclos, the managing director of Rigazio France, S.A., Lyon. The Milan top management would not receive copies of any of these reports, but would receive a monthly profit and loss summary, with comments explaining major deviations from the subsidiary's planned profit for the period.

The preparation of the budget formulas had progressed far enough by mid-year to persuade Mr. Spreafico to try them out on the September cost data. A top management meeting was then scheduled in Milan to discuss the new system on the basis of the September reports. Mr. Duclos and Mr. Forclas flew to Milan to attend this meeting, accompanied by the controller of Rigazio France and a production supervisor responsible for some thirty cost centers in the Lyon factory.

Mr. Enrico Montevani, Società Rigazio's managing director, opened the meeting by asking Mr. Spreafico to explain how the budget allowances were prepared. Mr. Spreafico began by saying that the new system was just in its trial stages and that many changes would undoubtedly be necessary before everyone was satisfied with it. "We started with the idea that the standard had to be adjusted each month to reflect the actual volume of production," he continued, "even though that might mean that we would tell the factory they were doing all right when in fact they had large amounts of underabsorbed overhead. In that case the problem would be that we had failed to provide enough volume to keep the plant busy, and you can't blame the foremen for that. When you have fixed costs, you just can't use a single standard cost per hour or per ton or per unit, because that would be too high when we're operating near capacity and too low when we're underutilized. Our problem, then, was to find out how overhead cost varies with volume so that we could get more accurate budget allowances for overhead costs at different production volumes.

"To get answers to this question, we first made some preliminary estimates at headquarters, based on historical data in the accounting records both here and in Lyon. We used data on wage rates and purchase prices from the personnel and purchasing departments to adjust our data to current conditions. Whenever we could, we used a mathematical formula known as a 'least squares' formula to get an accurate measure of cost variability in relation to changing volume, but sometimes we just had to use our judgment and decide whether to classify a cost as fixed or variable. I might add that in picking our formulas we tried various measures of volume and generally took the one that seemed to match up most closely with cost. In some cost centers we actually used two different measures of volume, such as direct labor hours and product tonnage, and based some of our budget allowances on one and some on the other.

Exhibit 1

OVERHEAD COST SUMMARY—COST CENTER 2122

September
(in francs)

	Std. Allowance at Normal Volume (500 hrs, 25 tons)	Budgeted at Actual Vol. (430 hrs, 23 tons)	Actual, Month of September	Over (Under) Budget
Supervision	180	180	145	(35)
Indirect labor	1,500	1,360	1,610	250
Waiting time	105	90	177	87
Hourly wage guarantee	70	60	30	(30)
Payroll taxes, etc.	1,614	1,416	1,504	88
Materials and supplies	150	129	141	12
Tools	750	645	638	(7)
Maintenance	1,600	1,536	1,876	340
Scrap loss	2,110	1,941	2,456	515
Allocated costs	5,260	5,260	5,305	45
Total	13,339	12,617	13,882	1,265
Per ton	533.56	548.57	603.57	55.00

These estimates were then discussed with Mr. Forclas and his people at Lyon, and the revised budget formulas were punched into tabulating cards for use in monthly report preparation.

"Although you have a complete set of the cost center reports, perhaps we might focus on the one for cost center 2122, labeled Exhibit 1. You

Exhibit 2

FLEXIBLE BUDGET FORMULA—COST CENTER 2122

(in francs)

	Allowance Factors		
	Fixed Amount per Month	Variable Rate	Remarks
Supervision.....................	180	—	Percent of foreman's time spent in cost center
Indirect labor..................	500	2.00/DLhr.	—
Waiting time..................	—	.21/DLhr.	Wages of direct labor workers for time spent waiting for work
Hourly wage guarantee..........	—	.14/DLhr.	Supplement to wages of workers paid by the piece to give them guaranteed minimum hourly wage
Payroll taxes, etc...............	204	2.82/DLhr.	Payroll taxes and allowances at 30 percent of total payroll, including direct labor payroll*
Materials and supplies...........	—	.30/DLhr.	—
Tools.........................	—	1.50/DLhr.	—
Maintenance...................	800	32.00/ton	Actual maintenance hours used at predetermined rate per hour, plus maintenance materials used
Scrap loss.....................	—	84.40/ton	Actual scrap multiplied by difference between materials cost and estimated scrap value per kilogram
Allocated costs.................	5,260	—	Actual cost per month, allocated on basis of floor space occupied

* Budgeted direct labor at standard volume, 500 hours at fr. 7.00 per hour; actual direct labor cost for September was 3053 francs.

can see that we have used two measures of volume in this cost center, direct labor hours and product tonnage. During September we were operating at less than standard volume, which meant that we had to reduce the budget allowance to fr. 12,617, which averaged out at fr. 548.57 per ton. Our actual costs were almost exactly ten per cent higher than this, giving us an over-all unfavorable performance variance of fr. 1,265, or fr. 55 per ton.

"I know that Mr. Duclos and Mr. Forclas will want to comment on this, but I'll be glad to answer any questions that any of you may have. Incidentally, I have brought along some extra copies of the formulas I used in figuring the September overhead allowances for cost center 2122, just in case you'd like to look them over."

Questions

1. Do you agree with Mr. Spreafico that 548.57 francs per ton (see Exhibit 1) is a more meaningful standard for cost control than the "normal" cost of 533.56 francs?
2. Comment on the variances in Exhibit 1. Which of these are likely to be controllable by the foreman? What do you think the production supervisor should have done on the basis of this report?
3. What changes, if any, would you make in the format of this report or to the basis on which the budget allowances are computed?
4. In developing the budget allowances, did Mr. Spreafico make any mistakes that you think he could have avoided? Does his system contain any features that you particularly like?

CASE 21–2. MAMMOTH MANUFACTURING COMPANY

The Mammoth Manufacturing Company was a large producer of manufactured metals parts. It produced stampings, machined castings, and assemblies of stamped and machined parts for the automobile industry, the appliance industry, the tractors and implements business, and several other types of manufacturers and assemblers all over the United States. The company produced few parts for direct sale to the consumer. Instead, the parts were included in the final assembly of a consumer product such as an automobile or a home appliance sold by Mammoth's customers.

The Mammoth Manufacturing Company had 41 manufacturing plants spread out over the country. Total sales were in excess of one-half billion dollars.

The Cost Control System

For many years, Mammoth had no cost control system worthy of the name. The plants had an historical cost system and reports were submitted monthly to the central office in Cleveland, Ohio. Nothing much was done with these reports and, as long as the plant managers met their production commitments, no one bothered much about costs. In the 1970s, however, competition became quite severe in the type of products Mammoth produced. As a consequence, profit margins were reduced drastically and the management of the company began looking around for means of improving their competitive position. Manufacturing cost control was an obvious area. The management decided that they must install a system of control over their manufacturing costs.

Several people with experience in standard costing and budgeting were hired to develop and install a cost control system in the manufacturing plants. Each manufacturing plant was considered to be a cost responsibility center, with the plant manager responsible for meeting his cost targets.

At each plant, industrial engineering departments were established and labor standards were set for each part. The accounting department at each plant was expanded to include a budgeting section. This section was responsible for developing flexible budgets to cover manufacturing overhead costs in accordance with instructions from the corporate controller's staff.[1]

The Budget Analysis Department

Under the corporate controller, at the central staff in Cleveland, was the Budget Analysis Department. It was the responsibility of this department: to establish timetables for budget submission; to provide forms and instructions so that the budgets would be prepared in a uniform manner; and to analyze the budget proposals and recommend whether they should be accepted or not. This was to insure a uniform "task" in each budget. The Budget Analysis Department also had responsibility for prescribing the budget performance reports. Each month the direct labor and overhead cost performance of each plant was analyzed and the results summarized for management.

Results of the Control System

Almost from the beginning the effect of the new control system was to reduce manufacturing costs significantly. Part of these savings came from the industrial engineering studies required to set the labor standards. Part of the savings resulted from the analysis of overhead costs that was required to prepare the budgets. Often, it became evident on analysis

---

[1] Material costs were controlled by a different system and will not be considered in this case.

that certain costs were seriously out of line. Much of the savings came because the system made the plant managers and the line foremen cost-conscious. The system, however, was not installed without problems and the purpose of this case is to describe three situations that occurred during the initial period of installation.

SITUATION 1: DEFINITION OF FIXED EXPENSE

Several of the people in the Budget Analysis Department came from a large automobile company where the flexible budget equation was calculated by using the budgeted costs at two volumes: zero and standard volume. The budgeted expense at zero volume was defined as the "level of costs that would be required with a six months' shut down". This resulted in a low fixed cost and, consequently, a high variable cost. Since the variable cost per unit was relatively high using this method, the

Exhibit 1

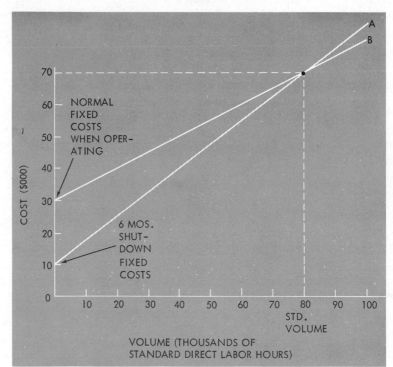

Line A shows the relation of budgeted expense to volume assuming that there is a fixed cost at zero volume of $10,000. This is the estimated fixed cost that would be incurred after a six month's shutdown.

Line B shows the relation of budgeted expenses to volume assuming that there is a fixed cost at zero volume of $30,000. This is the estimated normal fixed cost incurred when the plant is operating.

At a standard volume of 80,000 hours, the total budgeted expense is estimated to be $70,000. Note that at less than SV, Line B gives the greater budget authorization. At more than SV, Line A provides the higher budget.

reduction in budgeted cost for each unit below standard volume was also high. This meant that when a plant was operating below standard volume, the budget allowance was squeezed. On the other hand, when volume exceeded standard, the budget authorization would be relatively high. This relationship is shown in Exhibit 1.

The argument for using this method was that it forced costs down when volume fell and the company really needed the cost savings, whereas, when volume was above standard, the company could afford to be a little more liberal about expenditures because they were earning increased profits from the additional volume.

Questions

1. What do you think of the method of determining the budget equation used by the automobile company?
2. How do you think the budget equation should be calculated at Mammoth?

SITUATION 2:   REASONABLE AND CONSISTENT "TASK"

The Budget Analysis Department was responsible for analyzing the proposed budget from each plant and recommending to top management whether it should be accepted as proposed, accepted with adjustment, or rejected. The ideal budget was one that could be attained if plant management was consistently efficient. The variance from budget, then, represented the extent of the plant's inefficiency.

It was important not only that the approved budget represent an efficient "task," but that the degree of "task" be consistent among the divisions. Although each plant's budget performance was analyzed individually, comparison among the plants was inevitable. If the budget levels did not represent a consistent task, some managers would be judged unfairly.

One of the principal problems facing the Budget Analysis Department was how to insure that the approved budgets included reasonable task and that the degree of task was consistent among the divisions. This problem was made particularly difficult because the plants realized that it was to their benefit to have a "loose" budget since they were being evaluated against it. Furthermore, no absolute standards existed. Overhead rates differed because of differences in automation, in facilities, in location, and so forth. Also, it was not possible to compare plants directly. No two plants produced exactly the same product line. Even where production processes were similar, there were enough differences because of geographic location, type of equipment, and mix of products that direct comparisons were not meaningful.

Question

How would you solve the problem described above if you were the manager of the Budget Analysis Department? The constraints within which you must work are:

a. The Budget Analysis Department consists of thirty analysts, varying in experience from one to ten years.

b. Each Plant Budget Department consists of a supervisor and three to five analysts. The budgeting people, however, tend to identify themselves with the plant rather than with the central controller's office.

SITUATION 3:   THE OAK PARK PLANT

The Oak Park Plant produced machined parts and assemblies almost exclusively for the automobile industry. At the time that the budget system was first being introduced, a new plant manager, Mr. Lou Hart, was placed in charge of the Oak Park Plant. Hart came from one of the large automotive manufacturers where he had developed a reputation as a "cost-cutter".

Hart went to work on cost-cutting at Oak Park with vigor. His first budget proposal was 15 percent less than the previous year's actual expense, adjusted to a comparable volume of production. Although the budget represented substantial reduction in all areas of cost, Hart's proposal represented a 25 percent reduction in indirect labor.

The Oak Park Plant's actual costs for the first year of the budget system (also Hart's first year with the company) were *10 percent less than budget*. In other words, Hart's actual overhead costs, for his first year as manager of the Oak Park Plant, were about 25 percent less than the preceding year's, at comparable volumes. Because of this performance Hart was given a special award by the president of Mammoth.

Hart's proposed budget for his second year was 10 percent less than his first year's actual costs. The proposed indirect labor budget was now about one half of the amount being spent when Hart first took over the Oak Park Plant. Hart's actual costs continued to be better than budget until the autumn of his second year.

The Oak Park Plant had been producing the same parts, with only slight modifications, for the past several years. During Hart's second year at Oak Park, almost all of the automobile companies made drastic changes in the design of the parts that were being produced at the Oak Park Plant. Hart was faced with the necessity of changing over nearly every production line in the plant. This process was made particularly difficult because one of the automobile producers failed to finalize several designs until very close to the time that production on the parts was supposed to begin. Hart had reduced his staff so drastically that he did not have nearly enough manufacturing and industrial engineers to handle the changeover. Furthermore, his supervision was spread so thin that, even where the changeover was accomplished, trouble developed on several lines and production was severely curtailed. As a result, Hart failed to meet production schedules on several major parts, and consequently, the business was given to competitors. By the time the production had been straightened out, the Oak Park Plant had lost nearly half of its business. Needless to say, Hart was replaced.

Question

How do you make sure that a budget system does not motivate a manager to take too drastic cost-cutting action?

CASE 21–3. WHIZ CALCULATOR COMPANY

In August 1973 Bernard Riesman was elected president of the Whiz Calculator Company to fill the vacancy created by the departure of the former chief executive. Mr. Riesman had been with the company for 5 years, and for the preceding 2 years had been vice president in charge of manufacturing. Shortly after taking over his new position, Mr. Riesman held a series of conferences with the controller in which the general subject under discussion was budgetary control. The new president thought that the existing method of planning and checking on selling costs was particularly unsatisfactory, and he requested the controller to devise a system which would provide better control over these costs.

The Whiz Calculator Company manufactured a complete line of electronic calculators, which it sold through branch offices to wholesalers and retailers, and to government and industrial users. Most of the products carried the Whiz brand name, which was nationally advertised. The company was one of the largest in this rapidly growing and highly competitive industry.

Under the procedure then being used, selling expenses were budgeted on a "fixed" or "appropriation" basis. Each October the accounting department sent to branch managers and to other executives in charge of selling departments a detailed record of the actual expenses of their departments for the preceding year and for the current year to date. Guided by this record, by estimates of the succeeding year's sales and by his own judgment, each department head drew up and submitted an estimate of the expenses of his department for the succeeding year, detailed as to main items of expense. The estimates made by the branch managers were sent to the sales manager, who was in charge of all branch sales. He determined whether or not they were reasonable and cleared up any questionable items by correspondence. Upon approval by the sales manager, the estimates of branch expenses were submitted to the manager of distribution, Mr. Melmed, who was in charge of all selling, promotional, and warehousing activities.

The manager of distribution discussed these figures and the expense estimates furnished by the other department heads with the executives concerned, and after differences were reconciled, he combined the estimates of all the selling departments into a selling expense budget. This budget was submitted to the budget committee for final approval. For control purposes, the annual budget was divided into twelve equal amounts, and actual expenses were compared each month with the budgeted figures. Exhibit 1 shows the form in which these monthly comparisons were made.

Mr. Riesman believed that there were two important weaknesses in this method of setting the selling expense budget. First, it was impossible for anyone to ascertain with any feeling of certainty the reasonableness of the estimates made by the various department heads. Clearly, the expenses of the preceding year did not constitute adequate standards

Exhibit 1
BUDGET REPORT CURRENTLY USED

Branch Sales and Expense Performance					
Date: October 1973		Branch A		Mgr:	N. L. Darden
	This Month				
	Budget†	Actual	Over*-Under	% of Sales	Over*-Under Year to Date
Net Sales	190,000	160,000			
Executive Salaries	2,000	2,000	—	1.25	—
Office Salaries	1,150	1,134	16	0.71	1,203
Salesmen's Compensation	11,400	9,600	1,800	6.00	2,802*
Traveling Expense	3,420	3,127	293	1.95	1,012*
Stationery, Office Supplies and Expense	1,042	890	152	0.56	360
Postage	230	262	32*	0.16	21
Light & Heat	134	87	47	0.05	128
Subscriptions and Dues	150	112	38	0.07	26
Donations	125	—	125	0.00	130
Advertising Expense (Local)	1,900	1,800	100	1.12	1,200*
Social Security Taxes	291	205	86	0.13	27*
Rental	975	975	—	0.61	—
Depreciation	762	762	—	0.48	—
Other Branch Expense	2,551	2,426	125	1.52	247*
Total	26,130	23,380	2,750	14.61	3,420*
† 1/12 of 1973 budget.					

against which these expense estimates could be judged, since selling conditions were never the same in two different years. One obvious cause of variation in selling expenses was the variation in the "job to be done," as defined in the sales budget.

Second, selling conditions often changed substantially after the budget was adopted, but there was no provision for making the proper corresponding changes in the selling expense budget. Neither was there a logical basis for relating selling expenses to the actual sales volume obtained or to any other measure of sales effort. The chief executive believed that it was reasonable to expect that sales expenses would increase, though not proportionately, if actual sales volume were greater than the forecasted volume; but that with the existing method of control it was impossible to determine how large the increase in expenses should be.

As a means of overcoming these weaknesses the president suggested the possibility of setting selling cost budget standards on a fixed and variable basis, a method similar to the techniques used in the control of manufacturing expenses. The controller agreed that this manner of approach seemed to offer the most feasible solution to the problem, and he therefore undertook with the cooperation of the sales department a study of selling expenses for the purpose of devising a method of setting reasonable standards. Over a period of several years, the accounting department had made many analyses of selling costs, the results of which had been used in determining the proper bases for allocating costs to products, customers, functions, and territories, and in assisting in the solution of certain special problems, such as the problem of determining how large an individual order had to be in order to be profitable to the company. Many of the data which had been accumulated for these purposes were helpful in the controller's current study.

The controller was convinced that the fixed portion of selling expenses–in other words, the portion which was independent of any fluctuation in sales volume–could be established by determining the amount of expenses which had to be incurred at the minimum sales volume at which the company was likely to operate. He therefore asked Mr. Melmed, the manager of distribution, to suggest a minimum volume figure and the amount of expenses which would have to be incurred at this volume level. A staff assistant was assigned the task of studying the past sales records of the company over several business cycles, the long-term outlook for sales, and sales trends in other companies in the industry. From the report prepared by his assistant Mr. Melmed concluded that sales volume would not drop below 45 percent of the current capacity of the factory.

Mr. Melmed then attempted to determine the selling expenses which would be incurred at the minimum volume. With the help of his staff assistant, he worked out a hypothetical selling organization which in his opinion would be required to sell merchandise equivalent to 45 percent of factory capacity, complete as to the number of persons needed to staff each branch office and the other selling departments, including the advertising, merchandise and sales administration departments. Using current salary and commission figures, the assistant calculated the amount of money which would be required to pay salaries for such an organization. The manager of distribution also estimated the other expenses, such as advertising, branch office upkeep, supplies and travel, which he thought would be incurred by each branch and staff department at the minimum sales volume.

The controller decided that the variable portion of the selling expense standard should be expressed as a certain amount per sales dollar. He realized that the use of the sales dollar as a measuring stick had certain disadvantages in that it would not reflect such important influences on costs as the size of the order, the selling difficulty of certain territories, changes in buyer psychology, and so forth. The sales dollar, however, was the measuring stick most convenient to use, the only figure readily available from the records then being kept, and also a figure which all the individuals concerned thoroughly understood. The controller believed that a budget which varied with sales would certainly be better than a budget which did not vary at all. He planned to devise a more accurate measure of causes of variation in selling expenses after he had an opportunity to study the nature of these factors over a longer period of time.

As a basis for setting the initial variable expense standards, using a

Exhibit 2

BUDGET FOR "OTHER BRANCH EXPENSE," BRANCH A

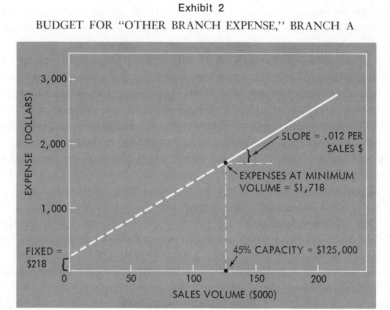

technique called linear regression the controller determined a series of equations which correlated actual annual expenditures for the principal groups of expense items for several preceding years with sales volume. Using these equations, which showed to what extent the principal expense items had fluctuated with sales volume in the past, and modifying them in accordance with his own judgment as to future conditions, the controller determined a rate of variation (i.e., slope) for the variable portion of each item of selling expense. The controller thought that after the new system had been tested in practice, it would be possible to refine these rates, perhaps by the use of a technique analogous to the time-study technique which was employed to determine certain expense standards in the factory.

At this point the controller had both a rate of variation and one point (i.e., at 45 percent capacity) on a selling expense graph for each expense item. He was therefore able to determine a final equation for each item. Graphically, this was equivalent to drawing a line through the known

Exhibit 3

BUDGET REPORT PROPOSED BY CONTROLLER

Expense Budget Report			Branch: A Manager: N. L. Darden Date: October 1973			
	Budget Factors		*This Month*			*Year to Date*
	Fixed	*Variable*	*Stnd Act* ~~*Budget*~~	*Actual* ~~*Actual*~~	*Over* Under* ~~*Variance*~~	*Over* Under*
Net sales			160,000	160,000		†
Executive Salaries	2,000	—	2,000	2,000	—	
Office Salaries	110	.0051	926	1,134	208*	
Salesmen's Compensation	—	.0600	9,600	9,600	—	
Traveling Expense	568	.0142	2,840	3,127	287*	
Stationery, Office Supplies, and Expense	282	.0042	954	890	64	
Postage	47	.0010	207	262	55*	
Light and Heat	134	—	134	87	47	
Subscriptions and Dues	10	.0008	138	112	26	
Donations	20	.0005	100	—	100	
Advertising Expense (Local)	150	.0100	1,750	1,800	50*	
Social Security Taxes	42	.0013	250	205	45	
Rental	975	—	975	975	—	
Depreciation	762	—	762	762	—	
Other Branch Expense	218	.0120	2,138	2,426	288*	
Total	5,318	.1091	22,774	23,380	606*	

† The controller had not recalculated budgets for previous months, and figures were therefore not available for this column.

point at the slope represented by the rate of variation. The height of this line at zero volume represented the fixed portion of the selling expense formula. The diagram in Exhibit 2 illustrates the procedure, although the actual computations were mathematical rather than graphic.

The selling expense budget for 1974 was determined by adding to the new standards for the various fixed components the indicated flexible allowances for the 1974 estimated sales volume. This budget was submitted to the budget committee, which studied the fixed amounts and the variable rates underlying the final figures, making only minor changes before passing final approval.

The controller planned to issue reports each month showing actual expenses for each department compared with budgeted expenses. The variable portion of the budgeted allowances would be adjusted to correspond to the actual volume of sales obtained during the month. Exhibit 3 shows the budget report which he planned to send to branch managers.

One sales executive privately belittled the controller's proposal. "Anyone in the selling game," he asserted, "knows that sometimes customers fall all over each other in their hurry to buy, and other times, no matter what we do, they won't even nibble. It's a waste of time to make fancy formulas for selling cost budgets under conditions like that."

Questions

1. From the information given in Exhibits 1 and 3, determine insofar as you can, whether each item of expense is (*a*) nonvariable, (*b*) partly variable with sales volume, (*c*) variable with sales volume, or (*d*) variable with some other factors.
2. What bearing do your conclusions in Question 1 have on the type of budget that is most appropriate?
3. Should the proposed sales expense budget system be adopted?
4. If a variable budget is used, should dollar sales be used as the measure of volume?

CHAPTER 22

ANALYZING AND REPORTING PERFORMANCE

This chapter describes methods of identifying several types of variances between planned results and actual results, it discusses how these variances should be interpreted, and it describes how they are reported, along with other information, as a basis for management action.

OVERVIEW OF THE ANALYTICAL PROCESS

In most situations, actual revenues and costs do not correspond to planned revenues and costs. Management wants to know not only *what* the amounts of the differences between actual and planned results were but also, and more importantly, *why* these differences occurred. Analytical techniques that are helpful in identifying the causes of the differences between actual results and planned results are discussed in this section. Essentially, these techniques decompose the total difference between actual and planned performance into several elements, each of which is called a variance. Having identified how much of the total difference is attributable to each type of variance, management is in a position to fix responsibility and to ask relevant questions. The answers to these questions may suggest the need for corrective action.

In a given company the techniques used to analyze the differences between actual and budgeted performance depend on management's judgments as to how useful the results are likely to be. Some companies do not use any formal techniques; others use only a few of those described here; and still others use even more sophisticated techniques. There are no prescribed criteria beyond the general rule that any technique should provide information that is worth more than the costs involved in developing the information.

Structure of the Analysis

We shall refer to the data with which actual performance is being compared as the *budgeted* data because, as emphasized in Chapter 21, a carefully prepared budget is usually the best indication of what performance should be. The same techniques can be used to analyze actual performance in terms of any other basis of comparison, such as performance in some prior period, or performance in some other responsibility center. Although our principal focus is in analyzing the performance of responsibility centers in a business company, the same general approach can be used for analyzing any situation in which inputs are used to produce outputs.

In earlier chapters, we have used the term *variance* for the difference between actual costs and standard costs. We shall now broaden the meaning of this word to include the difference between the actual amount and the budgeted amount of *any* revenue or cost item.

An *unfavorable* variance is one whose effect is to make actual net income lower than budgeted net income. Thus, an unfavorable revenue variance occurs when actual revenue is less than budgeted revenue, but an unfavorable cost variance occurs when actual cost is higher than budgeted cost. Corresponding statements can of course be made about favorable variances.

In looking at the business as a whole, attention ultimately is directed to the "bottom line," that is, at the amount of the net income. If in a certain company budgeted net income in April was $100,000 and actual net income was only $80,000, the $20,000 variance indicates that something went wrong in April. It does not, however, indicate *what* went wrong. In order to take effective action, management needs to identify the variances in specific items that together explain the total unfavorable variance. These items can be grouped into three categories, each of which corresponds roughly to an area of responsibility within a company:

1. Gross margin variances, which are the responsibility of the marketing organization,
2. Production cost variances, which are the responsibility of the production organization, and—
3. Other variances, which are the responsibility of top management and its principal staff units.

GROSS MARGIN VARIANCE

Gross margin is the difference between sales revenue and cost of goods sold. In calculating both actual and budgeted gross margin, the goods sold are costed at their *standard* unit costs, rather than at their *actual* unit costs. (Differences between actual and standard unit costs are production cost variances and are described in the section on that topic.) The total gross margin variance is the difference between the actual and budgeted gross margins. It can be decomposed into three components:

1. The *selling price variance*, which arises because the actual selling price per unit was different from the budgeted selling price per unit.

2. The *sales volume variance*, which arises because the actual sales volume, in terms of number of units, was different from the budgeted sales volume.

3. The *mix variance*, which arises because some products had higher unit margins than others and the actual proportion of products with various unit margins was different from the budgeted proportion.

We shall first describe how to isolate the selling price and sales volume variances. In order to defer the description of the mix variance, we shall assume in these calculations that all products had the same unit margin.

Selling Price and Sales Volume Variances

If actual gross margin in April was $9,900 and budgeted gross margin was $10,000, there was an unfavorable gross margin variance of $100. This $100 is explainable in terms of a variance in unit selling prices and/or a variance in sales volume. The rules for isolating the effect of these two components are as follows:

1. The *selling price variance* is the difference between the actual unit margin[1] and the budgeted unit margin, multiplied by the *actual* number of units.

2. The *sales volume variance* is the difference between the actual sales volume (in units) and the budgeted sales volume, priced at the *budgeted* unit margin.

The *net variance* (or *total variance*) in gross margin is the algebraic sum of the selling price and sales volume variances. It follows that having found either the selling price or the sales volume variance, the other can be found by subtracting this variance from the net variance. The net variance is also, of course, the difference between actual and budgeted gross margin.

The application of these rules is illustrated in Illustration 22–1, which is a diagram of this situation:

	Actual	Budgeted
Unit gross margin	$ 11	$ 10
Volume, units	900	1,000
Gross margin (unit margin × volume)	$9,900	$10,000

---

[1] Although the amount is referred to as a price variance, it actually represents the difference between unit selling prices and unit cost of goods sold. This point will be discussed later on in this section.

Illustration 22–1

DIAGRAM OF SALES PRICE AND VOLUME VARIANCES

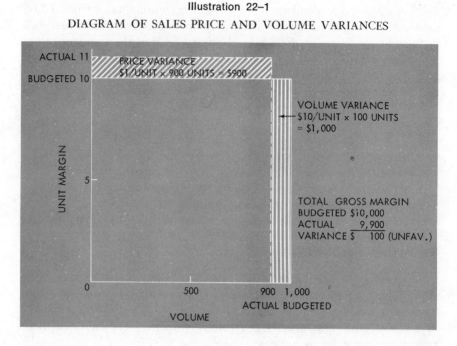

In the diagram, the solid rectangle indicates the budgeted gross margin (1,000 units × $10 per unit = $10,000), and the dotted rectangle indicates actual gross margin (900 units × $11 per unit = $9,900). The variances are the areas where the two rectangles do not coincide. The *selling price* variance is 900 units times $1 per unit, or $900; it is favorable because actual unit margin was higher than budgeted unit margin. The *sales volume* variance is 100 units times $10 per unit, or $1,000; it is unfavorable because actual sales volume was less than budgeted volume. The net variance is the algebraic sum of these two variances, or $100 unfavorable; this is also the difference between actual gross margin and budgeted gross margin.

The calculations are repeated in terms of the rules given above:

1. (Actual Margin   − Budgeted Margin)   ×   Actual Volume   = Price Variance
         ($11   − $10)   ×   900   = $900
2. (Actual Volume   − Budgeted Volume)   ×   Budgeted Margin = Volume Variance
         (900   −   1,000)   × $10   =   −$1,000
3. Actual Gross Margin − Budgeted Gross Margin   = Net Variance
         $9,900   − $10,000   =   −$100

These equations are set up in such a way that a *plus* (i.e., algebraically positive) result means a favorable variance and a *minus* (i.e., algebraically negative) result means an unfavorable variance, but it is easier to use common sense to determine whether the variance is favorable or unfavorable than it is to remember these relationships.

Joint Variance. The diagram in Illustration 22–1 shows clearly the nature of the variances when one of the variances is favorable and the other is unfavorable. The situation is less clear, however, when *both* the variances are favorable or when *both* are unfavorable. The nature of the difficulty is illustrated by Illustration 22–2 which shows the same

Illustration 22–2

DIAGRAM OF A JOINT VARIANCE

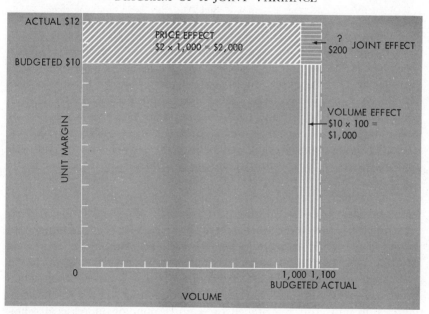

budgeted performance as in Illustration 22–1, but actual performance in a month when both the margin variance and the volume variance were favorable, as follows:

	Unit Margin	Volume	Gross Margin
Actual	$12	× 1,100	= $13,200
Budgeted	10	× 1,000	= 10,000
Net variance			$ 3,200 (favorable)

In this situation, the favorable net variance of $3,200 arose partly because the actual unit margin was $2 higher than the budgeted unit margin and partly because the actual volume was 100 units more than the budgeted volume. *At least* $2,000 is a price variance because the 1,000 budgeted units were sold at the $2 higher margin, and *at least* $1,000 is a sales volume variance because the 100 units of additional volume had a budgeted margin of $10 per unit. There remains $200 of variance to be explained, however. As shown in the upper right-hand corner of Illustration 22–2, this $200 results from the *combination* of the higher unit margin and the larger volume. This *joint variance* is *not* reported separately. The rules stated above have the effect of assigning this $200 as a price variance, as can be seen from this calculation:

1. (Actual Margin − Bud. Margin) × Actual Volume = Price Variance
         ($12   − $10)   ×   1,100   = $2,200
2. (Actual Volume − Bud. Volume) × Bud. Margin   = Volume Variance
         (1,100   −   1,000)   × $10   = $1,000

Assignment of the joint variance as a price variance arises solely because of the way in which the above rules are stated. It would be equally plausible to construct rules such that the joint variance became part of the sales volume variance. It would also be possible to construct rules such that part of the joint variance became a price variance and the remainder became a sales volume variance, but these rules are so complicated that few companies think it worthwhile to use them. It is important that whatever rule is selected be used consistently throughout the company.

WHY WORK WITH MARGINS? Since gross margin is the difference between sales revenue and cost of goods sold, the question arises as to why the variances for each of these items are not isolated separately, rather than combining them as was done above. Although it is possible to make such a separation, there are two reasons why this is less useful. First, net income is affected by the *difference* between unit selling prices and unit costs, rather than by either item taken by itself. If an increase in unit costs is matched by a corresponding increase in selling prices, there is no effect on net income. The job of the marketing organization is to maintain an appropriate margin between costs and selling prices. Secondly, the effect of a change of one unit in sales volume on net income is measured by the gross margin for that unit, rather than by the selling price taken by itself or the cost taken by itself.

EXAMPLE: Assume this situation:

	Budget			*Actual*			*Variance*
	Units	*Unit Amount*	*Total*	*Units*	*Unit Amount*	*Total*	
Sales........	1,000	$25	$25,000	900	$25	$22,500	$2,500 (U)
Standard cost of goods sold.......	1,000	15	15,000	900	15	13,500	1,500 (F)
Gross margin.	1,000	$10	$10,000	900	$10	$ 9,000	$1,000 (U)

It could be said that the variance caused by the fact that actual sales volume was 900 units rather than the 1,000 units budgeted was an unfavorable sales variance of $2,500 and a favorable Cost of Goods Sold variance of $1,500, but this is confusing. It is particularly confusing to think of a decrease in sales volume as causing a favorable variance. The real effect of the volume decrease is best measured by the gross margin per unit, in this case $10, times the number of units; that is, because of the decrease of 100 units in volume, net income was decreased by $1,000.

Note that although labelled as a selling price variance, the variance discussed above is actually a variance related to unit gross margins. It is sometimes, and more accurately, called a "unit margin" variance, rather than a selling price variance.

FURTHER DECOMPOSITION OF VARIANCES. It is sometimes possible to break down the margin variances even further, and since these variances are usually the most important causes of changes in net income, further breakdowns are worthwhile. The volume variance can be subdivided if data are available on total sales of a product by all companies. From these data, a given company can compute its *market share*, that is, the percentage of its sales to total industry sales. Variances caused by changes in total industry sales reflect general economic conditions, whereas variations caused by changes in market share are the responsibility of the company's own marketing organization. Similarly, the selling price variance can sometimes be decomposed into the portion attributable to general price movements and the portion attributable to the company's own pricing tactics.

Mix Variance

When a company sells several products having different gross margins, the total gross margin is influenced by the relative proportions or "mix" of high-margin to low-margin products that are sold. The difference in gross margin caused by the difference between the proportions assumed in the budget and the actual proportions sold is the *mix variance*. This variance did not show up in the preceding examples because we assumed all products had the same unit margin, nor would it show up in a multiproduct situation if the actual and budgeted unit margins were the *average* of those for all products. It does show up when the variances for each product are calculated separately.

The portion of the mix variance attributable to each product is calculated from the difference between the actual quantity sold and the budgeted *proportion* for that product, that is, the quantity that would have been sold if that product's sales had been the budgeted percentage of actual sales volume. The mix variance is the sum of these amounts for all products.

The calculations are illustrated in Illustration 22–3. The assumed

situation is the same as that in Illustration 22–1, except that we now assume that the company makes three products, each with a different gross
margin. In the budget, it was planned that 30 percent of sales would be
in Product A, which has a relatively low unit margin, and 30 percent
would be in Product C, which has a relatively high unit margin. In the
period, actual sales of the low-margin Product A were only 20 percent
of the total and actual sales of the high-margin Product C were 40
percent of the total. The actual mix was thus "richer" than planned, and
this produced a favorable mix variance.

The amount of mix variance accounted for by each product and the
total are calculated in Section B of Illustration 22–3, and the selling price
variance is calculated in Section C. Note that the sum of the mix and
selling price variances calculated in this fashion is $900, which is the same
amount as the selling price variance in Illustration 22–1, which was computed on the basis of an average margin.

Use of the Mix Concept. The mix concept is often used in analyzing
gross margin variances. It is important to know to what extent the total

Illustration 22–3
COMPUTATION OF MIX AND MARGIN VARIANCES

A. Assumed Situation

	Budget				Actual			
	Volume		Unit			Volume		Unit	
Product	%	Units	Margin	Total	%	Units	Margin	Total
A	30	300	$ 9.00	$ 2,700	20	180	$ 9.50	$1,710
B	40	400	10.00	4,000	40	360	11.00	3,960
C	30	300	11.00	3,300	40	360	11.75	4,230
Total	100%	1,000	$10.00	$10,000	100%	900	$11.00	$9,900

B. Computation of Mix Variance

Product	Actual Volume	− Budgeted Mix*	= Difference	× Budgeted Margin	= Mix Variance
A	180	270	−90	$ 9.00	−$810
B	360	360	0	10.00	0
C	360	270	90	11.00	990
Total	900	900		Mix Variance	$180

* This is the budgeted volume percentage for each product applied to total actual volume (e.g., 30% × 900 = 270).

C. Computation of Price Variance

Product	Actual Margin	− Budgeted Margin	= Difference	× Actual Volume	= Price Variance
A	$ 9.50	$ 9.00	$0.50	180	$ 90
B	11.00	10.00	1.00	360	360
C	11.75	11.00	0.75	360	270
			Total Price Variance		$720

variance was caused by changes in the "richness" of the sales mix, that is, by the proportion of high-margin products. It has wider applicability, however. In general, a mix variance can be developed whenever a cost or revenue item is broken down into components, and the components have different unit prices. When a price variance is computed by use of an average price, we do not know whether the variance is caused by a true difference in prices, or whether it is caused by a change in the proportion of the elements that make up the total; that is, by a change in mix. For example, if instead of using the total number of direct labor hours and the *average* hourly wage rate in calculating the labor variances, we use the number of direct labor hours in each skill category and the hourly wage rate for that skill category, a labor mix variance can be developed.

Some chemical companies and other companies whose manufacturing process consists primarily of combining several raw materials into finished products compute a material mix variance. Most companies do not compute material and labor mix variances, however. They have decided that the additional information is not worth the cost of calculating it.

PRODUCTION COST VARIANCES

In describing production cost variances, we shall deal with each of the three elements of production cost: direct labor, direct material, and factory overhead.

Direct Labor Variances

The standard (i.e., budgeted)[2] direct labor cost of one unit of product is constructed essentially by multiplying the standard time (e.g., standard number of hours) required to produce that unit by a standard rate per unit of time (e.g., standard wage rate per hour). Total standard direct labor cost for *an accounting period*, such as a month, is found by multiplying the standard direct labor cost per unit by the actual number of units of product produced in that period. When employees are paid on an hourly basis, actual direct labor cost for the period is the product of actual hours worked times the actual labor rate per hour. These relationships suggest that it is possible to break the variance between actual and standard direct labor costs into two components:

1. The variance caused by the fact that actual *time* differed from standard time; this is the *labor quantity variance* or *usage variance;* and
2. The variance caused by the fact that actual *labor rates* differed from standard labor rates; this is the *labor price variance* or *rate variance.*

---

[2] In the discussion of direct labor and direct material we shall use "standard" rather than "budgeted," because the former is more common. In this context, they have the same meaning.

A commonly used pair of rules for isolating the effects of these components follows:

1. The *usage variance* is the difference between standard hours and actual hours, priced at the standard rate per hour.
2. The *rate variance* is the difference between the standard rate per hour and the actual rate per hour, multiplied by the actual number of hours.

The *net* variance (or *total* variance) in labor costs is the algebraic sum of the usage and rate variances. The net variance is also the difference between the actual direct labor cost and the standard direct labor cost.

The standard number of hours is the standard number of hours for the products *actually produced* in the period. It is found by cumulating the standard unit labor hours for each of the units produced. It is *not* the number of hours which may have been planned for the period as shown in the operating budget unless actual production volume is the same as planned volume.

As was the case with margin variances, if both the usage and rate variances are unfavorable or if both are favorable, a joint variance will occur. The effect of these rules is to assign the joint portion of the variance to the rate variance.

A sample calculation is described below. The situation is as follows:

	Actual	Standard
Hours required for units produced............	1,000	900
Wage rate per hour.......................	$ 5	$ 4
Direct labor cost........................	$5,000	$3,600

In this situation, the unfavorable net variance is $5,000 − $3,600 = $1,400. The $1,400 variance is partly the result of the high wage rate and partly the result of the longer time required. The above rules segregate the effect of each factor, as follows:

1. (Standard hours − Actual hours) × Standard rate = Usage variance
       (900   −   1,000)   × $4   =   −$400
2. (Standard rate − Actual rate) × Actual hours = Rate variance
       ($4   − $5)   ×   1,000   =   −$1,000

INTERPRETATION OF THE DIRECT LABOR VARIANCE. The reason for attempting to break down the total direct labor variance as described above is that the labor rate variance is often evaluated differently from the labor usage variance. The rate variance may arise because of a change in wage rates for which the foreman in charge of the responsibility center cannot be held responsible, whereas the foreman may be held entirely responsible for the usage variance, because he should control the number of hours that direct workers spent on the production for the period.

This distinction cannot be made in all cases, for there are many situations in which the two factors are interdependent. For example, the fore-man may find it possible to complete the work in less than the standard number of hours by using workers who earn a higher than standard rate, and he may be perfectly justified in doing so. Even so, the use of the technique described above may lead to a better understanding of what actually happened.

Direct Material Variances

The variance between actual and standard direct material costs can be broken down into what are commonly called *material usage variance* and *material price variance* by the same technique as that described above for direct labor. The material usage variance is also called the *yield variance*. The rules given above for direct labor are used for direct material simply by changing a few words. For example:

	Actual	*Standard*
Quantity (pounds) used in the period.........	1,000	900
Price per pound........................	$ 5	$ 4
Material cost..........................	$5,000	$3,600

The *usage* or *yield* variance is 100 pounds times $4 a pound, or $400, and the *price* variance is $1 a pound times 1,000 pounds, or $1,000; both variances are unfavorable.

In many companies, as described in Chapter 16, the cost accounting system is constructed so that the material price variance is isolated when material is purchased and placed in raw materials inventory. Raw Materials Inventory is debited at standard cost, Accounts Payable (or Cash) is credited at actual cost, and the difference is debited or credited to Material Price Variance. In such a system, the difference between the actual material cost and the standard material cost *is* the usage variance; it need not be calculated separately.[3]

As was the case with direct labor, the separation of direct material into its price and usage components facilitates analysis and control of direct material costs. The price variance is the responsibility of the purchasing department, whereas the usage variance is the responsibility of the department that uses the material.

SPOILAGE AND REWORK. The material usage variance shows the difference between the actual quantity and the standard quantity of material *put into* the manufacturing process. If the product itself does not pass inspection at the end of the production process or at some intermediate

---

[3] If actual raw material used is of a different *quality* than that specified in the standard (and hence has a different standard unit price), a sort of price variance is created. Ordinarily, no attempt is made to separate out this variance from the pure usage variance.

stage, it must either be discarded or sent back to have the defect corrected. If discarded, the labor, material, and overhead costs accumulated on it up to that point constitute *spoilage*. If sent back for correction, the extra *rework* cost is also a cost associated with substandard products. The cost of spoilage and rework is usually classified as an item of factory indirect cost or overhead cost. As such, it is encompassed by the discussion of overhead costs, which is in the next section.

Overhead Variances

The net overhead variance is the difference between total actual overhead cost incurred in a period and total absorbed overhead cost for that period. It can be decomposed into a production volume variance and a spending variance.

PRODUCTION VOLUME VARIANCE. The production volume variance is caused by the presence of fixed costs. Because overhead costs are comprised in part of fixed costs, *unit* overhead costs are greater at low volumes than they are at high volumes. Thus, if the actual volume is different from the budgeted volume, a volume variance arises.

In order to measure the production volume variance, the cost-volume relationship described in Chapter 17 must be recalled. In Illustration 22–4, the line marked "budgeted" cost shows this direct, but less than proportional, relationship between costs and volume. Costs at any volume are

Illustration 22–4

BUDGETED, ABSORBED, AND ACTUAL COSTS

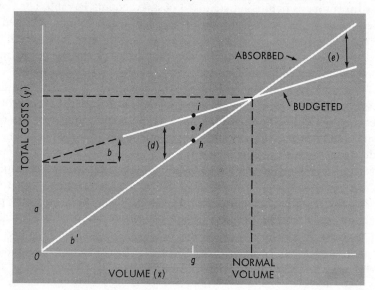

expected to be the fixed amount per period, *a*, plus the variable rate per unit of volume, *b*, times the number of units of volume, *x*.

The overhead rate used to allocate overhead costs to products is determined by choosing one level of volume, which is called the *standard* or *normal volume*, and dividing budgeted total costs at that volume by the number of units of volume. Thus, if the overhead variable budget equation is $500 per period +$1 per unit, and if standard volume is 1,000 units, total budgeted overhead costs for 1,000 units are $1,500, and the overhead rate is $1.50 per unit. Alternatively, the overhead rate can be calculated as follows:

	Overhead Rate
Variable costs per unit (at any volume)	$1.00
Fixed costs per unit at 1,000 units ($500 ÷ 1,000)	0.50
Total overhead rate	$1.50

At any volume, overhead costs would be *absorbed* or *applied* as part of full product costs at the rate of $1.50 per unit. The line of "absorbed" cost on the diagram shows the total amount of overhead costs that would be absorbed at various volumes. Note that at standard volume, budgeted costs equal absorbed costs, but that at any other volume budgeted costs are different from absorbed costs, as indicated by the spread between the two lines. At lower volumes, costs are expected to be *underabsorbed*, as indicated by the amount *d*, and at higher volumes they are expected to be *overabsorbed*, as indicated by the amount *e*. They are under-absorbed or overabsorbed *because* actual volume differs from standard volume; hence, this amount is the volume variance. The production volume variance results solely from the fact that actual volume in a given period differed from the volume that was used in setting the overhead rate, that is, the standard volume. Also, the production volume variance is attributable solely to the fixed component of the overhead rate; variable overhead costs per unit are, by definition, unaffected by the volume level.

SPENDING VARIANCE. If, whatever the volume level, the actual overhead costs incurred in a period were the same as the budgeted costs *for that volume*, as shown in the variable budget, the net overhead variance would be entirely attributable to volume. For many reasons, however, actual costs are not likely to be the same as the amount of costs budgeted at the volume level for the period. The difference between actual costs and budgeted costs at the actual level of volume in the period is called the *spending variance*.

The spending variance for overhead costs has the same significance as the *sum* of the usage and price or rate variances (i.e., the *net variance*) for direct material cost and direct labor cost. Indeed, it would be possible to decompose the spending variance into usage and price components in the same manner as was described for these direct costs. Most companies do not do this for overhead costs, however, because they do not find this additional breakdown worthwhile.

CALCULATION OF OVERHEAD VARIANCES. The overhead variance, as shown in the accounting records, is the algebraic sum of the volume variance and the spending variance. In order to understand how each variance is calculated, refer again to Illustration 22–4, which shows these variances graphically. From the relationship indicated there, the procedure for calculating the amount of the variances can be discerned. The situation illustrated in that exhibit is one in which actual costs are at the point marked f, and actual volume is g; that is, actual volume is below standard volume, and actual costs are below the costs budgeted at the actual volume but they are higher than absorbed costs. Absorbed costs at the actual volume are the amount h, and budgeted costs at the actual volume are the amount i. Note that budgeted costs are the amount of costs budgeted for the volume level actually attained in the period. The following relationships will hold:

The *net overhead variance* is the difference between absorbed costs, h, and actual costs, f. In the example, the variance is unfavorable. As is stated above, the net overhead variance is also the algebraic sum of the volume variance and the spending variance.

The *production volume variance* is the difference between absorbed costs, h, and budgeted costs, i. In the example, this variance is unfavorable.

The *spending variance* is the difference between budgeted costs, i, and actual costs, f. In the example, this variance is favorable.

EXAMPLE: Assume that:

Actual volume in an accounting period is 900 units of product.

Actual overhead costs are $1,380.

The variable budget formula is $500 per period plus $1 per unit of product.

The overhead rate is $1.50 per unit of product.
Then:

Budgeted cost at the actual volume = $500 + $1(900) = $1,400
Absorbed cost at the actual volume = $1.50 × 900   = $1,350
Total variance (unfavorable)   = $1,350 − $1,380 = −$30
Volume variance (unfavorable)   = $1,350 − $1,400 = −$50
Spending variance (favorable)   = $1,400 − $1,380 = $20

USE OF THE OVERHEAD VARIANCES. Presumably, the manager is responsible for the spending variance in his responsibility center. Because the variable budget cannot take account of all the noncontrollable factors that affect costs, however, there may be a reasonable explanation for the spending variance. The existence of an unfavorable variance is therefore not, by itself, grounds for criticizing performance. Rather, it is a signal that investigation and explanation are required.

In some situations the manager may also be responsible for the volume variance; for example, his failure to obtain the standard volume of output may result from his inability to keep products moving through his department at the proper speed, or production quality problems may have hurt sales volume. The volume variance is more likely to be someone else's responsibility, however. It may result because the sales department was unable to obtain the planned volume of orders, because some earlier department in the manufacturing process failed to deliver materials as they were needed, or because vendors did not deliver raw material when it was needed.

In appraising spending performance, the analyst should look behind the total spending variance and examine the individual overhead items of which it consists. The total budgeted cost is the sum of the budgeted amounts for each of the separate items of cost. A spending variance can and should be developed for each important item; it is the difference between actual cost incurred and the budget allowance for that item. Attention should be focused on significant spending variances for individual elements.

OTHER VARIANCES

Conceptually, it would be possible to decompose the total variance in items of selling, general, and administrative expenses into volume and spending components, as was done for factory overhead costs, but ordinarily this is not done. Instead, the differences between actual and budgeted amounts are simply listed. Most of these expense items are discretionary costs, and the expectation is that the budgeted amounts will be adhered to regardless of volume fluctuations; isolation of a volume variance under these circumstances would not be appropriate.

COMPLETE ANALYSIS

As a way of summarizing the techniques described thus far in this chapter, the complete analysis of a simple situation is shown in Illustration 22–5. The income statement (Section A) shows a variance between actual and budgeted income of $59. (For simplicity, all amounts except *unit* costs and margins are in thousands; thus a volume of 200 means 200,-000 units, and $59 means $59,000.) The question is: What accounts for this $59 variance? The answer to this question is given in Section B, which decomposes the total variance into elements. The remainder of the Illustration shows how each of these elements was found.

Illustration 22–5

COMPUTATION OF VARIANCES

A. Income Statements

	Budget	Actual	Variance
Sales....................................	$540	$551	
Less: Standard cost of goods sold...........	440	418	
Gross margin at standard cost................	$100	$133	$ 33
Less: Manufacturing variances..............	0	82	(82)
Gross margin............................	$100	$ 51	$(49)
Selling and administrative expense............	40	50	(10)
Income before Taxes.......................	$ 60	$ 1	$(59)

B. Summary of Variances

Selling price.....................................	$ 38
Sales volume....................................	(5)
Net margin......................................	$ 33
Material price...................................	$(16)
Material usage..................................	4
Labor rate......................................	(8)
Labor usage....................................	(24)
Overhead volume................................	(15)
Overhead spending..............................	(23)
Net manufacturing..............................	$(82)
Selling and administrative........................	$(10)
Income Variance................................	$(59)

( ) = unfavorable.

C. Gross Margin Variances

	Sales (Units)	Unit Margin	Total Margin
Underlying data:			
Budget.........................	200	$0.50	$100
Actual.........................	190	0.70	133
Net margin variance.................			$ 33

Selling price variance:

(Actual unit margin − Budgeted unit margin) × Actual units = Price variance
($0.70 − $0.50) × 190 = $38

Sales volume variance:
(Actual volume − Budgeted volume) × Budgeted unit margin = Volume variance
(190 − 200) × $0.50 = ($5)

D. Cost Variances

Underlying Data, Costs

Item	Standard	Actual
Production volume	200 units	170 units
Direct material	2 lbs./unit at $0.20/lb.	320 lbs. at $0.25 = $80
Direct labor	0.4 hrs./unit at $2.00/hr.	80 hrs. at $2.10 = $168
Overhead	$100 + $0.50 per unit	$208

Computation of Cost Variances

(1) *Material price variance:*
(Standard price − Actual price) × Actual quantity = Material price variance
($0.20 − $0.25) × 320 = ($16)

Illustration 22–5 (*continued*)

(2) *Material usage variance:*
    (Standard quantity − Actual quantity) × Standard price = Material usage
                                                            variance
        (340*   −   320)   × $0.20   = $4
  * 170 units at 2 lbs. per unit.

(3) *Labor rate variance:*
    (Standard rate − Actual rate) × Actual hours = Labor rate variance
      ($2.00   − $2.10) ×   80   =   ($8)

(4) *Labor usage variance:*
    Standard hours − Actual hours × Standard rate = Labor usage variance
      (68*   −   80) × $2.00   =   ($24)
  * 170 units at 0.4 hours per unit.

(5) *Overhead volume variance:*
    Absorbed overhead: 170 units × $1 per unit* $170
    Budgeted overhead: $100 + ($0.50 × 170 units) 185
        Volume variance .... $(15)
  * Overhead rate = [$100 + ($0.50 × 200 units)] ÷ 200 units = $1.00 per unit.

(6) *Overhead spending variance:*
    Budgeted overhead (as above) $185
    Actual overhead 208
        Spending variance .... $(23)

Gross Margin Variances

The first step in the computation is to analyze the difference between budgeted and actual gross margins. This part of the analysis is shown in Section C. The unit margin is the difference between *standard* unit cost of goods sold (which was $2.20) and selling prices. Budgeted selling price was $2.70 per unit, and actual selling price was $2.90 per unit, so the budgeted unit margin was $0.50 and the actual unit margin was $0.70.

The selling price variance is determined by multiplying the actual sales quantities for each product by the difference between actual and budgeted unit margins. (In the interest of brevity, a mix variance is not shown.)

The sales volume variance is the loss or gain in gross margin that results from a difference between actual and budgeted sales volume.

The algebraic sum of the selling price variance, $38, and the sales volume variance ($5) is the $33 shown as the variance in gross margin on the income statement.

Note that margin variances are favorable when actual is greater than budget, which is of course the opposite situation from cost variances.

Cost Variances

Next we turn to an analysis of the cost variances. Note that, as shown in Section D, actual production volume (170 units) is less than actual sales volume (190 units), the difference being made up out of inventory which is carried at standard cost. Carrying the inventory at standard cost means that expense variances are treated as period costs and charged directly to cost of goods sold during the period in which they occur. The labor, material, and manufacturing overhead variances described earlier in the chapter are calculated in Section D. Their algebraic sum equals the $82 unfavorable cost variance noted on the income statement.

An examination of the $10 unfavorable variance in selling and administrative expenses completes the analysis of the income variance. This is not shown; it would consist of an analysis of the amount of and reasons for differences between the budgeted amount and the actual amount for each category of expense.

CONTROL REPORTS

Types of Reports

Reports on what has happened in a business are useful for two general purposes, which may be called information and control, respectively.

Information reports are designed to tell management what is going on. They may or may not lead to action. Each reader studies them to detect whether or not something has happened that requires looking into, and if nothing of significance is noted, which is often the case, the report is put aside without action. If something does strike the reader's attention, an inquiry or an action is initiated. The information on these reports may come from the accounting system, but it may also come from a wide variety of other sources.

Control reports are of two general types. One is intended to report on *personal* performance, and the other to report on *economic* performance. The first type reports on the performance of operating managers, that is, the heads of responsibility centers. The essential purpose of such a report is to compare actual performance in a responsibility center with what performance should have been under the circumstances prevailing, in such a way that reasons for the difference between actual and standard performance are identified and, if feasible, quantified. The second and quite separate type of analysis shows how well the responsibility center has performed as an economic entity. Such analyses are made periodically, but not as frequently as monthly, of profit centers and investment centers. Such analyses require the use of full cost accounting rather than responsibility accounting; in fact, the report looks the same as an income statement for a separate business would look.

The control report may show that the responsibility center manager is doing an excellent job, considering the circumstances, but if the profit center is not producing a satisfactory profit, (or the investment center, an adequate return) action may be required regardless of this fact. There are therefore two essentially different ways in which the performance of a responsibility center is judged. First, there is the report which focuses on the manager's responsibility for turning in an actual performance that corresponds to the commitment he made during the budget preparation process. *Behavioral* considerations are important in the use of this report. Second, there is the analysis of the responsibility center as an economic entity. In such an analysis, *economic* considerations are dominant. The following discussion is limited to reports of the first type.

Content of Control Reports

EFFECTIVENESS AND EFFICIENCY. The performance of a responsibility center manager can be measured in terms of the effectiveness and efficiency of the work of the responsibility center. By *effectiveness*, we mean how well the responsibility center does its job— that is (to quote the dictionary), the extent to which it produces the intended or expected results. *Efficiency* is used in its engineering sense—that is, the amount of output per unit of input. An efficient machine is one which produces a given quantity of outputs with a minimum consumption of inputs, or one which produces the largest possible outputs from a given quantity of inputs.

Effectiveness is always related to the organization's objectives. Efficiency, per se, is not related to objectives. An efficient responsibility center is one which does whatever it does with the lowest consumption of resources; but if what it does (i.e., its output) is an inadequate contribution to the accomplishment of the organization's objectives, it is ineffective.

EXAMPLE: If a department that is responsible for processing incoming sales orders does so at a low cost per order processed, it is efficient. If however, the department is sloppy in answering customer queries about the status of orders, and thus antagonizes customers to the point where they take their business elsewhere, the department is ineffective; the loss of a customer is not consistent with the company's goals.

In many responsibility centers, a measure of efficiency can be developed that relates actual costs to some standard—that is, to a number that expresses what costs *should be incurred* for a given amount of output. A budgeted cost or a standard cost is such a standard. Such a measure can be a useful indication of efficiency, but it is never a *perfect* measure for at least two reasons: (1) recorded costs are not a precisely accurate measure of resources consumed, and (2) standards are, at best, only approximate measures of what resource consumption ideally should have been in the circumstances prevailing. Each of these limitations has been discussed in earlier chapters.

In an expense center, effectiveness cannot be measured in monetary terms; effectiveness, if measured at all, must be measured in nonmonetary terms such as units of product produced, because, by definition, there is no monetary measure of output in an expense center. In some profit centers a monetary measure of effectiveness is possible. When a primary goal of the whole organization is to earn profits, then the contribution to this goal by a profit center is a measure of its effectiveness. This is so because in a profit center, both outputs (i.e., revenues) and inputs (i.e., costs) are measured in monetary terms; profit is the difference between them.

Since the amount of profit is influenced both by how effective a manager is and also by how efficient he is, the profit in a profit center measures *both* effectiveness and efficiency. When such an overall measure exists, it is unnecessary to determine the relative importance of effectiveness versus efficiency. When such an overall measure does not exist, however, it is feasible and useful to classify performance measures as relating either to effectiveness or to efficiency. In these situations, there is the problem of judging the relative importance of the two types of measurements. For example, how do we compare two maintenance managers, one who incurs higher costs than he should but has an excellent record of keeping equipment in tip-top condition, and the other who incurs lower but also has a poor record of equipment breakdowns? The former is more effective but less efficient than the latter.

Profit is, at best, only an approximate measure of effectiveness and of efficiency for several reasons: (1) monetary measures do not exactly measure either all aspects of outputs or all inputs, for reasons already given; (2) standards are not accurate; and (3) at best, profit is a measure of what has happened in the short run, whereas we are presumably also interested in the long-run consequences of decisions.

Criteria for Control Reports

Criteria that should govern the content of control reports are:

1. Reports should be related to personal responsibility.
2. Reports should compare actual performance with the best available standard.
3. Reports should highlight significant information.
4. Reports should be timely.
5. Information should be communicated clearly.
6. Reports should be integrated.
7. Reports must be worth more than they cost.

As a basis for discussing these criteria, we shall use the set of control reports shown in Illustration 22–6.

Focus on Personal Responsibility. Responsibility accounting provides information that meets the criterion that reports should be related to personal responsibility. Responsibility accounting also classifies the costs assigned to each responsibility center according to whether they are controllable or noncontrollable. Many control reports, including those in Illustration 22–6, show only controllable costs; nevertheless, some of them contain noncontrollable costs for information purposes.

In order to facilitate analysis and corrective action, the total amount of controllable cost is classified by item (also called *object*, or *natural element*, or *function*). Indirect labor, supplies, power, heat, overtime premiums, and spoilage are examples from the long list of cost elements that might be useful in a given situation.

Appropriate Standards. Standards used in control reports are of three types: (1) predetermined standards or budgets, (2) historical standards, or (3) external standards.

Predetermined standards or budgets, if carefully prepared, are the best formal standards; they are the basis against which actual performance is compared in many well-managed companies. The validity of such a standard depends largely on how much care went into its development. If the budget numbers were arrived at in a slipshod manner, they obviously will not provide a reliable basis for comparison.

Historical standards are records of past actual performance. Results for the current month may be compared with results for last month, or with results for the same month a year ago. This type of standard has two serious weaknesses: (1) conditions may have changed between the two periods in a way that invalidates the comparison; and (2) when a manager is measured against his own past record, there may be no way of knowing whether the prior period's performance was acceptable to start with. A foreman whose spoilage cost is $500 a month, month after month, is consistent, but we do not know, without other evidence, whether he is consistently good or consistently poor. Despite these inherent weaknesses, historical standards are used in many companies.

External standards are standards derived from the performance of other responsibility centers. The performance of one branch sales office may be compared with the performance of other branch sales offices, for example. If conditions in these responsibility centers are similar, such a comparison may provide a useful basis for judging performance. The catch is that it is not easy to find two responsibility centers that are sufficiently similar, or whose performance is affected by the same factors, to permit such comparisons on a regular basis.

Highlighting Significant Information. The problem of designing a good set of control reports has changed drastically since the advent of the computer. When data had to be collected and reported manually, great care had to be taken to limit the quantity of information contained

Illustration 22–6

PACKAGE OF CONTROL REPORTS

A.   First (or, lowest) Level Report

Drill Press Department (Foreman)	Actual		(Over) or Under Budget	
	June	Year to Date	June	Year to Date
Output:				
Standard direct labor hours..........	1,210	6,060	105	501
Direct labor cost:				
Amount.........................	$3,860	$22,140	$ 360	$1,140
Time variance....................			622	1,807
Rate variance....................			(262)	(667)
Controllable overhead:				
Setup costs......................	1,187	7,224	(265)	90
Repair and rework................	520	2,916	180	91
Overtime premium................	484	2,748	(75)	(704)
Supplies.........................	215	1,308	(121)	(210)
Small tools......................	260	1,521	160	(82)
Other...........................	644	3,888	91	195
Total.......................	$3,310	$19,605	$ (30)	$ (620)

B.   Second Level Report

Production Department Cost Summary (General superintendent)	Amount		(Over) or Under Budget	
	June	Year to Date	June	Year to Date
Controllable overhead:				
General superintendent's office.......	$ 1,960	$ 12,300	$ (115)	$ (675)
Drill press........................	3,310	19,605	(30)	(620)
Screw machine.....................	3,115	18,085	90	(135)
Punch press.......................	5,740	33,635	(65)	(640)
Plating...........................	1,865	9,795	(175)	825
Heat treating.....................	3,195	18,015	210	35
Assembly.........................	5,340	35,845	(625)	(1,380)
Total.......................	$24,525	$147,280	$ (710)	$(2,590)

	Standard		Variance	
	June	Year to Date	June	Year to Date
Direct labor:				
Drill press........................	$ 3,860	$ 22,140	$ 360	$1,140
Screw machine.....................	5,240	31,760	540	1,560
Punch press.......................	3,720	23,850	215	940
Plating...........................	1,410	7,370	155	1,410
Heat treating.....................	1,630	8,510	180	390
Assembly.........................	11,260	68,340	1,570	(310)
Total.......................	$27,120	$161,970	$3,020	$5,130

[To Section C.]

Illustration 22–6 (*continued*)

[From Section B.]

| C.   Third Level Report | | | (*Over*) or | |
| Factory Cost Summary (Vice president of production) | *Amount* | | *Under Budget* | |
	June	*Year to Date*	*June*	*Year to Date*
Controllable overhead:				
Vice president's office..............	$ 2,110	$ 12,030	$ (315)	$ 35
General superintendent's office.......	24,525	147,280	(710)	(2,590)
Production control.................	1,235	7,570	(125)	(210)
Purchasing......................	1,180	7,045	95	75
Maintainance....................	3,590	18,960	(235)	245
Tool room......................	4,120	25,175	160	(320)
Inspection......................	2,245	13,680	180	(160)
Receiving, shipping, stores..........	3,630	22,965	(70)	(730)
Total......................	$42,635	$254,705	($1,020)	$(3,655)
	Standard		*Variance*	
	June	*Year to Date*	*June*	*Year to Date*
Direct labor........................	$27,120	$161,970	$3,020	$5,130

in reports because the cost of preparing them was relatively high. By contrast, the computer can spew out vast quantities of information at a relatively low cost. A computer can print out more figures in a minute than a manager can assimilate in a day. Thus, the current problem is to decide on the *right type* of information that should be given to management. To provide managers with less information than they need is bad, but to deluge them with information that they do not need is almost as bad.

A management control system should operate on the *exception principle*. This principle states that a control report should focus management's attention on the relatively small number of items in which actual performance is significantly different from the standard; when this is done, little or no attention need be given to the relatively large number of situations where performance is satisfactory.

TIMING OF REPORTS. The proper control period, that is, the period of time covered by one report, is the shortest period of time in which management can usefully intervene and in which significant changes in performance are likely. The period is different for different responsibility centers and for different items of cost and output within responsibility centers. Spoilage rates in a production operation may be reported hourly, or oftener, because if a machine starts to function improperly the situation must be corrected at once. Certain other key cost elements of a production cost center may be measured daily. Reports on overall performance, particularly those going to top levels of management, usually are on a monthly basis, as in Illustration 22–6. Top management does not have either the time or the inclination to explore local, temporary problems.

The other aspect of report timing is the interval that elapses between the end of the period covered by the report and the issuance of the report itself. Obviously, this interval should be as short as is feasible.

CLARITY OF COMMUNICATION. Since a control report is a communication device, it obviously is not doing its job unless it communicates the intended message clearly. This is much easier said than done. There is room for much misunderstanding in interpreting the meaning of the numbers on a report. Those who are responsible for designing control reports are therefore well advised to spend much time in choosing terms that convey the intended meaning and in arranging the numbers on the report in a way that emphasizes the intended relationships.

INTEGRATED REPORTS. Monthly control reports should consist of an integrated package; that is, the reports for lower level responsibility centers should be consistent with and easily relatable to summary reports that are prepared for higher level responsibility centers, and these in turn should be consistent with the summary report for the whole company.

Parts B and C of Illustration 22–6 illustrate this process of summarization. Part B is a control report for the next higher level in the organization hierarchy. The drill press department, which is one of several departments for which the general superintendent is responsible, appears as one line on this report. Part C is a control report for an even higher level, the total production operation.

COST OF REPORTING. A reporting system, like anything else, should not cost more than it is worth. Unfortunately, there are great difficulties in applying this statement to practical situations. Although researchers are attempting in various ways to measure the value of management information, they have not had much, if any, success.

At least one practical statement can be made: If no one uses a report, it is not worthwhile. Useless reports are not uncommon. They come about because a new problem area created the need for a report at some earlier time and although the problem area disappeared, the report continued. It is therefore worthwhile to review a company's set of reports from time to time and eliminate reports that are no longer needed. A report structure, like a tree, is often better if it is pruned.

Use of Control Reports

The first question to be raised about a comparison between actual and planned performance is: of what use is it? A manager's performance can be measured only *after* he has performed; but at that time the work has already been done, and no subsequent action by anyone can change what has been done. How, therefore, can a control report actually control performance? There are two good answers to this question.

First, if a person knows in advance that his performance is going to be measured, reported, and judged, he tends to act differently from the way he would have acted had he believed that no one was going to check up on him. (Anyone who has received grades in school should appreciate the importance of this point.)

Second, even though it is literally impossible to alter an event that has already happened, an analysis of how a person has performed in the past may indicate, both to that person and to his superior, ways of obtaining better performance in the future. Corrective action taken by the person himself is important; the system should "help the person help himself." Action by the superior is also necessary. Such action ranges in severity from giving verbal criticism or praise, to suggesting specific means of improving future performance, to the extremes of firing or promoting the person.

In addition, the comparison between actual and planned performance may indicate that the plan itself needs to be revised.

FEEDBACK. In both its effect on the manager and in its effect on the plan, a control report is a *feedback device*, as indicated in Illustration 22–7. The term, feedback, comes from electrical engineering, where it

Illustration 22–7

USE OF PERFORMANCE REPORTS

refers to electrical circuits that are arranged so that information about a mechanism's current performance is fed back in such a way that the future performance of that mechanism may be changed. A thermostat is a feedback device; if the temperature of a room drops below a pre-scribed level, the thermostat senses that information and activates the furnace; the furance then makes heat that increases the room temperature. In an engineering diagram, the circuitry and associated control apparatus is called a *feedback loop.*

Control reports are feedback devices, but they are only one part of the feedback loop. Unlike the thermostat, which acts automatically in response to information about temperature, a control report *does not by itself* cause a change in performance. A change results only when man-agers take actions that lead to change. Thus, in management control, the feedback loop requires both the control report *plus* management action.

THE CONTROL PROCESS

There are three steps in the control process:

1. *Identify* areas that require investigation.
2. *Investigate* these areas to ascertain whether action is warranted.
3. *Act*, when investigation indicates the need for action.

Identification

The control report is useful only in the first step in the process. It suggests areas that seem to need looking into. Although significant variances between actual and budgeted performance are a signal that an investigation may be warranted, they are not an *automatic* signal. The manager interprets the numbers in the light of his own knowledge about conditions in the responsibility center. He may have already learned, from conversations or personal observation, that there is an adequate explanation for the variance, or he may have observed the need for corrective action before the report itself reaches him. Some managers say that an essential characteristic of a good management control system is that reports should contain no surprises. By this they mean that man-agers of responsibility centers should inform their superiors as soon as significant events occur and should institute the necessary action imme-diately. If this is done, significant information will already have been communicated informally to the superior before he receives the formal report.

INTERPRETATION OF VARIANCES.   A variance is meaningful only if it is derived from a valid standard. Although it is convenient to refer to "favorable" and "unfavorable" variances, these words imply value judg-ments that are valid only to the extent that the standard is a valid measure of what performance should have been. Even a standard cost may not be an accurate estimate of what costs "should have been under the circumstances." This situation can arise for either or both of two reasons: (1) the standard was not set properly, or (2) although set properly in the light of conditions existing at the time, those conditions have changed so that the standard has become obsolete. An essential first step in the analysis of a variance, therefore, is an examination of the validity of the standard.

ENGINEERED AND DISCRETIONARY COSTS. The manager must also distinguish between items of engineered costs and items of discretionary costs. With respect to engineered costs, the general rule is "the lower they are, the better." The objective is to spend as little as possible, consistent with quality and safety standards. The supervisor who reduces his engineered costs below the standard amounts usually should be congratulated. With respect to discretionary costs, however, the situation is quite different and much more complicated. Often, good performance consists of spending the amount agreed on, for spending too little may be as bad as, or worse than, spending too much. A factory manager can easily reduce his current costs by skimping on maintenance or on training; a marketing manager can reduce his advertising or sales promotion expenditures; top management may eliminate a research department. None of these actions may be in the overall best interest of the company, although all of them result in lower costs on the current reports of performance.

In short, the proper interpretation of a control report involves much more than a look at the size of the variances. In order to determine what, if any, investigation should be made, the manager brings to bear all his experience regarding the work of the responsibility center, all the information that he has obtained from informal sources, and his intuitive judgment or "feel" for what needs attention.

Investigation

The existence of variances of significant size raises questions in the manager's mind, and he next takes steps to find out the answers to these questions. The president does not say to the sales manager, "You had an unfavorable sales volume variance; *therefore,* you performed poorly." Rather, he asks: "*Why* did you have an unfavorable sales volume variance?" In other words, the manager does not look upon an unfavorable variance as an automatic basis for criticism, nor on a favorable variance as an automatic basis for praise. Rather, he regards the variances as pointing to situations for which an explanation of underlying causes is required. He seeks to find these causes, and only after he has found them does he act.

In this chapter we have said that the individual variances indicate the *cause* of the difference between actual and budgeted performance. In one sense, they do indicate causes; the material price variance shows how much of the total variance was caused by a difference between actual and standard material prices. The variances do not, however, indicate *why* the difference between actual and standard occurred. Was an unfavorable material price variance the consequence of lack of diligence on the part of the purchasing department in finding the vendor who offered the lowest price, or was it the consequence of an increase in the market price of the material? Variance analysis does not reveal these *underlying causes*. It does reveal the areas in which further investigation is needed in order to determine what the underlying causes were. Usually, an investigation of possible significant areas takes the form of a conversation between the head of a responsibility center and his superior. Based on his investigation, the manager decides whether further action is required. The superior and the manager should agree on the positive steps that will be taken to remedy unsatisfactory conditions revealed by the investigation. Equally important, if investigation reveals that performance has been good, a "pat on the back" is appropriate.

Of course, in many situations, no action at all is indicated. The superior judges that performance is satisfactory, and that is that. The superior should be particularly careful not to place too much emphasis on short-run performance. An inherent characteristic of management control systems is that they tend to focus on short-run rather than long-run performance; that is, they measure current profits rather than the effect of current actions on future profits. Thus, if too much emphasis is placed on results as shown in current control reports, long-run profitability may be hurt.

SUMMARY OF COST CONSTRUCTIONS

In Part II we have discussed three types of accounting information:

1. Full cost accounting.
2. Differential accounting.
3. Responsibility accounting.

In connection with each type, we have described several types of costs, to the point where the distinction among them may have become confusing. Illustration 22–8, which is a brief description of each type, may help to clear up these distinctions.

For purpose of emphasis, we repeat two points that have been made previously:

1. Each of the three types of management accounting information is used for a different purpose. One must first understand the purpose for

Illustration 22–8

SUMMARY OF COST CONSTRUCTIONS

Full Cost Accounting	*Differential Accounting*	*Responsibility Accounting*
Direct: Costs traceable to a cost objective. *Indirect*: Costs not traceable; an equitable portion is allocated to the cost objective. *Full*: Direct costs + Indirect costs.	*Variable*: Costs which vary proportionately with *volume*. *Fixed*: Costs which do not vary with volume. *Semivariable*: Costs which vary with volume, but less than proportionately. Can be decomposed into variable and fixed components.	*Engineered*: "Right" amount can be estimated by engineering methods. *Discretionary*: Amount subject to manager's discretion. *Committed*: Cannot be changed in the short run.
Capital: Asset to be amortized over several future periods. *Product*: Direct + indirect *factory* cost of product. *Period*: All other costs; expenses of current period.	Composition depends on the nature of the specific problem.	*Controllable*: Manager can exercise significant influence (not complete control). *Noncontrollable*: Other costs. Includes committed and allocated costs.
Full costs are either historical costs or estimated future costs.	Differential costs are always estimated future costs.	Responsibility costs are either historical costs or estimated future costs.

which information is to be used in a given situation and then select the information that is appropriate for that purpose.

2. Although the three types of management accounting information are discussed separately, collectively they comprise the overall management accounting system. This system contains raw data that are used to construct full cost information, differential information, or responsibility information. Each of these types of information is then used for the purpose for which it is relevant.

SUMMARY

The difference between budgeted net income and actual net income can be decomposed into a number of variances, each of which helps to explain why the income variance occurred.

The essential purpose of control reports is to compare actual performance in a responsibility center with what performance should have been under the circumstances prevailing, in such a way that reasons for the variances between actual and expected performance are identified. A control report identifies areas that require further investigation. The first step of the control process is to study the report to identify such areas. The second step is to investigate each of these areas, usually in a meeting with the manager of the responsibility center involved. The third step is to take action if, after appropriate investigation, action appears to be warranted. This action should include praise, as well as criticism.

CASES

CASE 22–1. PROBLEMS IN THE ANALYSIS OF GROSS MARGIN AND DIRECT COSTS

PROBLEM A

In preparing its annual budget, Company A budgeted sales of Product 1 at 5,000 units. This product had a budgeted price of $15 per unit, and standard unit cost of $8. Actual sales of this product turned out to be $72,000 for 4,500 units.

Required:

1. What was the net gross margin variance?
2. What was the selling price variance?
3. What was the sales volume variance?

PROBLEM B

Company B makes three products. Budgeted and actual sales and margins for these products were as follows:

	Budget		Actual	
	Unit Sales	Unit Margin	Unit Sales	Unit Margin
Product 1..........	3,000	$4.00	2,500	$4.20
Product 2..........	2,000	7.00	3,000	6.50
Product 3..........	5,000	3.00	4,000	2.90
	10,000	$4.10	9,500	

Required:

1. Calculate the mix variance.
2. Calculate the price variance.

3. Calculate the volume variance (based on the $4.10 budgeted average unit gross margin).
4. What is the net gross margin variance?

PROBLEM C

Company C calculates direct cost variances monthly. For May, the following data apply to its two products:

	Standard Material per Unit	Standard Labor per Unit	Units Produced in May
Product 1.............	5 lbs.	3.5 hrs.	700
Product 2.............	7 lbs.	5.0 hrs.	600

Actual usage in May was 8,000 lbs. of materials and 5,150 hours.

Required:

1. Calculate the material usage variance in pounds and the labor quantity variance in hours.
2. If the standard materials price is $20 per lb. and the standard wage rate is $5 per hr., restate the variances from Question 1 in monetary terms.

PROBLEM D

Company D makes a product for which you are given the following per unit information for June:

	Standard	Actual
Material.........	50 lbs. @ $3/lb.	60 lbs. @ $2.80/lb.
Labor..........	12 hrs. @ $4/hr.	10 hrs. @ $4.10/hr.

The company produced 1,000 units in June.

Required:

1. Calculate the material usage and price variances.
2. Calculate the labor quantity and rate variances.
3. Speculate as to what may have caused this particular pattern of variances.

PROBLEM E

Company E makes a product which has the following standard materials cost per 100 pounds of finished product:

60 lbs. of material X @ $.50/lb..............	$30.00
40 lbs. of material Y @ .75/lb..............	30.00
100 lbs. of materials with total cost............	$60.00

As materials were not normally spoiled during production, these standards included no allowance for waste.

During October, actual quantities and costs were as follows:

Material X:	used 5,500 lbs. @ $.50/lb. =	$2,750
Material Y:	used 4,500 lbs. @ $.80/lb. =	3,600
	10,000 lbs.	$6,350
Actual finished product:	9,800 lbs.	

Required:

Compute the materials variances for October. (Hint: this problem contains a mix variance, analogous to the gross margin mix variance in Problem B.)

CASE 22–2. PROBLEMS IN THE ANALYSIS OF OVERHEAD COST

PROBLEM A

The overhead rate is $2 a ton. Budgeted overhead cost at 3,000 tons a month is $8,000 and at 7,000 tons is $12,000. Actual overhead cost in September is $9,000, and actual volume is 5,000 tons.

Required:

1. On a graph, show absorbed costs and expected costs.
2. State the following:
   a. Standard volume.
   b. Budgeted nonvariable cost.
   c. Budgeted variable cost per ton.
   d. Costs absorbed in September.
   e. Volume variance in September.
   f. Spending variance in September.
   g. Net variance in September.

PROBLEM B

The formula for budgeted overhead costs is $y = \$5,000 + \$1$ per unit. Standard volume is 5,000 units a month. Actual overhead expense in March is $11,500, and output in March is 6,000 units.

Required:

1. Standard volume.
2. Budgeted nonvariable cost.
3. Budgeted variable cost per unit.
4. Cost absorbed in March.
5. Volume variance in March.
6. Spending variance in March.
7. Net variance in March.

PROBLEM C

The forecast year's overhead expense for an expected volume of 180,000 pounds of a product is as follows:

$$
\begin{aligned}
&\text{Nonvariable overhead} \ldots\ldots\ldots\ldots\ldots\ldots\ldots\ldots \$\ 36,000 \\
&\text{Variable overhead} \ldots\ldots\ldots\ldots\ldots\ldots\ldots\ldots\ldots\ 108,000
\end{aligned}
$$

In May, output was 10,000 pounds and actual overhead expense was $7,700. Determine (*a*) the budget line, (*b*) standard volume, (*c*) standard overhead per unit, and (*d*) the overhead variances.

PROBLEM D

In June overhead volume variance was 0 and spending variance was a debit of $600. In July overhead volume variance was a debit of $800, but spending variance was 0. June actual overhead expense was $7,000 for an output of 800 tons. July's expense was $5,600, and output was 600 tons. In August output was 900 tons and actual overhead expense was $7,100. What was the budget figure for August? How much was absorbed in August? What can you say of variances for August?

PROBLEM E

Overhead was charged to product at 75 percent of direct labor dollars. According to the budget, overhead should be $5,600 for a direct labor payroll of $8,000 and $6,800 for a direct labor payroll of $10,000. If actual overhead costs turned out to be $6,000 and $7,000, respectively, at these two volumes, what were the variances? What was the budget formula? What was standard volume for the company?

PROBLEM F

Department 12 of the Hudson Company manufactured rivets and no other products. All rivets were identical. In August Department 12 made four million rivets. The company used a standard cost system plus a variable budget for overhead expense. Standard unit overhead charges (i.e., standard unit costs for overhead) were determined by dividing budgeted costs at an expected average volume by the number of rivets (in thousands) which that volume level (i.e., rate of capacity) represented.

Certain cost information is shown in the following table, and you are requested to fill in the blank spaces. The clue to the expected average volume necessary to fill in the blanks in line 3 can be found by a close analysis of the relationships among the figures given for allocated service and general overhead.

Dept.12	Actual Cost, August	Std. Chg. per 1,000 Rivets	Total Std. Cost, August*	Overhead Budget, August	Overhead Budget Formula
Direct labor.........	$10,500	$3.00	$	Not Used	
Direct material......	22,000	5.00	20,000	" "	
Department direct overhead expense..	9,500	...	.....	$ 9,200	$6,000 per month plus $0.80 per thous. rivets
Allocated service and general overhead...	5,000	1.00	4,000	5,000	$5,000 per month
Total.........	$47,000	$ ...	$	$14,200	

* Standard charge per thousand rivets times August volume of 4,000,000 equals total standard cost.

Required:

1. Fill in the blanks.
2. What was the expected average volume (in terms of rivet output) at which the standard unit overhead charge was determined?
3. Explain as much of the difference between total actual costs and total standard costs as you can on the basis of the information given.

CASE 22–3.   BROADSIDE BOAT BUILDERS, INC.

Located in Cornish, New Hampshire, Broadside Boat Builders served boaters using New England waters with a small, lightweight fiberglass sailboat capable of being carried on a car roof. While the firm could hardly be considered as one of the nation's industrial giants, its burgeoning business had required it to institute a formal system of cost control.

Pat Decatur, Broadside's president, explained, "Our seasonal demand opposed to a need for regular, level production means that we must keep a good line of credit at the bank. Modern cost control methods and consistent inventory valuation procedures enhance our credibility with the bankers and more importantly have enabled us to improve our methods and procedures. Our foremen have realized the value of good cost accounting and the main office has, in turn, become much more aware of problems in the barn."

Broadside's manufacturing and warehouse facilities consisted of three historic, New England barns converted to make eleven-foot "Silver Streak" sailboats. The company's plans included the addition of fifteen- and eighteen-foot sailboats to its present line. Longer-term plans called for adding additional sizes and styles in the hope of becoming a major factor in the regional boat market.

The "Silver Streak" was an open cockpit, day sailer sporting a main-sail and small jib on a seventeen-foot, telescoping, aluminum mast. It was ideally suited to the many small lakes and ponds of the region and after three years it had become quite popular. It was priced at $450 complete.

Manufacturing consisted basically of three processes: molding, finishing, and assembly. The molding department mixed all ingredients to make the fiberglass hull, performed the actual molding, and removed the hull from the mold. Finishing included hand additions to the hull for running and standing rigging, reinforcement of the mast and tiller steps, and general sanding of rough spots. Assembly consisted of the attachment of cleats, turnbuckles, drain plugs, tiller, and so forth, and the inspection of the boat with mast, halyards, and sails in place. The assembly department also prepared the boat for storage or shipment.

Mixing and molding fiberglass hulls, while manually simple, required a great deal of expertise, or "eyeball," as it was known in the trade. Addition of too much or too little catalyst, use of too much or too little heat, or failure to allow proper time for curing could each cause a hull to be discarded. Conversely, spending too much time on adjustments to mixing or molding equipment or on "personalized" supervision of each hull could cause severe underproduction problems. Once a batch of fiber-glass was mixed there was no time to waste being overcautious or it was likely to "freeze" in its kettle.

With such a situation, and the company's announced intent of expanding their product line, it became obvious that a standard cost system would be necessary to help control costs and to provide some reference for foreman performance.

Davey Jones, the molding department foreman, and Rick Ober,

Broadsides' accountant, agreed after lengthy discussion to the following standard costs:

Materials—Glass cloth—120 ft² @ $ .40	=	$48.00
Glass mix — 40 lbs @ $ .75	=	30.00
Direct labor—Mixing — 0.5 hrs @ $4.00	=	2.00
—Molding 1.0 hrs @ $4.00	=	4.00
Indirect costs—Absorb at $3 per hull*	=	3.00
Total cost to mold hull	=	$87.00

* The normal volume of operations for overhead derivation purposes was assumed to be 450 hulls per month. The estimated monthly indirect cost equation was: Budget = $1.44 × hulls + $702.

Analysis of Operations

After several additional months of operations, Mr. Ober expressed disappointment about the apparent lack of attention being paid to the standard costs. Molders tended to have a cautious outlook toward mixing too little or "cooking" too long. No one wanted to end up throwing away a partial hull because of too little glass mix.

In reviewing the most recent month's production results, Mr. Ober noted the following actual costs for production of 430 hulls:

Materials:

Purchased	60,000 ft² glass cloth @ $.39/ft²
	20,000 lbs glass mix @ $.76/lb
Used	54,000 ft² glass cloth
	19,000 lbs glass mix

Direct labor:

Mixing 210 hrs @ $4.10/hr
Molding 480 hrs @ $4.00/hr

Overhead:

Incurred $1,400

Before proceeding with further analysis, Ober called Jones to arrange a discussion of variances. He told Ms. Decatur, "Maybe we should look into an automated molding operation. Although I haven't finished my analysis, it looks like there will be unfavorable variances again. Jones insists that the standards are reasonable, then never meets them!"

Ms. Decatur seemed disturbed and answered, "Well, some variances are inevitable. Why don't you analyze them in some meaningful manner and discuss your ideas with Jones. He is an expert in molding whose opinion I respect. Then the two of you meet with me to discuss the whole matter."

Questions

1. Determine the molding department's direct cost and overhead variances. Why do you think they occurred?
2. Do you think Broadside's standards are meaningful? How would you improve them?

CASE 22–4. COTTER CO., INC.

In preparing its annual profit plan, the management of the Cotter Co., Inc., realized that its sales were subject to monthly seasonal variations, but expected that for the year as a whole the profit before taxes would total $240,000, as shown below:

	Annual Budget	
	Amount	Percent of Sales
Sales......................................	$2,400,000	100
Standard cost of goods sold:		
Prime costs............................	960,000	40
Factory overhead.......................	840,000	35
Total standard cost..................	$1,800,000	75
Gross margin............................	$ 600,000	25
Selling and general overhead................	360,000	15
Income before taxes......................	$ 240,000	10

Management defined "prime costs" as those costs for labor and materials which were strictly variable with the quantity of production in the factory. The overhead in the factory included both fixed and variable costs; management's estimate was that, within a sales volume range of plus or minus $1,000,000 per year, variable factory overhead would be equal to 25 percent of prime costs. Thus the total factory overhead budgeted for the year consisted of $240,000 of variable costs (25 percent of $960,000) and $600,000 of fixed costs. All of the selling and general overhead was fixed, except for commissions on sales equal to 5 percent of the selling price.

Mr. Cotter, the President of the company, approved the budget, stating that, "A profit of $20,000 a month isn't bad for a little company in this business." During January, however, sales suffered the normal seasonal dips, and production in the factory was also cut back. The result, which came as some surprise to the president, was that January showed a loss of $7,000.

Operating Statement
January

Sales......................................		$140,000
Standard cost of goods sold.............		105,000
Standard gross margin..................		$ 35,000
Manufacturing variances:..............	Favorable or	
	(Unfavorable)	
Prime cost variance..................	$(3,500)	
Factory overhead:...................		
Spending variance................	1,000	
Volume variance..................	(12,500)	(15,000)
Actual gross margin..................		$ 20,000.
Selling and general overhead..........		27,000
Loss before taxes.....................		$ (7,000)

Questions

1. Explain, as best you can with the data available, why the January profit was $27,000 less than the average monthly profit expected by the president.
2. What is Cotter's monthly breakeven volume?
3. What was Cotter's January production level?
4. How much did finished goods inventory change in January?
5. What were actual overhead costs in January?

CASE 22–5.   DAWKINS MANUFACTURING COMPANY

Early in January, 1974, the cost report shown in Exhibit 1 was submitted to Mr. Peter Dawkins, president of the Dawkins Manufacturing

Exhibit 1

COMPARISON OF MANUFACTURING COSTS
Metal Frame Department

	1972	1973	Variance, 1973 over 1972
Raw materials...................	$1,070,000	$1,232,000	$162,000
Direct labor.....................	260,000	270,000	10,000
Department overhead:.............			
Indirect labor..................	100,000	20,000	(80,000)
Supervision....................	20,000	20,000	—
Power.........................	8,200	9,500	1,300
Depreciation...................	30,000	100,000	70,000
General overhead................	232,000	264,500	32,500
Total....................	$1,720,200	$1,916,000	$195,800

Company. This report was for the frame department which was one of the primary producing departments in the company. Mr. Dawkins was alarmed by the report because of the increase in cost. He commented that the only area of efficiency seemed to be in the use of indirect labor. Mr. Dawkins requested an investigation of the situation, which produced the following additional information.

The department made two types of metal frames which were used in the construction industry. The primary difference in the types was their size. The larger size of frame, called the J frame, required more material than the small frame (S frame), but less direct labor time was required because of an automatic assembly process which had not yet been adapted to the small frames. The department supervisor said that the J frame required about two units of raw material (primarily metal stripping), whereas the S frame required only one unit. The supervisor indicated that these quantities were based on normal operating efficiency. An investigation of the storeroom records showed that 560,000 units of raw materials had been issued during 1973, whereas 535,000 units had been issued during 1972.

The direct labor requirement was the opposite of the raw material. A J frame required about one half the amount of labor time as did the S frame. The foreman estimated that, under normal working conditions, the department should produce about ten J frames per labor hour. The direct labor in the department was about the same insofar as the level of skill required, and the average wage rate per hour was $5.00. Failure to schedule work properly and failure to provide adequately for absenteeism (primarily the responsibility of the personnel department) sometimes resulted in a night shift which was paid a 10 percent premium. The policy of the company was to avoid night shift work if at all possible.

While the price of raw materials had gone up in 1973 about 10 percent (a unit of raw material cost $2.00 in 1972), the basic direct labor rate stayed about the same. An investigation of the payroll showed that about 52,000 direct labor hours were actually paid for during 1973, while about 50,500 hours had been paid in 1972. The actual direct labor rate did vary from the $5.00 rate because of some night shift work and also because in February, 1973, some workers were transferred into the frame department to cover excess absenteeism due to a mild influenza epidemic. These transferred workers received a wage rate somewhat higher than the average for the frame department.

An investigation of the general overhead revealed that this cost was an assigned cost. The company's practice was to assign the general administration overhead (the cost of such departments as accounting, personnel, general factory management, and engineering) to producing departments on the basis of total direct and indirect labor dollars (excluding supervision). The total general overhead for the company was $1,150,000 in 1973 and $1,160,000 in 1972. The total direct and indirect labor cost for all producing departments was $1,260,000 in 1973 and $1,800,000 in 1972.

During 1973, the company purchased and installed some portable conveyers which made it possible to release several material handlers who made up the largest element of indirect labor. The desirability of the equipment had been assessed by using a ten-year economic life, and this period was chosen for depreciation purposes. A full year's depreciation had been included for 1973.

The power cost was assigned to the frame department by using the unit cost of power as determined by the power service department. In 1972, this cost was 1.6 cents ($0.016) per kw-hr, whereas the rate went up to 1.8 cents in 1973 because of an increase in the cost of fuel used to make the power. The foremen of the power department and the frame department agreed that power consumption was highly dependent on direct labor hours. The frame department foreman said that a fairly good rule of thumb that had been used in the past was ten kw-hrs of power for every hour of direct labor. He said that if power were used efficiently, this rate of consumption should be attainable.

A check of the production reports showed that production of completed frames for each of the two years was as follows:

	1972	1973
S Frames	150,000	150,000
J Frames	180,000	200,000

Questions

1. Explain, insofar as possible, the significance of and reasons for the increase in costs.
2. In general, how would you rate the efficiency of the metal frame department in 1973?
3. Can you suggest a better way of reporting costs for the department in the future?

CASE 22–6. C. F. CHURCH MANUFACTURING COMPANY

The C. F. Church Manufacturing Company was established in 1898 for the purpose of manufacturing toilet seats. The executives had devoted considerable effort to the development of a quality product, to widespread advertising of the product, and to the realization of economical manufacturing methods.

The manufacturing processes were quite simple. First, the seats were shaped out of wood at a branch plant. They were then shipped to the main plant, where they underwent the particular finishing processes required. Some units were sprayed with paint, but the best seats were coated with cellulose nitrate sheeting..After the seats were coated, the rough edges were filed and the seats were sanded, buffed, and polished. Finally, hinges and rubber bumpers were added, and the seats were packed for shipment. Most operations were performed by hand with the aid of small machines, such as paint spray guns and buffing wheels.

1. Accounting

COLLECTION OF MATERIAL AND LABOR COST. A major part of the work required in the cost system was the orderly accumulation of data on actual and standard costs. The procedure in regard to materials used was as follows. When an order for a particular style of finish was started through the factory, the foreman of the department that performed the first operation received a manufacturing order. On the basis of this order, the foreman filled out a stores requisition slip for the materials necessary to manufacture this order. Items listed on this requisition subsequently were priced, and their purchase cost was entered on the requisition by the cost department on a last-in, first-out basis. (Inasmuch as raw material was purchased infrequently in large contract lots, this procedure was not difficult.) When seats were ready to be assembled and packed, the foreman in the assembly department made out an assembly order (Exhibit 1), which included a requisition for hinges, screws, bumpers, cartons, and fillers. These issues of materials were also costed at last-in, first-out. The totals of the requisition slips for the month served as the basis for credits to the respective materials inventory accounts and a debit to the Work in Process account for the cost of material put into process.

The direct labor debit to Work in Process was equally straightforward. Daily, each productive employee made out a time and production report (Exhibit 2) on which he recorded the factory order number, the operation, the time spent on each operation, and the number of pieces that he had finished. A clerk in the payroll department entered the correct piece rate or hourly rate and made the proper extension. The total of the direct labor thus computed provided the credit to the Accrued Wages account and the debit (for direct labor) to Work in Process.

STANDARD BURDEN SCHEDULE (ANNUAL). The debit to Work in Process for manufacturing expense was based on annual estimates of the relation of burden expenses to direct labor costs for each department. These annual estimates were made so that for each department there was available a schedule of standard burden expenses at varying possible rates of capacity utilization. Exhibit 3 illustrates such a schedule for the coating department, Department No. 3.

Exhibit 1

ASSEMBLY ORDER No. 6291
Coated

Date August
Shipping Order No. _____
Work Order No. _____
Plate No. 2000
Quantity 100

Seats 2,000 - 917
Covers 2,000 - 917

Hinges 2,000

Special Instructions

FOR COST DEPT. ONLY	UNIT COST		AMOUNT	
Material	5	51	551	00
Labor		92	92	00
Burden	1	90	190	00
Total Cost	8	33	833	00

REQUISITION No. 6291
Hinges – Screws – Bumpers

Date August

DESCRIPTION	QUANTITY
Hinges 2,000	100
Screws 3/4 x 7	
Screws 5/8 x 7	400
1 1/4 x 8	200
Brass Ferrules	
Bar Bumpers	200
Tack Bumpers	200

Delivered by

	UNIT COST	AMOUNT	
Hinges			
Screws			
Screws			
Ferrules			
Bar Bumpers			
Tack Bumpers			

REQUISITION No. 6291
Cartons – Fillers

Date August

DESCRIPTION	QUANTITY
Cartons 25	100
Fillers	200
800	
214	100
105	
Blocks	

Delivered by

	UNIT COST	AMOUNT	
Cartons			
Filler No. 1			
No. 105			
No. 800			
No. 214			
Blocks			

Exhibit 2

FORM C-STR 7918		C. F. CHURCH MFG. CO.							
		Time and Production					Date *August* —		
Employee No. **3/3**		Name							
Order No.	Oper. No.	TIME			Labor or Piece Rate	No. Pieces	Cost		✓
		Started	Finished	Elapsed					
2068	31	7:20	12:00	4.8	2.30	350	8	05	
2068	31	1:00	4:20	3.4	2.30	250	5	75	
							13	80	

The process used to prepare the standard burden schedules was as follows:

1. Determine 100 percent capacity of each department in terms of direct labor hours and direct labor dollars by theoretically loading each unit of productive machinery and equipment with the number of workers required to operate it, together with the necessary productive employees on floor or bench work. Consider, however, the normal sales volume of different types of products and limitations as to type of equipment in any one department that affect the capacity of the plant as a whole. For example, output might be limited to the capacity of the coating and spraying departments.

2. Establish burden expense allowances for each department, considering four general classifications: indirect labor, indirect supplies, fixed charges, and charges from nonproductive departments.

3. Base allowance for indirect labor and indirect supplies on the past year's experience, making adjustments if necessary for changes in wage rates and the prices of supplies. Compute these projections first for the 100 percent capacity determined above, and from this point use a sliding or graduated scale for the lower percentages of capacity. Give due recognition to the fact that some of these costs do not vary at all with production, that others vary in the same ratio as production, and that others, although variable, do not move proportionately with the rate of actual plant activity.

4. Prorate power expense according to the number of horsepower

hours used and metered in the respective departments; water expense (after consideration is given to any special demands for water in particular departments, such as steam) according to the number of employees; insurance, taxes, and depreciation with reference to the net book value of buildings and equipment. Charge directly to the department involved specific insurance that definitely can be assigned to an individual department, such as automobile insurance on trucks in the shipping department or boiler indemnity for the steam department.

5. Distribute the total expense of nonproductive departments such as steam, general plant, shipping, and plant administration to the productive departments on the most logical basis: steam according to floor area, general plant and plant administration according to direct labor hours, and shipping according to direct labor dollars. The estimated cost of defective work for the whole plant was distributed to operating departments on the basis of the expected distribution of direct labor dollars. This item of expense was included in the total of "Charges from other departments," shown at the bottom of Exhibit 3.

6. Revise the standard burden schedules only for a general increase or decrease in wage rates or material costs or an important change in the manufacturing processes.

STANDARD BURDEN RATE. After the burden expense schedule was prepared, executives estimated the percentage of capacity utilization expected during the coming year. The standard burden rate was the rate shown on Exhibit 3 for the estimated percentage of capacity. For example, it was estimated that during the year the coating department would operate at an average of 80 percent of capacity. The standard burden rate for the coating department was therefore 200 percent of direct labor, as shown at the bottom of the 80 percent column in Exhibit 3. The other columns in Exhibit 3 were used for control purposes, as described subsequently.

ACTUAL BURDEN COSTS (MONTHLY). Actual burden costs incurred during the month were charged to the Burden account in the general ledger and to an appropriate detail account in a burden subsidiary ledger. There was a detail account for each item listed in Exhibit 3 (supervision, general labor, and so forth) in each department. Service department and other overhead costs were allocated to the producing departments. At the end of the month, the amount of "absorbed burden" was calculated by multiplying the burden rate for each department by the actual direct labor cost of the department for the month. In the coating department, for example, the actual direct labor for August was $5,915.60, and this multiplied by 200 percent gave $11,831.20, the absorbed burden. (Note that the rate used was the burden rate determined annually, *not* the burden rate under the column in Exhibit 3 that relates to the actual volume of the current month.)

Exhibit 3

BURDEN DEVELOPMENT, DEPARTMENT NO. 3

	100%	95%	90%	85%	80%	75%	70%	65%	60%	50%	40%
Indirect labor:											
01 Supervision	775.00	775.00	775.00	775.00	775.00	775.00	775.00	775.00	775.00	775.00	775.00
08 General labor	625.00	595.00	565.00	530.00	500.00	470.00	440.00	405.00	375.00	315.00	250.00
10 Idle and lost time											
11 Guaranteed rate cost	375.00	356.00	338.00	319.00	300.00	281.00	263.00	244.00	225.00	188.00	150.00
16 Overtime bonus	100.00	100.00	95.00	90.00	85.00	85.00	80.00	75.00	50.00	25.00	25.00
19 Repairs and maint.—M and E	175.00	175.00	165.00	165.00	160.00	160.00	160.00	150.00	150.00	100.00	100.00
Total indirect labor	2,050.00	2,001.00	1,938.00	1,879.00	1,820.00	1,771.00	1,718.00	1,649.00	1,575.00	1,403.00	1,300.00
Indirect supplies:											
31 Repairs and maint.—M and E	25.00	25.00	25.00	20.00	20.00	20.00	20.00	20.00	15.00	15.00	10.00
35 Acetone and isotone	1,625.00	1,545.00	1,465.00	1,380.00	1,300.00	1,220.00	1,140.00	1,055.00	975.00	815.00	650.00
37 Sandpaper and sand-belts	11.00	10.00	10.00	9.00	9.00	8.00	8.00	7.00	7.00	5.00	4.00
38 Glue and cement	775.00	736.00	700.00	660.00	620.00	580.00	540.00	500.00	465.00	385.00	310.00
41 Consumable supplies	125.00	120.00	112.00	106.00	100.00	94.00	88.00	81.00	75.00	63.00	50.00
42 Loose and hand tools	50.00	48.00	45.00	43.00	40.00	38.00	35.00	33.00	30.00	25.00	20.00
46 Miscellaneous	15.00	14.00	14.00	13.00	12.00	11.00	10.00	9.00	9.00	7.00	6.00
Total indirect supplies	2,626.00	2,498.00	2,371.00	2,231.00	2,101.00	1,971.00	1,841.00	1,705.00	1,576.00	1,315.00	1,050.00
Fixed charges:											
65 Insurance—bldgs. and equip.	21.58	21.58	21.58	21.58	21.58	21.58	21.58	21.58	21.58	21.58	21.58
66 Insurance—L. and C.	161.00	152.00	145.00	137.00	128.70	121.00	113.00	105.00	97.00	80.00	64.00
68 Power	27.00	26.00	24.00	23.00	21.60	21.00	19.00	18.00	16.00	14.00	11.00
69 Water	17.25	17.25	17.25	17.25	17.25	17.25	17.25	17.25	17.25	17.25	17.25

70 Taxes—city and town	28.68	28.68	28.68	28.68	28.68	28.68	28.68	28.68	28.68	28.68
71 Taxes—social security	530.00	504.00	477.00	450.00	424.27	398.00	371.00	345.00	318.00	265.00
72 Depreciation	81.25	81.25	81.25	81.25	81.25	81.25	81.25	81.25	81.25	81.25
73 Provision for vacations	725.40	725.40	725.40	725.40	725.40	725.40	725.40	725.40	725.40	725.40
78 Group insurance	112.70	112.70	112.70	112.70	112.70	112.70	112.70	112.70	112.70	112.70
80 Pensions	420.36	420.36	420.36	420.36	420.36	420.36	420.36	420.36	420.36	420.36
Total fixed charges	2,125.22	2,089.22	2,053.22	2,017.22	1,981.79	1,947.22	1,910.22	1,875.22	1,838.22	1,766.22
Total direct expense	6,801.22	6,588.22	6,362.22	6,127.22	5,902.79	5,689.22	5,469.22	5,229.22	4,989.22	4,484.22
Charges from other departments	9,435.37	9,333.33	9,240.12	9,140.56	9,032.28	8,945.27	8,826.90	8,751.83	8,630.42	8,440.11
Total expense	16,236.59	15,921.55	15,602.34	15,267.78	14,935.07	14,634.49	14,296.12	13,981.05	13,619.64	12,924.33
Direct labor dollars	9,375.00	8,906.00	8,437.00	7,969.00	7,500.00	7,031.00	6,562.00	6,094.00	5,625.00	4,687.00
Burden rate	173%	179%	185%	191%	200%	208%	218%	229%	242%	276%

Note: The rightmost (final) column of the original reads:
28.68 | 212.00 | 81.25 | 725.40 | 112.70 | 420.36 | Total fixed charges 1,694.22 | Total direct expense 4,044.22 | Charges from other departments 8,235.38 | Total expense 12,279.60 | Direct labor dollars 3,750.00 | Burden rate 327%

The absorbed burden for all departments was debited to Work in Process and credited to the Burden account. Any balance remaining in the Burden account was then closed to Loss and Gain. In August, for example, actual burden was $45,914.98, absorbed burden was $45,904.44, so $10.54 was debited to Loss and Gain.

STANDARD PRODUCT COSTS. Deliveries from work in process to finished goods were recorded by completion in the factory of the assembly order (Exhibit 1). On the lower left corner of that form there was space for the cost department to fill in the standard cost per unit and the total amount of standard cost for the order, and the total of these standard costs entries for a month was credited to the Work in Process account and debited to Finished Goods Inventory.

The standard costs per unit mentioned in the previous paragraph were prepared for each product in the form illustrated in Exhibit 4. Because the lines on the standard cost sheets were arranged by successive operations, they showed the cumulative cost of a product at the completion of every operation as well as the final cost at which the product was delivered to finished goods inventory. For each operation and for the total cost there was a breakdown that showed separately the standard costs of materials, labor, and burden. The method of arriving at these costs is described below.

Standard materials costs consisted of a predetermined physical amount per unit priced at the expected purchase price for each classification of raw stock or of finished parts stock. Standard labor costs for the various piece-rate operations were simply the current piece rates; in the case of daywork operations, they were the quotients obtained by dividing the daywork rate by an estimated attainable average output. Standard burden costs were found by multiplying the departmental burden rate selected for the year by the standard labor cost for the operation concerned. For example, the standard cost sheet for a style calling for a coated finish might show for an operation in the coating department a standard labor charge of $0.079. As indicated above, operations in the coating department for the year were estimated to be at 80 percent of capacity, which for the coating department meant a burden rate of 200 percent of productive labor. Thus, the standard burden cost for the operation with a labor charge of $0.079 was set at 200 percent of this amount, or $0.158.

These standard product costs were used to price deliveries into finished stock, to cost work in process inventory, and to transfer production between accounts. Once the standard costs were prepared, it was expected that they would remain constant except for alterations necessary to reflect a significant change in the manufacturing process, a change in wage rates or in the price of materials, or the selection of a new normal percentage of operating activity that determined the unit allowance for burden.

Exhibit 4

STANDARD COST				

DATE   January 1   PLATE NO.   2000

Description	Material	Labor	Burden	Total
Receive woodwork	1.17	0.004	0.008	1.182
Insp. and hand sand		0.012	0.024	1.218
Bottom coat	0.542	0.038	0.076	1.874
Trim T.B. and O.F. seats		0.011	0.022	1.907
Sand edges T.B.C.F. out		0.003	0.008	1.918
Sand edges T.B.C.F. in		0.003	0.008	1.929
Inspect		0.012	0.024	1.965
Top coat	0.543	0.079	0.158	2.745
Shave		0.010	0.020	2.775
Sand edges—upright belt		0.005	0.014	2.794
Sand seats and covers		0.039	0.107	2.940
Inspect and file		0.015	0.030	2.985
Dope		0.004	0.008	2.997
Buff seats and covers		0.108	0.208	3.313
Inspect		0.012	0.024	3.349
Buff repairs		0.044	0.085	3.478
Trademark		0.007	0.014	3.499
Drilling		0.004	0.008	3.511
Total seat	2.255	0.410	0.846	3.511
Total cover No.	1.983	0.399	0.826	3.208
Total seat and cover	4.238	0.809	1.672	6.719
Assemble		0.032	0.064	6.815
Cleanup polish		0.033	0.066	6.914
Seal end of carton		0.006	0.012	6.932
Inspect and wrap		0.034	0.068	7.034
Seat, label, and pack		0.010	0.020	7.064
Bar bumpers	0.043			7.107
Tack bumpers	0.019			7.126
Screws 1¼–8	0.047			7.173
Hinge	1.04			8.213
Carton and filler 2—No. 1	0.125			8.338
Total Cost	5.512	0.924	1.902	8.338

VARIANCES. At the end of each month's accounting period, a physical inventory of raw materials, supplies, work in process, and finished goods was taken. For this inventory, raw materials and supplies were priced on the basis of last-in, first-out purchase cost, and work in process and finished goods were priced according to the standard cost sheets described above. The difference between the inventory thus determined and the book balance of each inventory account was closed into Cost of Goods Sold. The most important of these differences was for work in process inventory.

A work in process statement (Exhibit 5) was prepared each month. This report showed the beginning inventory at standard cost plus actual

Exhibit 5

Work in Process

Period Ending August   Order No. GENERAL

Detail		Amount		
Balance from Last Period			158	597	19
DIRECT MATERIALS			76	338	21
DIRECT LABOR					
1 Varnish					
2 Spray	2	990	25		
3 Coating	5	915	60		
4 Filing		998	83		
5 Sanding	1	637	53		
6 Buffing & Polishing	6	175	78		
8 Assembling and Packing	4	788	60		
Total Direct Labor			22	506	59
BURDEN					
1 Varnish					
2 Spray	6	180	50		
3 Coating	11	831	20		
4 Filing	1	937	73		
5 Sanding	4	489	05		
6 Buffing & Polishing	11	888	76		
8 Assembling and Packing	9	577	20		
10 Shipping					
Total Burden			45	904	44
TOTAL COST			303	346	43
Less Deliveries at Cost			222	386	74
BALANCE IN PROCESS			80	959	69

DELIVERIES AT COST

Date		Amount			Date		Amount			Date		Amount		
8/31	Del.	220	876	63										
	Var.	1	259	07										
	Defect.		251	04										
	Net	222	386	74										

direct materials, actual labor, and actual absorbed burden added during
the period in each department. From this total cost figure, there were
subtracted the actual deliveries to finished goods as indicated on the
completed assembly orders, less products transferred from Finished
Goods back to Work in Process for reworking, both costed at standard

Exhibit 6

SUMMARY OF ENTRIES TO INVENTORY ACCOUNTS

August

Raw Materials
(Several accounts according to nature of material)

$151,204 Balance	$76,318.21 Requisitions, priced at last-in, first-out cost (debit to Work in Process).
$343,640.19 Purchases at invoice cost (credit to Accounts Payable).	$138.32 Adjustment to physical inventory (Dr. or Cr.).
$1,101.67 Materials salvaged from returned goods (credit to Cost of Goods Sold).	

A physical inventory of all raw materials was taken each month and the difference between inventory and book balance written off to Cost of Goods Sold.

Work in Process

$158,597.19 Balance	$220,894.24 Deliveries to finished goods at standard costs (debit to Finished Goods).
$76,318.21 Direct materials from requisitions priced at last-in, first-out cost (credit to Raw Materials).	$251.04 Defective work, from defective work order (debit to Burden).
$22,506.59 Direct labor from payroll summary (credit to Accrued Wages).	$1,259.07 Adjustment to physical inventory (Dr. or Cr.).
$20.00 Materials purchased not usually carried in inventory (credit to Accounts Payable).	
$17.61 Transfers from finished goods for reworking or alteration, at standard cost (credit to Finished Goods).	
$45,904.44 Absorbed expense (earned burden) from burden summary sheet (credit to Burden).	

Finished Goods

$429,682.73 Balance	$400,954.09 Shipment at standard costs (debit to Cost of Goods Sold).
$220,894.24 Deliveries to finished goods at standard costs (credit to Work in Process).	$17.61 Transfers to work in process for reworking or alteration at standard cost (debit to Work in Process).

A physical inventory was taken of all work in process every month. This was priced and totaled according to standard costs at last operation performed; the difference between the inventory and balance in the Work in Process account, representing the cost variation, was written off to Cost of Goods Sold.

cost. The resulting Balance in Process was the book value of work in process and was compared with the figure obtained by valuing, at standard, the results of the physical inventory. Any difference indicated by this comparison constituted the variance of actual cost from standard and was closed to Cost of Goods Sold. The physical inventory balance at standard constituted the debit to Work in Process at the beginning of the next month. If this Work in Process variance was large, its causes were investigated and action was taken accordingly.

A descriptive summary of the inventory accounts is given in Exhibit 6.

2. Control of Burden Expenses

BUDGETED BURDEN EXPENSES. The Church company used the departmental burden schedules to set bogeys for the foremen and supervisors who were responsible for incurring expenses. A knowledge of the actual amount of direct labor for each productive department made it a simple matter to determine which column of figures to use as the bogey standard for evaluating the spending performance of each foreman. For example, the coating department (Exhibit 3) might be expected to operate, on the average, at 80 percent of capacity, but in any one month the actual operations might vary considerably from this average. Thus, if direct labor dropped to $7,031, the foreman would be expected to spend only $580 for glue and cement rather than the $620 allowable at the average operating level. For nonproductive departments, the column selected was the one that listed the expenses expected for the percentage of capacity nearest the average operating level of all productive departments.

COMPARISON OF ACTUAL AND BUDGET. The departmental comparisons of the actual burden expenses, by accounts, with the appropriate budgeted allowance for that volume, are illustrated in the departmental budget sheet, Exhibit 7. The August budgeted expense figures for the coating department are based upon an output level of 65 percent of capacity. This figure was arrived at by comparing the actual direct labor expense for the month, amounting to $5,915.60, to the closest corresponding direct labor expense, $6,094, which is under the 65 percent column shown on Exhibit 3. (Exhibit 7 is a standard form, and only those lines that are pertinent to the operations of the coating department are filled in on the example shown.)

Exhibit 7 also showed two items over which the foreman had no control. Other Overhead expenses was the total amount of fixed charges allocated to the department on the basis of the percentage distributions described earlier. Defective Work was the total amount of defective work budgeted ($600) and actual ($251.04) for the *entire plant*, and it bore no relation to the work done in the coating department. The amount allocated to each department for defective work was not shown

Exhibit 7

			Budget	Actual Expense	Over or Under Actual	
		C. F. CHURCH MFG. CO.				
		HOLYOKE				
		Analysis of Overhead Expenses				
	DEPARTMENT #3 Coating				Month August	
			1	2	3	
1		INDIRECT LABOR				1
2	01	Supervision	775 00	756 00	19 00	2
3	04	Truck Drivers & Helpers				3
4	06	Shipping				4
5	08	General Labor	405 00	171 22	233 78	5
6	09	Repair and Rework				6
7	10	Idle and Lost Time		1 77	(1 77)	7
8	11	Guaranteed Rate Cost	244 00	28 14	215 86	8
9	16	Overtime Bonus	75 00	32 98	42 02	9
10	19	Repairs & Maint. & Mchy. & Equip.	150 00	38 26	111 74	10
11	17	Vacations		46 00	(46 00)	11
12	21	Paid Holidays				12
13		Total	1649 00	1074 37	574 63	13
14		INDIRECT SUPPLIES				14
15	31	Repairs & Maint.--Mchy. & Equip.	20 00	360 18	(340 18)	15
16	33	Repairs & Maint. Trucks				16
17	35	Acetone & Isotone	1055 00	739 48	315 52	17
18	36	Buffing Compounds & Buffs				18
19	37	Sandpaper & Sandbelts	7 00	9 60	(2 60)	19
20	39	Labels, Tape, etc., Glue & Cement	500 00	734 71	(234 71)	20
21	40	Shipping Cartons				21
22	41	Consumable Supplies	81 00	55 54	25 46	22
23	42	Loose & Hand Tools	33 00	13 55	19 45	23
24	46	Miscellaneous	9 00	7 51	1 49	24
25		Total	1705 00	1920 57	(215 57)	25
26		OTHER OVERHEAD expenses:				26
27		Insurance, power, taxes, social				27
28		security, depreciation, group				28
29		insurance & pension	1875 22	1472 46	402 76	29
30						30
31		DEFECTIVE WORK	600 00	251 04	348 96	31
32						32
33		DIRECT LABOR	6094 00	5915 60	178 40	33
34						34
35						35
36						36
37						37
38						38
39						39
40						40

on Exhibit 7 because the basis of allocation was considered too arbitrary. The amounts for both Other Overhead expenses and for Defective Work were shown in the Analysis of Overhead Expenses principally as a matter of information for the foreman. They were not considered as being controllable by the foreman.

Each month the accounting department prepared Exhibit 8, summarizing the actual, budgeted, and absorbed burden costs for each operating department. The amount shown as Actual Expense was obtained by adding the Charges from Other Departments ($8,362.13 for the coating department) to the other burden items shown in Exhibit 7 (excluding defective work). The Budgeted Expense was the total burden for each department as shown on the burden development sheets (Exhibit 3) at

Exhibit 8
BURDEN SUMMARY AND STATISTICS

Plant—Holyoke   Period Ending—August 31

Dept. No.	Description	Direct Labor	Actual Expense	Budgeted Expense	Loss or Gain on Budget	Absorbed Expense	Over- or Under-absorbed
1							
2	Spray	2,990.25	6,464.64	7,103.64	639.00	6,180.50	(284.14)
3	Coating	5,915.60	12,829.53	13,981.05	1,151.52	11,831.20	(998.33)
4	Filing	998.83	2,590.83	2,190.20	(400.63)	1,937.73	(653.10)
4–I							
4–C							
4–5							
5	Sanding	1,637.53	3,907.74	5,243.47	1,335.73	4,489.05	581.31
6	Buffing	6,175.78	11,275.76	10,750.25	(525.51)	11,888.76	613.00
7							
8	Assemble and pack	4,788.60	8,846.48	8,998.58	152.10	9,577.20	730.72
9							
10							
11							
12							
14							
15							
	Total Plant	22,506.59	45,914.98	48,267.19	2,352.21	45,904.44	(10.54)

Year to Date

Dept. No.	Description	Direct Labor	Actual Expense	Budgeted Expense	Loss or Gain on Budget	Absorbed Expense	Over- or Under-absorbed
1							
2		22,071.46	44,718.50			45,643.78	925.28
3		50,512.16	104,611.39			101,024.32	(3,587.07)
4		9,077.03	21,509.51			17,618.52	(3,890.99)
4–I							
4–C							
4–5							
5		13,660.61	35,648.86			37,443.73	1,794.87
6		51,978.12	98,119.96			100,057.88	1,937.92
7							
8		30,878.48	62,125.19			61,756.96	(368.23)
9							
10							
11							
12							
14							
15							
	Total Plant	178,177.86	366,733.41			363,545.19	(3,188.22)

Exhibit 9

SUMMARY OF PERFORMANCE IN THE COATING DEPARTMENT

	April		May		June		August	
	Actual	(Over) or Under	Actual	(Over) or Under	Actual	(Over) or Under	Actual	(Over) or Under
Indirect labor:								
01 Supervision................	811	(36)	782	(7)	756	19	756	19
08 General labor.............	654	(124)	558	(28)	418	22	171	234
10 Idle and lost time........	.....	.....	.....	.....	.....	.....	2	(2)
11 Guaranteed rate cost.....	313	6	154	165	50	213	28	216
16 Overtime bonus..........	63	27	45	45	37	43	33	42
19 Repairs and maint.—mchy. and equip.....	89	76	30	135	35	125	38	112
17 Vacations................	.....	.....	.....	.....	.....	.....	46	(46)
Total................	1,930	(51)	1,569	310	1,296	422	1,074	575
Indirect supplies:								
31 Repairs and maint.—mchy. and equip.....	5	15	85	(65)	176	(156)	360	(340)
33 Repairs and maint.—trucks...........	.....	.....	.....	.....	.....	.....	.....	.....
35 Acetone and isotone......	1,300	80	1,134	246	1,031	109	739	316
36 Buffing compounds and buffs......	.....	.....	.....	.....	.....	.....	.....	.....
37 Sandpaper and sandbelts....	10	(1)	14	(5)	5	3	10	(3)
39 Labels, tape, etc., glue and cement......	575	85	462	199	182	358	735	(235)
40 Shipping cartons........	.....	.....	.....	.....	.....	.....	.....	.....
41 Consumable supplies......	66	40	116	(10)	48	40	56	25
42 Loose and hand tools.....	37	6	14	29	10	25	14	19
46 Miscellaneous...........	27	(14)	9	3	9	1	8	1
Total................	2,020	211	1,834	397	1,461	380	1,922	(217)
Other overhead expenses: Insurance, power, taxes, social security, depreciation, group insurance, and pension.	1,456	561	2,014	3	1,836	74	1,472	403
Defective work.............	391	209	656	(56)	594	6	251	349
Direct labor...............	7,812	157	8,024	(55)	6,599	(36)	5,916	178

the applicable level of operations (65 percent for the coating department in August).

The amount of Absorbed Expense was computed by applying the *annual* burden rate to the direct labor in each productive department, as explained in the preceding section.

In the opinion of the management the entries in the column headed Loss or Gain on Budget could be considered a measure of the effectiveness of departmental supervision, whereas the amount Over- or Underabsorbed was influenced both by efficiency and by the volume of production.

The departmental overhead budget constituted the point of real control over expenditures. At the end of each month, the president met with the cost supervisor and the foremen to discuss spending. At these meetings the foremen were encouraged to discuss their performance as indicated by the budget report. When the system was first installed, the cost supervisor did most of the talking, but with increasing familiarity with the costs for which he was responsible, each foreman gradually became "cost conscious," and after a short time each foreman knew approximately what his monthly performance would be, even before he saw the budget comparison report.

The foreman in charge of the coating department was particularly interested in controlling the overhead costs under his jurisdiction. Every month he discussed the analysis of overhead expenses with the factory manager and the cost supervisor to evaluate with them the performance of his department. During the first week of September, he received the analysis of overhead expenses for August (Exhibit 7), and he checked all the items carefully to learn if there were any costs out of line with his expectations for that month. He copied the August figures onto a sheet (Exhibit 9) on which he had previously summarized the figures for recent months (except for July, which included a vacation shutdown). After he felt that he had a good idea of his cost position, he arranged for a meeting with the factory manager and the cost supervisor to review the situation with them.

Questions

1. What are the major purposes of the standards developed by the company?
2. How does the company develop standard burden rates? How often do *you* think they should be changed?
3. What steps are involved in the development of the standard cost sheet (Exhibit 4)? How accurate do you judge the figures to be?
4. What are the possible causes of the $1,259.07 credit to Work in Process labeled "adjustment to physical inventory" in Exhibit 6?
5. Explain so as to distinguish them clearly from one another, the figures

$12,829.53, $13,981.05, and $11,831.20 shown for the coating department on Exhibit 8.

6. If you were the cost supervisor, what evaluation would you make of the performance of the foreman in the coating department in controlling his overhead costs? About which items in Exhibits 7–9 would you be likely to question him?

7. In the coating department for the month of August, what is the variance attributable to "Charges from Other Departments"? Of what significance is this variance to (*a*) the coating department, and (*b*) the service departments that created these charges? Should this variance be included in the burden summary and statistics report?

APPENDIX TABLES

Table A

PRESENT VALUE OF $1

Years Hence	1%	2%	4%	6%	8%	10%	12%	14%	15%	16%	18%	20%	22%	24%	25%	26%	28%	30%	35%	40%	45%	50%
1	0.990	0.980	0.962	0.943	0.926	0.909	0.893	0.877	0.870	0.862	0.847	0.833	0.820	0.806	0.800	0.794	0.781	0.769	0.741	0.714	0.690	0.667
2	0.980	0.961	0.925	0.890	0.857	0.826	0.797	0.769	0.756	0.743	0.718	0.694	0.672	0.650	0.640	0.630	0.610	0.592	0.549	0.510	0.476	0.444
3	0.971	0.942	0.889	0.840	0.794	0.751	0.712	0.675	0.658	0.641	0.609	0.579	0.551	0.524	0.512	0.500	0.477	0.455	0.406	0.364	0.328	0.296
4	0.961	0.924	0.855	0.792	0.735	0.683	0.636	0.592	0.572	0.552	0.516	0.482	0.451	0.423	0.410	0.397	0.373	0.350	0.301	0.260	0.226	0.198
5	0.951	0.906	0.822	0.747	0.681	0.621	0.567	0.519	0.497	0.476	0.437	0.402	0.370	0.341	0.328	0.315	0.291	0.269	0.223	0.186	0.156	0.132
6	0.942	0.888	0.790	0.705	0.630	0.564	0.507	0.456	0.432	0.410	0.370	0.335	0.303	0.275	0.262	0.250	0.227	0.207	0.165	0.133	0.108	0.088
7	0.933	0.871	0.760	0.665	0.583	0.513	0.452	0.400	0.376	0.354	0.314	0.279	0.249	0.222	0.210	0.198	0.178	0.159	0.122	0.095	0.074	0.059
8	0.923	0.853	0.731	0.627	0.540	0.467	0.404	0.351	0.327	0.305	0.266	0.233	0.204	0.179	0.168	0.157	0.139	0.123	0.091	0.068	0.051	0.039
9	0.914	0.837	0.703	0.592	0.500	0.424	0.361	0.308	0.284	0.263	0.225	0.194	0.167	0.144	0.134	0.125	0.108	0.094	0.067	0.048	0.035	0.026
10	0.905	0.820	0.676	0.558	0.463	0.386	0.322	0.270	0.247	0.227	0.191	0.162	0.137	0.116	0.107	0.099	0.085	0.073	0.050	0.035	0.024	0.017
11	0.896	0.804	0.650	0.527	0.429	0.350	0.287	0.237	0.215	0.195	0.162	0.135	0.112	0.094	0.086	0.079	0.066	0.056	0.037	0.025	0.017	0.012
12	0.887	0.788	0.625	0.497	0.397	0.319	0.257	0.208	0.187	0.168	0.137	0.112	0.092	0.076	0.069	0.062	0.052	0.043	0.027	0.018	0.012	0.008
13	0.879	0.773	0.601	0.469	0.368	0.290	0.229	0.182	0.163	0.145	0.116	0.093	0.075	0.061	0.055	0.050	0.040	0.033	0.020	0.013	0.008	0.005
14	0.870	0.758	0.577	0.442	0.340	0.263	0.205	0.160	0.141	0.125	0.099	0.078	0.062	0.049	0.044	0.039	0.032	0.025	0.015	0.009	0.006	0.003
15	0.861	0.743	0.555	0.417	0.315	0.239	0.183	0.140	0.123	0.108	0.084	0.065	0.051	0.040	0.035	0.031	0.025	0.020	0.011	0.006	0.004	0.002
16	0.853	0.728	0.534	0.394	0.292	0.218	0.163	0.123	0.107	0.093	0.071	0.054	0.042	0.032	0.028	0.025	0.019	0.015	0.008	0.005	0.003	0.002
17	0.844	0.714	0.513	0.371	0.270	0.198	0.146	0.108	0.093	0.080	0.060	0.045	0.034	0.026	0.023	0.020	0.015	0.012	0.006	0.003	0.002	0.001
18	0.836	0.700	0.494	0.350	0.250	0.180	0.130	0.095	0.081	0.069	0.051	0.038	0.028	0.021	0.018	0.016	0.012	0.009	0.005	0.002	0.001	0.001
19	0.828	0.686	0.475	0.331	0.232	0.164	0.116	0.083	0.070	0.060	0.043	0.031	0.023	0.017	0.014	0.012	0.009	0.007	0.003	0.002	0.001	
20	0.820	0.673	0.456	0.312	0.215	0.149	0.104	0.073	0.061	0.051	0.037	0.026	0.019	0.014	0.012	0.010	0.007	0.005	0.002	0.001	0.001	
21	0.811	0.660	0.439	0.294	0.199	0.135	0.093	0.064	0.053	0.044	0.031	0.022	0.015	0.011	0.009	0.008	0.006	0.004	0.002	0.001		
22	0.803	0.647	0.422	0.278	0.184	0.123	0.083	0.056	0.046	0.038	0.026	0.018	0.013	0.009	0.007	0.006	0.004	0.003	0.001	0.001		
23	0.795	0.634	0.406	0.262	0.170	0.112	0.074	0.049	0.040	0.033	0.022	0.015	0.010	0.007	0.006	0.005	0.003	0.002	0.001			
24	0.788	0.622	0.390	0.247	0.158	0.102	0.066	0.043	0.035	0.028	0.019	0.013	0.008	0.006	0.005	0.004	0.003	0.002	0.001			
25	0.780	0.610	0.375	0.233	0.146	0.092	0.059	0.038	0.030	0.024	0.016	0.010	0.007	0.005	0.004	0.003	0.002	0.001	0.001			
26	0.772	0.598	0.361	0.220	0.135	0.084	0.053	0.033	0.026	0.021	0.014	0.009	0.006	0.004	0.003	0.002	0.002	0.001		0.001		
27	0.764	0.586	0.347	0.207	0.125	0.076	0.047	0.029	0.023	0.018	0.011	0.007	0.005	0.003	0.002	0.002	0.001	0.001		0.001		
28	0.757	0.574	0.333	0.196	0.116	0.069	0.042	0.026	0.020	0.016	0.010	0.006	0.004	0.002	0.002	0.002	0.001	0.001				
29	0.749	0.563	0.321	0.185	0.107	0.063	0.037	0.022	0.017	0.014	0.008	0.005	0.003	0.002	0.002	0.001	0.001	0.001				
30	0.742	0.552	0.308	0.174	0.099	0.057	0.033	0.020	0.015	0.012	0.007	0.004	0.003	0.002	0.001	0.001	0.001	0.001				
40	0.672	0.453	0.208	0.097	0.046	0.022	0.011	0.005	0.004	0.003	0.001	0.001										
50	0.608	0.372	0.141	0.054	0.021	0.009	0.003	0.001	0.001	0.001												

Table B

PRESENT VALUE OF $1 RECEIVED ANNUALLY FOR N YEARS

Years (N)	1%	2%	4%	6%	8%	10%	12%	14%	15%	16%	18%	20%	22%	24%	25%	26%	28%	30%	35%	40%	45%	50%
1	0.990	0.980	0.962	0.943	0.926	0.909	0.893	0.877	0.870	0.862	0.847	0.833	0.820	0.806	0.800	0.794	0.781	0.769	0.741	0.714	0.690	0.667
2	1.970	1.942	1.886	1.833	1.783	1.736	1.690	1.647	1.626	1.605	1.566	1.528	1.492	1.457	1.440	1.424	1.392	1.361	1.289	1.224	1.165	1.111
3	2.941	2.884	2.775	2.673	2.577	2.487	2.402	2.322	2.283	2.246	2.174	2.106	2.042	1.981	1.952	1.923	1.868	1.816	1.696	1.589	1.493	1.407
4	3.902	3.808	3.630	3.465	3.312	3.170	3.037	2.914	2.855	2.798	2.690	2.589	2.494	2.404	2.362	2.320	2.241	2.166	1.997	1.849	1.720	1.605
5	4.853	4.713	4.452	4.212	3.993	3.791	3.605	3.433	3.352	3.274	3.127	2.991	2.864	2.745	2.689	2.635	2.532	2.436	2.220	2.035	1.876	1.737
6	5.795	5.601	5.242	4.917	4.623	4.355	4.111	3.889	3.784	3.685	3.498	3.326	3.167	3.020	2.951	2.885	2.759	2.643	2.385	2.168	1.983	1.824
7	6.728	6.472	6.002	5.582	5.206	4.868	4.564	4.288	4.160	4.039	3.812	3.605	3.416	3.242	3.161	3.083	2.937	2.802	2.508	2.263	2.057	1.883
8	7.652	7.325	6.733	6.210	5.747	5.335	4.968	4.639	4.487	4.344	4.078	3.837	3.619	3.421	3.329	3.241	3.076	2.925	2.598	2.331	2.108	1.922
9	8.566	8.162	7.435	6.802	6.247	5.759	5.328	4.946	4.772	4.607	4.303	4.031	3.786	3.566	3.463	3.366	3.184	3.019	2.665	2.379	2.144	1.948
10	9.471	8.983	8.111	7.360	6.710	6.145	5.650	5.216	5.019	4.833	4.494	4.192	3.923	3.682	3.571	3.465	3.269	3.092	2.715	2.414	2.168	1.965
11	10.368	9.787	8.760	7.887	7.139	6.495	5.937	5.453	5.234	5.029	4.656	4.327	4.035	3.776	3.656	3.544	3.335	3.147	2.752	2.438	2.185	1.977
12	11.255	10.575	9.385	8.384	7.536	6.814	6.194	5.660	5.421	5.197	4.793	4.439	4.127	3.851	3.725	3.606	3.387	3.190	2.779	2.456	2.196	1.985
13	12.134	11.343	9.986	8.853	7.904	7.103	6.424	5.842	5.583	5.342	4.910	4.533	4.203	3.912	3.780	3.656	3.427	3.223	2.799	2.468	2.204	1.990
14	13.004	12.106	10.563	9.295	8.244	7.367	6.628	6.002	5.724	5.468	5.008	4.611	4.265	3.962	3.824	3.695	3.459	3.249	2.814	2.477	2.210	1.993
15	13.865	12.849	11.118	9.712	8.559	7.606	6.811	6.142	5.847	5.575	5.092	4.675	4.315	4.001	3.859	3.726	3.483	3.268	2.825	2.484	2.214	1.995
16	14.718	13.578	11.652	10.106	8.851	7.824	6.974	6.265	5.954	5.669	5.162	4.730	4.357	4.033	3.887	3.751	3.503	3.283	2.834	2.489	2.216	1.997
17	15.562	14.292	12.166	10.477	9.122	8.022	7.120	6.373	6.047	5.749	5.222	4.775	4.391	4.059	3.910	3.771	3.518	3.295	2.840	2.492	2.218	1.998
18	16.398	14.992	12.659	10.828	9.372	8.201	7.250	6.467	6.128	5.818	5.273	4.812	4.419	4.080	3.928	3.786	3.529	3.304	2.844	2.494	2.219	1.999
19	17.226	15.678	13.134	11.158	9.604	8.365	7.366	6.550	6.198	5.877	5.316	4.844	4.442	4.097	3.942	3.799	3.539	3.311	2.848	2.496	2.220	1.999
20	18.046	16.351	13.590	11.470	9.818	8.514	7.469	6.623	6.259	5.929	5.353	4.870	4.460	4.110	3.954	3.808	3.546	3.316	2.850	2.497	2.221	1.999
21	18.857	17.011	14.029	11.764	10.017	8.649	7.562	6.687	6.312	5.973	5.384	4.891	4.476	4.121	3.963	3.816	3.551	3.320	2.852	2.498	2.221	2.000
22	19.660	17.658	14.451	12.042	10.201	8.772	7.645	6.743	6.359	6.011	5.410	4.909	4.488	4.130	3.970	3.822	3.556	3.323	2.853	2.498	2.222	2.000
23	20.456	18.292	14.857	12.303	10.371	8.883	7.718	6.792	6.399	6.044	5.432	4.925	4.499	4.137	3.976	3.827	3.559	3.325	2.854	2.499	2.222	2.000
24	21.243	18.914	15.247	12.550	10.529	8.985	7.784	6.835	6.434	6.073	5.451	4.937	4.507	4.143	3.981	3.831	3.562	3.327	2.855	2.499	2.222	2.000
25	22.023	19.523	15.622	12.783	10.675	9.077	7.843	6.873	6.464	6.097	5.467	4.948	4.514	4.147	3.985	3.834	3.564	3.329	2.856	2.499	2.222	2.000
26	22.795	20.121	15.983	13.003	10.810	9.161	7.896	6.906	6.491	6.118	5.480	4.956	4.520	4.151	3.988	3.837	3.566	3.330	2.856	2.500	2.222	2.000
27	23.560	20.707	16.330	13.211	10.935	9.237	7.943	6.935	6.514	6.136	5.492	4.964	4.524	4.154	3.990	3.839	3.567	3.331	2.856	2.500	2.222	2.000
28	24.316	21.281	16.663	13.406	11.051	9.307	7.984	6.961	6.534	6.152	5.502	4.970	4.528	4.157	3.992	3.840	3.568	3.331	2.857	2.500	2.222	2.000
29	25.066	21.844	16.984	13.591	11.158	9.370	8.022	6.983	6.551	6.166	5.510	4.975	4.531	4.159	3.994	3.841	3.569	3.332	2.857	2.500	2.222	2.000
30	25.808	22.396	17.292	13.765	11.258	9.427	8.055	7.003	6.566	6.177	5.517	4.979	4.534	4.160	3.995	3.842	3.569	3.332	2.857	2.500	2.222	2.000
40	32.835	27.355	19.793	15.046	11.925	9.779	8.244	7.105	6.642	6.234	5.548	4.997	4.544	4.166	3.999	3.846	3.571	3.333	2.857	2.500	2.222	2.000
50	39.196	31.424	21.482	15.762	12.234	9.915	8.304	7.133	6.661	6.246	5.554	4.999	4.545	4.167	4.000	3.846	3.571	3.333	2.857	2.500	2.222	2.000

Table C

PRESENT VALUE OF SUM-OF-YEARS' DIGITS DEPRECIATION

Years of Useful Life	2%	4%	6%	8%	10%	12%	14%	15%	16%	18%	20%	22%	24%	26%	28%	30%	35%	40%	45%	50%
3	0.968	0.937	0.908	0.881	0.855	0.831	0.808	0.796	0.786	0.764	0.745	0.726	0.707	0.690	0.674	0.658	0.621	0.588	0.558	0.531
4	0.961	0.925	0.891	0.860	0.830	0.802	0.776	0.763	0.751	0.728	0.706	0.685	0.665	0.646	0.628	0.611	0.572	0.538	0.507	0.479
5	0.955	0.914	0.875	0.839	0.806	0.775	0.746	0.732	0.719	0.694	0.670	0.647	0.626	0.606	0.588	0.570	0.530	0.494	0.463	0.435
6	0.949	0.902	0.859	0.820	0.783	0.749	0.718	0.703	0.689	0.662	0.637	0.613	0.591	0.570	0.551	0.533	0.492	0.456	0.425	0.398
7	0.943	0.891	0.844	0.801	0.761	0.725	0.692	0.676	0.661	0.633	0.606	0.582	0.559	0.538	0.518	0.500	0.458	0.423	0.392	0.366
8	0.937	0.880	0.829	0.782	0.740	0.702	0.667	0.650	0.635	0.605	0.578	0.553	0.530	0.508	0.488	0.470	0.429	0.394	0.364	0.338
9	0.931	0.869	0.814	0.765	0.720	0.680	0.643	0.626	0.610	0.580	0.552	0.527	0.503	0.482	0.462	0.443	0.402	0.368	0.338	0.313
10	0.925	0.859	0.800	0.748	0.701	0.659	0.621	0.604	0.587	0.556	0.528	0.502	0.479	0.457	0.437	0.419	0.378	0.345	0.316	0.292
11	0.919	0.848	0.786	0.731	0.682	0.639	0.600	0.582	0.565	0.534	0.506	0.480	0.456	0.434	0.415	0.397	0.357	0.324	0.297	0.273
12	0.913	0.838	0.773	0.715	0.665	0.620	0.580	0.562	0.545	0.513	0.485	0.459	0.435	0.414	0.394	0.376	0.338	0.306	0.279	0.257
13	0.907	0.828	0.760	0.700	0.648	0.602	0.562	0.543	0.526	0.494	0.465	0.439	0.416	0.395	0.376	0.358	0.320	0.289	0.264	0.242
14	0.902	0.818	0.747	0.685	0.632	0.585	0.544	0.525	0.508	0.476	0.447	0.421	0.398	0.377	0.358	0.341	0.304	0.274	0.250	0.229
15	0.896	0.809	0.734	0.671	0.616	0.569	0.527	0.508	0.491	0.459	0.430	0.405	0.382	0.361	0.343	0.326	0.290	0.261	0.237	0.217
16	0.890	0.799	0.722	0.657	0.601	0.553	0.511	0.492	0.475	0.443	0.414	0.389	0.367	0.346	0.328	0.312	0.277	0.248	0.225	0.206
17	0.885	0.790	0.710	0.644	0.587	0.538	0.496	0.477	0.460	0.428	0.400	0.375	0.352	0.332	0.315	0.298	0.264	0.237	0.215	0.196
18	0.880	0.781	0.699	0.631	0.573	0.524	0.482	0.463	0.445	0.413	0.386	0.361	0.339	0.320	0.302	0.286	0.253	0.227	0.205	0.187
19	0.874	0.772	0.688	0.618	0.560	0.510	0.468	0.449	0.432	0.400	0.372	0.348	0.327	0.308	0.291	0.275	0.243	0.217	0.196	0.179
20	0.869	0.763	0.677	0.606	0.547	0.497	0.455	0.436	0.419	0.387	0.360	0.336	0.315	0.296	0.280	0.265	0.233	0.208	0.188	0.171
21	0.863	0.754	0.666	0.594	0.535	0.485	0.442	0.424	0.406	0.376	0.349	0.325	0.304	0.286	0.270	0.255	0.224	0.200	0.181	0.164
22	0.858	0.746	0.656	0.583	0.523	0.473	0.431	0.412	0.395	0.364	0.338	0.315	0.294	0.276	0.260	0.246	0.216	0.193	0.174	0.158
23	0.853	0.738	0.646	0.572	0.511	0.461	0.419	0.401	0.384	0.354	0.327	0.305	0.285	0.267	0.252	0.238	0.208	0.186	0.167	0.152
24	0.848	0.729	0.636	0.561	0.500	0.450	0.409	0.390	0.373	0.344	0.318	0.295	0.276	0.258	0.243	0.230	0.201	0.179	0.161	0.147
25	0.842	0.721	0.626	0.551	0.490	0.440	0.398	0.380	0.364	0.334	0.308	0.286	0.267	0.250	0.236	0.222	0.195	0.173	0.156	0.142
30	0.818	0.683	0.582	0.504	0.442	0.393	0.353	0.336	0.320	0.292	0.269	0.249	0.232	0.216	0.203	0.191	0.167	0.148	0.133	0.120
35	0.794	0.648	0.542	0.463	0.402	0.355	0.317	0.300	0.286	0.260	0.238	0.220	0.204	0.190	0.178	0.168	0.146	0.129	0.116	0.105
40	0.771	0.616	0.507	0.428	0.368	0.323	0.286	0.271	0.257	0.233	0.213	0.196	0.182	0.170	0.159	0.149	0.129	0.114	0.102	0.093
45	0.749	0.586	0.476	0.397	0.339	0.296	0.261	0.247	0.234	0.212	0.193	0.178	0.164	0.153	0.143	0.134	0.116	0.103	0.092	0.083
50	0.728	0.559	0.448	0.370	0.314	0.272	0.240	0.227	0.214	0.194	0.176	0.162	0.150	0.139	0.130	0.122	0.106	0.093	0.083	

Source: From tables computed by Jerome Bracken and Charles J. Christenson. Copyright © 1961 by the President and Fellows of Harvard College. Used by permission. See page 626 for explanation of use of this table.

INDEX

INDEX

A

Absorbed overhead costs; *See* Overhead
Absorption costs, 250
Accelerated depreciation; *see* Depreciation
Account categories, 35
Account flow chart, 440–41
Account form of balance sheet, 32
Accounting
  defined, 7
  language, 11–12
  limitations on, 397
  preconceptions about, 8
Accounting alternatives, 394–97
Accounting changes, treatment of, 387
Accounting numbers, characteristics of, 424–28
Accounting period, 53–54
Accounting principles, criteria for, 13–14
  source of, 14–15
Accounting Principles Board, 15
Opinions
  No. 5, 196 n
  No. 6, 198 n
  No. 8, 235 n
  No. 9, 68 n, 283 n
  No. 10, 127 n
  No. 11, 266 n
  No. 12, 206 n
  No. 15, 284, 291 n
  No. 16, 297, 300 n
  No. 17, 213 n, 301 n
  No. 18, 304, 313
  No. 19, 315
  No. 20, 387 n
  No. 21, 128 n, 269 n, 270 n
  No. 25, 283 n
  No. 26, 272 n
  No. 29, 196 n
  No. 30, 242 n, 283 n
  No. 31, 386 n

Accounting Principles Board—*Cont.*
Statements
  No. 3, 245
  No. 4, 7 n, 24 n, 37 n, 40 n, 56 n
Accounting Research Bulletin No. 43, 38 n, 177 n, 210 n, 224 n, 249 n, 282 n, 294
Accounting Research Study No. 7, 395 n
Accounting Terminology Bulletin No. 1, 12 n
Accounting Trends and Techniques, 16, 132 n, 169 n, 301 n, 321 n
  depreciation, 204 n
Accounts
  adjusting entries, 92–95
  chart of, 89
  closing entries, 96
  nature of, 86
  ruling and balancing, 97
Accounts payable, 40
Accounts receivable, 38
  aging, 133
  bad debt expense, 95, 130–36, 138
  cash budget, 733
  write-off, 134
Accretion, 211
Accrual accounting, 73
Accrued expenses, 41
Accrued revenue, 58
Accumulated depreciation, 95
Acid-test ratio, 361
Acquisition, 296
Activity related basis of allocation, 457
Adjusting entries, 92
Aging accounts receivable, 133
Agricultural commodities, revenue measurement, 126
All-inclusive income statement, 60
Allocation, nature of, 453–54
  of costs, bases for, 456–58
  of indirect costs, 452–63

This book has been set in 10 point Janson with 10 point Caledonia Bold, leaded 2 points, and 9 point Janson, leaded 2 points. Part numbers are in 18 and 42 point Helvetica Medium and part titles are in 24 point Helvetica Regular. Chapter numbers are in 14 and 24 point Helvetica Regular and chapter titles are in 18 point Helvetica Medium. The size of the type page is 27 x 45½ picas.